Tonya

ⓗanging out.

in

england

other titles in the

(H)angingout.

series:

europe

spain

france

ireland

italy

Hangingout in england

First Edition

A Balliett & Fitzgerald Book

Hungry Minds™

Best-Selling Books • Digital Downloads • e-Books • Answer Networks
e-Newsletters • Branded Web SItes • e-Learning

New York, NY ✦ Cleveland, OH ✦ Indianapolis, IN

Balliett & Fitzgerald, Inc.
Project Editors: Liz Barrett, Kim Wyatt, and Kristen Couse
Production Managers: Maria Fernandez, Mike Walters
Production Editor: Paul Paddock
Map Artist: Darshan Bhagat
Line Editors: Will Tizard, Kevin McLain, Sarah Kizis, Eric Ducker, Amy
Leibrock, Julia French, Jennifer Purdy
Copy Editors: Carolyn Keubler, Christopher Tinney
Proofreaders: Jodi Brandon, Fran Manushkin, Donna Stonecipher,
Shoshanna Wingate.
Associate Editors: Nathaniel Knaebel, Chris Varmus, Alix McNamara,
Lauren Podis
Editorial Intern: Joanna Cupano
Cartographer: Roberta Stockwell

Published by
Hungry Minds, Inc.
909 Third Avenue
New York, NY 10022

ISBN: 0-7645-6246-0
ISSN: 1531-1546

Book design: Sue Canavan and Mike Walters

Special Sales: For general information on Hungry Minds' products and
services please contact our Customer Care Department within the U.S.
at Tel 800-762-2974, outside the U.S. at Tel 317-572-3993 or Fax 317-
572-4002.

For sales inquires and reseller information, including discounts, premium
and bulk quantity sales, and foreign-language translations, please contact
our Customer Care Department at Tel 1-800-434-3422 or Fax 317-572-
4002.

5   4   3   2   1

CONTENTS

england

backmatter

maps

a disclaimer

Please note that prices fluctuate in the course of time, and travel information changes under the impact of the many factors that influence the travel industry. We therefore suggest that you write or call ahead for confirmation when making your travel plans. Every effort has been made to ensure the accuracy of information throughout this book and the contents of this publication are believed correct at the time of printing. Nevertheless, the publishers cannot accept responsibility for errors or omissions or for changes in details given in this guide or for the consequences of any reliance on the information provided by the same. Assessments of attractions and so forth are based upon the authors' own experiences and therefore, descriptions given in this guide necessarily contain an element of subjective opinion, which may not reflect the publisher's opinion or dictate a reader's own experience on another occasion. Readers are invited to write the publisher with ideas, comments, and suggestions for future editions.

Your safety is important to us, however, so we encourage you to stay alert and be aware of your surroundings. Keep a close eye on cameras, purses, and wallets, all favorite targets of thieves and pickpockets.

Please write to:
Hanging Out in England, First Edition
Hungry Minds, Inc.
909 Third Avenue
New York, NY 10022

foreword

m ost of us have had the experience of going to a new school or moving to a new neighborhood and not knowing a soul there, not knowing the laws of the land, feeling lost and uncool. But if you're lucky, someone comes along who invites you in and shows you where the action is. The same can be said for travel—unless you're committed to seeing Europe through the moving tinted window of a tour bus, pretty soon you're going to want to get past the initial strangeness and get with it. And to really be able to do that, you need someone or something to help you along, so that what could have been just another cute postcard turns into a new chapter in your life.

Going to Europe is infinitely more complicated—and ultimately more rewarding—than just going on a road trip. Without some help, you may repeatedly find yourself surrounded by a numbed-out tour group, scratching your head and wondering what all the fuss is about. We sent out our teams of writers with just that in mind. Go to where the action is, we instructed them, and tell us how to find it.

Of course we tell you how to see all the cultural and historical goodies you've read about in art history class and heard about from your folks, but we also tell you where to find the party, shake your butt, and make friends with the locals. We've tried to find the hottest scenes in Europe—where traditions are being reinvented daily—and make these guides into the equivalent of a hip friend to show you the ropes.

So, welcome to the new Europe, on the verge of mighty unification. The European Union (EU)—and the euro's arrival as a common currency—is already making many happy, others nervous, and setting the entire continent abuzz with a different kind of energy. As the grand tour of Europe meets the Info Age, the old ways are having to adjust to a faster tempo.

But even as the globe is shrinking to the size of a dot com, Europe remains a vast vast place with enough history and art and monuments to fill endless guides—so we had to make a choice. We wanted the *Hanging Out Guides* to live up to their title, so we decided to specialize and not only show you the best spots to eat, shop, sightsee, party, and crash, but also give you a real feeling for each place, and unique but do-able ways to get to know it better. So we don't cover *every single* town, village, and mountaintop—instead, we picked what we felt were the best and serve them up with plenty of detail. We felt it was crucial to have the room to go deeper, and to tip you off as to how to do the same, so that after you see the sights, you'll almost certainly end up in a place where you'll get to know the secret to the best travel—the locals.

Aside from the basics—neighborhoods, eats, crashing, stuff (shopping), culture zoo (sightseeing stuff), and need to know (the essentials)—we cover the bar scene, the live music scene, the club scene, the gay scene, the visual arts scene, and the performing arts scene, always giving you the scoop on where to chill out and where to get wild. We take you on some beautiful walks and show you great places to hang (sometimes for no money). Things to Talk to a Local About actually gives you some fun conversation openers. Fashion tells you what people are wearing. Wired lists websites for each city—some general, some cool, some out-of-the-way—so you can start checking things out immediately. It also takes you to the best cybercafes in each place. Rules of the Game lays out local liquor and substance laws and also gives you the vibe on the street. Five-0 does a quick sketch of cops in each city. Boy meets Girl dares to speculate on that most mysterious of travel adventures. And Festivals & Events lists just that. We also take you out to all the best outdoor spots, where you can hike, bike, swim, jump, ski, snorkel, or surf till you've had enough.

Our adventurous team of writers (average age, 24) and editors let you in on the ongoing party. We want to make sure that your time abroad is punctuated by moments when you've sunk deep enough into the mix (or danced long enough to it), so that you suddenly get it, you have that flash of knowing what it's like to actually *be* somewhere else, to live there—to hang out in Europe.

introduction

from the Magna Carta to the mosh pit, it seems like everything Western started in England. Even today, fashion and musical trends often start on this side of the pond before heading west. Think miniskirts and Dido.

So before you get here, you already know a lot about the place. You've seen the changing of the guard, Princess Di's wedding, the Beatles crushed by screaming mobs. But England is not what you think it is. Forget your images of Buckingham Palace and buckets of fish and chips. England is a land of contrasts. Yes, England has cutting-edge fashion and a world-class club scene. But they also have funky food and funky weather. This opposition is present in the people, too. You've got the stiff-upper-lip Brit, dedicated to tradition and order, and the cheeky hooligan who likes to pound pints and talk football (that's soccer to you Yanks). Remnants of Victorian excess are everywhere, stuffy and flamboyant in that peculiar British way. Just step inside a pub to see the other side.

There about 60 million people in England, and not all of them are, well, what we think of as British. OK, so there are tea drinkers, fish and chips eaters, and garden tenders. But there as many ravers, artists, and mountain climbers. And the nightlife kicks booty. With over 5,000 pubs in London's city limits alone, you would indeed be crawling if you tried to have a drink in each one of them. In between pubs, you can fortify yourself with a meat pie or a jacket potato. But vegetarians can find grub too, thanks to the influx of immigrants that have diversified England's farthest reaches. Curry, anyone?

england

England is a playground. It's a Merchant-Ivory production, a Hugh Grant comedy, *Sid & Nancy*, and *Pee-Wee's Big Adventure* all rolled into one. And not only does everyone speak your language—although you might not always understand what they are saying—the Brits love to party.

When you're planning your trip, think of England in four parts: **the South, the North, Central,** and, of course, **London.** Your hipster resume would not be complete without a trip to London. Europe's largest city is more electric and energetic than it's been in years. Some say that it has surpassed New York in terms of sheer energy, outrageous fashion, and a nightlife that is second to none. The city is like a great wheel, with Piccadilly Circus at the hub and dozens of communities branching out from it. London is a conglomeration of neighborhoods, each with its own personality. When you need a break from clubbing, check out the freak show at London's Camden, head to an art gallery on Bankside, or go shopping in Soho.

Shopping is actually huge all over England, and flea market freaks will be in heaven. Whether you are looking for museum quality stuff or fun junk, you'll find it—from outlandish shoes to royal kitsch. Browse antique shows, markets, fairs, stalls, and car boot sales to find that oh-so-British keepsake to take home.

Outside of London, for English of the partying variety you'll want to head to **Bristol, Manchester, Liverpool, Leeds,** or **Newcastle. Birmingham, Liecester,** and **Nottingham** are worth a look if you're in Mid-England. Once sooty post-industrial towns, these places now gleam with shiny new clubs, and music spills in to the streets. In fact, you'll be hard pressed not to notice the music, and it can be worth traveling from London to hear a fresh DJ at a club like Liverpool's Zanzibar or Manchester's Planet K. From punk to trip-hop, it all started here, too.

Let's not forget the British Rock 'n' Roll Invasion and Manchester Northern Soul. Gender benders and trend starters hail from every corner of the country, and you'd be hard pressed to name a song on the *Billboard* charts that doesn't contain a riff from the Beatles, the Rolling Stones, Eric Clapton, Led Zeppelin, The Who, The Clash, The Sex Pistols, or David Bowie. And the imports keep coming: think Oasis, Fatboy Slim, Radiohead, Beth Orton, and darling Dido, all Brits.

If your idea of a good time doesn't involve a pint, there are plenty of other ways to get busy. You can hike across the country over greener-than-green hill and dale, or take in a New Age hot spot like Glastonbury. Walk across the otherworldly moors and understand the Bronte sisters desperate obsession. Watch clouds and write poems in Wordsworth's rambling country, once you get away from the crowds, that is.

Wander through unspoiled seaport villages and toss back a pint with salty dogs. Surf the southwest coast and then sleep over in a quainter-than-quaint village lined with cobblestone streets. Go island tripping off the **Northumbria coast.** Despite England's oft-reputation as an industrial blight, nature is plentiful.

Even in urban areas, you can take a breather. Pack a picnic basket and punt down a charming, historic river in historic **Oxford** or **Cambridge.**

Yes, they are student towns, but of the world leader variety versus party hound (Although Bill Clinton went to Oxford as a Rhodes Scholar...). Take in a bookstore and make your brain much, much larger before you head to your next den of iniquity.

If you are into the way-back machine, there is always the history. England is older than dirt. Walk along **Hadrian's Wall,** the Roman fortification built in AD 122 to keep the riffraff out. Check out small towns where thatched roofs and more sheep than people are the order of the day. Visit villages that eerily haven't changed in hundreds of years, like **Castle Combe.** If it's higher ground you seek, the cathedrals of England will not disappoint; York Minster is one of the greatest in the country. And you can't swing a cat without hitting a castle. **Windsor Castle,** England's largest, is the best place to watch the Changing of the Guards. **Northumbria** rules if you're looking for crumbly castles ala Braveheart.

The English definitely have a penchant for the bizarre, and little pockets of weird and wild abound. Want to see the world's largest pencil? Done. Gather with goths at a museum dedicated to all things Dracula or take a ghost walk in **York.**

The myths and legends of literature also loom large. Visit Shakespeare's stomping grounds, the alleged burial site of the Holy Grail and Arthur and Guinevere, the home of *The Canterbury Tales,* Robin Hood, and Alice in Wonderland. And let's not forget **Stonehenge,** the mysterious circle of rocks allegedly the site of Druid ceremonies (it was actually there waaaay before the Druids—the truth is no one is really sure what went down there). While you're wandering, check out **Avebury,** another famous bunch of rocks, that you can actually walk among and touch.

Now about the bare necessities: First, the food. At some point in your journey, you may feel like you have only two choices: fried or fried. Although you might have found some nifty curry stand or vegetable market, the regional food, well, let's just say it isn't why you came. But there are specialties worth having. You can eat cheddar cheese where it originated and drink a pint of the sublime Newcastle Brown Ale in its hometown. Cheers!

Sure, it rains in England. But you'll rarely get a true downpour, and certainly nothing to keep you from your plans. Summer is the best time weather-wise, and it's also the time to hit lots of outdoor festivals. Just count on a wee bit of rain and a chill. Even indoors, Brits consider chilliness wholesome, so bring a jumper (that's a sweater to you Yanks).

B & Bs are everywhere, and they are not like the precious places you find in the States. No, in England, Ma & Pa really open up their house and rent a room. They are often the best bet and you get to hang with the real deal.

Outside of the larger cities and especially in the North, transportation can be tricky. It's best to have your routes well planned—know how you are getting where and when—unless you have time to burn.

Finally, in a country as steeped in tradition as it is in anarchy, it's a good idea to keep a few things in mind. One word you will hear a lot is "sorry," meaning "excuse me." You'll hear it as people brush past on the street, or in the pub. The other important word to know is "queue." Londoners don't line up, they queue up. Everywhere you go, you'll see people in lines. Nobody just jumps on a bus in London; they queue up at the bus stop. Don't be rude, Yank. Get in line.

Beneath the British formality, the people are usually very friendly, particularly if you survive the first five minutes of the hazing (in other words, being called a Yank). It's not an insult. Be polite—minding your ps and qs (at first) will get you invited to the party.

You might take some habits home with you: an afternoon cup of tea, or good manners, for example. You'll also leave England with a better sense of your own country and cultural traditions. And it is Europe, after all, so you'll learn a little bit about how the world is put together.

One last thing: Don't mention the American Revolution.

the best of england

Glastonbury festival [Wiltshire & Somerset]: Experience three endless summer days of unequalled English hedonism with the Glastonbury Festival: an extravaganza of music, theater, and the arts.

Clubbing in Bristol [Wiltshire & Somerset]: Bounce from one club to the next on Bristol's party packed quayside. Strut up the gangway of **Thekla,** one of Bristol's trendiest clubs aboard a docked boat, and chill out to a view of twinkling lights.

Media [Nottingham]: This place tops the list of happening clubs to get your groove on. Every week at its Renaissance party, there's a different lineup of world-class DJs. The queue's so fantastically long you'll think you're at the most popular club in London, not in a city with 1/40th the population.

Gay and Lesbian Pride Festival [Birmingham]: For gays and straights alike, this party is the best weekend festival around. It has special street fair events, and a Miss Camp Pride parade that attempts to compare itself with Sydney's Gay Mardi Gras.

Oldham Street [Manchester]: Home to some of the best clubs around, like **Planet K,** and the focus of the Northern Soul musical movement, this street provides everything you need for a night of extreme partying.

Don't overlook **Affleck's:** Four floors of shops that focus on everything you can't find anywhere else is ingeniously combined with a couple of bars featuring mostly Brit pop. The building takes up an entire city block and brings new meaning to the words "block-party."

Cream and Zanzibar [Liverpool]: Although **Cream** is the best-known club in the area, it is also the most crowded with the worst music. If you are out to drink and rub shoulders with as many people as possible, this is the place for you. If you like room to dance, a crowd that will boogie along with you, and some excellent music, head to **Zanzibar.**

Newcastle-Upon-Tyne [Northumbria]: It's truly the gem of the north as far as partying goes, and nothing can really live up to the weekend scene here. On Friday and Saturday nights, the streets are lined with peeps decked out in fashion's finest who are coming or going from bar to club to bar.

Leeds [Yorkshire]: In the past few years the cosmopolitan resurgence of the north has created dynamic changes in this city's life. Once a town that slept after 5pm, the city now comes alive at the end of the workday, with new clubs, bars, and performance spaces opening up weekly.

CULTURE

Alice's Shop [London]: Browse the shop that was the inspiration for the "Old Sheep Shop" in the Alice in Wonderland books. Filled with lots of wonderful stuff, including rare editions of the books and a complete chessboard with all the famous characters.

Blenheim Palace [Oxfordshire & Cambrideshire]: Wander the splendor of Winston Churchill's birthplace, where the current Duke of Marlborough lives, and check out the library where Sylvester Stallone got married.

Lincoln Cathedral [Central England]: Definitely the best cathedral in Central England, the word amazing doesn't describe the awe-inspiring impact this grandiose structure has on its visitors. The spiky organ is especially striking, as is the cathedral's beautiful golden exterior when it is lit up and shines brightly like a magnificent star in the night sky.

Warwick Castle [Central England]: This castle is rumored to be the best castle in all of England. That's a bold statement. Horror fans might like to visit the castle because it's allegedly haunted, and contains a dungeon of medieval torture equipment.

Barber Institute of Fine Arts [Birmingham]: Some say this is the finest small art museum in England. It's meticulous inside, and it contains priceless paintings by famous artists like van Gogh.

St. Ann's Well and Buxton Opera House [Buxton]: For a small town, Buxton truly provides for the culture hungry. Built in imitation of Bath, there is no shortage of great architecture and high-class entertainment. The **Buxton Opera House** attracts shows that are normally reserved for the large cities, and touring the bathhouses is an interesting view into the history of this tiny town. It is also rumored that the baths around **St. Ann's Well** will someday be reopened, adding spa resort to the list of sophisticated pastimes in Buxton.

Tate Gallery [Liverpool]: London was the only mainstay of cultural interests until Liverpool decided to get in on it, and they have managed with great success. This gallery honestly represents innovation in art, featuring only what is new and interesting in the contemporary art world.

Grasmere [Lake District]: For centuries, literary giants have come to the Lake District to find inspiration, and one of the best known of these greats is William Wordsworth. He spent most of his life in Grasmere and the town is a veritable shrine to the man and his work. Everything from his gravesite to the desk where he composed most of his later work is on display for you to view.

Hadrian's Wall [Northumbria]: Here you can actually experience the vastness of the Roman Empire and the lasting affect they had on their lands. This 73-mile wall at one time stretched from coast to coast to block invaders from the north. It remains only a fragment of the height that it once was, but its magnificence remains.

York [Yorkshire]: Culture seeps through every crack of this city. The history and class of this town are apparent in the architecture and the people. Even the bars and pubs hold onto their historical backgrounds with pride, adamantly opposing change and constantly reviving their individual roles in the making of this great city. Make sure you check out the York Minster. The ornate detail and sheer extravagance of this building is every bit as shocking as the fact that it took about 300 years to complete. It inspires awe each time you catch even a glimpse and is truly one of humanity's greatest feats.

outdoors

Adventure Caving [The Mendips]: Crawl through the Cheddar limestone caves outfitted in carabiners and boilersuits, or go outside and do a spot of abseiling on the vertical drops of the jagged Mendip hills.

Hiking on the Isle of Wight [The Southeast]: The unspoiled terrain of West Wight offers some spectacular walking paths that make it seem as if you are standing on the edge of the continent. Hike to the Needles, three giant chalk pinnacles that stick out of the water off the end of the island.

The Cotswold Way [Central England]: This trail is easily Central England's top dog of outdoor activities. Start your walk in the thatched-roofed house town of Chipping Campden and you'll pass through green lush fields dotted with grazing sheep and cows. Be sure to pause for a moment to take in the fresh country air and enjoy the views of distant valleys and hilltops.

Stanage Edge [The Peak District]: Three miles of sheer rock makes these cliffs a rock-climbers dream. Famous for its infinite number of climbing possibilities and its ability to accommodate for all skill levels, Stanage Edge offers the best climbing in England.

Glenridding [The Lake District]: This town was made for hikers. Its close proximity to Helvellyn, the only mountain of its height in England with a razor sharp summit, attracts hikers from all over the country and is thankfully exclusive to this group of people. Unless you are a nature lover, fond of beautiful mountains, crystal lakes, and breathtaking views, there is no reason to visit this tiny outdoor oasis.

Pennine Way [The Peak District]: At 270 miles, this long distance trail is often tackled in order to overcome its difficulty as much as it is to experience the history from which it stems. Once the northbound path taken by Roman troops, it now passes entirely through northern England ending just over the Scottish border.

Warkworth Castle and Hermitage [Northumbria]: Sometimes the best is the most secret and in the case of castles this holds true. Although it isn't surrounded by unbelievable natural beauty, this castle is extremely well preserved and the details that remain intact are truly amazing. There is also a nearby hermitage that was carved by hand out of a limestone cliff and was occupied by a practicing monk for most of his life.

Shoreline Walk [Northumbria]: Along the Northumbrian coast you will find the most beautiful of England's shorelines, and the stretch of calm seas and crystal sands between Bamburgh and Seahouses is a perfect representation of the rest of the area. This four-mile stroll is serene and comforting.

Rievaulx Abbey [Yorkshire]: The mile-long walk from Helmsley is the perfect preparation for the majestic ruins. What is so impressive about these ruins are the spaces between the stones; the arches are seemingly suspended in the air with nothing but their own resistance to crumbling to keep them from falling.

weird and bizarre

Castle Coombe [Central England]: Visit a picture perfect town with only one short street in the south Cotswolds that hasn't changed its appearance in 200 years.

Stonehenge & Avebury [Wiltshire & Somerset]: Gaze at the world famous, mysteriously built stone circles of Stonehenge, and walk among and touch the stones at Avebury, where the circles are eight times as big.

Salamander's [Derby]: Talk about one stop-shopping. Here you can enjoy a cheese sandwich, get your tongue pierced, and buy wind chimes all at the same place.

Nine Ladies Stone Circle [Matlock]: Whether you arrive at daytime, when there are mostly hikers and the occasional dreadlocked protestor, or during a full moon, when a ceremony of drums and a coven of dancing witches and wizards is the norm, the inherent spookiness of this Peak District attraction will stick with you for a long time.

Well Dressings [Peak District]: Once a Pagan ritual, this celebration of drinking wells couldn't be suppressed by the Catholic Church and has been adopted by some as a Christian holiday. For one weekend during the summer, some Peak District towns decorate the town well with flowers and other organic material in honor of the gift of life provided by this substance.

Homes of Football [Ambleside]: If you can't get to a game of football, go see the closest thing to it: papier-mache models of spectators and players displayed among the most famous moments in football history. Nothing short of weird, these 3-D re-creations of actual scenes at recent football games are a most impressive display of football fanfare.

Ghost Walks [York]: This animated version of York's past is more like a live action horror film than a history lesson. Even if history is of little interest to you, this walk is well worth the time. Spectacular performers bring the spooky and mysterious past to life, providing an unusual view into the city.

City Walls [Berwick-Upon-Tweed]: Once protecting this valuable port city from invaders by sea, the buried walls of Berwick now create an almost alien landscape. Worn down by years of water and wind erosion the walls are now grassy mounds that rise and fall with the same frequency as a sound wave. The drops between mounds are so sharp they necessitate warning signs and restricted areas to prevent someone from taking a 20-foot plunge.

London and Environs

London and Environs

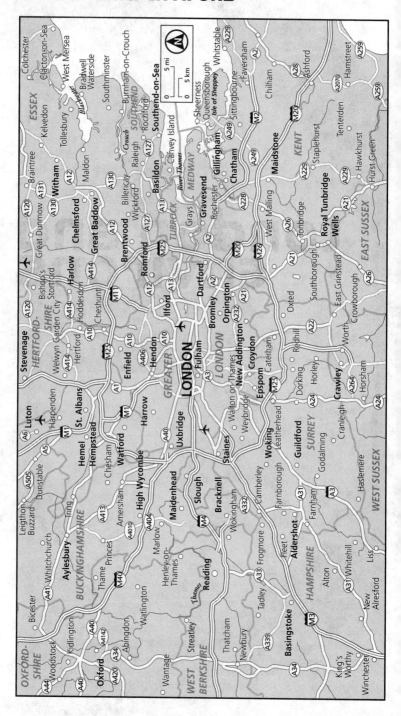

Even on vacation, the concrete jungle of London can become a bit overwhelming, even for the most die-hard urbanites. So, be it a bright, sunny weekend afternoon (if you're lucky enough to have one in London), or just a day when breathing some fresh air seems essential, hop on a train for a day trip away from the hurly-burly. The attractions closest to London that offer a hearty taste of the British countryside are **Richmond** and **Windsor.**

Richmond is like an extended suburb of London, with a similar vibe to London's Chelsea neighborhood. Nestled next to the Thames, the town center is designed in a circular manner, so that once you wander around a bit—it's like déjà vu—you'll inevitably come back to where you started. Filled with chi-chi shops and restaurants, this is where the posh set resides. Richmond is good for shopping, walking along the river, or having an extended lunch outside at one of the waterfront cafes.

The famed **Kew Gardens** is one stop before Richmond on the train, so it can be combined quite conveniently with Richmond for a good day trip. Kew's beautiful and massive botanical garden features trees and plants from all over the planet. There is a Ginkgo biloba tree, which was planted in the 1760s; a whole flower bed of South African flora and a collection of Japanese bamboo, to name but a few. The greenhouses contain madly exotic plants, including citrus and tropical fruits, teas, and sacred lotus, and a number of ponds and monuments in the gardens provide an ideal setting to walk around in or to relax on the grass.

Windsor, on the other hand, is chock-full of history, not to mention pinstriped Eton boys. And if you're hankering to see how royalty lives, **Windsor Castle** is the Queen's second major residence, after Buckingham Palace. You won't be alone in your quest, as there are always hordes of tourists about. For some calmer moments, the river offers good walkways and boat trips, as well as bonding opportunities with the swans.

If you only have time or energy for a one-day trip out of London, go to Windsor, as you will be immersed in a wealth of English culture at its most traditional. There are also plenty of mellow mainstream pursuits if you're not in the mood for the cultural shtick. You can riffle through the shops selling clothes, records, books, and gifts, lunch at restaurants or tea rooms, drift into art galleries, or simply roam about the bustling streets.

Getting around the region

All the London environs are easily accessible by train, and since you won't be too far afield, the cost can be kept low. The travel time is under an hour, and everything in each place is within walking distance, so if you get an early start on the day, you'll have of plenty of time to explore all the major attractions. A good day can be had by taking the commuter rail train to Richmond and Kew, stopping first at Kew and spending a few hours in the gardens, then hopping back on the train to Richmond for shopping, lunch on the river, and a walk or boat ride. If you want to visit both places, you can do the Richmond/Kew Gardens trip in one day, but plan to devote a full day to Windsor.

▶▶ROUTES

Kew and Richmond are each about a half-hour trip from London if you take the North London Rail line from the West Hampstead commuter rail station (across from the tube station; £2.70 day return). Or, a decidedly slower method is to take the **tube** to Kew Gardens (Zone 3, second to last stop on the southwest District line) and Richmond (Zone 4, last stop on the southwest District line).

For **buses** to Richmond and Kew from London, get on one of the District line buses that leave from Fulham Broadway and stop at both Kew and Richmond (bus 391). Contact the **London Transport Travel Information** for more journey-planning advice, times, and fares *(Tel 0207/222-12-34 and 0207/233-01-01; www.transportforlondon.co.uk)*.

TRAVEL TIMES

All times by train

	London	Kew Gardens	Richmond	Windsor
London	-	:35	:20	:40
Kew Gardens	:35	-	:05	:45
Richmond	:20	:05	-	:35
Windsor	:40	:45	:35	-

If you're feeling extra adventurous, you can take a **boat** to Richmond on the Thames from Westminster Pier, which leaves about seven times a day. The service, however, can be erratic, due to varying water levels. The trip takes about an hour and a half depending on tidal conditions. For more details on the boat trips, call *Tel 0207/79-30-20-62 or 0207/79-30-47-21*. The trip costs £8 for an adult single and £12 return. The boat ride is definitely fun, not to mention relaxing, with beautiful scenery en route.

To go to Windsor from London, leave from **Waterloo** or **Paddington stations** in London. The trip lasts about 50 minutes (£5.90 day return). Windsor has two train stations and the service is frequent to both.

Green Line coaches *(Tel 0208/668-72-61; Bus 700, 702; Same day round-trip ticket £7)* to Windsor run from Hyde Park Corner in London and take about an hour and a half. The bus drops you near the Parish Church, across the street from the castle.

London

Having given birth to the Swinging '60s, the Sex Pistols, and all-night raves, London could easily rest on its party laurels, but instead the city is the pacesetter for the 21st century—and now you don't even have to know some secret password to find the good parties. Those days are done, as are the days of the strict 11pm shutdown of bars and pubs that gave London nightlife its peculiar character. Beginning in 1993, late-night licenses were granted to a few bars, starting what many hope will be a complete overhaul of London's ancient drinking laws. It was around the same time that the government also started cracking down on E-fueled warehouse parties, passing a law against people dancing to "repetitive beats," moving raves into clubs and special-event halls. The outcome of this epic battle between the forces of youth culture and the status quo is still undecided, but the lines of division are pretty clear.

London is in fact two cities in one: an exciting, fast-paced, international center of fashion, music, and club culture; and the remains of one of Europe's most powerful empires, trying to preserve (and promote) some of its former glory. And while the government looks to the future, eagerly throwing money at wacko monuments to England like the Millennium Dome, most Londoners take greater national pride in the treble victory of the football (soccer) powerhouse, the Manchester United. The two Londons coexist, creating a weird rhythm between them, as thousands of partiers and barflies run from pub to bar to club before everything shuts down around midnight. Sometimes the two faces of the city can even intersect, as when the austere **National Portrait Gallery** [see *culture zoo*, below] hosted a huge show of rock 'n' roll photography.

But in the city that now modestly calls itself the "New Capital of Europe" (perplexing the European Union even further), the relentless bone of contention for revelers is still the absurd curfew. Happily, a bunch of spots do have late-licenses, letting them stay open until 1am, 3am, and sometimes 6am: **The End, Ministry of Sound,** and **Bar Rhumba** [see *club scene,* below] are all there for diehards.

Despite the shortage of early-morning action, London's shockingly vibrant nightlife has only expanded and diversified in recent years, with tons of clubs, concerts, and bars ready to drain your wallet. Jazz, rock, punk, techno, trance, tribal, neo-psychedelic-whatever—all co-exist happily side by side, in addition to a rapidly developing Asian and world-beat scene. The new London is as cosmopolitan as it's ever been, back on the cutting edge of the art, music, and fashion worlds—and there's actually good food now (some of it even English, for chrissake). The vibe is definitely upbeat. To get the lowdown on just about everything, pick up a copy of *Time Out* at any newsstand. It lists everything from films to special sales and comes out each Wednesday. Smaller magazines like *Sleaze Nation* also contain listings and can be found in many of the trendy shops off Oxford Street. The 411 on raves and one-off parties is generally publicized on fliers, which get stuck on walls and piled high by the doors of many shops. Just remember though, this city ain't cheap, so keep an eye on what you spend (definitely in pubs, where it's easy to lose track) if you want to get to know London's myriad personalities.

four things to talk to a local about

1. **Middle America:** The English are absolutely intrigued by the vast, flat expanse of America that's just overflowing with homicidal/suicidal kids, hysterically ignorant yokels, and guys with big mullet hairstyles. True or not, the stereotype comes up a lot when locals realize you're from across the pond.
2. **Football:** Just don't call it soccer. Ask a local to explain the special thrill when a big game ends in a tie.
3. **Movies:** Most kids have a recent favorite, whether it be American extravaganzas or local flicks.
4. **Raving Back in the Day:** Many Londoners enjoy reminiscing about the heady days before everybody figured out that lots of sketchy drugs and loud music probably aren't that good for the head.

The English have a reputation for being standoffish, but they're actually generally friendly and love to talk, especially to people from the "colonies," and *especially* after a few pints. You've really got nothing to lose striking up a conversation, and hey, they speak English! Your only risk might be getting snagged on the end of a sharp wit. Just don't get too riled up if you think someone's picking on you; they're probably just "taking the piss out of you"—a national sport. Favorite subjects to ridicule Americans about include our penchant for oversize clothing and our slang—but, like, *duuude*, people in glass houses...[see *say what?*, below].

neighborhoods

While it appears to have been built with little to no planning, there is some semblance of structure within London's sprawl. The city center is usually divided into the City, the spot where London began, and the **West End,** a cluster of neighborhoods most people consider the city's true center. Many of the major tourist spots are in a small area just north of the Thames River and are easily walkable. **Trafalgar Square** is a good place to orient yourself, with the **National Gallery,** the **National Portrait Gallery** [see *culture zoo,* below, for both], **Nelson's Column,** and all that other good stuff (including pesky pigeons) at hand. To the north is **Soho,** thronged both day and night by a mix of tourists and locals, with hundreds of quirky little boutiques, record stores, pubs, and clubs to check out. Due south is **Whitehall,** home to all the grand official buildings including **No. 10 Downing Street** (home of the Prime Minister), and further south is **Westminster** of **Westminster Abbey** fame [see *culture zoo,* below].

Southwest takes you past the **ICA** [see *arts scene,* below] and beautiful **St. James Park** to **Buckingham Palace;** you keep going south to reach stylish **Chelsea,** where famous artists from Oscar Wilde to Mick Jagger lived once, and where rich yuppies live now, in spectacular houses. Northwest of Chelsea is **Kensington,** named for the palace nearby. Some of London's best shops, and its only Urban Outfitters, are along **Kensington High Street.** For a funky bit of shopping, **Portobello Road,** in nauseatingly famous **Notting Hill,** west of Kensington, has a weekend market as well as a host of cool shops and bars.

West of Trafalgar is the super-swanky shopping area bordered by **Regent** and **Piccadilly** streets. Further west there's more luxurious living and shopping in **Mayfair** and **Park Lane** until you reach the truly enormous **Hyde Park** [see *great outdoors,* below].

Just north of Trafalgar, **Theaterland**—a clot of big, glitzy theaters along **Shaftesbury Avenue** and **Leicester Square**—also has more than its fair share of bars, restaurants, and tourists. London's small but lively **Chinatown** is just north of Leicester Square, and a short walk east gets you to trendy **Covent Garden,** crammed with bars and shops appealing to teenagers and upscale artsy-fartsy types alike. **Bloomsbury,** home of the **British Museum** [see *culture zoo,* below] and London University, sits just north of Covent Garden and Soho. Kind of dull at the moment, the

12 hours in london

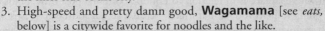

1. Skip the tourbuses, climb atop the nearest **double decker** and let it show you London's sometimes cluttered and confusing charm from on high.
2. Visit the **Victoria and Albert** [see *culture zoo,* below] so you can appreciate the finer side of the city.
3. High-speed and pretty damn good, **Wagamama** [see *eats,* below] is a citywide favorite for noodles and the like.
4. Narrow and unassuming, Berwick Street, in the heart of Soho, is lined with some of London's best record shops, like **Selectadisc** [see *stuff,* below].
5. No trip to London is complete without purchasing some ludicrously priced clothes, the best of which can be found in and around Covent Garden's **Neal Street** [see *stuff,* below].
6. Not even the East Village compares to the slightly played-out freak scene at the **Camden Market** [see *stuff,* below].
7. Go see some legit. With literally more theaters than one could visit in a year, there's bound to be something worthwhile being performed [see *arts scene,* below].
8. An integral part of the English social fabric, drinking in the pub is critical to seeing England as the locals do—slightly blurry and spinning [see *bar scene,* below].
9. The birthplace of rave culture, London's clubs top America's biggest and best with both hands tied. **The End** [see *club scene,* below] is one of the coolest, not to mention the loudest.
10. Wind up the night with a few friends and some beers on top of **Primrose Hill** [see *hanging out,* below], a popular park with a kick-ass view of the city's historic skyline.

neighborhood owns a place in literary history as home to the moody, randy geniuses of the Bloomsbury Group, including Virginia Woolf, Bertrand Russell, and John Maynard Keynes. Farther north, popular with crusty punkers as well as colorful ravers, the streets of **Camden Town** (aka Camden) are cluttered with young people shopping the crowded market or stumbling from one local pub to another.

To the east, on the south side of the Thames, **Bankside** houses big draws like the **Museum of the Moving Image,** the **Design Museum,** the spankin' new **Tate Gallery of Modern Art** [see *culture zoo,* below, for all three], and the **Globe Theatre** [see *arts scene,* below].

For its gritty appeal and a bounty of hipster hangouts like **Dogstar** [see *bar scene,* below], **Brixton,** in South London—at the very end of the Victoria line of the Tube—is well worth the schlep. A largely Caribbean neighborhood, Brixton is notoriously dangerous, but the almost complete absence of handguns makes it seem less so in comparison to equally famous spots in New York or L.A. Also worth checking out are some neighborhoods on the make, including North London's **Islington,** a grownup version of Camden, and nearby **Stoke Newington,** which has a multi-culti vibe along **Church Street.**

The city is sectioned into boroughs and postal districts, delineated by combinations of letters and numbers posted on the wall-mounted signs about town (WE6, SE4, etc.). They're actually directional markers telling you where a place is in relation to London's original post office. Not that it's going to help you all that much, because actual addresses doesn't seem to be regulated in any way. Some places don't even have numbers. To make matters worse, most people just use the neighborhood name to locate themselves. That's why people mean Camden Town, not the larger borough of Camden, when they tell you to check out the shopping in Camden.

Thankfully, the omnipresent Tube goes just about everywhere (but shuts down at midnight), and buses will get you to the more secluded sections of the city. Just tell the driver your destination, and he'll not only stop at the appropriate spot, but point you in the right direction. Walking can be a pain, but it's your best bet in clogged and crowded Soho, Leicester Square, and Covent Garden. All too familiar with the difficulties of finding and getting to where they need to be, Londoners rely on their beloved taxi drivers—not to be confused with minicab drivers [see *need to know,* below]—who must spend two whole years in training to gain *The Knowledge* of the streets. For those without the time or inclination to memorize every back alley in town, there is the **London A-Z.** Known as the "A to Zed," this indispensable book maps out the whole city, with a street-finding index in the back. Don't worry about looking like a tourist whipping yours out on the street; most locals have at least one copy, too. If you really can't find what you're looking for, just ask somebody; Londoners live in a heavily touristed city, but they're secretly proud of it and bear few grudges against confused travelers.

hanging out

Sprawling as well as plagued by lousy weather, London lacks landmark hangouts like Astor Place and St. Mark's in New York's East Village. Sure, there are places like Leicester Square and Neal Street, always crammed with mad people, but there are few places famous for just plain chillin'. Fortunately, people are friendly for the most part, and often quite interested in what visitors think of their town. A note to Yanks: Curiosity aside, many English people assume young American tourists are uncouth goofballs (now, where would they get *that* idea?), so try to muster a little polish when making new friends.

only here

So, you know the steering wheel is on the right side, chips are fries, and there's more nudity on TV. But a lesser-known idiosyncratic attraction is London's pirate radio scene. Anyone with a cell phone and a transmitter can set up shop *Pump Up the Volume*–style. While few of the stations have broadcasters as scandalous as Hard Harry, most play different types of dance music, interspersed with shout-outs and commercials for upcoming events. Pirate radio enjoys de facto legitimacy by virtue of its popularity. **Freak FM 101.8** and **Kool FM 94.6** are two popular broadcasts specializing in garage and jungle.

For skaters, there's **South Bank,** which is right opposite the Strand on the Thames by Waterloo Bridge. This patch of concrete underneath the National Film Theater is an all-weather favorite of skateboarders, in-line skaters, and their hangers-on, who artfully outmaneuver the corporate types out for their lunchtime jog.

If the risk of grievous bodily harm is too much to stomach, another nice place to relax and enjoy a spot of good weather is **Regents Park.** Accessible by Tube (*Regents Park* stop), this expanse of gardens houses the London Zoo as well as a boating lake. Oh yeah, and you can drink beer in public, so why not unwind with a nice cold one?

Or try North London's **Primrose Hill,** just across Prince Albert Road from the northern edge of Regents Park. Much smaller and significantly less spectacular, the hill sports one of the best views of downtown London you can find. The view does the skyline justice only at night, though, when the park becomes home to lots of small groups of young people getting wasted one way or the other. The only catch is getting there directly. While the *Swiss Cottage, St. John's Wood,* and *Chalk Farm* Tube stops all put you within a few blocks, a visit requires a short walk and your trusty *A-Z.*

For meeting people late at night, nothing really compares to a wander through **Soho.** Convenient to just about every night bus and minicab operator in the city, the Soho streets between Tottenham Court Road and Leicester Square stay crowded long after most bars have closed. Both locals and tourists wander around in search of munchies at the Chinese restaurants on Lisle Street, the many kebab stands, the 24-hour **Café Bohème** [see *bar scene,* below], or the **Burger King** on Tottenham Court Road and Oxford Street.

Despite the range of places to go at all hours, London is still mostly an early city. The social hub of the city, its pubs, are the places to schmooze for most locals, even those too young to drink. Most pubs (stylish theme bars aside) are local joints visited by regulars who've been drinking and watching football (soccer) together year after year. For the indispensable English experience, head to the neighborhood pub on the night of an important football match. The crowds, the cheers, and the beer raining out of upheld pint glasses is a truly pagan religious experience. If the dive around the corner is just too awful to bear, try **Flask** *(77 Highgate West Hill; Tel 0208/340-72-60; Tube to Highgate; 11am-11pm Mon-Sat, noon-10:30pm Sun; AE, MC, V)* by Hampstead Heath, or **Sir Richard Steele** *(97 Haverstock Hill; Tel 0207/483-12-61; Tube to Belsize Park or Chalk Farm; 11am-11pm Mon-Sat, noon-10:30pm Sun; No credit cards)*. Both of these North London pubs capture the multigenerational community vibe in the comforting surroundings of traditional English pub decor.

bar scene

Drinking verges on sport for the English, who consume alcohol to such excess that bars' taps sometimes actually go dry before midnight. No great pastime is without its shrines, and London has thousands of bars and pubs that elevate getting wasted to new heights. Pubs are also, of course, the places to sample pub grub, which varies in quality but almost always seems to have some kind of internal organ in it.

boy meets girl

Since so much of London's social scene revolves around getting pissed, pickups are often heavy-handed. If the club is loud, you can even forget about pickup lines. From the boy's perspective, the modus operandi is basic:

1) Casual chitchat shouted into the woman's ear
2) A drink is offered
3) Maybe a dance (if venue permits)
4) If steps 1-3 have gone well, numbers are exchanged.

But it's important to remember that English gals aren't shy about getting what they want, either. Though many expect the man to make a move, British women are less reserved than many puritanical Americans when it comes to romance. All that said, it's important to recognize when to kick game and when to step back. For starters, neighborhood pubs are not the place to aggressively mack. Save the James Bond act for a bustling club or bar, where the vibe is more conducive to meeting and greeting. If the bar scene is too intimidating, raves and clubby spots are filled with eager and inebriated people of all persuasions looking for love—or at least its convincing imitation.

A scuzzy, dingy pub right in midst of the Camden Market **The Elephants Head** *(224 Camden High St.; Tel 0207/485-31-30; 11am-11pm Mon-Sat, noon-10:30pm Sun; No credit cards)* is a punk version of the traditional local, serving greasy sandwiches alongside beer and booze. It's populated by a hodgepodge of elderly alcoholics and mohawked punks trapped in 1977, so there's little chance of bumping into a group of camera-toting tourists while sipping a pint here (so stash that camera!).

The World's End *(174 Camden High St.; Tel 0207/482-19-32; Tube to Camden Town; 11am-11pm Mon-Sat, noon-10:30pm Sun; No credit cards)* is an oft-mentioned, classic piece of the Camden scene. Catering to a raucous and inexplicably immense mob of indie-rocking teens and college-age misanthropes, the pub serves the standard food and drinks. But after the quaint front area, the decor veers into the bizarre—the back bar resembles some sort of dream town with mock storefronts and streetlights. As at all pubs, the hours favor compulsive and early drinking, both rooms filling up with throngs of punters by early evening.

Housed in a truly amazing space, **Dogstar** *(389 Coldharbour Lane; Tel 0207/733-75-15; Tube to Brixton; Noon-2:30am Mon-Thur, noon-4am Fri, Sat, noon-12:30am Sun; AE, MC, V)* puts most bars to shame and is well worth the trip to Brixton. High ceilings, a large bar, a good number of spacious tables, and an *X-Files* pinball machine all make for a comfortable, uncramped vibe. Well-priced double shots and a wide selection of standard beers are the main attractions—and the rotating lineup of DJs never hurts. The tunes tend toward house, with a smattering of techno and electronica thrown in, although Dogstar neither looks nor feels like a rave. Beware of bigger crowds and cover charges on weekends.

Known mostly as a nightclub, **Bar Rhumba** [see *club scene*, below] also has a fantastic happy hour from 5pm till 9pm, before things get really swinging at night. Both the bar and the nearby booths get packed with cool and friendly regulars drawn by reasonable prices and excellent music, ranging from soul to hip-hop to jungle and back. The decor is pretty plain, but the nice vibe makes Bar Rhumba a worthwhile stop for a drink or three. A smartly fashionable dress code is enforced only on Saturday nights.

Dark and airy, the **Beat Bar** *(265 Portobello Rd.; Tel 0207/792-20-43; Tube to Ladbroke Grove; 11am-11pm daily; No credit cards)* is a long and narrow hipster pub near the end of trendy Portobello Road. Even with quirky art exhibits and a slew of DJs spinning anything from hip-hop to jungle to Latin jazz, this bar is mysteriously uncrowded. The simple food is good, the staff groovy, and the few customers funny and amicable. Ideal for catching a drink while scouring the markets and shops in Notting Hill.

Attracting a diverse, clubby clientele, **Junction** *(242 Coldharbour Lane; Tel 0207/738-40-00; Laughborough Junction Rail or Bus P4, 35, 45, 345; 4pm-midnight Mon, till 11pm Tue, Wed, till 2am Thur, Fri, noon-2am Sat, noon-midnight Sun; AE, MC, V)* serves up a good range of well-priced beers, especially during the lengthy happy hours: all day on Mondays and from 4pm to 8pm all other nights. Music runs the gamut of DJ-driven styles, with regular appearances by both lesser-known talents as well as big

london pub crawl

One of the dandiest ways to explore the city, other than aimless wandering around the West End, is to set aside an evening for a classic, leisurely pub crawl. This one begins at Piccadilly Circus and ends in Covent Garden. After exiting the Tube station, head right on Shaftesbury Avenue. A block and a half along, on the righthand side, **Bar Rhumba's** evening happy hour beckons. Crowded with cool and friendly locals of the New Media, scenester variety, Rhumba exudes a vibe of cultivated hipness. Soak it up over a pint or two, then bounce out the door and continue right until you hit Wardour Street. Hang a left and keep going until you reach gay Soho's main drag, Old Compton Street; take a right. Keep going till you come to Frith Street; go left and walk a couple of blocks until you reach **Garlic and Shots,** on the right. Stop in for a quick "bloodshot" against a background of grinding industrial tunes, then head back out to Old Compton Street to resume your course toward Charing Cross Road. One block before you get to that bustling avenue, stop in at **Café Bohème** to rinse the garlic taste out of your mouth with the after-work crowd. Then head back out to Charing Cross Road and take a left. Cross at the circle and walk down Earlham Street for about two blocks until you come upon the busy shopping area around Neal Street. Just before you get to that pedestrian walkway, duck into the basement space of the **Freedom Brewery** to sample some of London's finest microbrews amid stark modern surroundings. By the time you've had enough of the elitist brew, not to mention the elitist patrons, it may be time to call it a night. Just hang a right on Neal Street, walk two blocks to Covent Garden station and head home, drunk and not, mind you, too disorderly [see *bar scene,* above and below, for all bars mentioned].

names like Bassment Jaxx. The huge crowds are always up for it, and their enthusiasm seems to have taken a toll on the scruffy interior. Most nights have no cover charge, and it's pretty reasonable when it's required.

The somewhat precious microbrew craze sweeping the States has hit England now, too. **Freedom Brewery** *(41 Earlham St.; Tel 0207/240-06-06; Tube to Covent Garden; 10:30am-midnight Mon-Sat, noon-11:30pm Sun; www.freedombrew.com; MC, V)* offers four different kinds of boutique beers brewed on site, in the basement of the Thomas Neals shopping center in trendy Covent Garden. The bar's staff seem hipper than the yuppie customers. But the beers are quite good, as is the low-key, moderately priced Italian food.

Down along the banks of the Regents Canal, off Camden High Road, **Dingwalls** *(Camden Lock; Tel 0207/267-15-77; Tube to Camden Town; 7:30pm-12:30am Mon-Thur, 7pm-midnight Fri, Sat; No credit cards)* is a massive indoor/outdoor bar with a bumping nightclub and an upstairs comedy club on the premises. It's lovely on a warm summer night, with a number of outdoor tables set under parasols, and if the weather or crowds seem inhospitable, there's plenty of room indoors. The club space,

five of the best pubs

Hitting the local pub is as much a part of your average Brit's lifestyle as eating and sleeping, and even though London is much more sophisticated than the rest of Britain, the same applies here when it comes to passion for the pub. And although you can't swing a dead cat without hitting a pub in the city, there are a few that are just superior when it comes to ambience, location, and/or history. **Freemason's Arms** *(32 Downshire Hill; Tel 0207/433-68-11; Tube to Hampstead; 11am-11pm weekdays and Sat, noon-10:30pm Sun)* is right next to the Hampstead Heath and down the road from Hampstead High Street. It has a wonderful garden with benches that is perfect for a sundowner or a lazy weekend mid-afternoon pint. **The Clifton** *(96 Clifton Hill; Tel 0207/624-52-33)*, in nearby St. John's Wood, is much more formal in decor with drapes and armchairs, lending the feel of sitting in a library. Another North London suburb, Maida Vale, has the **Warrington** *(93 Warrington Crescent; Tel 0207/286-29-29; Tube to Maida Vale; 11am-11pm Mon-Sat, noon-10:30pm Sun; All major credit cards)* as its local. Apart from the fussy decorative lamps, porch columns and glazed tiles at the entrance, the huge saloon bar inside is a great place to grab a pint and take it outside to the many small tables and chairs on the sidewalk. **Ye Olde Cheshire Cheese** *(145 Fleet St.; Tel 0207/353-61-70; Tube to Blackfriars; Open till 9pm daily)* is olde England at its best. This 1667 tavern is set in the heart of what used to be London's newspaper hub. Once there, take a stroll down Fleet Street, which has a lot of great old buildings. And finally, the **Cow Saloon Bar** *(89 Westbourne Park Rd.; Tel 0207/221-00-21; Tube to Bayswater, Edgeware Rd., or Lancaster Gate)* is a popular one for its buzzy ambience attributable to its small size, as well as the outdoor garden.

london

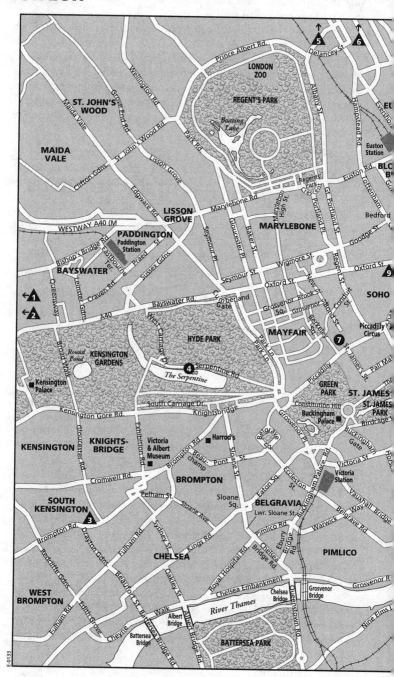

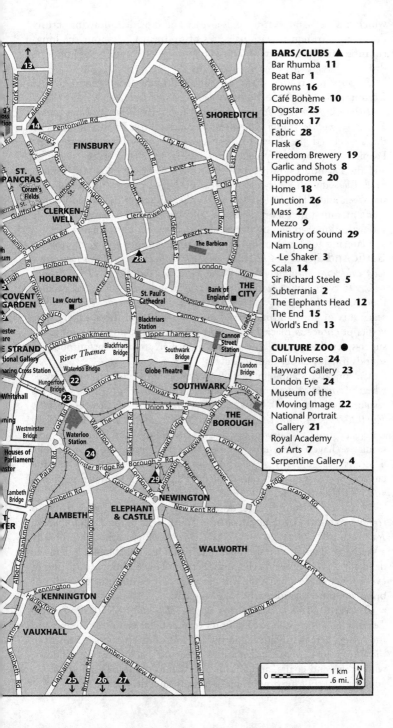

BARS/CLUBS ▲

Bar Rhumba **11**
Beat Bar **1**
Browns **16**
Café Bohème **10**
Dogstar **25**
Equinox **17**
Fabric **28**
Flask **6**
Freedom Brewery **19**
Garlic and Shots **8**
Hippodrome **20**
Home **18**
Junction **26**
Mass **27**
Mezzo **9**
Ministry of Sound **29**
Nam Long
 -Le Shaker **3**
Scala **14**
Sir Richard Steele **5**
Subterrania **2**
The Elephants Head **12**
The End **15**
World's End **13**

CULTURE ZOO ●

Dalí Universe **24**
Hayward Gallery **23**
London Eye **24**
Museum of the
 Moving Image **22**
National Portrait
 Gallery **21**
Royal Academy
 of Arts **7**
Serpentine Gallery **4**

which has a separate entrance, is sweaty and crowded, drawing scruffy dudes and women in various states of undress. Check out the long-running Metalheadz party on Sundays for a good sampling of London's drum 'n' bass scene.

Smack-dab in the thick of Soho's thriving bar scene on Old Compton Road is **Café Bohème** *(13-17 Old Compton St.; Tel 0207/ 734-06-23; Tube to Leicester Sq.; 8am-3am Mon-Wed, 24 hours Thur-Sat, 9am-midnight Sun; AE, MC, V)*, a classy little Paris-style brasserie that's a relaxed alternative to the packed bars that abound in the area. People lounge on comfy couches, as well as on chairs on the sidewalk, and the bar offers a respectable assortment of drinks plus tasty French food. Blessed with a late-night license, the bar stays open till 3am during the week and all night long on weekends. Although the fashion police aren't manning the door, the music and crowd tend toward an upscale sophistication, typified by the regular evening jazz performances.

Catering to the seemingly incompatible yuppie and goth crowds, **Garlic and Shots** *(14 Frith St.; Tel 0207/439-19-11; Tube to Tottenham Court Rd.; 5pm-midnight Mon-Wed, 6pm-1am Thur-Sat, 5-11:30pm Sun; MC, V)* serves a huge selection of beer, booze, and garlic-saturated Swedish food. Cramped seating and a soggy downstairs bar serve it up, while a scary mix of goth and industrial music blares from the speakers. The vodka of choice is Black Death, and the bar's most popular shot is the super-spicy "bloodshot." A vampire's nightmare, this indoor/outdoor bar sounds much weirder than it really is.

Celebrated restaurateur Terence Conran is known for his love of space when it comes to designing the latest hipster food spot (i.e., all of his restaurants are massive). **Mezzo** *(100 Wardour St.; Tel 0207/314-40-00, Fax 0207/314-40-40; Tube to Leicester Sq./Piccadilly Circus; AE, MC, V)* is no exception. It's fairly pricey to eat here and the food is nothing spectacular, so have a drink or two at the bar, as the atmosphere is unbeatable. There is a large bar upstairs and a smaller one downstairs, where the chances of snagging a table are higher. It's a great spot for meeting friends and it's right in the heart of Soho.

If you're a cocktail fanatic, do not waste your time on flash bars. Go straight to **Nam Long-Le Shaker** in South Kensington *(159 Brompton Rd.; Tel 0207/373-19-26 or 0207/370-35-81)* which, although primarily a Vietnamese restaurant, has a bar that is a lot less lethal looking than the drinks it serves. Enter the Flaming Ferrari. This bad boy, consisting of every imaginable spirit that will get you wasted and quickly, will not bring you fond memories the following day.

Browns *(82-84 St. Martin's Lane; Tel 0207/497-50-50; Tube to Leicester Sq.)* is another of London's very popular chain restaurants but the atmosphere is still great, and the bar area of this particular Browns in the West End/Covent Garden area is open and spacious by the windows, with tables and chairs, and affords a view into the restaurant. It's also a good central spot for pre-theater or after-theater drinks.

LIVE MUSIC SCENE

As in most of the rest of the world, London's rock 'n' roll scene is gradually vanishing underneath a massive pile of records and samplers. That isn't to say that long hair and power chords have completely disappeared, but rather that they're no longer at the heart of London's massive music scene. But a glance at the listings for concerts and shows in any of this town's numerous newspapers and magazines proves that Londoners do love a good concert. Seemingly every band of import passes through town, from the biggest arena-rock groups to the most way-out world-music ensembles. While shows take place in small clubs tucked away in the labyrinth of London's streets, several major venues consistently book the best and brightest on the national and international scene. At the smaller places, expect to pay £3 to £10.

Less conventional bands avoid the über-venues in favor of cooler concert halls like **Brixton Academy** *(211 Stockwell Rd.; Tel 0207/924-99-99; Tube to Brixton; Hours vary; MC, V)*, in South London, which packs in thousands for shows ranging from Lauryn Hill to the Chemical Brothers. The space is intimate, but there's still enough of it to stand around and look cool in.

Another London venue housed in a converted theater, **Shepherds Bush Empire** *(Shepherds Bush Green; Tel 0207/771-20-00; Tube to Shepherd's Bush; Hours vary; MC, V)* offers a decent atmosphere, better acoustics, and box seats available for booking. Dedicated to musical variety, the Empire hosts everything from Sebadoh to world music performances. It's owned and operated as a counterpart to South London's **Clapham Grand** *(Clapham Junction, St. John's Hill; No phone; Clapham Junction train station via Waterloo or Victoria; Hours vary; MC, V)*, a fairly standard rock venue.

FIVE-O

The English hear all the stories about lawlessness and police brutality and wonder how Americans manage to stay alive. Their own impressions of the police are far more benign. While Scotland Yard doesn't have the reputation of being the friendliest police force on Earth, the officers are generally courteous and patient with tourists. Nevertheless, they can and will bust people for their misbehavior. If you don't wind up drunk and pantless in Leicester Square, or decide to roll joints on the Tube, you shouldn't have any trouble. Use your head, don't steal, and treat the officers with the respect they will probably accord you, even as they arrest you.

One of the biggest of England's concert arenas, the legendary **Wembley** *(Empire Way; Tel 0208/902-09-02; Tube to Wembley Park)*, is closed for renovation until 2002.

Another internationally known venue is the **Royal Albert Hall** *(Kensington Fore; Tel 0207/589-82-12; Tube to S. Kensington; AE, MC, V)*, which plays host to loads of big-name acts in addition to regular opera performances. The venue itself is an enormous Victorian concert hall, suitably extravagant for the range of glitzy, heavy-hitting events it hosts year-round. They're in the process of a renovation, and many hope it'll sharpen the sometimes spacey acoustics.

Everything from swing to free jazz can be found in London, but two venues consistently get recommended by the locals. The first is the legendary **Ronnie Scott's** *(47 Frith St.; Tel 0207/439-07-47; Tube to Tottenham Court Rd.; 8:30pm-late daily; £5-20 cover; AE, MC, V)*, London's most respected jazz venue. Small and hazy with cigarette smoke, the club hosts two nightly shows by some of jazz's leading heavyweights. Vibes virtuoso of the '70s Roy Ayers recently held down two weeks of nightly gigs, but the music often treads less funkified territory.

If the traditional jazz-joint vibe at Ronnie Scott's doesn't tickle your fancy, head to the **Jazz Café** *(5 Parkway; Tel 0208/963-09-40; Tube to Camden Town; 7pm-1am Mon-Thur, 7pm-2am Fri-Sat, noon-4pm/7pm-midnight Sun; Cover £6-18; www.jazzcafe.co.uk; MC, V)* for a more new-school experience. While still booking big names like McCoy Tyner, the Jazz Café will also reel in performers like Fred Wesley and Lynn Collins of James Brown fame. The smooth, modern space is cool and accessible, as is the balcony restaurant. The food is equally modern (European) and pretty good.

club scene

While mainstream pop music has spiraled down into Boyband Hell, London's underground scene has created some of the most progressive and exciting music of the past decade. Styles ranging from tech-house to neurofunk aren't just for ravers in wacky clothes any more. Clubbing is a national pastime for the English, and London is unquestionably the place. *Time Out* lists what's on where, but less commercial events advertise via fliers, which can be had at pretty much every club/bar/shop in the city. Dress codes, attitudes, and door policies vary from place to place, as do the peak times to groove. For more options, check out the mixed parties listed in the Gay Scene [see below].

A good number of London's most beloved DJs work at dance record shops like **Black Market** [see *ground zero of the club scene,* below], so a visit to any one of London's gazillion vinyl emporiums may offer the chance to rub elbows with a spinning star.

Bar Rhumba *(36 Shaftesbury Ave.; Tel 0207/287-69-33; Tube to Piccadilly Circus; 5pm-3:30am Mon-Thur, till 4am Fri, 7pm-6am Sat, 8pm-2am Sun; Cover £3-12; MC, V)* heats things up until well after midnight with a fantastic sound system, top talent, and a clientele of cool regulars.

genrefication

Unless you've taken some interest in the whole electronica frenzy, the array of musical styles, from house to hardcore, is really confusing. Evolved out of the dance music of the '70s and '80s, today's styles derive from disco, hip-hop, and early electronic geniuses like Kraftwerk and Stockhausen. Here's a simple breakdown of some of dance music's ever-multiplying subgenres:

House: A direct descendant of disco, house music is named after the Chicago club where its earliest fans went dancing. Today, house can be soulful and smooth or hard and futuristic. It's always recognizable by strong, disco-y beats.

Techno: Also imported from America's Midwest, techno has taken London by storm. Utilizing all sorts of electronic gadgetry, producers have married synthetic sounds and rhythms to the steady bounce of house music.

Garage: House music's soulful cousin, garage is currently all the rage in London. Using soulful vocals, MC raps, and deep bass lines, garage is faster and more in-your-face than house.

Big Beat: Fusing techno production with the funky beats of hip-hop, big beat/breakbeat is the most accessible style of dance music. Artists like Prodigy and Fatboy Slim have made this style extremely popular.

Jungle/Drum 'n' Bass: Drawing from sources as diverse as dub, reggae, hip-hop, jazz, and techno, jungle and drum 'n' bass utilize staccato beats and tearing bass lines to devastating effect. The lighter sounds known as intelligent are a good deal easier on the ears of the uninitiated.

Trance: Recognizable by its trademark buildups, trance is like melodramatic techno, energetic but often repetitive.

Hardcore: Lost somewhere between techno and jungle, hardcore is fast and pounding. Less funky than drum 'n' bass, it's like techno on speed.

Movement Thursdays, hosted by drum 'n' bass luminaries Bryan G and Ray Keith, is one of the best in England. While things get moving on the dance floor, the bar keeps up a mellower blend of hip-hop and soul. Also check out the Monday night party hosted by James Lavelle of UNKLE fame, who spins jazz and funky stuff to a less rowdy crowd. The vibe is

Rules of the Game

Although England's drinking age is 18, the only aspect of the liquor law that's strictly enforced regards drunk driving. So it looks like you can take a beer onto the streets without fear. As for recreational drugs, they're all illegal. Hash is commonplace, since it's relatively cheap, and hard drugs are around, but most party-goers seem to be happy with some drinks and the old club favorite, E. In fact, about three million English people roll face every weekend. When they're in season, magic mushrooms grow wild in Hampstead Heath. Needless to say, drugs of any type are risky, so don't buy any crap from sketchy strangers on the street, and be careful mixing intoxicants. Most clubs either provide EMTs or can sort you out with the medical attention you need. Scary, huh?

chilled-out, focusing more on the music and social scene than on fashion or connections. Cool but within reach of those tired of the relentless pursuit of trendiness, Bar Rhumba is a standout.

Another venue with a strong reputation among the party people is **The End** *(18 West Central St.; Tel 0207/419-91-99; Tube to Tottenham Court Rd.; 10pm-3am Tue-Thur, till 5am Fri, till 7am Sat, 8pm-4am Sun; No credit cards),* the undisputed clubber's club, boasting one of the best sound systems in England. Massive crowds jam the dance floor each night. The music tends toward the rave-oriented, with house, jungle, techno, and garage all well represented alongside chiller sounds and hip-hop. Its location not far from Soho and the rest of the West End guarantees a slightly pricey cover (£8 to £13), but it's well worth it.

Another destination for those in search of well-heeled hedonism is the world-famous **Ministry of Sound** *(103 Gaunt St.; Tel 0207/378-65-28; Tube to Elephant and Castle; 10:30pm-6am Fri, midnight-9am Sat; Cover £10-15; No credit cards),* London's answer to the bygone New York superclub. Featuring internationally renowned DJs spinning uptempo house, techno, trance, and breaks, Ministry attracts a decked-out mob of seriously intoxicated clubbers stoked to dance until dawn. The downsides include occasionally brutal cover charges and choosy bouncers enforcing the smart dress code.

The Scala *(275 Pentonville Rd.; Tel 0207/833-20-19; Tube to King's Cross/St. Pancras; 8pm-2am Mon-Thur, 10pm-5am Fri, Sat, 7pm-midnight Sun; www.scala-london.co.uk; No credit cards)* does it all—food, drinks, cinema, theater—but it remains best-known for its club nights. Just north of collegiate Bloomsbury in a drab part of town, Scala's multiple floors and varied attractions draw a down-to-earth crowd of punters and hotties. The club's featured musical styles are eclectic, with Thursday night *Scratch* parties bringing top hip-hop to London, complete with some of the best break dancing this side of *Beat Street*. Other nights offer up anything from reggae to alt theater.

Subterania *(12 Acklam Rd.; Tel 0208/960-45-90; Tube to Ladbroke Grove; 8pm-2am Mon-Thur, 10pm-3am Fri, Sat, 8pm-midnight Sun; AE, MC, V)*, deservedly has a strong rep for booking quirky acts in its unusual space. Located underneath the elevated train tracks at the tail end of Portobello Market, this club aggressively supports up-and-coming talent like hip-hoppers Company Flow and also established acts like Israel Vibration. It's one of London's more consistently bumping venues, featuring a strong roster of hip-hop, dance, and R&B nights as well as one-off concerts and parties. When they aren't drinking, the patrons throng to the circular dance floor. There are a few tables and chairs set in odd nooks and crannies along the walls for those too shy to get funky.

Housed on an upper floor of what was once a gigantic church, **Mass** *(St. Matthews Church, Brixton Hill; Tel 0207/738-52-55; Tube to Brixton; 10pm-6am Fri-Sat, 6pm-1am Sun; MC, V)* is split into two rooms, one of which has a large stage. The other room features a balcony overlooking a downstairs dance floor and DJ booth. The dress code is street style and the diverse crowd couldn't care less. The music tends towards the dark and gritty, with both DJs and bands representing on the weekends. Known for going late, the party doesn't even get really packed until after other bars and pubs have closed down for the night. Highlights include the monthly installment of Bar Rhumba's *Movement* party, as well as the funky hybrid of Indian instrumentation and electronic energy at *Air Swaraj*.

Hit happenin' EC1 with a night at **Fabric** *(77A Charterhouse St.; Tel 0207/490-04-44; Tube to Farringdon; Open regular club days and hours; www.fabric-london.com)*, which, along with Home, are two of the newer clubs to hit London's larger-than-life clubbing scene, with the intention of seducing a range of clubbers not only in the 18-24 division. The three dance floors are outfitted with audiovisual technology to make the most jaded DJ weep, including satellite-ready plasma screens. If you need a break from the deep house, U.S. garage, breakbeats, and drum 'n' bass, there's an escape route via an elevator to the roof terrace.

Home *(1 Leicester Sq.; Tel 0207/964-19-99; Tube to Leicester Sq.; Open regular club days and hours)* is spread luxuriously over seven floors, with a top-floor restaurant, a members bar below—named aptly enough for the cooler-than-thou 'At Home'—a club bar, and the main event, a double-volume, 1,200 capacity dance space. There's also another dance floor as well as a multimedia cafe (why not?), but the devoted 'homies' go Home more for the trancey house and garage, not to mention the appeal of Saturdays with resident DJ Paul Oakenfeld.

If you're not a lover of garage, and perhaps are not even too sure what that means when it doesn't refer to the place where you put your car, and are longing for some good, old-fashioned disco (i.e., mainstream dance tunes), both the **Hippodrome** *(Charing Cross Rd.; Tel 0207/437-43-11; Tube to Leicester Sq.; Thur-Sat)* and **Equinox** *(Leicester Sq.; Tel 0207/437-14-46; Tube to Leicester Sq.; Open regular club days and hours)* on Leicester Square, have going what you're craving. The Hippodrome is majorly untrendy when it comes to what's hot in London now, but it can't be beat for a larger-than-life laser, lights, dancers-in-a-cage-type feel. You'll probably bump into more tourists here than at Fabric, for instance, but at least when the Backstreet Boys come on the sound system, you'll know you're among kindred spirits.

arts scene

Having spent the past decade dragging itself out of the doghouse, London has rebounded big time. Art, music, film, fashion, and food have become some of London's hottest cultural exports—including Saatchi's *Sensation* that created all the hoopla in New York—attracting all manner of artists and fashionistas to its galleries, boutiques, and special events, like the incomparably stylish biannual London Fashion Week.

bookworms

Though the literary scenes London once hosted—like Dr. Johnson's or Virginia Woolf's—no longer exist, the city does have a bookish side. In addition to being more articulate than most Americans, it would appear that the English read more, too. One of the newer and cooler celebrations of the English scene is the **Clerkenwell Literary Festival** *(www.clerkenwell.barts.com),* held each July. Sponsored by artsy heavy hitters like David Bowie, the festival is a multimedia celebration of new and old works and their connections to the rest of London's vibrant arts scene. Held in venues as diverse as Dickens' house and **Turnmills** [see *gay scene,* below], the festival includes films and performances by DJs and groups like the Beta Band. Readings and the like take place every day in a variety of changing venues all over the city. Check *Time Out* or **Waterstone's** bookstore [see *stuff,* below] for specs.

The highbrow and lowbrow mix pretty comfortably here, as witnessed by the yearly furor over the prestigious Booker prize. Everyone argues over the final outcome—in 1977, Chairman Philip Larkin threatened to jump out a window if Paul Scott's *Staying On* didn't win (it did)—and the result is almost always unpopular with the critics. This distinctly eggheaded passion is matched only by the excitement generated at betting shops when people wager on the outcome of this literary event. Booker and bookies—a match made in England's green and pleasant land.

ELEMENTS of design

From the outrageous window displays of Carnaby Street to the sleek interiors of Ian Schrager's latest hotel, London cool is never more present than when it involves interior design. There are a coupla spots to check out on a day's wandering that offer a taste of what some of the hottest designers about are up to. The aforementioned Ian Schrager has two hotels in the city: **St. Martin's Lane** *(45 St. Martin's Lane, off Trafalgar Square)* and the **Sanderson** *(50 Berners St, off Oxford St.).* The windows in the rooms of St. Martin's change color according to the preference of each guest, so at night you're ensured a dazzling rainbow effect from the street below. At his other hotel, off Oxford Street, the lobby and Purple Bar are definitely worth a scope. From sparsely placed funky bits of furniture, including a replica of Dali's lips, to the reception counter that has some kind of luminescent screen covering it with a naked figure that walks across, to the elevators that feel as if you've stepped into the galaxy, the Sanderson has so many novelties and gimmicks that you can be entertained without even checking in. Off Brick Lane [see *five of the best ethnic eats,* below] is a cluster of stores selling clothes, furniture, and housewares but, above all, selling design elements. **Eat my Handbag Bitch** *(6 Dray Walk, 91-95 Bridge Lane; Tel 0207/375-31-00; www.eatmyhandbagbitch.co.uk)* is certainly not your most conventional of store names, and the 20th-century vintage stuff inside isn't either. Two doors down is the **World Design Laboratory,** which is more like a carnival ride than a shop. In order to actually get inside, you have to walk through a dark tunnel (with musical accompaniment) into a room lit so brightly you might need to grab some ultra-trendy sunglasses in one of the cabinets to shield your eyes. In this temple of weirdness, the odd pair of jeans hangs on a rack from plastic, see-through pipes that make it appear as if they're floating in mid-air. For some more conventional consumer fun, the chain store **Muji** (which means 'no brand goods' in Japanese) *(187 Oxford St.; Tel 0207/437-75-03)* and 77 King's Rd.; Tel 0207/352-71-48; Branches all over; Prices vary for goods from £1 to over £100)* sells everything from tank tops to erasers. The rich display of stationery, kitchenware, furniture, and toiletries illustrates typical Japanese flair when it comes to effortlessly combining minimalism, functionality, and elegance in anything.

festivals and events

Although annual street festivals like the **Caribbean Notting Hill Carnival** *(3 days during the Bank Holiday Weekend in late Aug; Tel 0208/964-05-44)* and **Greenwich and Docklands Festival** *(mid-July; Tel 0208/305-18-18)* and music festivals such as the **London Fleadh** *(One day in mid-June; Finsbury Park; Tube to Finsbury Park),* modern Irish and Celtic extravaganza, and the South Bank's **Coin Street Festival** *(through July and Aug, along the South Bank in venues such as Oxo Tower Wharf, Gabriel's Wharf, and the Riverside Walkway; Tel 0207/401-22-55)* promise mayhem in certain parts of the city, the real action lies in the English countryside, which hosts several Woodstock-scale festivals between May and September.

Touted as the best of the festivals, **Homelands** *(End of May; The Bowl in Matterley Estate, Winchester; Tel 0208/963-09-40; www.home lands-uk.com)* has eight arenas featuring the freshest European and American electronic acts like the Chemical Brothers and DJ Shadow.

Glastonbury *(End of June; Worthy Farm, Pilton, Somerset; Tel 0906/708-08-08; www.glastonbury-festival.co.uk):* A rock 'n' roll extravaganza hosting 200,000 fans, Glastonbury is the most diverse of the summer jams. The festival features music ranging from indie rock to jazz to reggae on nine stages. Other attractions include food stalls, a kids' area, and acres of muddy English farmland.

Big Day Out *(Second week of July; The National Bowl, Milton Keynes):* While heavy metal may have suffered a severe loss of popularity in the States, English fans still turn out in droves to feel the

▶▶VISUAL ARTS

In addition to the major museums and galleries, London has established itself as a place of contemporary innovation. When bad boys like Damien Hirst are already part of the art establishment, the door opens even further for new talent to push the boundaries.

One of the biggest of these edgy arts spaces is the **Slaughterhouse Gallery** *(63 Charterhouse St.; Tel 0207/490-08-47; Tube to Farringdon or Barbican; 11am-6pm daily; Free admission).* Located opposite a meat market in Clerkenwell, the gallery's name is a reminder of the underground space's former use.

Slightly more pleasant is the massive studio complex **Delfina** *(50 Bermondsey St.; Tel 0207/357-66-00; Tube to London Bridge; 10am-5pm Mon-Fri, 2-5pm Sat, Sun; Free admission).* This four-year-old studio/gallery/restaurant grants free studio spaces to international as well as British artists, which has its obvious risks as well as rewards....

noise. Located 45 minutes outside of London, Big Day Out books big names like Metallica and Marilyn Manson alongside their English counterparts.

Womad *(End of July; Rivermead Centre, Reading; Tel 01225/744-494; realworld.on.net/womad):* Started by Peter Gabriel, Womad is a multiday world-music smorgasbord. In addition to performers from across the globe, the festival features international food and art displays. More family-friendly than most, Womad features a children's area and swimming pool.

Be aware that these festivals face steep competition from at least a dozen similar events scheduled each summer. Due to the scale and quantity of the festivals, locations, lineups, dates, and even the events themselves are subject to change or cancellation. **National Express** *(Tel 08705/010-104, www.nationalexpress.co.uk)* runs special bus trips to and from many of the bigger events, with prices included in the entry fee.

The **Bishopstock Blues Festival** *(Last week of May for a couple of days; Bishop's Court Palace, Exeter, Devon; Tel 01392/875-220, Fax 01392/876-528)* is billed as the UK's premier blues festival and is set in the grounds of an 850-year-old Gothic Revival palace. Last year's highlight was John Lee Hooker, and the organizers set a limit on allowing only 5,000 people in per day, so you gotta know this is a fairly sought-after event. The relaxing vibe comes catered and with full bar facilities.

Whitechapel Open Studios *(Whitechapel High St.; Tel 0207/522-7878; Tube to Aldgate East; 11am-5pm Tue-Sun, 11am-8pm Wed; Free)* is a great place to check out East London's edgy talent. They show a variety of media, most of it cool, some of it sexy, and all of it provocative.

The **White Cube** *(2 Duke St.; Tube to Green Park; www.whitecube.com)* and now the **White Cube 2** *(48 Hoxton Sq., Shoreditch; Tube to Liverpool St., bus to Shoreditch)* are two ultra-white, ultra-bright modern little art exhibition spaces. White Cube 2 consists of one very brightly top lit room in the lovely, tucked-away Hoxton Square, with two giant brick and glass front doors making a dramatic opening statement. Much like the **Saatchi Gallery** (see *culture zoo*, below), they both showcase lots of the controversial contemporary British artists, such as the aforementioned Hirst.

While not strictly on the artistic fringe, the **Cartoon Art Trust** *(67-68 Hatton Garden; Tel 0207/405-47-17; Tube to Chancery Lane or Farringdon; 10am-5pm Mon-Sat, noon-5pm Sun; Free admission)* has a cool schedule of rotating shows dedicated to historic as well as modern cartoon art.

▶▶FASHION

As one of the world's most fashionable cities, London starts trends and creates styles. Top designers like Jean-Paul Gaultier regularly scope out what the kids are wearing on the street for inspiration, and the rest of the world looks to the biannual **London Fashion Week** *(for information and tickets: Tel 0120/342-64-12, Fax 0120/342-64-11, www. londonfashionweek.co.uk)*

Taking place in February and September, London's biggest fashion event features around 140 designer collections worn by the world's top models. Held in a large tent, this three-ring fashion circus has become the most important style event outside Paris or Milan, featuring luminaries such as Alexander McQueen, Hussein Chalayan, Nicole Farhi, and Tristan Webber. Although attendance at some shows is by invitation only, many events organized around Fashion Week are open to the public.

▶▶PERFORMING ARTS

It's no surprise there's a full range of theater and dance in London, for every budget and taste. And if that's not for you, there are plenty of movie theaters. Listings can be found in *Time Out* as well as the weekend supplements of London's major newspapers. Prices vary from expensive to astronomical, but discounts are often available to students and young people. Booking through services like **Globaltickets** *(Tel 0207/734-45-55)* can sometimes get you into sold-out West End events, but often with a hefty premium. For bargain tickets, check the **Half-Price Ticket Booth** in Leicester Square on the day of show. Your best bet is to call the venue ahead of time to book (this applies to movies, too).

London's crawling with theaters. Big, glitzy productions take place in the West End, which stretches from Piccadilly Circus, along Shaftesbury Avenue, to Covent Garden and the Strand. If Andrew Lloyd Webber doesn't light your wick, loads of Shakespearean theater, opera, and fringe events provide excellent alternatives.

The **Barbican Centre** *(Silk St.; Tel 0207/638-88-91; Tube to Moorgate or Barbican; £12-42; AE, MC, V)* has regular seasons by both the Royal Shakespeare Company and the London Symphony Orchestra. The monolithic arts complex also houses a three-screen cinema and gallery spaces.

Funky and unconventional performances combine with avant-garde art, photography, dance and cinema at the **ICA** *(The Mall; Tel 0207/930-36-47; Tube to Charing Cross or Piccadilly Circus; MC, V)*, which also hosts lectures and club nights. Recent events included a large retrospective of films by Andrei Tarkovsky as well as an exhibition of goth photographer Floria Sigismondi's work.

Serious theatergoers stick to the off-West End scene. **The Bush** *(Shepherds Bush Green; Tel 0208/743-33-88; Tube to Goldhawk Rd.; MC, V)* has a reputation as a top theater committed to up-and-coming writers. Getting seats can be tricky, due to the theater's tiny size and its immense popularity.

Maybe the most significant off-West End theater, the **Royal Court** (*Sloane Sq.; Tel 0207/565-50-50; Tube to Sloane Sq.; MC, V*), is scheduled to return to its home in Sloane Square after a lengthy exile for renovations. Known as the top venue for new writers, the works performed here often raise a few eyebrows.

Virtually all of England's professional dancers make their living in London. Among the many dance troupes and companies, standouts include the Royal Ballet, the Adzido Pan-African Dance Ensemble, and the Richard Alston Dance Company.

The top venue for ballet is the **Royal Opera House** (*Bow St.; Tel 0207/304-40-00; Tube to Covent Garden; AE, MC, V*), a gorgeous, grand old theater that is the home of the Royal Ballet. Be prepared to pay up big-time (over £40) for tickets.

Contemporary and brand-new works are consistently strong at **The Place** (*17 Duke's Rd.; Tel 0207/387-00-31; Tube to Euston; MC, V*), which hosts the Richard Alston Dance Company as well as performers from around the world.

The newly renovated **Sadler's Wells Theatre** (*Rosebery Ave.; Tel 0207/863-80-00; Tube to Angel; £8-35; AE, MC, V*) also has a strong reputation built on its eclectic schedule of local and international talent. The theater also hosts seasons by the English National Ballet.

Smokers and the people who love them should check listings to see if there's a movie worth seeing at the **Notting Hill Coronet** (*Notting Hill Gate; Tel 0207/727-67-05; Tube to Notting Hill Gate; MC, V*). This theater is probably the last in London to allow smoking in the auditorium. It shows mostly American flicks, which debut a couple of months after their Stateside premieres.

For all the blockbusters, check out the **Empire** (*Leicester Sq.; Tel 0207/369-17-22; Tube to Leicester Sq.; MC, V*), or the **Odeon Marble Arch** (*10 Edgeware Rd.; Tel 01426/914-501; Tube to Marble Arch; MC, V*), home of London's largest screen.

Art-house pictures and foreign films are fixtures at the Barbican Centre and the ICA [see above for both]. Both of these multimedia venues feature film series as well as one-off oddities.

gay scene

When there was a terrorist attack on the popular Admiral Duncan bar in the heart of gay Soho, there was a public outpouring of sympathy and rage. So, while intolerant lunatics can exist everywhere, the general attitude toward gay life here is accepting and supportive. London's queer population is visible and vocal, and the gay community has loads of bars, clubs, shops, and services in and around Soho. Although there are plenty of exclusively gay clubs and bars around town, mixed nights are currently enormously popular, allowing circuit boys and the straight girls who love them (and every other combo) to party together. In addition to *Time Out* and the handful of widely available free gay mags, hotlines like the **Gay and Lesbian Switchboard** (*Tel 0207/837-73-24; 24 hours*) and the

London Lesbian Line *(Tel 0207/251-69-11; 2-10pm Mon, Fri, 7-10pm Tue-Thur)* provide info on all types of goings-on around town.

Organizations like **Outrage** *(Tel 0207/439-23-81)* and **Stonewall** *(Tel 0207/336-88-60)* are very active on issues like legal inequality and homophobia. Additionally, large events like the annual Gay and Lesbian **Mardi Gras** *(Tel 0906/302-27-79; www.londonmardigras.com for dates and info)* and the **Lesbian and Gay Film Festival** *(National Film Theatre, South Bank; Tel 0207/928-32-32; Tube to Waterloo)* provide ample opportunities to party with a purpose (who could ask for more?). Check the free weekly Pink Paper, available at newsstands and many shops in Soho, for more info.

As one of the battlefields in the struggle for gay rights, the **Admiral Duncan** *(54 Old Compton St.; Tel 0207/437-53-00; Tube to Leicester Sq.; 11am-11pm Mon-Sat, noon-10:30pm Sun; No credit cards)* stands as a rainbow-festooned declaration of gay resistance to intolerance. Reopened after the tragic bombing that tore the place apart, this traditional gay bar is a lively and crowded refuge for gay London.

Noted as one of the few gay bars with a happy hour, **Bar Code** *(3-4 Archer St.; Tel 0207/734-33-42; Tube to Picadilly Circus; 1pm-midnight Mon-Thur, till 1am Fri, Sat, till 10:30pm Sun; No credit cards)* gets really out of control between 5:30 and 6:30pm. Packed with young folks getting as trashed as possible, so you'll never notice the lack of decor. While some might mind the scuzzy upstairs, few seem to mind the downstairs dance floor, which is lit mainly by a charmingly sorry set of disco lights.

Walking the length of the bar at **Compton's of Soho** *(51-53 Old Compton St.; Tel 0207/479-79-61; Tube to Leicester Sq.; Noon-11pm Mon-Sat, noon-10:30pm Sun; MC, V)* almost guarantees a visual undressing by other patrons, as the place is overwhelmingly patronized by men on the prowl. With loud music and aggressive come-ons aplenty, this place will disappoint those in search of a quiet pint and good conversation.

Known mostly as a gay man's hangout, Soho also has a few lesbian-only haunts. The first and best-known is **Candy Bar** *(4 Carlisle St.; Tel 0207/494-40-41; Tube to Tottenham Court Rd.; 5pm-midnight Mon-Thur, till 2am Fri, 2pm-2am Sat, 1-11pm Sun; No credit cards)*. Occupying two floors, this compact and stylish bar is teeming with friendly dykes enjoying the uncommonly man-free surroundings.

Some of the most popular DJs in London are regulars at gay clubs and club nights. One venue which consistently draws top talent to its gay nights is **Heaven** *(Villiers St.; Tel 0207/930-20-20; Tube to Charing Cross or Embankment; 10:30pm-5am daily; No credit cards)*. Renowned for its dance floor, this 2,000-capacity club attracts way more boys than girls, though that may not be the case on mixed nights.

Ranking a close second on the gay club-ometer are the Trade parties rocking the **London Astoria** *(157 Charing Cross Rd.; Tel 0207/734-69-63; Tube to Tottenham Court Rd.; 5am Sat night till late Sun afternoon; No credit cards)*. A massive and legendary party renowned in gay and straight circles, *Trade* is a fierce end to a debauched weekend, full of sweaty, wide-eyed clubbers hoping Monday never comes.

The ever-popular **Turnmills** *(63 Clerkenwell Rd.; Tel 0207/250-34-09; Tube to Farringdon; Late-license hours; No credit cards)*, one-time host of Trade, still has the occasional gay event. A staple of London's club scene, Turnmills has several different hangs, from classy coffee bar to a two-level dance floor in the big room.

Capitalizing on the current trend toward mixed clubbing, **Freedom** *(60-66 Wardour St.; Tel 0207/734-00-71; Tube to Tottenham Court Rd.; 11am-3am Mon-Sat, till 11pm Sun; MC, V)* attracts a super-trendy mob of fashion types with its futuro-loungey interior and posh cocktails. The sweaty dance floor downstairs comically mixes shirtless men flexing their pecs and girls attempting to dance in too-tight dresses.

CULTURE ZOO

If culture could kill, you'd be dead in London. The Empire stretched far and wide, grabbing loads of great loot along the way. So it's all here, and your greatest problems will be time and money. There's so much history and culture here, you could spend your whole life exploring it. Here are the greatest hits—plus a few old & moldies we had to throw in, against our better judgement.

The little-known White Card, which can be purchased at Tourist Info booths [see *need to know*, below], entitles you to wander a slew of museums freely for three or seven days and might end up saving you a bundle. You can probably sneak out (if so inclined) and see all the corny royal stuff while your hip friends are still sleeping off a hangover.

The most recent exciting cultural news in London has been the development of the city's South Bank. Much press has been devoted to the new Tate Museum of Modern Art, the Millennium Bridge (the first Thames crossing built in a century), by Sir Norman Foster, that links Bankside with St. Paul's Cathedral, and the London Eye (the massive big wheel that moves continuously very slowly). Shakespeare's Globe has also recently undergone a refurbishment and the oldest working theater in the United Kingdom, the Old Vic, is also here. There's also no shortage of trendy places to have a bite, a beer, or do some shopping. Oxo Tower Wharf and Gabriel's Wharf are two spots for these sorts of pursuits. To get to Bankside, get out at the Black Friars, London Bridge, Southwark, or Monument Tube stops.

In Shakespeare's time, there were tons of pubs, theaters, and inns here, making the South Bank area a lot more bustling and seedy. People would look across the Thames River (as the masses couldn't read in those days) and if there was a flag on the flagpole, that meant that there was a show on that day. Today, you can just pick up a program from the Globe Theatre, or check on the web.

Tate Modern *(Bankside Power Station, The Queen's Walk; Tel 0207/887-88-88, Fax 0207/887-88-98; 10am-6pm Sun-Thur, 10am-10pm Fri-Sat; www.tate.org.uk/modern; Free admission except for special*

down and out

In a city as expensive as London, keeping amused without breaking the bank is pretty difficult. Window shopping never costs a penny, and just walking around markets like Camden is an activity unto itself. Plenty of the museums and galleries, like the **Slaughterhouse Gallery,** the **Cartoon Art Trust**, the **Tate Gallery,** the **National Gallery,** and the **British Museum** [see *arts scene,* above, and *culture zoo,* below] charge no entrance fee, providing culture on the cheap. Weather permitting, London's parks are ideal for walks or lazy picnics. At night, the view from **Primrose Hill** [see *hanging out,* above] will take your mind off any and all financial problems. Then there are bars like **Dogstar** [see *bar scene,* above], with no cover during the week and double shots for the price of a single. Imagination and some self-restraint go a long way in London. If your budget is still getting you down, find an orange crate to stand on and vent your frustrations at **Speakers Corner,** where whining (and shouting and gesticulating wildly) have become a cultural institution [see *culture zoo,* below]. Then, after dark, head to the center of **Piccadilly Circus** and sit by the fountain. Either gaze at the huge electronic billboards and watch the moveable feast go by, or strike up a chat with some other West End wanderer. The fountain is always brimming with hangers-out.

shows): This behemoth of a building is matched inside by quadruple-volume spaces and massive iron sculptures by Louise Bourgeois. The actual gallery rooms on the third and fifth floors are by and large a bit pokey, though. Divided up into themes (instead of in chronological order or according to 'isms'), the paintings and sculptures deal with History/Memory/Society, Nude/Action/Body, Landscape/Matter/Environment, Still Life/Object/Real Life, and 'Between Cinema and a Hard Place.' At times, the magnificent panoramic views visible through the floor-to-ceiling glass windows outdo the art on display. Especially the sight of St. Paul's Cathedral directly ahead.

Shakespeare's Globe Theatre *(21 New Globe walk, opposite the Bankside Pier; Tel 0207/401-99-19 or Tel 0207/887-88-88, Fax 0207/902-15-15; 9am-noon daily May-Sept, 10am-5pm daily Oct-Apr; Performances May 12-Sept 24; www.shakespeares-globe.org; £7.50, £6 students; Tickets £5-£26):* Here you'll find the biggest exhibition devoted to the world of Shakespeare from Elizabethan times to today. Documenting everything from blueprints to corsets, the more interesting part of the building is the actual theater, which is open only in summer, when the Shakespeare productions are performed. The original site of the theater is around the corner, where there is a plaque and some informational boards. The Globe has been reproduced as closely as possible to an Elizabethan theater, and the tour guides will tell you (since they're often asked) that *Shakespeare in Love* was not filmed here. For the movie, the theater was reproduced in Shepperton Studios.

The Rose *(56 Park St., off the Globe walk; Tel 0207/593-00-26; Open daily; www.rdg.ac.uk/Rose/; £3, £2.50 students):* Just around the corner from the Globe Theatre is the archaeological site of the theater where plays by Henslowe, Shakespeare, and Marlowe were performed. Built in 1587, this was the first theater on Bankside. Its remains were discovered in 1989 and are being excavated and conserved. Since there is only a sound and light show at the site illustrating the story of The Rose, a brief walk by would probably suffice.

London Eye *(Riverside Building, County hall, Westminster Bridge Rd.; Tel 0870/500-06-00 for pre-bookings; 9am-10pm Apr 1-Sept 10, 10am-6pm Sept 11-Mar 31; www.british-airways.com/londoneye; £7.45 Jan-May, £7.95 June-Dec):* The big wheel you see looming over the Thames with cable cars attached to it is not a temporary carnival attraction, it's the spanking new observation wheel, which turns continuously all day long and provides panoramic views of the city. Arrive early or prepare to languish in endless lines for a chance to hop on the contraption.

Dalí Universe *(County hall, Riverside Building; Tel 0207/620-24-20; Tube to Waterloo or Westminster; 10am-5:30pm daily; www.daliuniverse.com; £8.50, £6 students):* If you're a Dalí enthusiast, this is definitely worth a visit since it is the first permanent commercial Dalí exhibition in the world, comprising four galleries of over 30,000 square feet. The collection of about 500 sculptures and drawings includes the Mae West sofa (the giant red lips), and a selection of dripping clocks. Located right next to the London Eye, the galleries make for a surreal contrast to the super-symmetrical engineering of the big wheel.

Hayward Gallery *(Tel 0207/960-42-42; 10am-6pm daily, till 8pm Tue-Wed, 10pm Fri; www.hayward-gallery.org.uk; £6, £4 students):* This modern art gallery merits a mention since it is the largest public art space in the UK. It features everything from modern masters to contemporary names, showcasing controversial exibits similar to those at the Saatchi Gallery.

The **Design Museum** *(Butler's Wharf, Shad Thames; Tel 0207/378-60-55; www.designmuseum.org; Tube to Tower Hill or London Bridge, then short walk; 10:30am-6pm Mon-Fri, noon-6pm Sat, Sun; £5.25, £4.50 students):* A monument to all things usefully beautiful (i.e., functional art), it is vastly more appealing than the over-touristed Tower of London, which sits just across the Thames. Unless you have a thing for old prisons, you creepy thing. (If you do, however, make sure to go first thing in the morning so you don't get crushed with the other creepies.)

Serpentine Gallery *(Kensington Gardens; Tel 0207/298-15-15; Tube to Knightsbridge, Lancaster Gate or South Kensington; 10am-6pm*

not your average religious experience

Hawksmoor's Christ Church in Spital-fields, near the market, is considered by many to be one of London's most beautiful churches. It was designed by Nicholas Hawksmoor and Sir Christopher Wren, one of England's most famous architects (he was responsible for St. Paul's Cathedral). Constructed between 1715 and 1759, the church falls into the English Baroque style and features a dramatic Georgian steeple rising from a grand portico. The Parish church **St. Martin-in-the-Fields** *(Trafalgar Sq., Tube to Charing Cross; Open daily 10am-6pm, free lunchtime conceruts daily at 1pm, candlelit recitals in the evenings)* was designed by James Gibbs and dates from the 18th century. However, there has been a church on this site since the 13th century, so the name derives from the time when the site actually was in the fields, between Westminster and the City. The white stone exterior and elaborate spire come into their own at night when floodlit. **Shri Swaminarayan Mandir** *(105-115 Brentfield Rd., Neasden, just off the North Circular Rd.; Tube to Neasden; Tel 0208/965-26-51; Open 9am-noon and 4-6pm Apr-Oct and Nov-Mar; £2)* is Europe's first traditional Hindu Temple. Built in 1995, it is a replica of the Akshardam temple in western India. It was created with 26,300 pieces of limestone and marble crafted by over 1,500 sculptors in India, and then shipped to London to be erected, all at a cost of about £10 million. The **Central Mosque** *(Tube to St. John's Wood)*, on the western side of Regents Park, is the largest Islamic Center in Britain. First opened in 1978, the building has a minimalist design with a couple of dazzling touches such as the minaret and the golden dome, which was designed by Frederick Gibberd. The oldest surviving Parish church in London, built between 1123 and 1250, and possibly the most beautiful, **St. Bartholomew The Great** *(Enter through Tudor-style gate called Smithfield Gate, at the cloth fair; Tube to Barbican)* also has a movie star résumé: It made appearances in *Four Weddings and a Funeral* and *Shakespeare in Love*.

daily; www.serpentinegallery.org; Free admission): Back in the center of the city and certainly worth a detour if you're in Hyde Park, this gallery is the exhibition site for contemporary artists. The structure was a tea pavilion in 1934 and now houses modern art exhibits that change every two to three months. A recent, particularly interesting exhibit, called *The*

Greenhouse Effect, illustrated the links between the display of nature in the gardens and the display of nature in the gallery by turning the Serpentine into a conceptual greenhouse. Sculptures included *Bird,* a small skeleton of a bird made from the artists' fingernail parings and superglue, as well as a full-size apple tree in a mound of dirt in the entrance. The most interesting exhibit, though, was an aviary with live parrots inside that were trained to learn the sounds of an extinct language. These are the only living 'speakers' of the language of the Maypure—a Caribbean Indian tribe that was annihilated by a neighboring tribe.

Saatchi Gallery *(98a Boundary Rd.; Tel 0207/624-82-99; Tube to Swiss Cottage or St. John's Wood; Noon-6pm Thur-Sun; £4):* Bankrolled by ultra-wealthy advertising kingpin Charles Saatchi, the gallery exported its *Sensations* and hosts bizarre exhibitions and installations, including a room half-filled with sump oil. The tree-filled suburban location of this venue (in the quiet, upmarket St. John's Wood) stands in contrast to its wide-open space of oddities, illusions, and eye-openers.

St. Paul's Cathedral *(St. Paul's Churchyard; Tel 0207/236-41-28; Tube to St. Paul's; Open 8:30am-4pm Mon-Sat, galleries open 9:30am-4pm Mon-Sat; Cathedral £4 adults, galleries £3.50 adults):* Famous for the wedding of Charles and Diana in 1981 (watched by over 900 million people all over the world), this cathedral is an indelible part of the London skyline. The present building dates back to 1675. In 1666, the great fire of London destroyed St. Paul's and, as a result, the great architect of the day, Sir Christopher Wren, was appointed to design a new cathedral. The great dome became the symbol of English survival during the blitz or WWII.

Westminster Abbey *(Parliament Sq.; Tel 0207/222-51-52; Tube to Westminster or St. James's Park; 9:15am-3:45pm Mon-Fri, 9:15am-1:45pm and 4pm-4:45pm Sat; £5 adults, £3 students):* A tour through this focal monument of English political and religious life will teach you more than you ever wanted to know about medieval British history. Most of England's kings and queens have been crowned here and many have been buried here, including Elizabeth I.

Kensington Palace *(Kensington Palace Gardens; Tel 0207/937-95-61; Tube to High St. Kensington, Queensway, or Bayswater; 10am-5pm daily in summer, 10am-4pm daily in winter; £8.50 adults, £6.70 students):* Supremely luxurious and rich with history, this is the one-time home of Princess Diana and well worth a visit for royal buffs and those with delusions of grandeur.

Houses of Parliament and **Big Ben** *(Bridge St. and Parliament Sq.; Tel 0207/219-42-72 House of Commons, Tel 0207/219-31-07 House of Lords; Tube to Westminster; House of Commons: from 2:30pm Mon, Tue, from 3:30 Thur, from 9:30am Wed, from 11:30am Thur; House of Lords: from 2:30pm Mon-Wed, from 3pm Thur; Free admission):* Standing gloriously on the Thames, these buildings add another striking aspect to the city's skyline. Benjamin Clock is about as characteristic of England as the Statue of Liberty is of New York. Visiting the House of Commons is a unique experience. The debates are certainly colorful and watching Tony Blair in action is a somewhat surreal experience.

British Museum *(Great Russell St.; Tel 0207/636-15-55; Tube to Tottenham Court Rd. or Holborn; 10am-5pm Mon-Sat, noon-6pm Sun; www.britishmuseum.ac.uk; Free admission):* There's something for everyone in this giant storehouse of goodies gotten (and misbegotten) during the days of the Empire. It features around six million exhibits, not to mention the mummies!

Victoria and Albert Museum *(Cromwell Rd.; Tel 0207/938-84-41; Tube to S. Kensington; Noon-5:45pm Mon, 10am-5:45pm Tue-Sun; £5 adults, £3 students, free admission after 4:30pm):* Possibly the biggest museum devoted to applied arts, here is housed a gigantic collection of Asian art, modern design objects, and seven legendary tapestries by Raphael.

Museum of the Moving Image *(South Bank; Tel 0207/928-35-35; Tube to Waterloo; 10am-6pm daily; £6.25):* Beginning with shadow puppetry and optical toys from back in the day, the campy chronology is re-created in the flesh by costumed actors, and is at once informative and bizarrely entertaining.

Barbican Centre *(Silk St.; Tel 0207/382-71-05; Tube to Moorgate or Barbican; 10am-6:45pm Mon, Thur-Sat, till 5:45pm Tue, till 7:45pm Wed, noon-6:45pm Sun; £5):* Despite being written off as a wannabe Pompidou Center, here you will find some high-caliber contemporary art and photography exhibits in its main galleries. A recent David Bailey exhibit had huge Rolling Stones portraits staring down.

The Wallace Collection *(Hertford House, Manchester Sq., just north of Oxford St.; Tel 0207/935-06-87; Tube to Bond St. or Baker St.; 10am-5pm Mon-Sat, 2-5pm Sun; www.demon.co.uk/heriatge/wallace; Free admission):* Housed in a historic London town house, and not that well known to the visiting masses, this is formerly one of the world's most extensive private collections. It was made public in 1897 and contains an eclectic combination of work from several centuries: medieval and renaissance, European and Oriental arms and armor, Dutch genre painting, 18th and 19th English and French painting, furniture, and porcelain. However, the highlight of the museum is *The Swing* by Fragonard, painted in 1767. If you've ever studied art history, you've probably heard of this little, sparkling gem. Upon order of the family who bequeathed the collection, nothing has ever been added or loaned, thus reserving it as one of the greatest collections ever made by an English family.

National Gallery *(Trafalgar Sq.; Tel 0207/747-28-85; Tube to Charing Cross, Leicester Sq., Embankment, or Piccadilly Circus; 10am-6pm daily, till 9pm Wed; Free admission except for special shows):* Sure it's old hat, but what a hat! This is truly one of the great art museums of the world, with spectacular stuff spanning eight centuries. Da Vinci, Rembrandt, Van Gogh, they're all here, struttin' their stuff.

National Portrait Gallery *(St. Martin's Place; Tel 0207/306-00-55; Tube to Charing Cross, Leicester Sq.; 10am-6pm daily; Free admission):*

A fine art album, this gallery displays a broad range of headshots, from the old and stodgy to the new and wacky. Check out Warhol's take on Queen Elizabeth.

Royal Academy of Arts *(Piccadilly; Tel 0207/300-80-00; Tube to Green Park or Piccadilly Circus; 10am-6pm daily, until 8:30pm Fri; www.royalacademy.org.uk; £7-8 admission, £5 students):* If you're in London during the months of May till August, check out the annual Summer Exhibition. Featured are rooms with hundreds of little paintings cluttered together on the walls as well as modern sculptures, drawings, and architectural models. One room is usually dedicated to the work of an individual artist while another sculptor is chosen to exhibit a large piece or pieces in the front courtyard of the building. The majority of the works are for sale and there are prizes awarded to the artists.

Tate Gallery *(Beside the Thames, Millbank; Tel 0207/887-80-00; Tube to Pimlico; 10am-5:50pm daily; Free admission):* Along with the new Tate Gallery of Modern Art, the entire contents of the original have been reorganized, so that instead of the conventional art-museum structure that follows chronological order, the two Tates are designed thematically. In addition, the Tate Gallery now houses only British art—as well as work by some famous visitors to the city—as the modern art collection has been moved to the new Tate. Be sure to catch the misty Turners and the God-drunk Blakes.

modification

If pain (the good kind, silly) is on your travel itinerary, stop by **Hair By Fairy** *(8-10 Neal's Yard; Tel 0207/497-07-76; Tube to Covent Garden; 10am-6pm Mon-Sat, closed Sun; No credit cards)* for ear work or body piercing. Don't worry, the shop is registered with the local health authorities and the piercers all have first-aid training.

Or try **Into You** *(244 St. Johns St.; Tel 0207/253-50-85; Tube to Farringdon; Noon-7pm Tue, Wed, Fri, noon-9pm Thur, till 6pm Sat; AE, MC, V for jewelry, piercing, no credit cards for tattoos),* an East London clearinghouse for all things pointy and primitive. This specialty studio will pierce or tattoo you almost anywhere, for a price.

Still another alternative is **Sacred Art** *(148 Albion Rd.; Tel 0207/254-22-23; Tube to Angel, bus 73; 11:30am-6:30pm Mon-Fri, 11am-6pm Sat; No credit cards)* in Stoke Newington. Located in North London, this modern mecca for all types of body-mod is known as the best in London.

Traveling takes its toll on one's appearance. Luckily, **Theorem** *(4 Cross St.; Tel 0207/354-97-13; Tube to Angel or Highbury Islington; 9am-7pm Mon-Sat; No credit cards)* can transform the wack-est hairstyle into something special. Phone ahead for an appointment and prices.

great outdoors

While lunch-break joggers usually hit the Millennium Mile on the South Bank of the Thames, the paths of **Regents Park** *(Tube to Regents Park),*

by foot

London may be one of Europe's largest cities, but the interesting sections of the city are within walking distance of one another. One of the best routes begins at the **Museum of the Moving Image** [see *culture zoo,* above] on the South Bank of the Thames. After zipping through the chronology of cinema, head out the door and down to the Millennium Mile, a park along the river's edge. Before heading off to the right, check out the skateboarders at **South Bank** [see *hanging out,* above]. The first big draw is the **Oxo Tower** *(Tel 0207/401-22-55; 11am-6pm daily),* directly accessible from the footpath. This arts development houses several galleries, shops, and restaurants. The best attraction, however, is the observation gallery on the eighth floor (open until 10pm). A few more minutes' walk down the path takes you by the **Tate Gallery of Modern Art.** Occupying an enormous space along the river bank, the museum houses the modern art collection of the **Tate Gallery** [see *culture zoo,* above, for both Tates]. Next comes the historic **Globe Theatre** [see *arts scene,* above], Shakespeare's famed playhouse. Still farther along, a few twists and and turns take walkers past **The Clink** *(Clink St.; Tel 0207/378-15-58; Tube to London Bridge; 10am-6pm daily; £4; No credit cards),* a prison-turned-museum full of displays about torture. The last stop along the Mile is the **Design Museum** [see *culture zoo,* above]. Cross the Tower Bridge to the north bank and zip past the dreadful lines at the **Tower of London** to reach the nearby Tube station.

Hyde Park *(Tube to Knightsbridge),* and **Hampstead Heath** *(Tube to Hampstead)* are where non-corporate joggers jog. A run, a power walk, or even a plain old saunter through Regents or Hyde Park will not only be a good dose of oxygen to counter London's pollution, but it's also an aesthetic treat. Regents is one of London's most genteel parks, offering boating, a bandstand, a cafe, and an open-air theater, which dates back to 1932. At the center is a lovely rose garden surrounding a small duck-filled pond with connecting Japanese bridges. The London Zoo is located in Regents Park, and even if you don't go in, the sight of giraffes sticking out of the top of the fence as you walk by is a weird sight in the middle of London. To the north of Regents Park, the 206-foot-high **Primrose Hill** *(Prince Albert Rd.; Tube to Camden Town)* is good for a quick climb and sharp intake of oxygen. Once at the top, it's prime positioning for kite-flying, picnicking, or just checking out the view of the city. Hyde Park, one of the biggest in the world, also has its fair share of gardens, ponds, trees, and a 41-acre lake called the Serpentine, where you can row or (ye gads!) swim. In-line skating is very big in Hyde Park. Not only is there a wide, flat stretch along the Serpentine, but also on many other paths that diverge into the green. Hampstead Heath is great for walking and the patches of grass get packed with picnickers, particularly on Sundays. Some of the heath is very wild, which makes for a nice contrast to London's heavily manicured parks, such as Regents. If you saw *Notting Hill* with Hugh Grant and Julia Roberts, you'll remember **Kenwood House** *(Hampstead Lane, Hampstead Heath; Tube to Hampstead; Open daily 10am-6pm Apr-Oct, 10am-4pm Nov-Mar; Free admission)* as the setting of the Henry James movie that Julia's character was starring in. Dating from the 17th century, the house was re-vamped in the 1760s for the Earl of Mansfield. The last private owner of the house was the Earl of Iveagh, an avid collector of 17th and 18th century art. When he died, he bequeathed the Rembrandts, Vermeers, van Dycks, and Gainsboroughs to the nation and they're now on public display here. Other highlights include the oval library, dating from the 18th century. The gardens, apart from acting as Hollywood locations, are also used for the occasional music concert.

Green Park is very small in comparison to the ones mentioned above, but it's a convenient spot to walk through if you're at the Royal Academy [see *culture zoo,* above] and want to get to Buckingham Palace, since it links Piccadilly with The Mall. In summer, there are stripy deck chairs laid out. Not to mention that the park is situated right next to The Ritz Hotel, so it's worth a quick look for the associated glamour, at any rate. Linked to Green Park is **St. James's Park,** an equally beautiful stretch of manicured gardens with black swans in the river. The best feature of St. James's is the bridge: If you stand in the middle of it, you have a unique view of Buckingham Palace on one side and Whitehall on the other. Rental bikes are available at **Bikepark** [see *need to know,* below] in Covent Garden for £10 the first day, £5 the second, and £3 each successive day. And if all that sounds too tiring to your hungover ears, you can always chill out in one of the deck chairs scattered around the lawns.

Head to **Slam City Skates** *(16 Neal's Yard; Tel 0207/240-09-28; Tube to Covent Garden; 10am-6pm Mon-Sat; MC, V)* for info on events and competitions, and rentals.

If and when all the pubs, clubs, and bars start to get boring, call **Adrenalin Village** *(Chelsea Bridge Tower, Queenstown Rd.; Tel 0207/731-59-58; Tube to Sloane Sq., then bus 137; Noon-5pm Wed, Fri, 11am-6pm Sat, Sun; MC, V)* to book a bungee jump over Battersea Park. The price tag is £50.

If you suddenly get the hankering to glide on water, both **Docklands Watersports Club** *(Gate 16, King George V Dock, Woolwich Manor Way; Tel 0207/511-70-00; Tube to N. Woolwich Station)* and **Royal Docks Waterski Club** *(Gate 16, King George V Dock; Tel 0207/511-20-00; Tube to N. Woolwich Station)* provide all the necessary equipment. The former rents jet skis, while the latter has wakeboards as well as plain old water skis. Given the proximity to central London, don't expect crystal-blue waters or beautiful, bikini-clad beachgoers.

city within a city

Once the seat of the British Empire, London has a diverse population from all corners of the globe. While many internationals have assimilated seamlessly into English society, ethnic communities still pepper the city, creating their own rhythms and keeping London lively.

Concentrated in the north, London's Jewish community is visible in Golder's Green, where most of the city's Orthodox population resides. Aside from the synagogues and religious resources available in the area, this neighborhood beyond Hampstead also has the best bagels and delis in all of London. Sites of interest include the **Jewish Cemetery** *(Hoop Lane; Tube to Golder's Green; 8:30am-5pm Mon-Fri, Sun),* a burial ground in use since 1895.

Much of London's Arab community shares the area around Queensway in Bayswater with the city's second-largest Chinese community (Chinatown is the biggest). Busy and prosperous, this stretch of shops and cafes is minutes from the big thoroughfare of Edgeware Road. The closest Tube station is Paddington.

On the way out of the prosperous central region of London, beyond the City, lies the infamous East End. Though renowned as a rough-and-tumble area plagued by crime and racism, London's eastern sectors aren't all dangerous. Spitalfields, an East End neighborhood, is home to much of the city's Indo-Pak population, as well as a bunch of artists. Accessible from Liverpool Street station, the area's markets, shops, and restaurants are among the best in East London. Check out Brick Lane on a weekend, when it's jammed with the local subcontinentals shopping and hanging out.

Most visible in Brixton, London's West Indian population is among the largest outside the Caribbean. Having come in the 1950s, the Afro-Caribbean community has kept a foothold in the area, which has become a hot spot for London's hipsters. The site of riots during the '80s, Brixton, located in South London, is plagued by racial problems and has a reputation for being dangerous. Both of these impressions seem a bit off when you visit the busy market along Electric Avenue just a few feet from the Brixton Tube station. The **Brixton Market** is open every day but Sunday, from 8:30am to 5:30pm, till 1pm Wednesdays.

STUFF

The good news: London offers unbelievable shopping. The bad news: Everything costs way, way, too much money. Numerically, prices are equivalent to those in the U.S., only the currency is nearly twice as precious. So, unless you're a trust-fund baby or a newly minted web tycoon, shopping can be dangerous to your finances.

Although it's famed for its markets, there's more to London's shopping scene than the funky threads hawked at the Camden and Kensington markets. Boutiques from Soho to Covent Garden peddle the newest styles and designers, while bigger shops on Oxford Street and Kensington High Road offer more civilized shopping. And shoe fanatics and fetishists of all stripes will find their salvation on Neal Street, which sells footwear unlike anywhere else on earth.

If clothes aren't your bag, the mecca of DJ culture has everything for music junkies, from rare funk to unreleased promo vinyl. London's music superstores, like **Virgin** [see *stuff, below*], sell current albums alongside thousands of high-priced CDs. For more cutting-edge stuff, stick to the specialty shops.

▶▶USED AND BRUISED

For 18-hole oxblood Docs or the most outlandish orange nylon drawstring cargo pants, look no farther than **Camden Market** (*Camden High Rd. and Chalk Farm Rd.; Tube to Camden Town; 9am-6pm weekends; No credit cards at most stalls*), a hipster version of Marrakech. Visiting this indoor/outdoor market is an experience, not an activity. If all the bustle makes you hungry, dozens of vendors sell falafel, pad thai, and French fries for cheap.

Portobello Market (*Portobello Rd.; Tube to Notting Hill Gate; all day Fri and Sat*) in trendy Notting Hill (if you've seen the movie *Notting Hill,* it's the market that Hugh Grant walks through) is a great market to browse after brunch on a weekend. Head to the end of the market, away from the gate, to rummage for more vintage clothes and less fussy antiques.

The two lesser known markets, Brick Lane and Old Spitalfields, also offer some good finds. **Brick Lane** (*Brick Lane; Tube to Liverpool St.; market on Sun only*) sells vintage clothes and cheap cleaning products (not exactly the most likely of combos). It's also a good opportunity to check out the old Truman Brewery, which has now become a hangout and workspace for the local fashion, arts, and design crowds. Even though this is a primarily Bangladeshi community, there are an inordinate amount of funky design and furniture shops [see *elements of design,* above] on and off this strip.

Old Spitalfields (*Columbia Rd.; Sun*) is on the site of a once famous fruit and veggie market but now sells arts and crafts, old clothes, young designer labels, candles, organic produce, books, flowers, furniture, and food. If it's flowers you're after, though, head to Columbia Road, which on Sunday morning, comes alive with flowers, herbs, and all types of greenery.

ground zero of the club scene

London may have hundreds of vinyl and dance specialty shops, but only one enjoys the loyal following of **Black Market Records** *(25 D'Arblay St.; Tel 0207/437-04-78; Tube to Tottenham Court Rd.; 11am-7pm Mon-Sat; MC, V)*. Started in 1987, this Soho shop has been at the center of the rave scene from the beginning. While the upstairs section specializes in house, garage, and hip-hop, the basement area sells a top selection of jungle and drum 'n' bass. Five daily deliveries of fresh stock flesh out the selection to include the joints every DJ needs to have.

With a staff that includes top DJs like Nicky Blackmarket, Clarkie, and Ray Keith, Black Market is an important testing ground for new styles and sounds. Staffers know what works in the mix, and patrons often rely on them for advice. On the rare occasions when the store doesn't stock what you are looking for, staffers often volunteer to sell their personal copies—and if that isn't love, what is?

Adding to Black Market's phenomenal reputation, staffers run two record labels out of the upstairs offices. Azuli Records is the house imprint, while Kartoonz releases drum 'n' bass. Releases are available in the shop and other dance outlets. Other draws include the huge number of fliers and advertisements for the best raves and clubs in London, a selection of underground mix tapes, the army of celebrity customers, and the loudest shop sound system in the United Kingdom.

▶▶**DUDS**

Skipping preppiness for the edgy looks of London's youth scenes, **Mash** *(73 Oxford St.; Tel 0207/434-96-09; Tube to Tottenham Court Rd.; 10am-6pm Mon-Sat, noon-5pm Sun; MC, V)* stocks a complete array of street, skate, and club clothing for both men and women. In addition to jeans, cargos, combats, fleeces, hoodies, and workwear, Mash sells skateboards, sneakers, videos, backpacks, and jewelry.

Keeping it real on the streetwear tip, but going for a more fashionable market, is the perennially cool **Red Or Dead** *(41-43 Neal St.; Tel 0207/379-75-71; Tube to Covent Garden; 10:30am-7pm Mon-Fri, 10am-6:30pm Sat, noon-5:30pm Sun; www.redordead.co.uk; MC, V)*. Selling shoes, accessories, and the clothes to go with them, Red Or Dead is a favorite of London's trendoid women, but they sell a small assortment of men's clothes too.

In the same vein, **Diesel** (*43 Earlham St.; Tel 0207/497-55-43; 10:30am-7pm Mon-Wed, Fri, Sat, till 8pm Thur, till 6pm Sun; AE, MC, V*) also works hard to make exceptional versions of everyday clothing. Housed on three floors abutting the pedestrian chaos of Neal Street, Diesel is always crowded with fashion-hungry men and women frantically racing to grab up the wares.

Importing the latest baggy and expensive gear from New York, **Home** (*39 Beak St.; Tel 0207/240-70-77; Tube to Oxford Circus; 10:30am-6:30pm Mon-Wed, Fri-Sun, 11am-7pm Thur; homesoho@aol.com; No credit cards*) sells American labels like Triple 5 Soul and cartoony designs by Paul Frank alongside courier bags and a selection of sneakers from the past 20 years.

The French are looking to hip-hop style! Run by a French hip-hop enthusiast, **Regular Store** (*Earlham St.; Tel 0207/240-26-25; Tube to Leicester Sq.; 11am-7pm Mon-Sat, 1-5:30pm Sun; www.regular_store. co.uk; MC, V*) sells a range of futuristic urban streetwear, watches, bags, and kicks. The basement record shop provides the perfect soundtrack—in French or English.

▶▶FOOT FETISH

The English may rate poorly regarding dental hygiene, but they outclass the competition when it comes to footwear of all varieties. While Camden High Street has its fair share of shoe stores, any serious shoe shopper should head to Neal Street, which has more cool shoe stores than any other strip in town.

The first name in shoe stores, **Shelly's** (*14 Neal St.; Tel 0207/240-37-26; Tube to Covent Garden; 10am-6pm Mon-Sat, 11am-5pm Sun; AE, MC, V*) sells a wild array of footwear. The styles are current, but the futuristic sneakers and boots, from Acupuncture to Vans, aren't quite cutting-edge by the time they reach Shelly's.

The clunky and crazy designs available just down the street at **Swear** (*61 Neal St.; Tel 0207/240-76-73; Tube to Covent Garden; 10am-6:30pm Mon-Sat, noon-5pm Sun; MC, V*) are at times out of this world. Wide, bubbling soles are a must, and the shoes feature unusual accents like liquid-filled bubbles emblazoned with the Swear logo. Not for the faint of heart or feet.

JD Sports (*33-34 Carnaby St.; Tel 0207/287-40-16; Tube to Oxford Circus; 10am-6:30pm Mon-Fri, till 7pm Sat, 11am-5pm Sun; MC, V*) carries the newest Air Jordans, but its strength is the selection of classic Adidas, Nike, New Balance, and Puma trainers. JD's stock of old-school sneakers and running shoes is absolutely unbeatable.

▶▶LOTIONS AND POTIONS

The idea of **Lush** (*123 King's Rd.; Tel 0207/376-83-48; Tube to Sloane Sq.; 10am-7pm Mon-Sat, noon-6pm Sun; www.lush.co.uk*), a chain of stores across England selling fresh, handmade cosmetics, is not one whose product idea is supremely original, yet Lush has perfected it. With bowls of chunky mixtures that resemble oatmeal more than face masks, and huge rounds of soap that look like giant cheeses, you will be enraptured by the multi-sensory experience to be had here—even if you're faithful to Neutrogena.

▶▶BOUND

From Shakespeare to Johnson to Orwell, London has always fostered a love of words. For the latest readings and such, check *Time Out* for listings. Some events will, of course, be advertised in bookstores, and one of the best for info and also for its stock is **Waterstone's** *(121-129 Charing Cross Rd.; Tel 0207/324-42-91; Tube to Tottenham Court Rd.; 9:30am-8pm Mon-Sat, noon-6pm Sun; MC, V),* which has branches everywhere in addition to the one listed here. Charing Cross Road (between Tottenham Court Road and Leicester Square) is lined with bookstores, and everything from the latest bestsellers to antiquarian and second-hand books can be found on these sometimes sleek, sometimes dusty shelves. All the major names are here: Waterstone's, Foyle's, Blackwell's and Borders, as well as some lesser known ones such as Bookends and Lovejoys. Head lower down toward Leicester Square, for the rare books.

For those with a taste for traditional English lunacy, **Foyle's** *(113-119 Charing Cross Rd.; Tel 0207/437-56-60; Tube to Tottenham Court Rd.; MC, V),* hasn't changed much in 50 years and has some out-of-the-way titles.

The American megastore **Borders** *(203-207 Oxford St.; Tel 0207/292-16-00; Tube to Tottenham Court Rd.; 8am-11pm Mon-Sat, noon-6pm Sun; AE, MC, V)* is good, if predictable, and has a cafe and music store to boot.

The cramped and chaotic **Compendium** *(234 Camden High St.; Tel 0207/485-89-44; Tube to Camden Town; 10am-6pm Mon-Sat, noon-6pm Sun; MC, V)* has everything from obscure poetry to critical theory on the shelves. The staff is knowledgeable and polite, so don't be shy.

Another beloved London bookshop is **Murder One** *(71-73 Charing Cross Rd.; Tel 0207/734-34-85; Tube to Tottenham Court Rd. or Leicester Sq.; 10am-7pm Mon-Wed, till 8pm Thur-Sat; AE, MC, V),* the one-stop crime and suspense specialty store. The land that gave us Sherlock Holmes is still enthralled by whodunits and mysteries of all stripes.

▶▶TUNES

The 'zines and fliers that pile up in heaps by the cashiers in **Selectadisc** *(34 Berwick St.; Tel 0207/734-32-97; Tube to Tottenham Court Rd.; 9:30am-7pm Mon-Sat; AE, MC, V)* are important documents of London's music scene. To find the records people buzz about, just browse the racks of CDs and vinyl.

For more historic sounds, try **Reckless Records** *(30 Berwick St.; Tel 0207/437-42-71; Tube to Tottenham Court Rd.; 10am-7pm daily; MC, V),* two adjacent storefronts devoted to used and hard-to-find vinyl. The first shop sells soul, funk, reggae, hip-hop, and dance music, while the second sells jazz, blues, and rock.

Ray's Jazz Shop *(180 Shaftesbury Ave.; Tel 0207/240-39-69, Fax 0207/240-73-75; 10am-6:30pm Mon-Sat, 2-5:30pm Sun; rays.*

jazz@dial.pipex.com; Access, V, MC) is a superb place for a jazz lover. You can feel the store's history as you walk in, among the stacked shelves and racks of new and used LPs and CDs. The shop stocks everything from early jazz to funk records, and there are also books, magazines, and cassettes. Ray's is also a good place to find out about upcoming gigs and to pick up listings (look for the free *Jazz Guide*).

When time is of the essence, just stop by the gargantuan **Virgin Megastore** *(14-16 Oxford St.; Tel 0207/631-16-14; Tube to Tottenham Court Rd.; 10am-9pm Mon-Sat, noon-6pm Sun; AE, MC, V).* This behemoth of a record store has not only a gazillion CDs, tapes, and records, but a fun selection of fiction and nonfiction, movies, and video games too. Located right outside the exit from the Tube, the store could very well bankrupt you before the shopping trip along Oxford Street even begins.

EATS

While the younger, trendier contingent may have put London back on the global culinary map, huge segments of the population turn up their noses at organic radicchio salad, preferring a greasy plate of fried fish and chips. Most of the good restaurants still steer well clear of traditional English cuisine, and London's diverse population offers ample alternatives to the almighty pub grub. In addition to countless Indian restaurants and balti houses, London has a fair number of Chinese restaurants in Soho. Kebab stands abound, often outselling their Western fast-food competition through larger portions and later hours. A good one to check out is the Cafe Metro on Camden High Street, right by Camden Town Tube.

Healthy stuff like organic produce and noodley dishes have become wildly popular here, the new health awareness even sparking national hysteria over genetically modified food (hmmm, maybe there is something wrong with eight-pound talking tomatoes...). The change in attitude has created a vast market for healthful California-esque cuisine, but ironically, the rising health consciousness of English diners hasn't convinced most restaurants to prohibit smoking at the table. And make sure to see if service is included in the check before tipping the waiter (usually 10 to 15 percent, depending).

▶▶**CHEAP**

Although a virtual infinity of kebab restaurants peppers London's commercial streets, they occupy wildly varying culinary territory.

Blending the cuisine of the Middle East with the cafe vibe of Paris, **Cafe Diana** *(5 Wellington Terrace, Bayswater Rd.; Tel 0207/792-96-06; Tube to Notting Hill Gate or bus 12, 52, 94; Entrees from £5; No credit cards)* is perfect for a quick lunch before heading toward Portobello Road or into Kensington Gardens. Cafe Diana also looks Parisian, until you notice that the walls are completely concealed behind a mass of portraits of Princess Di. With mostly indoor seating and just a couple of small

say what?

Cockney isn't the only kind of slang in England. Everyday conversation is full of words and phrases that are meaningless to the uninformed. To sound like a local, fake an accent and be sure to drop the following sayings:

Geezer: No, it's not a senior citizen. A "geezah" is the English equivalent of "dude." Achieve "Diamond Geezer" status, and you have hit the big time.

Bloke: A person of the male persuasion, as in: "That bloke is a geezer."

Bird: The English term for people of the female persuasion, as in: "Did you see that bird kick that bloke in the huevos?"

Draw: Also known as chuff, gear, spliff, or marijuana, as in: "That bird stole my draw and ran off with me brother!"

Bloody: An English substitute for "damn," as in "Where's me bloody draw, dammit?"

Safe: Not used as an umpire's judgment in England—something is "safe" when it's cool.

Sorted: A slang term originally used in an antidrug campaign, the situation is "sorted" when all is going well.

Wicked: Slightly different than its usage in New England, as in: "That party was safe, I mean it was bloody wicked!"

Mate: You know you're in when someone calls you "mate" instead of "that Yank bastard."

Shag: If a hottie wants to shag you senseless, be very happy. That means they want to do the wild thing all night.

Snog: Make out.

Tosser (pronounced 'tos-sa'): If someone calls you a tosser or, even worse, a "giant tosser," you are clearly not making friends down at the local pub.

Nutter (pronounced 'nut-ta'): A nutter is someone a few sandwiches short of a picnic. If you have a tendency to do tequila slammers in your spare time, you may be deemed by some to be a nutter.

Taking the piss: If you're taking the piss out of someone, you're making fun of him or her because they're a big, fat wanker (equivalent to tosser).

Bollocks: Bullshit. But, if something is "the dog's bollocks," that means it's very cool indeed.

sidewalk tables, Cafe Diana attracts mostly local folks and probably more than a few royal-watchers.

Another unusual take on the kebab shop is the studenty **Groovy Grub** *(52 Tavistock Place; Tel 0207/713-09-03; Tube to Russell Sq.; "Morning"-midnight daily; Entrees from £3.50; No credit cards)*. Keeping things copacetic, the staff serve up the obligatory falafels and gyros, with chicken, burgers, and a rainbow trout in "groovy sauce" (whatever that is) for the more adventurous. Located on a boring street in a neighborhood lacking streetlife, Groovy Grub is ideal for those staying at the **Generator** or **Crescent Hotel** [see *crashing*, below, for both], but probably doesn't warrant a schlep across town (which defeats the purpose of budget eating).

If something more well-rounded tickles your fancy, London has a good number of all-you-can-eat buffet joints in Soho's compact Chinatown. **Mr. Au** *(47-49 Charing Cross Rd.; Tel 0207/437-74-72; Tube to Leicester Sq.; 11am-11:30pm daily; Entrees from £4.90; No credit cards)* is a good choice for gluttons and tightwad tourists. Right in the thick of it at Leicester Square, Mr. Au is where the action is. For a reasonable price, you can gorge yourself on a variety of soups, rolls, stir-fries, and noodle dishes. Of course, you sacrifice any semblance of atmosphere—unless, that is, you consider the sound of chewing ambience. Mr. Au is a favorite of drunken tourists racing to gobble their food to get back onto the streets of the West End.

Yet, sometimes you need a real meal for not a lot of loot. For good, cheap food made to order, head to South London's **Noodle House** *(426 Coldharbour Lane; Tel 0207/274-14-92; Tube to Brixton; Noon-11:30pm Mon-Thur, till midnight Fri, Sat; Entrees from £5; No credit cards)*. This super-cheap Vietnamese restaurant on one of Brixton's most happening streets is both popular and delicious, serving a wide variety of appetizers and entrees, noodled or noodle-free, for veggies and omnivores alike. The food, like the restaurant, is simple and no-nonsense, with a couple of little flourishes, like a fresh juice selection, to distinguish it from the run-of-the-mill noodle spot. A popular stop before a night of drinking or clubbing, Noodle House gets a bit crowded in the later evening, so come early to avoid the crunch.

Within the maze of streets that inhabit Covent Garden lies tranquil Neal's Yard. The square is lined with stores selling alternative products and outdoor cafes, the best of which is **Neal's Yard Salad Bar** *(2 Neal's Yard; Tel/Fax 0207/836-32-33; Tube to Covent Garden; About £4)*. This tiny restaurant with its rickety outdoor tables and heated lamps was the first vegetarian cafe in the Yard, opening in 1982, and the daily variety of veggie and vegan dishes are soul food par excellence, not to mention outstanding value.

The Portuguese fast food chicken chain **Nando's** *(O2 Centre, Finchley Rd.; Tube to Finchley Rd.; Tel 0800/975-8181; About £3 for burgers, £6 for meal combos; www.nandos.co.uk)* was brought over to the

five of the best ethnic eats

London is just as multicultural as New York, and the same dazzling array of ethnic restaurants can be found here. But if you're in the mood for a casual, quick bite but still want an international flavor, head to these ethnic gems: **Yo! Sushi** *(O2 Centre, Finchley Rd.; Tel 0207/431-44-99; Noon-11pm daily; www.yosushi.co.uk; £2.50 and up depending on color-coded dish)* is a ubiquitous chain of eat-and-run sushi restaurants. There is a circular bar along which a conveyer belt runs carrying a variety of color-coded (according to price) dishes. If the one you want isn't there, one of the chefs in the center of the bar will be happy to whip it up for you. Highlights include the salmon maki rolls, the chicken yakitori, and the salmon yakitori. The other novelty of this place is the motorized drink cart that winds its way around the restaurant making comments, such as "OK, OK, I'm here. Do you think I'm a bus or something?" But be sure you don't step in its path because it won't hesitate in exclaiming "Out of my way, sucker!"

Solly's *(148A Golders Green Rd.; Tel 0208/455-21-21; Tube to Golder's Green; Less than £5 for take-out orders)* in Golders Green is the always busy archetypal Israeli food joint set in a predominantly Jewish neighborhood. It is only because the falafels are to-die-for that anyone would put up with the abuse that comes with ordering at Solly's. (Think Soup Nazi.)

Ranoush Juice *(43 Edgeware Rd.; Tel 0207/723-59-29; Tube to Marble Arch; 9pm-3am daily; £4 starter)* is one of those Lebanese quickie hot spots that only locals know about. This is because it's well hidden

UK after enormous success in South Africa, where the restaurant is based. As a result, you're bound to hear more than one or two South African accents if you pop in to sample the delicious combos on offer with their signature *peri peri* sauce. There are also delicious veggie burgers.

▶▶**DO-ABLE**

While the budget eats in London are nothing to get too excited about, there is plenty of excellent food available for just a few pounds more. Ground rules for finding good food at decent prices: Eat adventurously, and avoid all American chain restaurants. While most pubs serve food during the day and evening, similarly priced, significantly better fare can be found in restaurants around the city. Operating a four-restaurant chain, **Wagamama** *(11 Jamestown Rd.; Tel 0207/428-08-00; Tube to Camden Town; Noon-11pm Mon-Sat, 12:30-10pm Sun; www.wagamama. com; Entrees £10 and under; AE, MC, V)* presents itself as the restaurant of the future: fast, cheap, and delicious. Located off the main streets of Camden, the newest branch of this fantastically popular chain (the name

in a clump of similarly sounding restaurants (all ending in 'noush'), in the not too aesthetically enhanced Edgeware Road. The spread of Mediterranean fare to be found here, not to mention the freshly squeezed fruit juices, is, simply put, out of this world. Rush there as soon as you can. If you're craving more Lebanese, Shepherd's Market in Mayfair is a good little area to bounce from one spot to the next. **Brick Lane,** very near Petticoat Lane, is the strip to sate all your Bangladeshi and Indian cravings. The road is home not only to one curry joint after another, but also to an outdoor market on the weekends (see *used and bruised,* above). For the most misshapen but delicious pizza, go to **La Pizzeria** *(Sydney St., off the King's Rd.; Tel 0207/376-76-00; Tube to Sloane Sq.; Open daily; No credit cards)* in the Chelsea Farmer's Market. The open kitchen also doles out big bowls of pasta and risotto. The only catch with this restaurant is that on weekends the line stretches around the block and there is a ridiculous cover charge of £1 per person (which is usually reserved for a tablecloth charge or coat keeping, not for a casual pizza picnic setup), but do take it off the bill if you see fit (a 12.5 percent tip is also included).

The other ultra-popular spot in the Chelsea Market is **The Market Place** *(Chelsea Farmer's Market; Tel 0207/352-56-00; 9:30am-5pm daily winter; 9:30am-11pm daily summer).* Especially good on a sunny weekend afternoon, the menu is casual and homely with sprinklings of South African culinary tidbits.

means "selfish" in Japanese) is just as "Futurama" as the other three, featuring an undulating green metal and glass wall. Inside, staff takes orders on handheld Trekkie computers, whisking generous portions of Japanese noodles and dumplings to your place at the crowded picnic-style tables within minutes. While the quasi-cafeteria thing is a bit wacky, the hordes of hipsters mobbing the restaurant don't seem to mind at all.

Tactical *(27 D'Arblay St.; Tel 0207/287-28-23; Tube to Tottenham Court Rd. or Oxford Circus; 9am-11pm Mon-Fri, noon-11pm Sat; Entrees £10-18; No credit cards)* serves up more conventional eats in cool surroundings. A bar, cafe, coffeeshop, and bookstore in one, Tactical's eclecticism makes it a standout. Serving a rotating menu of sandwiches, beers, and coffees alongside a motley assortment of edgy and subversive books, Tactical is a hipster's paradise. Don't plan on getting too much reading done, unless you can concentrate while the freshest New York hip-hop booms out of the speakers. Definitely a cool place to chill while in the neighborhood, especially on Sundays, when they have a live DJ.

To die for desserts

The Hampstead High Street is one of the nicer high streets in London, and this is in part due to **La Creperie de Hampstead** *(Perrin's Lane, midway off the High Street; Tube to Hampstead; 11:45am-11pm Mon-Thur; 11:45am-11:30pm Fri-Sun; Savory crepes £3; sweet crepes £2),* a tres petite creperie that has been selling crepes that melt perfectly in your mouth available with milk, dark, or white Belgian chocolate, for 20 years. A sign on the stand warns: 'Belgian chocolate is absolutely divine but may ooze out when you bite.' Mmmm.

For sticky toffee pudding that you simply will not believe, **The House on the Hill** *(Rosslyn Hill, lower Hampstead High St.; Tel 0207/435-80-37; Tube to Hampstead; Daily till midnight; Dessert £5; All major credit cards)*—also in Hampstead—is the place to get it. The House, as it is referred to by locals, is also a restaurant and bar serving the North London hipsters. The best time to drop in, however, is after dinner for a cappuccino and the aforementioned heavenly sticky stuff. The ubiquitous restaurant chain **Dome** *(35A-B Kensington High St; Tube to High Street Kensington; Tel 0207/937-66-55; Daily till 10:30pm; Dessert £4; All major credit cards)* serves a dessert called Banoffi Pie. Now, you will find Banoffi Pie at other London eateries, but do not be fooled. None of these pathetic attempts will in any way compare to the real deal on offer at Dome. An orgasmic combination of caramelized condensed milk and bananas balancing precariously on a ginger cookie–type base, this is *the* stuff.

The ubiquitous **Pizza Express** *(39 Abbey Rd.; Tel 0207/624-55-77; Tube to Kilburn Park; 11:30-midnight daily; www.pizzaexpress.co.uk; Entrees from £10-18; AE, MC, V),* with dozens of branches across London, sounds like a chain of takeout joints—but Pizza Hut it ain't. This hugely popular chain fully deserves its good rep. The menu offers a range of personal pizzas as well as salads topped with the fine house dressing (which is also sold in bottles). It's popular with most Londoners, so expect to see all sorts dining together in London's original pizzeria. The upscale St. John's Wood location is near to both the happening **Saatchi Gallery** [see *culture zoo,* above], and the legendary Abbey Road crossing, immortalized on the cover of the Beatles album.

Another good bet is **Nontas** *(16 Camden High St.; Tel 0207/387-45-79; Tube to Mornington Crescent; Noon-3pm, 6:30pm-midnight Mon-Sat;*

Entrees from £10; MC, V), a little Greek restaurant that is so relaxed it feels like dining in somebody's home. They serve authentic Greek food without the kitschy statues and broken pottery, and the dishes are perfectly prepared and seasoned. In addition to the food, diners also enjoy a hilarious combo of Greek music and classic '60s tunes performed by the proprietor himself.

Also in the area is **Sauce** *(214 Camden High St.; Tel 0207/482-07-77; Tube to Camden Town; Noon-11pm Mon-Sat, till 4pm Sun; Entrees from £6; MC, V)* an organic bar and restaurant. Minimal and white, the restaurant is warmed by colorful tablecloths and excellent paintings. The bar is willing and able to amuse the odd twenty- or thirtysomething put off by veggie burgers with lentils, nuts, and seeds.

Cranks *(17-19 Great Newport St.; Tel 0207/836-52-26; Tube to Leicester Sq.; Open daily)* is London's well-known health food restaurant chain. Cranks used to be much more organic in feel, with long wooden benches and huge buffets with loads of mushy bowls, whereas now it's much more sleek and colourful in that bright and plastic way. But despite the fact that the quality of the grub has deteriorated somewhat, it's still a sure thing for healthier fast food, although it is fairly costly.

Similar to Pizza Express, **Ask** *(121-125 Park St., off Oxford St.; Tel 0207/495-77-60; Tube to Bond St. or Marble Arch; 5:30-10:30pm; £10; All major credit cards)* is also one of the usual suspect restaurants that seems to have a branch or two in every suburb of London. The food is as imaginative as can be expected from a run-of-the mill pizza/pasta spot, but it is consistently delicious. The restaurants are minimalist, but elegantly decorated with a modern, bright feel. Although the pizza Fiorentina at Pizza Express can't be beat, the penne with tuna at Ask is just as good.

▶▶SPLURGE

As with anywhere else, it usually takes lots of money to get a first-class meal in London. **Mr. Kong** *(21 Lisle St.; Tel 0207/437-73-41; Tube to Leicester Sq.; Noon-3am daily; Entrees £10-25; MC, V),* on Chinatown's main drag, is an exception to the rule. Serving Cantonese food, it makes its reputation on the daily and chef's specials. Talk things over with the waiter, who can recommend obscure and tasty dishes. Although the decor is equivalent to any ghetto wok in America, authentic Chinese food of this caliber is a rare find in London or anywhere else.

For those wanting something posh, London has no shortage of trendy gourmet restaurants. A standout is **Axis** *(1 Aldwych; Tel 0207/300-03-00; Tube to Temple, Covent Garden, or Charing Cross; Noon-3pm Mon-Fri, 5-11:30pm Mon-Sat; Avg entree £25; AE, MC, V),* housed in the **One Aldwych** hotel. Blending influences from Europe and Asia, Axis (though its name is odd in a city that got Blitzkrieged) serves an excellent selection of fusion cuisine. A meal may be costly, but the service and the exquisite ambience, complete with a vertigo-inducing cityscape mural, confirm that it's money well spent. As in the rest of One Aldwych, simplicity and good taste prevail.

An expanse of cream and gold with giant palms in brass urns and slowly revolving fans greets you as you enter. To the right is a conservatory with more greenery, and all around the walls are lined with original photos of gents on elephant-back out to bag a tiger. The air is laden with the sweet, sour, and heady scents of a thousand spices. Yes, you're in curry heaven. **The Bombay Brasserie** *(Courtfield Rd.; Tel 0207/370-40-40; £10-20 per entree)* is the restaurant of **Bailey's Hotel,** on Gloucester Road, conveniently located directly opposite the Tube station. The menu is exquisite, so the best time to visit is at the all you can eat Sunday lunchtime buffet (book early). True, there are better curries in London, and at better prices, but the atmosphere here is like nowhere else, so you don't resent the price.

Beach Blanket Babylon *(45 Ledbury Rd; Tel 0207/229-29-07; Open daily; Starters £4.95-11, Entrees £11.50-35)* in trendy Notting Hill is a candlelit Gaudiesque paradise complete with multicolored, glistening, mirrored mosaics, twisting spiral staircases held together by chains, and a cavernous seating arrangement that juts out of the stone walls. The menu is pretentious in the extreme, but certainly varied (rabbit, Thai, prawn curry, squid, gravlax, foie gras, red meat, and chicken), and the atmosphere is superb and surreal. This is a perfect spot to hide away with that desirable someone in its many nooks and crannies. If your wallet is not busting at the seams, at least down a drink in the overcrowded bar and take a peek around.

Tucked behind London's answer to Madison Avenue—Sloane Street—is a kitchen serving some of the best Italian in town. **Sale e Pepe** *(9/15 Pavilion Rd.; Tel 0207/235-00-98 or Tel 0207/235-01-14; Tube to Knightsbridge)* is run by actual Italians, and the taste of the heaped bowls of spaghetti and endless breadsticks will stay with you long after you've paid the check.

crashing

Even the thriftiest travelers will find it next to impossible to survive on less than about £50 a day in London. Much of that money will inevitably go toward lodgings, which of course range from simple to opulent. If the latter is to your liking, understand that you're gonna drop some cash for that luxury. Luckily, even London's least expensive accommodations are comfortable and fairly convenient. The tourist office will help you make a reservation if you show up without a plan.

▶▶**CHEAP**

The cozy **Ashlee House** *(261-265 Gray's Inn Rd.; Tel 0207/833-94-99, Fax 0207/833-96-77; Tube to King's Cross/St. Pancras or Bus 10, 46, 91, 73, 214, 19 to King's Cross; info@ashleehouse.co.uk; £36 single, £24 double, £15 dormitory; No credit cards)* is just blocks from the King's Cross/St. Pancras Station, which has seven different subway and train lines and a number of city buses. It hosts loads of young tourists from all over the world, so there's no lack of company in the clean-but-styleless dorms or the smoky lobby. Breakfast of the cereal-and-coffee variety is included, and kitchen facilities are available for other meals. Coin laundry, common showers, and single-sex bathrooms let you preserve some dignity while living out of a backpack.

Situated in a neighborhood that's a favorite among both Australian tourists and leather-clad gays, the **YHA Earl's Court Youth Hostel** *(38 Bolton Gardens; Tel 0207/373-70-83, Fax 0207/835-20-34; Tube to Earl's Court, Bus C1, N97 to Earl's Court; Desk open till 11pm; earlscourt_@yha.org.uk, www.yha.org.uk; £21 dormitory; AE, V, MC)* is sure to be a blast. The hostel features a smoky little common room with cable TV and a pay-per-use Internet station as well as a garden, kitchen, laundry facilities, phone cards, tickets, and money exchange. The bathrooms and showers are shared, though they aren't coed. Drawbacks include the distant location and a bizarre musty smell that permeates the entire building. Hmmm....

Probably the strangest hotel in the universe, the **Generator** *(Mac-Naughten House, Compton Place; Tel 0207/388-76-66, Fax 0207/388-76-44; Tube to Euston or Russell Sq., or Bus 10, 30, 73, 91 to Euston; generator_@lhdr.demon.co.uk, www.lhdr.demon.co.uk; £38 single, £26 double, £20.50 dormitory; V, MC)* is decorated in industrial style. It's billed as a place to meet and hang out with other young travelers—probably because the bland and cramped rooms drive most patrons to retreat to the common areas on the main floor, which include several bars and restaurants. Each floor has single-sex toilets and showers, and each dorm has its own washbasin and mirror. The hotel also offers breakfast, tourist advice, and packed lunches.

There area a few other reliable and affordable options: **The Palace Hotel** *(31 Palace Court; Tel 0207/22--5628, No Fax; £12 dorm, £15 quad, £17 triple, £18 double; shared bathrooms No credit cards)* is in the heart of Notting Hill just off of the Notting Hill Gate tube stop. They have a mall kitchen and game room, as well as free tea and coffee in the morning. Or park hyour bones at **Enrico House** *(77079 Warwick Way; Tel 0207/233-7538, Fax 0207/233-9995; £45 double w/o bath, £450 double w/shower; v, MC)*, around a half-mile southeast of Victoria Station. A full English breakfast is included in the price of a room.

▶▶DO-ABLE

The greatest asset of the **Shaftesbury Hotel** *(65-73 Shaftesbury Ave.; Tel 0207/434-42-00, Fax 0207/437-17-17; Tube or Bus 14, 19, 38 to Piccadilly Circus; £70 single, £85 double, £119 single suite; AE, V, MC)* is its location, smack-dab in the heart of Theaterland and Soho. The rooms are clean and conservative, but there are ample distractions outside the windows, which open onto crowded streets lined with theaters and restaurants.

Located in popular Notting Hill across from Johnny Depp's new digs is the odd little **Gate Hotel** *(6 Portobello Rd.; Tel 0207/220-707, Fax 0207/221-91-28; Tube or Bus 12, 27, 28, 31, 52, 94 to Notting Hill Gate; gatehotel@globalnet.co.uk, www.users.globalnet.co.uk/~cufra/pages/gatehotel._html; £60 single, £78 double; AE, V, MC)*. Run by a hysterically funny couple, the Gate is a most pleasant place to stay. In addition to attractions like the Portobello Road Market, the hotel

London

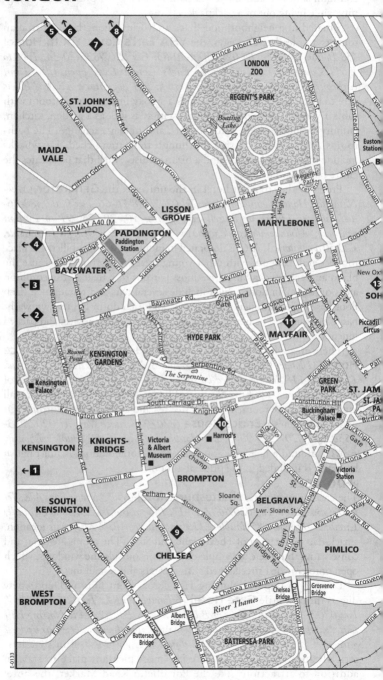

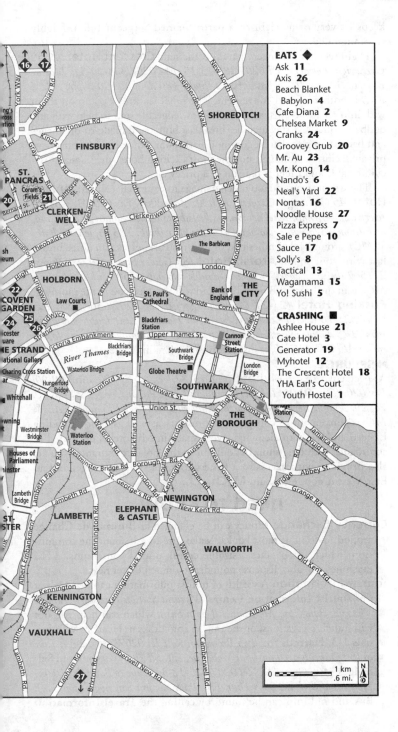

EATS ◆

Ask **11**
Axis **26**
Beach Blanket
  Babylon **4**
Cafe Diana **2**
Chelsea Market **9**
Cranks **24**
Groovey Grub **20**
Mr. Au **23**
Mr. Kong **14**
Nando's **6**
Neal's Yard **22**
Nontas **16**
Noodle House **27**
Pizza Express **7**
Sale e Pepe **10**
Sauce **17**
Solly's **8**
Tactical **13**
Wagamama **15**
Yo! Sushi **5**

CRASHING ■

Ashlee House **21**
Gate Hotel **3**
Generator **19**
Myhotel **12**
The Crescent Hotel **18**
YHA Earl's Court
  Youth Hostel **1**

keeps its very own celebrity, a parrot named Sergeant Bilko. Highly recommended.

Definitely not a swingers' paradise, the staid **Crescent Hotel** *(49-50 Cartwright Gardens; Tel 0207/387-15-15, Fax 0207/383-20-54; Tube or Bus 10, 30, 73, 91 to Euston; £42 single, £80 double, £90 triple; AE, V, MC)* is both cozy and convenient. The hotel features a common room with info on attractions, as well as a knowledgeable staff to help with any oddball requests. A stay includes breakfast buffet and made-to-order eggs and bacon. Singles share a common bathroom, while larger rooms have private facilities. Although not the most exciting hotel, the Crescent is a comfortable and friendly bargain in a pricey city.

These spots won't do too much damage to your wallet either: **Jenkins Hotel** *(45 Cartwright Gardens; Tel 0207/387-2067, Fax 0207/383-3139; reservations@jenkinshotel.demon.co.uk; Tube to Russell Square, Kings Cross, or Euston; £62 double w/o bath, £72 double w/bath, £83 triple with bath; V, MC)*, around 1 1/2 miles east of Regents Park, gives you a free breakfast with your room. **Arofsk Hotel** *(83 Gower Street; Tel 0207/636-2115; Tube to Goodge Sgreet; £44 double w/o bath, £58 double w/bath; v, MC)*, is in the heart of Bloomsbury and will also feed you in the morning. **Rusking Hotel** *(23-24 Montague Street; Tel 0207/636-7388, Fax 0207/323-1662; Tube to Russel Square or Holborn; £60 double w/o bathroom, £75 double w/bathroom, £75 triple w/o bathroom, £85triple w/bathroom; AE, DC, MC, V)*, is just south of the Jenkins Hotel.

▶▶**SPLURGE**

A spectacular space, **Myhotel** *(11-13 Bayley St.; Tel 0207/667-60-00, Fax 0207/667-60-01; Tube to Tottenham Court Rd. or Goodge St., Bus 10, 24, 29, 73; guestservices@myhotels.co.uk; £155 single, £195 double; AE, V, MC)* is convenient to collegiate Bloomsbury as well as Soho. Blending Eastern and Western elements, every space in Myhotel is decorated in accordance with feng shui. In addition to this polar reassurance, you are also provided with access to a fitness room, a stylish lounge, and an East/West fusion restaurant, **MyChi.**

need to know

Currency Exchange Money can be changed at **Bureaux de Change** around town or at most banks. Make sure to ask about the commission, which often takes a sizable chunk out of your funds. ATM machines will also dispense pounds, at a much better rate.

Tourist Information A wealth of tourist information can be found at the **Tourist Information Centre** *(Victoria Station Forecourt; Tube to Victoria; 8am-7pm Mon-Sat, till 5pm Sun)*, which can help you out with hotel reservations, or the smaller info desks in **Heathrow Terminals 1-3, Harrods** *(87-135 Brompton Rd.; Tel 0207/730-12-34; Tube to Knightsbridge; 10am-6pm Mon, Tue, Sat, till 7pm Wed-Fri)*, and **Selfridges** *(400 Oxford St.; Tel 0207/629-12-34; Tube to Bond St.; 10am-7pm Mon-Wed, till 8pm Thur, Fri, 9:30am-7pm Sat, noon-6pm Sun)*. Bus and rail info can be found by calling the **Travel Information**

Centre Hotline *(Tel 0207/222-12-34),* or by visiting their desks at Heathrow, Victoria, Piccadilly Circus, Oxford Circus, Euston, and King's Cross/St. Pancras stations.

Public Transportation Most attractions are accessible by subway or bus. The subway, known as the **Tube,** is fast and convenient, but it's closed after midnight. A series of night buses, designated by the prefix "N," pick up the slack. Fares for the Tube vary from 80p to £3.10 depending on how many of the six zones you plan to travel through. Multi-day passes called **Travelcards** *(£17.60-34.90 for unlimited use),* available at the Tube stations, grant varying degrees of flexibility. The best deal is the weekly travel pass, which grants access to the Tube and all buses. Bus fares start at 70p and rise depending upon distance traveled. Taxis are widely available, and the drivers are legendary for their knowledge of the city. Look for the taxi's distinctly large silhouette barreling down the road and flag it down—they're available if the yellow bar on top is lit. Many taxis accept credit cards in lieu of cash. Still another option is London's minicabs, private car services that vary wildly in price and dependability. A reasonable service is **Addison Lee** *(Tel 171/387-88-88).*

American Express Presuming you accidentally left home without it, get a replacement card here *(192 Victoria St.; Tel 0207/828-45-67; Tube to Victoria; 9am-5:30pm Mon-Fri, till 4pm Sat).*

Health and Emergency For emergencies: *999.* Call *Tel 0208/900-10-00* for doctors on-call 24 hours a day. **Charing Cross Hospital Emergency Room** *(Fulham Palace Rd., Hammersmith; Tel 0208/846-12-34)* is also open 24 hours.

Pharmacy Get the pills for all types of chills or spills at **Bliss** *(5 Marble Arch; Tel 0207/723-61-16; Tube to Marble Arch; 9am-midnight daily).*

Telephones City codes: *207* and *208*; Directory assistance: *192*; International operator: *155.* Pay phones accept coins or calling cards, available at any off-license (convenience store).

Airports London's three international airports are **Heathrow** *(Tel 0208/759-43-21; www.baa.co.uk),* **Gatwick** *(Tel 01293/535-353; www.baa.co.uk)* and **Stansted** *(Tel 01279/680-500; www.baa.co.uk).* By far the largest and busiest, Heathrow is connected to town by both the Tube and the speedy **Heathrow Express** *(Paddington Station; Tel 0845/600-15-15; £10; Trip takes 15 minutes; 5:10am-11:40pm daily every 15 minutes).* On your way out of town, additional time can be saved by checking in for your flight at Paddington Station. From Gatwick, get into town via the **Gatwick Express** *(Victoria Station; Tel 0990/301-530; Trip takes 35 minutes; 5am-11:45pm daily, then hourly through the night; £9.50).* While this is the most expensive way to the airport next to taxis (which will run you £35-45 plus tip from any of the airports), it is both fast and reliable. The speediest route from Stansted is via **Stansted Skytrain** *(Liverpool St. Station; Tel 0345/484-950; Trip takes 45 minutes; Every 30 minutes 5am-midnight Mon-Sat, 7am-midnight Sun; £10.70).*

wired

Along with all the porn and bootleg music on the Internet, a number of excellent websites about London are floating around in cyberspace.

www.bta.org.uk: The official site of the British Tourism Authority, regarding all things touristy in London and the rest of England.

www.timeout.co.uk: The web version of the omnipresent bible of London culture.

www.london.eventguide.com: Listings of arts events, restaurants, and hotels.

www.albemarle-london.com: Dedicated to London's glitzier West End productions, this site has listings, top-ten lists, news, and online booking.

www.s-h-systems.co.uk/london.html: In addition to comprehensive hotel listings by neighborhood, this site has local weather, car rental service, and exclusive discounts on accommodations.

www.sorted.org/london: A website devoted to London's hedonistic nightlife. Listings and info are provided alongside DJ bios and loads of links to related sites.

www.guardian.co.uk: The online version of London's popular daily, *The Guardian*.

www.multimap.com: Organized by postal code, this site can provide comprehensive street maps of the entire city.

www.grafcafe.com: A cool site with tons of cool flicks of London's finest aerosol villains.

www.urban75.com: "Underground" website with info on raves, drugs, direct action (protests), and lots of other cool shit to read.

www.neonlit.co.uk: A comprehensive site devoted to England's literary scene brought to you by the good folks at *Time Out*.

www.hostels.com: For a complete listing of hostels in London.

Trains The first step for any rail journey out of London is a call to the **National Rail Enquiry Line** *(Tel 0345/484-950)*. Schedule information for all of England's numerous rail services can be found there. Fares tend to be very reasonable, and even the most distant points are accessible within a few hours. Trains to the south coast of England leave from **Charing Cross Station.** Those bound for the east, from **Fenchurch Street.** Those heading to the northeast and Scotland, from **King's Cross.** Trains to East Anglia leave from **Liverpool Street.** Trains to the Midlands leave from **Euston.** **Paddington** serves the southwest and South Wales. **St. Pancras** sends trains out to the north of England. The south, Kent, and the Sussex coast are accessible via **Victoria.** Lastly, trains for the Dorset

www.hotelnet.co.uk: For a complete listing of hotels in London.

www.thisislondon.com: Updates, listings, events guides, and info on everything London-related.

www.londontransport.co.uk: This site deals with the Tube and bus network, and includes useful maps.

www.pti.org.uk: This website deals with the entire UK transport system, including info on rail, coach, air, ferry, and metro travel.

www.artsfestivals.co.uk: Directory of all the arts festivals in the UK with dates and useful contact numbers.

www.uktw.co.uk: Online theatre bookings for the forward planner.

www.countryside.gov.uk: Good assemblage of info on national trails, areas of beauty, wilderness areas, and national parks in the country.

For e-mail and a Vampire (beet, carrot, and orange juice), try **Juice** *(7 Earlham St.; Tel 0207/836-73-76; Tube to Leicester Sq.; 10am-10pm Mon-Sat, till 8pm Sun; No credit cards)* a Covent Garden juice bar and cybercafe. Because of the natural food and juice selection, the regular customers look less pasty than your average Net-head.

From the creator of easyJet.com and easyRentacar.com comes the ultra-cheap, super-easy chain of Internet cafes **easyEverything.com** *(9-16 Tottenham Court Rd., Oxford St. end; Tel 0207/907-78-00; Tube to Tottenham Court Rd.; Open daily 24 hrs; www.easyeverything.com)*. With five supermarket-sized stores open in central London all the time offering computer access for as little cash as £1, this is revolutionizing the concept of the Internet cafe internationally. In addition to web surfing, Microsoft Office 2000 software is available now as well, at the same price.

coast, the south, and the **Eurostar** *(Tel 0990/186-186)* train to Paris and Brussels can be caught at **Waterloo Station.** Tickets can be booked in advance or purchased at the station with cash, check, or credit card. However, prices and ticketing are complicated and are subject to change without notice.

Bus Lines Out of the City The main bus service to points outside London is **National Express** *(Tel 0990/898-989)*. Buses depart from **Victoria Coach Station** *(Buckingham Palace Rd.; Tel 0207/730-34-66)*. As with most services in England, special pricing is available for students. The bus service also provides special coaches to and from some of Britain's major summer festivals and concerts [see *festivals and events,* above].

Bike Rental Bikes can be rented from **Bikepark** *(14 Stukeley St.; Tel 0207/430-0083; Tube to Covent Garden; 7:30am-8:30pm Mon-Fri, 8:30am-6:30pm Sat; AE, MC, V)*. It's £10 the first day, £5 the second, and £3 each successive day.

Scooter Rental There's something European about getting around by moped. To get putting, call **Scootabout** *(King's Cross; Tel 0207/833-46-07; Tube to King's Cross; 9am-6pm Mon-Fri, till 1pm Sat; MC, V)*. Thankfully, insurance and a helmet are included in the rental fee.

Laundry Convenient location and standard coin-operated facilities make **Duds 'n' Suds** *(49-51 Brunswick Shopping Centre; Tel 0207/837-11-22; Tube to Russell Sq.; 8am-9pm Mon-Fri, 9am-8pm Sat, Sun; No credit cards)* the ideal laundromat near Soho and the rest of the West End.

Internet See *wired*, above.

everywhere else

kew gardens

London's **Kew Gardens** is actually a scientific research center brilliantly disguised as botanical gardens. You can visit Kew year-round, and it's a good place to go on the same day as Richmond, as it's one stop before it on the train [see *need to know,* below]. The gardens span 300 acres, so if you feel like oxygenating the lungs, this is the place to do it. The site encompasses lakes, greenhouses, walks, garden pavilions, and museums, and there are also plenty of patches of grass to lie down and read on—meditative oases where you can just plain chill.

The huge glass-domed **Palm House** is a supremely beautiful example of Victorian architecture. It overflows with tropical rain-forest plants and trees—once you step inside, the tropical humidity hits you head-on. Up above you'll see the trees touching the high ceiling, and the huge fanlike leaves hanging over the pathways. All that's missing are a couple of loincloth-sporting natives to make it feel like you're really wandering the Amazon.

Downstairs, the Palm House's **marine display** shows off a wide variety of algae (more interesting and better looking than you'd ever guess) and features colorful tropical fish. There's also a tank filled with sea horses that bob up and down in the water like rusks dunked in tea.

The **Pagoda,** on the east side of the gardens, is a 10-story circular structure that has no practical function (you can't go in), but was designed purely to give visual punch to the landscape. The red pillars at the base and the red railings on the balconies on each level do create a stunning picture. Very near the Pagoda is the **Japanese Gateway** that overlooks a big Zen-type garden. On the path leading west toward the lake you'll find a little duck pond, and a bit farther west beyond the lake is the bamboo garden.

Another of the large greenhouses worth going into is the **Princess of Wales Conservatory,** near the main gate in the northern part of the gardens. This structure, with multilayered, jutting roofs, houses a giant water lily (in summer) that floats on the pond, as well as the weirdest-looking giant flytraps. The flytraps attract flies by stinking of rotten meat, if you can believe there's a plant that can smell that bad. Once the flies are lured inside, they are used as pollinators and then spat back out the plant's mouth!

It's a good idea to call ahead [see *contact info*, below] and find out what is in season in the gardens, as the wide variety of flowers bloom during different months.

need to know

Contact Info *Tel 020/89-40-11-71;* Online at *www.kew.org.*

Hours/Days Open The gardens generally open at 9:30am, but it's best to call ahead for seasonal hours. Guided tours leave from the **Victoria Gate Visitor Centre** at 11am and 2pm daily, March to October; 11am daily and noon on weekends, November to February; and are closed Christmas and New Year's Day.

Cost Admission is £5 for adults, £3.50 for students.

Directions and Transportation Take the **District line Tube** or **South West Trains/Silverlink** rail from London to either Kew Gardens Station or Kew Bridge station, respectively. From either of the two stations it is a short, well-marked walk to the gardens.

richmond

South of the Thames you'll find Richmond, a very wealthy area where mega-punters, such as Jerry Hall, have homes. Widely considered to be an outlying southwest suburb of London, posh Richmond is actually within an outer borough of London called **Richmond-upon-Thames,** located in the county of Surrey. But you don't need much money to steal away to this place for an afternoon and banish the chaos of metropolitan life—even for just a few hours.

Since Richmond lies on the **Thames,** it has beautiful river walks and an abundance of cafes and benches lining the water. The walking paths are narrow, however, so you may be competing with cyclists for space on the weekends.

Or, you can rent a rowboat at one of the boating stations near the **Richmond Bridge.** Just go straight to the river, pop into one of the informal rental sheds, and introduce yourself [see *need to know,* below].

Richmond has a charming and low-key **town center** filled with cutesy shops selling knickknacks, along with the major chain stores that you'd find on any English High Street—**W. H. Smith, Next, Whittards, HMS.** Slightly off from the town center is the **grass commons,** lined with pubs along one side. This huge field is a great place to chill out and watch a cricket game or toss a Frisbee in the summer. A relaxing low-cost afternoon can be spent walking around the window-shopping-friendly town, followed by a long walk along the Thames, and rounded out by a lazy lunch at one of the riverside restaurants. It's a superb place to spend a Sunday afternoon away from the pollution and noise of London, possibly in combination with a trip to Kew Gardens.

Richmond is easily accessible from London by train. You can reach it on the Tube (last stop on the District line going southwest), but that takes a lot longer than getting a day return (from the West Hampstead rail station, not the Tube stop, which is across the road). A round-trip ticket costs £2.70 and the trip takes about a half-hour each way. After exiting the train station, turn left—there's only one exit out of the train station so you can't miss it—and walk southwest along the **Quadrant.** It's a short 5- to 10-minute walk into the center of town. Once you get there, it doesn't take more than a few minutes to walk around the whole town or down to the river.

If the skies turn gloomy, there are two cinemas—**Richmond Film-house** (3 Water Lane; Tel 0208/332-00-30; Buses 190, 65) and **Odeon** (72 Hill St.; Tel 0181/315-42-18; Buses 65, 490, H33, H37, 397, 191)—showing mainstream Hollywood flicks.

Eats

Once you've worked up a thirst walking, cycling, or boating on the river, a great place to have lunch is right next to it at **Pitcher & Piano** (Next to the Richmond Bridge; Tel 0208/332-25-24; Noon-11pm Mon-Fri, 11am-11pm Sat, 11am-10:30pm Sun; Sandwiches £4-9, main courses and salads £6-8; V, MC with £5 min). Although P&P is a chain restaurant, this particular one is different from the others. It's light and bright and has a wonderful gazebo-like structure in the middle, which gets packed to the windowpanes on Sunday afternoons. On this day of rest, patrons relax and read the newspapers that are strewn about the couches and tables.

Richmond is not short on restaurants, and all of the usual suspects make an appearance: **Café Rouge** (248 Upper Richmond Rd. West, Tel 0208/828-88-97 and 7a Petersham Rd.; Tel 0208/332-24-25), **Café**

TO MARKET

If you're looking to enjoy a leisurely picnic on the green, pick up your supplies in the town center at **Marks & Spencer** (13 George St.; Tel 0208/948-00-44; 9am-7pm Mon-Thur, till 8pm Fri, 8:30am-6:30pm Sat, 11am-5pm Sun) or **Tesco** (29 George St.; Tel 0208/910-75-00; 24 hrs Mon-Fri, till 10pm Sat, 11am-5pm Sun).

Pasta *(20 Hill St.; Tel 0208/940-89-51),* **Caffe Uno** *(15-17 Hill Rise; Tel 0208/948-62-820),* and **Dome** *(26 Hill St.; Tel 0208/332-25-25).*

If you are interested in a picnic lunch, there are two major supermarkets [see *to market,* above].

need to know

Tourist Information The **TIC** is located at the Old Town Hall *(Whittaker Ave.; Tel 0208/940-91-25, Fax 0208/940-68-99; information. services@richmond.gov.uk).*

Health and Emergency Emergencies: *999.* **West Middlesex University Hospital** *(Twickenham Rd., Isleworth, Middlesex; Tel 0208/560-21-21)* is the closest hospital for urgent care. It occupies a site close to the Thames and within easy access to Richmond.

Telephone Dial *8* for outer London, and the town's code is *020.*

Boat There are plenty of rental places to choose from along the river. Among them, **Richmond Boat Hire** *(Next to Richmond Bridge; Tel 0208/948-82-70; £3.50 per hour, £10 weekdays, £15 weekends with a £20 deposit per boat)* is in the center of town, and can set you up with a rowboat.

Bike/Moped Rental If you'd like to take a spin around town, **The Original Bike Hire Company** *(Tel 0800/013-80-00; £12 per day or £4.50 per hour)* rents bikes from Richmond Park in the car park at Roehampton Gate.

windsor

Day-tripping to Windsor will satisfy any remaining royal cravings you might have and give you a double dose of traditional English culture.

Home to the famous **Windsor Castle** (second residence of the royal family) and the nearby **Eton College** (where English royalty and the just-plain-posh go to study), Windsor is perfect for a day's exploration. About 31,000 folks live here, but be prepared: Windsor is packed in the summer, and its charming small-town character diminishes a bit.

The castle dominates the center of town from its lofty position atop **Castle Hill** and is visible from every point in central Windsor. It's quite a behemoth to behold as you walk south up curving **Thames Street.** Many streets in Windsor offer fine examples of Victorian and Georgian architecture, particularly south of the castle. The oldest part of town is located immediately opposite **Henry VIII Gate** (the exit of the castle), where the cobblestoned streets hail from the 17th century. The **Parish Church** and the **Guild Hall** were both built by famed English architect Sir Christopher Wren in 1690. Other historic jewels include the **Old King's Head** on **Church Street,** which has a plaque recording the execution warrant for Charles I in 1648. The building is also reputed to be the place where Shakespeare wrote *The Merry Wives of Windsor.* Another building to check out, if you're a royal enthusiast, is the **house of Nell Gwynne,** Charles II's favorite mistress. An interesting tidbit about the geography of Windsor: According to the *Guinness Book of Records,* **Queen Charlotte Street,** directly across from the TIC [see *need to know,* below], is the shortest street in England.

Windsor's main shopping drag is **Peascod Street,** which leads west off **High Street.** It's not the most amazing shopping experience in the world, with the usual stores (Laura Ashley, Next, and Monsoon among them) and a couple of local bookshops, namely Methvens and Hammicks. Off Peascod, you will find the mall-like **King Edward Court Shopping Centre** *(Tel 0800/923-00-17; 10am-6pm Mon-Sat, Thur till 7pm, 11am-5pm Sun)* and, near that, the small, half-enclosed center that holds the **Windsor Central** train station (there are two train stations in town; the other is **Windsor & Eton Riverside**), a couple of upmarket boutiques (such as Daks, Hobbs, and Jaeger), and restaurants.

Everything in Windsor is within walking distance. As you come out of the Windsor & Eton Riverside station onto **Datchet Road,** there are two options: Follow Datchet south, where it turns into Thames Street, up the hill to the shops; or turn right (northwest) onto the **Windsor Bridge** that leads to Eton.

Eton is spread across the top of High Street and its side streets. After crossing the bridge, you'll enter **Eton High Street,** where you'll find lots of antique shops and art galleries.

Opposite Eton College is **South Common Lane,** which, if you follow to the end, away from Eton High St., will lead you to a collection of massive green fields, sprinkled with tall trees and wildflowers—a scene straight out of a Van Gogh painting. One of the footpaths goes off to the right and leads you in a circle past Eton College's **sports field,** from where you have a great view of the back of the glass art studio on Common Lane—a blast of modern architecture in the midst of such pastoral tranquility. On the walk to the fields, you'll be able to mingle with the Eton boys (only during term times, of course, April 26-July 2,

eton boys' duds

Except for the tails and pinstripe pants, some of the boys have slight variations in their uniforms. If you're a keeper (captain) of any of the school's sports teams, house captain, or a member of sixth-form select (meaning a scholar), then you can wear stick-ups (bow tie and a winged collar). If you're a member of pop (a prefect), then you're allowed to choose your own colored waistcoats as well as special trousers and bow tie, à la Prince William.

windsor

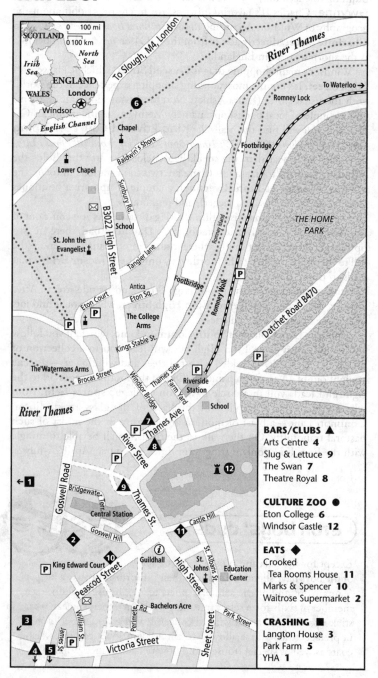

SCOTLAND

0 — 100 mi
0 — 100 km

North Sea

Irish Sea

ENGLAND

WALES　London

Windsor

English Channel

River Thames

To Slough, M4, London

To Waterloo →

Romney Lock

Footbridge

6

Chapel

Baldwin's Shore

THE HOME PARK

Lower Chapel

Sunbury Rd.

B3022 High Street

School

St. John the Evangelist

Tangier lane

Footbridge

Romney Island

Romney Walk

P

Antica
Eton Sq.

Eton Court

P

The College Arms

P

Kings Stable St.

Datchet Road B470

The Watermans Arms

Brocas Street

Windsor Bridge

Thames Side

Farm Yard

Thames Ave.

Riverside Station

P

School

River Thames

← 1

Goswell Road

Bridgewater Terr.

River Stree

P

7

8

9

12

Central Station

Goswell Hill

2

Castle Hill

11

P

King Edward Court

Guildhall

10

i

St. Johns

St. Albans St.

Education Center

Peascod Street

Bachelors Acre

Perimeter Rd.

3 ←

James St.

William St.

P

Victoria Street

Sheet Street

Park Street

High Street

4　5

BARS/CLUBS ▲
Arts Centre **4**
Slug & Lettuce **9**
The Swan **7**
Theatre Royal **8**

CULTURE ZOO ●
Eton College **6**
Windsor Castle **12**

EATS ◆
Crooked
　Tea Rooms House **11**
Marks & Spencer **10**
Waitrose Supermarket **2**

CRASHING ■
Langton House **3**
Park Farm **5**
YHA **1**

Sept 6-Oct 1) outfitted in their traditional uniforms of tails, black pin-stripe pants, and white bow ties.

Windsor Bridge, which joins the town center and Eton, is a lovely spot to pause and look at the view to the east and west, as the river forms a clearing.

The **Thames river walk** is a good place to feed the gangs of ducks and swans. (These swans are vicious during mealtime and will dash out of the water and waddle toward you if they think you're being stingy.) There are also several points along the Thames to rent boats and to book either a half-hour or a two-hour river trip [see *need to know,* below]. A bit touristy, but worthwhile if you just want to chill and float down the Thames.

bar, live music, and performing arts scene

Nightlife in Windsor is, admittedly, not rife with excitement, but two of the more hopping bars include the **Slug & Lettuce** *(5 Thames St.; Tel 01753/864-405; 11am-11pm daily)* and **The Swan** *(9 Mill Lane, corner of Datchet Rd. and the pedestrian road that leads to Windsor Bridge; Tel 01753/862-069; 6-11pm daily).* The Slug & Lettuce has a modern feel with its stripped wood floors and sleek wine bar. You're likely to meet the young and trendy, both locals and visitors. The Swan, however, is a much noisier, rough-and-tumble English pub with tables on the sidewalk. Here you'll find a more down-home, local crowd, which is likely to be a bit older.

The Arts Centre *(Corner of St. Leonards and St. Marks Rd.; Tel 01753/859-336; Box office 10am-11pm Tue-Sat, 7-10:30pm Sun; Handling fee £1.50; MC, V)* has a theater, a bar, and a live music venue that features folk, jazz, rock, and world. There are regular folk nights, as well as a rock week, and jazz on Tuesdays.

The Arts Centre lures a younger crowd than the **Theatre Royal** *(Thames St.; Tel 01753/853-888; Box office 10am-8pm Mon-Sat; MC, V, Switch),* which is the main venue in town for big productions from London's West End (think: *Les Miserables, Saturday Night Fever*) and is across the street from the castle.

culture zoo

Both Windsor Castle and Eton College will leave you with an unforget-talbe sense of the pomp and ceremony of traditional aristocratic British culture. To see royalty on a big scale, visit the 1,000 rooms of the world's largest inhabited castle. And you don't have to be a student of one of the most famous schools in the world to get a feel for the smart and elegant Eton. Simply walk around the college grounds and take in the buildings, which are grandiose for a secondary school.

Windsor Castle *(Castle Hill; Tel 01753/869-898; Last admission for State Apartments 4:30pm Mar-Oct; 3:30pm Nov-Feb; Castle closes 5:15pm Mar-Oct; 4:15pm Nov-Feb; Evensong in St. George's Chapel 5:15pm daily,*

*closed Sun; Changing of the guard held 11am daily, except Sun Apr-June, usu-
ally in the Quadrangle, on alternate days the rest of the year outside the Guard-
room in the Lower Ward, near the exit; £10.50 adults, no student concessions):*
The royals' home away from home has been inhabited by British royalty
for 900 years and is an official residence of the queen. When she is staying
in the castle, her personal flag flies from the Round Tower in the center of
the castle grounds. The castle is a working palace and official engagements
are still held in many of the rooms showcased on the tour. Because it is a
functioning royal venue, sometimes certain areas are restricted to visitors.
Nevertheless, the State Apartments, the Gallery, Queen Mary's Dolls'
House, St. George's Chapel, and the Albert Memorial Chapel are always
accessible when the castle is open for visitors. Some of the more interesting
rooms on the palace tour are the State Room in the Waterloo Chamber, as
well as the numerous bedrooms, dressing rooms, and drawing rooms that
both the queen and prince have in separate wings of the castle.

The State Room is massive with a long table in the center, used for
dining with heads of state. The high ceilings combined with the portraits
on the walls and all the space make it appear grand indeed.

If you have a penchant for pistols and swords, the entry room to the
State Apartments will not disappoint. The long rifles, hand pistols, and
knives of all shapes seem to span history.

The grounds surrounding the castle are lovely to wander around in,
especially the North Terrace, which offers magnificent sweeping views of
the town below.

Eton College *(Tel 01753/671-177; Visiting hours seasonal according
to terms: 10:30am-4:30pm daily; Mar 29-Apr 17 and June 29-Sept 4,
2pm-4:30 April 18-June 28 and Sept 5-29; Terms open 2pm Apr 26-July 2;
Sept 6-Oct 1; Closed May 15, 31, June 30; Admission £3, tours £4, Admission includes access to School Yard, College Chapel, Museum of Eton Life,
and Brewhouse Gallery; visits@etoncollege.org.uk):* This exclusive school
was founded in 1440 by Henry VI and is one of the oldest, most established, and most respected boarding schools in the country. If you don't
plan on visiting Cambridge or Oxford, your stop here will at least give
you a feel for posh, English, boys-only schooling. The library is housed in
a domelike structure and the college chapel is similar to the King's Chapel
at Cambridge University—one of the most ornate chapels in England.
You can take a guided tour or just poke around on your own. A single
building called Eton College houses the chapel, School Yard, Museum of
Eton Life, and Lower School.

EATS

If you want to grab a cheap, fresh sandwich to eat on one of the benches
that line the castle walls on High Street, go to **Waitrose** *(32 King Edward
Court; Tel 01753/855-577; 8:30am-7pm Mon-Wed, Sat, till 8pm Thur,
till 9pm Fri, 11am-5pm Sun),* located in the pedestrian square of the King
Edward Court Shopping Centre, or **Marks & Spencer** *(130 Peascod*

St.; 9:30am-5pm Mon, 9am-5:30pm Tue, Wed, 9am-6:30pm Thur, 9am-6pm Fri, 8:30am-6pm Sat).

Thames Street is crammed with the usual fast-food joints like Burger King and Pizza Hut, and there are also chain restaurants for a quick snack in the Windsor & Eton Central Station shopping enclave. **The Crooked Tea Rooms House** *(Market Cross Houses, 51 High St.; Tel 01753/857-534; Avg tea fare £2-4)* is the Leaning Tower of Pisa of tearooms. This Hansel and Gretel-esque house is lopsided, with slanted doorways at the front and back. The original Crooked Tea House was built in 1687, but was knocked down and rebuilt in 1718. The wood used for the beams wasn't treated properly at the time, and the result is the crooked appearance that remains its hallmark today. It's a good place for tea cakes, scones, and crumpets that even the queen would be happy to nosh on.

crashing

There are a few expensive hotels and more reasonably priced B&Bs in Windsor, but none particularly stand out. The **information center** *(24 High St.; Tel 01753/743-907)* has an accommodation-booking service for a fee of £2 or £3.

▶▶CHEAP

There isn't an independent hostel in town, but there is a **YHA** *(Edgeworth House, Mill Lane; Tel 01753/861-710, Fax 01753/832-100; 1-mile walk from Windsor & Eton Central, 1-mile walk from Riverside station; Reception open at 1pm Mar 1-Dec 23; closed Dec 24-Jan 2; £7.40 under 18, £10.85 adults; windsor@yha.org.uk; MC, V).* There are anywhere from two to 22 beds per room. You can hang out in the lounge, TV room, or self-catering kitchen anytime, as there's no lockout, or use the showers, drying room, bicycle and luggage storage, laundry, Internet access, and grounds. Packed breakfasts are available upon request.

▶▶DO-ABLE

Situated next to a church on a large, quiet, leafy street, **Langton House** *(46 Alma Rd.; Tel 01753/858-299; £40-50 double; No credit cards)* was built in the early 1900s. It is centrally located, only a few minutes' walk from the town center and the castle. All rooms have TV and hairdryers, as well as access to a small kitchen area with fridge, toaster, microwave, tea- and coffee-making facilities, and complimentary cookies. Private bathrooms are available.

Park Farm *(St. Leonards Rd.; Tel 01753/866-823, Fax 01753/850-869; £35 single, £40 double, £65 family room; park.farm@virgin.net)* is a small B&B with hairdryers, tea- and coffee-making facilities, and color TV in all the rooms. En suite bathrooms are available.

need to know

Currency Exchange Most of the major banks, including **Nat West** *(12 High St.; Tel 01753/854-321)*, **Lloyds** *(2 Thames St; Tel 01753/850-507)*; **HSBC** *(5 High St.; Tel 01753/232-600)*, and **Barclays** *(29 High*

St.; Tel 01753/223-605) are near or on High Street. Four other banks are located on Peascod Street. Their hours tend to be the same (9:30am-5:30pm Mon-Fri, 9:30am-4pm or 5pm Wed, 10am-noon Sat).

Tourist Information The **information center** (24 High St.; Tel 01753/743-900; 10am-4pm Mon-Fri, 10am-5pm Sat, 10am-4pm Sun) offers an accommodation-booking service (Tel 01753/743-907) [see crashing, above], books, guides, maps, and souvenirs. Located above the TIC, the small "Town and Crown" exhibition (open daily; £1 adults) displays the development of the town and castle over the ages.

Public Transportation Local **buses** are available (Tel 01753/524-144) to take you around Windsor.

Health and Emergency Emergency **police, fire,** or **ambulance: 999;** **local police station** on Alma Road (Tel 01753/831-990). The nearest hospital is **Wexham Park Hospital** (Slough; Tel 01753/633-000, Fax 01753/691-343), about 10 minutes by taxi from the city center.

Pharmacies There's a **Boots** (113 Peascod St.; Tel 01753/864-378) in town.

Trains and Buses There are two train stations: **Windsor & Eton Riverside** station (Southwest trains from London Waterloo every half hour daily, hourly on Sun; 50 minutes; Tel 02380/213-600 or 01703/213-600; £5.90 day return) and **Windsor & Eton Central** (Trains run from London Paddington, and change at Slough, about 50 minutes). **Green Line coaches** (Tel 0208/668-72-61; Bus 700, 702; same-day round-trip ticket £7) run from Hyde Park Corner in London and take about an hour and a half. The bus drops you near the Parish Church, across the street from the castle. You can also catch a connection from **Heathrow** to Windsor, which is only about 15 minutes away (Tel 01753/524-144).

Postal There is a **post office** (38-39 Peascod St.; Tel 01753/861-451) where you can mail off your postcards of the castle.

oxfordshire &
cambridgeshire

oxfordshire & cambridgeshire

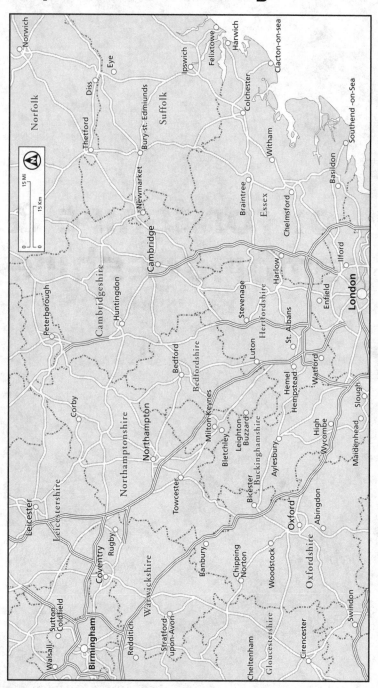

The main attractions in Oxfordshire and Cambridgeshire are, as their names obviously suggest, the two famous universities there: Oxford and Cambridge. Both of the schools occupy beautiful little storybook towns and of course, both of the towns are also party places because students like to party. But don't forget, these aren't *Animal House* types; they're much more like Ivy Leaguers from Harvard and Yale. Oxford is probably the best party town of the two, if only by sheer volume—it has more clubs, bars, and pubs than laid-back Cambridge.

The city of Oxford is home to Britain's equivalent of Harvard: **Oxford University.** It's the place to go if you're drawn to the arts; famous alumni include John Donne, Harold Macmillan, T.E. Lawrence, and Lewis Carroll. The campus buildings are architecturally and historically magnificent, but Oxford is very much a modern city. Its packed, polluted streets are crammed with parcel-burdened locals rushing around during their lunch breaks. The age of the place is evident in a variety of businesses, including the Mitre pub, found in one of Oxford's most historical 17th-century buildings, and Alice's Shop, the inspiration for the illustrator's "Old Sheep Shop" in *Through the Looking Glass.*

Located a short drive from Oxford is the grand **Blenheim Palace,** home of the current Duke of Marlborough and, more importantly, the birthplace of one of the greatest Brits of all time, Winston Churchill. **Henley-on-Thames** is the epitome of an English country town and the stomping ground of the hatted elite, whose most important business seems to be looking prim and proper as the boats glide by during the annual summer Royal Regatta. It's a major photo op for aspiring *paparazzi* and royal-watchers.

The **River Thames** flows through the central and south part of Oxfordshire, and the chalk **Chilterns** extend in a beech-clad ridge for 40 miles from the Thames Valley to St. Albans in Hertfordshire. The northern side of the county borders the **Cotswolds,** an area full of tranquil little countryside villages that look like cover photos for travel guides to rural England.

The town of **Cambridge** is the focal point of Cambridgeshire. The buildings on Cambridge University's campus dominate the skyline. Cambridge is smaller and quainter than Oxford, though it also has often been described as the dullest and ugliest provincial town in England. The students get around by bicycle and sprawl out on The Backs, a meadow surrounded by a river, gardens, and campus buildings, during the midday heat. There is a definite rivalry between the two universities, mirroring the Harvard-Yale feud. Oxford and Cambridge compete in an annual boat race similar to the American duo's annual football game. One activity not to be missed in Cambridge is punting down the rural **River Cam**—that means "rowing" to yanks—after which you should go listen to the boys' choir in the King's College Chapel; if you can't get into the angelic voices of a bunch of English schoolboys, you could always try to imagine what the same songs might sound like, sampled by Puff Daddy.

Cambridge sits on the edge of the **Fens,** flat land that covers the rest of the county. A mecca for painters, the brooding landscape of the Fens has lots of narrow, straight roads, churches dropped into the middle of

TRAVEL TIMES

Times by train unless otherwise indicated * By road.	Oxford	Cambridge	Ely	Blenheim Palace	Henley-On-Thames	London
Oxford	-	3:35	4:00	:35*	1:10	1:10
Cambridge	3:35	-	:15	4:10 (train to Oxford, then bus)	3:15	1:15
Ely	4:00	:15	-	4:35 (train to Oxford, then bus)	3:40	1:25
Blenheim Palace	:35*	4:10 (bus to Oxford, then train)	4:35 (bus to Oxford, then train)	-	1:45	1:45

nowhere, twisted willows with huge split trunks from years of pollarding, and a decidedly dodgy history.

Ely Cathedral, a 15-minute train ride from Cambridge, rises from fen country like a phoenix with its skyscraper-like spires. The 15-mile flat pathway between Cambridge and **Ely** is perfect ground for cycling.

getting around the region

The best way to get around Oxfordshire and Cambridgeshire is to start at each of their prominent locations: Oxford and Cambridge, respectively. Frequent train and bus service makes getting to both places from London a piece of cake. From Oxford there are frequent trains and buses to Henley via Twyford. To get to Blenheim Palace, take a local bus from Oxford's main depot to Woodstock, stopping at the palace en route. From Cambridge there are regular trains as well as campus buses to Ely. Trains are usually quicker and more pleasant, because you get to glide through the English countryside, but buses are always a cheaper option and tend to run more often. Both transportation systems are highly efficient in England and offer numerous changes, stops, and routes. There are always offices at the depots where the staff will help you map out your route. You also can get maps, timetables, and brochures.

▶▶ROUTES

To see each region fully, it makes sense to use London as your starting point. From Oxford, spend a few hours at **Blenheim Palace** (a short distance away) and then go back to **Oxford** to head off for **Henley**.

If you're planning to use Oxford as your base, visit Henley first, as it lies between Oxford and London.

Go from London to **Cambridge** and then make a simple train change to **Ely**, and you will be able to see both of these towns in a day trip, if need be.

oxford

Oxford University has a boozing legacy that is almost as impressive as its academic reputation. The tradition of a "sconcing" started here several centuries ago and is still popular today. A "sconce" is basically a challenge in which one student dares another to stand on a bench—or a dining hall table—and chug a yard of ale, all in one go. If he succeeds, he can return the challenge, and so on, until no one is left standing or the loser has no more money to pay the bill. Originally, students were sconced to embarrass them for using bad manners at the dinner table; today they do it, apparently, just to get blitzed.

Oxford isn't just about students though. It's a full-fledged city, bustling with urban energy. With 120,000 permanent residents plus thousands more students and tourists, you'll encounter plenty of very busy people going about their daily lives.

The quintessentially European-city trait of the very old mixing with the mod is indelibly marked on Oxford: The buses and cars that clog the main streets—and the pollution that goes along with the traffic—are quite incongruous with the elegant buildings that were here long before cars were invented; there are shiny new bars as well as tiny pubs that date back to the 13th century; fast-food chains sit right next to 15th-century college buildings. It's a stark contrast, though it is kind of funny to hear the Colonel speak with an English accent.

England's private universities are broken up into numerous individual colleges; Oxford's 35 are sprinkled throughout town and you can tour them any time of the year. Both the beaten path and the areas off the beaten path are practically jammed with beautifully constructed college buildings. You can get a neck cramp gazing up at the gargoyles and the "dreaming spires" reaching up toward the sky. Oxford is actually known as "The City of Dreaming Spires." Remember those sandcastles you used to make by dribbling wet sand through your fingers? That's what some of the spires look like, except they're stuck on top of magnificent, sand-colored stone buildings instead of outrageous sandy beaches. Most of the older colleges look almost like castles or fortresses with huge, arched wooden doors that look as though Prince Charming might ride through any minute. The most accepted explanation for the fortress-style doors is that they were actually constructed for the protection of the students. Many moons ago, the townsfolk of Oxford apparently got fed up with the rowdy college students and decided to retaliate with a riot of their own, perhaps living out the fantasy your downstairs neighbors have every time you throw a party. The college doors supposedly were built in response to the riots. Or at least that's how one legend has it.

The grandest of the colleges are New, Merton, University, Trinity, and Christ Church. Christ Church is the must-see, but don't explore only one college. If you have time for only two, make sure to also see the sprawling grounds of Magdalen College. Of the newer colleges, Keble is one of the few that's dressed to impress: It might strike you like a huge brick monstrosity at first, but wander inside and check out the huge quad and the chapel, which houses the painting "The Light of the World."

Oxford also has quite an impressive list of alumni; seven of the university's "Union Society" officers have gone on to become British prime ministers. The Union Society is a student group modeled on the British House of Commons and holds weekly debating matches. The members of each team sit on rows of benches facing each other, exactly as it's done in the House—the debates are hugely confrontational and aggressive. Another former student, the poet Percy Bysshe Shelley was actually expelled from the university after publishing a pamphlet called *The Necessity of Atheism.* University College (the university's oldest and most

for whom the bell tolls

Mandatory heavy drinking isn't the only university custom in Oxford. Christ Church College has a more sober one: Every night at 9 the bell in Tom Tower rings 101 times for each of the original 101 students of the college, whose curfew back then was 9pm. This incessant ringing has inspired a variety of ghost stories, but more common reactions range from a splitting headache to the desire to become a bell-tower sniper.

oxford

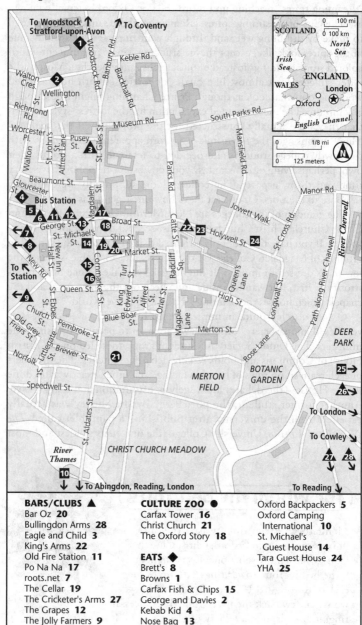

BARS/CLUBS ▲
Bar Oz **20**
Bullingdon Arms **28**
Eagle and Child **3**
King's Arms **22**
Old Fire Station **11**
Po Na Na **17**
roots.net **7**
The Cellar **19**
The Cricketer's Arms **27**
The Grapes **12**
The Jolly Farmers **9**
The Zodiac **26**
Yes But **6**

CULTURE ZOO ●
Carfax Tower **16**
Christ Church **21**
The Oxford Story **18**

EATS ◆
Brett's **8**
Browns **1**
Carfax Fish & Chips **15**
George and Davies **2**
Kebab Kid **4**
Nose Bag **13**

CRASHING ■
Bath Place Hotel **23**

Oxford Backpackers **5**
Oxford Camping
  International **10**
St. Michael's
  Guest House **14**
Tara Guest House **24**
YHA **25**

creatively named college), which originally tossed his arse out, is now in possession of a statue of him, in memoriam of his death by drowning in 1822. The statue was made in Italy (where he died) and was meant to stay there—until, of course, they realized that the stone the statue was made out of wouldn't survive the climate. So where did they send it? To Shelley's old pals, the folks who kicked him out of University College! Of course, he *is* immortalized in stone as limp and dead, so maybe they just took the statue for a big post-mortem belly laugh. Oxford is also famous for its Rhodes scholars—Bill Clinton was one—who study in the center for social and political studies, a green-domed building you'll pass on a tour of the campus.

To check local diversions that don't involve dead poets or notorious former U.S. presidents, pick up some of Oxford's publications with listings of what's going on around town. There's *This Month in Oxford,* available at the tourist office, to guide you through all of your cultural desires, plus *Oxford Freebie, Inside, Orbit* or *Pulse*—available at many pubs—to lead you into the temptation of a more decadent lifestyle. And there's always the *Daily Information,* a large neon sheet of paper that's tacked to most store fronts; it will give you a day-to-day breakdown. There's never a shortage of places to check out: theme nights at clubs, exhibits at the MOMA, films at the cinema, plays, etc., Get to it.

neighborhoods

Oxford is a pleasant city to walk around in. Everything is pretty much intermingled in the city: Colleges, shops, museums, and theaters are within a stone's throw of each other. Between **St. Giles** on the west, **The High** on the south, **Longwell Street** on the east, and **Broad** on the north, the university buildings pretty much dominate the area. You won't find major businesses in this tight section, as it is more geared toward being the "living space" of the town.

If you take the bus to Oxford, you'll arrive at Gloucester Green, the Oxford bus station, which is in the town center. From there, it's just a 5-minute walk east to the shops and major attractions. There are also waiting taxis, if you've got a bunch of gear and you don't want to lug it around on foot.

If you come in by train, it's a 15-minute walk east to the center of town and the major attractions. There's a taxi stand outside the station; buses to other parts of town also stop there.

If you want to hoof it from the train station off **Botley Road,** walk east down **Park End Street,** which branches into **New Road.** This street eventually meets up with **Queen Street,** which turns into the High Street (known to the locals as "The High") where you'll find all the shops, restaurants, and the **Carfax Tower** [see *culture zoo,* below]. If you go left (north) instead of right off Park End Street into **Worcester Street,** you'll come almost immediately to the Tourist Information Center on Gloucester Green, a really cool open square lined with shops, newsstands, and small coffee bars. This place is crawling with people, due to the proximity of the bus station and TIC, so there's often a bustling atmosphere. Proceed right (east) onto **Beaumont Street,** which leads into **Cornmarket Street,** one of the main drags. OK, so you're wandering down Cornmarket on a lovely spring day: What can you expect to see besides the majesty of Christ Church's Tom Tower looming in the distance? Well, first of all, if it's a lovely spring weekend, good luck doing anything that resembles wandering. Push, shove, prod, poke your way through the panhandlers, tourists, students, and people from neighboring villages out for a day of shopping. Once you learn to deal with that, however, the atmosphere can be quite invigorating: If the sun is shining in England, everyone's spirits generally lift and you'll see people walking in step to the string quartet or the funky band that's playing on the street.

At night Cornmarket remains the main drag, but the scene changes immensely. Now you've got the famous singing drunken Englishmen to contend with, as well as scantily clad club-going girls (which can be a good thing, right?). Needless to say, if you party all the time (at least until 2am), then wandering the noisy streets will be a blast. Be careful, though: These people have had a lot to drink and they're liable to hurl at any moment. Watch where you step.

Going north, Cornmarket turns into St. Giles, which leads to northern Oxford where large Victorian houses abound but are now mostly divided into apartments for students and other assorted academic types.

hanging out

There's no doubt that Oxford is dominated by academia—the student population is around 15,000 all told. And the best places to find them are, of course, the coffee shops and cafes. Chat up a cutie in the line outside High Street's **Harvey's of Oxford** while you're waiting for the legendary cherry-apple flapjacks, or grab a seat beside that twentysomething hottie at **Café Coco,** a lively and chic brasserie off The Plain (a traffic circle, southeast of the city center) on Cowley Road.

If you'd rather just kick back and not make conversation, there's always a garden waiting for you. All the colleges have them, though a lot of the more well-known, touristy colleges either charge a fee or won't let you in at all. But if you're wily and can slip past the porters, you'll be rewarded with a heaven of greenery. Just don't walk on the disturbingly well-manicured lawn of the quad, as they certainly frown upon that (although it's been said that Virginia Woolf once had a great time doing it). And if you can't get into the much-coveted and highly elusive grounds of Magdalen College, head across the street to the Botanic Gardens, where there's a delightful maze of flowers, benches and fountains. Have a picnic!

For an escape from all that pretty crap, head to the neighborhood down Cowley Road, all the way at the end of High Street, and experience the more familiar, nitty-gritty type of college setting. Here you'll find the **Zodiac** [see *club scene,* below] as well as coffee shops, kebab houses, and funky little shops that smell of incense and sell fun, cheap stuff ranging from Indian sari material, spiked bracelets, or old curtains to used clothes, weird appliances, and anything you can dream up. There's even a naughty sex shop.

bar scene

When it comes to drinking, Oxford has been doin' it and doin' it and doin' it well for at least eight centuries before you were born. You thought you drank a lot last weekend? Imagine the amount of beer college students would consume in 800 years. The university has been known to house secret drinking societies, and a lot of the pubs here rival the colleges for their longevity. Oxford shares its country's healthy attitude toward drinking all day, but it also shares its laws against drinking all night. Like all of England, pubs usually open at 11am Monday to Saturday (noon on Sundays) and close at the ridiculous hour of 11pm (10:30 on Sundays). You won't believe it until the first time you hear the clang of the last-call bell ringing out your doom at 10:45pm

If old stuff makes you all tingly, make sure you have a pint at **The Bear** (*Alfred St.; Tel 01865/721-783; 11am-11pm Mon-Sat, noon-10:30pm Sun*), dating back to 1242 and hangin' tough as Oxford's oldest pub.

All the University's colleges have their own bars, serving up government-subsidized liquor. Ah, what kind of heavenly land have we alighted in?! If you're down and out, or a bit on the cheap side, or just want to hang with some students, throw on a college scarf and do your impersonation of an Oxford student to get great deals on your pints, which are normally around £2 to £2.50 at pubs. Take a look at the college bar listings at *http://users.ox.ac.uk/,skug/handbook/Pubs* and click on "college bars A-M" and "New" for a description of each. Be bold and walk right on in, even if you're not a student—the worst they can do is throw you out.

school's out forever!

If you're here around the end of June, you might notice that many Oxford students start dressing suspiciously alike, and rather oddly. What is this strange phenomenon that incites them to dress in suits and white bow ties? At the end of their third and final year of rigorous Oxford education, "finalists" take their last batch of exams at the Examination Schools on High Street, and all throughout the city, you'll see students whizzing by on their bicycles on their way to the exam schools, wearing the traditional, test-taking garb which even includes the stereotypical gown and mortarboard cap. Check out their lapels: A white carnation means "No one can help me now because I am about to start writing the essays that will determine what the last three years of my life were worth"; a red carnation, on the other hand, means "Man, am I gonna be pissed in a few hours! Clear the path, I'm headin' to the pub!" If you would like to see more of this phenomenon, go around to the back of the exam schools by following the cobbled Merton Street and the crowds of students with "Congrats" balloons. Once here, you might think that *NSync is about to come rushing out and blow you a personal kiss, but what you are witnessing is actually just a crowd of friends waiting for their finalists to finish. After three years of busting their butts, these finalists get the rock-star treatment, complete with screaming fans, confetti, and sprays of champagne (although security frowns on that and runs around handing out fines). It's definitely a wild scene. For more wildness, continue to follow the crowds, which will probably end up at the King's Arms Pub to further annoy the staff with demands for beer and refusals to drink it on the premises. The outdoor tables are definitely full, so the next logical place is the Bodleian Library. Yes, drink and revel on the steps in the company of the Nine Muses (whose statues grace the roof of the building), or just that weird drunk guy who always seems to be shouting in people's faces.

The pubs in Oxford are generally pretty lively: You'll see raucous students and timid tourists even in the ones where the town drunks rule. Probably the most popular pub among students is **The King's Arms** *(40 Holywell St.; Tel 01865/242-369; 11am-11pm Mon-Sat, noon-10:30pm Sun; V)*, attached to and owned by Wadham College. The outdoor tables are always filled, even in the winter, so venture inside and explore all the little rooms that branch off from the main barroom. One's a relatively unexciting coffee room, good for tea and sandwiches and cakes at reasonable prices; others sport leather couches and a feeling that maybe you should be wearing a smoking jacket. Hey, where's my pipe?

Just try and find **The Turf** *(Bath Place, off Holywell St; Tel 01865/243-235; 11am-11pm Mon-Sat, noon-10:30pm Sun; V)*, I dare you! It's actually one of the most popular pubs in Oxford with people of all sorts, despite the fact that it's almost hidden down a long, narrow alley that makes you feel kind of like you're being led to your death as opposed to heading out for a pint or a good ol' fashioned piss-up with your mates. To get there, either take the narrow right turn off of Holywell Street going east, onto Bath Place, or go down the alley (St. Helen's Passage) from New College Lane, passing under the lovely Bridge of Sighs. Once you're there, you'll find a low-ceilinged, quaint, and cozy old English tavern furnished with old-as-the-hills wooden tables. It's lively inside as well as outside year-round, as they have big charcoal braziers alight, keeping everyone warm, or at least fighting with each other to get near the heat.

There are two pubs a hop, skip, and jump (across a major road with no safe place to cross) from each other, The Lamb and Flag and The Eagle and Child, which will probably fulfill all of your North Oxford pub crawl desires. **The Eagle and Child** *(49 St. Giles; Tel 01865/310-154; 11am-11pm Mon-Sat, noon-10:30pm Sun)*, aka "the bird and the babe," is a narrow pub popular with the students of north Oxford colleges like St. John's. It's also famous for having been the meeting place of the Inklings, an Oxford writing group that included J. R. R. Tolkien (*The Hobbit* "premiered" here) and C.S. Lewis. There are no magical closets, but there's a nice garden terrace. Across the street is **The Lamb and Flag** *(12 St. Giles)*, a big 500-year-old pub with plenty of beer a-flowing and frequent drink specials on such treats as vodka and Red Bull or double Jack Daniels and soda. It may be big, but you're going to have to fight your way to the bar on the weekends.

If you're looking to hit the sauce, another pub with good deals on the hard stuff is **The Hobgoblin** *(108 St. Aldates; Tel 01865/250-201; 11am-11pm Mon-Sat, noon-10:30pm Sun; V, MC)*. A double shot of your heart's desire goes for around £2.20, so drink along with the weird (but fun) mix of Pembroke college students and old drunken regulars. Try and count the excess of beer mats plastered to the walls and ceiling around the bar. (You won't win a prize or anything, we just wanted to see if you would actually do it....)

For someplace with a bit of an older, quieter crowd, try **The Head of the River** *(Abingdon Rd. at the Folly Bridge; Tel 01865/721-600; 11am-11pm Mon-Sat, noon-10:30pm Sun; V)*, on the Isis River. It tries to be a little classier than the average piss-up pub and the drink prices reflect that, but in the end a pub is a pub is a pub, right? The best part about it is the tables right on the river, which is overwhelmingly popular with summer tourists. When we say right on the river, we mean it: There's nothing protecting your drunk arse from stumbling right into the water. There is, however, a big, old-fashioned crane at the water's edge (you can read the story of it inside the pub); maybe they'll get it working again and pull you out by your panties.

There definitely won't be any tourists at **The Bookbinders** (Canal St.), our out-of-the-way pick for soaking up some Englishness sans people asking the way to Christ Church. Come complain about the rain with the locals. It's a quiet North Oxford pub near the canal and in the old factory district of the town, with friendly staff and old townie regulars. There are checkerboards painted on the tables, but the best part is the free monkeynuts (aka peanuts): There's a huge barrel full of them, so stick your hand in and start eatin'.

If your plan to buy five drinks at 10:45 and drink them really fast didn't do the trick, there are a few bars that are usually open past 11pm. **thirst** (Park End St.; Till midnight Sun-Wed, till 1am Thur-Sat) is still quite new, but it's already the hip place to be. It's dim and thumping, like a good bar should be, with really nice cocktails and sleek furniture like shiny tables, just low enough to the ground that they practically beg you to dance on them. The drinks are expensive (around £5), but live a little— or at least pretend to be an Oxford student and try to get the bartenders to give you your drink for £3.95. If you really can't pretend, head to happy hour at **The Duke of Cambridge** (Little Clarendon St.) between 5 and 7 or 8pm, depending on the season and their feelings of rivalry toward the Beat Cafe across the street. Drinks (normally around £6) are half-price no matter who you are. The Duke is also a hip later-night hangout but a little more subdued in its decor than thirst and therefore more attractive to the older cool crowd. Since nothing makes you look more suave than holding a martini glass, try one of their many varieties: We recommend the apple.

If you like drinking in the house of the Lord, **Freud's** (Walton St.; Tel 01865/311-171; Till midnight Mon, Tue, till 2am Wed-Sun; Cover £3 Sat night) is the place to be. It used to be a church, and its stained-glass windows are still in place. It's big and beautiful, but the drinks are way too expensive for what you get and the atmosphere has an inexplicable high school cafeteria feel. Maybe it's the rows of tables on a black and white checkered floor.

Sick of all things English? Craving some Aussie hops? Try **Bar Oz** (8 Market St.; Tel 01865/248-388; All major credit cards), an Australian bar with a sports pub feel to it. Bar Oz also serves inexpensive pub food [see eats, below].

In one of the oldest buildings in Oxford, you'll find a warm pub called **The Grapes** (7 George St.; Tel 01865/793-380). On the first Monday of each month at 7pm they have a South African night, where SA foods (such as boerewors rolls, sausage made from beef and a combination of local spices) are served. If you like red meat, are partial to beer-guzzling, and enjoy watching a spot of sport, you'll fit right in.

LIVE MUSIC SCENE

Venues for good jazz, folk, or pretty much any other type of live music aren't prolific in Oxford—Radiohead and Supergrass took off and pretty much haven't looked back. You might have to go for more of a club scene if you're looking for live entertainment. The music venues are scattered about the city, so you may need to hop in a cab or take one of the City-line buses.

If it's Wednesday, check out **The Old Fire Station** [see *club scene,* below], which has live music—usually indie. Live jazz, blues, and local bands also play here.

The recently renovated **Bullingdon Arms** *(162 Cowley Rd.; Tel 01865/244-516; Bus 51 to Cowley Rd.; Till 2am Fri, Sat)* has live music gigs throughout the week and good Guinness. Tuesday is jazz night.

Showcasing jazz and blues groups is **The Cricketer's Arms** *(43 Iffley Rd.; Tel 01865/726-264; Bus 52 to Cowley Rd.; 11am-11pm Mon-Sat, noon-10:30pm Sun, food served noon-2pm).* The pub is decorated with photos of cricket and jazz players.

The relatively new **roots.net** *(27 Park End St.)* is your best bet for really out-there stuff, ranging from DJs to modern Irish folk music. The interior is pretty interesting too: It features a huge fake tree, with branches spreading all around the bar.

CLUB SCENE

It's 11pm. You've got a buzz going and the pub's kicked you out. What do you do? Follow the crowds and join a queue for one of Oxford's clubs, which stay open till the not-so-wee hours of the morning (i.e., 2am). The scene here is pretty much geared toward drunken college students ready to bump it. Hell, even the townsfolk are looking to bump it, and it's just a matter of time before you get freaked to a Top 40 hit. However, in its defense, Oxford's scene is completely unpretentious and therefore freeing and fun. Obviously you're not going to find a hot London club here, but you'll never get the feeling that you're just not cool enough to breathe. Dress up, dress down, wear as little as possible if you're a woman—just leave your pretentions at home and *dance.*

OK, we've established that you're gonna get freaked. So where's it going to be? The most notorious club in Oxford is **The Zodiac** *(190 Cowley Rd.; Tel 01865/420-042; 7:30pm-2am Mon-Fri, 9pm-2am Sat; www.the zodiac.demon.co.uk; £3-10 cover).* All of its standard club nights are good, but the most fun have to be the nights that don't take themselves so seriously: Monday night's *Atomic 80s* and Thursday night's *Cheasy Listening,* when its finally OK to admit that you dance to Tom Jones in your underwear when no one's looking. Also look out for *Transformation Club,* consisting of dance, trance, and drum 'n' bass, on Saturday.

Look for live jazz, '70s cheese, and more at **The Old Fire Station** *(40 George St.; Tel 01865/794-494; £6 Fri, Sat, ladies free before 10:30pm,*

£4-6 other nights, music cover begins at 9pm). A DJ spins a variety of music, including '70s disco, every night in a big open space with a bar, dance floor, and tables by the windows. This venue also holds a theater, art museum, and science museum.

Like the one in Cambridge, **Po Na Na** *(13-15 Magdalen St.; Tel 01865/249-171, Fax 01865/790-422; 9pm-2am Mon-Sat; dave@ponanaox. fsnet.co.uk, www.ponana.co.uk)* is a Moroccan-themed club with changing events that are listed on its website. Fridays and Saturdays are *Weekend Vibes* here, where the selection of music is as diverse as possible, from funk to Latin, jazz, hip-hop, and drum 'n' bass. If you don't want to groove on the sweaty dance floor, lounge on the plush cushions surrounding the tables and wait for someone to offer to peel some grapes for you.

Previously called The Dolly, **The Cellar** *(Frewin Court, Cornmarket St.; Tel 01865/244-761; 5-11pm Mon-Wed, 5pm-2am Thur-Sat; Cover after 10pm, gigs most nights)* boasted huge crowds right from the start, although some people complain that it's become a schoolboy hangout. It's pretty low-key on weekdays: People relax on couches and sip drinks while listening to a variety of music, giving it more of a bar/lounge vibe than a club vibe. However, it gets packed on the weekends, with plenty of sweaty bodies packing in to dance to a mixture of breakbeat, hip-hop, garage, and house, spun by resident and guest DJs. Look for it down a little alley off of Cornmarket Street.

Although it has been closed for renovations for some time, **Yesbut** *(29 George St.; Tel 01865/726-036; 8pm-2am Mon-Sat)* once housed, and will hopefully house again, the night of the hipsters: *Strange Fruit*. This cocktail bar with tiny dance floor transformed every Wednesday night from the "Yes (please-grab-my) But" to a haven for indie-lovers, playing

wired

www.oxfordcity.co.uk: A hip, easy-to-navigate site that lists all the bars, clubs, galleries, museums, and theaters in the city. It gives clear contact information for each place as well as links to sites detailing the history of some of these places.

www.cherwell.org: The online edition of Oxford University's student independent newspaper.

www.dailyinfo.co.uk: Another good all-around site dedicated to informing tourists of every aspect of Oxford, from restaurants to news to current events.

The **Internet Exchange** *(8-12 George St.; Tel 01865/241-601; www.internet.exchange.co.uk; from 3p per minute)* is part of a UK-wide chain of Internet cafes.

bloke snogs bird

With all this talk of clubs like "Shark End" or the "Yes (please-grab-my) But," you might be making a list of places to avoid. Don't bother, and don't be scared: Most clubs in Oxford have a high incidence of bad come-ons, but you can at least prepare yourself for what's in store by becoming familiar with the lingo:

Snogging: Making out, probably in a dark corner somewhere.

Pulling: Picking out a lucky person in the crowd at a club, zeroing in on them with your beady little eyes and doing whatever it takes to get them to come home with you or at least give you a snog. Can also be used in the sense of "Get your coat. You've pulled."

Sharking: Trying really, *really* hard to pull.

Most of these terms exist because of one overwhelmingly used vocabulary word in Britain: *pissed.*

Now that you know, you can defend yourself. Knowledge is power.

everything from Pulp to Elvis Costello to New Order to Pavement to—well, they describe it as "Off-Kilter Indie, Post-rock, and Eclectica." Put on some horn-rimmed glasses and Daryl K's and get down!

For something more traditionally sleazy, try the **Park End Club** *(37-39 Park End St.; Tel 01865/250-181; Mon, Wed-Sat),* playfully referred to as "Shark End." What's "sharking," you ask? Well, it's kind of like "pulling": Both terms connote insinuating yourself into someone's path and commencing from there to try and get them to come home with you, or at least make out with you in the corner; sharking simply implies that the offender is way more determined. Park End just had loads of money sunk into it and now it has four floors of good, cheesy fun with carpeting that will remind you of a Howard Johnson's lobby. This place is the old standby for (usually) Wednesday night student night: There will be a huge queue for certain, packed with sparkly girls and randy boys.

ARTS SCENE

Oxford has a rich array of theaters, which fits perfectly with its rep as an academic and arts-inclined school. The theaters are all within walking distance of one another once you're in the middle of town. The MOMA is a delightful little museum and very do-able in a short period of time.

▶▶VISUAL ARTS

The **Museum of Modern Art** *(30 Pembroke St.; Tel 01865/722-733, Fax 01865/722-573; 11am-6pm Tue-Sun, till 9pm Thur; £2.50 adults,*

£1.50 students, free Wed 11am-1pm and Thur 6-9pm; www.moma.org.uk) is an awesome white gallery space with small rooms in front that lead up the stairs to double volume spaces and slanted ceilings with skylights. Usually, the main gallery rooms feature one exhibition that is part of a national or international tour. Not too long ago it was black and white photography, mostly photojournalism, but they showcase paintings as well. There is also a cafe and bookshop in the building.

▶▶PERFORMING ARTS

A lot of famous international stars started their thespian careers at Oxford. Highly acclaimed British actors Richard Burton, Emma Thompson, and John Cleese all performed here, not to mention Hugh Grant, as a student.

Located behind The Oxford Playhouse, the 50-seater **Burton Taylor Theatre** *(Gloucester St.; Tel 01865/793-797; www.burtontaylor.co.uk; No credit cards)* is the studio theater to The Playhouse and puts on mostly student productions in comedy, contemporary, drama, and new writing. While the box office accepts only cash and checks, you can charge tickets, up to 30 minutes before the show, at the Oxford Playhouse box office.

It is said that in the late sixties, Richard Burton and Elizabeth Taylor used **Bath Place Hotel** [see *crashing,* below] as a secret rendezvous when Burton was acting at the **Oxford Playhouse** *(11-12 Beaumont*

the oxford connection

Oxford's literary associations would make any budding writer tingle with excitement. Not only did Lewis Carroll, who dreamed up Alice, call Oxford home, but so did Colin Dexter, creator of Inspector Morse— now a well-known television character. J. R. R. Tolkien, mastermind behind the *Lord of the Rings,* was actually born in South Africa but went to Exeter College at Oxford. It might even seem English comes from Oxford—never mind England—since lots of things that are used as a reference for the "Queen's English" seem to have the word "Oxford" somewhere along the line: the *Oxford English Dictionary,* for instance. There is an old debate about whether or not the 17th Earl of Oxford was, in fact, the author of all that is credited as being Shakespearean. The Oxfordian theory that the court insider and lifelong confidante of Queen Elizabeth was the real Shakespeare, does little more than rile the academe. An "oxford" is also traditionally a low-cut shoe laced or tied over the instep, a soft durable cotton or synthetic fabric, or a breed of large, hornless sheep.

St.; Tel 01865/798-600; 2:30pm matinees, 7:30pm daily, 8pm Fri; £8-22; All major credit cards). These days, this space presents more mainstream drama, contemporary dance, and music performances. Recently redeveloped, the Playhouse is Oxford's main theater. English acting legends such as John Gielgud and Judi Dench have performed here with visiting companies. John's *Arthur* co-star, Dudley Moore, also performed here as a student, along with Rowan Atkinson, aka Mr. Bean.

Decorated with big faces on the facade outside and a painted ceiling inside, the domed **Sheldonian Theatre** *(Broad St.; Tel 01865/277-299; 10am-12:30pm/2-3:30pm Mon-Sat; £1.50 adults)* seats 1,500 in a structure designed and built in the style of a Roman theater by Christopher Wren between 1664 and 1668 while he was a professor of astronomy at the university. Today it's used for concerts, university ceremonies, and other events. Information for these events can also be obtained by calling the Oxford Playhouse.

Nothing like the one in Harlem, **The Apollo Theatre** *(George St.; Tel 01865/243-041; £5 for students, up to £50)* puts on large, modern productions of comedy, ballet, opera, and drama.

The **Old Fire Station** [see *club scene,* above] features student productions, although not as many as the Playhouse. Mostly, however, there's professional theater here.

Movie theaters in town include the downtown mainstream three-screen **ABC** *(George St.; Tel 01865/251-998 for recorded info, 0541/550-501 for bookings),* and around the corner from the Apollo, near St. John's College, is the two-screen **ABC** *(Magdalen St.; Tel 01865/251-998, 0541/550-509 for bookings).* The independent two-screen cinema with a bar/cafe is **Phoenix Picture House** *(57-58 Walton St.; Tel 01865/554-909),* about a 20-minute walk northwest of the town's center. For indie cinema, old favorites like *Wayne's World,* and truly bizarre old movies about cat people, head to **The Ultimate Picture Palace** *(Jeune St.; Tel 01865/245-288),* a 25-minute walk east of the town's center. This is a one-theater affair, which makes it feel oddly like a porno theater.

▶▶LITERARY SCENE

Since Oxford is home to one of the greatest universities in the world, many a famous writer has studied and lived here. Therefore, it is not surprising that there is an excess of bookshops and libraries. One bookshop, **Blackwell's** [see *stuff,* below], is particularly well-known. Established in 1879, this branch is the flagship store of a national chain of over 80 shops, and is one of the largest in the world. From the bookshop, Blackwell's leads literary walking tours *(2:30pm Tue, 11am Thur, 11am and 2:30pm Sat; £5 adults, £4 students)* around the city and university, highlighting spots of literary and historic interest. But lest you're expecting ye olde bookshoppe, be forewarned: A Starbucks-esque coffeeshop has been installed.

Lewis Carroll, author of the classic *Alice in Wonderland,* lived in Oxford and worked at the university as a math tutor. One of the stores in the city, **Alice's Shop** [see *stuff,* below] was used as the inspiration for *Through* *the Looking Glass.* The book's illustrator, Sir John Tenniel, visited the shop to sketch it as the "old sheep shop" in the book. Alice Liddell, the little girl on whom the character Alice was based, lived opposite the shop at Christ Church, where her father was dean.

There are more books than you can shake a stick at (5 million, to be exact) at the **Bodleian Library** *(Catte St.; Tel 01865/277-224; Guided tours 10:30am, 11:30am, 2 and 3pm Mon-Fri, 10:30 and 11:30am Sat Mar-Oct; no morning weekday tours Nov-Feb; £3.50 adults, free admission to 15th-century Divinity School, 17th-century Old Schools Quadrangle, and Exhibition Room).* It's a copyright library, which means that they have a right to receive a copy of every book printed in England. And that's a lot of books, mister. Where do they keep them all and how do the students get to them, you ask? Well, most of the volumes are kept in intricate passages that run under Broad Street; students must order their book and wait for the little underground librarians to find it for them; then the book is sent up on a conveyor belt. Needless to say, after all this trouble, students are not allowed to take books out of the library: There's always a guard on duty checking for sticky fingers. It's an amazing thought, isn't it? Underneath your feet are shelves upon shelves of books and some mole-people digging them up for students who may or may not actually want to read them....

The building is a magnificent sight in itself, made of sanded stone like most of the buildings in Oxford, but it differs from the rest of the architecture in that it has huge pillars marking the front entrance, on Broad St. The roof is the home to statues of the Nine Muses, seven made of stone and two of fiberglass (if you look really close, you can see that the fiberglass ones are lighter in color). These were attached to the roof after a "slight" accident in which two of the large, very heavy figures fell from the top of the building.

If you go up the steps and into a large graveled courtyard, you'll have to pass through another doorway to get to the quadrangle; once there, try to observe the sign that says "Silence Please," as Oxford University does actually have students who do study sometimes. You might want to peep into the huge windows to get a look at this phenomenon, but you won't see anything: Something about the way the light hits the windows turns them a spectacular opaque gold. Take a tour of this place because you won't be able to see it any other way.

For more library fun, go behind the Bodleian and check out the Radcliffe Camera with its huge dome. Unfortunately, you can't go in as a tourist (students and faculty only!), but at least be sure to get a look at it.

gay scene

When most people think of Oxford, they probably think of a really straight-and-narrow old boys' network with no room under their smartly buttoned-up shirts for alternative lifestyles. That's a highly debatable point, but definitely don't expect to find a gay mecca when you get to

Oxford: The scene at most clubs is aggressively heterosexual. However, while the scene is still quite repressed, progress is being made: There are a few places that cater specifically to the gay party crowd, a gay community center, and an Oxford University Lesbian Gay Bisexual Society. You can visit their website *(http://users.ox.ac.uk/,lgbsoc/)*. For links on what's happening around town, try *www.chch.ox.ac.uk/jcr/gayox.htm.*

One of Oxfordshire's first gay and lesbian pubs, **The Jolly Farmers** *(20 Paradise St.; Tel 01865/793-759; Noon-11pm Mon-Sat, 12:30-10:30pm Sun)* features occasional bouts of comedy as well as male strippers and drag shows. The students do tend to make it a bit rowdier than it might be otherwise, which is probably a bit of an annoyance to the locals, but maybe the strippers like it.

Opened in 1991 by Sir Ian McKellan, **The Northgate Center** *(St. Michael's St.; Tel 01865/200-249; Events 8-11:30pm Thur, 10pm-2am Fri, 1-5pm/10pm-2am Sat)* is Oxford's LGB community center, run mostly by volunteers as a co-op funded by donations and membership fees. It houses a dance floor, a cocktail bar, a cafe, a library, and a counseling center; on the weekends it becomes one of the two clubs in town that host gay nights. Thursday night is *Boyzone* (the name says it all), Friday night is women only, and Saturday is mixed all day. You need to be a member or with a member to get in, so either join up or make friends real fast at one of the local pubs.

The other gay night in Oxford, *Loveshack,* happens at the **Coven II** *(Oxpens Rd.; Tel 01865/242-770; 10pm-2am Fri)* on Fridays. This place used to be more officially gay in a shiny leather type of way, but now *Loveshack* is all that's left of a ruined empire. Oh, how the mighty have fallen into one night of house and cheesy pop. Don't be discouraged, though: *Loveshack* is pretty popular (mostly with men) because, as with all clubs in Oxford, the cheese is what makes it fun.

CULTURE ZOO

People come to Oxford and Cambridge primarily to participate in the collegiate atmosphere of the town: to gaze at the beautiful architecture, so steeped in history and tradition, and to punt down the River Isis or Cam, depending which town you're in. However, even if you have no interest in the university, Oxford offers some good cultural expeditions, such as a trip up the Carfax Tower (which requires a minimal amount of mental activity), or a look at the classical artworks of the Ashmolean Museum.

Carfax Tower *(Carfax crossroads; Tel 01865/792-653; 10am-5:30pm daily Apr-Oct, 10am-3:30pm Nov-Mar; £1.20 adults, concession rates available):* Walk up the 99 steps of the 72-foot-high tower for a great 360-degree view of Oxford's "dreaming spires." Standing at the center of the old city—known as the four ways—the tower is all that remains of St. Martin's Church, demolished in 1896. On the east facade, the clock is adorned with two mechanical "quarter boys" that hit the bells every quarter hour.

If you haven't had a heart attack from all the stair-climbing yet, you can also climb up into the Saxon Tower of St. Michael at the North Gate, also on Cornmarket Street, or into the tower of The University Church of St. Mary the Virgin on the High Street, which has a spectacular 360-degree view from a tiny, tiny little balcony that wraps round the tower. It's also fun from the street to look up at the little ant people who have braved the narrow stone stairs and hopefully aren't thinking of spitting on you.

Christ Church *(St. Aldates; Tel 01865/276-492; 9am-5pm Mon-Sat, 1-5pm Sun; Services 8am, 10am, 11:15am, 6pm Sun, 7:30am, 6pm Mon-Fri; £2.50 adults, £1.50 students):* The largest and grandest of Oxford University's colleges, it is also the location of England's smallest Anglican cathedral, known to locals as "The House." The House also has the added fame of being the only church in the world to be both a cathedral and a college chapel. As you walk into the college's grounds, there are wonderful gardens on the right. Inside, the most interesting room is the Hall, a huge room with long dining tables where both senior and junior members of the college have meals. The walls are packed with portraits of college alumni through the ages. The portraits of various Christ Church men who have achieved prominence include Prime Ministers William Gladstone and Anthony Eden; Charles Dodgson (better known as Lewis Carroll), the author of *Alice in Wonderland;* philosopher John Locke; and founder of Pennsylvania, William Penn. So, all in all, the students have plenty of time to worry about great expectations while they're having their bangers and mash.

The Oxford Story *(6 Broad St.; Tel 01865/728-822; 9:30am-5pm daily Apr-Oct, 9:30am-5:30pm daily July, Aug, 10am-4:30pm Nov-Mar, till 5pm weekends; www.heritageattractions.co.uk; £5.70 adults, £4.70 concession):* This attraction aims to give an introduction to the rich history of the 900-year-old city, mainly highlighting the history of the university. You take your seat and ride in a motorized cart that takes you on an audiovisual tour. It also shows some of the people that were Oxford scholars and have since become masters of the universe, such as Bill Clinton, Tony Blair, and Margaret Thatcher.

The Ashmolean Museum *(Beaumont St.; Tel 01865/278-000; 10am-5pm Tue-Sat, 2-5pm Sun and bank holidays, till 8pm Wed, May-July; Free admission, recommended donation of £2):* This museum of art and architecture may not be reputed as one of the premier museums in Europe, but don't blow it off—it has some interesting stuff; plus, it's free. It houses ancient Egyptian, Greek, Islamic, and Chinese relics, as well as pottery, sculpture, and even paintings by some of the big boys: Monet, Manet, Renoir, Bonnard, Picasso, and van Gogh (pronounced by the English as "Van Goff"). For English culture gone wrong, check out Oliver Cromwell's death mask and the lantern used by the famous traitor, Guy Fawkes. If you're in Oxford around November 5, you'll be sure to see plenty of fireworks commemorating the foiling of his 17th-century attempt to blow up the king.

modification

For a wide range of hairdressing services, head to **Anne Veck** *(33 St. Clement's St.; Tel 01865/727-077; anne@anneveckhair.com)* which not only offers the standard cut and blow dry (£24 girls, £15 guys), but hair extensions and Cyber Imaging, so you can see what you would look like before you go wild and crazy.

city sports

A long-running tradition for visitors in both Oxford and Cambridge is to experience the fine art of punting. This is also the water transportation of choice. A punt is a wide canoe-shaped boat, which is broad, square, and flat on both ends. The person delegated to do the rowing plunges the flat-edged pole deep into the riverbed and this propels the boat along the river. If you're going to be visiting Cambridge as well, go punting there, as the picture-perfect setting is much more serene for this kind of activity. Otherwise, rent or be chauffeured in a punt, or hire a row or electric boat on the Cherwell and the Thames (called the Isis in Oxford). Boathouses are located at **Magdalen Bridge** *(Tel 01865/202-643)*, **Bardwell Road** *(Tel 01865/515-978)*, and Folly Bridge, St. Aldates, and can be rented between April and October.

stuff

Though it's impossible to imagine why you'll ever want to shop in one more gigantic chain store, they're all here in the city's principal shopping streets: Queen, Cornmarket, and Magdalen. There are indoor malls on Queen and Cornmarket as well. Shop for less generic stuff along the short strip of St. Ebbes and the narrow alleyway, North Parade. Browse on Broad Street, Turl Street, and the High Street for old and new books, gifts, souvenirs, antiques, jewelry, rare maps, and prints. Head to Cowley Road for funkier stuff, or, on the opposite end of the spectrum, head to Little Clarendon Street for some cool, higher-priced stuff.

▶▶DUDS

If you're looking for some Oxford University duds, there's no shortage of shops peddling the requisite sweatshirts, T-shirts, scarves, etc. Opposite Trinity College, **Flags** *(18 Broad St.; Tel 01865/722-258, Fax 01865/792-395; 9am-5:30pm daily; All major credit cards)* is an all-out Oxford University clothing mart, selling nothing but the college's gear.

The **University of Oxford Shop** *(106 High St.; Tel 01865/247-414, Fax 01865/724-379; 9am-5:30pm Mon-Sat; shop@oushop.com, www.oushop.com; Most credit cards accepted)* is a close second as an Oxford wear specialist. They sell prints, ceramics, official sweatshirts, T-shirts, rugby jerseys, and ties emblazoned with the university's name.

▶▶BOUND

For some *Alice in Wonderland* delight, head to **Alice's Shop** *(83 St. Aldates; Tel 01865/723-793; 10:30am-5:30pm Mon-Sat; 11am-4:30pm Sun)*, a store completely devoted to Alice paraphernalia. Look for rare

fashion

Most people around the world choose to wear a coat when the temperature dips below 40 degrees. Many wear one in even slightly warmer weather. Yet nobody seems to have informed the young women of Oxford University of this phenomenon— these girls will brave any weather wearing only the tiniest skirt and tight, tight shirt. While guys tend to dress either really hip and Dieseled-out—or, more likely, in the standard English-guy look of button-down shirt (with or without sweater) and fitted trousers (remember, "pants" means undies)—the girls head to stores like Miss Selfridge or Topshop to pick up the least amount of material possible for their next night out clubbing. And a jacket is out of the question: Not only will it cramp their style, but it will force them to wait on the coat-check queue and pay at least a pound to have it stashed. Another Oxford fashion phenomenon is the going-to-a-ball look. Almost every college and society at the university throws a ball at one time or another, and you'll almost always see girls in tight fancy dresses wandering around with—or looking for—guys in tuxes. (Oxford is probably one of the few cities in the world in which every 19-year-old guy owns a tuxedo.)

and modern illustrated (mostly affordable), editions of the Lewis Carroll books as well as Alice and the crew in the shape of chess pieces, plates, pictures, etc. [see *arts scene,* above].

The flagship branch of **Blackwell's** *(48-51 Broad St.; Tel 01865/792-792, Fax 01865/794-143; 9am-6pm Mon and Wed-Sat, 9:30am-6pm Tue, 11am-5pm Sun; oxford@blackwellbookshop.co.uk, www.blackwell.co.uk/book-shops)* is a huge, multilevel shop selling every book imaginable, from recent bestsellers to classics [see *literary scene,* above].

Oxford University Press *(116-117 High St.; Tel 01865/242-913, Fax 01865/241-701; 9am-6pm Mon-Sat; bookshop@oup.co.uk; AE, MC, V)* has an extensive range of Oxford University Press titles.

▶▶HOW BAZAAR

The **Covered Market** *(Mon-Sat),* in between Market Street and Carfax, was started in the late 1700s as a response to a general wish to clear the 'untidy mess and unsavory stalls' from the main streets. John Gwynn, the architect of Magdalen Bridge, drew up the plans and designed the High Street front with its four entrances. Today, the scope of what's available in the market has broadened substantially since its Victorian beginnings.

You can shop at a variety of colorful stalls and small shops selling all types of clothes, housewares, meat, fish, cheese, fruits and vegetables, records, and flowers. There are also cakes in an open store where you can watch the decorators in action through the window. The market entrance is on the High Street and in Golden Cross (the medieval courtyard of the former Cross Inn, which opens off Cornmarket Street).

The **open-air market at Gloucester Green** (just behind the bus station) hosts a food and clothing market every Wednesday and an antiques market on Thursdays.

EATS

Food in England, especially in Oxford, is expensive any way you slice it, and going out to eat someplace where there's waiter service is a once-in-a-while luxury affair. Fortunately, there are plenty of other options: Almost every pub serves food (most meals will run you about £5 or £6), it's just a matter of when. Some serve for only a few hours in the afternoon, others serve in the afternoon, then stop, then serve again in the evening. The latest time pubs will serve food is usually 9:30pm, so after that it's either a sit-down place, fast food, or a kebab van [see *mystery*

mystery meat

Ever seen a group of guys standing around a van in tuxes, eating food out of Styrofoam containers? You will in this town, and what's more, after a night of clubbing, you'll likely join in and indulge in one of Oxford's fast-food phenomena: the kebab van. You'll find them all over the city, including St. Aldates, opposite Christ Church (they have the best chips in town and they know it, so you'll get a little less for your £1), St. Giles, Broad Street, George Street, and more. The meat may scare you, but there are plenty of people who have eaten the chicken or lamb kebabs and lived to tell the tale. There are other options, though, if you don't like mystery meat: chips with vinegar, jacket potatoes with all sorts of toppings, pita with hummus, veggie burgers, etc. These places are really popular, trust us: Before long you'll find yourself hankering for a hunk of something from a mobile food vendor. After all, there's no 7-Eleven in England to satisfy your late-night cravings. And when these vans drive off at 3:30am, that's it, buster.

meat, above]. Just one word of advice: Stick to either English, French, Indian, or Lebanese cuisine. That means, basically, stay away from anything Chinese or Italian, at least in Oxford.

▶▶**CHEAP**

As a testament to its student concentration, Oxford has nearly every fast food imaginable. Since the places listed here are all pretty hole-in-the-wall-ish, they'll all be open pretty much from 9:30am-5:30pm daily, except for Carfax Fish and Chips.

Head to **Bretts** *(Park End St.)* near the train station for burgers; **Carfax Fish and Chips** *(Carfax Passage, off the High St.; till midnight Mon-Fri)* for, you guessed it, fish and chips. Hit up established and unpretentious **George and Davies** *(Little Clarendon St.)* for ice cream and bagel sandwiches, and **Kebab Kid** *(Gloucester Green)* for a lamb, chicken, or veggie kebab served in naan bread.

Among the pubs, you can either stick with the biggies like the **King's Arms** [see *bar scene,* above] which has a coffee room offering sandwiches for around £2 or £3 until 5pm. There is also a separate bar for ordering hot food (served from noon-3:30pm and 5-9:30pm), like traditional pies or hamburgers or grilled chicken, as well as cold salads and quiches. If you can't handle the 30-minute wait for your food at dinnertime, try **The Turf** [see *bar scene,* above], the other monster among popular Oxford pubs. Chances are they've already run out of one of your choices, but hopefully they'll have the black bean burger and some chips waiting for you. The Turf serves food from noon-3pm and 6:30-9:30pm.

For a pub option that feels a bit more like a restaurant, try the **Wig and Pen** *(9-13 George St.),* where you order at the bar but they actually bring you your food! It's standard pub fare that's really nothing special, except for one glorious thing: They serve nachos. The formerly mentioned **Bar Oz** [see *bar scene,* above] on Market Street also serves decent, inexpensive pub food (around £3.75). Choose from beef, chicken, or veggie "Barbie Burgers." Or try the nachos, baguettes, and pita pouches. They also have entrees of pasta, steak, chicken, and chili. A specialty of the place is the spicy twisters (fries to you) topped with some indescribable condiment.

▶▶**DO-ABLE**

Oxford's vegetarian mainstay is **Nose Bag** *(6-8 St. Michael's St.; Tel 01865/721-00-33; 9:30am-5:30pm Mon, till 10pm Tue-Thur, till 10:30pm Fri, Sat, till 9pm Sun; lunch under £6, dinner under £7.50),* in the center of the city. A wide range of home-cooked veggie dishes are served here. For dessert, pop downstairs to The Saddlebag Cafe for cakes and coffees to go.

Although a chain, **Browns** *(5-11 Woodstock Rd.; Tel 01865/311-415; 11am-11:30pm Mon-Sat, noon-11:30pm Sun; All major credit cards)* is decidedly un-chain-like. The one here is very popular with the students, and it's just a 10-minute walk north of the town center. The spacious room is filled with ceiling fans, plants, and generous-sized booths. The overall look is that of an understated brasserie. The food is good, and the atmosphere is great (it's always packed). You're probably looking at £20 for a main entree, a couple of drinks, dessert, and coffee—and if you just have an entree, it could be as low as about £10. Come here for breakfast, lunch, dinner or just a casual, lingering drink.

There's an abundance of great Indian restaurants in Oxford (as in most parts of England...). They're up and down the High Street, down Cowley Road, in the center of town, everywhere—just close your eyes and choose. One of the best is **Chutney's** *(36 St. Michael's St.; Tel 01865/724-241)* with its tasteful, contemporary interior and amazing appetizers—order the thin, crispy appetizer bread and get a dazzling array of chutney on a lazy susan.

▶▶**SPLURGE**

The Oxford landmark on the Cherwell River, **Cherwell Boathouse Restaurant** *(Bardwell Rd.; Tel 01865/552-746; Bus to Banbury; Noon-2pm/6-9:30pm Tue-Sat, noon-2pm Sun; Dinner from £20.50; Sun lunch £19.50; Closed Dec 24-30; AE, DC, MC, V)* offers an intriguing fixed-price menu. The cooks change the fare every two weeks to take advantage of the availability of fresh veggies, fish, and meat. Enjoy starters like toasted pine nut and cranberry dressing. For an entree, you may opt for a tress of sole and salmon with pasta and a tomato and herb salsa, or free-range loin of pork with port and dried plums. For dessert, try the lemon and almond roulade.

The English may indeed harbor a distaste for the French, but they do allow froggy cuisine on their bland little island. Oxford has a handful of French restaurants that carry a bit more of a price tag, once you tack on a bottle of wine and some dessert. Try **Cafe Rouge** *(11 Little Clarendon St.; Tel 01865/310-194)*, an adorable bistro with an excellent (and generously portioned) gallette with butter beans.

crashing

The Oxford Backpackers is a fun place to stay if you're looking for some communal traveler bonding. Otherwise, there aren't a lot of decent, inexpensive crashes in the city center. You'll probably have to venture farther north or south, or book way in advance for the centrally located B&Bs.

The TIC [see *need to know*, below] does do accommodation bookings for a £2.50 fee, plus a 10 percent refundable deposit.

▶▶**CHEAP**

Oxford Backpackers *(9a Hythe Bridge St.; Tel 01865/721-761; Open till midnight; £11 dorm beds; www.hostels.co.uk)* is a fun hostel near the train and bus stations with "musical showers" and videos. The reception area is big and open with a bar and tables where everyone hangs out and plays games. There are some rooms with four beds, but the rest have eight to 14 beds.

The more subdued **YHA** *(2a Botley Rd.; Tel 01865/727-275, Fax 01865/176-402; 24-hour access; £11 plus £2 membership fee; oxford@ yha.org.uk, www.yha.org.uk; AE, V, MC, Delta, Switch)* is right behind Platform 2 of the railway station. It has 185 beds, a lounge, TV room,

only here

In may other European cities, May Day is sort of a socialist workers day, where you're likely to see parades with red flags and shouting labor unionists who don't seem to realize that communism does not appear to be the wave of the future. But in Oxford, May Day is a huge celebration of the pagan rites of spring. People stay up all night (whether they're having a party with friends or searching for the possible impromptu rave in Port Meadow, North Oxford) in order to make it to Magdalen Tower at 6am. The college choir sings from the top of the tower to hordes of spring-ushering revelers, some of whom try their best in their drunkenness to jump into the Cherwell River. Everyone bonds in the dim morning light to the sound of beautiful music, and then scrambles to the nearest pub to devour a huge, greasy, traditional English breakfast, watch the Morris Dancers jig their ode to fertility, and keep up their 12-hour-long beer buzz.

cafeteria, kitchen, cycle shed, luggage store, and laundry facilities. Breakfast, dinner, and packed lunches can all be purchased.

For camping enthusiasts, **Oxford Camping International** *(426 Abingdon Rd.; Tel 01865/246-551; Bus 35 or 36 from St. Aldates; £4.20 per tent, £4.50 per person)* has 84 sites with toilet and laundry facilities.

▶▶**DO-ABLE**

St. Michael's Guest House *(26 St. Michael's St.; Tel 01865/242-101; £40-50 double)* is almost interminably full, so it must be doing something right. Or maybe it's just its extremely central location, just off Cornmarket Street, that makes it so popular. In any event, book well ahead, if possible. None of the rooms here are have private baths, but there is a sink in each room as well as a tea maker.

Something like a cross between a hostel and a basic B&B, **Tara** *(10 Holywell St.; Tel 01865/202-953; £20 single, £38 double)* is another popular spot, located on a charming old street in central Oxford. Many of the rooms even overlook colleges. There's a basin and TV in each room, and a communal guest kitchen.

▶▶**SPLURGE**

Set in a cluster of 17th-century cottages in an even more beautiful courtyard in the heart of the city is the **Bath Place Hotel** *(4-5 Bath Place; Tel 01865/791-812, Fax 01865/791-834; www.bathplace.co.uk; bathplace@compuserve.com; Double rooms for single occupancy from £90, doubles from £95, four-posters from £135, doubles with sitting room from £125, triple occupancy from £130; All major credit cards).* This little charmer has rooms with four-post beds and timber-beamed ceilings, among other romantic touches (all rooms are en suite with minibar, TV, and complimentary fruit bowls).

need to know

Currency Exchange Carfax is the central locale for banks. **Barclays** is at 54 Cornmarket Street *(9:30am-5:30pm Mon, Tue, Thur, and Fri, 9:30am-5pm Wed, 10am-noon Sat)*.

Tourist Information The **TIC** *(The Old School, Gloucester Green; Tel 01865/726-871; 9:30am-5pm Mon-Sat, accommodation service till 4:30pm)* offers a selection of maps, guidebooks, and souvenirs. Also, info and booking for guided walking tours and bus tours, as well as an accommodation-booking service for a £2.50 fee.

Public Transportation There are two reliable bus services: **Oxford Bus Company** *(395 Cowley Rd.; Tel 01865/785-400)* operates on green Park and Ride buses that travel the north-south and east-west routes through the city. **Stagecoach** *(Unit 4, Horsepath, Cowley; Tel 01865/772-250)* operates on blue and cream minibuses and red and gray coaches. City buses leave from the corner of Cornmarket and Queen streets.

There are plenty of taxis to be had in Oxford, although you can't hail them just anywhere on the street. There is a taxi rank on Gloucester Green for transportation from the bus station, and another taxi rank forms at night to cart home the drunks on the corner of Cornmarket and Queen. There is a taxi stand for **A1 Taxis** *(Tel 01865/240-000, 01865/242-424)* off of St. Aldates, down the alley next to the Hobgoblin Pub; the stand and its waiting room are open 24 hours. A1 seem to have competitive rates, but you'll find no shortage of numbers all over the city, including **ABC Taxis** *(Tel 01865/775-577)*.

American Express Pick up another green card at your friendly AMEX office *(4 Queen St.; Tel 01865/792-066; 9am-5:30pm Mon, Tue, Thur, Fri, 9:30am-5:30pm Wed, 9am-5pm Sat, 11am-3pm Sun)*.

Health and Emergency Emergency: *999*. **Police** are located at St. Aldates and Speedwell streets *(Tel 01865/266-000)*. **John Radcliffe Hospital** *(Headley Way; Tel 01865/741-166; Bus 13B or 14A)* is near the YHA. Go east on the High Street past The Plain traffic circle. Continue down St. Clement's and turn left into Headley Way, right after Marston Road.

Pharmacies For all your pharmaceutical needs, try the **10 O'clock Pharmacy** *(59 Woodstock Rd.; Tel 01865/515-226; Till 10pm daily)* or **Boots the Chemist** *(151a Cowley Rd.; Tel 01865/243-633; 8:30am-5:30pm daily)*.

Telephone City code: *01865*.

Trains There are regular services from London Paddington, Slough, and Reading *(Tel 0345/484-950; £14.20 day return fare)*. The trains run twice an hour during the week with journeys taking just under an hour. Call for schedule and fare info.

Bus Lines Out of the City The **Oxford Tube** *(Tel 01865/772-250; www.stagecoach-oxford.co.uk;)* is a fairly new bus service that runs from Oxford to London every 12 minutes daily, year-round. Buy your ticket from the driver on board. There's also the 24-hour **Oxford Express** *(Tel 01865/785-400),* which goes to central London, plus Heathrow and Gatwick airports.

Boat See *city sports,* above.

Laundry Clean-o-Fine *(66 Abingdon St.; 8am-9:30pm Mon-Fri, 7:30am-9:30pm Sat, Sun)* will make your duds so.

Postal Mail your postcards and packages from the **P.O.** *(102-104 St. Aldates St.; Tel 01865/202-863; 9am-5:30pm Mon-Fri, 9am-6pm Sat).*

Internet See *wired,* above.

cambridge

Home to one of the most prestigious universities in the world, Cambridge is loaded with both students and their most common mode of transportation: the bicycle. About 105,000 people live here year-round, and close to 16,000 students bring a party vibe to the night spots when school is in session. But don't get your after-dark hopes up; this is a place where the history and architecture lessons are first and parties, second. Sorry, Ibiza it ain't.

What you're supposed to come here for are striking spires and turrets, drooping willows hanging over narrow cobblestone lanes, and the river **Cam** winding its way luxuriously around the city center. Most of the college buildings were built during the 15th and 16th centuries, but the university's oldest jewel dates back to 1284.

Spending a day in this city's ancient seat of learning is a collegiate dream come true for the non–rocket scientists among us. The school's amazing alumni roster includes Isaac Newton, John Milton, and Stephen Hawking.

The colleges are spread throughout the city and some are more worthy of a visit than others. These are the ones to visit: **King's, Trinity,** and **St. John's** [see *culture zoo,* below]. But a walk on the grounds of any of the colleges at the university is an inspiring experience, simply because they are all so gorgeous.

Cambridge's age-old tradition is punting [see *city sports,* below]. On a sunny day, there is nothing more sublime than being punted down the River Cam by a strapping Cambridge lad, or simply by your own muscle-power. With bridges, weeping willows, colleges, and gardens all around, it's a damn fine sight and a great way to see Cambridge.

cambridge

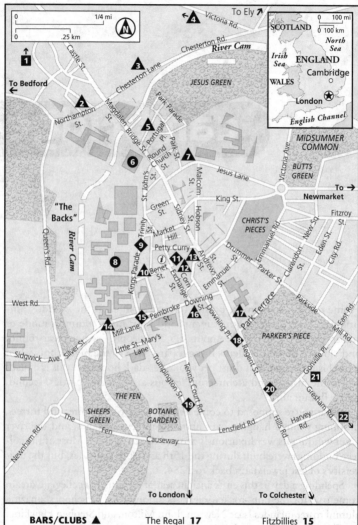

To Ely ↗

Victoria Rd.

SCOTLAND
Irish Sea
North Sea
ENGLAND
WALES
London
English Channel
Cambridge

0   100 mi
0   100 km

Chesterton Rd.
River Cam
JESUS GREEN

Chesterton Lane

Castle St.

To Bedford ←

Northampton St.
Magdalen Bridge St.
Portugal

Park Parade

Round Church St.
St. John's St.

"The Backs"

Queen's Rd.
River Cam

West Rd.

Park St.
Malcolm St.
Jesus Lane
King St.

MIDSUMMER COMMON
BUTTS GREEN

To → Newmarket

Fitzroy St.

Victoria Ave.

Green St.
Sidney St.
Hobson St.

Trinity St.
Market Hill
Petty Curry
Kings Parade
Benet St.
Corn Exchange St.

CHRIST'S PIECES

Andrews St.
Emmanuel St.
Drummer St.

Emmanuel Rd.
Parker St.
Clarendon St.
New Sq.
Eden St.
City Rd.

Downing St.
Pembroke St.
Mill Lane

Little St. Mary's Lane

Trumpington St.

Sidgwick Ave.
Silver St.

THE FEN
SHEEPS GREEN

The Fen

Newnham Rd.

BOTANIC GARDENS

Tennis Court Rd.

Park Terrace
PARKER'S PIECE

Parkside
East Rd.
Mill Rd.

Gonville Pl.
Gresham Rd.
Harvey Rd.
Hills Rd.

Regent St.

Lensfield Rd.
Causeway

To London ↓

To Colchester ↓

0   1/4 mi
0   .25 km

Cambridge is not all about academics and the past, though, so if you've got a modern-day dot.com venture in mind, know that old-time Cambridge is now touted as a high-tech outpost. Megapunter Bill Gates, who decided in 1997 to fund a research center here, once made the claim that Cambridge was becoming "a world center of advanced technology."

Cambridge's main newspaper, the *Cambridge News,* has an excellent "what's on" section which gives listings of all the happenings in town, including theater, clubs, bars, and music. *Varsity,* Cambridge University's student newspaper, also lists events.

neighborhoods

If you're arriving by train, it's about a 15- to 20-minute walk into town, or 10 minutes by bus (the buses run from the railway station into town every 10 to 15 minutes). You might be slightly concerned because the initial view of Cambridge is a bit discouraging (all cheap B&Bs and plain brick houses), but after about 15 minutes, once you've passed the cricket grounds and the huge glass facade of the YMCA, things will start to look up. What appeared to be just another dull, if not downright ugly, small town gradually morphs into the quaint, serene university village you've heard so much about.

From the **Drummer Street** train station, turn onto **Station Road** which quickly branches off to the right into **Tenison Road** (where you'll find the **YHA** [see *crashing,* below]). If you stay on Station Road past Tenison, it'll link up with **Hills Road,** which turns into **Regent Street,** and continues in a northwestern direction. This route leads you to the city center and the bus station. The center of town is a small cluster of streets packed with restaurants and shops. This is where you'll want to hang out, and **King's Parade** is where you'll want to go first, as it's the central strip. The university buildings mostly lie in this vicinity with tea rooms, cafes, and shops scattered in between. **The Backs** (college lawns), the Fitzwilliam Museum, and the riverside pubs are also a hop, skip, and a jump from King's Parade. The main streets run north-south (King's Parade, **St. Andrews Street**) with smaller but treasure-trove-packed streets cutting them horizontally (**Market, Wheeler,** and **Downing streets**). Note that the main streets change names approximately every 250 yards (**Trinity** into King's Parade into **Trumpington,** and **Sidney** into St. Andrews into Regent, for example).

The central bit of Cambridge is easily walkable, but eventually you may want to rent a bike [see *need to know,* below] so you can blend in with the natives.

hanging out

The Backs, where the lawns of the colleges sweep down to the River Cam, are a perfect spot to relax with the students among the patches of wildflowers (and the occasional farm animals roaming around). It's not that easy to mingle—most people just sit and read or eat their lunch by themselves or in little groups—but you may be able to strike up a conversation or two. If not, take the opportunity to chill out in this idyllic setting and pull out this awesome guidebook to read while you're munching on your sandwich.

Another pretty, grassy spot is the gardens east of Queen's Road along the river. You can hang out on the bridges and watch the punters pass by below, or scope out the view of the colleges.

bar scene

Since thousands of students live in Cambridge, there is no shortage of drinking spots, mostly on Castle Street, where you can throw a pint down the hatch. On weekends, students take a break from being scholastic superstars and indulge in the *Castle Street pub run,* which, very simply, entails hitting as many of the watering holes as possible and getting shit-faced.

During the day when the weather is good, visit the **Anchor** *(Silver St.; Tel 01223/353-554; 11am-11pm Mon-Sat, 1-10:30pm Sun)* which is located right on the river at The Steps.

The Regal *(38-39 St. Andrews St.; Tel 01223/366-459; 11am-11pm Mon-Sat, noon-10:30pm Sun)* is the largest pub in Great Britain at 10,000 square feet. But, apparently, size doesn't matter, as some locals hold the opinion that The Regal is "shit." (Most likely they have a problem with the Regal's modern vibe and prefer the more studenty and laid-back feel of the pubs on Castle Street.) Despite that less-than-encouraging endorsement, the pub often bulges beyond capacity in the evenings to the sounds of the jukebox. With a building cost of £3 million, The Regal's developers

you wanna flitch?

Every spring, couples of Dunmow, a village not far from Cambridge, take part in a mock trial with a jury of six singles from the same town. If the couple prove that for a whole year and one day they have "not wished themselves unwed"—in other words, that no plates have been flung across the room at an unsuspecting spouse—the reward is a chunk of bacon, a "flitch." In 1104, this was a serious event; it was made civil law in 1855. Nowadays though, the Dunmow Flitch Trials resemble more of a major sporting-event-cum-Jerry Springer extravaganza: They're held only every four years and they're televised. The next Dunmow Flitch Trials will be on Saturday, July 10, 2004.

clearly knew they wouldn't have trouble finding customers in Cambridge. The beer here is cheap, but you can't get unique brews except during one of the beer festivals that happen a couple of times a year, when 50 of the pub's finest hops come out to play.

Another slick bar that believes size does, indeed, matter, is the **Rat and Parrot** *(3-8 Downing St.; Tel 01223/304-357; 8am-11pm Mon-Sat, noon-10:30pm Sun; All major credit cards)*. It has a whopping 7,050 square feet split up among three floors. They're all pretty much the same, with lots of tables and stools. It has a big outside deck as well, where you can mix with the crowd and enjoy a drink on summer nights. It's not a wonderful place to have beer, though, as there are no hand pumps or ales.

The Eagle *(Benet St., off the King's Parade [Benet turns into Wheeler St.]; Tel 01223/505-020; Noon-2:30pm/5:30-8:45pm daily)* is one of the oldest pubs in Cambridge and its history pretty much testifies to that. The folks at the pub were first to hear about Watson and Crick's little DNA double helix announcement, and the Eagle's ceiling was scratched with the initials of British and American pilots during WWII. Serving local ales made by hometown brewmaster Greene King, there's also a wide-ranging pub menu.

Known for its dazzling array of delicious cocktails, the **Maypole** *(Portugal Place, between Bridge and New Park Sts.; Tel 01223/352-999)* near the ADC Theatre, likes to show them off in its lengthy happy hour (5-11pm).

LIVE MUSIC SCENE

There's a decent mix of music in Cambridge, in both small and large venues. Check local papers for a gigs guide before going out.

Not only does **Venue** *(66 Regent St.; Tel 01223/367-333)* serve great modern international cuisine [see *eats,* below], there's live music every Friday and Saturday and every night in December. Local and national musicians play jazz, classical, blues, and contemporary music.

If you're in town on a Friday, head to the **Fresher & Firkin** *(16 Chesterton Rd.; Tel 01223/324-325)* for its most popular night. Situated on the northern side of Jesus Green (so a bit out of the city center), it has a combination of weekly music nights sprinkled with comedy and party events.

If you're an Irish folk fan, **The Geldart** *(1 Ainsworth St.; Tel 01223/355-983),* in the east of town, won't disappoint with their Thursday night "rocking shamrocks."

The **Corn Exchange** *(3 Parsons Court, Wheeler St.; Tel 01223/357-851, Fax 01223/329-074; Box office open 10am-6pm Mon-Sat, 10am-9pm on show nights; www.cornex.co.uk)* is Cambridge's largest venue for arts and entertainment. It mainly plays host to major rock and pop bands—original members of '80s pop group Spandau Ballet's played here recently. But it also features classical concerts, opera, and jazz, and the occasional dance and theater performances.

club scene

The pub scene beats the club scene in Cambridge, because when it comes to drinking, the English (especially the kids) don't like to f—k around. This is evidenced by the pub/club ratio. The clubs mentioned below are popular venues, but none of them are ultra style. The rule is don't show up in your ripped jeans, but you don't need to wear your shiniest duds either. Show up at around 10:30-11pm so you'll have a chance to hit one or two of the town's pubs beforehand.

The clubs listed here are all within walking distance of one another in the center of the shopping district. You can take in more of the university's buildings as you stumble between them in the wee hours.

Labeled as the mainstream, cheesy club in town, **Fifth Avenue** *(Heidelberg Gardens, Lion's Yard; Tel 01223/364-222, Fax 01223/351-456; www.fifthavenue.f9.co.uk; Cover varies)* still manages to pack 'em in with different music every night. On Mondays there's '70s, '80s and early '90s (£3.50 before 10:30pm, £4 after). Shake it down on Thursday's international night with salsa and Europop, or come on in on Saturdays for classics blasting from the speakers (£6.50 before 11pm, £7.50 after).

There's no dress code at the **Fez** *(15 Market Passage; Tel 01223/519-224, Fax 01223/519-226; 9pm-2:30am Mon-Thur, 9pm-3am Fri, Sat; thefezclub@cambridgecity.fsnet.co.uk, www.ponana.co.uk; Free Mon & Wed before 9pm)* which features different styles of music every night. On Saturdays there's funk and house, and Fridays showcase 'esoteric' guest DJs.

On the first Saturday of every month at **Po Na Na** *(7a Jesus Lane; Tel 01223/323-880, Fax 01223/323-285; ponana@cambridgecity.freeserve.co.uk, www.ponana.co.uk; 7pm-midnight Mon, 8pm-midnight Tue-Thur, 7pm-midnight Fri, Sat; Happy hour till 10pm Mon-Thur, till 9pm Fri, Sat; £1.50 Mon-Thur, £3-£4 Fri, Sat),* American guest DJs spin house and garage. If you've been aching to learn how to salsa, head to the club on Mondays from 7-9pm for classes, for only £5.

arts scene

Cambridge's performing arts scene outpaces its visual arts scene. The two art places in town, one museum and one gallery, both are cool, but there are more theaters with a broader mix of productions than art exhibition spaces.

▶▶VISUAL ARTS

The Fitzwilliam is noted for its permanent collection of antiquities from ancient Egypt, Greece, and Rome. If you have a penchant for modern art, you'll want to check out Kettle's Yard.

Housed in a gorgeous two-story building a few minutes' walk south of the city center is the **Fitzwilliam Museum** *(Trumpington St.; Tel 01223/332-900, Fax 01223/332-923; 10am-5pm Tue-Sat, 2:15-5pm Sun; 11am-5pm Sun, May only; fitzmuseum-enquiries@lists.cam.ac.uk, www.fitzmuseum.cam.ac.uk; Admission free),* where the main art collection in town resides. Upon entering, notice the large overhead dome with skylights that set the dramatic mood for the multitude of rooms, each dedicated to a specific genre or a period of art. Notable collections include both the English and continental collections of ceramics and porcelain, as well as the modern art located upstairs. By the way, this is your chance to see some masterpieces—paintings by Rubens, Monet, Renoir, and Hogarth, to name a few. There are also frequent temporary exhibitions, plus lectures and events, so check a program at the front desk for details.

The lovely glass box that is **Kettle's Yard** *(corner of Castle and Northampton Castle Sts.; Tel 01223/352-124; 11:30am-5pm Tue-Sun; mail@kettlesyard.cam.ac.uk, www.kettlesyard.co.uk; Admission free)* is the smaller and strictly modern art gallery in town. The Yard part of this gallery space features a changing exhibition every few months. Their permanent modern art collection of painting, sculpture, glass, and ceramics is in the adjoining House and is open from 2-4pm. *The Shape of Living,* one of the first exhibitions in 2001, focuses on Serge Chermayeff, one of the major figures of modernist architecture and design in Britain and the U.S. The development of his ideas is traced through his own houses, the design of his furniture, and his relationships with artists such as Henry Moore during the '30s.

A past exhibition examined 'a life of letters': David Kindersley was an alphabetician who moved later in his life to central Cambridge. Kindersley's stone cutting and street signage are a familiar part of the Cambridge cityscape today and his work also extended to major architectural commissions, including the gates to the new British Library.

▶▶PERFORMING ARTS

There's no shortage of stage action in town, from student Shakespearean productions to touring West End sound and light shows. If you'd rather sit through a movie than a play, there's both a big mainstream cinema as well as an excellent art house venue.

The Junction *(The Cattle Market, off Clifton Rd.; Tel 01223/578-000 or 511-511; bookings@junction.co.uk/spiral@junction.co.uk, www.junction.co.uk; Box office open noon-6pm Mon-Sat; Adults from £6, concession from £5)* is a lively and eclectic arts and entertainment venue with everything from live music acts to nightclub events. They also showcase comedy, dance, theater, and digital arts.

The **Cambridge Arts Theatre** *(6 St. Edwards Passage; Tel 01223/503-333, Fax 01223/578-929; Box office open 10am-7:45pm Mon-Sat, 6-7:45pm Sun, performance days only; boxoffice@cambarts.demon.co.uk, www.cambridgeartstheatre.com; Adults from £5, £2 off concessions; MC, V, AE, Switch)* is a lively venue for drama, dance, comedy, and music, featuring a lot of productions from London's West End. It was also the theatrical stomping ground of Emma Thompson and John Cleese in their student days.

If you'd rather see some amateur theater by university students, walk on over to the **ADC Theatre** *(Park St.; Tel 01223/503-333; Box office located at the Cambridge Arts Theatre; info@adc-theatre.cam.ac.uk, www.adctheatre.cam.ac.uk),* which puts on two shows a night at 8 and 11. From musical Shakespeare to Oscar Wilde adaptations to comedy shows, there's a full range of stuff for the young scholars to demonstrate what they can do in the non-academic department.

The **Cambridge Arts Picture House** *(38-39 St. Andrews St.; Tel 01223/504-444, Fax 01223/578-937; opens at noon daily; enquiries@ picturehouse-cinemas.co.uk, www.picturehouse-cinemas.co.uk; £3.50-5 adults)* shows the best art house (e.g., *Europa Europa, The Golden Bowl*) releases, as well as some silent films. For the latest mainstream films, there is an eight-screen **Warner Village** multiplex on the first floor of the Grafton Center *(East Rd.; Tel 01223/460-441; www.warnervillage.co.uk; Adults from £3.30, concession rates available)*.

gay scene

There's a strong gay community feel at **The Town and Gown** *(Pound-hill, just off Northampton St.; 11am-11pm daily, noon-10:30pm Sun; Tel 01223/353-791)* and the **Five Bells** *(126-128 Newmarket St.; Tel 01223/314-019; 11am -11pm daily, noon-10:30pm Sun)*, which has a huge beer garden—always an essential in the summer.

culture zoo

People come to Cambridge primarily to absorb the collegiate atmosphere of the town, gaze at the beautiful architecture, and punt down the river. Most people get around on bicycles, so you'll be able to look up at the structures without nearly choking from traffic pollution, as you might do in Oxford.

King's College, Trinity College *(Noon-2pm Mon-Fri, library; 3-5pm daily, hall; 10am-5pm daily, chapel)* and **St. John's College:** These are the main Cambridge colleges and all three charge a £3.50

---

festivals and events

Cambridge is home to the super-smart, but naming their inter-college boat races the "May Bumps" seems a bit inconsistent with that, since they're held in June. After the bumping, Cambridge becomes decidedly empty when students go on their "long vac." However, there are still festivals happening, even if it's only the tourists who are bumping into one another. **The Strawberry Fair** *(First Sat in June; www.strawberry-fair.org.uk)* is, contrary to its name, a celebration of local arts, crafts, and music, but also features stalls selling world foods. **The Folk Festival** *(July 27-29; www.cam-folkfest.co.uk/)* has a lineup of internationally renowned musicians including, at last year's festival, Joan Baez.

entrance fee (the rest of the colleges are free). With admission, you get to walk around the inner grounds of the colleges, which often include pretty gardens and open courtyards. Admission to the college chapels and the libraries is also included.

King's College Chapel *(King's Parade; Tel 01223/331-100; 9:30am-3:15pm Mon-Sat, 1:15-2:15pm Sun):* Apart from a visit to any of the Cambridge colleges, this is the cultural highlight of the town. From King's Parade, the large Gothic building appears to be substantial, but nothing extraordinary. That is, until you step inside and have the unique experience of being surrounded by four walls of solid stained glass. The enormous space and color make it a heavenly setting for listening to the church's boys' choir—but be sure to gulp an espresso first, or their lilting tones could send you into a blissful sleep.

modification

Cambridge Piercing Studio *(200 Mill Rd.; Tel 01223/506-312, 01223/244-006; 10am-5pm Mon, Tue, Fri, and Sat, 10am-6pm Wed, Thur)* testifies to having a piercing room "private and akin to an operating theatre in both looks and levels of hygiene." Piercings range from a £10 nose stud to a £40 bar through a spot in the genital region. Since most of the bits on the bod being pierced here seem to be in areas your average person wouldn't voluntarily put a hole in, this place is definitely not for the faint-hearted.

great outdoors

If you do but one energy-exerting exercise in Cambridge (we're talking about activities in the daylight hours), it must be punting. This is a quintessentially English experience. There are several locations willing to rent you a punt for an hour or two. Either go to The Steps or The Bridge, both quayside points next to River Cam in The Backs area. There you'll find **Scudamore's** *(Moat House, Granta Place; Tel 01223/359-750; £8 per boat self-hire, chauffeured trips available as well).* Or you can go to the Silver Street Bridge, between King's Parade and Queen's Road, and get a punt at **Granta Punt Hire Company** *(Newnham St.; Tel 01223/301-845; 9:30am-dusk daily; granta.boats@lineone.net; £8 per hour self-hire, £6.50 per person, £22 minimum per boat, for hour-long student-chauffeured punting tour through colleges).* You can also rent regular canoes or rowboats here.

If you enjoy walking, take advantage of the **Fens land** surrounding Cambridge, which is as flat as a pancake. From Cambridge you can find (ask at the TIC [see *need to know,* below] if you can't) a wonderful long-distance path to walk as part of the **Fen Rivers Way**, which stretches for nearly 50 miles between Cambridge and King's Lynn. The Fens landscape is dissected by the rivers, dykes, and embankments that trickle slowly across the Fenland into the Wash. From Cambridge, the walk follows the River Cam through pastures and approaches Ely, 27 km away. Here, it joins the River Great Ouse, which it follows all the way to King's

Lynn and the Washes. You can bring a picnic lunch to ward off any hunger pangs.

STUFF

▶▶BOUND

Heffers *(20 Trinity St.; Tel 01223/568-568)* bookstore has six branches: They sell stationery (at 19 Sydney Street), children's books (30 Trinity Street), paperbacks and video (31 St. Andrews Street), and art and graphics (15-21 King Street). The music store is at 19 Trinity Street, and sells classical and pop cassettes, CDs, and choral college music so you can learn to sing like those boys in the King's Chapel. Catch Heffers also in the Grafton Shopping Centre, where you can pick up their new fiction and non-fiction titles. If you're Heffered out, there's also **Cambridge University Press** *(1 Trinity St.).*

Try **G David** *(16 St. Edward's Passage; Tel 01223/354-619)* for antiquarian editions and hardbacks, and the **Haunted Bookshop** *(9 St. Edward's Passage; Tel 01223/312-913)* for travel, illustrated, out-of-print children's books, and first editions. For art and architectural books, head downstairs at **Deighton, Bell & Co.** *(13 Trinity St.; Tel 01223/568-568)* and upstairs for more antiquarian as well as second-hand books.

▶▶MALL RATS

A variety of shops, an eight-screen cinema, and a food court are available at the multilevel glass-domed **Grafton Shopping Centre** *(East Rd.; 9:30am-5:30pm Mon-Sat, till 7:30pm Wed, 11am-5pm Sun).* From the upper-level coffee shop you can sit and sip java while watching the shoppers mill about below.

EATS

The tearooms can be a bit stuffy but there are a bunch of them, so there are plenty of chances to enjoy a yummy scone and jam. If you'd rather, head over to a more studenty coffeeshop like the Copper Kettle and munch a pastry. If you're truly hungry there is no shortage of pubs selling the usual pub fare—jacket potatoes, sandwiches, soups, and salads.

Lining Cambridge Market Square are lots of little restaurants that provide a good position to watch the open market. There is also the local **Prêt-a-Manger,** whose coffees and delicious pre-made sandwiches serve as an easily transportable lunch if you're going to **The Backs** [see *hanging out,* above].

▶▶CHEAP

The quintessential student grub magnet in town is **The Copper Kettle** *(4 King's Parade; Tel 01223/365-068; £5 hot lunch).* This Tudorish-style coffeeshop sells daily homemade specials as well as cakes, pre-made sandwiches, rolls, and pastries. There are also some chunky vegetarian quiches hanging out with the predominantly red-meat dishes.

The only vegetarian restaurant in Cambridge, **Rainbow** *(9a King's*

Parade; Tel 01223/321-551; 9am-9pm daily; £6) is tiny, but the vegan and veggie dishes are well worth the squeeze.

Cambridge seems to do well with bakeries, and the French patisserie **Fitzbillies** *(52 Trumpington St.; Tel 01223/352-500; 9am-5:30pm Mon-Thur, till 9pm Fri, Sat, 11:30am-4:30pm Sun; £3 for entrees)* is no exception. With a cafe upstairs, this is the place to indulge in some Chelsea buns and cake (try the chocolate, which is a student favorite), as well as pies and sandwiches.

▶▶DO-ABLE

If you can't make it to the **Rat and Parrot** [see *bar scene,* above] for drinks, go there to catch a bite for lunch or dinner. From all-day brunch (average £3) to meat, chicken, and fish entrees (average £5.50), there's probably something here that'll please you. The extensive menu also features sandwiches, starters, Mexican platters, pasta, salads, and burgers; not to mention the mouth-watering selection of desserts and specialty coffees.

Rolling Stone Bill Wyman's **Sticky Fingers Café** *(26-28 Regent St.; Tel 01223/358-478; Noon-11:30pm Mon-Sat, noon-midnight Sun)* is worth a stop if you're a Stones fan—the walls are covered with the band's memorabilia. This, the third Sticky Fingers, opened in July 1997.

If you'd like to eat and then listen to tunes [see *live music scene,* above], check out **Venue** *(66 Regent St.; Tel 01223/367-333; 5:30-11:30pm Mon-Sat, till 9:30pm Sun; average for three-course a la carte meal £25, two-course set meal £14.50, snacks £5).* A two-course set menu is available Sunday to Thursday from 5:30-7:45pm, and there's also an a la carte menu available every evening. If you're on a tight budget, there's also a snack menu, with most items less than £5, available in the cocktail bar upstairs.

In every other decent-sized town in southern England, there is a

TO MARKET

You'll find luscious fruits and veggies at the stands in Cambridge Market Square, located in Lion's Yard, a pedestrian shopping district. The market doesn't have set hours but pretty much goes on from 10am-5pm every day with a craft market on Sundays. This market has great produce and during the day—it really adds a market feel to Cambridge. If you're the least bit homesick for a slice of American (though who knows why you would be), there's something soothingly Norman Rockwell about a student cycling home with shining red apples in the bicycle's basket!

Browns, and they're all pretty much the same. But the **Browns** *(23 Trumpington St.; Tel 01223/461-655, Fax 01223/460-426; 11am-11:30pm Mon-Sat, noon-11:30pm Sun; £8 for lunch entree; AE, MC, V)* here is one of the town's most popular eating places among the students, locals, and tourists. This becomes apparent as you wait and wait for a 1 o'clock table on the weekends. Although not mega-pricey, a relaxing lunch with a couple of drinks, dessert, and coffee can set you back about £20. Try the delicious salmon fishcakes. This is a good pit stop after the Fitzwilliam, a bit farther up and across the street.

▶▶SPLURGE

Located near Jesus Green, **Twenty Two** *(22 Chesterton Rd.; Tel 01223/351-880; 7:30-10:30pm; About £25; AE, MC, V; Reservations required)* is a local gem. The homey-yet-elegant Victorian dining room offers a fixed-price menu featuring whatever's freshest in the market. White onion soup and sautéed breast of chicken with thyme jus are just a few of the chef's creations, and there is always something for the discriminating vegetarian.

crashing

There are a slew of B&Bs near the train station on Tenison Road, but they're not very close to the center of town. So, if time is not of the essence and you're happy to cruise around a bit and see what's available, try not to stay in this area as it is completely lacking in atmosphere. In fact, Cambridge is probably one of the few towns whose YHA is far from any action whatsoever.

The TIC [see *need to know,* below] will book rooms for a £3 fee and a 10 percent deposit if you show up in person.

▶▶CHEAP

There is one hostel in town, the local **YHA** *(97 Tenison Rd.; Tel 01223/354-601, Fax 01223/312-780; 24-hour access; Dorms £11.90 adults, £8.20 under 18, about £3 more with breakfast, £27 double, £37 triple, £49 four beds, £61 five beds, £70 six beds; cambridge@yha.org.uk, www.yha.org.uk; V, MC, Delta and Switch).* It is a 15- to 20-minute walk from anything vaguely appealing, but it has a nice lounge and TV room, and is fully stocked with a games room, smoking room, cafeteria, self-catering kitchen, laundry and Internet facilities, bicycle store, and a courtyard garden.

The **YMCA** *(Queen Anne House, Gonville Place; Tel 01223/356-998; £22 single, £36 double)* offers clean, generous-sized rooms in a convenient location between the town center and the train station.

There is a **Camping and Caravanning Club** site *(19 Cabbage Moor, Great Shelford; Tel 01223/841-185; Cambus bus 102 or 103 from the bus station on Drummer St.; Open Mar-Oct; £5.20 per person, £5.20 pitch fee)* 3 miles south of the city center. It provides tent-dwellers with flush toilets and showers.

In the north of the city, the basic **Carpenter's Arms** *(182 Victoria Rd.; Tel 01223/351-814; £8 per person)* has two six-bed dorms. It's located

wired

Cambridge isn't wired for the Internet in a major way. It's somewhat ironic, actually, that the one Internet cafe that everyone goes to resembles a library more than anything, with shelves of second-hand books lining the walls. Near the hostel, the Internet cafe **CB1** *(32 Mill Rd.; Tel 01223/576-306; 10am-8pm Mon-Sat, 11am-7pm Sun; www.cb1.com)* charges 10p a minute.

www.cambridge-news.co.uk/tourism: Comprehensive Cambridge information site: accommodation listings, venues, etc.

www.latindance.fsnet.co.uk/salsa.htm: List of salsa venues and news around town.

www.varsity.cam.ac.uk: Cambridge University's student newspaper online.

www.cam.ac.uk/CambArea: Great list of links for everything related to Cambridge, provided by the University's website.

above a pub, so you can drink to your heart's content knowing that your bed is a short trip (no pun intended) up the stairs.

▶▶DO-ABLE

Near the train station, there is a string of basic B&Bs on Tenison Road, all offering the same type of accommodation. The **Six Steps Guest House** *(93 Tenison Rd.; Tel 01223/353-968, Fax 01223/356-788; £25-40 single, £40-70 double; sixsteps@aol.com;)* offers rooms with private bath, cable TV, and phones.

The Conifers *(213 Histon Rd.; Tel 01223/311-784; £48 per night; maureenkent.213@camnews.net)* has just one twin room, with private bath and its own entrance leading onto a private garden and terrace. There is also a galley kitchen outfitted with microwave, fridge, and a dining table and chairs for your private use. This B&B is within walking distance from the city center.

With a great location, the **Arundel Hotel** *(53 Chesterton Rd.; Tel 01223/367-701, Fax 01223/367-721; Bus 3 or 5; £69-96 double, including continental breakfast; AE, DC, M, V)* has clean and comfortable rooms with king or twin beds plus compact bathrooms with plenty of shelf space. If you want a room overlooking the River Cam and Jesus Green, you'll pay the higher rate. A coin-operated launderette is on the premises, as well as a bar and restaurant and a garden with outdoor tables for drinks in warm weather.

▶▶SPLURGE

In a good spot overlooking the River Cam, the **Cambridge Garden House Moat House Hotel** *(Granta Place, Mill Lane; Tel 01223/259-988, Fax 01223/316-605; £154-209 single, £184-239 double; £79-134* *single, £158-213 double off-peak; revcgh@queensmoat.co.uk; MC, V, AE, Delta)* will pamper you well. The compact bathrooms are fitted with shower stalls. There is a leisure club in the hotel that is free for guests, with a pool, Jacuzzi, and gym.

need to know

Currency Exchange There is a **Barclays** and a **Lloyds** *(3 Sidney St.; 9am-5pm Mon, Tue, Thur, Fri, 9:30am-5pm Wed, 10am-1pm Sat)*, both on Sidney Street, and Abbey National, Midland, NatWest, TSB, and Nationwide are on St. Andrews Street. There is also a **Thomas Cooke** *(8 Andrews St.; Tel 01223/366-141; 9am-5:30pm Mon-Sat)*.

Tourist Information The **TIC** *(The Old Library, Wheeler St.; Tel 01223/322-640; Fax 01223/457-588; 10am-6pm Mon-Sat, 11am-4pm Sun Apr-Oct; 10am-5:30pm Mon-Fri, 10am-5pm Sat Nov-Mar; tourism@Cambridge.gov.uk)* is in the back of the Guildhall and sells maps and postcards and offers an accommodation-booking service.

A tourist reception center for Cambridge and Cambridgeshire is operated by **Guide Friday Ltd.** at Cambridge Railway Station *(Tel 01223/364-44; 9:30am-6pm daily, till 3pm in off-season)*. The center, on the concourse of the railway station, sells brochures and maps. Also available is a full range of tourist services, including accommodations booking and guided tours of Cambridge that leave the center daily.

Public Transportation **Stagecoach Cambus** *(100 Cowley Rd.; Tel 01223/423-554; 50p-£2)* operates in the city and local area. The **bus station** *(Drummer St.; Ticket booth open 8:15am-5:30pm Mon-Sat)* is located roughly midway between Christ's College and Emmanuel College.

American Express You'll find AMEX services near the banks on Sidney Street *(25 Sidney St.; Tel 01223/351-636; 9am-5:30pm Mon, Tue, Thur, Fri, 9:30am-5:30pm Wed, 9am-5pm Sat)*.

Health and Emergency Emergency: *999.* The police and fire stations are in Parker's Piece, a square bordered by Parkside, Park Terrace, Regent Street, and Gonville Place, 5 minutes from the bus station *(Police Tel 01223/358-966; Fire Tel 01223/324-320)*.

The main hospital, **Addenbrooke's,** is approximately a mile and a half south of Cambridge on Hills Road, at the bottom of Hills Road *(Tel 01223/245-151; Bus 4, 5, 99, 113; about £2.50 by taxi)*.

Pharmacies There's a **Boots the Chemist** in town *(65-67 Sidney St.)* as well as a **Lloyds Chemist** *(54 Burleigh St.; Tel 01223/352-917)*.

Telephone City code: *01223.*

Trains The train station *(Station Rd.; 5am-11pm daily)*, is roughly a 15-minute walk from the center of town. Regular trains run between London's King Cross and Liverpool Street stations, and the Cambridge station at Station Road. The trip takes an hour, £14.60 return. To get to Ely *(£4.20 return from Cambridge),* or any of the other stops along the Fen Rivers Way, take one of the regular trains that operate between Cambridge and King's Lynn *(Tel 0345/484-950 for timetables and info).*

Bus Lines Out of the City There are **National Express** buses running hourly between London's Victoria station and Cambridge's Drummer Street station (both the local and national stations operate out of this facility), taking about 2 hours. You can get to Ely or any of the other stops along the Fen Rivers Way on a bus service connecting Cambridge with King's Lynn *(Tel 01223/423-554 for timetables and info).* For information on any other bus-related details—schedules, routes, prices—call or e-mail **Cambridge Coach services** *(Tel 01223/423-900; enquiries@cambridgecoaches.co.uk).*

Bike/Moped Rental **Cambridge Cycles** *(61 Newnham St.; Tel 01223/506-035)* or **Geoff's Bike Hire** *(65 Devonshire Rd.; Tel 01223/365-629; 9am-6pm daily Apr-Sept; 9am-5:30pm daily Oct-Mar; £4.50 for three hours, £7 for a day, £10 for two days, £12 for three days; £25 deposit)* are both good for rentals. Geoff's also offers guided cycle rides along the quietest paths in and around the town by a Cambridge graduate *(2pm Tue, Wed, Thur, 10am Sat, Apr-Sept; Approx. 2 1/2 hours; £9.50 including bike hire).*

Laundry The cutely named **Clean Machine** *(22 Burleigh St.; Tel 01223/578-009; 7am-9:30pm daily)* will take care of all your laundry needs.

Postal Send that postcard of the university to your mom from the **post office** *(9-11 St. Andrews St.; Tel 01223/323-325; 9am-5:30pm Mon, Tue, Thur, Fri, 9:30am-5pm Wed, 9am-12:30pm Sat).*

Internet See *wired,* above.

everywhere else

ELY

Ely is a pretty little town 16 miles—a brief train trip—away from Cambridge. Its main feature is the looming Ely Cathedral, but if you don't have time to actually go into town, the train ride in itself offers a great opportunity to see the Fens, the characteristic flat, green landscape of this area. The windmills and inns are easily seen from far away due to the region's flatness—and you'll really notice the ecclesiastical high points such as the cathedral.

If you do make it into town, you'll get an eyeful as you walk toward this medieval colossus poking high above the trees and buildings. On the far side of the cathedral is a park with lots of rolling hills and trees, a great place to sit or stroll if you have some time to kill.

Ely is the second smallest town in England, so you're in no danger of getting lost. If dropped at the railway, walk northwest along Station Road up toward the cathedral (the road name changes, but keep going straight). It's about a 10-minute walk, and the cathedral is on the right. Taxis are also available for £2 or £3.

If you arrive by bus, simply head south toward the cathedral. The bus stops at Market Street, the main shopping street. It's a 6- or 7-minute walk to the cathedral.

The Tourist Information Center [see *need to know,* below] is a 5-minute stroll from the cathedral, and just west of the landmark. You can walk alongside the Palace Green to the signed black and white Tudor-style building. The main shops of Ely are located in the High Street, Market Street, Forehill, and Market Square area.

CULTURE ZOO

The TIC [see *need to know,* below] offers a combination ticket for the cathedral, Cromwell House, Ely Museum, and the Stained Glass Museum for £8 adults, £6 students.

Ely Cathedral *(The Chapter House, the College; Tel 01353/667-735; 7am-7pm daily in summer, 7:30am-6pm daily in winter, till 5pm Sun in winter; £4, £3.50 students):* This is a must-do if you're a into cathedrals, Benedictine monasteries, or medieval domestic architecture. The near-legendary founder of this cathedral was Etheldreda, the wife of a Northumbrian king who established a monastery on the spot in 673. The present structure dates from 1081. Inside there is a stained-glass museum which houses a collection of more than a hundred panels of glass dating from the 10th century to modern times.

Oliver Cromwell's House *(29 St. Mary's St.; Tel 01353/662-062; 10am-5:30pm daily Apr-Sept; 10am-5pm Mon-Sat, 10:15am-3pm Sun Oct-Mar; £2.70 adults, £2.20 students):* If you're looking for some low-key culture, you'll find it here. Cromwell is a legend of the Civil Wars of 1642-1649 as a political and military leader, and his house is a quaint building worth admiring from the outside. Inside, the display includes period rooms decorated in the 17th century domestic style of Cromwell's day, as well as exhibitions including wax figures and even a "haunted" bedroom. The Tourist Information Center is also located here.

eats

There're the usual fish-and-chips options here; the best of the bunch is **Ely Fish Bar and Restaurant** *(52-54 St. Mary's St.; Tel 01353/666-204; Varied hours daily).* If you've had enough of battered cod, grab a sandwich at **Lunchbox** *(Market St.; Tel 01353/650-115; 9am-4pm daily).*

The Almonry Restaurant & Tea Rooms *(Tel 01353/666-360; Meals start at £4.50)* is housed in the medieval college building on the north side of the cathedral. It has a comfortable tearoom that's licensed to sell drinks, and you can take your drink out to a garden seat in good weather.

crashing

You'll probably want to head back to Cambridge to catch some z's more cheaply, but if for some reason you end up staying in town, there is a fine B&B, **23 Egremont Street** *(23 Egremont St.; Tel 01353/664-557; £23 single, £18 double; Flexible breakfast times)* a 5-minute walk from the city's center (northeast of the cathedral). There's a spacious garden at the rear with views of the cathedral.

Situated a 5-minute walk from the cathedral is **The Castle Lodge Hotel** *(50 New Barns Rd.; Tel 01353/662-276, Fax 01353/666-606; £35 single, £25-27.50 per person double; www.castlelodge@ely.org.uk).* A good selection of freshly cooked meals, including some vegetarian choices, is served in the dining room.

need to know

Currency Exchange All the major banks appear in Ely. There's a **Barclay's** *(28 High St.; Tel 01353/663-548)* with an ATM near the cathedral.

Tourist Information Situated in Oliver Cromwell's house, the **TIC** *(29 St. Mary's St.; Tel 01353/662-062; 10am-6pm daily Apr-Sept; 10am-5pm Mon-Sat Oct-Mar)* is situated near the cathedral. If you show up in person, the TIC can book accommodations for a £2 charge, plus a 10 percent deposit.

Health and Emergency Emergency: *999.* **Princess of Wales Hospital** *(Lynn Road; Tel 01353/652-162)* is available for small injuries.

Pharmacies Lloyd's Chemist *(19 High St.; Tel 01353/669-946)* is conveniently located near the cathedral.

Trains There are frequent express trains to and from Cambridge, on the lines between King's Lynn, Norwich, and Peterborough. From Cambridge, it is possible to catch a train to any major hub, including a direct train to London's Liverpool Street station *(Tel 0345/484-950 or 08457/484-950 for info)*.

Bus Lines Out of the City Campus buses run frequently between Cambridge and Ely *(Tel 01223/423-554 for info)*.

Postal The post office is located in **Lloyd's Chemist** [see *pharmacies,* above].

blenheim palace

Here's a good question for *Who Wants to be a Millionaire:* What grand luxe palace was Winston Churchill born in and Sylvester Stallone married in? Answer: Blenheim Palace, England's answer to Versailles. Queen Anne gave money to the first duke of Marlborough, John, to build the palace after he beat the French and Germans in the Battle of Blenheim in Bavaria, on the banks of the Danube. The palace is loaded with riches: antiques, porcelain, and oil paintings.

Try to get Rosalind Templeman as your guide for the tour that's included in the admission fee. She's smart and funny and has lots of good gossip about the place. The palace is open only in summer when the royal family in residence retreat to their summer home. For an extra £4 you can view their private apartments.

The library is one of the palace's most impressive rooms, with its fine stucco ceiling decoration and portraits of Queen Anne, King William II, and the 1st Duke of Marlborough, and is even rented out for special occasions (like Sly's wedding). Also, anyone may play the Willis organ at the north end of the library. Be sure to note the color photographs of the family on the tables, which are quite a contrast to the backdrops of oil portraits on the walls behind them. This gives this historical palace a surprising modern touch and is another reminder that, yes, royalty really does live here. You can also go into the room where Churchill was actually born—adjacent to which there is now a Winston Churchill museum.

Outside you'll find the perfect pastoral complement of sheep and cows wandering the abundant grounds. The crisp fresh country air makes the lakeside walk in the gardens to the Grand Cascade especially inviting.

From the outside cafe, go down the steps to the single bench by the water—a peaceful setting to enjoy lunch or just relax. From there, go up one flight of steps to the dusty path and walk down. In the gardens there is a circular rose garden featuring beds of red, pink, and white roses and towering trees.

need to know

Contact Information *Tel 01993/811-325, Fax 01993/813-527;* Online *www.blenheimpalace.com.*

Hours/Days Open The Palace is open 10:30am-5:30pm daily; the pleasure gardens, Marlborough Maze, and the Butterfly House are open 10am-6pm daily. The whole place closes down from November to mid-March.

Cost Admission is £9.50 for adults, £7 for students.

Directions and Transportation Take bus X50, 20a, 20b, or 20c from Oxford Gloucester Green station. Buses leave every 30 minutes Mon-Sat, at varying times. Call the Oxford station [see **oxford,** above] for schedules.

henley-on-thames

A perfect day trip from Oxford or London, Henley is an archetypal English town on the eastern edge of Oxfordshire. With the river **Thames** winding its way between lush green banks dotted with boats of all kinds, it's like walking into a Seurat painting of a waterfront scene. The Tudor-style architecture in town complements the aesthetic, but Henley revolves around the river, where the famous Royal Regatta has been held during the first week of July since 1839.

The course was originally used for the first Oxford/Cambridge University boat races, and the Henley Royal Regatta is now one of the country's premier racing events. It even attracts international competition, drawing oarspeople from around the world who find it both challenging *and* entertaining. Anyone can come to the annual 5-day event and watch up to 100 races each day, scheduled as frequently as every 5 minutes. For more information on the regatta, go to *www.hrr.co.uk.*

The Henley Festival, a riverside arts and music event held for four nights the week after the regatta is far less known, but often really fun to attend.

You would think it's obligatory to rent boats in Henley, considering that the river often looks like a big-city traffic jam—especially on a Sunday afternoon. You can rent rowboats as well as barges, punts, skiffs, and motorized canoes. You can even take a ride on a Japanese dragon canoe, complete with inspirational drumming. Stop by the town's largest and oldest outfitter, **Hobbs & Sons, Ltd.** *(Station Road Boathouse; Tel 01491/572-035; Daily Apr-Oct; £7 small, £8 large, £16-25 motor boats),* established in 1870, to find the right vessel for you. They also have a shop that sells virtually any nautical item you'd ever need, even if it's just a kicky straw boater's hat.

If you'd prefer to stay off the water, take the riverside walk that passes over a bridge and through little cascades and water mills, then leads through wide, open fields.

eats

Grab a ploughman's lunch, fish and chips, or salad at **The Angel on the Bridge** *(Thameside; Tel 01491/410-678, Fax 01491/410-727)*, a pub in a hotel next to the Henley Bridge. It's definitely the best-positioned restaurant in town, with a fun view of the river.

crashing

It's a bit spendy to stay over in Henley-on-Thames; it's best to make arrangements elsewhere. To stay over during the regatta, you'll need to make arrangements *way* in advance.

If you get stuck here, the most affordable option is **Shepherd's** *(Rotherfield Grays; Tel/Fax 01491/628-413; Closed Christmas week; £40-54 double (reduced for stays of 3 days or more), breakfast included; No credit cards)*, a very charming vine-covered country home standing on 8 acres of parkland. The decor is what you'd expect from an English country home: antiques and chintz as far as the eye can see....

need to know

Tourist Information The **TIC** *(Town Hall, Market Place; Tel 01491/578-034, Fax 01491/411-766; 10am-7pm daily Apr-Oct; 10am-4pm daily Oct-Mar; www.henley-on-thames.com)* can supply you with literature on the Royal Regatta.

Health and Emergency Emergency: *999*. Police *(Kings Rd.; Tel 01491/410-600)*.

Telephone City code: *01491*.

Trains Thames trains have an hourly service to Twyford from London Paddington. From there connect to Henley. Call *Tel 0345/484-950* for departure times or other info.

Bus Lines Out of the City Buses leave London Victoria for Reading. From there take local **bus 328** or **329** to Henley. There are buses from Oxford to London Heathrow via Henley. Call *Tel 0990/808-080* for info.

Postal Postal services are available inside **Martins Newsagent** *(2-4 Bell St.; Tel 01491/573-599)*.

the
southeast

the southeast

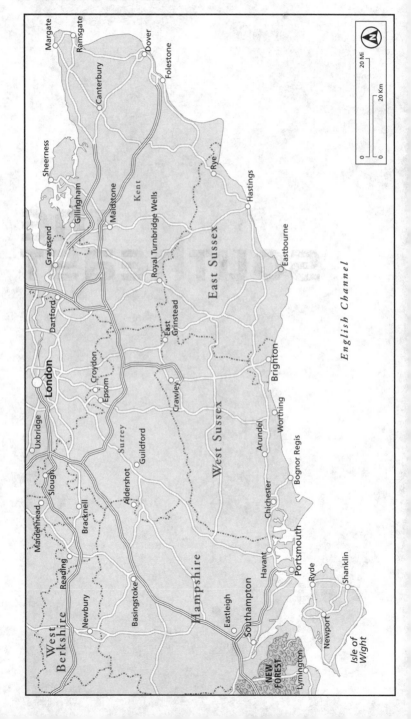

here begins the book of the Tales of Canterbury," reads the first line of the prologue Geoffrey Chaucer's classic *Canterbury Tales.* "Folks long to go on pilgrimages, and palmers to visit foreign shores and distant shrines, known in various lands; and especially from every shire's end of England they travel to Canterbury...."

When Chaucer wrote these words, it is doubtful he imagined the throngs of modern-day pilgrims, otherwise known as tourists, who travel to Canterbury in large numbers every year. This small city, along with the White Cliffs of Dover, are the county of Kent's main attractions. Considered the religious center of England, the mesmerizing Canterbury Cathedral has been rebuilt and enlarged so many times that it encompasses all styles of medieval architecture. The famous cliffs are worth a look if you're driving down the coast to East Sussex. The ancient seaport of Rye, southwest of Dover, is enchanting with its narrow, cobblestoned streets and 16th-century timbered houses. It's also home to one of England's oldest inns, The Mermaid Inn, where even the Queen Mother has crashed, as well as the Flushing Inn [see **Rye,** below] restaurant—a foodie's dream. All this, and a bag of chips, is compacted into a walled village that sits atop a cliff with panoramic views of the surrounding marshes.

Hastings couldn't be more different, with its garish seaside attractions, rough pebble beaches, and mobs of foppish British holiday-makers—in other words, a typical East Sussex scene. Hastings and the tiny nearby town of **Battle** form part of "1066 Country" (named for the 1066 Battle of Hastings)—a fact you will not quickly forget with the legion of promotional signs everywhere. You can stand on the actual grounds of the famous battle where William the Conqueror defeated King Harold for England's throne, and then walk around the abbey that William built to commemorate the dead. The highlight of East Sussex, however, is the cork-popping excitement of **Brighton,** a town first made popular by the 19th-century Victorians. Today, Brighton boasts some of the hottest and trendiest clubs in the country (apart from London, of course), including the largest gay club on the south coast. Lots of young people escape the concrete jungle of London to work in Brighton for the summer, so you're pretty much guaranteed to hook up with some like-minded hedonists while in town.

Traveling west from 1066 Country, you'll get to the most central southern county of England: **Hampshire.** Hampshire is an interesting

TRAVEL TIMES

Times by train unless otherwise indicated **Involves boat crossing	Brighton	Hastings	Battle
Brighton	-	1:20	2:15
Hastings	1:20	-	:15
Battle	2:15	:15	-
Rye	1:15	1:45	1:30
Canterbury	2:40	1:40	2:05
New Forest	2:25	4:00	3:50
Isle of Wight	1:35**	2:25**	2:10**

mix of naval ports and forests, as well as people. Jane Austen's books (think *Sense and Sensibility* and *Pride and Prejudice*) are populated with the Hampshire-inspired middle-class, and the general human spirit she wrote about remains here today. There are lots of rural pleasures to explore in Hampshire—complete with tiny cottages and thatched roofs—but the focal point is the **New Forest,** the largest remaining unenclosed tract of forest in England and a wonderful place for walking, bicycling, and horseback riding. There are also several cutie little seaside villages away from the gorse and heather of the New Forest, one of which, Lymington, links by ferry to the **Isle of Wight,** once Queen Victoria's summertime stomping ground, and now host to tons of boating events and festivals. It features miles and miles of paths and sandy beaches. The maritime bases of **Portsmouth** and **Southampton** are also vital transportation hubs. The old port of Portsmouth is brimming with English naval history, and Southampton has been a flourishing port for centuries, having launched both the *Mayflower* and the *Titanic*. **Winchester** is the capital of the

	Rye	Canterbury	New Forest	Isle of Wight	London
	1:15	2:40	2:25	1:35**	:50
	1:45	1:40	4:00	2:25**	1:35
	1:30	2:05	3:50	2:10**	1:20
	-	1:30	2:10	2:40**	:15
	1:30	-	4:00	2:40**	1:25
	2:10	4:00	-	1:55**	1:45
	2:40**	2:40**	1:55**	-	2:00**

ancient kingdom of Sussex, and was also the headquarters of the Anglo-Saxon kings during part of their 500-year reign in the Middle Ages. Winchester is home to the legendary Round Table of King Arthur and the Cathedral, of which some parts date back to 648 A.D. As you might have already guessed, the nightlife in these towns isn't really hopping—there are some great old pubs, but no cutting-edge music scenes. Save your clubbing shoes for Bristol and come here to experience Ye Olde England at its Ye Oldest.

getting around the region

The best way to get around the southeast is by train, bus, or a combination of the two. Trains are usually faster and more pleasant, with the added bonus of letting you glide through the magnificent English countryside, but buses are always a cheaper option and tend to run more frequently. Both transportation systems are highly efficient in England and offer numerous changes, stops, and routes. Each depot has an office with a friendly staff who will help you plan your route and load you up with maps, timetables, and pamphlets so you can carry on a little spontaneous exploring, too.

▶▶ROUTES

The best route for packing in the cities and towns of the southeast would start at Rye or Canterbury (each an easy train trip from London) and proceed to Hastings on one of the frequent trains or buses. From Hastings, take the train to Battle, hang out for a few hours, and then head back to Hastings to pick up a connection to Brighton.

There are no direct rail lines to Hastings and Rye from London. You must change trains at Tunbridge Wells and Ashford, respectively. You can take a direct bus from London to Hastings, so this may be your best bet.

Each of these towns is directly accessible by bus from London, so you don't have to plan a single route that goes through all of them if your time is limited. You can choose a few places as day trips and remain based in London. Brighton also makes a convenient base for planning day trips in the surrounding countryside.

Getting around Hampshire is a different story; you need to go by water for part of your trip. Take a train or bus to one of the closest points, such as Lymington, Southampton, or Portsmouth, and then hop on a ferry to the Isle of Wight. If you're planning on traveling to the New Forest first, take the Lymington ferry, since Lymington is located in the New Forest.

Southampton is on the same bus line as Brighton and Hastings (the London-Weymouth line) and serves as a direct link from the southeast to the Isle of Wight. The New Forest is just a few stops beyond Southampton, so you have the option of heading there as well.

The quickest direct route from London to the Isle of Wight is to take a train or bus to Portsmouth (the bus trip is only about 20 minutes longer than the train), or to Southampton (about an hour by train, two and a half hours by bus). The Isle of Wight is an easy ferry trip from either Portsmouth or Southampton.

To get to one of the New Forest towns—Ashurst, Beaulieu Road, Brockenhurst, or Sway—carry on a few train stops beyond Southampton. Alternatively, get off at Southampton and take one of the many bus connections to the New Forest.

brighton

Brighton is a town that does not take itself too seriously. Bette Davis allegedly said about a passing starlet, "There goes the good time that was had by all." The same might be said as one pulls out of the Brighton train station. The slutty appeal of "London by the Sea" comes from its unabashed gaudiness disguised as ritzy glamour—something like a Versace-clad woman wearing crotchless underwear. This is not to say that the most prudish will be forced to let their hair down in Brighton, but there is a rampant livin' it, lovin' it party feeling in town. Pick up a free copy of *The Latest* or *The Source* for current local listings.

neighborhoods

The Lanes, North Laine, Kemptown, and the **waterfront** are the major spots for sampling the moveable feast that is Brighton. From the train station, walk south down **Queen's Road** till you reach the clock tower. If you make a left onto **North Street,** and you'll hit the Lanes, a cluster of narrow pedestrian streets that are the oldest in town. If you carry on straight Queen's Road will become **West Street,** and eventually you'll hit **King's Road** and the pebbly beaches of the waterfront. If you want to head straight to North Laine, one of the funky, happenin' areas, go back up Queen's Road and head east on **North Road. Kemptown,** the center of gay life in Brighton, is located east of **Old Steine Street** and stretches all the way to the **Brighton Marina.** Note that many streets and roads are named after directions that don't actually correspond with their directions on a compass. Be particularly careful not to get North Road and North Street confused.

brighton

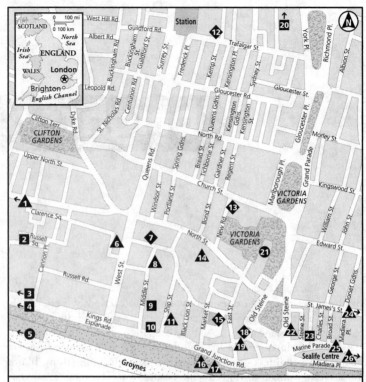

BARS/CLUBS ▲

Catfish Club **25**
Enigma **11**
Honeyclub **17**
Fishbowl **19**
Lanes End **14**
Revenge **22**
Richard's Brasserie **1**
The Escape **26**
The Hop Poles **8**
The Western Front **6**
The Zap **16**
Zanzibar **24**

CULTURE ZOO ●

Royal Pavilion **21**
West Pier **5**

EATS ◆

El Mexicano **13**
Havana
  Restaurant & Bar **7**
Krakatoa **18**
Room 101 **12**
The Strand **15**

CRASHING ■

Baggies Backpackers **3**
Brighton Backpackers **10**
Friese Green **9**
Cosmopolitan Hotel **23**
Oriental Hotel **4**
The Valentine
  House Hotel **2**
YHA **20**

hanging out

Grab some greasy fish & chips (if you haven't yet done this on the English coast, you should be ashamed of yourself) on Palace Pier and wander through the halls and halls of arcades, watch the rides at the end of the pier, or simply sit on a bench and try not to get rampaged by the giant seagulls. The grassy strip along the waterfront's King's Road is a good place to chill, kick a football, or toss a Frisbee.

bar scene

Brighton has plenty of options for those looking to down a few pints before they hit the clubs. Decorated in a great minimalist style, **The Hop Poles** *(13 Middle St.; Tel 01273/710-444; Noon-7pm Mon-Sat, noon-5pm Sun; V, MC)* is a relaxed, modern pub near the waterfront. It has an outdoor seating area with benches and tables where you can enjoy the cheap eats on the menu.

Seriously funky in its decor, **Fishbowl** *(74 East St.; Tel 01273/777-505; Open till 11pm)* in the Lanes has a very "fishy" interior. The place is decorated predominantly with silvery blue scales, and the beer taps are stuck into the mouths of fiberglass fish. Fishbowl offers full table service and a good cocktail menu.

Though owned by the same people as Fishbowl, **The Western Front** *(11 Cranbourne St.; Tel 01273/725-656; Noon-7pm Mon-Sat, noon-6pm Sun)* has a completely different atmosphere. Just off Churchill Square, this sprawling bar covers two large floors. Here, long wooden tables rest amid decorative cacti and other desert paraphernalia. The Western Front's proximity to the shops and its laid-back atmosphere and snack menu make it a perfect mid-afternoon hangout for students and local working folk alike.

A popular weekend hangout, **Lanes End** *(54-55 Meeting House Lane; Tel 01273/729-729; Fri, Sat from 8pm)* is a cafe/bar/restaurant occupying a long space with wooden floors and counters. The lounge bar is hopping on

boy meets boy or girl meets girl

Second only to London in the size of its gay population, Brighton is sort of like New York's Chelsea district. Don't expect flamboyance like you'd find in New York City, though. This is still England, after all, and, apart from summer festivals and the actual gay venues, you'd be pretty perceptive to pick up that Brighton has a bustling gay community at all.

wired

H and C Computers *(109 Western Rd.; Tel 01273/772-882, Fax 01273/772-883; 9am-9pm Mon-Sat, 11am-6pm Sun; £1 for 15 min., £1.50 for 30 min., £2.50 for 60 min.; robinc@handc.co.uk, www.handc.co.uk)* is a computer store with Internet access upstairs at very cheap rates. As an added bonus there's free coffee and Ice Cool Orange.

Opposite Waitrose, near Churchill Square, you'll find **Mail Boxes Etc.** *(91 Western Rd.; Tel 01273/706-020, Fax 01273/706-030; 9am-6pm Mon-Fri, 10am-4pm Sat; 8p per min. first 15 min., 4p per min. after; info@010.mbe.uk.com, www.mbe.uk.com)* a much less hip alternative.

www.brightonline.co.uk: Listings of pubs, clubs, and football-related information

www.zelnet.co.uk: Extensive listings of every hedonistic pursuit in Brighton.

www.thelatest.co.uk: Full what's on listings.

www.gay.brighton.co.uk: This site documents the history of the gay community in Brighton and lists all the famous gay people who have lived here.

Friday and Saturday nights, and there is live jazz on Sundays from 6pm to 9pm. The blue cocktail bar in the loft is open till 1am on Fridays and Saturdays, but you have to be a member (or with one) to get in. So, if you want to be whisked off to the cool, blue, cushion-strewn haven upstairs, pick up a member and play the part of the delightful companion for the evening.

Fridays and Saturdays at the **Catfish Club** *(The Madeira Hotel, Marine Parade; Tel 01273/698-331; 11am-2am; £3.50 admission Fri, £4 Sat)* are serious soul events that have been running for the past five years. The venue is a bit like a scout hall, but the music and diverse crowd are superb. It's packed with soul aficionados, hen-night frolickers, wide boys (those loud, obnoxious, low-grade, flashy types), and grannies.

LIVE MUSIC SCENE

A popular dining spot with locals, **Richard's Brasserie** *(102/106 Western Rd.; Tel 01273/720-058; 9:30am till late daily)* is a restaurant that also has two bars featuring live jazz music. The restaurant is near the West Pier, not far from the suburb of Hove. If you head to Hove Lagoon Watersports, this might be a good place to stop for a bite before heading back into Brighton.

The name is slightly misleading because this isn't really a true jazz club, but **The Jazz Place** *(10 Ship St., below Enigma; Tel*

01273/328-439; Cover £2.50-5, depending on the day) plays some great music. The schedule has Latin jazz on Mondays, hip-hop on Wednesdays, and *Roots Garden* on Tuesdays—a long-running roots reggae night for irie fun. Fridays are jazzier, with dance-floor type jazz, Saturdays are house-oriented. The bar holds a mere 200, so arrive early.

club scene

You can barely swing a cat in Brighton without hitting a club, so you'll hardly be stuck for late-night fun. Most are open till 2am and some even 5am. If you're into a particular kind of music or party, check *The Source* for daily listings of what's on at the clubs. Big with students, **Enigma** *(10 Ship St.; Tel 01273/328-439; Cover £3.50-5.50, depending on the day)* offers a wide variety of music: breakbeat on Tuesday, drum 'n' bass on Wednesday, jazz/electronica on Thursday, soul on Friday, and underground funk on Saturday. Enigma's not far from where Marine Parade becomes King's Road.

Midway between the two piers sits **Honeyclub** *(214 King's Rd. Arches; Tel 01273/202-807; Till 4am Mon-Sat, 1am Sun; Cover £2-10, depending on day),* a feast of campy club goodies—from Monday's disco infernos to Sunday's funky house sessions, and a lot of house, garage, soul, and big beats in between. Don't miss Friday's *Kinky Booty* parties *(10:30pm till late; £6 with special invite, £7-8 without),* when Miss Bossy Boots and Miss Daisy Vegas lead the glitzy girls and gorgeous guys into some fresh, frivolous fun.

Brighton's longest-running club—and still one of its most well-known—**The Zap** *(King's Rd. Arches; Tel 01273/202-407; Till 3am or*

festivals and events

Every May for about three weeks, Brighton bursts with more activity than usual during the **Brighton Festival** *(12a Pavilion Buildings, Castle Sq.; Tel 01273/700-747; www.brighton festival.org.uk).* This is England's largest arts festival, featuring music from opera to modern world bands, visual arts, theater and dance performances, films, a circus, street parades, and outdoor markets.

Throughout summer, a full range of activities around the city feature events in the arts, sports, and outdoors. In July, a **gay pride parade** takes place, with a different theme every year. Last year was *Glam & Glitz,* a celebration of the silver screen. Pick up a free *Summer Events* program at the TIC or call Brighton and Hove Council's Outdoor Events Office *(Tel 01273/292-711).*

4am Sat; Cover £3-9 depending on night) plays drum 'n' bass, techno, and house. Each night has a different theme, like '80s hits Mondays with cheap tequila shots (get in before 11pm and pay £2 instead of the £3 cover), and '70s Tuesdays when you get in free if you're dressed in '70s garb.

Freshly refurbished, **The Escape** *(10 Marine Parade; Tel 01273/606-906; £6 admission Fri, Sat)* is Brighton's most luxurious and plush venue. Saturday night's *Dolly Mixers* (all the DJs are female) are a bit cheesy, but the rest of the nights, including *Indie Tuesdays* and *Garage Thursdays,* are good fun.

Arts Scene

▶▶PERFORMING ARTS

Located in the Lanes, Brighton's most vibrant arts venue, **Komedia** *(Gardner St.; Tel 01273/647-101; www.komedia.dircon.co.uk),* serves up theater, comedy, cabaret, music, late bars, and a brasserie. **The Brighton Dome** *(29 New Rd.; Tel 01273/709-709, www.brighton-dome.org.uk)* has been recently refurbished to reinstate itself as Brighton's central arts venue. Located right next to the Pavilion Theatre and Corn Exchange, the Brighton Dome features contemporary music as well as jazz, Latin, and world. It also showcases traveling productions and dance, and has the London Philharmonic and the Bristol Philharmonic as its resident orchestras.

Right behind the **Royal Pavilion** [see *culture zoo,* below], the **Theatre Royal** *(New Rd.; Tel 01273/328-488; Prices vary depending on show; V, MC, AE, Switch)* is Brighton's main stage for West End productions featuring big stars.

For classic, foreign, and cult films, **Duke of York's** *(Preston Circus; Tel 01273/602-503; £5 admission, £3.50 before 6pm Mon-Fri, £4.50 before 6pm Sat, Sun)* is Brighton's plush art-house theater. For mainstream Hollywood, the eight-screen **Odeon** *(West St.; Tel 0870/505-00-07)* on the seafront is a better bet.

gay scene

Brighton's gay dance clubs rival the rest in terms of size and sheer decadence. The predominant gay area is Kemptown, jokingly referred to as "Camp Town." Most of the action takes place on St. James's Street and Old Steine. Two publications cover the gay community in Brighton; the glossier *Gay Times* costs £2.50, and *Capital Gay* is free. Both can be picked up at any newsagent.

The main gay party spot and the south's largest gay club is **Revenge** *(32-34 Old Steine; Tel 01273/606-064; 9pm-2am Mon-Sat; Cover £4-6),* located in Kemptown, near Marine Parade. This huge space rocks with a serious sound system, two bars, and two dance floors. It's disco night on Thursdays; '70s, '80s, and '90s music on Fridays; and *Choice Choonz* on Saturday. The most popular night is

Friday—known as *Lollipop*, an unabashedly trashy extravaganza hosted by three drag queens.

For a more laid-back experience, go to **Zanzibar** *(129 St. James St.; Tel 01273/622-100; Open daily)*, one block north of Marine Parade, off Manchester Street. The bar's vibe is friendly and casual, but not boring. There are always video jockeys playing and drink promotions to try.

For a mellow and slightly strange pub experience, **The Regency Tavern** *(32 Russell Square; Tel 01273/325-652; 11am-11pm daily)* is popular with gay and straight alike and close to the waterfront. The decor is bizarre, with green-and-white striped wallpaper and gaudy gold cherubs everywhere. It definitely evokes the campy style of the Regency period.

CULTURE ZOO

Royal Pavilion *(Tel 01273/290-900; 10am-6pm daily June-Sept; 10am-5pm daily Oct-May; £4.90 adults, £3.55 students):* If you want to see opulence like you've never seen before, you've come to the right place. Henry Holland and John Nash, the architects who built this "Fantasy of the Orient," surely did not subscribe to Mies van der Rohe's principle of "Less is more." The architects' interest in Indian marble mosques and palaces, as well as Chinese decor, led to this gold-chandeliered spectacle with dragons aplenty and patterns galore. The Royal Pavilion was a royal residence between 1787 and 1845, coinciding with the years of the Regency period in the arts (1785-1830). This was a rich creative period, a time when renowned poets like Byron, Keats, Shelley, Blake, Coleridge came out to play, joined by painters like Constable, Turner, and Lawrence. If you want to visit the Royal Pavilion, you'll find it near the waterfront, not too far from **Palace Pier** [see *hanging out,* above].

West Pier: Also not far from Palace Pier is what was once the beauty queen among piers. Closed in the '70s, West Pier is today a decaying, haunting landmark on the beachfront. If you look at it for a while, you can almost hear the organ-grinder music that must have emanated from its gracious domes. Now, thanks to a lottery grant, the pier will undergo rehabilitation.

modification

Interested in changing your look a bit? There are numerous tattoo and piercing establishments in town—some as scary inside as their names suggest. Near the Royal Pavilion, there's **Angelic Hell** *(2c North Rd.; Tel 01273/697-681; 11am-6pm Mon-Sat, noon-6pm Sun; No credit cards)* and the **Blue Dragon Tattoo Studio** *(2 North Rd.; Tel 01273/624-278; 11am-5pm Mon-Sat)*. Just up the road from the West Pier, you'll find **Perforations Body Piercing Studio** *(16a Little Preston St; Tel 01273/326-577; Noon-5:30pm Mon-Sat; No credit cards)*. And on Boyces Street, across from the Middle Primary School, is **Temple Tatu** *(9 Boyces St.; Tel 01273/208-844; Noon-6pm Tue-Sat; No credit cards)*. If you want service in the comfort of your hotel room, a technician from **Piercing Scream** *(Flat 2, 30a Adelaide Cresent, Hove; Tel 01273/321-245; Call for appointment Mon-Sat; V, MC, Switch, Delta)* will come to you.

The list of hair salons goes on and on, but two of note are Kensingtons and The Point, both in North Laine. A well-established hairdressing salon, **Kensingtons** *(9 Kensington Gardens; Tel 01273/673-686; 10am-4:45pm Mon-Fri, 9:30am-5pm Sat; Guys £20, girls £24; Cash or check only)* serves the city's rich array of clientele, from local students to London media folk. For an Indian head-and-shoulder massage with your cut, head to **The Point** *(16 Glouster Rd.; Tel 01273/693-833; 9am-6pm Mon, Wed, Sat, 9am-9pm Tue, Thur; Guys £16.50, girls £22; All major credit cards except AE)* and get special treatment from the friendly and attentive staff. The salon also sells its own products.

city sports

For all things water sports, check out **Hove Lagoon Watersports** *(Kingsway, Hove; Tel 01273/424-842; Call for prices; www.hovelagoon.co.uk)*. The shop is actually located in the town just to the west of Brighton on the seafront, but it is the place to go. Here you can rent equipment and go out on your own, or take a variety of courses, such as dinghy sailing, catamaran sailing, kite surfing, mako powerboating, windsurfing, waterskiing, and wakeboarding—whew!

stuff

The Lanes and East Street are where it's at when it comes to picking up choice antiques, jewelry, clothes, hats, and shoes. Upper North Street and Portland Road, near the clock tower, are good strips for antiques. The whole area of Western Road, North Street, and the sleek shopping center in Churchill Square (Western Road going eastward becomes North Street, after Churchill Square) is upscale store territory. North Laine is the funky bohemian center, packed with over 300 stores in less than half a square mile. Everything artsy, from African drums to '70s kitsch, is available here. Head down to the Artists' Quarter on the beachfront and dig around for prints, paintings, and artworks made from driftwood and wrought iron.

preceding the pashmina

The 19th-century Regency period was big in Brighton and left its mark on more than just the architecture. Let's take fashion, for instance: Shawls of Paisley, as they were called, were in fashion for about a hundred years, coinciding with the Regency period. The trend began when the woven Kashmir shawls first caught the collective international fashionista's eye, and soon European manufacturers were copying the style. During this time, millions were woven and embroidered from Kashmir and Persia to Austria, Paris, the U.S., and the UK. The output of shawls woven at Paisley, in Scotland, though, was the most prolific, which is how "Paisley" came to be a well-known sartorial term. The finest and softest fleece, called *shah tus* (king's wool), came from beneath the coarse outer hair of the underbelly of the wild central Asian goats. This particular underbelly fleece was used only for the very best shawls—the majority of which were from domesticated pashmina goats. These goats grew the hair to protect themselves from the harsh cold of the Himalayan region— much like the Sloanies today drape themselves in pashminas to protect their trendy bods from the London cold. Contrary to today, however, when pashminas come in every color of the rainbow, the best fleece in those days was left natural-colored, and only the darker fleece was dyed.

▶▶FUNKY DUDS
Brighton is the place to pick up an outfit perfect for your next Halloween party or cabaret evening. **Revamp Fancy Dress** *(11 Sydney St.; Tel 01273/623-288; 10am-5:30pm Mon-Fri, 10am-6pm Sat; All major credit cards)* is bursting with wacky party outfits, '60s and '70s boots, masks, wigs, makeup, balloons, and (lest we forget) tiaras.

▶▶BAZAAR
Browse the more than 50 stalls in the **Brighton Flea Market** *(31a Upper St. James's St.; Tel 01273/624-006; 9:30am-5:30pm Mon-Sat, 10:30am-5pm Sun)* in Kemptown. You might find a treasure among all the antiques, bric-a-brac, and collectibles.

▶▶MALL RATS
Brighton's main commercial shopping center is in **Churchill Square** *(Tel 01273/327-428; 9:30am-6pm daily, Thur till 8pm)*. With 83 stores under one huge, skylit roof, this place houses many of the mainstream clothes stores, like H&M, and the big bookstores, like Borders. If

the onslaught of consumerism makes you peckish, a variety of restaurants and cafes inside offer a bite to eat and a place to rest your weary bones.

€aTS

North Laine is brimming with sidewalk cafes and coffeeshops. On Palace Pier, you'll find a strip of fast-food stalls selling every type of junk food your heart could possibly desire, from fish & chips to doughnuts and ice cream. In general, sit-down restaurants accept most major credit cards, the exceptions being AmEx and Diner's Club. Dinner is usually served till around 10pm.

▶▶CHEAP

Near the waterfront you'll find **The Hop Poles** [see *bar scene,* above], where the average entree costs £4-4.50. Pop in for a drink and standard fare, like burgers and sandwiches, or try the more exotic international offerings, like Thai chicken curry and Spanish chorizo casserole.

Billing itself "positively vegan, definitely organic, and absolutely fabulous," **Room 101** *(101-102 Trafalgar St.; Tel 01273/704-000; 11am-11pm Mon-Sat, 11am-10:30pm Sun, food available till 9pm; Big snacks £2.95, little nibbles £2.75)* is one of Brighton's newest herbal-junkie paradises. Listen to soul, funk, and hip-hop in the minimalist atmosphere while sipping on organic wines, lagers, or ciders—and even get massaged (hands only) on Saturdays. On Sundays, there's an unconventional "take on English high tea, with reflexology or aromatherapy and a cuppa," for £3. Located near the train station.

For a little taste of Mexico, eat at **El Mexicano** *(7 New Rd.; Tel 01273/727-766; Noon-11pm Sun-Thur, noon-midnight Fri, Sat; Starters £2.75-4.90, entrees £5.50-11; elmexicano@youtopia.co.uk, www.elmexicano.co.uk; All major credit cards).* This wonderfully colorful restaurant has good, cheap *comida,* from *botanas* (snacks) to over-stuffed tortillas and burritos.

▶▶DO-ABLE

Located in the Lanes is **Krakatoa** *(Poole Valley; Tel 01273/719-009; Noon-11pm Tue-Sun; Sushi £3-4, entrees £5-6),* a good local spot for the sushi connoisseur. Krakatoa serves modern Japanese food in a small room with wooden tables and benches.

Serving an international menu, **The Coach House Café Bar/ Restaurant** *(59 Middle St.; Tel 01273/719-000; Noon-10pm Mon-Sat, noon-9:30pm Sun; Entrees £7-11; www.angelfire.com/id/coachhouse; V, MC)* is beautifully decorated with fork and knife artwork on the walls. The food is reasonably priced and good, and the setting is comfortable. Go there on Sunday for the popular fixed-price lunch.

▶▶SPLURGE

With its earth tones and sleek, geometric furniture, **Havana Restaurant and Bar** *(32 Duke St.; Tel 01273/773-388; 11am-10:30pm daily; Entrees £11.50-25; All major credit cards)* looks straight out of New York or L.A. Located near the intersection of North and West streets, Havana is a great place to go for a drink before dinner, and to watch the passing people parade on the street in this very quaint yet bustling part of town. The food is delicious, but at London prices, it should be.

A cozy little bistro hidden away off Bartholomew Square, **The Strand** (*6 Little East St.; Tel 01273/747-096; 6-10pm Mon, 12:30-10pm Tue-Thur, Sun, 12:30-10:30pm Fri, Sat; Entrees £9-15, 3-course set menu £12.95; All major credit cards*), has lots of fish on the menu in a rustic, intimate setting.

crashing

There are lots of choices for accommodations in Brighton, especially for backpackers and those looking for a cute, but not too pricey, B&B. The waterfront is loaded with ludicrously expensive hotels, and only a few charge rates that aren't ultra-extravagant. Brighton tends to lack anything between reasonable B&Bs and smart, sophisticated megaliths. The **Visitor Information Centre** [see *need to know,* below] will make you reservations for a small fee.

▶▶CHEAP

There are four youth hostels in town, three of which are centrally located. Book ahead since Brighton tends to be busy year-round.

If you're looking for a funky interior, **Brighton Backpackers** (*Corner of King's Rd. and Middle St.; Tel 01273/777-717, Fax 0123/887-778; £10-11 dorm beds, £55-60 per week, £25 doubles; stay@brightonbackers.com; No credit cards*) is the place for you. The dorm rooms contain four to eight beds, and the doubles are a good value at £12.50 per person. The location is great—right on the seafront—and you'll never go hungry with a 24-hour diner-style restaurant located underneath the hostel. Bonus: Brighton Backpackers is staffed with a bunch of international babes.

Down the road is **Friese Green** (*20 Middle St.; Tel 01273/747-551; Open 24 hours, services 9am-midnight; £9 dorm beds, £15 per person for double with shared bath, £50 per week; www.friese-green.demon.co.uk; No credit cards*), which is slightly cheaper for a dorm bed. Pretty much midway between the train and the coach stations, the hostel is filled with lots of international, friendly people, many of whom come to work in Brighton for the summer.

Baggies Backpackers (*33 Oriental Place; Tel 01273/733-740; Reception 9am-9pm; Dorm beds from £9, £25 double; www.cisweb.co.uk/baggies*) is a bit farther from the train and bus stations, but is located on a picturesque road off the seafront. This hostel has a large living room with a TV and couches. Even if you check out early, they let you hang out in the hostel until you leave.

The **YHA** (*Patcham Place, London Rd.; Tel 01273/556-196, Fax 01273/509-366; Reception 1-11pm Mar-Oct; 5-11pm Nov-Feb, closed Mon, Tue in winter; £10 per night, £9 with valid student ID, £6.90 under 18; brighton@yha.org.uk, www.yha.org.uk; V, MC, Delta, Switch*) is located 3 miles from the center of Brighton in a wonderful house across from open parkland. Bus 5A runs every 20 minutes from Churchill Square or outside the Royal Pavilion, and National Express coaches from London stop in front of the hostel. The YHA is well-equipped with a lounge, TV room, game room, cafeteria and self-catering kitchen, on-site parking, bicycle shed, lockers, laundry facilities, foreign currency exchange, and National Express coach tickets for sale. English breakfast, packed lunch, and dinner are also available. If you're a late-night partier, be warned! This YHA has an 11pm curfew.

▶▶DO-ABLE

Most of the B&Bs stand cheek-by-jowl on Regency Square just off King's Road next to the water. Right behind Regency Square, the smaller and quieter Russell Square is also filled with pretty guesthouses. The B&Bs are all pretty similar in terms of price and amenities, so if you arrive without a reservation, going door to door is a viable option.

If you plan ahead, try to book a room at the small and jazzy **Oriental Hotel** *(9 Oriental Place; Tel 01273/205-050, Fax 01273/821-096; £25 single Sun-Thur, £30 Fri, Sat, £54.50 double Sun-Thur, £69.50 Fri, Sat, one room with four bunk beds for £100, singles share bathrooms, doubles are en suite; info@orientalhotel.co.uk, www.brighton.co.uk/hotels/oriental; All major credit cards except AE, DC).* With walls dipped in Mediterranean blue paint, and decorated with terra-cotta pots, tall mirrors, and tapestries, the Oriental Hotel is an enjoyable and relaxing environment. Little touches like small bottles of sparkling mineral water in the rooms and a stack of magazines in the funky coffeeshop make this little hotel a standout. Breakfast is included and is delicious—especially the vegetarian choice.

One of the B&Bs in Russell Square is the **Valentine House Hotel** *(38 Russell Sq.; Tel 01273/700-800, Fax 01273/707-606; £40-55 double, £5 off without breakfast; All major credit cards),* a romantic little guesthouse with decorative window boxes and canopies over the beds. Hot breakfast is served in the hotel-style dining room that, except for the muzak, is cute in a gaudy sort of way. The proprietor, John Valentine, is charming and the setting is peaceful.

▶▶SPLURGE

Situated in New Steine, one of Brighton's famous seafront garden squares, is the family-run **Cosmopolitan** *(29-31 New Steine, Marine Parade; Tel 01273/682-461, Fax 01273/622-311; £24-40 per person depending on room and season, some singles and all doubles have private baths; Two-night minimum stay; www.cosmopolitanhotel.co.uk; All major credit cards).* The spacious rooms all have color TVs, telephones, and radios, and some have four-poster beds. The hotel bar (as well as some of the rooms) has views of the beach and Palace Pier. The lounge serves free hot drinks all day long.

need to know

Currency Exchange Banks (with ATMs) line North Street, near Old Steine; also near North Street is a **Thomas Cook** *(58 North St.; Tel 01273/325-711; 9am-5:30pm Mon-Sat, 10am-5:30pm Wed, closed Sun).*

Tourist Information The staff at the **Visitor Information Centre** *(Bartholomew Sq.; Tel 01273/292-589/99; brighton tourism@brighton-hove.gov.uk, www.tourism.brighton.co.uk)* will help you make hotel reservations, for a small fee. If you want to book for yourself, call the local, 24-hour hotline at *Tel 0345/573-512* for an accommodation guide.

Public Transportation There is a good local bus system, **Brighton & Hove Bus Company** *(Tel 01273/886-200),* with buses every few minutes on the main routes and plenty of city center bus stops. The new **metro** system has different color-coded buses for different routes. In the central area, there is only one fare (80p), whatever the distance.

American Express If you found you've left home without it, get thee to **American Express** *(82 North St.; Tel 01273/321-242 or 01273/203-766; 9am-5:30pm Mon-Sat, 9:30am-5:30pm Wed, closed Sun).*

Health and Emergency Emergency: *999.* The **police station** *(John St.; Tel 01273/606-744)* is a 5-minute walk from the Royal Pavilion. The **Royal Sussex County Hospital** *(Eastern Rd.; Tel 01273/696-955),* is in the eastern outskirts of Kemptown.

Pharmacies Late-night chemists open till 10pm every day of the year are **Ashtons** *(98 Dyke Rd.; Tel 01273/325-020)* and **Westerns** *(Coombe Terrace, Lewes Rd.; Tel 01273/605-354).*

Telephone City code: *01273.*

Trains There are frequent trains between Brighton and London Victoria or King's Cross stations. The fastest service takes only 49 minutes to **Brighton's train station** *(Terminus Rd., city center; Tel 0345/484-950).*

Bus Lines Out of the City Frequent buses leave from London's **Victoria Coach station. National Express** inquiries: *Tel 0990/808-080.*

Bike/Moped Rental There is a bicycle route along the seafront, on Victoria Gardens and Lewes Road, as well as many bike racks throughout the city center. The Visitor Information Centre stocks guides for cycling in the surrounding countryside. If you know where you want to go and just need the wheels, try **Freedom Bikes** *(108 St. James's St.; Tel 01273/681-698; 9:30am-5:30pm Mon-Sat May-Oct; £10 per day, £50 deposit per bike).* Another option is **Sunrise Cycle Hire** *(West Pier Promenade, King's Rd.; Tel 01273/748-881; 10am-6pm daily Mar-Sept; £12 full day, £8 half day, £20-40 deposit depending on bike),* where you can rent a tandem or a quad bike.

Laundry A laundromat, cleverly named **The Laundromat** *(5 Palace Rd.; Tel 01273/327-972; 8am-8pm daily),* is located near the Children's Hospital.

Postal Send those tacky seaside postcards from the local **post office** *(51 Ship St.; Tel 01273/573-209)* off Prince Albert Street, in the Lanes.

Internet See *wired,* above.

hastings

Hastings is quite hideous when you roll into the train station. If you're coming from Rye, you will be bitterly disappointed by the contrast in scenery. However, downtown Hastings, which is the initial point of entry, is entirely different from Hastings up on the hill and in the Old Town. Downtown, there is an ugly maze of pedestrian malls lined with both cheap, tacky, shops and sleek, upscale stores and shopping centers. The hills that slope up from the center of town are stacked with rows of identical houses, giving the city a sense of bland uniformity. But before you decide to turn and run, make a beeline for the Old Town, which is affectionately called "the twittens" by the locals. There, cozy restaurants and stone houses and inns adorned with flower boxes line the narrow streets. The other two spots that make Hastings worth more than a 5-minute visit are **West Hill** and **East Hill.** The views from both hills, which face each other, are simply spectacular. Although West Hill is highly residential, the homes don't obstruct the view. From here, the outline of **Hastings Castle** [see *culture zoo,* below] appears to be floating in the sky. To the left and far below is **The Stade,** a beach with fishing boats sitting on the shore. East Hill, a conservation area, offers similarly awsome views.

The road along the **beachfront** is your typically depressing southeast English coastline: pebbly beach on one side, amusement arcades on the other. However, Hastings has outdone itself in the level of gaudiness achieved here. Hastings is one of those places that most young people flee as soon as they are old enough to, leaving behind a mass of teenagers who look as if they're stuck in the 1980s, and who will get out, too, just as soon as they can. Despite this less than aggrandizing description, Hastings remains a popular holiday destination for the English, and, somewhat surprisingly, many people do live here and like it. It is also a convenient place to stay if you are on a tight budget and still want to visit Rye without the burden of pricey accommodations.

Pick up a free copy of *The Entertainer* and *Ultimate Alternative,* monthly publications of local arts and entertainment listings and news.

neighborhoods

From the train station, walk left on **Devonshire Road,** which meets up with **South Terrace.** Go south toward the water and you will hit the **Priory Meadow** shopping complex and the surrounding maze of pedestrian streets. South Terrace comes to a T at **Queen's Road,** one of the main streets in downtown Hastings. Continuing south toward the waterfront (take left off South Terrace), Queen's Road will fork. Take the left fork, **Albert Road,** which will take you to the beachfront. To get to **West Hill,** take a left onto **Castle Hill Road** just before you hit the waterfront. Castle Hill Road runs up a very steep hill and is hell to walk up if you're wearing a heavy backpack. If you would like to venture straight into **Old Town,** head left on the water-front till you see **George Street** branching off to the left. This road leads you into "the twittens" and away from the loud arcade games. The Old Town nestles under the shadow of West Hill, which you can also access from here on the long and winding **Croft Road.**

hanging out

The **West Hill** is the best place to chill out on the grass or to sit on the flat rocks at the edge and look out over the town below. This is also a perfect spot to fly a kite or have a picnic. It is quiet and uncrowded, and at sunset, the view from **Castle Hill Road** of the sun melting into the rows of houses is absolutely incredible. Both West Hill and East Hill are accessible via trolley service, which travels from the top to the center of town for 40p each way. This is a quicker and—on the uphill trip—a decidedly less strenuous option (but only the octogenarian crowd uses the West Hill trolley). The East Hill trolley is the steepest railway car in Britain, and since it doesn't travel through a tunnel, the view is amazing. Pick up the trolley for West Hill on George Street. For East Hill, get the trolley on Rock-a-Nore Road.

wired

www.entertainer2000.co.uk or **www.ua10 66.co.uk:** For arts and entertainment listings and news in the area.

www.observeronline.co.uk: The online edition of the Hastings newspaper.

www.hastings.uk.net: An interesting site containing information and history about the town.

hastings

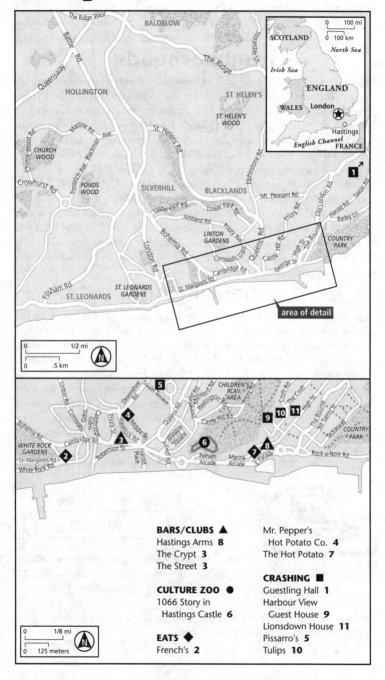

BARS/CLUBS ▲
Hastings Arms 8
The Crypt 3
The Street 3

CULTURE ZOO ●
1066 Story in
  Hastings Castle 6

EATS ◆
French's 2

Mr. Pepper's
  Hot Potato Co. 4
The Hot Potato 7

CRASHING ■
Guestling Hall 1
Harbour View
  Guest House 9
Lionsdown House 11
Pissarro's 5
Tulips 10

bar and live music scene

Beer and the blues seem to go hand in hand in Hastings. Located on a street just off the old town, the **Hastings Arms** *(2 George St.; Tel 01424/722-208; Music starts at 9pm, food served between noon-3pm/6-9pm)* has live blues every Monday, from mostly local bands, and lots of tables where you can enjoy dinner or drink while listening.

The spot for more serious jazz and blues is **Pissarro's Jazz and Blues Café Bar** [see *crashing*, below]. The bar features local and international musicians on Thursday, Friday, and Saturday evenings, as well as at Sunday lunch, with no cover.

club scene

There are only a couple of clubs worth mentioning, but they're right next door to each other so bar-hopping is a breeze even when you're down to a full stagger. Bonus: Both clubs have different music every night.

The Crypt *(Havelock Rd.; Tel 01424/444-675; 9pm-2am Thur-Sat; www.the-crypt.co.uk)* has theme parties most nights of the week: Thursday is *Back to the Future*, blasting '80s hits and serving tequila for 80p (yes, 80p). Friday is the *Six Million Dollar Disco* with groovin' '70s funk and breakbeat. Saturday is the *Big Mix-Up* with both DJs and live bands.

festivals and events

Old Town Carnival Week *(www.1066.net/carnival/)* is the much-anticipated annual pleasure spectacle of Hastings each August. OK, it ain't Mardi Gras in the Big Easy, but they do have a carnival queen who joins the mayor to lead the opening-ceremony prcession, which winds its way to the finals of the Old Town Crier competition. Included in the week's festivities is a treasure hunt, but, on this particular treasure hunt, the hunters go in costume to all 15 pubs in the Old Town. Kind of like Halloween meets St. Patrick's Day.

Coastal Currents is an art festival that goes on throughout the month of September. The focus of the festival is to take art out of its conventional viewing locations and put it in places you wouldn't necessarily associate with an art exhibit, such as hospitals and car parks.

Hastings Week commemorates the October 14 Battle of Hastings, with historical reenactments and a ceremonial raising of William the Conqueror's flag, the "Gonfalon." Along with fireworks from the castle up on the East Hill and the bonfire finale on Hastings Day, this is super-ultra 1066 mania, though it's tough to imagine why anyone but the Brits would really care.

A coffee bar during the day, **The Street** *(53 Robertson St.; Tel 01424/424-458)* serves up a combination of DJs and cheap cocktails Thursdays through Saturdays between 8pm and 9:30pm. It has a more laid-back atmosphere than the Crypt, and caters to a younger clientele. The **Dime Bar,** inside the Crypt/Street complex, makes for a good pit stop before the revelry at the Crypt begins.

CULTURE ZOO

1066 Story in Hastings Castle *(Castle Hill Rd., West Hill; Tel 01424/781-111, Fax 01424/781-186; 11am-3:30pm daily Oct-Mar 26; 10am-5pm daily Mar 27 through Sept; £2.50 students):* On the West Hill

hastings stars

Hastings has had its fair share of innovators and eccentrics. Here is a handful: John Logie-Baird (1888-1946) came to live in Hastings at age 35. Before inventing the television in 1924, he listed damp-proof socks and soup among his creations. Elizabeth Blackwell (1821-1910) was the first woman to qualify as a doctor and have her name registered in the British Medical Register. Prior to moving to Hastings, she opened a "dispensary" in 1853 in New York, which proved to be a forerunner to the contemporary private practice. Barbara Bodichon (1827-1890) formed the first ever women's Suffrage Committee, touring the country and holding meetings. One of her speeches converted Lydia Becker, who would become the movement's future leader, to the cause. Although Grey Owl (1888-1938) was born in Hastings as Archibald Belaney, he would become one of the greatest contributors to Canadian conservation, having been a prolific writer and lecturer on the Canadian north. Henry Rider Haggard (1865-1936) was an agriculturalist, as well as a colonial administrator in South Africa, who was best known for his famous novel *King Solomon's Mines.* He wrote over 40 popular books, including three additional novels set in Africa and all published in 1887. Marianne North (1830-1890) thought of the idea to present her paintings to Kew Gardens *and* provide the building to house them in. It opened in 1882 and today houses 832 of her oil paintings. And finally, Biddy the Tubman, born in 1879, performed—appropriately enough—in a tub in the sea between Hastings Pier and the former Queen's Hotel, delighting onlookers with his wet 'n' wild antics.

overlooking the town below, you can walk around and touch the majestic, jagged remains of the first Norman castle built by William the Conqueror. Before the castle was built, William and his troops briefly stationed themselves on this spot before going to kick some ass in the Battle of Hastings (which confusingly was not fought in Hastings, but in the town of Battle [see below]).

CITY SPORTS

The **East Hill** is a conservation area encompassing 300 acres of coastline, cliffs, and woods. It also offers a breathtaking 7-mile circular walk. There is also a golf course on the hill. Either hike up the hill or take the railway car lift from Rock-a-Nore Road in town.

Danceworks *(St. Clements Church House, Croft Rd., Old Town, opposite Tulips B&B)* is an adult community dance group where locals choreograph and perform modern dance routines at performing spaces around town. Classes are held in the studio in the Old Town.

STUFF

▶▶FOOT FETISH
For good prices on all the major brand names like Dr. Martens, Cat, and Skechers, take your tootsies to **Shoe Shuffle** *(11 Castle St.; Tel 01424/465-455; 9am-5:30pm Mon-Sat, 10:30am-4:30pm Sun; Shoes £5-69.99; V, MC, AE)*.

▶▶MALL RATS
The Priory Meadow Shopping Centre, in the middle of downtown, just a short walk from both the train station and the beach, serves up all the major chain stores like Top Shop, WH Smith, and Tower Records.

EATS

You'll find plenty of fast food and fish & chips in Hastings, but you can get cheap and tasty food of the not-fried variety as well.

▶▶CHEAP
At 10pm, **The Street** [see *club scene,* above] turns into a club, but between 10am and 5pm it serves cheap eats at the bar and its small outside tables. Expect bagels, baguettes, and salads for about £3 each.

For hot baked potatoes with a wide range of fillings, try **Mr. Pepper's Hot Potato Co.** *(Priory Meadow Shopping Centre, opposite BHS and in the wall of Littlewoods; Tel 01424/434-788; 8:30am-6pm Mon-Sat, 10am-5pm Sun)* in the downtown area or **The Hot Potato** *(28 George St., Old Town; Tel 01424/461-941; Noon-8pm Sun-Thur, noon-midnight Fri, Sat)* in the Old Town.

▶▶DO-ABLE
French's *(The America Ground, 24 Robertson St.; Tel 01424/421-195; Food served noon-4pm; Entrees £4.50; All credit cards)* is located in the better-looking section of downtown—you'll know it by its distinct black facade. During the day, the tables are filled with the business lunch crowd,

but come nighttime, it turns into a young, trendy pub. The menu is mostly standard pub fare, and there are daily specials such as steaks and a variety of pies.

▶▶**SPLURGE**

Röser's *(64 Eversfield Place; Tel 01424/712218; Noon-2pm Tue-Fri, 7-10pm Tue-Sat; Entrees £14.95-19, fixed-price lunch £19.95, fixed-price dinner £22.95; Reservations required; Closed last two weeks of Jan; V, MC, AE, DC),* set in a brick-fronted Victorian row house, is a pleasant surprise in the gastronomic wasteland of southern England. Gerald Röser, the best chef in East Sussex, changes the menu about every three weeks—past entrees have included medallions of venison in a savory red wine sauce; fresh, locally caught sea bass served Mediterranean-style with olive oil, lemon juice, and capers; and, in season, wild-boar chop with lentil sauce. Service is first-rate, as is the wine list.

crashing

Near the train station and downtown shopping, Cambridge Gardens is packed with cheap B&Bs, but none of them are particularly wonderful and the area is soulless. If you want to be near the train station, go to Pissarro's. But, if you're not fussy about being close to the town center, definitely go a little further out into the Old Town or up the West Hill. The TIC [see *need to know,* below] will book your rooms for £2.

▶▶**CHEAP**

The only hostel in the area is 3 miles (5 km) from the Hastings town center en route to Rye. Set on 3-acre of gardens, the **Guestling Hall** *(Rye Rd., Guestling; Tel 01424/812-373, Fax 01424/814-273; Hastings to Rye buses 711 and 346 pass the hostel, departure points for 711 are Hastings Railway Station, Breeds Place in the town center, and opposite the Boating Lake in the Old Town, 346 departs from Queens Rd.; Reception opens at 5pm; Closed Dec 19-Jan 27; Open Jan 27-Feb 28 except Sun, Mon, May 1-June 30 except Sun, July 1-Aug 31 daily, Sept 1-Oct 31 except Sun, Mon, Nov 1-Dec 20 Fri, Sat only; £9.80 adults, £6.75 under 18)* is affiliated with the YHA and has mostly large dorm rooms of 9-, 10-, and 12-bed rooms, two 4-, and two 6-bed rooms. It's a good idea to book in advance.

The Marina Lodge Guest House *(123 Marina St., St. Leonards; Tel 01424/715-067; £15-22; Some rooms with private bath; V, MC, AE, EC)* is set in a charming 19th-century town house directly across the road from the sea. Three of the B&B's seven rooms have stunning views of the sea, and they all have color TV, central heating, and coffee/tea.

Windsor Hotel *(Warrior Square Gardens, St. Leonards; Tel 01424/422-709; £18, singles with shared bath, £37, doubles with private bath; V, MC)* is located in Warrior Square Gardens, the formal centerpiece of St. Leonards. Sometimes you'll be lulled asleep—or jarred awake—by the live music wafting up from the bandstand on the square.

▶▶**DO-ABLE**

A small, basic hotel, **Pissarro's** *(10 South Terrace; Tel 01424/421-363, Fax 01424/431-602; Twins, doubles, and singles en suite; Singles £25,* *doubles £45; All major credit cards)* is situated near the train station and downtown shops. It has a restaurant serving French/Mediterranean food and a bar with an extensive wine list, continental beers, and local ales.

Superbly located in a narrow street in the Old Town, close to restaurants, pubs, and the waterfront, **Tulips** *(27 Croft Rd., Old Town; Tel 01424/712-511, Mobile 07971/934-879; 3 doubles, 1 single, £17-18/person)* is such a good deal, it's almost unbelievable. The rooms are spacious—one of the doubles is simply enormous—and they all come with their own sinks.

Run by a fun Scottish couple, the **Harbour View Guest House** *(21 Priory Rd., West Hill; Tel 01424/721-435, Mobile 07957/909-521; £20 per person, single or double, not en suite; No credit cards)* is located up on the West Hill in a building that can only be described as gracious. The sea-facing rooms have a gorgeous view, and breakfast is included in the price of the room. Best of all, one of the hosts, Andy, will cook you whatever you'd like for breakfast, and tell you hilarious stories while you eat.

▶▶SPLURGE

A beautiful medieval B&B, **Lionsdown House** *(116 High St., Old Town; Tel 01424/420-802, Fax 01424/420-802; £23.50-30 per person, £41-46 for two people, each room has an en suite or private bathroom; V, MC, Switch, Delta)* is decorated with exposed timbers and inglenook fireplaces that date back to 1450 A.D. The Tudor fireplaces and antique furniture make for a romantic and cozy atmosphere, and the rooms all have added luxuries like bathrobes, toiletries, and hairdryers.

need to know

Tourist Information Located in Queen's Square, next to the Priory Meadow Shopping Centre, this very helpful **TIC** *(Tel 01424/781-111, Fax 01424/781-186; 8:30am-6:15pm Mon, Fri, 8:30am-5pm Tue-Thur, 9am-5pm Sat, 10am-4:30pm Sun; info@hastings.gov.uk, www.hastings.gov.uk)* will book your accommodations for £2, deducted from the bill wherever you wind up staying. They also have racks of pamphlets, maps, and books.

Public Transportation Stagecoach South Coast Buses *(Tel 0870/243-3711; www.buses.org.uk)* operates the local public transport service. Their office, which also has copies of the current schedule, is behind the Town Hall, close to the Priory Meadow Shopping Centre.

Health and Emergency Emergency: *999.* Accident and emergency help: *01424/758-106.* Police non-emergency: *0845/607-0999.*

Telephone Local code: *01424.*

Trains There are frequent **trains** from London (Charing Cross or Victoria Station) to Ashford via Hastings. The trip takes between 90 minutes and 2 hours. There's also frequent service between Hastings and Battle, and Hastings and Rye. The train station in Hastings is on Havelock Road, just north of the town center, about a half-mile from the shore. For rail information, call *Tel 0345/484-950.*

Bus Lines Out of the City National Express buses *(Tel 0990/808-080 for information)* run regularly between London's Victoria Station and Queen's Road in Hastings.

Postal There is one main **post office** *(13-15 Cambridge Rd.; Tel 01424/464-243; 8:45am-5:30pm Mon, Thur, 9am-5:30pm Fri, Sat).*

battle

Battle has one **main street** with the Battle Abbey standing proudly at the top of it. Along with the towns of Hastings and Rye, Battle forms part of "1066 Country," named in reference to the Battle of Hastings, which took place on October 14, 1066, in the town of Battle. Apart from a couple of pleasant tearooms where you can grab an after-history-lesson refreshment, there is nothing going on in town, so it's not even worth wandering down the main street after you've toured the battlefield and the abbey. If you visit Battle, make it a day trip from one of the larger towns in the area.

Battlefield and **Battle Abbey** *(Battle; Tel 01424/773-792; Opens at 10am, but closing times vary, till 6pm summer, till 5pm fall, till 4pm winter; £4 adults, £3 concessions, includes audio tour):* The actual battlefield where the Normans fought the Saxons is beautiful. The battle was fought when Duke William of Normandy invaded England to fight Harold, the King of England, for the throne. After William won, he had the abbey built to commemorate the battle and atone for the deaths of the English who lost their lives. The abbey was completed in 1094, and four French St. Benedictine monks founded a community that lived there for nearly 500 years, until the church was demolished in 1538. Today, much of the abbey lies in ruins, but you can tour the buildings that remain standing, some of which are still in use.

You can take a 45- or 60-minute audio tour of the battlefield and the abbey to see points of attack and retreat and the spot where King Harold died, and you'll hear a narrative of events from the perspectives of King Harold's mistress, a Norman knight, and a Saxon Thane. Every weekend from July 22 to October, eight soldiers in costumes of chain-mail armor patrol the area. On the 14th and 15th of October, they present a full-on reenactment of the Battle of Hastings.

During the first two weeks of July, the town of Battle hosts a **Mixed Arts Festival** featuring youth performances, drama events, classical concerts, lunchtime concerts, street theater, and live music in the ancient Battle pubs. Contact the Battle Tourist Information Centre [see *need to know,* below]. The festival's hotline opens in April *(Tel 01424/773-322; battletic@rother.gov.uk).*

In late May, there is a two-day **Battle Medieval Fair** that bills itself as a "packed program of medieval mayhem." But if you read the find print, you'll see that their idea of "mayhem" is actually a combination of street entertainment that culminates in traditional maypole dancing. It's no rave, but it is a fun way to kill an afternoon if you're into street fairs. There's also mummers' plays; music; open arts, crafts, and produce markets; and a grand procession.

need to know

Tourist Information The **TIC** is a stone's throw from the abbey *(88 High St.; Tel 01424/773-721; 10am-6pm daily Apr-Sept; 10am-4pm Mon-Sat, 10am-2pm Sun Oct-Mar).*

Trains The **train station** in Battle is a stop on the London-Hastings line. From Hastings, it's about a 15-minute trip. Call *Tel 0345/484-950* for info.

Bus Lines Out of the City In summer, frequent **buses** run to Battle from Hastings and Rye. Call *Tel 0990/808-080* for info.

rye

There really are just two reasons to go to Rye: to check out the cool Georgian architecture and to chill for an afternoon. An upscale village that doesn't cater to backpackers, Rye is a small, cobblestoned town high up on a hill above the **Romney Marsh,** the **Rother, Brede,** and **Tillingham** rivers, and green fields as far as the eye can see. An ancient port, Rye played a vital role as a trading center when the sea surrounded it like a moat. In the 13th and 14th centuries, the French frequently attacked Rye, culminating with the town almost being burned to the ground in 1377. Today Rye is one of the most beautiful towns in southern England. As is the case in any upscale village, many of the stores specialize in selling arts and crafts, like the one that makes handmade collectors' teddy bears, and one that creates hand-decorated figurines and tiles. There are also loads of cute coffeeshops and small bookstores. But its true charm lies in the Georgian houses, stone timbers, and winding streets that will surprise you like an unexpected gift every time you turn the corner. The square around the church is completely cobblestoned and a great spot to relax and take in the quiet beauty of the town. The streets off the square are lined with picturesque medieval cottages that edge down to the cliffs and offer dramatic views. If you want to do a little research before you come, *www.rye-sussex.co.uk* has a fairly comprehensive list of places for food and drink, accommodation, and shopping, and gives a brief history of Rye.

bar and live music scene

Although not known for its party atmosphere, Rye has a few pub offerings.

Consisting of three pretty unspectacular rooms, **Ypres Inn** *(Gungarden, past the Rye Museum, or up the stairs from Fishmarket Rd.; Tel 01797/223-248, Fax 01797/227-460 11am-11pm Mon-Sat,*

rye

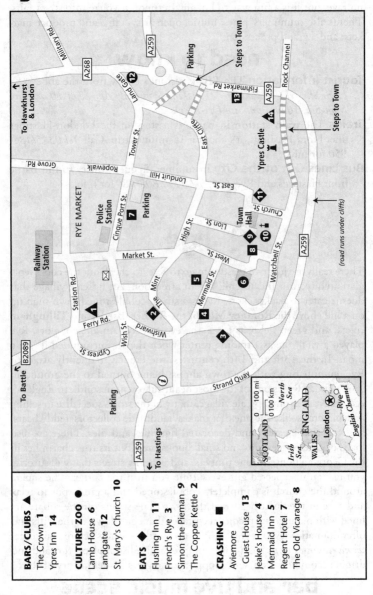

noon-10:30pm Sun) has a nice big garden outside, furnished with benches. Inside, you can nosh on some decent pub food while watching rugby, cricket, or football on TV. Sunday night is live blues night, with mostly local bands.

On Fridays and Saturdays a DJ spins at **The Crown** *(Ferry Rd.; Tel 01797/223-372),* but on the other nights the young locals who fill this sports bar while away their time playing pool and hitting the arcade games, while choosing from the wide range of beers on tap.

ARTS SCENE

▶▶VISUAL ARTS

Rye has plenty of antiques shops, small art galleries, and potters in its nooks and crannies, selling every sort of fine craft from oriental rugs, cushions, and furniture to handmade glass and timepieces. Rye has also been home to famous artists including Paul Nash (1889-1946), a surrealist painter who is one of the major British war painters.

To see the work of regional artists, visit **Rye Art Galleries** *(Easton Rooms, 107 High St. and Stormont Studio, Ockman Lane, off East St.; Tel 01797/222-433 or 223-218, Fax 01797/225-376; Open daily; Free admission).* It has a changing program of exhibitions, featuring artists living and working in the region. A selection of work from the permanent collection is always shown along with traveling exhibitions.

CULTURE ZOO

St. Mary's Church *(Contact Rev. Martin Sheppard for info; Tel 01797/222-430; Tower open 10am till dusk, weather permitting; £2 adults):* The most interesting detail at this site is the graffiti on the wall. It's not spray-painted, mind you, but scratched into the interior pillars by delinquents from hundreds of years ago. The 17th-century English writing is cool to check out—notice the difference in the way *W* was written. On top of the church, the tower offers an incredible lookout spot. Fields of rape (yellow flowers) are visible in the distance to the west, and marshlands stretch out to the east. To get to the tower, walk up a narrow pathway that was built in Kate Moss proportions, and then climb an equally skinny and rickety couple of flights of stairs. On the

the art of smuggling

The whole coastline from the southeast to the southwest of England was a smuggling haven during the 18th century. Among the more notorious smuggling gangs were the Groombridge and the Hawkhurst. Hawkhurst consisted of the biggest badasses of Kent and certainly the most efficient: It was said that upon being called for a smuggling run, 500 mounted and armed men could be assembled within the hour. Hawkhurst, their headquarters, was only 13 miles from Rye, and often they would hang out and drink in the Mermaid Inn with their loaded guns and pistols on the tables. Perhaps they were discussing diversion tactics, such as putting boots on their horses' hooves and pointing the horseshoes backward so that customs then followed the tracks in the wrong direction.

way up you'll first pass through the Ringing Chamber, containing one of the oldest church turret clocks still functioning in England (still running with its original works), built around 1561. When the bell is ringing, you can see the machinery operating. Then, climb into the Bell Chamber, which consists of eight bells, each weighing 5 tons and inscribed with a rhyme. The bells are rung often for services and weddings by a local band of bell-ringers.

Lamb House *(2-6pm Wed, Sat, Apr-Oct; £2.50 admission):* If you're a fan of Henry James, you can visit the digs he lived in between 1898 and 1916. Now a national monument, it was also home to writer E. F. Benson for a while.

The Landgate: Originally four gateways were built in Rye to fortify the town from invasion. Built in 1329, this is the only one remaining. Now it serves only as a pretty arch over the street; a chamber and two towers make up the gate, but there used to be a drawbridge and portcullis as well. At high tide, the sea surrounded Rye on three sides, and the only means of entry was through the Landgate.

modification

For some Aveda-style bliss, go to **Rye Retreat** *(Cinque Ports St., near the police station; Tel 01797/223-359; 9am-6pm Mon-Thur, 9am-9pm Fri, 9am-6pm Sat; Haircut and blow-dry £20-40, highlights £45-60, manicure £15.50, pedicure £19.50, facial £30-50).* This modern hair salon also offers city-style skincare treatments, including facials, manicures, and pedicures (using Aveda products, of course).

great outdoors

The **1066 Country Walk** is a well-known, 31-mile walk from Pevensey to Rye via Battle including links to Hastings and Bexhill. During the 15-mile Rye-Battle leg, there are spectacular views of the Brede Valley and coast from atop some of the hills. If the exertion leaves you ready for a little refreshment, stop at Carr Taylor Vineyards at Westfield and sample one of their well-known English wines, like England's first Method Champeniose (champagne).

Rich in wildlife, **Rye Harbour Nature Reserve** *(Warden, 2a Watch Cottages, Winchelsea; Tel 01797/223-862; Free information and guided walks leaflets)* is an area of sea, salt marsh, sand, shingle, and pools. There are footpaths leading to four bird-watching points and to Henry VIII's Camber Castle, which you can see from the tower in St. Mary's Church [see *culture zoo*, above].

STUFF

▶▶SURF GEAR

You'd think Rye was a bit of an odd place to find a surf store, but **Waves Surf Shop** *(The Landgate Arch, Tower Forge; Tel 01797/225-880)* has been here for years, selling all the major brands, such as Quicksilver, Rip Curl, O'Neill, and Reef clothing and accessories—presumably for those heading off to Hastings and its beach.

EATS

▶▶CHEAP

Established in 1920, **Simon the Pieman** *(Lion St., right by the Rye Church; Tel 01797/222-207; 9:30am-4:30pm Mon-Sat)* is "the oldest tearoom in Rye." With a sumptuous window display of cakes, candy, fudge, cookies, and pies, Simon also serves a lunch menu of snacky sandwiches.

▶▶DO-ABLE

Although it won't break the bank, **The Copper Kettle** *(34-35 The Mint; Tel 01797/222-612; From 6pm Mon-Fri, closed Wed, from 12:30pm Sat, Sun Oct-Feb; From 6pm Mon-Fri, from noon Sat, closed Sun Mar-Sept; Closing hours depend on how busy they are; £6-9 fish and meat entree)* is one of Rye's premier restaurants. The proprietors proudly display their collection of 80 liqueurs, ports, brandies, and malt whiskies in the window. A highlight here is oysters from nearby Whitstable.

Near the quay in a house that looks as if it belongs on a shipwrecked beach is **French's Rye** *(The Strand; Tel 01797/227-080; 11am-3pm Tue, Wed, 11am-3pm/7-11pm Thur-Sat, 11am-4pm Sun; Avg entree £5; No credit cards)*. It serves baguettes and burgers in a laid-back setting, and has live music on Sundays.

▶▶SPLURGE

Specializing in fish and seafood, **The Flushing Inn** *(4 Market St.; Tel 01797/223-292; Three-course fixed-price dinner £24-30; Two three-course* *fixed-price lunch menus £14.50 vegetarian, £15 non-vegetarian; V, MC, AE)* has been run by the Mann family since 1960. It is one of those glossy, food magazine–style restaurants that attracts foodies from all over, some of whom may never have heard of Rye otherwise. If dinner is not a possibility, try the much-cheaper lunch, or sample something from the overflowing dessert menu. From October to April, the restaurant holds regular gourmet evenings, or, as they prefer to call them, "Gastronomic Occasions!" Ignore the name, enjoy the food.

crashing

Rye is not known for inexpensive accommodations, but there are a select number of places that will allow you to stay in this pricey village and not blow your whole budget while doing so. There are several luxury hotels and B&Bs; the best among the latter include Jeake's House and The Old Vicarage, a pink building in the church square. If you're having difficulty finding a place to stay, go to nearby Hastings, a less desirable but much more economical option, and visit Rye on a day trip. The TIC will help you book your rooms, for a small fee [see *need to know*, below].

▶▶CHEAP

The Crown [see *bar and live music scene*, above] has one room available upstairs in the pub. A superb value for two or three people, the room has a double bed and a single bed all in the same room, and the rate is only £20.

The basic and generic **Regent Hotel** *(42 Cinque Ports St.; Tel/Fax 01797/225-884; Singles from £20, doubles from £32, all rooms with private baths and color TVs)* is centrally located and provides private parking.

The quaint and rustic **Cliff Farm** *(Military Road, Iden Lock; Tel 01797/280-331; Closed Dec-Feb; 3 rooms, £15 per person, shared bath, includes full English breakfast; No credit cards)* provides cozy accommodations on a 4.5-acre farm 2 miles east of Rye.

▶▶DO-ABLE

Run by an exceptionally charming and interesting woman named Dawn Keay, the **Aviemore Guest House** *(28-30 Fishmarket Rd.; Tel/Fax 01797/223-052; £20 single, £36 double, £36 two twin beds all sharing two bathrooms, £41 double en suite, £41 twin en suite, 10 percent discount on stays between 3-6 nights excluding July and Aug, and minimum stay of two nights during those months; aviemore@lineone.net; Most major credit cards, except DC; Parking available)* is a little B&B offering a great value. Apart from serving both continental and hot breakfasts, Dawn will provide you with a hand-drawn town map and advise you on restaurants and things to do. All the rooms have color TVs, and sinks are available in the rooms not en suite. There is also a lounge downstairs with books and games.

▶▶SPLURGE

Walking up Mermaid Street, you can't miss **The Mermaid Inn** *(Mermaid St.; Tel 01797/223-065, Fax 01797/225-069; Twin and doubles from £70 per person, singles and family rooms available, all en suite; mermaidin nrye@btclick.com; All major credit cards)*, one of England's oldest and prettiest inns on one of England's oldest and prettiest streets. This dollhouse of a hotel has been a Rye steadfast for centuries and was the headquarters of the notorious Hawkhurst gang of smugglers. The hotel is perfect for a romantic getaway, especially if you book a room with one of their famous four-poster beds. If you're a royal family fanatic, you can stay in Dr. Syn's Bedchamber (£80), the room that the Queen Mother stayed in on her trip to Rye. If you can't afford to stay here, definitely come take a look at it anyway, as the entrance, two lounges, bar, restaurant, and terrace are spectacularly quaint.

need to know

Currency Exchange Banks line the High Street.

Tourist Information Located at Strand Quay, the **TIC** *(Tel 01797/226-696, Fax 01797/223-460; 9am-5:30pm daily Apr-Oct; 10am-1pm weekdays, 10am-4pm weekends Nov-Mar)*, has details on restaurants, public transport, and entertainment. The staff will help you make hotel reservations for a £2 booking fee and a 10 percent deposit of the first night's bill (which will be applied to your total bill). It is fully stocked with souvenir paraphernalia as well.

Public Transportation Everything in town is within walking distance and the roads are narrow and windy in most parts, so there isn't a local bus system. **Taxis** are available, though. Try **Sean's** taxis *(Tel 01797/225-774)* or **David's** taxis *(Tel 01797/230-388)*.

Trains The **train station** *(Station Rd.; Tel 0345/484-950)* is a short walk from the center of town. There are frequent Connex South Central services from London (£17.60 one way) and Brighton. Also a direct hourly service will get you to Hastings (£3.20 one way) and Ashford.

Postal There is a **post office** *(Cinque Ports St.)* between Ferry Road and Market Street.

canterbury

Canterbury is one of only two cities in Kent. The other city is Rochester, which is nothing special. As a result, Canterbury is the partying, shopping, and cultural epicenter of the county, but the cultural and aesthetic aspects of Canterbury far outweigh the partying or shopping experiences to be had here.

Walking around town, you'll feel like you've stepped out of a time machine. The narrow streets lined with Tudor-style buildings and the remains of the stone fortification wall that once encompassed Canterbury give the small city an unmistakably medieval feel. Canterbury is said to be the second-most-visited place in England, and this fact becomes all too apparent when you step onto the High Street. The combination of a New York–style throng of people and the rickety dwellings with new

canterbury

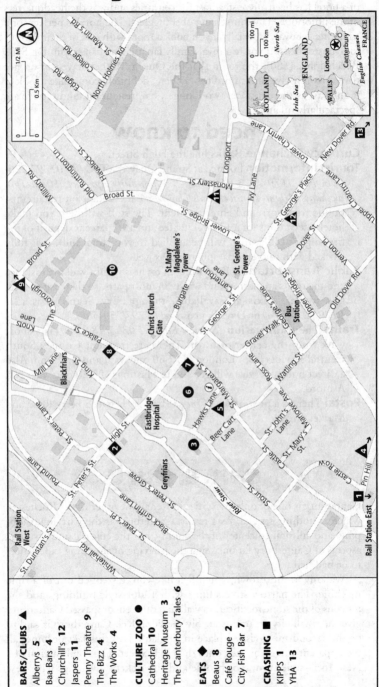

N

1/2 Mi
0.5 km

North Sea

SCOTLAND
Irish Sea
ENGLAND
WALES
London
Canterbury
English Channel
FRANCE

Lower Chantry Lane
New Dover Rd.
13
Upper Chantry Lane
St. George's Place
St. Martin's Rd.
North Holmes Rd.
College Rd.
Edgar Rd.
Military Rd.
Havelock St.
Old Ruttington Ln.
Broad St.
Monastery St.
Longport
Ivy Lane
11
Lower Bridge St.
Dover St.
12
St. George's St.
Vernon Pl.
The Borough
9
Knots Lane
10
St. Mary Magdalene's Tower
Canterbury Lane
St. George's Tower
Old Dover Rd.
Broad St.
Palace St.
Christ Church Gate
Burgate
St. George's St.
Upper Bridge St.
Bus Station
Mill Lane
8
King St.
Blackfriars
Gravel Walk
St. George's Lane
Ross Lane
Watling St.
7
St. Margaret's St.
6
5
Hawks Lane
Beer Cart Lane
Marlowe Ave.
St. John's Lane
Eastbridge Hospital
3
2
High St.
Castle St.
St. Mary's St.
4
St. Peter's Lane
St. Peter's St.
Greyfriars
St. Peter's Grove
Pound Lane
Rail Station West
St. Peter's Pl.
Black Griffin Lane
River Stour
Stour St.
Castle Row
Pin Hill
1
Rail Station East
Whitehall Rd.
St. Dunstan's St.

BARS/CLUBS ▲
Alberrys **5**
Baa Bars **4**
Churchill's **12**
Jaspers **11**
Penny Theatre **9**
The Bizz **4**
The Works **4**

CULTURE ZOO ●
Cathedral **10**
Heritage Museum **3**
The Canterbury Tales **6**

EATS ◆
Beaus **8**
Café Rouge **2**
City Fish Bar **7**

CRASHING ■
KIPPS **1**
YHA **13**

chain-store signs hanging from the rafters makes it feel like you're in a medieval town suddenly catapulted into the 21st century.

Apart from being England's religious mecca—made legendary through Chaucer's story of the journey of a ragtag group of people to the shrine of Thomas à Becket, the slain archbishop of Canterbury—this town is also home to the Christ Church University College and the University of Kent (UKC).

Unless otherwise noted, all the places written up in this chapter are located in the town center. For info on what's happening and price specials, pick up a free copy of the weekly *What Where When* from the visitor information centre (VIC) on St. Margaret's Street [see *need to know,* below].

neighborhoods

Canterbury has a small **town center** that can easily be explored in the span of a few hours. The **River Stour** runs through the western part of town, intersecting **Rheims Way,** which leads into the **A2** (the highway back to London). The two main streets are the **High Street,** which runs east to west, and **St. Margaret's Street,** which intersects the High Street, where the visitor information center and **The Canterbury Tales** [see *culture zoo,* below] interactive museum are located.

Most of the chain stores are on the High Street, which becomes **St. George's Street** farther east, and then **St. George's Place.** To the west, the High Street becomes **St. Peter's Street,** and then farther along, **St. Dunstan's Street.** Walking north up St. Margaret's Street, the streets narrow into **Mercery Lane,** and then open up to the sight of the spectacular **Canterbury Cathedral** [see *culture zoo,* below]. The feeling is similar to the thrilling experience of walking through the tunnel in a baseball stadium, with darkness pressing in all around you, until you suddenly burst out into the open air and onto the playing field.

Canterbury's center is small, so it's easy and pleasant to get around by foot. There aren't many cars, due to the narrow streets and masses of pedestrians.

hanging out

Where St. Peter's Street meets St. Peter's Place (where it becomes High Street), the West Gate stands in the middle of the road as a magnificent architectural reminder of the city's history. Walk across the road to the left of the West Gate, and you will enter a stretch of grass bordered by a huge patch of flowers, and next to that the Great Stour river, which is actually more of a stream (at least in this part). This picturesque piece of the city looks just like a picture-postcard Cotswold town in the middle of England. Follow the stream and it will take you to large, open lawns dotted with trees, where students lounge on the grass. This is a great place to chill or go for a riverside walk.

St. Peter's Street, before you reach the West Gate, is lined with restaurants and pubs that have small tables outside, offering a great location to have a drink and watch the hordes.

wired

You can get online at **Blockbuster Internet Bar** *(1 New Dover Rd., across from Safeway; Tel 01227/472-745; 10am-11pm Mon-Sat; £3 per 30 min.; 10 percent student discount).*

For an extensive directory of pubs in Canterbury, as well as detailed descriptions and information, go to ***http://welcome.to/can terbury/ or www.canterburypubs.co.uk.*** For a virtual tour of the city, it doesn't get more thorough than ***www.hillside.co.uk/tour,*** which offers picks and descriptions of pretty much every block.

bar and live music scene

If you prefer bars to clubs, you're in for some good news, as there is no shortage of drinking holes in Canterbury. The late-night bar scene out-does the club scene in terms of choice and quality. Some have late night licenses (till 2am) and others have live music.

One of the better-known hangs is **Alberrys** *(38 St. Margaret's St.; Tel 01227/452-378; Noon-1am Mon-Sat, happy hour 5:30-7pm daily; www.alberrys.co.uk).* This snug wine bar and bistro is popular with the locals and offers a choice of wines and bottled beers. Alberrys is pretty much the established place to spend pleasure time in Canterbury, and that means everybody in the city knows about it.

Near St. Augustine's Abbey, **Jaspers Café-Bar** *(14 Church St.; Tel 01227/450-245; Till midnight 12am Mon-Thur, till 1am Fri, Sat),* is Canterbury's alternative to clubbing on the weekends. There's no beer on tap, but the bottles are reasonably priced.

If you're searching for the student crowd, go to **Penny Theatre** *(30 Northgate; Tel 01227/812-851; 11am-11pm Mon-Wed, till 1am Thur-Sat, till 10:30pm Sun).* Part of the "It's a Scream" chain, there are food and drink specials and discounts for students holding NUS cards. There are TVs tuned to sporting events and slot machine–type games.

With over 10 TV monitors and one big screen, **Baa Bars** *(15 Station Rd. East; Tel 01227/462-520; Till 2am Mon-Sat; £5 admission after 11pm)* is Canterbury's most serious sports bar. It even has sofas for more comfortable viewing. On Tuesdays, live bands (playing mostly rock) replace the TVs as the evening's entertainment. The bar tends to attract a younger crowd.

club scene

Since Canterbury is not a sprawling metropolis, there aren't that many nightclubs to choose from; the ones that are here are bound to be packed most weekends by tourists, students, or both. **Churchill's** *(St.*

George's Place; Tel 01227/761-276; Till 1am Mon-Wed, 2am Thur-Sat; Cover £3-5 after 9pm) is Canterbury's nightclub mainstay and the premier spot for some good, clean, mainstream fun. Not suprisingly, the music is commercial, Top 40 stuff. Mondays are student nights when you need a NUS card to get in. Wednesday is comedy night, with much of the talent coming in from London. The big nights are Friday and Saturday, when you should arrive before 9pm for free entry and cheaper drinks. Don't show up in jeans or sneakers, however, as the bouncers may not let you in. Apparently, this is not a strict rule, so if you're charming or very good-looking, you might be able to get away with it.

On Friday and Saturday nights, **Baa Bars** [see *bar and live music scene,* above] runs two clubs in the same building: **The Bizz** *(7-10:30pm under 18 on Fri, 10:45-2am over 18 on Fri, 9pm-2am Sat)* and **The Works** *(9pm-2am Tue-Sat, over 18 only).* If you get to Baa Bars earlyish, which usually means before 9pm, you don't have to pay the cover for the clubs. The three-tiered club features dance, house, garage, and pop on each of its dance floors.

ARTS SCENE

▶▶VISUAL ARTS

At the end of Palace Street is the **King's Gallery** *(28 Palace St.; Tel/Fax 01227/786-986),* specializing in the works of artists Sir William Russell Fling, L. S. Lowry, David Shepherd, and Helen Bradley. Formerly the old King's School shop (circa 1647), this gallery of contemporary paintings and watercolors is opposite the current school in the cathedral precincts. Included in the gallery's collection of original works are silkscreens, limited editions, engravings, and prints. However, the most outstanding feature of the gallery is best seen from the *outside* of the building: the slanted sideways doorway.

▶▶PERFORMING ARTS

The **Marlowe Theatre** *(The Friars; Tel 01227/787-787, www.marlowetheatre.com)* puts on popular musicals, mostly from London's West End. The smaller university theater on the UKC campus, the **Gulbenkian Theatre** *(Giles Lane; Tel 01227/769-075; www.ukc.ac.uk/gulbenkian),* puts on more independent fare, covering comedy, drama, music, and lectures. Recent productions have included an evening with BBC radio-show host Rabbi Lionel Blue, and a half-hour lecture series covers such greats as Byron and Aristotle.

For films, the mainstream movie cinema is **ABC** *(St. George's Place; Tel 01227/453-577; www.abccinemas.co.uk/pages/canterbury.html),* which houses two screens. Sometimes the late shows at 10:30pm are alternative flicks. On the flipside, go to the university campus for **Cinema 3** *(Gulbenkian Theatre, UKC campus, Giles Lane; Tel 01227/769-075; www.ukc.ac.uk/gulbenkian),* a smaller theater that shows more special-interest films, as well as some mainstream flicks.

CULTURE ZOO

Tourists come to Canterbury primarily to see the Canterbury Cathedral. In 1170, Archbishop Thomas à Becket was murdered in the cathedral, and, ever since, it has attracted thousands of pilgrims (including Chaucer's tale-spinning characters). The cathedral is also the headquarters of the Anglican Church. The other main attractions in town are the two Canterbury Tales exhibits: the Canterbury Heritage Museum and the Canterbury Tales Visitor Attraction. A Canterbury Museums ticket (or a "passport" ticket) will give you reduced price entry to these and other museums in the city, including the one inside the **West Gate** [see *hanging out,* above] and the Roman Museum.

Canterbury Cathedral *(Through Christ Church Gate, at Burgate and St. Margaret's St.; Tel 01227/762-862; 9am-5pm Mon-Sat winter; 9am-7pm Mon-Sat summer; 12:30-2:30pm/4:30-5:30pm Sun; £3 adults, £2 students; enquiries@canterbury-cathedral.org, www.canterbury-cathedral.org):* Impressive from the outside and massive on the inside, the cathedral could easily warrant an entire day's visit, but if the prospect of examining its crevices doesn't send you into fits of ecstasy, then just do the highlights. Look at the site of the shrine of Thomas à Becket, toward the very back of the cathedral and up the stairs, where a stone marks the actual spot where he was killed. An eternally burning candle stands at his tomb. Or visit the large crypts downstairs on the south side of the cathedral. Perhaps the most beautiful part of the cathedral is the open quads in the precincts outside. You can also see some of the remains of the ancient city wall around the cathedral grounds, including glorious arches and lovely, wild gardens. There are self-serve audio tours, with a map provided, and guided cathedral tours are also available.

The Canterbury Heritage Museum *(Stour St.; Tel 01227/452-747; 10:30am-5pm Mon-Sat all year, 1:30-5pm Sun June-Oct; £2.30 adults, £1.50 students):* Situated in a 14th-century building with a beautiful medieval oak-beam roof, this museum documents the history of the city from its Roman roots to the wartime blitz. It also includes a Rupert Bear gallery—if you know Rupert books from your childhood, this'll definitely be a nostalgic trip.

Canterbury Tales Visitor Attraction *(St. Margaret's St.; Tel 01227/479-227; 9:30am-5:30pm daily Mar-June, Sept-Oct; 9am-5:30pm daily July, Aug; 10am-4:30pm Sun-Fri, 9:30am-5:30pm Sat Nov-Feb; £5.50 adults, £4.60 students; www.heritageattractions.co.uk):* This attraction is a lot cheesier, but far more fun. Here Chaucer's 14th-century world has been re-created with the pilgrims of his *Canterbury Tales* in an interactive walking tour, which takes you from a London inn to Canterbury Cathedral. You're joined by the knight, the miller, the wife of Bath, the nun's priest, and the pardoner. The models are intricately designed, and the lights, smells, and sounds are very evocative. This is probably aimed more at children, but any big kid will have just as much fun, if not more.

Canterbury's Art Gallery *(Beaney Institute, first floor, High St.; Tel 01227/452-747; 10am-5pm Mon-Sat; www.canterbury-artgallery.co.uk; Admission free):* This gallery features many temporary exhibitions tied into Canterbury's heritage; one recent show had contemporary artists interpreting Chaucer's *Tales*. There are also showcases of both Kentish artists and national work.

STUFF

Don't waste your time shopping for clothes in Canterbury. The High Street has most of the stores, but they are the usual chains found on any High Street in England. If you're determined to shop, try the streets around Palace and Sun streets, and you may find some funkier stuff. Or, spend your time in a bookshop—after all, this is Chaucer country. Widely considered the father of modern English poetry and the modern English novel, Chaucer was writing in English (although when looking at the Middle English he used you'll have doubts) when Latin was the standard literary language in Western Europe.

▶▶BOUND

In a very old and quaint Tudor-style house, the **Canterbury Bookshop** *(23a Palace St.; Tel 01227/464-773; 10am-5pm Mon-Sat)* sells first- and secondhand books, prints, and lithographs. The highlight is a gold-leaf edition of Chaucer's *Canterbury Tales*.

Another good place to get a copy of the *Tales* is at the gift shop in the **Canterbury Tales Visitor Attraction** complex [see *culture zoo*, above]. Here you can choose from such a large variety of modern English translations that it would put Barnes & Noble to shame.

FESTIVALS and EVENTS

Since Kent is hops country, there are lots of local beers and ciders to sample. The annual **Kent Beer Festival** *(Merton farm on the outskirts of Canterbury three days in July; Free courtesy buses run regularly during the festival from the bus station)* is a legit opportunity to get trashed under the guise of discovering a new culture.

Beginning with a lantern street procession, the annual **Canterbury Festival** *(Various venues around the city, including the streets; Tel 01227/455-600; Two weeks in Oct)* is a mixed arts festival with visual and performing arts events around the city. Examples of recent festival events include opera and international choirs performing in the cathedral, and Jason Donovan in a production of the *Rocky Horror Picture Show* at the Marlowe Theatre.

▶▶TUNES

For the best selection and the cheapest prices, head to independent **Parrot Records,** on Upper Bridge Street. Other local spots include **Richard's Records** at the bottom of the High Street and **Canterbury Rock** at the far end of St. Dunstan's. Canterbury Rock is ideal for more specialized and alternative stuff. Parrot has the largest selection with a big vinyl stock. Richard's is a mix of the two.

EATS

Canterbury is not a particularly expensive place when it comes to gastronomic matters, and there are many little shops in which to get a quick, cheap snack and drink. Alternatively, the pubs are good places to indulge in some pub-style soul food. There are also some of the trusted restaurant chains, like Café Rouge on St. Peter's Street—a particularly big restaurant with tables outside. For a list of ethnic eats in Canterbury, pick up an *Out* cuisine pamphlet from the visitor information centre [see *need to know,* below].

▶▶CHEAP

For some typical English fast food on the go, grab some kebabs at **Jaspers Café-Bar** [see *bar and live music scene,* above], where the pizza is also very good.

   City Fish Bar *(30 St. Margaret's St.; Tel 01227/760-873)* is the place to go for some greasy fish & chips. It's also centrally located.

▶▶DO-ABLE

Popular with local residents, **Alberrys** [see *bar and live music scene,* above] is a cozy bistro offering a menu of homemade dishes that changes monthly, with entrees running £4.50-13.50. Lighter lunch fare, like salads, jacket potatoes, and sandwiches, is reasonably priced. For more substantial meals, there's a good selection of pastas, red-meat dishes, and (oddly enough) an extensive Mexican selection.

   Though it does not look like much, **Beaus** *(59 Palace St.; Tel 01227/464-285; 10am-6pm Sun-Tue, 10am-10pm Wed-Sat; £4-8 per entree; Most credit cards except AE)* is light and bright and serves a wide variety of delicious sweet and savory crepes. The ratatouille crepe is great for lunch, followed by the strawberry one for dessert. Or try it the other way around—what the hell, you're on vacation!

▶▶SPLURGE

The most distinguished restaurant in Canterbury, **Sully's** *(County Hotel, High St.; Tel 01227/766-266; 12:30-2pm daily, 7-10pm Mon-Sat, 7-9pm Sun; Fixed-price lunch £17-20, dinner £23-29.50; V, MC, AE, DC),* is fittingly set in the most distinguished hotel. Although the place doesn't have any windows and the decor is a bit dated (ca. 1965), the seating and comfort level are first-rate. Considering the quality of the ingredients, the menu offers good values. You can always count on a selection of traditional English dishes, but if that's what you wanted you'd still be at the pub—try one of the more imaginatively conceived platters instead. Start with a warm filo pastry tartlet of mushrooms and asparagus with a light pesto cream, followed with a peppered sea fish with a mango and vanilla relish, sautéed spinach and crisp parsnip matchsticks. Or you could go for the grilled lemon sole, or the roasted pheasant breast with kumquats served on lentils with caramelized apple and a mellow curry cream. Drooling yet?

Two miles from Canterbury along the A28 Ashford Road, the **Old Well Restaurant** *(Howfield Manor, Chatham Hatch; Tel 01227/738-294; Noon-2pm/7-9pm daily; Entrees £9.95-16.95; V, MC, AE)* serves excellent food in the chapel part of the old manor. The emphasis is on fresh, local ingredients and the atmosphere is homelike and friendly. You might start with a smoked haddock and parsley fish cake, and move on to sirloin steak with red-onion gravy, or breast of chicken wrapped in Parma ham and set on a smoked garlic mash.

crashing

Canterbury is definitely a do-able day trip from London, especially since there isn't much nighttime excitement to miss out on. There are many B&Bs and hotels, though, just in case you get stuck here overnight. A list is available at the VIC, where they will also kindly book your rooms.

▶▶**CHEAP**
Good news for late-night partiers, **KiPPS** *(40 Nunnery Fields; Tel 01227/786-121; Bus C4 from bus station, ask for Nunnery Fields/Prospect Place, near Canterbury East train station; 7:30am-11:30pm reception, open all year; £10.30-15; Kipps@FSBdial.co.uk, www.amush. cx/kipps; Credit cards accepted)* is, thankfully, without a curfew. The accommodations are hostel-like, from six-bedded dorms to twin and single rooms to family rooms where cots can be provided. Breakfast and snacks are available.

There's also a **YHA** *(54 New Dover Rd.; Tel 01227/462-911, Fax 01227/470-752; Access from 1pm, Mar 1-Jan 1, Feb; £7.40 under 18, £10.85 adults; canterbury@yha.org.uk)*, which has 6-, 12-, and 14-bed rooms, as well as one single and one double room. The YHA has laundry facilities, lockers, a self-catering kitchen, a lounge, and a Bureau de Change.

Another cheap option is **Hampton House** *(40 New Dover Rd.; Tel 01227/464-912; £20 single, £40 double, includes bath; No credit cards)*, a luxurious Victorian house with quiet, comfortable rooms. The friendly proprietors bring tea and coffee to your room in the morning before inviting you downstairs for a traditional English breakfast.

▶▶**DO-ABLE**
In the center of town, the **Three Tuns Inn** *(24 Watling St.; Tel 01227/767-371, Fax 01227/785-962; £35 doubles with shared bath, £50 doubles with private bath; V, MC, AE, DC)* gets most of its business from its lively pub. The old-fashioned inn, built on the site of an ancient Roman theater, has an aura of history about it; you can even sleep in the room where William and Mary stayed in 1679. The antique rooms have all been refurbished, with good comfortable beds.

The **Dickens Inn at the House of Agnes** *(71 St. Dunstan's St.; Tel 01227/769-668; £55 double, £39.50 for minimum two-night stay, all* rooms with private bath; www.dickens-inn.co.uk; V, MC), two minutes from the cathedral, provides comfortable, modern accommodations amid picturesque 13th-century surroundings. There is a restaurant and bar on site, famous for their extensive selection of whiskies, and a walled patio and garden.

Only slightly less historic is the 100-year-old **Clare Ellen Guest House** (9 Victoria Rd.; Tel 01227/760-205; £48-52 double, breakfast included; V, MC), 8 minutes from the center of town.

▶▶SPLURGE

The **County Hotel** (High St.; Tel 01227/766-266; £102.50-118 double, £180 suite; reservations@county.macdonald-hotels.co.uk; V, MC, AE, DC), has been around since the end of the Victorian era; opt for one of the period rooms, if possible. You'll feel like the duke, duke, duke of Earl.

need to know

Currency Exchange You can exchange money at the **major banks** in town, or use your ATM card at a cashpoint (also located inside and/or outside the banks). Try **Lloyds** (49 High St.; Tel 01227/451-681; 9am-5pm Mon-Fri, 9:30am-5pm Wed, 9:30am-12:30pm Sat) or **Thomas Cook** (14 Mercery Lane; Tel 01227/767-656; 9am-5:30pm Mon-Sat).

Tourist Information The **main tourist office** (34 St. Margaret's St.; Tel 01227/766-567; 9:30am-5:30pm Mon-Sat, 9:30am-5pm Sun, closed Sun in off-season) can help you with accommodations, sight-seeing, entertainment, transportation queries, or anything else you may need to know. They are also exceptionally well-stocked with pamphlets, info on walking tours, books, and other paraphernalia.

Public Transportation At night, the only means of getting around on wheels is by **taxi.** There are taxi stands at both train stations and outside McDonald's. **Stagecoach** operates buses in and outside of the city to neighboring towns, but there aren't night buses. The local buses operate out of the bus station on St. George's Lane.

Health and Emergency The **police** are located at Old Dover Road, outside the eastern city wall (Tel 01277/762-055). The **Kent and Canterbury Hospital** (Ethelbert Rd.; Tel 01227/766-877) is about a 20-minute walk from the city center. There are signs posted along Old Dover Road.

Telephone City code: 01227; national and local directory inquiries: 192.

Trains There are two train stations in Canterbury, each a 10-minute walk from the cathedral: **Canterbury East** (Station Rd. East, south of the city center) for services from London Victoria to Dover via Canterbury (85 min; Two trains per hour Mon-Sat, direct hourly service Sun); and **Canterbury West** (Station Rd. West, northwest of the city center) for slower services from London Charing Cross or Waterloo (90 min; direct hourly service Mon-Fri).

Ashford International Station is 25 minutes away, and from there you can catch the **Eurostar** to Paris (National Rail inquiries Tel 08457/484-950).

Bus Lines Out of the City   The main bus system in England is **National Express** *(Local info Tel 01227/472-082; www.nationalex press.com)*. Regular buses to London Victoria, Dover, and Ramsgate (London 2-3 hours, the latter two each a half-hour away) operate out of the bus station on St. George's Lane *(Tel 01227/472-082; ticket office 8:15am-5:15pm Mon-Sat)*.

Bike Rental   If you'd like to toodle around Canterbury on wheels, stop by **Byways Bicycle Hire** *(2 Admiralty Walk; Tel 01277/277-397; £10 per day; £50 deposit per bike)*.

Laundry   There is a **Laundromat** near Westgate Towers *(36 St. Peter's St.; Tel 01227-786-911; 8:30am-5:45pm Mon-Sat)*.

Postal   Pick up *Canterbury Tales* postcards? Drop them at the **post office** *(28 High St.; Tel 01227/475-280; 8:30am-5:30pm Mon-Sat)*.

Internet   See *wired*, above.

new forest

Stretching from the cliffs at **Barton-on-Sea** along the **Solent** to **Calshot,** the New Forest coast has many beaches and is a great place for scenic walks and water sports. But the New Forest area is known, first and foremost, for its ancient woodlands surrounded by wide, open heaths. The small fields of grass sprinkled throughout the New Forest terrain provide backup grazing for 3,000 ponies and 2,000 cattle, which, by ancient right, roam free in the forest. As you drive on the roads between the towns, you'll see wild ponies grazing at the sides of the road. The mystique and low-rise look of the land was probably the reason William the Conqueror chose the New Forest as a special hunting ground over 1,000 years ago.

The towns of the forest are bustling little centers that offer all the amenities of any small town, as well as good access points to explore the region. The main towns are **Burley, Brockenhurst,** and **Lyndhurst.** Alternatively, you can have more of a coastal experience in Barton-on-Sea, **Milford-on-Sea,** or **Lymington,** and take great walks from here along the tidal marshes.

The town of Lymington is not just a yachting mecca. It also offers easy access to the heath and gorse (little bushes with yellow flowers) and is a busy market town. **Quay Hill** is the cobblestone path that leads from the **High Street** through the old town shops, past the ancient cottages and Georgian homes, to the two marinas at the river's mouth, where you can sit in one of the pubs or take a boat ride [see below]. From Lymington, there is access to **Lepe Beach,** a popular surfing spot, and Calshot, where there is an activities center that offers clay-pigeon shooting, among other pursuits.

New Forest Cycle Experience (*Island Shop, 2-4 Brookley Rd., Brockenhurst; Tel 01590/624-204; 9:30am-5:30pm daily; £9.50-22 depending on type of bike; www.bikeshop.demon.co.uk; V, MC, Switch*) offers 10 off-road trails that they have designed to maximize the New Forest landscape.

Both **Country Lanes Cycle Center** (*The Railway Carriage, Brockenhurst station; Tel 01590/622-627; 9:30am-5:30pm daily Easter-end Oct; www.countrylanes.co.uk; £12 per bike per day; All major credit cards; Two forms of ID required*) and **Rent a Bike** (*Sway, Greencroft, Manchester Rd.; Tel 01590/681-876; 8am-8pm daily; £9-15 per day depending on bike; V, MC*), will deliver your bike to your campsite or hotel. While you're there, pick up a copy of the map *Cycling in the New Forest, The Network Map.*

In the two big marinas at Lymington, there are many shacks on the water where you can hire and charter boats, including the rental of a rib (a small, quick boat to whip around the harbor in). There are places to rent surfing, water-skiing, and kayaking equipment here as well.

Puffin Cruises (*Lymington; Tel 0850/947-618 booking and info, 01590/644-004 evenings*) is located in the Lymington town quay and offers a variety of river trips. There are 30-minute river cruises departing every half-hour from 10:30am, 1-hour Solent cruises, 2-hour trips to the Needles rocks and lighthouse off the Isle of Wight, as well as eight crossings daily to Yarmouth, on the Isle of Wight. There are also lunchtime and evening specials that offer a service to Yarmouth, two and a half hours ashore for lunch or dinner, and then a return to Lymington.

There are lots of riding stables in the area, and for horse riding in the forest, contact the **Sandy Balls Holiday Center** *(Godshill, Fordingbridge; Tel 01425/654-114; www.sandy-balls.co.uk).*

New Forest Water Park *(Tel 01425/656-868; Hucklesbrook Lakes, Ringwood Rd., Fordingbridge; 10am-9pm or dusk, weekends Apr, Oct, early Nov; Wed-Sun May and second half Sept; daily June to mid-Sept)* has two lakes for water sports and fishing and offers training programs and guidance on aqua rides, waterskiing, jetskiing, and wakeboarding.

arts scene

Art Sway *(Sway; Station Rd.; Tel 01590/682-260, Fax 01590/681-989; 11am-5pm Tue-Sun; info@artsway.demon.co.uk, www.artsway.demon.co.uk; Admission free)* is a little gem that's definitely worth a visit if you're in the foresty village of Sway for a couple of hours, or even if you're staying in nearby Lymington. This contemporary art gallery, with changing exhibitions of paintings, craft, sculpture, and film, features some avant-garde stuff that would be at home in any modern art gallery in London.

bar scene and eats

In Lymington town, **The Black Cat** *(Queens St.; Tel 01590/672-139; Open daily; Fri happy hour 7-9pm with 50p off any drink)* and **The Thomas Tripp** *(Corner of Queens St. and Stanford Rd.; No phone),* off the High Street, are popular and fun pubs. The Black Cat even has a DJ and karaoke. Standard pub fare is offered: sandwiches, baked potatoes, and hot meals like steak-and-kidney pie.

crashing

Feel like camping? There are many campsites in the New Forest and one of the good ones is **Hollands Wood** *(Located just off the A337 Lyndhurst-Brockenhurst Rd., 3 miles south of Lyndhurst; Tel 0131/314-65-05; advance booking required; open Mar 23-Sept 26; £7-12.50 Sun-Thur, £7.90-13.20 Fri, Sat depending on the season),* a 10-minute walk from Brockenhurst. Situated in oak woods, the campsite is spacious and level. The amenities include flush toilets, hot and cold water, a launderette, and showers, but no snack stand, so be sure to pick up your groceries in town first.

Chester Cottage *(Mt. Pleasant Lane, outskirts of Lymington; Tel 01590/682-259; £40 single, £45 double, with breakfast, ranges from £245-425 per week)* is a great self-contained two-floor cottage, but B&B service is available as well. Mostly it is rented week-to-week during the summer months. Located on a pretty, winding road with lots of farms, it's accessible to the forest, just a few minutes walk away, and the town center of

Lymington is close by if you have a car. There are tennis courts and a large garden on the grounds.

Pickings for cheap accommodations are really slim around here. Two other nearby options are **Whitemoore House Hotel** *(Southampton Rd., Lyndhurst; Tel 023/282-186; £25 per person; breakfast included; V, MC)* and **Caters Cottage** *(Latchmoor, Brockenhurst; Tel 01590/623-225; £42-£45 doubles with shared bath, includes full English breakfast; No credit cards).*

need to know

Tourist Information There are Visitor Information Centres open year-round in three of the forest towns: **Lyndhurst** *(Main Car Park, High St.; Tel 023/80-28-22-69; 10am-6pm daily Apr-Oct; 10am-5pm daily Nov-Mar);* **Lymington** *(New St.; Tel 01590/689-000; 10am-5pm Mon-Sat Apr-Sept; 10am-4pm Oct-Mar);* and **Ringwood** *(The Furlong; Tel 01425/470-896; 10am-4pm Mon-Sat Apr-June; 10am-5pm Mon-Sat July-Sept; 10am-4pm Mon-Sat Oct; 10am-3pm Wed, Fri, Sat Nov-Mar).* The **VIC**s can help with details on guided walks, bus tickets, maps, accommodation (they will even book a place elsewhere in England for you when you leave the New Forest), sights, and activities. The VICs' comprehensive website is at *http://www.the newforest.co.uk/services.asp.*

The **forestry commission** *(The Queen's House, Lyndhurst; Tel 01703/283-141, pre-recorded info line giving details of guided walks, road, and bridge works, as well as timber operations; Tel 01703/284-476)* has marked trails for various sights, including deer-watch and tall-trees trails.

Directions and Transportation There is a regular **rail service** between London Waterloo and Brockenhurst, with a connecting train to Lymington known locally as the "Lymington Flyer." Sway is on the Waterloo-Weymouth line, as is Southampton *(National Rail inquiries Tel 0345/484-950).*

Bus 56 leaves for the New Forest from Southampton every 30 minutes from Monday to Saturday and every two hours on Sundays, and stops at Totton, Lyndhurst, Brockenhurst, and Lymington *(Bus time information Tel 01202/673-555).*

If coming by **car,** the **M3** and **M27** make the southeast accessible from London; and the **M40** and the **A34** provide access from the Midlands.

It is difficult to get around the New Forest if you don't have a car, as there is no regular bus service between towns or even between the suburbs of a town and its center. As a result, it might be easier to stay in one of the larger central towns, such as Brockenhurst or Lyndhurst, where accommodation, restaurants, pubs, and access to the New Forest are all within walking distance of one another, not to mention the train station.

Lymington is a major town as well, and is a good spot for exploring some typical New Forest terrain. The nearby town of Sway is sweet, too, although you really need a car to stay here or you'll be taking taxis everywhere (£8 from Brockenhurst to Lymington, £5 from Lymington High Street to Mount Pleasant Lane [see *crashing,* below]). Call **Lymington Taxis** *(Tel 01590/672-842)* or **Allports Taxis** *(Tel 01590/679-792)* to help you get where you're going.

The Isle of Wight

Off the southern coast of England is the popular resort locale, the Isle of Wight. Compact in size, it measures 23 miles from east to west, and 13 miles from north to south. The summers are sunny, and the winters mild, which might be part of the reason more than 2 million visitors hit the Isle's shores each year. With its varied landscape—from chalk and sand-stone cliffs to sandy beaches, marshes, river estuaries, rolling chalk down-lands, ancient woodlands, and stonewalled fields—there is so much environmental stimulation that a trip around the island makes you feel as though you're visiting a few different places. The 17 miles of coastline and 60 miles of extended walking paths give you plenty of opportunity to take in the sights. The island is well sign-posted with over 500 miles of footpaths and bridle ways crisscrossing all over the place, so don't forget your walking shoes.

There are eight main towns, mostly near the edges of the island—except for Newport, which lies in the island's center. Each locale has a distinctly different feel from the next, both in what the town has to offer and in its appearance. For example, West Wight presents a more pristine and rugged coastal landscape, with downlands and undercliffs, whereas East Wight's touristy coastal scene is dotted with beach resorts.

Ryde, on the northeast "corner," is the largest town on the island, with a grand esplanade and seafront promenade, a marina, and loads of nightlife with its medley of restaurants and pubs. **Union and High streets** make for good shopping amid Georgian and Victorian buildings. The pier is nearly half a mile long, and the town sits next to 6 miles of sandy beaches. The seaside hamlet of **Seaview,** near Ryde, is particularly fetching.

Sandown and **Shanklin** are very similar; each town has a long, undi-vided stretch of beach and a family resort atmosphere with water sports and tacky entertainment. In the 19th century, Sandown was a fashion-able seaside resort, and there are still a lot of Victorian and Edwardian buildings. But it is definitely skippable; it's just another typically shabby English seaside towns. You'd be better off spending your time in Wight's natural wildness.

Shanklin has an undercliff promenade lined with small hotels, cafes, and amusements, as well as a cliffside elevator that connects the town center at the top of the cliff with the beach and esplanade below. The two things that make Shanklin stand apart from Sandown are its old village and the **Shanklin Chine,** a fissure in the cliff with a walking path next to a 40-foot waterfall.

the Isle of Wight

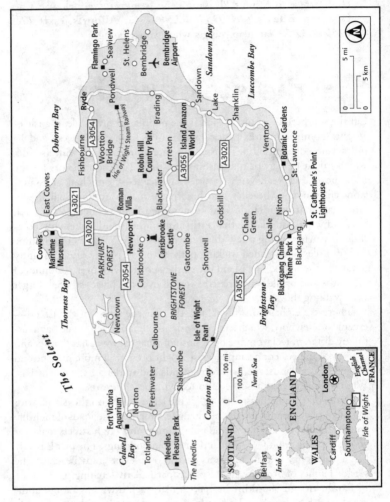

As you travel southward, you'll encounter **Ventnor,** a Victorian spa town with a Mediterranean feel. Built on a series of terraces beneath **St. Boniface Down,** the roads zigzag down to the sea. **Western Esplanade** has a half-sand, half-fine-shingle beach, and, above that, Ventnor Park offers sweeping views over the bay. Shopping-wise, you'll find antiques, gifts, and bric-a-brac. The restaurants cook up a lot of local seafood, including crab and lobster. Towns near Ventnor include **Bonchurch** (where Dickens wrote part of *David Copperfield*), **St. Lawrence,** and the thatched-roof village of **Godshill.**

Newport is the center of the island and also its major shopping area. The High Street here has many pubs, cafes, and restaurants, and the narrow back streets, combined with the wide squares and riverside quay, might make you forget that you're on an island at all.

West Wight is simply spectacular. From the rugged, white cliffs at **Freshwater,** to the multicolored cliffs at **Alum Bay,** this part of the island is so unspoiled and mind-blowing it makes you feel like you are standing on top of the world. A chairlift at Alum Bay will take you to the beach below. There are great coastal walks along the **Tennyson Trail** to **Tennyson Cross,** where the views of the Solent and Channel are matched only by the view of the three 100-foot, chalk rock Needles (the fourth one collapsed into the sea in the 18th century). Mysterious and silent, the Needles are daunting natural elements of the landscape, but they look as if they were planted there by some extraterrestrial. You can also take the open-top bus from the yachting and maritime center of **Yarmouth,** which sets out on nail-bitingly steep and winding roads that seem perilously close to dropping into the sea.

And finally, there are the other yachting and boating centers of **Cowes** and **East Cowes.** Cowes is in two parts, East and West, separated by the narrow River Medina and linked only by a chain ferry known as the floating bridge. West Cowes is better known since it holds the Royal Yacht Squadron and is the focus of Cowes Week. The flurry of events for this international regatta, held in early August, usually features the appearance of a few royals, numerous shore events, parades, and street theater,

The making of an island

Over a 100 million years ago, when Stone Agers wandered about, the Isle of Wight was not an isle at all but part of the southern English mainland. Some 40 million years later, the area was submerged underwater before it emerged as rock and land. About 10,000 years ago, Wight became an island when the sea level rose as the last Ice Age melted. The Romans came in 43 A.D. and called Wight "Vectis." Apart from the balmy weather—very conducive to al fresco pasta lunches—the Romans recognized the isle's strategic position for defending the invasion of southern England by foreigners. The Romans themselves had come with a legion of several thousand and met with little to zero resistance from the native Celts, who were few in number. During their four-century sojourn on the isle, the Romans built farms and villas; the remains of one were found on Cypress Road in Newport in 1926. Today, the islanders welcome invaders of the tourist variety and refer to them as "overners."

Royal Bengal, Chinese, and Siberian ones—as well as other wildcats. There's a pearl jewelry collection at **Isle of Wight Pearl Centre** *(Chilton Chine, Military Rd.; Tel 01983/740-352; 10am-5:30pm Mon-Sat, 10:30am-4:30pm Sun)* in Brightstone—the largest in England—where you can see craftspeople at work adding to the 35,000 pieces on display.

eats

There are plenty of places to eat on the island (got to keep the tourists happy!), ranging from the usual pub grub and takeaway to a few slightly better restaurants. As you might have guessed, seafood is the main attraction here.

▶▶CHEAP

At the **Royal Standard Pub** *(School Green Road, Freshwater; Tel 01983/753-227),* you can stuff your face with specialty roasts and meat pies, then wash it all down with lager or ale.

Set on a hilltop with the marina at its back, **Tonino's** *(8 Shooters Hill; Tel 01983/298-464; V, MC, AE)* serves classic Italian cuisine, including pasta dishes such as spaghetti with meat sauce (£6.95) and pizzas, from £6.50 for a basic Margherita to £14 for pizza topped with lobster and other fresh seafood.

Atop a cliff in Shanklin, **The Hideaway** *(Corner of St. Boniface Cliff Rd. and Cliff Path; Tel 01983/864-145; Cafe daily 10am-4pm, dinner Wed-Sat 6:30-8:30pm; Dinner reservations recommended; MC, V)* features a nautical interior and offers a great view over Sandown Bay. You might find vegetable chili, Boeuf bourguignonne, chicken in honey and Dijon mustard, or pork loin *forrestiere* on the menu.

▶▶DO-ABLE

If you want to eat with the yachtsmen near Cowes, go to the **Salty Seadog** *(Gurnard Marsh, a few miles west of Cowes; Tel 01983/200-330; Daily in summer; Thur-Sun in winter; £10-15 for entrees; www.salty seadog.co.uk).* This is a specialty seafood venue, so the summer menu features locally caught lobster, Bembridge crab, Solent sea bass, and mackerel. It also offers steaks and other meat dishes, plus some vegetarian options. The winter menu is more traditional—steak and kidney pie, Sunday roast, and all the other British faves.

crashing

The accommodation hotline for the whole island is *Tel 0500/867-979.* Also, the TICs will book a room for you free of charge [see *need to know,* below]. For info on campsites, pick up a copy of the *Official Camping & Touring Guide.*

There are only two youth hostels on Wight, one on the east side and one on the west.

▶▶CHEAP

Close to Alum Bay and the Needles, **Totland Bay YHA** *(Hurst Hill; Tel 01983/752-165, Fax 01983/756-443; Southern Vectis Bus 7/A Ryde-Newport-Yarmouth-Totland or 11, 12 from Newport via Calbourne or* all culminating in a blast of fireworks. Its High Street is filled with restaurants and clothing and gift shops, so you won't run short of chances to eat, drink, and shop if you end up here. East Cowes has a short promenade with views of the harbor.

The choices for getting around the island include traveling on bus and rail and, of course, bicycle [see *need to know,* below]. Bicycling is popular on Wight because of the constantly changing scenery, especially along the island's perimeter. The 62-mile Round-the-Island route will take you primarily along country lanes through towns and villages in about 5 to 8 hours. You can, however, pick it up or drop it at any point. The least hilly section is from Freshwater Bay to Cowes, and the hills are more in your favor, in general, if you go in a clockwise direction. Start at one of the corners of the island, either Cowes, Bembridge, Niton, or Freshwater Bay. There are many other bicycle routes on the interior of the island that go in all directions.

Pick up an **Official Pocket Guide** for descriptions of each town and its tourist sites, as well as for accommodation, restaurants, important phone numbers, and amenities listings. Also pick up a copy of the glossy magazine **Island Visitor** for in-depth articles on various aspects of the island that provide history and background. Its equally glossy counterpart, **Isle of Wight,** lists accommodation options with accompanying photos and details all the modes of transportation.

club and live music scene

Ryde, the island's largest town with a population of about 30,000, is one of the more popular spots to hang out. And if you make it to Sandown, you'll find one of the biggest nightclubs this side of the Solent.

There are two clubs in Ryde, Patsy's and The Balcony. Apparently Patsy's is where the teeny-bopper crowd hangs out, so head instead to **The Balcony** *(The Pavilion, Esplanade; Tel 01983/617-070),* housed in a complex that also has a bowling alley. For live music, try the **Royal Squadron** *(20 Union St.; Tel 01983/563-391),* which features local bands inside and has a pub on the outside of the building. The **Crown Hotel's pub** *(10 St. Thomas Sq.; Tel 01983/562-080),* at the top of Union Street, has live music from Sunday to Wednesday and hosts more rigorously selected local bands.

If you're on East Wight in Sandown you'll discover **Colonel Bogey's** *(Culver Parade, Sandown; Tel 01983/405-320; Free before 11pm, £1 after; info@bogeys.co.uk, www.bogeys.co.uk),* the biggest club on the island. There are various theme nights that change weekly, but every Tuesday is *Retro Night,* with the best of the '50s, '60s, '70s, and '80s, when pints are £1.50.

culture zoo

Most of the "cultural" attractions on the island are really nothing more than standard tourist sites. One highlight is the tiger and big cat sanctuary in the **Zoo** *(Yaverland's Seafront, near Sandown; Tel 01983/403-883 or 405-562; 10am-5pm daily),* where you can gaze upon 21 tigers—including white,

fEstivals and Events

There are several annual events on the island, including the **Walking Festival** *(Tel 01983/813-818)* in mid-May and the newly established **Cycling Festival** in mid-June. The Walking Festival goes on for two weeks and has grown to become one of the biggest walking festivals in the UK. Offering over 60 organized walks from easy to strenuous, there are also theme walks, such as night ghost treks or the insect trail at Cowes. The Cycling Festival also spans about two weeks and is similarly organized.

42 from Yarmouth; Reception opens at 5pm; £10.85 adults, £7.40 under 18) has 62 beds, with two to eight beds in each room. It has day access to the shelter. (Day shelter varies from hostel to hostel, but generally means just a dry area; for example a cycle shed, porch, or reception area.)

The other **YHA** *(The Firs, Fitzroy St., very close to train station; Tel 01983/402-651, Fax 01983/403-565; Reception opens at 5pm; £10.85 adults, £7.40 under 18)* is close to the waterfront in Sandown, and although very basic, without much of an atmosphere or comfort, it *is* clean. There are two to six beds per room. It has day access to the shelter and luggage storage.

Near Sandown is **Pier's View Guesthouse** *(20 Cliff Path, Lake; Tel 01983/404-646; £16 low season, £17 mid-season, £18 high season, includes breakfast; No credit cards)* with private baths. They also offer a "board" option, which provides an evening meal, as well as bed and breakfast.

On the opposite side of the island, the tiny, family-run **Sea House** *(Main Road, Yarmouth; Tel 01983/760-527; £15 per person)* has three rooms and one shared bath.

If you've ever dreamt of being rocked to sleep by gentle waves, book a room at **Island Charters** *(Barge Lane, Wootton Creek; Tel 01983/882-315; £16 per person; Closed Nov-Feb; No credit cards)*, which offers sleeper cabins inside ships moored in the Wootton estuary. The immensely friendly and in-love-with-his-work proprietor, John Gallop, will be glad to show you all there is to do on the island. At night, guests from all over the world relax on the decks of their boats and sip drinks while gazing up at the stars.

Dating from 1840, the **Chalet Hotel** *(The Esplanade, Ventnor; Tel 01983/852-285; Standard twins and doubles £44 Nov-Mar, £49 Apr-June, Oct, £53 July-Sept; Superior doubles £49 Nov-Mar, £55 Apr-June, Oct, £62 July-Sept; Family suites £65 Nov-Mar, £72 Apr-June, Oct; £82 July-Sept; Breakfast included)* is a Victorian house of great character in an unrivalled position on Ventnor's esplanade. Under new management, the hotel has been completely refurbished. All of the B&B's 12 rooms now have private baths, and all enjoy magnificent views of the sea and bay.

▶▶DO-ABLE

In Ryde, there's the **Dorset Hotel** *(31 Dover St.; Tel 01983/564-327; From £17.50 per person; www.thedorsethotel.co.uk; MC, V)*, which is central to town and a short walk to the sea. The hotel offers a licensed bar and swimming pool, and most rooms have a private bath.

Slightly to the south of Newport, about a 5- to 10-minute walk away from the town center, you will find **Magnolia House** *(Cypress Rd.; Tel 01983/529-489, Fax 01983/520-905; From £22 single; £19 doubles, private baths; Most credit cards)*.

need to know

Currency Exchange Most of the **major banks** are on the island, generally on the main street of every main town.

Tourist Information The **main tourist information center,** although there are several in the major towns, is the one in Shanklin *(67 High St.; Tel 01983/862-942; www.islandbreaks.co.uk)*. You will find **TICs** at Sandown *(8 High St.; 9am-5:30pm daily, 9am-5pm Sun)*, Ventnor *(34 High St.; 10am-3pm daily except Wed, Sun)*, Ryde *(Western Esplanade; 9am-5:30pm daily, 9am-5pm Sun)*, Yarmouth *(The Quay; 9am-5:30pm daily)*, Cowes *(Fountain Quay; 9am-5:30pm Tue-Sat, extended hours mid-July to end Aug)*, and Newport *(South St.; 9am-5:30pm daily, 9am-5pm Sun)*. The TICs can help you with maps of each town and walking/cycling route guides. They also offer free booking of 2accommodations.

Public Transportation Buy a one-day **Southern Vectis Rover** ticket for unlimited travel on **bus and rail** all around the island *(Tel 01983/827-005)*. All **car ferries and catamarans** are operated by **Wightlink** *(Tel 0870/582-7744; www.wightlink.co.uk)*.

Health and Emergency Emergencies: *999*. For police call *01983/528-000*. **St. Mary's Hospital** is located in Newport *(Parkhurst Rd.; Tel 01983/524-081)* off Medina Road, across from the prisons. All-night **emergency dental** treatment *(Tel 01983/524-081; 5pm-9am)* is also available.

Pharmacies There are plenty of drugstores on the Isle. In Ryde, go to **Boots The Chemists** *(170-172 High St.; Tel 01983/562-280; 9am-5:50pm Mon-Sat)*; in Sandown there's **Lloyds Chemists** *(17 High St.; Tel 01983/405-436; 9am-5:30pm Mon-Fri, 9am-1pm Sat)*. In Newport you'll find **Siddy's Ltd.** *(22 Carisbrooke High St.; Tel 01983/525-216, 9am-1pm/2-6pm Mon-Fri, 9am-1pm Sat)*, and in Cowes, try **Beken & Son** *(9 Birmingham Rd.; Tel/Fax 01983/294-467; 9am-6pm Mon-Fri, 9am-1pm Sat)*.

Telephone The local telephone code is **01983.**

Trains There is a short **railway** line between Shanklin and Ryde, stopping at Sandown, Lake, and Brading *(Tel 08457/484-950)*. The rail extension from Ryde Esplanade goes to Ryde Pier Head.

The **train station** at Portsmouth & Southsea has lines running north to London Victoria and Waterloo stations, as well as additional lines east and west. From Southampton Central *(Tel 023/80-33-40-10)* train station, trains lead north to London stations, and south to the New Forest area, Bournemouth, and Poole.

Boat The **Wightlink** ferry operates all ferry services *(Tel 0870/582-77-44; £5.30 one way, £8.40 return, cheaper day and half-day returns available; bookings@wightlink.co.uk, www.wightlink.co.uk)*. From Ryde Pier Head, you can catch the high-speed passenger catamaran to Portsmouth Harbor *(Tel 0870/582-77-44)*, which takes 15 minutes. From Ryde Esplanade, catch the **passenger Hovercraft** to Southsea *(Tel 01983/811-000)*. From Yarmouth, catch a **ferry** to Lymington *(Tel 0870/582-77-44)* in the New Forest, which links up with the same railway lines at Brockenhurst train station [see *trains,* above]. From West and East Cowes, there is a **ferry** to Southampton Central *(Tel 023/80-33-40-10)* train station.

For water-related rentals on East Wight, go to **Exterski** *(at the right of the pier in Sandown; Tel 01983/404-101; £20 one person, £22.50 two people, £25 three people)* for jet-ski hire and doughnut rides.

Bike/Moped Rental To rent a bike, call **Island Cycle Hire** *(17 Beachfield Rd., High St., Sandown; Tel 01983/407-030)* in East Wight or **Isle Cycle Hire** *(Wavells, the Square, Yarmouth; Tel 01983/760-219; 8am-6pm Mon-Sat, 8am-5pm Sun Oct-Apr; 8am-8pm daily May-Sept; £6 half day, £10 whole day)* in West Wight.

WILTSHIRE & SOMERSET

WILTSHIRE & SOMERSET

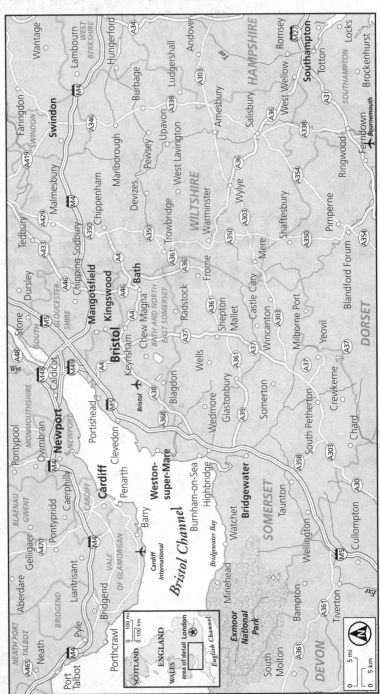

most people say it's crazy to go all the way to London and not visit **Stonehenge.** And they're right—sort of. You really should go there, but not just to see Stonehenge, which is much smaller than it looks in postcards and has fences all around it; you can't actually get inside the stone circle. So take a little time to check it out—it is, after all, one of the most famous prehistoric landmarks in the world—then head to **Avebury,** about 20 miles away, where the henge (the ditch built around the stones) is 16 times bigger than Stonehenge, and there are no restrictive fences. You can walk among the stones, touch them, talk to them, or sing a song to them if you feel like it—without the tour bus crowds you get at Stonehenge.

The whole area, from Stonehenge to **Exmoor National Park** on the east coast, is a great place to hang out for a while, not just because of it's stone-age monuments and natural beauty, but because of its outrageous party town, **Bristol,** and it's ancient Roman hot-tub heaven, the town of **Bath**. The region actually is a combination of two counties: Wiltshire and Somerset. Stonehenge and Avebury are in Wiltshire; Bristol, Bath, and Exmoor National Park are in Somerset.

Wiltshire's limestone and chalk landscape are common in the English countryside, along with rolling hills, fields, and hedgerows. You'll notice the limestone chalk when you come across one of Wiltshire's famous "white horses" carved into the hills. The general consensus is that Salisbury, situated among the lush marshes where the rivers Avon, Nadder, and Bourne meet, is the starting point of the West Country. Celebrated for its cathedral, with the tallest pinnacle in England at 404 feet, Salisbury is sprinkled with brick and tile-hung houses that have Georgian facades concealing medieval structures.

The legendary beauty and charm of this part of the country has been the backdrop for many movies and television programs. Part of the BBC adaptation of *Pride & Prejudice* was shot in **Lacock,** a well-preserved village owned by the National Trust. And **Castle Combe,** the southernmost village in the Cotswolds, provided the setting for the original *Dr. Dolittle,* starring Rex Harrison, rather than Eddie Murphy, in the title role. (Many of the villagers were extras, probably the most exciting thing to happen in years in sleepy little Castle Combe.)

THE LEY LINES THEORY

In the Romantic period in England, it was widely believed that the Druids constructed the famous stone circles of this region and worked their mojo here. The Druids were the spiritual leaders of the Celtic people. Local lore had it that Druids chose the locations for the stone circles to coincide with the intersection of "ley lines," bands of energy that crisscross the earth. The point at which two ley lines intersect is said to be imbued with tremendous power. Because the sites for the stone circles miraculously seem to be positioned on the same axis, it appears that ley lines link them all.

Whether the ley lines theory is true or the stones' position on the same axis is simply due to coincidence is impossible to say, but history belies the idea that Druids built the circles, because they weren't even around until long, long after the people of the Stone and Bronze Age had already constructed the sites, done whatever they were doing there, and died.

Once you cross into the neighboring county of Somerset, the undulating limestone hills of the **Mendips** begin, and the glinting waters of the **Bristol Channel** appear. Hidden in the Mendips, which are about 25 miles long and 5 miles wide, is a labyrinth of caves, including the glistening grottos at **Cheddar** and **Wookey Hole.** The towns of **Glastonbury, Street,** and **Wells** are bustling little villages steeped in history. Glastonbury is known for its abbey ruins and its reputation as a New Age healing haven; Street is famous for the shoemaking legacy of the Clark family; Wells is recognized for its cathedral.

Go wild in the Mendips outdoor-style. At **Cheddar Reservoir,** you can have it any way you want it: Whitewater canoeing and kayaking. surfing, surf-skiing (paddling out on a "flat" canoe, then catching a wave and riding it in, board-style), sailing, or wind surfing. **Mendip Outdoor Pursuits** *(Laurel Farmhouse, Summer Lane, Banwell, Weston-Super-Mare; Tel 01934/820-518 or 01934/823-666; 9am-5pm weekdays, often open on weekends)* provides instructors, equipment, and courses designed to suit all levels of experience. You can slso particaipate in assault courses (similar to obstacle courses) or orienteering (map reading abilities and speed are employed to identify as many flags, posts, or disks as quickly as possible on a land course) if you're not already involved in hiking or archery. (Did we mention caving, rock climbing, and abseiling?)

Once you cross over into Somerset and it's infamous party town,

Bristol, the scene changes. You can still go wild outdoors, but the summer sports tend to revolve around beer and bikinis during the day and aerobic club-hopping at night. Bath is a bit more sedate, but it wasn't always that way. The ancient Roman public baths, built on natural hot springs, are now closed for public use but must've been quite a scene when they were going strong, and are still a really cool spot to visit. Somerset's largest natural attraction is **Exmoor National Park,** with bleak, desolate moors similar to the plains in Devon's **Dartmoor Park** [see **Devon and Cornwall,** above]. Exmoor also has lush wooded valleys stretching out to stately cliffs that plunge into the Atlantic. Walk along most any part of the park's 620 miles of footpaths and you're likely to see Exmoor ponies, horned sheep, and red deer grazing the rolling hills.

getting around the region

Trains for Bristol (120 miles west of London) leave London Paddington every hour during the day, stopping at Bath (115 miles west of London, 13 miles southeast of Bristol) along the way. It takes roughly an hour to reach Bath from London; add a half-hour to get to Bristol. The trains from London stop at both train stations in Bristol—Temple Meads, in the center of town, and Parkway, on the city's northern outskirts.

The bus trip from London to Bath is about 2 hours long, and buses leave every other hour from London Victoria during the day. Buses bound for Bristol leave London Victoria about once an hour, and traveling time is about 2 hours. If you're planning to stay for a few days in the region, Bristol might be a convenient base as there is frequent bus service with easy connections to Bath (13 miles), Glastonbury (26 miles south of Bristol, 6 miles southwest of Wells), and Wells (21 miles southwest of Bath). From Wells, there are regular connections to Cheddar and Wookey Hole.

To reach Exmoor, there are several options: Trains from London go to Taunton (2 hours), Tiverton Parkway (2 hours), and Exeter (2 hours); or, from Bristol, take the Bristol-Plymouth line.

From Exeter there are four trains a day to Barnstaple on the Tarka line (1 hour). Buses leave daily from London for Barnstaple (5 hours), and Ilfracombe (5 hours). Buses also go from Plymouth and Bristol to Barnstaple. Once you're actually in the Exmoor district or on the border, there is a network of buses running between the towns of Minehead, Barnstaple, Ilfracomb, Dunster, and Williton. You also might enjoy one of the dozen specially designed scenic bus trips between smaller towns within the park.

Depending on where you arrive, you can take a cab or a bus, or walk to your final destination. Phone numbers for cabs are posted at the train or bus stations.

TRAVEL TIMES

Times by train unless
otherwise indicated
*By road

	Bristol	Bath	Lacock	Castle Combe
Bristol	-	:15	:40*	:30*
Bath	:15	-	:25*	:25*
Lacock	:40*	:25*	-	:10*
Castle Combe	:30*	:25*	:10*	-
Exmoor National Park	1:30*	1:50*	1:50*	1:40*
Stonehenge	1:25*	1:00*	:45*	1:10*
Avebury	:55*	:55*	:25*	:40*
Cheddar	:40*	:45*	1:05*	1:00*
Wookey Hole	:40*	:40*	1:05*	1:10*
Glastonbury	:50*	:50*	1:15*	1:15*

	Exmoor National Park	Stonehenge	Avebury	Cheddar	Wookey Hole	Glastonbury	London
	1:30*	1:25*	:55*	:40*	:40*	:50*	1:45
	1:50*	1:00*	:55*	:45*	:40*	:50*	1:40
	1:50*	:45*	:25*	1:05*	1:05*	1:15*	1:50*
	1:40*	1:10*	:40*	1:00*	1:10*	1:15*	1:45*
	-	2:10*	2:15*	1:05*	1:10*	:50*	3:20*
	2:10*	-	:30*	1:20*	1:10*	1:10*	1:40*
	2:15*	:30*	-	1:30*	1:35*	1:40*	1:40*
	1:05*	1:20*	1:30*	-	:20*	:20*	2:40*
	1:10*	1:10*	1:35*	:20*	-	:15*	2:40*
	:50*	1:10*	1:40*	:20*	:15*	-	2:40*

bristol

Bristol has the widest range of entertainment venues, attractions, and restaurants in the southwest. Add to the mix a student population of almost 12,000 and you've got an excellent place to experience some hard-core English-style clubbing. This is not to say that there aren't some lovely sections, such as the waterfront (known as "quayside," as opposed to the floating harbor, the proper name for Bristol's harbor), and the area between the city center and the indoor markets, with its winding streets and steep flights of stairs.

Since the city is quite big, with a population of about 370,000, it may be a good idea to get your bearings by doing the open-top guided bus, a hop-on, hop-off tour that stops at about 19 places around town (see *need to know,* below). It departs every 30 minutes in the summer and hourly during the rest of the year. You could also try one of the city's guided theme walks, which focus on spooky, historical, or natural sites [see *culture zoo,* below]. Or just pass on all of that, get a map, and find your own way around.

For entertainment options, pick up a free monthly copy of ***Bristol Entertainments*** at the TIC [see *need to know,* below].

neighborhoods

Bristol is divided into sections that can be categorized according to what they have to offer: The **Harborside** (city docks) and near it, **quayside,** with its restaurants and bars, is the best bit. **Welsh Back** runs along the water, parallel to **Queen's Square,** and is a center for sidewalk restaurants and pubs. (The river that runs through it is a center for swans and small boats.) Temple Meads Railway Station is east of the city center and the harbor. The **Avon Mead** complex, with restaurants, a multiplex cinema, and a bowling alley, is in south Bristol—not far from the train station.

From the train station, it's a 10-15 minute walk to the quayside and the **YHA** [see *crashing,* below]. To get there, walk down to **Bath Road** and cross over the **Redcliffe Way,** heading west past **St. Mary's Redcliffe Church** [see *culture zoo,* below] on the left. Go across the bridge and past Queen's Square on your right. Cross **Prince Street** and go straight onto **Narrow Quay,** turning left. The hostel is on the quayside.

A little bit past St. Mary's Redcliffe church is **The Grove,** a street that winds its way into the quayside. The Grove eventually meets up with Prince Street, and if you follow Prince Street northward, you'll get to the **Old City,** a densely packed section of restaurants, pubs, and shops;

where the students are

The two universities in town have distinctly different student scenes. **Bristol University (BU)** is a very public school (the equivalent of private in the States—in other words, very exclusive but not limited to members of the royal family or their peers). The student population is mostly wealthy and indulges in dinner parties at restaurants and bars such as Sevenshead, Bar Ha Ha, The Fine Line, and Casino (a favorite). The club scene for this lot consists mainly of Po Na Na, and the Square (a private club); some go to Lakota, the Silent Peach, and Wedgies on a Tuesday (when it's sports night) or Wednesday. The boys won't be seen darting around these nightspots in anything but Ralph Lauren, and it's strictly Jigsaw for the pashmina girls. They shop on Park Street and occasionally in Cribbs Causeway, but rarely in Broadmead—except for French Connection and Oasis. The girls flit off to Bath in their twin sets and pearls for more upscale shopping sprees, and to have their hair done at Hobbs. **The University of West England (UWE)** has its share of public schoolies too, but the scene swings much more to the down-to-earth side with more clubby and trendily dressed kids than the classic BU lot. The two groups are likely to meet up at Lakota, Po Na Na, and Club Loco, but you'll also find UWErs at Jester's comedy club or at house parties—a favorite. Dinner-wise, you'll find the UWE crew at more studenty hangouts like Browns, Café Blue, Mud Dock, and Hullabaloos, not to mention the ultra-cool coffeeshop on Park Street, Boston Tea Party. UWE also has a major sports scene; rowing is the most popular activity.

bristol

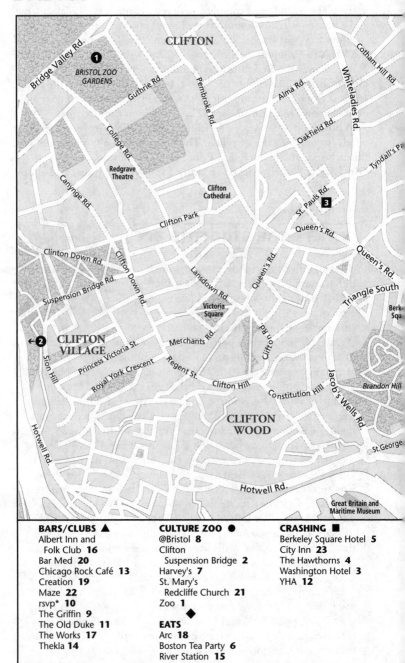

BARS/CLUBS ▲
Albert Inn and
 Folk Club **16**
Bar Med **20**
Chicago Rock Café **13**
Creation **19**
Maze **22**
rsvp* **10**
The Griffin **9**
The Old Duke **11**
The Works **17**
Thekla **14**

CULTURE ZOO ●
@Bristol **8**
Clifton
 Suspension Bridge **2**
Harvey's **7**
St. Mary's
 Redcliffe Church **21**
Zoo **1**
 ◆
EATS
Arc **18**
Boston Tea Party **6**
River Station **15**

CRASHING ■
Berkeley Square Hotel **5**
City Inn **23**
The Hawthorns **4**
Washington Hotel **3**
YHA **12**

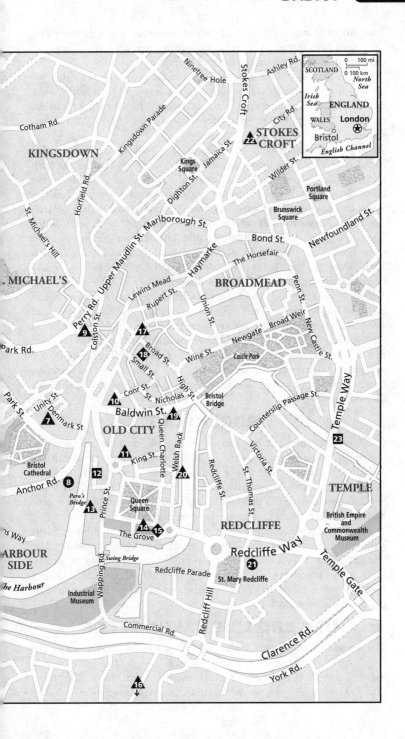

Baldwin and **Corn** are the most prominent streets. The Corn Street area has lots of bars, restaurants, and clubs—many of them housed in grand old buildings that were originally used by Bristol merchants.

A little bit east is the **Bristol Bridge** and the indoor markets that sell clothes, flowers, and fresh food. Even farther east and a bit north is the **Broadmead** shopping area [see *stuff*, below], home to the Galleries shopping center and all the main department stores (Bo-ring.). The bus station is also in this vicinity.

To get to the quayside from the bus station, walk south down **Lewins Mead**, take a left onto Baldwin Street (which will branch off to the left), and then take a right onto Prince Street. The hostel is on the right, on the quayside, about a 10- to 15-minute walk from the bus station. Baldwin Street also links up with **Colston Avenue** on its west side, which lies parallel to **St. Augustine's Parade**, a wide pedestrian strip with water fountains in its center, and the **Hippodrome Theatre** on one side [see *arts scene*, below]. At the bottom of St Augustine's, the road going right is **Park Street** [see *stuff*, below] which turns into **Queen's Road** and finally heads straight up into **Whiteladies Road** [see *bar and live music scene*, below]. A bit north of Whiteladies is **Clifton**, a suburb with an abundance of big Georgian houses, Regency terraces, colorful cottages, and tree-lined streets. **Victoria Square**, near the Downs, is especially lovely and worth a walk around. The **Clifton Suspension Bridge** [see *culture zoo*, below] is south of Clifton, next to **Clifton Village.** The Bridge goes over the River Avon, and at the bottom of the gorge is **Hotwells**, named after the hot wells that fed Bristol's once fashionable spa, which disappeared long ago.

hanging out

College Greene, a patch of grass between Park Street and the cathedral is heavily populated by students, who like hanging out next to Bristol's main drag with all the street buzz and funky clothing shops. Young locals also congregate or the quayside on weekend nights. There aren't many benches on the street, so people who spill out of the pubs onto the cobblestoned streets drink their pints standing in crowds.

Get mushy with your new favorite cutie at the lookout point on **Sion Hill**, where the view of the Clifton Suspension Bridge is awesome. The bridge also is a good romantic spot, especially late at night, when it's illuminated by thousands of tiny lights. During the day, check out the Downs (nearby), where fields of wildflowers and patches of forest are bound to put you "in the mood."

bar and live music scene

The student pub scene on Clifton's Whiteladies Road, also known as "the strip," stretches from the Downs to Queen's Road. It's lined with trendy bars and pubs that are open from early evening until 11pm. Clifton has the city's best cider pubs, where the drinks are so potent they're served by

wired

www.bris.ac.uk: The site of Bristol University.
www.thisisbristol.com: Online edition of the *Bristol Evening Post*.
www.bristol-city.gov.uk/museums: Bristol's museum site.
www.Bristol-city.gov.uk/events: Bristol City Council events guide.
www.nowuk.net: A gay site documenting what's on where in England, as well as chat rooms, dating services, and health-related info.

There is the **Internet Café** *(140 Whiteladies Rd.; Tel 0117/973-63-23; 10am-7pm Mon-Fri, 11am-6pm Sat; £2.50 for 30 min.)* and the industrial chic **Netgates Café** *(51 Broad St.; Tel 0117/907-40-40),* which has the added bonus of serving vegetarian and whole food, as well as tasty cappuccino.

the half-pint. Another magnet for nightspots is Corn Street, an area dotted with bars, clubs, and restaurants. Kingsdown, Cotham, and St. Michael's Hill also have some good pubs that offer both live music and a selection of ales and "real" beers. (We're not talking Budweiser here. Real beer is served from a still fermenting barrel of beer as opposed to a pressurized keg. It tastes somehow *fresher* than regular beer, but the quality may vary from pint to pint.) The Bristol-based **Smiles Brewery** *(Colston Yard; Tel 0117/929-73-50)* is located at the bottom of the hill next to the Christmas steps, and their beers can be sampled in the pub next door.

With its great space and excellent sound system, **The Fiddlers** *(Willway Street; Tel 0117/987-34-03, Fax 0117/987-33-69; 7:30pm-1am Mon-Wed, till 2am Thur-Sat, closed Sun; Cover £5-10)* is one of the city's foremost live music venues. The club plays host to local folk, roots, and blues bands as well as big-name international playas like Rhythm Republic, Cream, and Robert Plant.

Otherwise, there are the wine bars of Park Street and the live music venues of Bedminster. Check out the **Albert Inn and Folk Club** *(1 West St.; Tel 0117/966-19-68; Live music 8:30pm every Wed; Cover £3.50-7),* a tried-and-true Bristol institution featuring roots music ranging from acoustic blues and traditional English/Celtic tunes to singer-songwriters from all over the country and the U.S. On weekend nights, the waterfront area is alive—especially the strip outside **The Old Duke**—with young people milling about with their pints.

If you're in the city center, head to **rsvp*** *(14-16 Baldwin St.; Tel 0117/921-03-50),* a brightly colored restaurant and bar in a super-modern, split-level space with plenty of places to sit. There's live music or a DJ every night until 1am.

Café Blue *(Old Fire Station, Silver St.; Tel 0117/940-56-26; Cover*

FESTIVALS and EVENTS

The **St. Paul's Afrikan and Caribbean Carnival** on St. Paul's in July is a 1-day affair of Afro-Caribbean festivities and is the only all-night carnival in the country. This momentous street party includes DJs who blast reggae and hip-hop, as well as a costume parade along the streets.

Every year the Ashton Court Estate plays host to the **Bristol International Balloon Fiesta.** If you're not too keen on going up in the air, watch more than 150 brightly colored and specially shaped balloons take off.

£2.50) is the perfect pre-club hangout. The drinks aren't cheap, but the music is good. Even though it's more of a pub than a club, there is a dance floor where a DJ spins house on Fridays and Saturdays, and garage and hard house on Sundays. As its capacity is 300 people, it's a more intimate alternative to one of Bristol's mega-clubs.

Star and Garter *(33 Brook Rd.; Tel 0117/940-5552)* is a nice escape from the typical British pubs you've most likely visited to death. With a strong West Indian immigrant population, Star and Garter features reggae and dub DJs, cheap drinks, a welcoming crowd, and some mean domino games. Everyone is welcome.

If you're a jazz fan, you're in for a treat. **The Old Duke** *(King St.; Tel 0117/927-71-37; Music at 9pm nightly except Tue, also during Sunday lunch)* is perhaps one of the best jazz experiences you'll ever have. Different bands play every night to a clientele of genuine jazz-lovin' folks. Located next to **Bar Med** [see *eats,* below] in quayside, the club is walking distance from lots of restaurants and the youth hostel. The place has cool and odd decorating touches like old jazz posters plastered to the ceiling.

CLUB SCENE

Bristol takes clubbing seriously. In fact, the sheer number of clubs, coupled with the level of technology in the larger ones, could give some of London's hot spots a serious run for their money. The largest clubs are mostly in the Stokes Croft area northeast of the city center, and the waterfront is flooded with smaller clubs. To get there, walk across the bridge directly outside the YHA on Narrow Quay, turn right, and you'll find them in force; one after another, each a different color, each blasting different music, almost all sporting some kind of very self-important bouncer figure at the door.

Tuesdays are student nights everywhere in Bristol, which means everyone over 18 can get into the nightspots. (Some promoters require attendees to be 21 and over on other nights of the week.) Among them is the **Chicago Rock Café** *(The Watershed, Canons Rd.; Tel 0117/929-18-40; 11:30am-2am Mon, Thur, Sat, till 1am Tue, Wed, noon-11:30pm Sun)*. By day it's a restaurant/snack place, by night it turns into a bar/club with live DJs (and it continues to serve food).

The most interesting club on the waterfront has got to be **Thekla** *(East Mud Dock, The Grove; Tel 0117/929-73-42; Cover £5-8 depending on night, cheaper before 11pm; www.thekla.co.uk)*. It's a nightclub on a 173-foot coaster. In other words, a boat. This is probably one of the only times you'll want to "walk the plank," because you have to in order to get to the party. The view from the upstairs chill-out room and cafe is like looking out on the glistening lights of the French Riviera. Downstairs there's a stage and dance floor pumping a diverse range of music every night, from hip-hop to indie, with a sprinkling of hard house and '70s for good measure. Thekla has become well known for its drum 'n' bass *Drive-By* nights, where "nu skool jungle meets Old School chic."

Another notable spot is **Creation** *(13-21 Baldwin St.; Tel 0117/922-71-77; Fax 0117/925-27-41; creation@ukdanceclubs.co.uk, www.ukdance clubs.co.uk/clubs/creation.htm)*, a huge Ibiza-type setup with two elevated stands for professional dancers. The dance floor is huge and is overlooked by a glass-fronted VIP bar lounge. There is a large projection screen at the top of the club showing funky graphics. The music consists mainly of underground hard house tracks spun by various British DJs, but an occasional international guest can show up on the program. Dress smart and be ready for long lines.

With a capacity of 1,823, **The Works** *(15 Nelson St.; Cover £3, a gold card for £10 helps you skip the long queues to get in and get cheaper drinks)* features the latest technology in clubbing, like a revolving bar and a hydraulic staircase. On the weekends, there's a strict dress code (no jeans, look sharp!) and you have to be 21 to get in and groove to the dance cuts from the '70s and '80s.

Formerly called Club Loco, **Maze** *(Hepburn Rd., Stokes Croft; Tel 0117/923-29-20, Fax 0117/942-22-99; info@mazeclub.co.uk, www.maze club.co.uk)* is an attractive venue for DJs who want to spin for an attentive crowd. Tuesdays are disco, funk, soul, and hip-hop, with select drinks for only £1. Thursdays feature drum 'n' bass, Saturdays are all pop dance tunes, and on Fridays, it's hard house, and the club is open till 6am. There's also a smoking lounge inside where DJs grind out garage.

ARTS SCENE

While you can surely get your fill of history and art exhibits in Bristol, the performing arts are where it's at.

▶▶VISUAL ARTS

There are a few museums in Bristol that pay homage to famous architectural styles. **The Georgian House** *(7 Great Georgian St.; Tel 0117/921-13-62; Buses 1, 8, 9, 41-43, 54, 55, 80, and 99; 10am-5pm Wed-Sat)* is a beautiful Georgian (duh) town house furnished in the style of the period. **The Red Lodge** *(Park Row; Tel 0117/921-13-60; Buses 1, 8, 9, 41-43, 54, 55, 80, and 99; 10am-5pm Wed-Sat)* is an original Tudor lodge with one of the finest oak-paneled rooms in the west of England.

The **City Museum & Art Gallery** *(Queen's Rd.; Tel 0117/922-35-71; Buses 1, 8, 9, 41-43, 54, 55, 80, and 99; 10am-5pm daily)* is the primary museum in town, featuring artwork as well as historical and natural science displays. Temporary exhibitions focus on wildly differing themes, from a show demonstrating how to look after personal objects in our homes to black and white prints from the British Museum.

▶▶PERFORMING ARTS

For a taste of London's West End, catch one of the touring shows like *Fame, Rent, Annie,* or *42nd Street* at **The Hippodrome Theatre** *(St. Augustine's Parade; Tel 0870/607-75-00; Box office 8:30am-10pm Mon-Fri, till 9:30pm Sat, 10am-8pm Sun; Call for prices; www.Bristol-hippo drome.co.uk)*. Matinees are half-price—a great bargain considering you'd pay triple that to see a show in London. The Hippodrome also hosts one-off comedy shows.

Another of Bristol's premier entertainment venues is **Colston Hall** *(Colston St.; Tel 0117/922-36-86; Box office open on concert nights only 10am-10:30pm Mon-Sat, 5-10:30pm Sun; call for prices)* which has an eclectic program including classical, comedy, dance, pop, folk, and rock music.

Just off the harbor is historic King Street, home to the beautiful **Old Vic Theatre** *(King St.; Tel 0117/987-78-77, Fax 0117/949-39-96; Box office open 10am-8pm Mon-Sat, 10:30am-8pm Thur; Till 5:30pm July 17 to Sept 9; Closed Sat in Aug; £9.50 tickets, £6.50 concession Fri, Sat; bristol.old.vic@cableinet.co.uk, www.bristol-old-vic.co.uk)*. Opened in 1766, it is Britain's oldest working theater and has a history of almost continual use as a playhouse. There are behind-the-scenes tours every Friday and Saturday at 12:30pm (except in August). If you're a theater enthusiast, the tours are worth taking. The Old Vic is the centerpiece of an energetic arts center that includes the Theatre Royal, New Vic Studio and the New Vic Basement. Contemporary shows, comedy, dance, classical, and experimental theater are all featured here.

In the up-and-coming Gloucester Road area, there is a comedy club called **Jesters** *(140-142 Cheltenham Rd.; Tel 0117/909-66-55; Open 7:30pm, shows start 9pm, close 1am; www.jesterscomedyclub.co.uk; V, MC, Switch, Delta)*. Wednesdays through Saturdays the club features stand-up comedians, many who play in London as well. Every night after the show, Jesters becomes a disco, and on Mondays you can take salsa lessons. Booking in advance is recommended. Also in the area is the **Bristol Flyer Pub** *(96 Gloucester Rd.; Tel 0117/922-368)* which houses a small room called The Comedy Box above the main bar. Prepare to stand on a busy night.

One of two media centers in the quayside area, **Watershed** *(1 Canon's Rd., Harborside; Tel 0117/925-38-45, Fax 0117/921-39-58; Box office*

open 9am weekdays, 11am weekends; £4.50 adults, £3 students; info@water
shed.demon.co.uk, www.watershed.co.uk) screens a rotating cycle of art-
house films. It hosts several special events, including a gay and lesbian
film festival, a black film festival, and an animated short film festival. The
center also offers digital and photography courses, a cafe/bar, a shop, and
free sessions with the staff to discuss any aspect of digital, screen-based,
or photographic work.

Across the harbor, **Arnolfini** *(16 Narrow Quay; Tel 0117/929-91-91,
Fax 0117/925-38-76; 10am-11pm Mon-Sat [exhibitions till 7pm], noon-
10:30pm Sun and bank holidays [exhibitions until 6pm]; Admission varies;
www.arnolfini.demon.co.uk)* is Watershed's competition. Like the Watershed, the program at the Arnolfini encompasses dance, theater, music,
and visual arts. It's hosted the black film festival *Negritude,* the animated-
short film festival *Brief Encounters,* and *Wildscreen*—the "Oscars" of
wildlife filmmaking.

The smallest cinema in town is the **Arts Cinema** in King Square
(The Cube; Tel 0117/907-41-91), which specializes in cult films,
Hollywood classics, and the best of Bollywood. Watch out for double
bills, which in the past have included Buster Keaton and Marx Brothers
specials. The unique thing about this place is that it's located in what
looks like a suburban house in a residential 18th-century square, and
there's a bar inside where you can buy a drink to take to your seat. The
Odeon *(Union St., Broadmead; Tel 0117/929-08-82)* offers discounted
seats from Monday to Thursday, and screens contemporary and older
films. For more mainstream offerings, head to the genuine Art Deco–style
cinema, **ABC** *(Whiteladies Rd., Clifton; Tel 0117/973-36-40; £3.50
adults, £3 concessions and before 6pm),* in the student-heavy Whiteladies strip.

gay scene

The lively gay scene in Bristol includes everything from drinking and
dancing to hiking. To get yourself oriented, so to speak, call the Bristol
Lesbian & Gay Switchboard *(Tel 0117/942-08-42; 8-10pm daily)*.

Whether you want a relaxed drink with friends or are looking to hook
up with someone new, try one of the two bars at **The Griffin** *(41 Colston
St.; Tel 0117/927-24-21; 3-11pm Mon-Fri, noon-11pm Sat, noon-10:30pm
Sun; managers@thegriffinpub.co.uk, www.thegriffinpub.co.uk)*. The ground
floor bar is designed to create a warm environment conducive to drinking
and chatting, and the first floor is a bit darker and cruisier, in the style of
a Dutch leather bar, with discreet lighting and camouflage netting. Happy
hour is during the week between 4:30pm and 7:30pm, and on the weekends from 2-5pm.

culture zoo

Guided theme walks *(Book at the TIC; Tel 0117/946-222 booking, or
0117/926-07-67 info line; £3-4; Bristol@tourism.bristol.gov.uk, www.vis
itbristol.co.uk)*: If hotfooting about town is your thing, there are a

number of interesting guided walks, such as a tour of the historic inns and taverns of the city or a ghosts and ghouls tour. During the summer, various academics and specialists periodically offer **free history and wildlife walks** *(Contact City Museum & Art Gallery, Queen's Rd; Tel 0117/922-35-71; general-museum@Bristol-city.gov.uk, www.Bristol-city. gov.uk/museums)*.

Clifton Suspension Bridge Visitor Center *(Bridge House, Sion Place; Tel 0117/974-46-64, Fax 0117/974-52-55; Hours vary yearly, but are usually 10 or 11am till 4 or 5pm; £1.50 adults, same-day ticket concession for the SS Great Britain and the Open Top Bus; visitinfo@ clifton-suspension-bridge.org.uk, www.clifton-suspension-bridge.org.uk):* Bristol is indeed a culture zoo, largely due to Isambard Kingdom Brunel, an engineer whose first major commission—the Clifton Suspension Bridge—was given to him at the age of 25, after he won a contest to design a wrought-iron suspension bridge over the Avon Gorge. Subsequently, the bridge has become one of the most recognizable and famous landmarks in Britain and is included in every promotional picture of Bristol. Unfortunately, Brunel never got to see its completion, as he died prematurely, before the bridge was finished. To learn more, go to the visitor center near the bridge. It has displays illustrating the story of the bridge and explaining the engineering principles behind it.

SS Great Britain *(Great Western Dock, Gas Ferry Rd.; Tel 0117/926-06-80; 10am-5:30pm summer, 10:30am-4:30pm winter):* Brunel's innovative influence is still prevalent in other Bristol landmarks. He is the man behind the first ocean-going liners and the first ocean-going steam propeller–driven iron ship, the *SS Great Britain.* He also designed the Temple Meads train station, the first building you'll see in Bristol if you come in by train and the first comprehensive railway terminus.

@Bristol *(Harbourside, Tel 0117/915-10-00; £6.50 single ticket to Explore, Wildscreen, or Imax; £15.50 "All-Star Ticket" for all three over 1 or 2 days; Concession rates available; www.at-bristol.org.uk):* The newest complex in Bristol, this development is surrounded by cool bars, clubs, and restaurants on the waterfront. Inside the @Bristol, there's an interactive science center containing a virtual theater that explores atoms and molecules, a construction of a rainforest, and an Imax film theater. Outside the center is a large open space minimally filled with sculptures. At night, a huge mirrored disco ball (which you've gotta see to believe) reflects the bright blue lights that illuminate the space.

St. Mary's Redcliffe Church *(10 Redcliffe Parade West; Tel 0117/929-14-87; 7:30am-8pm daily; 8am-8pm summer weekdays, 8am-5:30pm winter weekdays):* There is a cathedral in Bristol, but a much more interesting ecclesiastical outing is St. Mary's, one of the best examples of medieval architecture in the country. Perched on the waterfront, the church was originally at the center of the shipping industry and the merchants of the port would begin and end their journeys here. Also, Admiral Sir William Penn (whose son William founded Pennsylvania) is buried in the south transept. The church is a striking aspect of the Bristol landscape and even a walk to look at it from the outside shouldn't be missed.

Bristol Zoo *(Clifton; Tel 0117/973-89-51; 9am-5:30pm daily in summer, till 4:30pm in winter; www.bristolzoo.org.uk)*: If you'd like to spend a day at the zoo, Bristol's features "Seal and Penguin Coasts," Gorilla Island, Bug World, Twilight World, the Aquarium, and the Reptile House.

Harvey's Wine Museum *(12 Denmark St.; Tel 0117/927-50-06; Call ahead for tour; V, MC, AE):* This is the birthplace of Harvey's Bristol Cream, one of the most popular sherries in the world. On display is a collection of 18th-century drinking glasses, antique decanters, corkscrews, bottles, silverware, and furniture. As is the case at any other distillery, you can sample the product; however, by no means are the wine cellars some sort of local watering hole. Harvey's is also one of the finest (read: most expensive) restaurants in the city [see *eats,* below].

modification

There are a bunch of tattoo parlors in town. **Art of Tattoo Time** *(88 North St.; Tel 0117/953-04-01)* in Bedminster, and **The Tattoo Studio** *(232 Cheltenham Rd.; Tel 0117/907-74-07; 10:30am-6:30pm Tue, Wed, Fri, and Sat; Noon-8pm Thur; No credit cards)* are among them. Take your bad hair day (or week or month...) to **Central Studio** *(Centre Gate, Colston Ave.; Tel 0117/929-23-48; 9am-late evening Mon-Sat; V, MC).*

city sports

For a stunning bird's-eye view of the city, contact **Bristol Balloons** *(Winterstoke Rd., South Bristol; Tel 0117/963-78-58; Flights leave from Ashton Court park late afternoon, evening or soon after dawn; £130 for one person, £120 per person for two or more people).* You'll get an aerial tour of the city on this 1-hour flight, including the stunning Clifton Suspension Bridge, the Avon Gorge, the waterside, the floating harbor, and the city center (the average flight is 10 miles). And afterwards, if your nerves are a bit shaky, you get chilled champagne (or orange juice if it's a bit early for you), as well as a commemorative flight certificate signed by the pilot. Another company that offers balloon flights from the same launch site is **The Big Balloon Co.** *(Tel 0117/954-22-99; £130 for one person, £120 each additional person),* but they don't offer any free booze.

There's an ice rink in the city center with classes offered by the **Bristol Academy of Ice Skating** *(Frogmore St.; Tel 0117/929-21-48; 10:30am-10:30pm daily; £3.80 Mon-Fri, £4.10 Fri, Sat nights; £1 skate rental; Students with ID £3.30 including rental).* There's a cafeteria and bar very conveniently located in the same complex.

stuff

The designated shopping area in town, **Broadmead** *(Tel 0117/925-70-53; www.bristolbroadmead.co.uk)* features large department stores, such as Marks & Spencer and Debenhams. Broadmead boasts that it is the largest shopping center in Southwest England, with over 400 shops. It's near the bus station in a part of town that is definitely one to miss if you are short on time.

▶▶DUDS AND CLUB GEAR

One of the main drags in town, Park Street is filled with clothing shops—mainly Bang Bang—and Urban Outfitter–type stuff—selling garb perfect for hitting the clubs.

▶▶MALL RATS

Located right in the middle of the Broadmead shopping area, **The Galleries** *(Tel 0117/929-05-69; 9am-5:30pm Mon-Sat, till 7pm Thur, 11am-5pm Sun; www.the-galleries.co.uk)* has over 100 stores with a lot of the High Street names. There's also a food court filled with the usual fast-food chains, which are OK for a snack, but save your appetite for the more interesting fare available quayside.

▶▶BAZAAR

The biggest market in the city, **St. Nicholas Market** *(Corn Exchange, Corn St.; Tel 0117/922-40-17)* is divided up into three sections: Exchange Hall Market, Glass Arcade, and the Covered Market. Exchange Hall contains a wide range of stalls selling everything from clothes and jewelry to secondhand books and crockery. It even hosts a psychic. For food, head through the hall to the Glass Arcade, where you'll find lots of well-known upmarket food brands. The Covered Market comprises a slew of small, wooden, self-contained units with similar sorts of goods as the Exchange Hall. The bazaar is definitely worth a stroll about even if you're not looking to shop.

EATS

Quayside is buzzing with places to eat. Just walk down Welsh Back and you'll spot them in a cluster. And Gloucester Road, whcih runs from the city center to the northern outskirts of town, is quickly catching up with Whiteladies Road in the number of cafes and new restaurants offering international cuisine. And if you're looking for a grocery store on the quayside, you're in luck [see *to market,* below].

▶▶CHEAP

Funky, Gaudí-inspired **Arc** *(27 Broad St.; Tel 0117/922-64-56; Soups £1.50, £2 with roll, £4 entrees; For lunch, £2 choice of three salads and a roll, £2.50 pizzas; 10% off takeaway orders)* has cheap eats, right in the center of town. You can munch on Thai green curry with basmati rice or a bowl of carrot and coriander soup. At lunchtime, the menu includes snack pizzas with organic bases, salads, and a selection of cakes for £1.

If you're shopping on Park Street and are feeling peckish, stop in **Boston Tea Party** *(75 Park St.; Tel 0117/929-86-01; 7am-10pm Tue-Sat, till 6pm Mon, 9am-7pm Sun; lunch entrees less than £5)*. Not only is it the ultra-hip cafe/restaurant about town, but it's cheap as well. Breakfasts are particularly excellent. The design of the place is based on the American West Coast coffeehouse, and the selection of brews does not disappoint.

TO MARKET

If you're staying near the water, you're close to a **Spar** supermarket *(42 Park St.; Tel 0117/925-17-90; 7am-11pm daily).*

Truth be told, no matter how much you may want to blend in with the country you're visiting, you're likely to end up with a hankering for a good old American burger and fries. That's where **Henry J. Bean's** *(93-95 Whiteladies Rd. Tel 0117/974-37-94; Noon-11pm daily; £5 platters; V, MC, AE)* steps in. With a lively student atmosphere, Henry J.'s is a nice place to relax, let down the hair, and have fun—oh yeah, did I mention you can get burgers and fries too?

Everybody has a place they go on Saturday morning to drown that hangover in a plate of cheap eggs and potatoes. In Bristol that place is the **York Café** *(1 York Place; Tel 0117/923-96-56).*

▶▶DO-ABLE

A light and bright restaurant and bar, **Bar Med** *(King St., Welsh Back; Tel 0117/922-18-46; Lunch entrees £5-6, tapas £2.50; V)* serves lunch food with a huge tapas menu. On weekend nights, the brightness turns multi-colored as the bar gets crowded and busy, and loud music plays upstairs. Shaped like a glass boat, the **River Station** *(The Grove; Tel 0117/914-44-34, Fax 0117/909-47-11; 9am-noon coffee and cake, noon-10pm food and drinks; Avg dinner entrees £6-7; V, MC)* sits right on the water. Beautiful and elegant, the menu is seafood-based and prices are reasonable—especially the take-away deli downstairs that serves delicious Middle Eastern snacks. Although most of the individual dishes are not that expensive, this is a place where you'll want to linger with a bottle of wine or two, coffee, and dessert, so the bill can add up.

Las Iguanas *(10 St. Nicholas St.; Tel 0117/927-62-33; Noon-3pm/5-11pm Mon-Sat; Entrees £7-11; V, MC, AE)* is a Latin-American tapas restaurant by day (and a good one too) and a raucous salsa bar by night. Take your pick.

▶▶SPLURGE

Harvey's Restaurant *(12 Denmark St.; Tel 0117/927-50-34, Fax 0117/927-50-01; Noon-2pm Mon-Fri, 7-10:45pm Mon-Sat; Entrees £17-20, fixed-price lunch £14.95-17.95, fixed-price dinner £32.95-39.95; Reservations required; V, MC, AE, DC),* located above Harvey's Wine Museum, is one of the finest restaurants in this part of England, serving award-winning modern classic French cuisine with hints of the Far East and Mediterranean. Try the pan-fried foie gras with apple and raisins for a starter, followed by pan-fried filet of beef with truffle mashed potatoes and mushrooms in a Beaujolais sauce, or roast farm pigeon with sautéed potatoes and an herb and sherry vinegar sauce. Naturally, they boast an extensive wine list, with the red wines of Bordeaux a particular specialty.

crashing

The price of accommodations in Bristol is opposite to what you'd expect: Rooms are cheaper on weekends than during the week. Most of the hotels jack up their weeknight prices in response to the influx of businesspeople who travel into the city to work. When the commuters leave town on the weekends, hotel prices come down to lure tourists. In the center of town, most of the rooms are in large chain hotels; a lot of them are fancy, and a lot of them are just plain expensive. And, strangely enough for a university city with so many young people, there is only one hostel. The University of Bristol offers a range of serviced and self-catering accommodations in Clifton or Stoke Bishop during school vacations. The Tourist Information Center will scour the lists and make accommodation bookings for you for a free of £3.

▶▶**CHEAP**

Occupying a converted warehouse with exposed brick walls and double volume ceilings, the **YHA** *(14 Narrow Quay; Tel 0117/922-16-59, Fax 0117/927-37-89; Open till late; £11.90 per bed in four- or six-bunk rooms, some w/ private bath; four family and twin rooms available; bristol@yha.org.uk, www.yha.org.uk; V, MC, Delta, Switch)* is surprisingly great for a hostel. It's located on the quayside, the rooms have wonderful views over the water, and it's right in the heart of club land, minutes away from downtown. The building has good facilities with a separate lounge, TV room, and game room. Additionally, there are laundry facilities and lockers in the bedrooms. Just to keep it from being too perfect, the staff and manager are far from charming and the hostel does not lend out towels: You have to buy them at £3.50.

   St. Michaels Guest House *(145 St. Michael's Hill; Tel 0117/907-78-20; £25 single, £35 double; V, MC)*, about 5 minutes from the city center, is a reliable and affordable spot for students, tourists, and everyone one looking for a place to crash. Rooms have cable TV, but the bathrooms are shared.

   The best of the university accommodations is **The Hawthorns** *(Woodland Rd., Clifton; Tel 0117/954-59-00, Fax 0117/923-71-88; Singles from £23.50, double/twins from £35.25; central-catering@bris.ac.uk, www.bris.ac.uk/depts/bursar/conf; V, MC)* with 73 singles, 26 double/twins, and 20 multiple bedrooms, more than half of which are en suite. The university also has multi-roomed flats available for weekly or weekend rentals.

▶▶**DO-ABLE**

If you're willing to go a few miles outside of town in order to cut down on some hotel costs, you should definitely try the **Oakfield Hotel** *(52-54 Oakfield Rd., Clifton; Tel 0117/973-36-43, Fax 0117/974-41-41; £28 single, £38 double; All rooms with bath; No credit cards)*. About a mile north in the town of Clifton, this meticulously kept B&B is simple, quiet, and well worth the money and the trip. Rooms include coffee makers and TVs.

The **Washington Hotel** *(St. Paul's Rd., Clifton; Tel 0117/973-39-80, Fax 0117/973-47-40; £36-63 single, £46-77 double/twin during the week; £23 per person in double/twin room from Fri-Sun; some rooms w/ private baths; V, MC, AE)* is bright and colorful. It also offers good amenities for a budget hotel, such as TV and radio in the bedrooms, and a comfy lounge area. The cost also includes a full English breakfast.

The modern **City Inn** *(Temple Way; Tel 0117/925-10-01, Fax 0117/907-41-16; £51.50 per room Mon-Thur, £44.95 per room Fri-Sun; bristolreservations@cityinn.com, www.cityinn.com; V, MC, AE)* is close to downtown and is a remarkably good deal. The suite rooms can hold a foursome, but they're affordable even if you're splitting the cost between two people. The hotel also has a fitness room and a funky, modern restaurant that serves food all day, including a special three-course menu for £12.95. The floor-to-ceiling windows in the rooms also allow a good view of Temple Gardens.

▶▶**SPLURGE**

Rated the best three-star hotel in the city, **The Berkeley Square Hotel** *(Berkeley Sq., Clifton; Tel 0117/925-40-00, Fax 0117/925-29-70; £49-96 single, £69-117 double/twin during the week, £34.50 per person in double/twin weekends, all rooms have private baths; All major credit cards)* is close to bustling Park Street [see *stuff*, above] in a peaceful Georgian square. The hotel was recently renovated and now each room has a wide-screen TV, CD player, and mini-bar.

NEED TO KNOW

Currency Exchange The main cluster of banks is in the **Broadmead** area.

Tourist Information The main tourist office is **The Annexe** *(Wildscreen Walk, Harbourside; Tel 0117/926-07-67 info or 0117/946-22-22 bookings, Fax 0117/929-77-03; 9:30am-5:30pm Mon-Sat, 11am-4pm Sun; bristol@tourism.bristol.gov.uk, http://tourism.bristol.gov.uk, www.visitbristol.co.uk)*. The staff at the TIC will make hotel reservations for a booking fee of £3, plus a commission of 10 percent of the first night's stay.

Public Transportation There is a good **bus system** in town. A ticket from the central downtown area to the Clifton area is £1.15 round-trip.

American Express There are two American Express locations: One is in the Broadmead area *(31 Union St.; Tel 0117/927-77-88; 9am-5:30pm Mon-Fri, 9am-5pm Sat)* and the other is in the west end *(74 Queen's Rd.; Tel 0117/975-17-51; 9am-5:30pm Mon-Fri, 9am-5pm Sat)*.

Health and Emergency The **police** are located near the Broadmead shopping district *(Nelson St.; Tel 0117/927-77-77)*. The main hospital is **Bristol Royal Infirmary** *(Upper Maudlin St.; Tel 0117/923-00-00)*, a few blocks north of the city center.

Telephone City code: *0117.*

Airports Bristol Airport *(Tel 01275/474-444)* is located on A38, just 9 miles from the city center. The easiest and cheapest way to get between Bristol and the airport is by public transportation on the **Bristol International Flyer** bus service run by **National Express** *(Tel 08457/808-080).* This service stops at both the Temple Meads Railway station and the bus station. The trip takes about 25 minutes. Buses run frequently between 5:30am and 10:30pm, and tickets can be bought on board (£5 adult return, £3 single).

Trains Frequent trains run from London Paddington to both stations in Bristol—Temple Meads in the center of town and Parkway Station, 6 miles out on the northern outskirts. Each trip takes just about 1 hour *(National Rail inquiries: Tel 0345/484-950).* Frequent bus service runs from the Parkway to the city center, but the fastest way to get there is via taxi *(Tel 0117/955-59-75 or 0117/953-86-38).*

Bus Lines Out of the City National Express *(Tel 0990/808-080)* buses depart hourly from London Victoria and take 2 hours. Bristol's bus station is a few minutes north of the city center on Marlborough Street.

Boat There are yellow and blue ferry boats that operate daytime round-trips on the harbor. **Bristol Ferry Boat Co.** *(Tel 0117/927-34-16; Daily Apr-Sept, weekends in winter; £1-3.50; enquiries@bristolferry boat.co.uk, www.bristolferryboat.co.uk)* does two routes that run from April to September: the Hotwells-City Center route and the City Center-Temple Meads route. Hotwells-City Center picks up at the Pump House, Nova Cottage, and makes several stops in the harbor and City Center. The City Center-Temple Meads route operates on weekends and school holidays. There is also morning commuter service between Hotwells and Temple Meads.

Bike/Moped Rental You can rent some wheels at **David Bater Cycles** *(12-14 Park St.; Tel 0117/929-73-68, Fax 0117/925-07-64; 9am-5:30pm Mon-Sat, open 10am Tue, closed Sun),* a full-service bike shop in the center of town.

Postal Post your packages at **The Galleries** *(Wine St.; Tel 0117/925-23-22; 9am-5:30pm Mon-Sat).*

Internet See *wired,* above.

bath

Just 115 miles west of London, Bath could easily be a day trip. But once the train rolls into the station and you're surrounded by the green Mendip hills on both sides, one day immediately begins to seem way too short for such a special place. Bath is enchanting. Even the center of town, which is often the ugliest part of a city, is beautiful here. All the buildings are built in the Georgian architectural style but are constructed from lime-stone, which gives the place a distinctly un-English feel. (A local building code mandates that every new building must be made from limestone to maintain the overall "look" of the city). There's also a lot of greenery in Bath. The numerous parks and the resplendent surrounding views look like perfect backdrops for *A Midsummer Night's Dream,* or any other whimsical Shakespeare play. The open squares and pedestrian malls of the city guarantee a relaxing, stop-to-soak-up-the-atmosphere kind of environment.

Apart from its physical beauty, Bath is famous for having Britain's only hot mineral springs. The Romans took advantage of nature's hot tub by building lavish baths, called *Aquae Sulis,* in 75AD. For almost 2,000 years, Bath has been a spa town that attracts all kinds of people. In the past, roy-alty and peasants alike soaked in the curative waters. Unfortunately, due to public-health concerns, it's no longer possible to take a dip in the hot springs, but a visit to admire the Roman architecture and beauty of the water is still more than worthwhile.

So, Bath, with its history and natural legacy, is now also a modern city with all the accompanying luxuries. You'll find every major shop you might find in London, plus an abundance of little boutiques, restaurants, cafes and bars, and a wide range of accommodation, sports, and sights. You'll find it hard to leave. Set aside a at least two to three days to explore the city and its environs, which include Stonehenge, Avebury, and Glastonbury.

As in many of the other major cities in England, you can take a hop-on, hop-off, double-decker bus tour. The bus stops at all the major tourist attractions in town and takes an hour, but the ticket (£8.50 adults, £6.50 students) is valid all day and offers discounts in certain restaurants and museums. This is a good option if you feel like getting your bearings from a tour guide, otherwise just skip it. It's easy to get around Bath by foot, and the local buses run frequently [see *need to know,* below].

For current information on entertainment listings, pick up a copy of *Venue* at the Tourist Information Center [see *need to know,* below].

neighborhoods

Walk out of the train station (the bus station is diagonally across the street to the left) and straight up **Manvers Street,** the street directly opposite the train station. Manvers Street soon turns into **Pierrepont Street.** (**Bath Backpackers Hostel** [see *crashing,* below] is on this street.) On the right is **North Parade Road,** a busy strip jammed with pubs, clubs, restaurants, and some hotels. Continue straight a bit more on Pierrepont and it joins a circular road with a traffic island in the middle, known as the **Grand Parade.** Turn left and walk down **York Street** and you will come to the square containing **Bath Abbey,** the **Roman Baths** [see *culture zoo,* below], and the information center. If you walk in a straight line down Grand Parade (the Parade Gardens will be below you on a grassy area next to the river) and continue to the right, you'll get to another cir-

wired

You can check your e-mail at **Click** *(19 Broad St.; Tel 01225/337-711; 10am-10pm daily; £3.50 per half hour, £5 per hour; www.click-cafe.com)*, a nice Internet cafe, but the rates are not cheap, so be quick about it. **Itchy Feet** *(Bartlett St.; Tel 01225/337-987; 10am-6pm Mon-Sat, 11am-5pm Sun; £1.50 per half hour)*, between George and Alfred streets, also offers Internet access.

www.thisisbath.com: Good site for news about the city provided by the *Bath Chronicle.*

www.bath.co.uk: Good for leisure listings, reviews, lists of shops and services. Check out "Best of Bath."

cular road with a traffic island. To the right is **Argyle Street**—which gives
you a good view of River Avon and the Pulteney Bridge—and to the left
is **Bridge Street.** Continue left on the circle, and Bridge Street meets up
with the **High Street.** Go north up High Street, which turns into **Walcot
Street,** and you'll find lots of shops, restaurants, and the **YMCA** [see
crashing, below]. A few minutes' walk up the High Street from Bath
Abbey and you'll see **Broad Street** branching off to the left. This is another
good street for restaurants, pubs, and shops.

The heart of town includes the square where the abbey and baths are
located, as well as the surrounding streets to the west and north such as
Westgate, Milsom, and **George streets.** The streets are linked by a "pedestrian precinct," which is a small network of roads where no cars are
allowed. These roads include **Union** and **Old Bond streets.**

The main park, Royal Victoria Park, and its **Botanical Gardens**
[see *hanging out,* below] are about a 20-minute walk from the center of
town in a northwestern direction. This is also where you'll find the **Royal
Crescent** [see *culture zoo,* below]. **Queen Square,** nearby, is a lovely
block surrounded by buildings and has benches on the grass. The streets
off of the square are very quaint and filled with treasures and pebble
stones.

hanging out

There aren't any spots where young hipsters over the age of 15 gather
to hang out and chill, but the center of town is linked with open
squares and pedestrian roads, and there are lots of benches where
people sit and read, eat, or people-watch. The big hangout for all the
14-year-olds in town is a skateboarding ramp in front of the botanical
gardens in Royal Victoria Park. It's a typical teen scene, some skate-
boarding and rollerblading like demons and others just standing
around looking cool. All of the parks around town are really pretty,
calm spots to relax, but the choice spot has to be the recreation ground
adjacent to the Pulteney Bridge. There are green-striped deck chairs
laid out on the lawn, similar to Green Park in London. For some
hanging out with added cultural kick, the **Prior Park Landscape
Garden** *(Ralph Allen Drive; Tel 01225/833-422 or 0891/335-242 for
24-hour recorded info; Badgerline buses 2 and 4 from Dorchester St.;
Noon-5:30pm daily, but hours vary from month to month; £3.80 adults)*
is a beautiful 18th-century landscaped garden created by Bath entrepreneur Ralph Allen, with creative advice from Lancelot Brown and
the poet Alexander Pope. Within the garden are the Palladian Bridge,
some lakes, and a wonderful view of the city.

bar scene

By law, most pubs are open between 11am and 11pm (10:30pm on Sundays), which means patrons must empty their cups by 11:20pm. But
recently enacted laws allow some pubs to stay open later, so check with
the proprietor about closing times.

bath

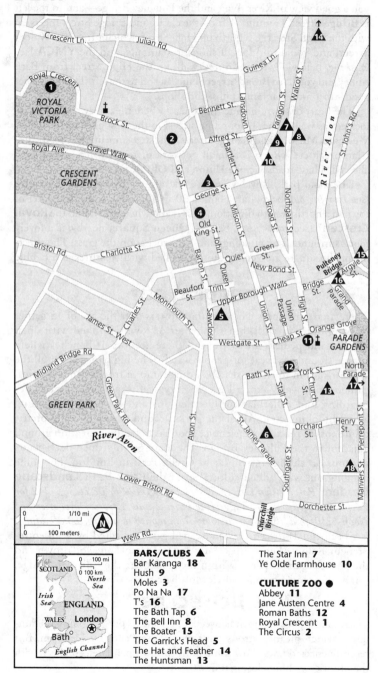

BARS/CLUBS ▲
Bar Karanga **18**
Hush **9**
Moles **3**
Po Na Na **17**
T's **16**
The Bath Tap **6**
The Bell Inn **8**
The Boater **15**
The Garrick's Head **5**
The Hat and Feather **14**
The Huntsman **13**

The Star Inn **7**
Ye Olde Farmhouse **10**

CULTURE ZOO ●
Abbey **11**
Jane Austen Centre **4**
Roman Baths **12**
Royal Crescent **1**
The Circus **2**

Though a few doors down from the Backpackers Hostel, **Bar Karanga** *(8-10 Manvers St.; Tel 01225/446-546, Fax 01225/480-937; Noon-2am Tue-Sun)* is otherwise quite far from any other hotspot in town. Thursdays are official pre-bar nights for *Saucy* at **Po Na Na** [see *club scene*, below], Fridays are *Fresh & Funky* with hip-hop, soul and R&B blasting on the loudspeakers. On Saturdays get three bottles of Stella Artois for only £5. If you prefer wine, from Thursday till Saturday bottles of house red or white are £5 each. On Sundays try out £10 jugs of Vodka Red Bull, a drink that recently made its debut in the States and is usually offered at raves.

    The Huntsman *(Terrace Walk; North Parade Passage; Tel 01225/428-812; Free before 10pm, £1 after)* is one of the only pubs in Bath with a late-night license till 2am. Though a bit grungy, it's extremely central and has tables on the street that give fantastic views of the parade of passing people.

    Close to the cinemas and around the corner from the Theatre Royal is **The Garrick's Head** *(6 St. John's Place, Sawclose; Tel 01225/318-368)*, which is reputedly haunted. Enjoy happy hour (5:30-6:30pm daily) at the pavement tables, and try the good, traditional, homemade food. The crowd here is predominantly theater-goers and actors, and it's always packed during show-time intermission.

    Founded in 1760, **The Star Inn** *(23 The Vineyards, off The Paragon; Tel 01225/444-437)* hasn't really changed since Victorian times, as you can see from the wood paneling and sepia-drenched decor. No games, no jukebox, just beer and conversation. Have a Bass, which is served here from a jug.

    Just off the Pulteney Bridge, **The Boater** *(9 Argyle St.; Tel 01225/464-211)* isn't the greatest-looking pub, but it does have an enormous garden (great in summer), Sky TV, and a jukebox. At its heart, it's a student magnet—rugby lads, in particular—with cheap drinks (£1.80 for beer, £1.70 for wine).

LIVE MUSIC SCENE

One of Bath's favorite music venues, **The Bell Inn** *(103 Walcot St.; Tel 01225/460-426; Mon and Wed nights, Sun lunch; No cover)* features regular live bands that play everything from jazz and blues to reggae and country. The long, narrow, 400-year-old room is covered in postcards from around the world which offer a welcome distraction if the band of the evening isn't quite up your alley. You're likely to find lots of students here.

    For an eclectic mix of jazz, funk, ska, and reggae, **The Hat and Feather** *(14 London St., top of Walcot St.; Tel 01225/425-672; No cover)* has live music playing or DJs spinning nightly and jam sessions upstairs.. This is Bath's ultraviolet-drenched, alternative music pub.

    Overlooking Bath, **Ye Olde Farmhouse** *(1 Landsdown Rd.; Tel 01225/316-162 or 420-944; Noon-11pm Mon-Sat, noon-10:30pm Sun, closed Wed)* features live jazz most nights between Tuesday and Sunday. There's a big-screen TV if jazz isn't your thing. You can also grab a pint of the locally brewed Bellringer here (the pub has its own brewery at the back).

festivals and events

For about 2 and 1/2 weeks every year during May and the beginning of June, the renowned **Bath International Music Festival** *(Box office at 2 Church St., Abbey Green; Tel 01225/463-362, Fax 01225/310-377; 9:30am-5:30pm daily during festival, tickets available after Apr 3; £1 discount students, 50 percent off under 20; info@bath festivals.org.uk, boxoffice@bathfestivals.org.uk, www.bathfestivals.org.uk)* takes over almost every venue in town. With a huge range of music on offer, including an extensive jazz program along with flamenco, choral music, Bulgarian, Scottish, and African traditional song, this festival draws a lot of visitors, so be sure to buy tickets early at the box office.

For about 2 and 1/2 weeks in May and June, the **Bath Fringe Festival** *(2 Church St., Abbey Green; Tel 01225/480-079; admin@bath fringe.co.uk, www.bathfringe.co.uk)* offers alternative entertainment from around the world. Events include Cuban and African percussionists, European contemporary dancers, workshops in vocals, theater, free street entertainment, and lots more arty, sometimes incomprehensible, stuff.

Recorded information on the major festivals and events is available *(Tel 09068/360-387, call is 60p per minute)*.

club scene

Tucked into the ground, **Moles** *(George St.; £4-5 cover for non-members)*, a block south of the Circus, offers top dance tunes with live music half the week; DJs play dance music the other half. This is definitely the spot for the big boys on the music scene, and there've been rumors that bands like Blur and Oasis have played here. It's a bit sparse in the decor department, the crowd is a bit older than other clubs—early twenties to mid-thirties—and the beer is not too expensive. Mondays are big beats and break techno; Tuesdays, it's all '70s and '80s hits; Wednesdays are funk; Thursdays feature either a band or a DJ; and Fridays, house and techno. Cheap drinks are also available on Fridays. The official policy at Moles is that you have to be signed in by a member, but this is not a hard-and-fast rule and you might as well give it a shot.

Po Na Na *(8-9 N. Parade; Tel 01225/401-115, Fax 01225/410-116; 9pm-2am Mon-Sat; Tue £1.50 students, £2.50 general; Wed £2 students, £3 general; Thur £1 students, £2 general; Fri £3 before 10pm, £5 after; Sat £2 before 9:30pm, £3 before 10pm, £5 after; Free Mon; scott@ponanabath.freeserve.co.uk, www.ponana.co.uk)*, just south of the Parade Gardens, is the place for a soul, funk, and house mix, played in a trendy Moroccan basement dive outfitted with tiger-skin seat covers, a great sound system, chill-out rooms, and a mostly student crowd. Bottles of beer go for about £2. Mondays are resident house; Tuesdays, top retro night; Wednesdays, house and garage; Thursdays, funk; and Friday, house and trance. Saturdays, it's funk again.

Top local DJs spin tunes you can talk over in the three bars at **Hush** *(Bladud buildings, Paragon; Tel 01225/446-288; £3 Sat after 10pm)* (hence the name). A few blocks east of the Circus, Hush is good as a pre- and post-club hangout, as it has lots of tables and chairs, a dance floor, a pool table, and a very chill atmosphere. It is also the proud owner of a late-night license so when it's open, it stays open till 2am.

When you're in the mood for cheesy, mainstream entertainment, **T's** *(Spring Gardens Rd., under Pulteney Bridge; Tel 01225/425-360; 9:30pm-2am Mon-Sat; £3-6)* is just the ticket. This underground tavern doesn't charge a fortune for cover or drinks, and the crowd is a happy, uncomplicated bunch. Student night is Thursday.

ARTS SCENE

▶▶VISUAL ARTS

Don't have much time, but still itchin' for some culture? Go to the **Victoria Art Gallery** *(Bridge St., next to Pulteney Bridge; Tel 01225/477-233, Fax 01225/477-231; 10am-5:30pm Tue-Fri, 10am-5pm Sat, 2-5pm Sun; Victoria-enquiries@bathnes.gov.uk; www.victoriagal.org.uk; Free admission)*, a fantastic little gallery that is easily do-able in an hour. The first floor has a changing exhibition every six weeks, while the second floor houses another traveling exhibition and a permanent collection of works by regional artists including Thomas Gainsborough (who lived at number 17 the Circus for a while) and Joseph M. W. Turner. The upstairs hallways are lined with local students' sculptures, some of which are covered in aluminum foil and stuck with green plastic insects.

▶▶PERFORMING ARTS

Bath's major theater and one of Britain's oldest, the **Theatre Royal** *(Sawclose; Tel 01225/448-844; Box office 10am-8pm Mon-Sat; shows 7:30pm Mon-Wed, 8pm Thur-Sat; 2:30pm matinees Wed and Sat; Tickets £9-25)* puts on mostly large-scale comedy, opera, and dance productions, (such as a theater version of *The Hobbit*), but it also shows some West End fodder. You can take a tour of the backstage on most Wednesdays and Saturdays, and before the midweek matinees you can even meet the actors and participate in a casual "Lunch & Listen" session. Also inside is the Vaults Gallery, which has both a changing exhibition and permanent display of the work of some of the world's leading theater designers. There is also a **Vaults Restaurant** *(Theatre Royal, Sawclose; Tel 01225/448-815)*, in the original vaults of the theater.

In the rear of the building, the **Ustinov Studio** is a narrow theater with a small stage that features comedy, drama, music, and dance. It is a major venue for the fringe stuff during the annual arts festival [see *festivals and events*, above].

To see a mainstream Hollywood flick, go to one of the three cinemas: **ABC** *(22-23 Westgate St.; Tel 01225/462-959; £4.60 adults, £3.30* students; www.abc-cinemas.co.uk;), **Little Theatre** *(St. Michael Place; Tel 01225/466-822; £4.20 adults, £2.70 students Mon-Fri)*, or **Robins** *(St. Johns Place; Tel 01225/461-506; £4.10 adults, £2.10 students)*, which are in proximity to one another, a few blocks west of the abbey. Catching a decent film there might be a bit tricky at times as they stick to the most mainstream of Hollywood schlock. Your best bet may be the Little Theatre, which does show some alternative picks.

gay scene

Located in a Georgian building near the bus station, **The Bath Tap** *(19 St. James Parade; Tel 01225/404-344; Noon-11pm Mon and Wed, 4-11pm Tue, noon-midnight Thur, noon-2am Fri, Sat, 2-10:30pm Sun; Lunch noon-2:30pm at the main bar; £2.50 Sat after 10pm; bathtap@bathtaponline.co.uk, www.bathtaponline.co.uk)* is Bath's premier gay and bisexual bar-cum-club for men and women. Its three floors are devoted to a variety of hedonistic pursuits. The main bar serves lunch and is the center of the action most nights. The lounge bar has lots of comfy seating with '70s and '80s music and a "nite bites" menu served between 10pm and 1am (definitely unconventional for any type of entertainment venue in England). The club bar is for dancing nights that go on till 2am. There are also daily activities: Mondays are for karaoke, with bottles of Champers going to those who don't empty the place; Tuesdays are cheap drinks nights; Wednesdays are drag quiz extravaganzas; and Fridays and Saturdays are heavy club nights with the DJs.

CULTURE ZOO

The two major cultural sights in Bath are the baths (of course), and the abbey.

The **Roman Baths** *(Abbey Churchyard; Tel 01225/477-785; 9am-6pm daily Apr-Sept; 9am-9:30pm Aug; 9:30am-5pm Oct-Mar; £6.90 adults, audio guides included):* There always seems to be a line outside waiting to join the mob of people inside, so try to get here early. The Romans first built their religious spa called *Aquae Sulis* around the three springs—the Great Bath, King's Bath, and Saerel—and people came to bathe in the water to cure ailments, to amuse themselves, or to relax. The waters in the three baths stay at a constant temperature of 46.5 degrees Celsius (116 degrees Fahrenheit). The most impressive thing about the baths is the durability of the Roman engineering. The original drains still work and water still travels from room to room. Inside the complex are also the ruins of the temple of Sulis Minerva, the Roman-Celtic goddess of the springs. A museum on the premises houses a daunting number of artifacts dating from the time the Romans founded the baths in 75 A.D. On display are treasures offered to the goddess, carvings from the classical temple, inscriptions of the local people of *Aquae Sulis,* and an interesting computer projection of how the whole development would have looked in ancient times. The museum has a bit too much stuff, and not all of it is gripping, but the springs and the actual Great Bath are gorgeous.

Bath Abbey *(Orange Grove; Tel 01225/422-462; 9am-6pm Mon-Sat Apr-Oct; 9am-4:30pm Mon-Sat Nov-Mar; 1-2:30pm/4:30-5:30pm Sun year-round; £2 requested donation):* Just across the square from the baths is a medieval church established in 1499. The church is worth a quick look around, if only to see an example of "perpendicular" architecture and to hear the organ, which is played several times a day, usually by people rehearsing for recitals. On the south side of the abbey under Kingston pavements are the **Heritage Vaults** *(Tel 01225/422-462; 10am-4pm Mon-Sat; £2 adults, £1 students).* These restored 18th-century cellars house a presentation of the history of the abbey site dating back to Saxon and Norman times.

Museum of Costume *(Assembly Rooms, Bennett St.; Tel 01225/477-789, Fax 01225/444-793; 10am-5pm daily; £4 adults, £8.90 combined entry to Museum of Costume and Roman Baths; costume-enquiries@bathnes. gov.uk; www.museumofcostume.co.uk):* Come wind your way through the evolution of fashion. Two hundred dressed mannequins and up to a thousand other costumes and accessories illustrate the changes in men's, women's and children's fashion since the 16th century. Along with a display of embroidered Elizabethan and Jacobean dresses, you can see the famous "silver tissue" dress, a rare example of court apparel made from cream-colored silk woven with silver thread, dating from the 1660s. Included in the exhibit is "Dress of the Year," which represents new ideas in contemporary fashion and could feature anyone from Armani to McQueen. Also take a look at the Assembly Rooms, where 18th-century society gathered to dance, play cards, and drink tea.

Holburne Museum of Art *(Great Pulteney St.; Tel 01225/466-669, Fax 01225/333-121; 11am-5pm Mon-Sat, 2:30-5:30pm Sun, closed Mon from Nov till Easter; www.bath.ac.uk/holburne; £3.50 adults):* It began its life as the Sydney hotel in the late 18th century, and was converted into the museum you see today in 1916. Jane Austen often visited the spot, which is located in the middle of the Sydney Pleasure Gardens. The Holburne now holds more of a specialist collection of silver, Italian bronzes, maiolica, porcelain, and Old Master paintings, among other *objets* from the collection of Sir William Holburne of 19th-century Bath.

Jane Austen walking tour *(Leaves 11am every day from the TIC [see* need to know, *below]; £3.50 adults, £2.50 students):* If you're a Jane Austen fan then you'll probably know that she lived in Bath for a bit (from 1801 to 1805), and set two of her novels, *Northanger Abbey* and *Persuasion,* here. You can take the 1 1/2-hour walking tour of the places Austen lived in, walked around, visited, and shopped at (tickets for the tour can be purchased at the TIC or from the tour guide). If you're still hankering for more Austen-abilia after the walk, check out the **Jane Austen Centre** *(40 Gay St.; Tel 01225/443-000; 10:30am-5:30pm daily; info@janeausten.co.uk, www.janeausten.co.uk)* for displays of the places that she depicted in her novels as well as images of her family and life in Bath. And if you're new to Jane Austen, pick up copies of her books at the gift shop.

only here

If you have only one evening in Bath, spend it doing the **Bizarre Bath** *(Tel 01225/335-124; £4.50, £4 students)* comedy walk. Not many interactive performances are this refreshingly wacky and funny. The walk leaves every night between Easter and September from outside the Huntsman Inn *(North Parade Passage; Tel 01225/428-812)* at 8pm, and no pre-booking is required. Just show up at the appointed time and prepare to laugh your ass off. The walk, which doesn't involve a lot of walking at all, lasts about 80 minutes, but is prone to running overtime, so don't make any fixed arrangements for afterwards. Giving a too-thorough description of the comedy walk would spoil the fun.

If you don't have a car but want to visit the nearby sites—like the stone circles, Lacock, and Castle Combe—go on the very intimate and entertaining **Mad Max Tour** *(Book at YMCA, Bath Backpackers Hotel, or TIC; 8:45am-4:30pm Mon-Fri; £15 per person excluding Stonehenge entrance fee and lunch; Maddy@mad max.abel.co.uk)*, named after the owner, Maddy's (supposedly mad) dog, Max. You'll be carted off to Stonehenge, Avebury, Lacock, and Castle Combe, with brief stops at Silbury Hill, as well as one of the famous Wiltshire White Horses [see *within 30 minutes,* below]. Other interesting tidbits from this tour include driving through the village of Box, where Peter Gabriel lives and has his recording studio. You'll start the journey on the 2.5-mile-long Batheaston Road, which is the most expensive motorway built in the UK, at a staggering £75 million. Ask when John is leading the tour, as you will not find a funnier, more charming, or more helpful tour guide. He does not stop cracking jokes, and has an enormous knowledge of the area and its history.

The Circus: At the end of Gay Street is John Wood's design of three crescents arranged in a circle with a carved frieze running around all of them. Soon after laying the foundation stone, Wood died, and his son—also named John Wood—finished the job. The younger Wood went on to design the Royal Crescent, a spectacular semicircular residential apartment building overlooking a large lawn in front of the Royal Victoria Park. The Circus is now designated a World Heritage Building.

No. 1 Royal Crescent *(Corner of Brock St.; Tel 01225/428-126; 10:30am-5pm Tue-Sun, mid Feb-Oct; 10:30am-4pm Tue-Sun, Nov):* This 18th-century townhouse has been restored, redecorated, and furnished to illustrate how it might have looked when it was first built.

CITY SPORTS

Pump those muscles on resistance machines and free weights at the **YMCA** *(International House, Broad St. Place; Tel 01225/325-913; 7am-10pm Mon-Fri, 8:30am-7pm Sat, Sun, and holidays; £4 per session, £3 if staying in YMCA, membership rates available for longer stays).* You can also break a sweat by playing in a pickup game of basketball, working out on cardio machines, or taking an aerobics and/or fitness class. After you exert yourself, relax in the solarium, sauna, or steam room (or any combination of the three).

In summer, drop by the North Parade **Cricket Ground,** south of N. Parade Road, and you might catch a match.

For something completely different, take a ride on a hot-air balloon from Royal Victoria Park. For information on flight times, contact **Bath Balloon Flights** *(24 Gay St.; Tel 01225/466-888, Fax 01225/336-167; 9am-5pm Mon-Fri, 10am-1pm Sat in summer).* This is a definite splurge activity; the cost for an individual is £125 per flight, £115 each for two to three people, and £103.50 each for four or more.

For those of you who like to jump off bridges, the **Adventure Café** *(5 Princes Buildings, George St.; Tel 01225/462-038; 9am-5pm Mon-Sat, 9:30am-4pm Sun)* has information about every sort of adrenaline-pumping activity in Britain. This is the place to find out where you can hurl yourself to near-death by bungee-jumping, skydiving, catapulting, or parascending. Or try something tame like rapid-running, micro-lighting, or pony-trekking. Who knows? You might end up participating in an adventure sport you've never heard of before.

STUFF

▶▶**BAZAAR**

Guildhall Market *(High St.; 9am-5:30pm Mon-Sat),* right across from the abbey, is a fantastic indoor market where you can buy specialty goods. The stalls offer goods like housewares and jewelry, or you can get a buzz at the cute, traditional barbershop with bright red walls. For beautiful homemade soaps (in exotic varieties like frankincense and myrrh with specks of gold) along with creams, oils, and big bowls of resin incense, don't miss **Lotus Emporium** *(Unit 9; Tel 01225/448-011; lotusemp@aol.com, www.lotusemporium.com).* The store will be expanding to include a space where people can watch the soaps being made.

There's a Saturday flea market on Walcot Street (just up from the Podium shopping center) which starts at 8am. Goodies for sale include products made by local craftspeople such as hand-blown glass, pottery, and handmade tiles.

▶▶**ANTIQUES**

Off Brock Street, leading to the Royal Crescent, is a lovely side street on the right called Margaret's Buildings, which is a good place to visit to scour for antiques.

▶▶**TRAVEL**

If you're preparing for some serious jet-setting, hotfoot it to **Itchy Feet** *(Bartlett St., between George and Alfred streets; Tel 01225/337-987)* for travel gear and guides. There's also a traveler's cafe and Internet access [see *wired,* above].

EATS

Bath has so many restaurants that you'll be hard-pressed to decide where to eat. Wherever you choose, get there early. Restaurants tend to stop serving dinner by 10 at the latest. (England may be in Europe, but the English have a lot to learn about the pleasures of Mediterranean-style, late-night dining.) Most sit-down restaurants accept all major credit cards, with the usual exceptions of American Express and Diner's Club.

▶▶**CHEAP**

If you've eaten enough traditional English breakfasts to last a lifetime, run to **La Baguette** *(3 Stall St.; Tel 01225/480-833; 8:30am-5:30pm Mon-Sat, 9am-5pm Sun)* for a hot 'n' cheap French breakfast of croissants, baguettes, or toasties (£1.60). Once you have a hot little toastie in your hot little hand, head for one of the benches in the middle of the street, or go sit in front of the abbey around the corner and listen to the street musicians. The tiny shop fills up quickly, so get there early.

A hop, skip, and jump from three movie theaters, the Theatre Royal, and the Ustinov Studio, the **Jazz Café** *(Kingsmead Sq.; Tel 01225/329-002; 8am-9pm Mon-Sat, 10:30am-4pm Sun; Everything on the menu is under £5)* is an Italian-style eatery with red-and-white-checkered table-cloths and a chalkboard listing the daily specials. The Jazz Café's claim to fame is that it serves homemade Italian "soul food" in a comfortable, non-fast-food environment. It's an amazingly good deal considering the location and the number and variety of veggie options. Despite its name, however, there is no live jazz.

A great place for lunch, the **Adventure Café** *(5 Princes Buildings, George St.; Tel 01225/462-038)* is a funky little coffeeshop that has tables outside on the street, and serves delicious hot and cold coffee drinks in tall glasses (£1-2). Adventure's the name of the game in the extremely imaginative sandwiches like the goat cheese melt with cranberry sauce and grapes on focaccia, served with side salad (£4.75). You can have your adventure in a regular sandwich, hot melted, or as a wrap.

For a greasy hamburger or veggie burger after the movies, **Mr. D's** *(37 Monmouth St.; Tel 01225/426-111; Open daily till 11pm; Avg dish £2)* is a tiny shop for quick, cheap grub.

▶▶**DO-ABLE**

An alleyway that leads somewhat indirectly to North Parade Road, North Parade Passage is jammed with restaurants, most of them on the more expensive side. One of the choice places on this street is **Sally Lunn** *(4 North Parade Passage, Tel 01225/461-634; 10am-10pm Mon-Sat, 11am-10pm Sun, closed Christmas; Morning coffee £4.50, lunch £5.50-10, dinner £10-15)*. Built in 1482, it is the oldest house in Bath and home of the Sally Lunn Bun. The entire menu is based on this bun, a type of white, puffy roll served with sweet or savory toppings. The restaurant and bun are named after a young French refugee who created the bun in 1680 while working as a cook in the restaurant. In the cellar there is a kind of museum where you can see remains of Roman, Saxon, and medieval buildings together with the restaurant's ancient kitchen.

For a pub dinner or lunch, head for the **Crystal Palace** *(Abbey Green; Tel 01225/482-666; 11am-4pm/6:30-9pm Mon-Sat, noon-5:30pm Sun; Avg entree £6.50)*. What this place lacks in culinary imagination and skill, it more than makes up for in friendliness and atmosphere. You have the choice of sitting inside, in the adjoining small room encased in glass, or in the garden, in the back, with benches and vine-laden beams overhead. Standard pub fare includes meat and fish main dishes, jacket potatoes, and sandwiches. If you're going for a potato, though, steer clear of the one with chicken tikka—it is dry and only confirms the belief that Indian-inspired cooking should remain in Indian restaurants.

For a lovely afternoon tea accompanied by a pianist or a trio of classical musicians, proceed to the **Pump Room** *(Abbey Churchyard; Tel 01225/477-000; 9am-6pm daily Apr-Sept; 9am-9:30pm Aug; 9:30am-5pm Oct-Mar; £3.85-9.95)*. This elegant dining room, which sits above the baths, serves cakes for tea, as well as breakfasts and lunches. It's been a local favorite since the 18th century, when society's elite came to socialize and partake of the spa water, which was thought to be curative. You can partake, too, for 50p a glass at the spa water fountain in the restaurant.

For vegetarians, **Demuth's** *(2 North Parade Passage; Tel 01225/446-059; 10am-10pm Sun-Fri, 9am-10pm Sat; www.demuths.co.uk)* is Bath's only licensed vegetarian restaurant, and apart from lots of veggie options for breakfast, lunch, dinner, and snacks, you can get organic wine as well

TO MARKET

A very big **Waitrose** supermarket *(The Podium, Northgate St.; Tel 01225/442-550; 8:30am-8pm Mon-Fri, 8:30am-7pm Sat, 11am-5pm Sun; V, MC)* sells pre-made sandwiches for about £2.50 and has an extensive self-service salad bar.

bath

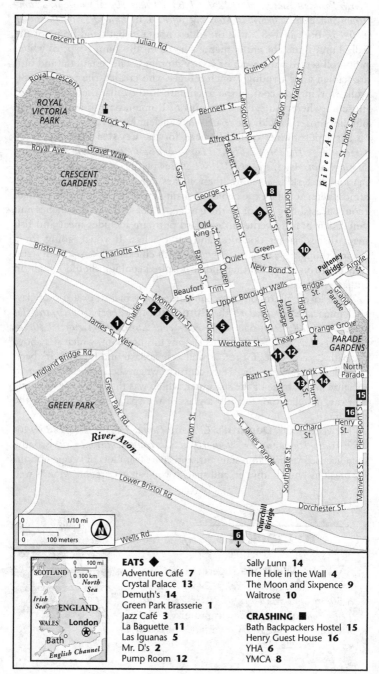

EATS ◆
Adventure Café **7**
Crystal Palace **13**
Demuth's **14**
Green Park Brasserie **1**
Jazz Café **3**
La Baguette **11**
Las Iguanas **5**
Mr. D's **2**
Pump Room **12**

Sally Lunn **14**
The Hole in the Wall **4**
The Moon and Sixpence **9**
Waitrose **10**

CRASHING ■
Bath Backpackers Hostel **15**
Henry Guest House **16**
YHA **6**
YMCA **8**

as organic teas and coffees. Specialties include roasted green olive and vegetable tart with goat cheese (£6.25) and hazelnut-lentil sausages with pesto mash (£9.50).

▶▶SPLURGE

While **The Moon and Sixpence** (6a Broad St.; Tel 01225/460-962; Noon-2:30pm daily, 5:30-10:30pm Mon-Thur, 5:30-11pm Fri, Sat, 6-10:30pm Sun; Entrees £8-14; AE, MC, V) isn't outrageously overpriced, it is a restaurant to eat at only if you're in the mood for a splurge. A truly delightful restaurant, located off Broad Street in a quiet, pebble-stoned nook, this is the place to take that special someone. Eat in the courtyard on a table dressed up with a white tablecloth and candles. Very romantic.

For some hot tamale action—both in the food and the wait staff—head to **Las Iguanas** (12 Seven Dials, Sawclose; Tel 01225/336-666, Fax 01225/311-733; Avg entree £7-10.50; www.iguanas.co.uk; All major credit cards). It's a good place to grab a bite before the theater or cinema, both of which are right around the corner. At dinner, tapas are served with the added excitement of not knowing whether your tequila slammer is loaded with chilies or not. There is a shopping list of different combo deals, some a la carte and some from the bar buffet. A three-course meal is available during the day for only £6. Between 5 and 6:30pm every day, prices are reduced by a pound on most of the menu.

The oldest restaurant in Bath, **The Hole in the Wall** (16 George St.; Tel 01225/425-242; Noon-10pm Mon-Sat; Set two-course lunch £7.50, extra course £3, plus a la carte; Dinner entrees average £15; AE, MC, V) is actually quite lovely. With its clean lines, earth tones, and informal atmosphere, it's a good place to sample an extensive list of cocktails, Belgian beers, and fine wines, but the food is a bit on the fussy side.

The **Green Park Brasserie** (Green Park Station, Green Park; Tel 01225/338-565; Dinner fixed-price menu £9.95 for two courses; All major credit cards) serves Anglo-French cuisine and boasts a wine list with over 40 wines from around the world. During the day, you can have coffee, a snack from the bar menu, or eat a la carte. And in the evenings on Thursdays, Fridays, and Saturdays, local musicians serenade you with live jazz. A good time to visit the Brasserie is for its jazz lunch on Saturdays and Sundays. Overall a good value spot, especially when the music's playing.

crashing

Bath has loads of B&Bs, most of them concentrated on North Parade and Pulteney roads to the east, and Upper Bristol Road to the west. B&B and hotel accommodations can be organized at the Tourist Information Office for a fee [see *need to know*, below]. Since Bath is such a tourist mecca, there are plenty of expensive hotels, most of which are centrally located.

▶▶**CHEAP**

If you're a fan of independent hostels that attract a grungy crowd, and you want to be near the train station, you will be in heaven at the **Bath Backpackers Hostel** *(13 Pierrepont St.; Tel 01225/446-787; Reception open 8:30am-midnight Mon-Fri, 8am-midnight weekends, no curfew; £12 per bed in mostly 6- or 8- bed rooms, £30 single, £20 per person double; stay inbath@backpackers-uk.demon.co.uk).* The hostel has some nice touches: each room is named after a musical genre ("jazz and blues"), and music is usually playing in the downstairs bar and pool room area. The four-story building is covered in colorful murals and the staff has a sense of humor (there's a House Rules sign on the wall in the TV room with instructions for guests of each nationality; Americans, for instance, are instructed to not "talk so loudly," and South Africans are told to "stop bragging about the Rugby World Cup '95"). But if you're into cleanliness, this isn't the place for you. This 60-bed hostel has only three showers and four toilets downstairs (a trek from the bedrooms), and they're not even in the same room. Expect a line for both. The dorm rooms are also not that big, but have a lot of beds in them and can be heated to temperatures that rival the inside of a furnace.

If the thought of a YMCA conjures images of a bunch of leather-clad dancing men with hairy chests, then you'll be surprised upon entering the **YMCA** in Bath *(International House, Broad St. Place; Tel 01225/325-900, Fax 01225/462-065; Open 24 hours daily; £11 dorms; £14 shared triples, twins, or bunk rooms, £13 for two or more nights; £15 single, £14 if two or more nights, includes continental breakfast; £5 refundable deposit for towels; dayinfo@ymcabath.u-net.com; V, MC, AE, DC).* Here, the staff could not be more proper. Luckily, this is not characteristic of the guests. The place feels as clinical as a hospital, but it's clean as a whistle and the prices for single rooms are comparable to regular hostel prices. The restaurant offers cheap food from 7am till 8pm every day, and there is a gym in the building *(Tel 01225/325-913; £3 per session if staying at the Y).* While lacking in any sort of ambience or warmth, the YMCA is an exceptionally good deal.

And finally, there's the ol' reliable **YHA** *(Bathwick Hill; Tel 01225/465-674, Fax 01225/482-947; Bus 18 or 418; Reception open 24 hours; Dorm beds £11 adult, £7.75 under 18; £31 double without bath, £36 with; £51 four-person rooms without bath, £56 with; £2 nightly surcharge non-members; bath@yha.org.uk; V, MC, Delta, Switch).* The hostel is not conveniently located—it's about a mile from the city center—but you're compensated with a wonderful view of the city. Housed in an Italianate mansion, the hostel is clean and provides a lounge with TV, a kitchen, a cafeteria, laundry access, a cycle store, and a foreign currency exchange. Its best feature is the large garden with seating area. English breakfast, packed lunches, and dinners are available.

▶▶**DO-ABLE**

Although not in the prettiest location, the **Henry Guest House** *(6 Henry St.; Tel 01225/424-052; £22.50-25 per person, includes full English* *breakfast; cox@thehenrybath.freeserve.co.uk; No credit cards)* is a stone's throw from the train and bus stations, and a 2-minute walk from the center of town. The eight rooms share three showers and two toilets. Each room has a color TV, as well as and tea- and coffee-making facilities. There is a pay phone in the hallway for guest use.

Dukes' Hotel *(53-54 Great Pulteney St.; Tel 01225/463-512, Fax 01225/483-733; £70-100 double, £120-140 family room, breakfast included; V, MC, AE)* is just a short walk from the heart of Bath. It's set in an elegantly restored building dating from 1780, and many of the original Georgian features, such as cornices and moldings, remain. Rooms, though smallish, are very comfortable, with firm mattresses on good English beds. Guests also relax in the refined drawing room or the cozy bar, where a traditional English menu is offered.

Built in 1789, **Laura Place Hotel** *(3 Laura Place, Great Pulteney St.; Tel 01225/463-815, Fax 01225/310-222; £68-88 double, £110 suite, breakfast included; V, MC, AE)* won a civic award for the restoration of its stone facade. Set on the corner of a residential street overlooking a public fountain, this very formal hotel has been artfully decorated with antique furniture and fabrics evocative of the 18th century. The rooms are medium-sized and very comfy and cozy, with small but well-equipped private bathrooms.

▶▶SPLURGE

Set on 7 acres of landscaped grounds, **Bath Spa Hotel** *(Sydney Rd., east of the city, off A36; Tel 01225/444-424, Fax 01225/444-006; £174-204 double, Sun-Thur, £219-31 Fri, Sat; £264-354 suites for two Sun-Thur, £289-369 Fri, Sat; www.bathspahotel.com, fivestar@ bathspa.u-net.com; V, MC, AE, DC)* is a stunningly restored 19th-century mansion. Rooms are handsomely furnished and plush without sacrificing country charm. Many rooms have old-fashioned four-post beds, and all have magnificent marble baths complete with deluxe toiletries. There are two fabulous restaurants on-site: Vellore, which serves excellent continental cuisine, and Alfresco, which offers a Mediterranean-style menu and garden seating in summer. There is also, as you might guess, a full health and leisure spa on the premises.

WITHIN 30 MINUTES

"Bury" is the derivation of the Saxon word meaning "fortification," and **Silbury Hill** (30 miles from Bath) was the largest manmade object in prehistoric Europe. Built 4,750 years ago, it took longer to build than Stonehenge. At a height of 130 feet, it looks just like a big mound to the naked eye, but hidden under the mud and grass is a six-tiered, chalk pyramid supported with timber frames. Why it was built and what it was used for remains a mystery, but the complex support structure suggests knowledge of engineering that is not expected of Neolithic people. Silbury Hill is located about 1 mile from the Avebury stone circle, and the Cherhill White Horse is right by the main road (A4) about 5 miles to the west of Avebury. There is regular daily bus service from Salisbury to

Avebury via Marlborough. If you have a car and want to drive, head out of Bath on the A4 going through Box, Chippenham, and Calne before reaching Avebury.

As long as you're in the car, you might want to go to **Cherhill White Horse,** although this isn't something to go out of your way to see. Located about 5 miles (a 5-minute drive) from Silbury, the 140-foot-long Cherhill White Horse was carved into the white chalk of the Wiltshire downs in 1780 by Dr. Christopher Alsop. There are a few of these white horses around Wiltshire, but this is one of the oldest and largest. The Cherhill White Horse stands next to **Landsdown Monument,** an obelisk erected in 1845 by Lord Landsdown, purportedly to commemorate the life of his cousin, Sir William Petty. (But Landsdown "accidentally" named it the Landsdown Monument after himself.)

need to know

Currency Exchange You can exchange money at the major banks in town or use your ATM card at a cashpoint (located inside and/or outside the banks). You'll find **Barclays** *(Westgate and Manvers Sts.)* and **Lloyds** *(Lower Borough Walls and 23 Milsom St.),* among many other banks.

Tourist Information The main tourist office is located at **Abbey Chambers** *(Abbey Church Yard; Tel 01225/477-101; Open daily all year; tourism@bathes.co.uk)* and offers tour tickets, maps, guides, and souvenirs. The staff will help you make hotel reservations for £2.50 plus a 10 percent deposit.

Public Transportation The bus station is off Manvers Street, very close to the train station. Buses in Bath are run by **Badgerline** *(Tel 01225/464-446)* and a trip around town averages £1 to £2. Or, buy a weekly ticket for £9.40. The bus station is close to the town center, so you'll have no trouble getting there on foot.

Health and Emergency **Royal United Hospital** *(Combe Park; Tel 01225/428-331)* is located 2 miles west of the city. Emergency: *999.*

Pharmacies Pick up your pharmaceuticals at **SAP Bowrey** *(87 Bradford Rd.; Tel 01225/833-640; 9am-6pm Mon-Fri, 9am-1pm Sat).*

Telephone City code: *01225.* If you're looking for a public phone, you will more than likely find one on North Parade.

Trains The Bath Spa train station is located at the south side of Manvers Street. Trains leave London Paddington daily once an hour, and the trip takes about an hour and 45 minutes, from there on to Bristol *(National Rail inquiries, Tel 0345/484-950).* The train station is close to the town center, so forgo the taxi and bus service. It's cheaper and quicker to walk.

Bus Lines Out of the City **National Express** *(Tel 0990/808-080)* coaches leave London Victoria every 2 hours daily and the trip takes about 3 hours. The Bath bus station is just a few steps from the train station. For exploration to nearby Glastonbury, Wells, Bristol, etc.

buy an adult day Explorer ticket (£5.30) from First Badgerline & City Line, which will save you a lot on individual tickets and is good for unlimited trips throughout the day.

Bike/Moped Rental Avon Valley Cycle Shop *(Tel 01225/442-442; 9am-5:30pm daily; Avg £14 per day)* is located behind the train station.

Postal There is a post office on High Street right before the junction where Broad Street branches off to the left.

Internet See *wired,* above.

everywhere else

lacock

About 12 miles southeast of Bath, Lacock is a small, picturesque village made up of four short streets that adjoin one other in a quintessentially English manner: by a pub. Besides that, there's a bakery, a post office, and a general store. The town is easy to take in during an afternoon, so you're best off making it a day trip from Bath. So why bother? Lacock is probably the most untouched, authentic old town you'll find in England. And they're doing their best to keep it that way: Lacock is almost entirely owned by the National Trust, and you can only live here if your ancestors did, or if you work in the area.

There are two sites of note in the town: the tithe barn and the blind house. Built in the 14th century, the tithe barn was used as a storage place for the one-tenth of the local grain that was collected to pay taxes. The blind house was used to lock up people who were unruly and "blind drunk" (hence the name). Parts of the BBC version of Jane Austen's *Pride and Prejudice* were filmed here.

Definitely try to have lunch at **The George Inn** (*4 West St.; Tel 01249/730-263; 10am-2:30pm/5-11pm Mon-Fri, 10am-11pm Sat-Sun; £3-12 entrees and lunch fare; MC, V*), the oldest pub in the village. Opened in 1361, it still has an original dog wheel, once used for spit-roasting. (The dog wheel wasn't used for roasting dogs. Rather, a dog was tethered to the center of the wheel and made to run, which turned a spit and made sure that the roasting meat cooked evenly.) There is also a big seating area outside the back entrance with benches.

Or go to **The Red Lion** (*The High St.; Tel 01249/730-456; 11am-2:30pm/6-11pm daily; Entrees £5.95-7.50*). Its main claim to fame is that it appeared *Pride and Prejudice*. They are also known for their homemade savory pies: steak and kidney, chicken and ham, beef and Stilton, and others. All desserts are homemade except ice cream.

need to know

Tourist Information There isn't a tourist office here, but in Bath you can request info on Lacock.

Directions and Transportation There are no trains or buses to Lacock, so you'll either have to get on an organized tour [see **Bath**] or hire a car. From Bath, take the A4 about 12 miles to the A350, then head south to Lacock. Another option is to book a mini-cab in Bath. The trip between Bath and Lacock costs about £18 each way, which could prove economical if you're traveling with a group.

castle combe

If you thought Lacock was quaint and pretty, you will not believe Castle Combe, the most southern—and most heavily touristed—Cotswold village. The village, which consists of only one street, has not changed its appearance in about 200 years. To understand this fully, go into the post office at the top of the street and look at an old postcard picture of the town. Then step outside and look down the street. Apart from the real-life version being in color, it is exactly the same. There are no businesses other than a few guest houses, B&Bs, and small souvenir shops. The castle itself has long since vanished. All the buildings, constructed in toy-town proportions, are made of mellow limestone with sloping roofs and flowers growing out of the stones. Sitting in the bottom of a small valley, the whole village looks as if it is being hugged by the hills. At the bottom of the street is a stream with a bridge over it where you can lean over and watch brown trout jump. This activity passes as entertainment in Castle Combe. Visiting Castle Combe is about drinking in the beauty of the village, which to many inhabitants and visitors alike is the prettiest in all of England.

The village got its name in the 11th century when a castle was built over the Combe (the Saxon word for valley). The castle was home to the lords of the land, and after it was destroyed in the 14th century, the Manor House was built for the baronial family. Over the years, the Manor House fulfilled a variety of functions, including serving as a hospital during World War II. Today it provides exclusive accommodations to travelers in its current incarnation as the **Manor House Hotel** *(Tel 01249/782-206, Fax 01249/782-159; £120-350 double, all rooms en suite; enquiries@manor-house.co.uk, www.manor-house.co.uk; MC, V, AE, DC)* and it is the place to stay if you're a mega-punter.

need to know

Tourist Information Not even a chance! Get info in Bath, at the tourist office there.

Directions and Transportation Castle Combe makes a nice day trip from Bath or Lacock (just be sure to pack a lunch). Like Lacock, there are no public trains or buses, so to get here you'll either have to take an organized tour [see **Bath,** above] or hire a car and take the A46 north 6 miles to A420, then head east to Ford following the signs north to Castle Combe. From Lacock, take the A350 north to Chippenham, then get on A420 west and follow the signs.

EXMOOr National Park

Exmoor is a bit smaller than Dartmoor National Park, covering 692 square kilometers (267 square miles), two thirds of which is in the county of Somerset and one third in Devon. Stretching from the **Brendon Hills** in the east, to **Combe Martin** in the west, the plateaus on the moor end up at England's tallest cliffs, which overlook the **Bristol Channel** coast. Inland, herds of wild ponies and red deer roam the grassy moorland, surrounded by wild purple heather and intersected by deep wooded valleys, known as combes.

Some of the sites and monuments in the park date back to the Bronze Age, including burial mounds and stone circles. There are Iron Age hill forts here as well, along with Roman fortlets, medieval castles, an ancient "clapper" bridge, farmsteads, and even some rural industrial sites.

Lynton and **Lynmouth** are the two largest settlements in the park, filled with traditional stone and slate buildings and a few ornate Victorians. The park has a wide range of routes to explore, from long-distance walks to nature trails to designated cycle and horseback trails. Fishing for salmon and trout in the fast-flowing rivers is also popular here.

Any time of year is good for visiting the park, but spring and autumn are sublime, as you can walk for miles and not see anyone else, then end your solitary day next to a roaring fire in a sociable local pub.

A particularly interesting walking route is the **Two Moors Way** *(www.devon-cc.gov.uk/prow/twomoors),* a 102-mile (163km) walk between **Ivybridge** on the southern edge of Dartmoor and Lynmouth on the north coast of Exmoor. The walk links both national parks, crossing from north to south, and passing through moorland and wooded terrain, as well as the unspoiled rural territory between the two. The distance makes it an ideal week-long expedition, with stops at park towns along the way.

Pick up a copy of the excellent and free *Exmoor Visitor* newspaper for information on everything to do in the park, including accommodation listings, activities, events, important numbers, write-ups of the towns, news, and a map. The leaflet *Now You're Really Walking (www.devoncc. gov.uk/prow/routes/)* lists the multitude of walks in Exmoor, a lot of them linking to the Two Moors Way.

crashing

For help finding guest-house, farm, or B&B accommodations, contact **Elaine Goodwin** *(Tel 01398/331-400, lodfin.farm@eclipse.co.uk)*, who runs the Exmoor Holiday Group out of her house. For low-cost hostel accommodation with a twist, there are camping barns with communal living and sleeping areas, cooking facilities, eating areas, toilets, and hot showers. The barns come equipped only with wooden bunks, so you need to bring your own sleeping bags. One such barn is **Woodadvent** *(Near Rockwater; Tel 01200/428-366; £3.75 per person)*, which is situated on a working sheep and beef farm near the village of Rockwater and was converted from the original farmhouse and cider barn. Woodadvent has two separate 12-person sleeping areas, each of which has a wood-burning stove and barbecue pit. From this site, there are four farm trails you can take to explore the area, and Rockwater is within walking distance. Near Dulverton, **Northcombe** camping barn *(Tel 01200/428-366; £4.50 per person or £60 for sole use per night; Up to 15-person capacity)* has been converted from an old water mill into two separate sleeping barns. You can also camp in the field behind the barn.

need to know

Tourist Information There are numerous village information agencies and five visitor centers *(www.exmoor-holidays.co.uk)* across the park: **Dulverton** *(Fore St.; Tel 01398/323-841; 10am-5pm daily Apr-Oct, limited winter opening; dulvertonvc@Exmoor-nationalpark.gov.uk)*, **Dunster** *(Dunster Steep; Tel 01643/821-835; 10am-5pm daily Apr-Oct, limited winter opening)*, **Combe Martin** *(Seacot, Cross St.; Tel/Fax 01271/883-319; 10am-5pm daily Apr-Sept, till 7pm at peak times, open mornings Oct)*, **Lynmouth** *(The Esplanade; Tel 01598/752-509; 10am-5pm daily Apr-July, Sept, Oct; 10am-6pm daily Aug, limited winter opening)*, and **County Gate** *(A39 Countisbury; Tel 01598/741-321; 10am-5pm daily Apr-Sept; 10am-4pm Oct)*.

You can also get information at the **Exmoor National Park administrative offices** *(Exmoor House, Dulverton, Somerset; Tel 01398/323-665, Fax 01398/323-150; 8:30am-5pm Mon-Fri; info@ exmoor-nationalpark.gov.uk, www.exmoor-nationalpark.gov.uk)*, in the southwest corner of the park.

Directions and Transportation There are many interesting bus routes to take through Exmoor, one of which is the **North Exmoor Visitor Bus** *(Three buses daily, 9:15am-6:30pm Mon-Sat May-Sept; £3)*, which leaves from Bancks Street in Minehead and does a scenic loop via Dunster, Timberscombe, Wheddon Cross, and Exford. Since there are a few buses operating during the day, you could have a walk or a pub lunch in whichever village you fancy, and then get back on another bus to go home. Pick up a copy of the *Exmoor by Public Transport Guide* at any one of the TICs listed above.

Trains serve Barnstaple, Exmoor's western gateway, from **Exeter St. David's** *(1-hour trip every hour; £10.10)*. You can reach Minehead,

EXMOOR NATIONAL PARK

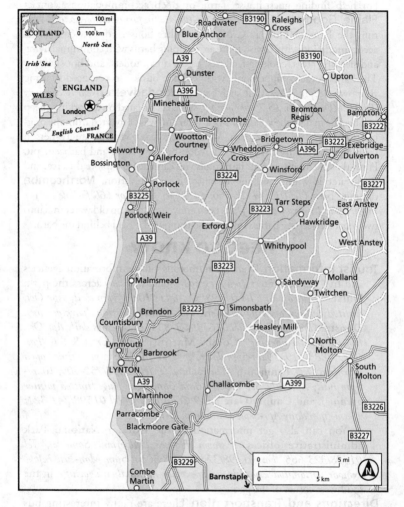

Exmoor's eastern gateway, by **Southern National** *(Tel 01935/476-233)* bus from Taunton. To get to Taunton, take the train from Exeter *(25 minutes; £7)*. Call **British Rail** *(Tel 08457/484-950)* for schedule and fare information.

STONEHENGE

Stonehenge, one of the most famous prehistoric structures in the world, has survived 500 years of wear and tear, including stones that have fallen, or been stolen to build houses and repair roads. But it was almost destroyed a few years ago by the British government, when the English Heritage decided to turn it into a $300 million theme park with a 3000-car parking lot and a huge visitor center with shops, restaurants, and a monorail to the stones. Fortunately a massive public protest put a halt to the plans and the ancient monument still stands isolated on the chalk downs in the flat **Salisbury plain,** in the middle of nowhere. Well, sort of: There is a huge parking lot and a highway leading up to it, but it's still beautiful and striking, even though the noise from passing cars makes it hard to get into a serene spiritual state.

Stonehenge was a spiritual center in prehistoric times and the focal point in a landscape filled with prehistoric ceremonial structures. The construction and development spanned a period of 1,500 years and was done in three main building stages. It remains a mystery how the people of the Stone and Bronze Age managed to bring the large stones to the site—a distance of 18.5 miles (30km) from the **Marlborough Downs**—and then lifted them into formation. It is widely thought that they moved the stones, which weigh up to 45 tons each, along the fields with wooden rollers. Once the stones reached the edge of the pit where they were to stand, they were levered into position by stone hammers buried around the base. It has been estimated that it would have taken 600 people a year to move one stone. The smaller Bluestones that sit inside the structure come from the Preseli Mountains in Wales, which are 239 miles (385km) away. The stones at Stonehenge were "dressed," which means they were battered into shape, so their appearance is more smooth and finished.

The design of the stones is widely thought to be in accordance with certain astronomical alignments. For instance, the main entrance is in the northeast, aligning with the sunrise on the summer solstice. During the summer solstice, the sun shines along the Avenue (the short path leading to the stones from the large Heel stone) at dawn and is centered on the so-called Altar stone. No one knows what festivities went on at Stonehenge during the Bronze and Stone Age periods, or the exact date when the Druids began their annual summer solstice celebrations here. Druidic ceremonies continued at Stonehenge up until the late 20th century, and crowds of curious onlookers would turn up to watch the proceedings. In 1984, Stonehenge was placed under the control of English Heritage—the group that wanted to turn it into a theme park—which banned the Druids from the site.

You really do have to see Stonehenge. Don't let the controversy or the parking lot stop you. It is probably smaller than you would expect, but absolutely beautiful, powerful, and unreal.

NEED TO KNOW

Contact Info Tel *01980/624-715*.

Hours/Days Open Stonehenge is open 9:30am-6pm daily Mar 16-May 31; 9am-7pm daily June 1-Aug 31; 9:30am-6pm daily Sept 1-Oct 15; 9:30am-5pm daily Oct 16-23; 9:30am-4pm daily Oct 24-Mar 15; closed Dec 24-26 and Jan 1.

Cost Admission is £4 for adults, £3 for students.

Directions and Transportation Stonehenge is located at the junction of A303 and A344/A360. From Bath, take A36 approximately 10 miles south, then A303 east to Stonehenge. From Salisbury, about 5 miles south of Stonehenge, take A36 northwest to the A303, then head east on A303 to Stonehenge.

Another option is to book a tour from Bath or Salisbury that will take you on a day trip of a bunch of the area highlights, including Stonehenge, Avebury, Lacock, and Castle Combe.

From Bath, **Mad Max Tours** [see **Bath,** above] runs a day trip with a pub stop for lunch. **Danwood** *(Tel 01225/429-381 for Stonehenge-only tour; £25; Tel 01373/465-965 for other tours; £14)* also runs Bath-based minibus tours to Stonehenge, Salisbury, Wells, and Cheddar.

Wilts & Dorset *(Tel 01722/336-855)* sends several buses to Stonehenge from Salisbury daily (depending on demand). You can pick up the bus from town or the train station. The train station is on the western outskirts of town, across the River Avon from the town center. The trip takes about 40 minutes, and a round-trip ticket costs £4.80.

avebury

After you've been zapped by the incredible Stonehenge vibe—but annoyed by the cars and the crowds—head north 20 miles to Avebury. The stone circle there is 16 times larger than Stonehenge, and anyone, even the Druids among you, can enter the circle, walk around, even touch the stones.

The construction of the stone circle at Avebury began about 4,500 years ago and spanned a period of about 300 years. The henge, the ditch that surrounds the stones, was dug out to a depth of 9 meters using deer antlers and shoulder blades of cattle—a task that is estimated to have taken 1.5 million hours of labor. Four entrance points were left, at approximately the north, south, east, and west of the formation. The stones that make up the Avebury circle were brought in from the Marlborough Downs, about 7 miles away. These stones were left "undressed" and, as a result, their wonderful rough texture and shape were left untouched.

Also, unlike Stonehenge, Avebury doesn't appear to have been built in accordance with astronomical alignments. Certain evidence found at Avebury, including the belief that the site lies on the ley line linked to the Beltane sunrise, indicates that this site may have been used for fertility rituals.

There is no formal entrance to the stone circles since they are in a massive public field, so you can go anytime and stay for however long you want.

The Henge Shop *(Tel 01672/539-229, Fax 01672/539-660; 9am-5:30pm daily)* is on the one main road in the town of Avebury, and is a good place to pick up holistic goodies such as dowsing rods and crystals, as well as books to study up on mystical topics.

need to know

Tourist Information Pick up a map and directions from the local **Tourist Information Center** *(Great Barn, Avebury; 9:30am-4:30pm Mon-Sat)*.

Directions and Transportation The most direct way to get to Avebury is to take a car. Avebury is located on A361 between Swindon and Devizes.

If you don't have a car, you can either take a train/bus combo, or book a tour that includes a visit to Avebury. The closest train station is 12 miles away in Swindon, which is on the London to Bath line. Bus 49 runs limited service from Swindon to Devizes and stops in Avebury.

From Salisbury, **Wilts & Dorset** *(Tel 01722/336-855)* runs two buses (5 and 6) three times a day Monday through Saturday, and twice on Sundays. The trip takes about an hour and 40 minutes, and costs £4.80 round-trip. Salisbury can be reached from London via Heathrow by a **National Express** bus *(Tel 0990/808-080),* which runs three times a day and is about a 3-hour trip. Trains run from Waterloo to Salisbury over 20 times a day; the trip takes about 1-1/2 hours.

From Bath, **Mad Max Tours** [see **Bath,** above] runs a day trip with a pub stop for lunch.

cheddar

Of course the first thing that comes to mind is cheese, and indeed, the process of making cheddar cheese *was* invented in this tiny town. But thanks to the limestone caves hidden in the **Gorge** (now visitor attractions), there is a lot more here than cheese. We're talking tourists. The town caters so much to the camera-toting crowd that it is like a bizarre little Cheese Land in Disney World—definitely not a place to go if you're on a diet. But if you are ready to brave the throngs for a taste of Cheddar, it's an easy day trip from Bath or Bristol.

The gorge is Britain's largest, splitting the **Mendip Hills** from top to bottom; it's about 1 mile long. It is believed today that the gorge was formed by summer meltwater during the various ice ages over the past 2 million years. Each ice age cut the gorge deeper and further molded its jutting-out planes. The limestone, into which the gorge was cut, was formed 280-345 million years ago. The cliffs on the south side of the gorge are almost vertical and range from 330 feet high (100 meters) to nearly 500 feet high (150 meters) in some places. You'll get a good view from atop the gorge on the circular cliff walk [see *city sports,* below].

CULTUre ZOO

Cheddar Caves & Gorge *(Tel 01934/742-343, Fax 01934/744-637; 10am-5pm May to mid-Sept; 10:30am-4:30pm mid-Sept to Apr; £7.50 adults, £5 students):* Admission to this attraction includes a short bus tour up the winding road of the inland cliffs, and access to other points of interest like Gough's Cave, Cheddar Man, Cox's Cave, Jacob's Ladder and Lookout Tower, and the Gorge Walk. Highlights that shouldn't be missed include **Gough's Cave,** a huge, beautiful cave dramatically lit to showcase its amazing stalagmites and stalactites. The dripping caverns—which look like the build-up of wax on a burning candle—were formed from the summer meltwaters of the last ice age. The tour guides will shine a flashlight high on the ceiling of Gough's Cave and point out bats sleeping there. The bats look like small, black dots, and you would definitely miss them if you didn't know they were there. Inside Gough's Cave is **Cheddar Man,** Britain's oldest complete skeleton (9,000 years old), which you can read all about and examine more closely in the exhibition upstairs. **Cox's Cave** is smaller than Gough's, with the calcite on the rocks that gleam in different colors.

The 1,090 acres of the Cheddar Gorge have been designated a Site of Special Scientific Interest, due to the unspoiled wilderness of grassland, heathland, woodland, and scrub. The Gorge is home to a number of rare plants found only in the Cheddar area, including the Cheddar Pink and Cheddar Bedstraw. And if butterflies are your bag, you'll find an abundance of them here—about 29 different species.

city sports

The 3-mile, circular cliff-top **Gorge Walk** is spectacular. It takes about 1-2 hours and will lead you to the tops of both sides of the gorge. Set in a conservation area, you can get up to the path by walking up **Jacob's Ladder,** a steep staircase of 274 gasp-inducing steps. You'll pass the **Lookout Tower, The Pinnacles** (the highest viewpoint over the Gorge), and the **Black Rock Nature Reserve** along the way. (For a good view of the surrounding area, including the Mendip Hills and Glastonbury Tor, climb up the Lookout Tower, where you can see all the way to Exmoor on a clear day.)

An exciting thing to do in Cheddar is **Adventure Caving** (*Book in office above Gough's Cave; Tel 01934/742-343, Fax 01934/744-637; Several trips daily, 10 people maximum per 1-hour trip; £10 adults*). Led by a caving leader, you'll be outfitted in carabiners, helmet, boilersuits, and Wellingtons (rubber boots). Then, caver's lamp in hand, you will tread deep into a system of "wild" caves beyond the well-lit caverns of Gough's Cave. You'll crawl for a while, lifeline down a 40-foot steel ladder, climb, clip onto a wire traverse, and crawl some more. Terms like "lifelining" and "clipping onto wire traverses" may sound pretty scary, but this expedition is intended to be an introduction to caving and is aimed at beginners (though reasonable fitness and a minimum height of 4'8" are required). You can also book spots at the same office for climbing the rock face and abseiling. Availability for the latter activities depends largely on the weather.

eats

Fat alert: Cheddar is not a good place to visit if you're watching your waistline. The town is stuffed with shops selling all kinds of sweets and goodies. But hey, you're on vacation.

The Cheddar Gorge Cheese Co. (*Tel 01934/742-810, Fax 01934/741-020; 10am-4pm daily, till later in high season; Admission valid all day*) is billed a craft village, but it is really a veritable feast of junk food. First you can watch the famous cheddar cheese being made on the premises by actual cheese makers, and listen to a talk on cheese-making in the little museum. Then you can sample the various cheddars in the store next door. There is also a fudge maker, lace maker, candle maker, spinner, cider jar maker, and potter, all of whom you can watch working and, if appropriate, sample their wares. In the pottery store, you can throw your own small pot for £1.50 with the *Ghost*-style help of the potter. Cider is also big in Cheddar, and a store inside the complex offers tastings.

If you're not too nauseated after all those samples, check out the small **Sweet Kitchen** (*Tel 0193/474-3810 or 0117/978-2074*) off the main road. You can watch sweet batter being pummeled, roasted, and made into bite-sized candies. And for dessert, the Cheese and Cider Barn (on

Cheddar

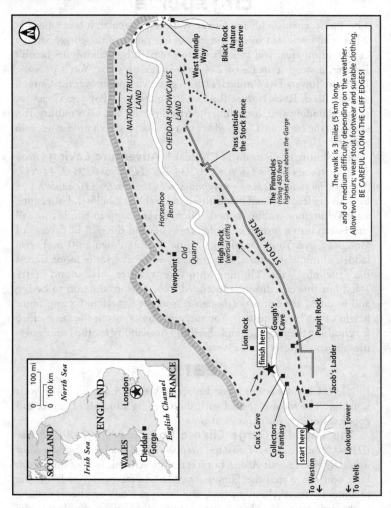

West Mendip Way

Black Rock Nature Reserve

NATIONAL TRUST LAND

CHEDDAR SHOWCAVES LAND

Pass outside the Stock Fence

The Pinnacles (rising 450 feet) highest point above the Gorge

Horseshoe Bend

Old Quarry

Viewpoint

High Rock (vertical cliffs)

STOCK FENCE

Lion Rock

finish here

Gough's Cave

Pulpit Rock

Jacob's Ladder

Cox's Cave

Collectors of Fantasy

start here

Lookout Tower

To Weston

To Wells

The walk is 3 miles (5 km) long, and of medium difficulty depending on the weather. Allow two hours; wear stout footwear and suitable clothing. BE CAREFUL ALONG THE CLIFF EDGES!

SCOTLAND

North Sea

Irish Sea

ENGLAND

London

WALES

Cheddar Gorge

English Channel

FRANCE

0   100 mi
0   100 km

the main road) serves great ice cream, with or without clotted cream. Although there is a huge variety of flavors to choose from, try the double chocolate, which gives Ben & Jerry's a serious run for the money.

crashing

Cheddar is really only fun as a day trip (Bath, Glastonbury, and Bristol are all within 30km), but if you want to stay over, you can pop into the YHA—it is surprising that Cheddar has one, considering its small size.

There are also a few places on the main road, and the TIC will help you book at no charge.

The **YHA** *(Hillfield; Tel 01934/742-494, Fax 01934/744-724; Reception open at 5pm; open most of year; £10.85 adults, £7.40 under 18; cheddar@yha.org.uk)* has 53 beds spread about mostly two-, four-, and six-bedded rooms. There is day access to the main room, kitchenette, shower, and toilets.

If you can't stomach the thought of yet another hostel, you can also try the **Chedwell Cottage** *(Redcliff St.; Tel 0193/474-3268; Rooms £30 for one person, £19 per additional person; V, MC, AE),* a clean, welcoming, 200-year-old B&B.

need to know

Tourist Information Located on the main drag, right in the middle of all the shops, is the **TIC** *(Tel 01934/744-071, Fax 01934/744-614).* The staff is exceptionally helpful and will advise you on bus connections out of Cheddar, as well as sights, accommodations, and history. Here you'll also find a lot of literature on things to do and see in the area.

Bus Lines Out of the City From Bristol take a bus from the main bus station to Weston Super Mare (it takes just under an hour), and from there catch the **First Badgerline** *(Tel 01934/621-201 or 0117/955-32-31)* 126 or 826 to Wells, which goes via Cheddar (takes about 25 minutes). From Bath, take a bus to Wells, via Cheddar. Buy an adult day Explorer ticket (£5.30) from **First Badgerline & City Line** *(Tel 01934/620-122),* which will save you a lot on individual tickets and is good for unlimited trips throughout the day.

WOOKEY HOLE CAVES

Two miles east of Wells lie the **Wookey Hole Caves.** These are spectacular, extensive caverns carved by the **River Axe,** which flows through most of the caves. Don't miss the **Witch's Parlour,** the largest unsupported rock dome in Europe. Exploration of the caves began in 1914, and only 25 caverns have been explored to date: Much of the site is under water, and diving techniques have just recently become sophisticated enough to allow for deeper exploration. Nobody knows how many more caverns are still waiting to be discovered.

The admission fee to the caverns also covers the 19th-century paper mill, where you can watch paper being made by hand—a 400-year-old tradition here—and even make it yourself. Cotton, denim, and hemp are pulped to make the paper, which is then hung on cow-hair ropes—strung one above the next and tied between rafters—in the 19th-century drying loft which is still in use today. Other attractions in Wookey Hole include an assortment of Edwardian amusements: a mirror maze, distorting mirrors, and a vintage penny arcade.

need to know

Contact Information Tel: *01749/672-243;* e-mail: *witch@wookey hole.demon.co.uk;* on line: *www.wookey.co.uk.*

Hours/Days Open The caves are open 10am-5:30pm daily from April to October, and 10am-4:30pm daily from November to March. They're closed December 17-25.

Cost Entrance to the caves is free, but a 2-hour tour will run you £7.20.

Directions and Transportation You can catch bus 171 to Wookey Hole from the Wells Bus Station in Princess Road four times a day Monday through Saturday. Times are as follows: 9:53am Mon-Fri, 10:11am Sat only, 11:11am Mon-Sat, 1:11pm Mon-Sat, and 2:11pm Mon-Sat. Wookey Hole is just 2 miles away, and the trip takes about 10 minutes.

glastonbury

When the Glastonbury Festival comes to town, pretty little Glastonbury becomes the grungiest hotspot of the English party circuit. It's also a haven for New Age hippies looking to revel in Old World charm and mystique. There is an age-old belief that Glastonbury is the fabled isle of Avalon. And according to Celtic mythology, it is the Island of the Blessed Souls and the resting place of King Arthur and his second wife, Queen Guinevere.

But wait, there's more! There's also the myth that Joseph of Arimathea brought the Holy Grail, containing Christ's blood, here. As a result, throughout the Middle Ages, Glastonbury was a major center of pilgrimage and today is the hub of all things holy as well as holistic, earning its reputation as the "Holiest Earthe in England."

But all you *really* need to know about is the three-day **Glastonbury Festival** *(Worthy Farm, Pilton, 8 miles from Glastonbury; Tel 01458/832-020; www.glastonburyfestivals.co.uk; advance tickets only)*, perhaps the most famous and popular of all the arts festivals in England. It features about 1,000 music acts, circus arts, mime, and theater, and attracts people from all over the world. Young, party-loving people flock here by bus, train, and car from all over, so book accommodations early. Fatboy Slim and Nine Inch Nails were among those on the 2000 playbill.

Sorry to say, the 2001 festival has been cancelled, due to rowdy gatecrashers at last year's festival (it's that kind of place). But you need to buy a ticket well in advance anyway, so start saving up for 2002!

culture zoo

Glastonbury has plenty of historic buildings and ancient sites, all within easy walking distance of one another.

Glastonbury Abbey *(Magdalene St.; Tel 01458/832-267;*

9:30am-6pm (or dusk, whichever comes first) daily; £2.50): The site of the first Christian church in England, the abbey is allegedly the home of King Arthur's tomb. Once one of the wealthiest and most prestigious monasteries in England, it was destroyed under Henry VIII, but the remaining ruins, circa 12th-13th century, are spectacular.

Glastonbury Tor: Southeast of Glastonbury Abbey is a 525-foot hill that has been deemed sacred since ancient times. A place of Christian pilgrimage since the Middle Ages, St. Michael's Tower, on the summit, is all that remains of a 14th-century church. To get to Glastonbury Tor, turn right at the top of the High Street, and continue up to Chilkwell Street. Turn left onto Wellhouse Lane and take the first right up the hill. The hike up will take you about 45 minutes, but in summer there is a Glastonbury Tor bus that costs 50p.

Chalice Well *(Chilkwell St.; Tel 01458/831-154; 10am-6pm daily, Apr-Oct; 11am-5pm daily Nov, Feb, Mar; Noon-4pm Dec, Jan; www.chal icewell.org.uk):* The allegedly healing waters of the well tie together all the myths surrounding Glastonbury. It is said to be the ancient red spring of Avalon, and Joseph of Arimathea is purported to have hidden the Holy Grail in its depths. The wellhead is the source of the spring and you can enjoy the healing waters at the old Healing Spa in King Arthur's Court. You'll also find colorful gardens and paths with pretty overhanging greenery.

crashing

If you're going to set up camp for the 3-day festival you may want to try staying at the **The Bear Inn** *(53 High St.; Tel 01458/442021; £63 per night, £70 luxury room, £30 weekends; V, MC, AE).* With comfortable, well-kept rooms and color TVs to boot, it's a solid pick.

The name says it all: **The Divine Light Center** *(15 St. Brides Close; Tel 01458/835-909; £20-25 per person; No credit cards)* is the clear choice for nurturing your inner hippie. This non-smoking, vegetarian B&B helps you connect with the "I AM." Seriously, and most importantly, the welcoming proprietors John and Meredith Flanagan provide comfortable rooms with private baths, TVs, and a self-serve kitchen.

need to know

Tourist Information The staff at the **TIC** *(9 High St.; Tel 01458/832-954, Fax 01458/832-949; 10am-5pm Sun-Thur, 10am-5:30pm Fri, Sat Easter-Sept; 10am-4pm Sun-Thur, 10am-4:30pm Fri, Sat off-season)* will help you make hotel reservations in person but not over the phone.

Bus Lines Out of the City The main bus stop in town is opposite the town hall on Magdalene Street, which is an easy walk from the center of town. There's a daily **National Express** bus *(Tel 0990/808-080)* from London Victoria Coach station at 6:30pm that arrives in Glastonbury at 9:55pm. There are buses every half hour from Monday to Saturday between Glastonbury and Bristol *(Tel 01179/553-231; Buses*

376 and 378), that also stop at Wells (6 miles away) and Street (2 miles away). If you're going to Wells or Glastonbury from Bath, take bus 175, which leaves every hour Monday to Saturday and every two hours on Sunday.

If you plan on visiting Wells, Glastonbury, and Street in one day, make sure to buy a one-day Explorer ticket for about £5.30 on First Badgerline & City Line buses, instead of spending double on individual tickets. You can buy them at the ticket window in the bus station.

devon &
cornwall

devon & cornwall

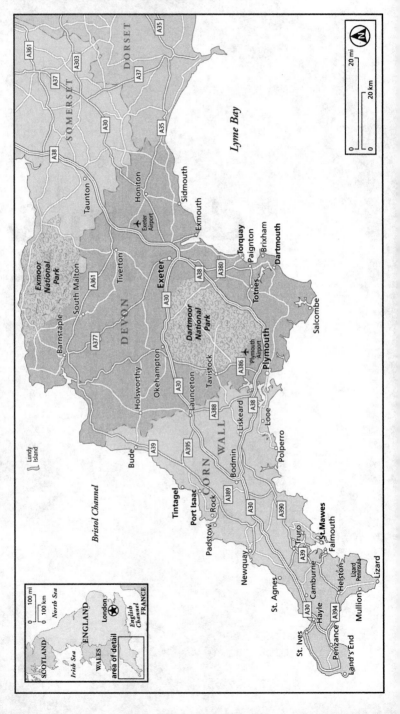

The neighboring counties of Devon and Cornwall share the sensational southwest coast of England. The beauty of both lies inland as well, where the pastoral landscape is covered in sheep, hedgerows (the English love hedgerows), fields of rape (the oddly named yellow flower), and rolling green hills. The hills are so green, in fact, that they look as if they've been colored in by a big green marker. All this natural beauty sound just too boring to be true? Don't worry, there's some nightlife too, mainly in surf-haven **Newquay**. Just keep reading....

What the English call their "Riviera" is the strip down from Torquay, on the southeast side of the country, which includes places like Clovelly and Paignton. But of all the seaside villages to visit, your best bet is **Salcombe**. It's beauty is so mesmerizing that it acts as a magnet for sun seekers along the English coast. Located on a small bay surrounded by an estuary, the sailing boats bob on the calm water and golden patches of beach twinkle in the sun.

The major natural attractions in Devon are its national parks: **Dartmoor** in the southeast and **Exmoor** [see **Wiltshire & Somerset region,** above] on the north coast. Dartmoor's open moorland is usually enshrouded in mist, but when it clears, the scores of prehistoric granite formations peep out, providing the only decoration on this bleak and isolated stretch of terrain. It's not all barren though. Parts of the park have streams running through wooded and boulder-strewn ravines. Lydford Gorge, for instance, boasts the 90-foot White Lady Waterfall.

From seaside entertainment to picturesque villages to ancient churches, Exmoor may have more aesthetic variety, but Dartmoor's flat planes of moor land need to be seen to be believed. The parks are connected by **Two Moors Way,** a walk that winds its way through 100 miles of contrasting countryside.

The two main bases usually used to explore the county are **Exeter** and **Plymouth,** which act as important transportation hubs. Exeter is built high on a plateau above the River Exe, encircled by sections of Roman and medieval walls and remains of the medieval water supply system beneath the city. Exeter's city center is crammed with shops and other amenities of any bustling city. Plymouth is rich in historical sites and naval importance. You can stand on the southern waterfront, known as the Hoe, where Sir Francis Drake finished his game of bowls as the Spanish Armada loomed on the horizon. The Eddystone lighthouse, with its carnival-esque red and white stripes, has been rebuilt on the shore from its previous position 14 miles out at sea. The people of Plymouth loved their lighthouse so much that when the sea threatened to completely destroy it, they had it dismantled stone by stone and moved to its present location on the Hoe. The city is focused around its harbor, as this is the largest naval base in Britain. The Barbican is the old section of town, featuring quaint streets bulging with pubs. If you're in a car, Plymouth is worth a quick stop on the way east.

Cornwall definitely struck it lucky when pieces of land were given out. Covering everything west of Launceton and south of Bude, it is evident when you look at a map why this jutting peninsula is called "the toe." Cornwall has a proud heritage removed from the rest of England. It has its own language, although not much used these days, and the regional foods are served with pride. Cornish cream tea has even been crudely copied in Devon as Devonshire cream tea, and not without a bit of sneering from the Cornish. Food is a big deal in this part of England—especially seafood and clotted cream. At first, this may seem an odd combo, but in a restaurant if you order crab followed by a dessert that causes your arteries to recoil in horror, you'll be tempted to take up permanent residence in Cornwall. And if you clean your plate, the Cornish people will be ready to adopt you as one of their own. There are also more notable seaside spots in Cornwall than in Devon.

You won't want to miss **Polperro,** an old fishing village to the extreme southeast, famous for its smuggling past. It is an enchanting jumble of cottages that resemble ships carved out of stone. This bit of the county has a different feel from the rest of Cornwall in that it's less modern and more like what you would imagine a fishing port of old might have been. **Penzance** is further west down the coastline from Polperro. Everything north of Penzance until you hit St. Ives forms one major chunk of Cornwall that could be explored in one go.

The desolate, awe-inspiring beauty of the coastal drive from St. Ives to **Land's End** (which is literally the end of England) makes the trip seem like a religious experience. The southwestern town of **St. Ives** is an artistic colony with two major museums—the Tate and the Hepworth—and myriad art galleries are hidden in its narrow streets.

St. Ives is also a surfing Mecca, with miles of golden sands, although it is not as well known for surfing as **Newquay,** the self-proclaimed "Surf Capital of Europe." Newquay's claim may stem from its position as the English hot spot on the professional surfers touring circuit. (The World Surfing Championships are usually held here when the UK is the host country.) In Newquay, all your wildest surfing and clubbing fantasies can come true. The beaches are incredible and the clubs almost rival them in size and scope, and the clientele for both take their summer break pleasure time seriously.

For a more genteel Cornish experience, **Rock** and **Padstow,** and the little harbor villages of **Tintagel** and **Boscastle**—all on the north shore—offer a more subdued, sophisticated getaway. The beaches that surround Rock and Padstow are beautiful wide strips of soft sand surrounded by unspoiled, grassy dunes and an estuary where boats are left stranded in the mud at low tide. This area of coast is a great place to explore by foot. Travelers usually start off at a northern point and walk all day south down the coastal path, eventually crashing at the first village they come to when they're too tired to continue. This is a wonderful way to see as much of the coast as possible, as well as a means to check out a bunch of the cute little seaside towns.

The northern coast of Cornwall features the unique Victorian public garden, **Longcross.** Located between Tintagel and Rock near **Port Isaac** (another gorgeous Cornwall bay), this coastal garden has a maze, a "secret garden," little granite fishponds, and fountains among its lush plants and shrubs. It may sound prissy, but it's worth a look, if only because it's so damn *English*.

getting around the region

The best way to get around the Southwest is by train or bus, or a combination of both. Trains are usually quicker, but only one excruciatingly slow railway line runs through the West Country: the London-Penzance route. This line makes stops at all the major cities along the way. Although the extensive bus system might prove more time-efficient and less annoying, the train trip down to Exeter and on to Plymouth is perhaps the most beautiful of all the southern English routes, and certainly worth the extra time. On the other hand, if you don't have a rail pass, the ticket price (£102 round trip, £26-46 one-way) can be crippling to your budget. The trip to Exeter takes about two hours by train (four hours by bus); the journey to Plymouth will take three hours by train (four by bus). The scenery along the way is wonderful, making the journey more than worthwhile.

From Exeter and Plymouth, extensive bus and cab connections will get you to the seaside hamlet of your choice. From Plymouth, take a bus to Salcombe (one hour). From Exeter, take the bus to one of the towns in Dartmoor or Exmoor. From Exeter and Plymouth, there are numerous bus and train connections to the seaside villages of Cornwall, with train stops at Bude, Newquay, St. Ives, Penzance, and Looe, and bus stops at Polperro, Padstow, Rock, Tintagel, and Boscastle.

If you're traveling alone, you might consider taking an organized tour where you'll meet (and hopefully bond with) other adventure seekers. Tours are designed to hit regional hot spots, with accommodations included, and can be an economical option. However, if you have plenty of time and want to get to less tourist-y places, the tours may not be ideal as they don't get to out-of-the-way spots.

A touring company dedicated to adventurous young travelers, **Road Trip** *(Tel 0800/0560-505; bookings@roadtrip.co.uk, www.roadtrip.co.uk; £79)* organizes weekend tours of both Devon and Cornwall. The "Devon Retreat" includes Exeter, Dartmoor, a trip on a steam railway, and a "ghosts and ghouls" haunted adventure. The "Cornwall Connection" explores

TRAVEL TIMES

Times by train unless otherwise indicated. *By road.	Salcombe	Dartmoor National Park	Polperro
Salcombe	-	:35	1:15*
Dartmoor National Park	:35*	-	1:00*
Polperro	1:15*	1:00*	-
St. Ives	2:15*	2:00*	1:25*
Rock	1:40*	1:15*	:50*
Padstow	1:40*	1:00*	:50*
Newquay	1:45*	1:30*	:55*

Newquay down to Land's End, Penzance, and St. Ives. The separate tours leave every Friday from central London and include accommodations. You travel in their "funky" minivans, equipped with TVs and VCRs to get you through the boring patches.

▶▶**ROUTES**

For exploration of Devon from Exeter or Plymouth, simply pick the seaside hamlet of your choice. For instance, from Plymouth, take a bus to Salcombe; or from Exeter, take a bus to one of the towns in Dartmoor or Exmoor.

The quickest route to visit all the Cornish highlights is to take a train from Plymouth to Looes (264 miles from London, 20 miles from Plymouth, via Liskeard) and then a bus or cab to Polperro. From there, go back to Looe, where you can catch the main rail line to St. Ives (319 miles from London, via St. Erth). From St. Ives, head on to Newquay by train (via Par) or by bus. From Newquay, there are buses to Padstow and Rock

St. Ives	Rock	Padstow	Newquay	London
2:15*	1:40*	1:40*	1:45*	4:05*
2:00*	1:15*	1:20*	1:30*	3:45
1:25*	:50*	:50*	:55*	4:35
-	1:10*	1:00*	:45*	5:20*
1:10*	-	:20*	:35*	4:40*
1:00*	:20*	-	:25*	4:45*
:45*	:35*	:25*	-	8:50*

(about an hour's trip). Buses to Tintagel and Boscastle run on the Bude to Wadebridge route, where you can also connect to a bus to Padstow. Train and bus schedules vary according to season, so pick up a copy at the stations.

The most efficient route for all the Cornish highlights is to take a train from Plymouth to Looe and then a bus or cab to Polperro. From there, go back to Looe, where you can catch the main line to St. Ives, and then Newquay (via Par), or take a bus between St. Ives and Newquay. From Newquay, there are buses to Padstow and Rock, and buses to Padstow and Rock between Bude and Wadebridge.

newquay

Newquay is known as "The Surf Capital of Europe," but if you're not a surfer, it won't take long until you will wish you were. Apart from the beaches, which are gorgeous, the town of Newquay is not much to look at. But it's loaded with bars and clubs and is definitely the place to party—even if you couldn't hang ten if your life depended on it. So if you need a break from English culture and sophistication, head here for some good, old fashioned, no-frills hedonism.

Pick up a copy of *Woz On* for £1 at the TIC [see *need to know*, below] for a detailed rundown on what's happening in Newquay's hotspots.

neighborhoods

Manor Road, which turns into **East Street** and then **Cliff Road,** is the main drag in town. A lot of the backpackers and surfing lodges are in the triangle between **Tower Road** and **Fore Street,** since it's a stone's throw from the major surfing spot, **Fistral Beach.** Other beaches in **Newquay Bay** are **Towan, Great Western, Tolcarne, Lusty Glaze,** and **Porth.**

Where to hang out? As if you had to ask. **Fistral Beach,** baby. Whether you're a surfer or just hoping to catch a glimpse of a Kelly Slater look-alike, this is *the* place. There are other beaches in Newquay, but this is the famous one. (The other beaches are quieter and more family-oriented.) Even in the pouring rain, the surfers are out in full force, bobbing on the waves while the drops come pelting down.

bar scene

The **Walkabout Inn** *(The Crescent; Tel 01637/853-000; open till 2am daily; www.walkaboutinns.co.uk)* is the laid-back, fun-lovin' Australian pub chain in the UK. Serving Aussie beers, wines, and regular pub food, this particular Walkabout has a spectacular view over Towan Beach below. The split-level design features small tables and chairs on the top floor and benches downstairs. There are TVs everywhere, including one giant screen, showing sports.

A typical surf bar–hopping expedition would begin at **The Red Lion** [see *eats,* below] for some warm-up rounds. Then head further down Fore Street to **The Sailor's Arms** *(11-17 Fore St.; Tel 1637/872-838, Fax 01637/852-497; 11am-11pm Mon-Sat, noon-10:30pm Sun).* When you're ready to move on to some hard-core bar action, **Sailors** *(service info same as The Sailor's Arms)* is next door and has a total of 4 bars as well as 24 video screens to get hypnotized by.

live music scene

The **Walkabout Inn** [see *bar scene,* above] has live bands on Friday, Saturday, and Sunday. They're usually traveling acts, including international rock groups. There's also a soloist (a guitarist who sings) on Monday through Thursday nights.

Another pub featuring local rock bands and lots of TVs is the **Newquay Arms** *(16 Bank St.; Tel 01637/878-887; summer 11am-11pm Mon-Sat, noon-10:30pm Sun; No cover),* in the heart of Newquay. This one also has a DJ every night and is packed during the day with

wired

There is a little cyber cafe, aptly named **Cyber Surf @ Newquay** *(2 Broad St.; Tel 01637/875-497; 10am-10pm daily; cybersurfnewquay@hotmail.com; 10p per minute),* across from the Somerfield supermarket car park. This is not a place to linger, however, as the rates are not cheap. There's also Internet access with better rates at **Emoceanl Surf** *(2 Gover Lane, near Towan Beach; Tel 01637/851-121; 9am-6pm daily; emoceanl@emocean.screaming.net; 5p per minute, No minimum charge).*
www.newquay-online.com: Dedicated to all things surfing related, from pics of Newquay surfer Russell Winter (both on the waves and with his shirt off), to info on booking summer classes online or designing your own custom-made board.

newquay

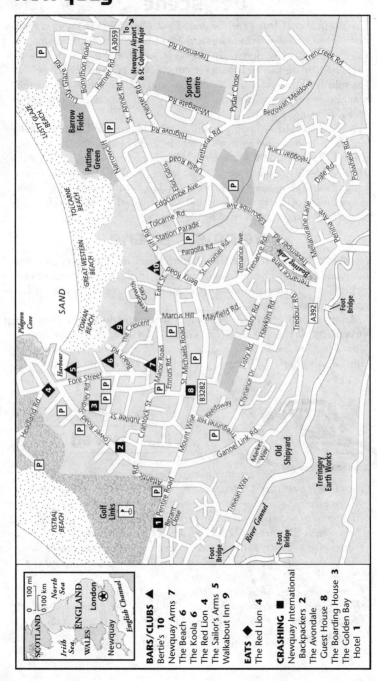

A3059
To Newquay Airport & St. Columb Major

Trencreek Rd

Trevenson Rd

Sports Centre

Bedowan Meadows

Pydar Close

Treloggan Lane

Dale Rd

Polwhele Rd

Penina Ave

Mellanvrane Lane

Trevemper Rd

Foot Bridge

A392

Tredour Rd

Old Shipyard

Treringey Earth Works

River Gannel

Foot Bridge

Foot Bridge

Trevean Way

Market Way

Gannel Link Rd

Treninnick Hill

Reedsway

Mount Wise

B3282

Chyniance Dr.

Hawkins Rd

Listry Rd

Trenance Rd

Trenance Lane

Boating Lake

Trenance Ave.

St. Thomas Rd

Berry Road

East St.

Mayfield Rd.

Marcus Hill

St. Michaels Road

Emnors Rd.

Manor Road

Jubilee St.

Crantock St.

Tower Road

Sydney Rd

Fore Street

Beach Rd

The Crescent

Trebarwith Cres

The Crescent

Pargolla Rd.

Station Parade

Tolcarne Rd.

Edgcumbe Ave.

Edgcumbe Ave

Cliff Rd.

Ulalia Road

Edward Eliot Gdns.

Narrowcliff

Trethellas Rd.

Hilgrove Rd.

Tretherras Rd.

Whitegate Rd.

Chester Rd.

St. Annes Rd.

Henver Rd.

Bonython Road

Lusty Glaze Rd.

Barrow Fields

Putting Green

LUSTY GLAZE BEACH

TOLCARNE BEACH

GREAT WESTERN BEACH

TOWAN BEACH

SAND

Pidgeon Cove

Harbour

Headland Rd.

Atlantic Rd.

Pentire Road

Bessant Close

Golf Links

FISTRAL BEACH

SCOTLAND
North Sea
Irish Sea
ENGLAND
WALES
Newquay
London
English Channel

0   100 mi
0   100 km

BARS/CLUBS ▲
Bertie's **10**
Newquay Arms **7**
The Beach **6**
The Koola **6**
The Red Lion **4**
The Sailor's Arms **5**
Walkabout Inn **9**

EATS ◆
The Red Lion **4**

CRASHING ■
Newquay International
 Backpackers **2**
The Avondale
 Guest House **8**
The Boarding House **3**
The Golden Bay
 Hotel **1**

young locals and visitors having a couple of pints, eating lunch, or watching sports on the telly. It gets especially crowded on rainy days. During the summer, the 80-seat beer garden is fantastic.

club scene

Newquay has nine clubs, an enormous amount for a town of 30,000. The young people who flock here are die-hard surfers by day, die-hard partyers by night. In general, people don't dress up to go out. It's a very dart-home-after-the-beach, jump-in-the-shower-and-into-your-slightly-more-formal-wear, and dart-back-to-the-club-circuit kind of vibe.

With a capacity of 2200, **Berties** *(East St.; Tel 01637/872-255; Hours vary; www.bertiesclub.co.uk; Cover varies, £3-10)* is the largest, most well-known nightspot in Newquay. There are three clubs within Berties, each featuring a different style of music. *Massive Mix,* held on Saturdays, has the Ultimate Commercial Mix happening in the main club, dance happening in Club 2 and '70s and '80s music in Club 3. Berties appeals to the international surfing crowd as well as the English locals who are hoping to hook some international booty. People don't dress up in Newquay, period, but you can't arrive in your surf duds, either. So, wear some pants that hang past the knee and a shirt with sleeves and everyone will be happy. It would seem that Berties is trying actively to appeal to the lowest common denominator (or there may just be a huge market for moistness here), as on Sunday, it holds a "Miss Wet T-Shirt" contest.

Two clubs are right off Towan Beach, on Beach Road. The music at **The Koola** *(Beach Rd.; Tel 01637/873-415; 7pm-2am; the.koola@virgin.net; No cover)* and **The Beach** *(1 Beach Rd.; Tel 01637/872-194; 9pm-2am Mon-Sat, 7:30pm-midnight Sun; www.beachclubnqy.co.uk; Cover varies, £4 and up)* attracts a slightly more ravey crowd. The Koola is another of the mega-clubs in Newquay, but this one focuses on hip-hop with occasional bouts of party mixes, house, garage, and funk. One of Newquay's newer clubs, The Beach has Ladies Night on Wednesdays, when girls get in free and guys pay £2.

modification

Steve's Tattooing and Body Piercing Studio *(4 Wesley Yard; Tel 01637/872-455),* off Beach Road, is the place to have holes punched and needles stuck into your bod.

city sports

Newquay is the place to "hang 10" and put your "toes to the nose" or whatever else it is one does with the "swell" according to surf lingo. In plain English: This is the place to learn to master the waves or at least improve your skills. Not only will you be able to choose from a variety of surfing schools, but the number of surf shops in town selling wet suits, boards, clothing, and other paraphernalia are reason enough to change Newquay's nickname to "The Surf Shop Capital of Europe."

boy meets surfboard

If you think we're exaggerating the prevalence of the surfing thing, you clearly haven't been in Newquay for long enough. But, if you're a girl who gets off on the thought of bronzed, blonde Adonises, then you might be a tad disappointed when you see the wetsuit-clad crew emerge from the deep blue here. The English are not traditionally blessed as a nation when it comes to natural, glowing looks. Not to say that there aren't fantastic exceptions (Jude Law is English, after all) but, as a whole, you're better off waiting till summer really hits in July and August, when the international hotties arrive in full force.

Reef Surf School *(9 Socotra Dr., Trewoon; Tel/Fax 07071/234-455; www.reefsurfschool.com; lessons from £20 for half day; free transport to and from destination)* is the first school in the UK to offer tandem surfing. How does it work, you ask? Well, picture yourself in the big ocean on a small surfboard (thankfully much wider, thicker, and stronger than standard boards), with the instructor standing behind you. He concentrates on balancing the board (which is the hardest part), so you can haul your ass into a standing position as the board is thrown forward by the weight of the ocean behind you. Hopefully he's very, very experienced. The actual school is about 15 miles inland.

In a stall on Fistral Beach, you can sign up for classes or rent equipment from the **British Surfing Association** *(Fistral Beach; Tel 01637/850-737; Tolcarne Beach; Tel 01637/851-487; May to October; colin@britsurf.demon.co,uk, www.britsurf.co.uk; £20 half-day lessons, £30 full-day lessons)*. Tolcarne Beach, the other location for lessons, is sheltered, making it a good place for beginners to start their surfing careers.

Water World *(Trenance Park; Tel 01637/853-829 info, 853-828 opening times and charges; martin@waterworld.prestel.co.uk, www.newquay waterworld.co.uk)* has a 25-meter swimming pool and a tropical fun pool with twisting water slides, including a 60-meter water flume. After you've had your workout in the pool or the gym, dance, or aerobics studio, head over to the cafe to grab some grub or to the bar to treat your sore muscles to a beer.

If regular surfing doesn't blow your skirt up, what about kite surfing? **Big Air** *(The Extreme Academy, on The Beach, Watergate Bay; Tel 01637/860-840, Fax 01637/860-877; bigair@watergatebay.co.uk)* is located on two and a half miles of sands between Newquay and Padstow, about five miles north of Newquay. Power kiting is one of the fastest-growing extreme sports in the UK and entails attaching yourself to a small parachute that is controlled like a kite. You can then either fly through the air holding the kite device, or surf while holding the kite, or sit in a cart on the beach which can go up to 50mph and hold the kite. It is designed to harness the wind so you can propel yourself forwards at a ferocious velocity.

The **Newquay Trail** is a recommended bicycle path that is part of the **Cornish Way,** a 180-mile long system of trails that wind through the Cornish countryside. Contact local guides Bridie Toft or Cheryl Cooper *(Tel 01832/322-320)* for more info and maps. Maps are also available at the TIC [see *need to know,* below]. Follow the quiet country roads through some gorgeous countryside to **Trerice** (a National Trust house and garden). After making your way through Newquay, you'll end up at the picturesque **Porth Reservoir.** From there you can then go on through **Colan Woods** to Padstow.

STUFF

▶▶SURF GEAR

When Bilbo opened in 1966, it was the first surf shop in Europe. Today Newquay is inundated with surf shops. Although the store does not sell boards anymore, it's still worth going to **Bilbo** *(6 Station Parade; 01637/878-882; 9:30am-5:30pm daily; V, MC)* for other surfing paraphernalia like wetsuits, accessories, and clothes. For boards, try Bilbo's umbrella company, **Boardwalk Surf Ltd.** *(17 Cliff Rd. Tel 01637/878-880, Fax 01637/879-000; 9:30am-5:30pm daily; V, MC).* Shape your own board at **Surfers Workshop** *(7 Toby Way; Tel 01637/871-837; open May-Oct; call for consultation),* off Tower Road, which also does board repairs.

EATS

There aren't any culinary highlights in Newquay. Places that are cheap and quick reign supreme. As a result, there are fast food joints everywhere you look.

Head to the surfing hangout **The Red Lion** *(Tel 01637/872-195; food served daily noon-9pm; most homemade specials less than £6)* at the junction of Fore Street, Tower, and Beacon roads for standard pub fare in terms of selection, but above average in terms of taste. For a healthier selection, try **Wilbur's Café** *(Fore St.; Tel 01637/877-805; hours vary, usually 10:30am-3:30pm; average £2; No credit cards),* just off Beach Road. Grab a homemade sandwich (made fresh each day) and a cheap slice of cake for dessert.

▶▶DO-ABLE

A couple of good options are located on Cliff Road, not far from the train station. **The Maharajah Indian Restaurant** *(39 Cliff Rd.; Tel 01637/877-377 or 01637/877-273, Fax 01637/ 851-900; 5pm-midnight daily; www.maharajah-restaurant.co.uk; entrees £5-9; MC, V)* offers an excellent selection at affordable prices, with chicken, veggie, and seafood dishes, all spiced up the way you like it. The atmosphere is casual-elegant, and the ocean views are so good they're downright distracting. Across the street, the creatively named **Mexican Cantina** *(38 Cliff Rd.; Tel 01637/851-700; 11am-11pm daily, 5pm-11pm off season; www. mexicancantina.co.uk; entrees £5-12)* offers spice of a different kind, from the usual enchiladas, burritos, and ultimate nachos to seafood and more exotic dishes like Tropical Tequila Chicken. Did someone say "tequila?" What's a Mexican restaurant without a tempting selection of fruity beverages (lime, strawberry, banana, and peach margaritas, £3.95, £11.95 for a pitcher)?

crashing

One thing to keep in mind when choosing hostels is that most of the surf lodges are inundated with English surfers and travelers, which can turn them into a bit of a rough scene at times (think Spring Break with a dash of soccer hooligan thrown in). That's why the Newquay International Backpackers only accepts international travelers (but English *surfers* can stay here), to keep the atmosphere more balanced. As far as B&B's and hotels go, there isn't anything special to say about them except that they are abundant. Head to the TIC for booking assistance.

▶▶**CHEAP**

Ray, the guy who runs St. Ives International Backpackers and **Newquay International Backpackers** *(69-71-73 Tower Rd.; Tel/Fax 01637/879-366; backpackers@dial.pipex.com, www.backpackers.co.uk/newquay; free shuttle service for bus, train, and airport; £8 Sep-Apr, £9 May, £10 Jun, £12 Jul-Aug, small dorm rooms, twins, doubles),* is a fantastic host. But the Newquay hostel differs from its St. Ives counterpart in a variety of ways. It is a lot cozier, with a small lounge and bar adjoining the pool room. There is a separate shower room and board store in the back, as well as a dining room next to the kitchen. Everyone watches movies together in the lounge at night or plays Jenga at the bar. Each room is named after a different city or beach, and the doors have been colorfully painted by hostel visitors who paid with their artistic abilities instead of cash. The atmosphere is warm and welcoming. It is a great place to pick up fellow travelers who are looking to bond and have a good time. It's also close to everything, most importantly Fistral Beach; there's an easy trail down to the surf.

A block from Newquay International Backpackers, **The Boarding House** *(4/6 Fernhill Rd.; Tel 01637/873-258; www.theboardinghouse.co.uk; £13 per person weekends May-end Sept and weekdays July and August, £10 during the week May-end Sept, £8-10 per person; includes breakfast and free tea/coffee all day, £3.50 evening meal; V)* is missing that grungy, bohemian feeling—unlike most hostels, it's very clean and offers good amenities. If you're looking for a place to stay but aren't into the communal atmosphere you get in a lot of hostels, this is the place. There is a licensed "Aussie" bar (the lodge is run by Aussie Richard Steel) that serves home-cooked evening meals and breakfasts. Complimentary coffee and tea are available all day.

▶▶**DO-ABLE**

The Golden Bay Hotel *(Pentire Ave.; Tel 01637/873-318; enquiries@gold enbayhotel.co.uk; £18-29 per person according to room and season, special* *during winter and spring £65 per person for four nights bed and breakfast; MC, V)* has twelve rooms with private showers or baths. The rooms are equipped with color TV and clock radio, and some of them have deluxe features such as king-size or four-poster beds. There are lunchtime snacks and bar snacks available at the bar, where you can enjoy (fairly distant) views of Fistral Beach, which is about 200 meters from the hotel. At the back of the hotel is the pretty Gannel estuary, also about 200 meters away.

Offering both basic and luxury rooms all en suite and all with TV, **The Avondale Guest House** *(St. George's Rd.; Tel 01637/872-234, Fax 01637/871-969; mark.philips@virgin.net, http://newquayguesthouse.com; £14-22 nightly per person, £85-120 weekly; accepts most major credit cards),* just off Manor Road, also has a lounge for its guests with color satellite TV and a bar. The staff will make you packed lunches on request.

A 5-minute walk from the Newquay train station, **Sea Shells** *(55 Fore St.; Tel 01637/874-582, Fax 01637/874-582; stokes@seashells36.freeserve.co.uk; from £16 per person depending on season, all doubles, some en suite; no credit cards)* is located at cliff's edge and a short walk from almost everything you need in Newquay. Breakfast is included in the price of the room.

▶▶**SPLURGE**

Tucked in the cliffs above the harbor, the **Harbor House Hotel** *(North Quay Hill; Tel 01637/873-040; alan@harbourhotel.co.uk, www.harbourhotel.co.uk; £31-36 per person depending on season; will pick you up from the rail station; V, MC),* has five rooms, all en suite, all with balconies, and all with views of the beaches and harbor. There is a lounge and a bar in the hotel, as well as a TV lounge with digital television. The rooms are individually decorated with antique beds and have bathrooms with showers. The hotel is a 5-minute walk from the town center, and the closest beach is Towan, a 2-minute walk away.

need to know

Tourist Info The **TIC** *(Marcus Hill; Tel 01637/871-345; 9am-6pm Mon-Sat, 9am-4pm Sun)* has free street maps and postcards and sells the *Woz On* for £1. The staff will help you make hotel reservations for a £2 booking fee.

Health and Emergency Emergency: *999.* **Newquay Hospital** *(St. Thomas Rd.; Tel 01637/893-600)* is located at the end of St. Thomas Road, off Mount Wise.

Pharmacies You'll find two **Kayes** *(East St.; Tel 01637/873-353; 9am-7pm Mon-Fri, 9am-6pm Sat, 10am-12:30pm Sun, daily till 9:30pm in summer* and *Narrow Cliff; Tel 01637/872-957; 8:30am-7pm Mon-Fri, 9am-noon Sat)* branches in Newquay.

Telephone City code: *01637*

Trains There are four trains a day between **Newquay** and **Par** (the offshoot of the London-Penzance line takes about 50 minutes between Newquay and Par, 5-1/5 hours between London Paddington and Par). The train station is off Cliff Road at **Tolcarne Road** in the center of town.

Bus Lines Out of the City Western Greyhound *(14 East St.; Tel 01637/871-871; enquiries@westerngreyhound.co.uk, www.westerngreyhound.co.uk)* provides as many as six buses each week to **St. Ives** (takes two hours), and one or two buses a week to **Padstow** (takes one hour). The bus station is located in the center of town on **East Street,** at the corner of Trebarwith Crescent.

Bike/Moped Rental Newquay Cycles and Bike Hire *(Unit 1, Wesley Yard, between Manor Rd. and Jubilee St.; Tel 01637/874-040 or 874-496, evening Fax 01637/851-600; www.newquaycycles.co.uk; £6 adult half day, £10 adults full day; delivery and pick-up of fewer than 4 bikes for £1)* specializes in Micmo and Dawes cycles. They also offer "cycle safaris" that include a picnic lunch or barbecue.

Postal Send those snaps of you hanging ten from the **post office** *(31-33 East St.; Tel 01637/873-364; 9am-5:30pm Mon-Fri, 9am-12:30pm Sat).*

Internet See *wired,* above.

everywhere else

salcombe

Ex-*Sunday Times* style columnist and London "It" girl Tara-Palmer Tomkinson once called Salcombe "Devon's answer to [France's upscsale] Cap d'Antibes." The sophisticated appeal of Salcombe is evident as you get your first view of the town. The hilltop streets packed with houses form a semi-circle around a glistening bay dotted with sail and power-boats. Picture-perfect, this small bay is engulfed by green, rolling hills and surrounded by little empty beaches. Well, actually, they're only empty till the warm weather hits—then they're as packed with vacationers as the rest of the town. Salcombe offers up some standard beach-town summer-time fun in a truly beautiful setting. Come soak in the rays and the views.

The "industrial area" of town, which is probably the loveliest industrial area you've ever seen, encompasses the section of town between the ice cream factory on Island Street [see *eats,* below] and the boat repair yard. This area was completely mud and water until the 1920s, when houses made of green hornblende stone were constructed on the site. You'll find most of the shops and restaurants in town on **Fore Street,** Salcombe's main street. The harbor is east of Fore and the streets running west of Fore make up the residential section of the small village.

In town, **Robinson Row** (off **Courtenay St.)** is a little path you can walk up to see a row of charming country cottages and flowers. Off Cliff Road and below the war memorial, **Cliff House Garden** is a relaxing spot to hang out and watch the boats in the estuary. The beaches across from the estuary on all sides, including **Small Cove, Mill Bay, Sunny Cove,** and **South Sands,** are easily accessible via ferry.

bar, live music, and club scenes

There are four pubs in town, all spread out on Fore Street, which gets packed in summer when tourists invade Salcombe en masse. The pubs are usually open from 11am till 11pm daily, and till 10:30 on Sundays, unless they have a late-night license allowing them to stay open till 2am.

salcombe

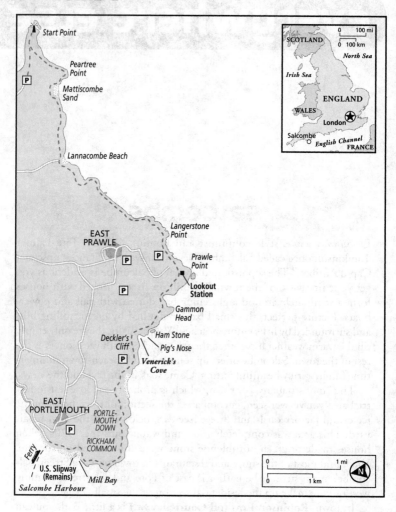

The pub with the most welcoming, comfortable atmosphere is **The Ferry Inn** *(The Ferry Steps, Fore St.; Tel 01548/844-000)*. Three stories high, it features a large waterside beer garden with good ales and pub grub.

The Marine hotel [see *crashing,* below] contains a slightly more expensive piano bar open in the evenings within a comfortable lounge overlooking the estuary. Most people in the hotel are part of the town's geriatric scene, and everyone is dressed to the nines, but the jazz and classical music they play is good enough to entice you for a pre-dinner drink or two. Plus, the view is superb.

For a laid-back, casual atmosphere, go to **Dusters Bistro** *(50 Fore St.; Tel 01548/842-634; closed on Tuesdays),* which has live jazz on Wednesdays and at Sunday lunch. The food is good, too.

The nearest nightclub, **Fusion** *(Union Rd., Kingsbridge; Tel 01548/857-021; double-decker bus service from Salcombe in summer; 10pm-2am Fri and Sat nights all year, Tues and Thurs in July and Aug; www.fusion2.co.uk; jeans OK; over 18),* is in Kingsbridge about 7 miles from Salcombe. The club is loaded with entertainment choices: three bars (one of which is a padded cell), a cyberbar with free Internet access, two small Sony Playstations, a Sega Dreamcast, and of course, dancing. Lots of young party-loving folk hang out here, though during the summer it gets packed with tourists, so it does become a bit of a meat

by foot

At the end of **Island St.,** head uphill on **Church St.** The houses on the right-hand side of the street were built for the area's coastguards, and if you look carefully, you'll see that the houses get smaller as you go uphill. They were designed this way so people always knew where the officer in charge lived: in the big house at the bottom. Continue a bit past the church, walk down the hill, passing the end of **Buckley St.**—whose name means "up above"—and turn right onto **Fore St.** You'll notice that some parts of the street are wider than others. The wide parts are where bombs fell during World War II and destroyed the 18th- and 19th-century buildings that once lined the street. Stop at **Victoria Inn** and look at the ornate old-fashioned water tap next to it. Until the early 1900s, this was one of only three public taps in town. Check out the "fishy" notice above. Now walk back the way you came, along Fore St., until you get to the **Fortescue Inn.** Turn right down **Union St.** to **Customs House Quay.** Opposite the lifeboat shop is the impressive **Customs House,** with a crest over the door. The house next door displays a typical feature of many of those on Fore St.: wooden slots on either side of the front door. These are where "breakwater boards" are inserted, because Fore St. has the tendency to flood during high tides. Walk back toward the Fortescue Inn and turn right under the arch. Notice the old gas lamp on your left, typical of those installed from 1866, when parts of the town first had street lighting. Walk past the quayside houses and back into Island St., but just before you enter, look right down **Thorning St.** at the old stone and wooden-boarded building. The hooks in the wall were once used for hauling in large animals when the building was a slaughterhouse.

market. If you're not in the mood to chitchat, grab a seat in Fusion's DVD cinema (complete with full bar) and catch a late-night cult flick. Or you could watch the fish or bubble tanks that dot the club.

arts scene

The annual exhibition of the **Salcombe Art Club** *(10:30am-1pm/2-4:30pm)* is held in a lovely loft studio by Victoria Quay. Here, a group of practicing regional artists exhibits its work for sale from Easter to October. During the winter, oil, watercolor, and printmaking classes are taught here. There are also occasional workshops and lectures.

culture zoo

The **Overbecks Museum and Garden** *(Sharpitor [see YHA, in crashing, below, for directions]; Tel 01548/842-893; garden 10am-8pm daily, 11am-5:30pm Sun-Fri Apr, July, Sep, daily in Aug, 11am-5pm Sun-Thur Oct; £4 adults, £2.80 garden only):* This is an especially convenient attraction to visit if you're staying at the YHA, as the museum and the hostel are in the same building. The exotic coastal garden overlooking the estuary is filled with sub-tropical plants such as banana, fig, and palm trees. The house within the garden contains Edwardian curios, such as a working 19th-century musical jukebox and an electrical "rejuvenating" machine. (Used in the 1920s and 1930s, this apparatus fed electrical pulses through the body in an attempt to improve circulation and prolong one's active life. Scary.)

modification

If you're in need of a haircut before heading for the action at Fusion, **Nicholas Hair & Beauty** *(Marine Hotel; Tel 01548/843-370)* can fill all your hair and beauty therapy needs. It's also conveniently located in the **Marine Hotel** [see *crashing,* below].

city sports

Name any outdoor sporting activity and you can do it in Salcombe. The **ICC Activity Centers** *(10 Island St.; Tel 01548/843-929; prices vary according to activity and duration)* and **ICC Splash Centre** *(South Sands Beach; Tel 01548/843-451; during July and August; info@icc-salcombe.co.uk, www.icc-salcombe.co.uk)* can set you up in pretty much any water sport, with or without instruction. Dinghy and keelboat sailing, kayaking, power boating, banana rides, donut rides, water skiing, wake boarding, and windsurfing are all available.

Not surprisingly, there are many places to rent or hire a boat in this seaside town. One good option is the **Salcombe Boat Hire** *(Booking office at Salcombe Fishmongers, 11 Clifton Place; Tel 01548/844-475)* for one-hour, four-hour, and daily rentals on self-drive 12-16ft. fiberglass boats. You can also rent Flyers, Dories, Spinners, and Cabin boats to suit your fancy.

For a good workout followed by a bit of pampering, check out the **The Marine** hotel, where you'll find an indoor swimming pool, sauna, spa pool, gym, and massage room [see *crashing,* below].

festivals/cool annual events

Every year in mid-June there are three days of boats and bands, plus a craft fair, skateboard workshop, face painting, juggling, and a range of open-air music events at the harbor in the **Salcombe Festival.** *(Contact the TIC for info on dates and the program—see need to know, below, for info.)* There is also a regatta in August in which all classes of sailing boats, such as Lasers, Salcombe Yawls, Toppers, and Merlin Rockets, compete. Locals and visitors alike take part in the events, which also include homemade raft races, dinghy races, and mud races, (where contestants race through a muddy bit of the estuary).

If a bit of outdoor rambling is more your speed, amble along the gorgeous 8-mile coastal walk between **Mill Bay** (across the bay from Salcombe) and **Start Point.** This path is a section of the longer South West Coast Path that stretches over 594 miles from Minehead to Poole. For a more manageable walk that will give you an exquisite taste of the Devon coastline, take the first two miles of the walk along rugged coastline and unspoiled forest paths. To get to Mill Bay, take the East Portlemouth ferry [see *need to know,* below] across the harbor, and take the ascending coastal route beginning at Mill Beach, with additional patches of beach turning up around every corner. In the warmer months, the path is lined with purple foxgloves and bluebells. When you finish at **Gara Rock,** you couldn't wish for a more pastoral setting to have a drink or lunch than the grounds of the **Gara Rock Hotel** [see *crashing,* below]. Take the forest route, which is a sheltered downhill path through a canopy of trees, back to Mill Bay from the hotel.

eats

Most sit-down restaurants in Salcombe accept all major credit cards, with the usual exception of American Express and Diner's. Dinner usually ends at around 10pm.

▶▶CHEAP

Accompanying the home-cooked snacks and meals at **The Fortescue Inn** *(Union St.; Tel 01548/842-868; noon-2pm/7-9:45pm daily; entrees £3-9)* is delicious, thick, homemade bread. The freshly battered fish is a house specialty in this intimate pub with low ceilings and dark wood furnishings. Although the food isn't the greatest, the value is good.

Move over Willie Wonka—**The Salcombe Chocolate Factory** *(Island St.; Tel 01548/842-260, Fax 01548/843-489; www.chocfactory.com)* sells every chocolate concoction you could imagine. From chocolate scented candles to chocolate-themed greeting cards to 500 grams of solid Belgian

TO MARKET

If you've got a place to cook up some dinner, visit **Salcombe Fishmongers** *(11 Clifton Place; Tel 01548/844-475)* to get fresh, locally caught fish including salmon, trout, shellfish, and squid.

slabs of the stuff. You can continue salivating upstairs in the actual factory, while watching the chocolate spinning and dripping off the machinery. Okay, so maybe it doesn't qualify as a balanced meal, but hey, you're on vacation, right?

Next door to the chocolate factory is the **Salcombe Dairy** *(Shadycombe Rd.; Tel 01548/843-228),* which sells traditional Devonshire ice cream and sorbets. The locally made ice cream is exceptionally creamy, catastrophic for the waistline but orgasmic for the taste buds.

▶▶**DO-ABLE**

Apart from the live jazz on Wednesday and Sunday, **Dusters Bistro** *(50 Fore St.; Tel 01548/842-634; open at 7pm daily except Tuesdays)* is known for its fresh fish, steaks, and vegetarian dishes. It's one of the more popular local hangouts, and has a pleasant, casual atmosphere.

For a perfectly laid-back Sunday evening, head to **Captain Flint's** *(82 Fore St.; Tel 01548/842-357).* This casual, colorful pizzeria has good fresh pastas, Aberdeen steaks, and pies with a wide range of toppings. This is a family restaurant, so you'll see more kids here than in other places.

If you're starving after walking along the Devon coast, **The Gara Rock Hotel** [see *crashing,* below] *(open from 9am-9pm daily; average lunch £4.75)* has a snack and a more substantial menu of lunchtime fare, such as vegetarian pizzas and jacket potatoes with toppings. The tables outside have a stunning view that will take your attention away from the awful food. Or, just have a drink or a cream tea in the lounge/bar inside.

For out-of-this-world Indian and Nepalese food, **Kukri** *(18 Fore St.; Tel 01548/844-233; entrees average £6; all major credit cards)* is the name of the game. It's a hole in the wall with zero atmosphere, but none of that will matter when the food arrives. The naan bread is especially good.

▶▶**SPLURGE**

Owned and run by Sally and Lesley, a spinster and a serial wife respectively, **The Spinster & The Serial Wife** *(Russell Court; Tel 01548/842-189; entrees average £5-14.50; all major credit cards except AE)* is a Salcombe favorite. The menu is varied, serving imaginative and sophisticated red meat, chicken, and fish dishes. The smart crowd here spends a bit more than average on a meal. As a result, it attracts an older crowd, tourists, or locals celebrating a special occasion.

crashing

Try not to land in Salcombe—especially at night—without arranging accommodations first, as it is difficult to find something by just walking around. There isn't a huge selection, and none of the accommodations are cheap compared to those in other towns along the coast. The staff at the TIC can help you book accommodations [see *need to know*, below].

▶▶CHEAP

The **YHA** (*Overbecks, Sharpitor, take ferry to South Sands from Salcombe, 10-minute walk up hill to Overbecks, follow signs for National Trust; reception opens at 5pm; Tel 01548/842-856, Fax 01548/843-865; £9.80 adults, £6.75 under 18)* is set in a pretty National Trust property of sub-tropical gardens. The hostel has one of each of the following: two-, six-, eight-, and fifteen-bed dorm rooms, as well as five four-bed rooms. Breakfast isn't included but there is a dining room with a self-catering kitchen on the premises. The YHA is technically about 2 miles from Salcombe, but taking the ferry over to South Sands beach makes the trip much quicker—the hostel is only a 10-minute walk from the beach.

If you're into camping, try **Alston Farm Campsite** *(Tel 01548/561-260, Fax 01548/561-260, £6-8 for two people in a tent or motor home, showers and WCs on site; no credit cards)*, located two miles south of Salcombe. Take a bus or taxi from the train station [see *need to know*, below].

▶▶DO-ABLE

Run by a lovely couple, Peter and Bernice, **Ria View** *(Devon Rd.; Tel/Fax 01548/842-965, Mobile 0467/665-321; basweet@onetel.net.uk; two doubles, one twin at £24 per person, one shower/bath to share for all three, but a toilet and basin in each room; no credit cards)* is a sweet and comfortable B&B that serves breakfast overlooking the water. Ask Peter to make you one of his delicious cappuccinos. The Green Room has a beautiful view of the town below and the estuary.

The Lodge Hotel *(Marlborough; Tel 01548/561-405, Fax 01548/561-111; info@thelodge.uk.com; all rooms en suite; £25-29 single, £50-58 double)* is conveniently close to the city center and easy to get to from bus and train transportation.

▶▶SPLURGE

As **The Marine** *(Cliff Rd.; Tel 01548/844-444, Fax 01548/843-109; info@menzies-hotels.co.uk, www.menzies-hotels.co.uk; from £65-115 per person depending on season, reduced rates Sun-Thurs; all rooms en suite; V, Switch, Delta, Access)* is the smartest hotel in Salcombe, it appeals to an octogenarian crowd more than anyone else. However, most of the rooms do have wonderful close-up views of the estuary from their balconies, and there is 24-hour room service, a hair and beauty salon, and a gym in the building.

Sitting in a gorgeous position high up on the cliff overlooking the sea is **The Gara Rock** *(East Portlemouth; Tel 01548/842-342, Fax 01548/843-033; take the summer coastal hopper 159 bus from Kingsbridge to Gara Rock; gara@gara.co.uk, www.gara.co.uk; rates vary according to* *season, and whether room is sea-facing or terrace-facing; from £31-44 per person per night; slight discount for stay longer than two nights; V, MC, AE, D, DIN).* This is a good rest stop or ending point on the coastal walk from Mill Bay, across from Salcombe [see *city sports,* above]. If you want to stay here the whole time you're in Salcombe, you can drive here. Coming by road from Kingsbridge, take the A379 towards Torcross and Dartmouth. At the town of Stokenham, turn right and follow the road to East Prawle (it's pretty clearly marked). Before entering Salcombe, turn right and take the road to Gara Rock and East Portlemouth. Bus service will also get you to the Gara Rock.

need to know

Currency Exchange Your banking options in Salcombe include **Lloyds** *(Fore St.; Tel 0845/303-0107; 9:30am-4:30pm Apr-Aug, 9:30am-4:30pm Sept-March, 24-hour ATM)* and **HSBC** *(Fore St.; Tel 01548/446-000; 9:30am-1pm Mon, Wed, Fri).*

Tourist Info Located off the northern end of Fore St., the **TIC** *(Market St.; Tel 01548/843-927, Fax 01548/842-736; 10am-2pm Mon-Wed, 2-5pm Thurs-Sat; info@salcombeinformation.co.uk, www.salcombein formation.co.uk)* is fully stocked with pamphlets and timetables. The staff is happy to assist you in booking accommodations, buses, and trains and providing sightseeing info.

Public Transportation Everything in Salcombe is within easy walking distance.

Health and Emergency Police, fire, ambulance or coastguard: *999* Police direct telephone line: *0990/777-444*

Pharmacies To clean up those surfing injuries, get to **Chris Carpenter Pharmacist** *(25 Fore St.; Tel/Fax 01548/842-293).*

Telephone: City code: *01548*

Airport The nearest **airports** are at **Exeter** *(Tel 01392/367-433)* and **Plymouth** *(Tel 01752/772-752),* which are about five miles from the city center. A taxi from either airport to town should run about £4-5.

Trains The nearest train stations are in **Totnes** (20 miles away) and **Plymouth** (25 miles away). You can take a taxi or a bus from Totnes or Plymouth [see *bus lines out of the city,* below]. There is one, slow train line that runs through Devon and Cornwall, which stops both at Exeter and Plymouth and from there branches off to various south west and southeast destinations. From **Plymouth** to **Paddington** station in London takes about three hours. If you're traveling on the weekend and are planning on buying a one-way ticket, inquire about getting a Weekend First class ticket, which is not that much more than a coach ticket *(£50 as opposed to £44).* The incremental cost is worth it for the additional room you'll have to spread out, the free newspapers, and a free beverage from the dining car. Call **National Rail** *(Tel 0345/484-950)* for rail inquiries.

Bus Lines Out of the City There are three buses a day leaving **Salcombe** for **Plymouth** (one hour ride), where you can catch a train or another bus to a number of destinations in southern England. Pick up a schedule from the TIC. A one-way bus ticket between Plymouth and Salcombe is £3.70. Alternatively, you could take a taxi to Plymouth, which costs about £32. If you're traveling in a group of five, this is a good value.

Boat There are three ferry services. The **East Portlemouth Ferry** *(Tel 01548/842-364; 85p one-way)* is a regular service connecting Salcombe and East Portlemouth across the estuary. The **South Sands Ferry** *(Tel 01548/561-035)* is a half-hourly service from South Sands to Salcombe town center. The third ferry links **Salcombe** with **Kingsbridge** *(Tel 01548/853-525 or 853-607),* as well as offers scenic excursions on the **"Rivermaid."** There are also daily one-hour estuary cruises from 11am-5pm on the **"Kirby"** *(Salcombe Boat Hire; 11 Clifton Place; Tel 01548/844-475).*

Postal The **post office** is across from the TIC *(corner of Courtenay and Market Streets; Tel 01548/842-536; closed Sat afternoons).*

dartmoor national park

The bleak and mournful moors of Dartmoor National Park, provided the sinister backdrop for the Sherlock Holmes mystery *Hounds of the Baskervilles,* but don't let fear deter you from visiting. The park is equally striking for its lush, wooded valleys with streams, making Dartmoor a dramatic setting for walking, bicycling, and horseback riding. (And fishing, too.) Known as the last great wilderness in England, this diverse landscape—covering 368 square miles (954 square km)—is divided by the **River Dart** and marked with stone outcrops, called *tors.* There are quite a few towns in and on the circumference of the park, linked by country lanes that wind through rolling farmland, where you can refuel or crash for the night. **North Bovey, Drewsteignton, Lustleigh,** and **Throwleigh** are pretty little villages with thatched cottages and medieval stone farmhouses; **Chagford,** near **Okehampton** on the north side, is a beautiful little village that was once a prosperous mineral trading center. The town itself still bustles with activity and has a surprising variety of shops and services. Other major spots include **Tavistock** on the western side, **Bovey Tracey** on the east, and **Princetown** in the center of the Park. Princetown is a bleak place, most famous for its prison.

A lot of people come to Dartmoor to check out the prehistoric remains, such as the standing stones from the Bronze Age and the hill forts and hut circles from the Iron Age, that are a ubiquitous part of the landscape. The high moor of the **Upper Plym** has the motherlode, though, with a concentration of Bronze Age and medieval remains. Remains of tin mines are also visible in many locations. Even if seeing the relics isn't the main focus of your trip, they're cool to keep an eye out for as you're hiking around.

dartmoor national park

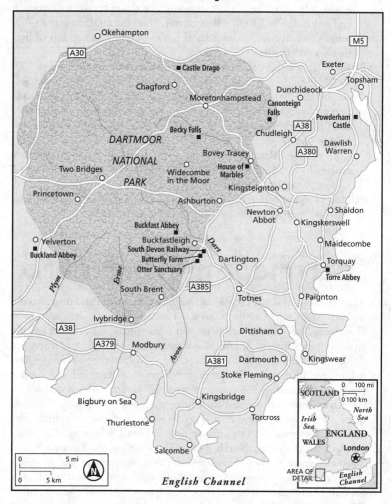

To the northeast is the **Teign Valley,** an area of steep rocky slopes with oak woodlands bisected by a salmon river. **Parke,** the eastern entrance at Bovey Tracey, is full of riverside meadows and mixed woodland that make for good shaded walking trails. On the western side halfway between Okehampton and Tavistock, **Lydford Gorge** *(The Stables, Lydford, Oke-hampton; Tel 01822/820-320; 10am-5:30pm daily Apr-Sept, 10am-4pm daily Oct)* is another highlight of the park. This dramatic 1.5-mile gorge makes for several woodland walks high above the River Lyd that shouldn't be missed. The biggie—a 3-mile circular route—starts near the 90-foot **White Lady Waterfall** then follows the river upstream through a steep, oak-wooded ravine to the **Devil's Cauldron,** where the river cascades into a series of whirlpools. There are also two separate shorter walks that still include dramatic waterfall views.

The town of Okehampton itself is no great shakes, but it's in a perfect position for some true moorish walks. If you arrive in mid-July, your trip will coincide with a weeklong arts festival that features jazz, theater, an arts exhibition, big bands, an orchestra, and a beer festival.

One well-marked trail you can hook up with in Okehampton is the **Tarka Trail** (180 miles, 290 km), a figure-eight route that links the moors on the north Devon coast with Okehampton. Another trail to consider is **The Dartmoor Way** (90 miles, 144 km), a circular route linking five of the major towns of Dartmoor: **Okehampton, Moretonhampstead, Ashburton, Buckfastleigh,** and **Princetown.** It passes through some of the most beautiful scenery of the park.

For fishing info on the rivers and secluded reservoirs, ask for the *Fishing Down in West Devon* pamphlet from the TIC. The TIC can also provide information on where to rent fishing equipment and the fishing permits needed for the reservoirs and rivers in the park. There are three golf courses four miles west of Okehampton [see *need to know,* below].

The park boasts bike routes to suit many styles, from gentle rides up quiet country roads to strenuous, heart-pounding off-road workouts. If you prefer a quiet and relatively flat ride, try **Abbeyford Woods,** a 3-mile off-road, circular route through forestry commission land. It is also easily accessible from Okehampton. The **Sticklepath and Okehampton cycle route** is a 30-mile circular route on quiet roads that travels through Hatherleigh and several small villages. This route links with the **Tarka Trail** and the town of Holsworthy to the **Black Torrington route,** a trail of 25 miles. Grab a cycling leaflet from the TIC, as well as a guide for bicyclists in Dartmoor.

Sprawling over 738 acres, **Roadford Watersports Centre** [see *need to know,* below] is the largest water sports facility in the region. Located between Okehampton and Launceston, to the south, it specializes in sailing, windsurfing, and canoeing courses and has safe training areas for beginners as well as more exciting conditions for seasoned sailors. It is open year-round, but hours vary so be sure to call before you go.

Certain areas of north Dartmoor are used for military training, and are (fortunately) closed to the public when the training includes live fire (that's guns, to us civilians).

Pick up a free copy of the excellent ***Dartmoor Visitor*** newspaper at the TIC [see *need to know,* below] for information on everything to do in the park, including accommodations listings, a guided walks program, events, important numbers, write ups of the towns, news, and a map. Also pick up the ***Okehampton Area Discovery Map,*** with a map on one side and lists of important numbers and descriptions of the walks and sites on the other.

EATS

The **White Hart Hotel** *(Fore St., Okehampton; Tel 01837/527-30 or 545-14; 10:30am-11pm; lunch £5-6)* is a lovely pub centrally located in the middle of town. Adjoined to a 17th-century coaching inn, it serves hot and cheap food, such as soups, jacket potatoes, and sandwiches, as well as starters and more substantial fare. There's also a variety of beer on tap. Self-service is another way to go while touring the park; groceries are available at **Farm Fare** *(26 North St.; Tel 01364/652-273; 8am-7pm Mon-Sat)* in Ashburton.

crashing

There is a **YHA** *(Klondyke Rd., Okehampton; Tel 01837/539-16, Fax 01837/539-65; call to book before 10am or after 5pm; okehampton@yha.org.uk; £10.85 adults, £7.40 under 18, £3.20 breakfast, £4.80 dinner, £2.80 packed lunch, and £3.65; V, Access)* that offers both hostel and camping accommodations, but it tends to fill up fast, so make reservations in advance. Located at the top of a steep road next to the now closed railway station, most rooms have four or six beds—some en suite; there's also a lounge and dining area, laundry facilities, games room, and shop that sells drinks, books, guides, gifts, and the like. You can also sign up for Dartmoor activities here.

On the same road leading to the hostel is **Meadow Lea** *(65 Station Rd., Okehampton; Tel 01837/532-00, Mobile 07747/140-374; £18 singles not en suite, £25 single person in double en suite, £38 doubles en suite, £50 and £45 family rooms including one double bed and two singles; No credit cards)*, a clean and comfortable B&B with televisions in all the rooms and a lounge downstairs. The house is on a quiet street, close to the main road in Okehampton.

need to know

Tourist Info The **Tourist Information Centre** *(White Hart Courtyard; Tel 01837/530-20, Fax 01837/552-25; www.Dartmoor-npa.gov.uk, www.dartmoor.co.uk)* in Okehampton is located off the main drag. The leaflet *Guided Walks and Activities* lists the current schedule of walks in Dartmoor.

For inquiries and bookings from this list, call the **High Moorland Visitor Centre** *(Tel 01822/890-414; 10am-5pm daily in season, 10am-4pm daily off season; £2.50-4.50 for guided walks, depending on length)*. The green-and-white *Dartmoor Public Transport Guide* is a good resource not only for bus and train timetables, but for descriptions of walks in the park as well.

Directions and Transportation There are four to five **buses** *(Devon Bus inquiries; Tel 01392/382-800 or 01271/382-800; DevonBus@devon-cc-gov.uk, www.Devon-cc.gov.uk/DevonBus)* on weekdays from Exeter St. David's into the park to Chagford and regular services to Okehampton *(£2.10 one way)*. If you want to go to Cornwall from Dartmoor, the best route is to take the Okehampton-Bude bus *(£2.50 one way)* and get a connection from there to Padstow, St. Ives, Newquay, etc.

The nearest **rail station** *(Western Nation rail; Tel 01752/222-666; local and national rail info, Tel 08457/484-950; Sunday only train service between Exeter St. David's and Okehampton rail station)* is also at

Exeter St. David's. The **Dartmoor Sunday Rover ticket** *(May 28-Sept 17; £5 adults)* is an exceptional value. Available only on Sundays and bank holidays during the summer, it offers unlimited travel for the day on most of the stops on the bus and train network in Devon and Cornwall, including the Devon Bike Bus route [see *rental*, below].

Rental Horseback riding is a cool way to explore the moors and woods of Dartmoor, and several stables are willing to rent you the horse to do it. **Skaigh Stables** *(Skaigh Lane, Sticklepath, Okehampton; Tel 01837/840-429; Rides at 10am and 2pm, arrive 15 minutes before ride begins; £12 per hour, £25 half day, £40 full day; book in advance for group rides)* offers beginner and advanced rides. **Eastlake Farm Riding Stables** *(Belstone, Okehampton; Tel 01837/525-13)* and **The Grange Equestrian Centre & Unistar Sporting Club** *(Northlew, Okehampton; Tel 01837/523-03; lesson £18 private, £12 per person joint, £10 per person group)* offer riding lessons, liveries, and clay shooting.

Okehampton's Adventure Centre *(The Station; Tel 01837/539-16)* is run out of the Okehampton YHA. It offers morning and afternoon trekking, water sports, and climbing trips. Call well in advance to make reservations.

If you'd like to sail, windsurf, or canoe, try **Roadford Watersports Centre** *(Tel 01409/211-507; call for prices and times; motor access from the A30)*.

Tee off at **Ashbury Golf Courses** *(4 miles west of Okehampton; Tel 01837/554-53; 7am-midnight daily; £14-18 green fees for 18-hole courses and £7-9 PAR 3 18 holes)*. They'll rent you golf clubs (what, you didn't bring your set over on the plane?) for a £5 deposit.

Bicycles can be rented from **Okehampton Cycles** *(Bostock Garden Centre, North Rd.; Tel 01837/532-48; road bike £9.50 per day, mountain bike £14.50 per day; MC, V)*. To bond with other bike nuts, you may want to look into the **Devon Bike Bus** *(Tel 01392/383-223; summer only with two timetables Tues-Sat and Sun/holidays; rbvis@devon-cc.gov.uk, www.devon-cc.gov.uk/DevonBus; no pre-booking; £5, 10p per cycle per journey)*, which operates as a local bus service and stops at a variety of places in Devon, including Okehampton, and takes you to the starting points for good bicycle trails in the area. You can hop on at any point (with your bike), get off, and ride back. Or ride until you're pooped and catch the bus back.

polperro

By now you've probably heard the words "quaint," "idyllic," and "picturesque" enough times that you're beginning to doubt whether there are any other adjectives to describe southern England. Well, when it comes to "enchanting," the town of Polperro *is* the definition. This ancient fishing port is so cute and small, you cannot quite believe that it isn't a film set or some painted facade. The Cornish language is still alive and kicking in Polperro, although not kicking very strongly. Some of the elder residents still speak it, and you'll see an occasional gate with signs written in Cornish on it. The town's name itself comes from the Cornish language: "Pol" is Cornish for "cove" or "pool," and "Perro" was probably someone's personal name. (However, some other sources say the name comes from the Cornish word "Pry," meaning mud or clay.)

The town center is tiny, with winding alleys lined on both sides by small white cottages (lots of them are for rent) and beautiful gardens. The hills that nearly surround the village in a semi-circle are covered in lush trees in various shades of green, with a few houses inserted in between. During high tide in the mornings, ducks and swans in the harbor swim right by the **Roman Bridge,** but in the afternoon and evening, brightly colored boats sit stranded in the mud (illustrating the second theory behind the town's name). The main streets of Polperro are equipped with pottery and curio shops, pubs, and lots of accommodations. Everything is within easy walking distance. This eye-candy of a village makes for a great one or two day trip, so you give yourself enough time to soak in the local flavor.

Six miles to the east, **Looe** is the nearest moderately sized town and, although pretty, it is nothing compared to Polperro. The nearest **train station** and **TIC** [see *need to know,* below] are located in Looe, so you may pass through the town on your way to Polperro.

bar and live music scenes

A popular hangout among locals, the **Blue Peter** *(Quay St.; Tel 01503/272-743; 11am-11pm most days, noon-10:30pm Sun; No cover; No credit cards)* is an intimate bar at the edge of the harbor. It's a great place to have a drink and relax any time of day or night. Especially good times to go are Saturday night or Sunday afternoon, when you can listen to live blues and jazz while enjoying a pint.

The Three Pilchards *(The Quay, Tel 01503/272-233; 11:30am-3pm/7-11pm Mon-Sat, noon-3pm/7-10:30pm Sun; No credit cards),* right next to the harbor, is frequented by locals and visitors alike. It's a large L-shaped room with a black oak interior and a fireplace that burns brightly at night. Sit in the window seat and listen to the talk of the villagers, even if you don't understand a word of their dialect.

culture zoo

The Olde Forge *(Mill Hill; Tel 01503/272-378; 10am-6pm daily Apr & Oct, 10am-9pm June-Sept; admission £2.50):* If you've been dying to see a somewhat cheesy animated feature about Cornish history, as told through seven different legends and folklore, check out the "Land of Legend and Model Village" in The Olde Forge. There's also a model railway and a replica of old Polperro. The Olde Forge has definite kitsch value, but if you don't have much time or are on a budget, skip it.

CITY SPORTS

There are two great cliff walks from town. If you walk past the Blue Peter pub on **Quay St.** [see *bar and live music scenes,* above] to the edge of the jagged rocks next to a small beach and make a right, you'll see a path that leads up the hill and winds round the corner up to the cliffs. To get to the other path, walk up **The Warren** on the other side of the harbor, where it splits in two: a coastal path and another grassy path labeled "Reuben's Walk." We'd recommend taking the prettier "Reuben's Walk", in part because it passes by a tiny white lighthouse that you can get up close and personal with.

EATS

▶▶CHEAP

The smell wafting from **Wrights** *(The Coombes; Tel 01503/272-217),* home to 45 flavors of "real" Cornish ice cream as well as traditional tin miners' pasties (one half of the pasty is steak and vegetable, the other half dessert), is heavenly. Located opposite the Claremont Hotel [see *crashing,* below] on The Coombes, you cannot miss the shop as you walk into town. It also sells regular vegetable and meat pasties and donuts.

   The Three Pilchards [see *bar and live music scenes,* above] serves pub grub ranging from sandwiches and jacket potatoes to curry, steaks, and salads. Prices range from £1.50 to £7.95.

▶▶DO-ABLE

A warm and casual restaurant, **The Polmary** *(The Coombes; Tel/Fax 01503/272-828; 10am-10pm daily; main courses £6.95-16.95; all major credit cards except AE)* serves everything, basically: fresh seafood, steaks, chicken, lamb chops, hot soups, and salads. It was recently opened by two couples who had no previous experience running restaurants, but their outstanding hospitality and efficiency make it seem as though they've been in the business forever.

   The Kitchen *(Fish na Bridge; Tel 01503/272-780; main courses £10.90-15; reservations required; V, MC),* once a wagon-builder's shop, is set in a lovely pink cottage about halfway down to the harbor from the parking area. Run by the husband-and-wife team of Vanessa and Ian Bateson (Vanessa makes all the desserts and bakes the bread), the restaurant offers homestyle English meals made from the freshest ingredients available. The menu changes seasonally and prominently features fresh fish. Typical dishes include sea trout with lemon-and-herb butter and breast of duckling with blueberry-and-Drambuie sauce. There's also a wide selection of vegetarian dishes.

▶▶SPLURGE

An elegant dinner venue, **The Cottage** *(The Coombes; Tel 01503/272-217; open for lunch daily except for Wed and Sat, dinner 7-9pm Mon-Sat; Avg. entree £11; all major credit cards except DIN, AE)* is a sweet little place with a pretty garden in the back that is open for lunch when the weather is good. You can also have a cream tea here during the afternoon or early evening.

crashing

Polperro's main road is lined with B&B's, and the stream next to the road has little bridges over it acting as driveways to the houses and guesthouses. It's more pleasant to stay right in the town center, though, as the atmosphere is great and you'll be nearer to the harbor.

One B&B on the Roman Bridge that we don't recommend is the **House on Props.** Although it looks adorable from the outside the place when we saw it wasn't all that clean and the rooms smelled musky. Worse, the rooms didn't have locks, even though anyone could get in from the bar downstairs. And it wasn't cheap. The best places in town are listed below.

▶▶CHEAP

High up and overlooking the harbor, **The Watchers** *(The Warren; Tel/Fax 01503/272-296; www.polperro.org; from £19 per person en suite)* offers a sensational view. (Don't worry, the walk up to it is not too arduous.) Rooms all have private baths, color TVs, and hairdryers. It's a surprisingly good value for being in the best location in town.

The Polmary *(The Coombes; Tel/Fax 01503/272-828; £17.50 per person with breakfast; two doubles, one twin, one bathroom; all major credit cards except AE)* offers standard accommodation above a lovely restaurant.

▶▶DO-ABLE

An elegant 8-room hotel right in the center of town is **The Old Mill House** *(Mill Hill; Tel 01503/272-362; £27.50-30 per person in family; double, twin and four poster rooms, £10 more if single, all en suite)*. There is a homely bistro in the hotel decorated with fishing nets and a bar serving homemade pub food.

New House *(Talland Hill; Tel 1503/272-206; regular rooms have shared bathrooms, £20 per person regular room, £22 per person suite, No credit cards)* overlooks the harbor of Polperro.

▶▶SPLURGE

It's the largest hotel in town, but the **Claremont Hotel** *(The Coombes; Tel 01503/272-241; B&B rates vary per person from £25.95-40 for a double en suite, £30.95-32.95 for a single, £67-78 for a family room that accommodates three to four people, £37-41 penthouse; discounts available if you eat in the hotel restaurant; all major debit and credit cards except DIN)* is still relatively small, with 12 rooms. Each room features a private bath with shower, tea/coffee making facilities, and color TV. Room 11 is the penthouse and is particularly nice, with lots of space and a skylight over the bed.

need to know

Tourist Info The nearest **TIC** is 6-mile bus trip away, in Looe *(Guildhall, Fore St., East Looe; Tel 01503/262-072; closed in winter months)*.

Public Transportation There are little red trams that ferry people down to the town center from the bus stop. This is more of a novelty ride than efficient transportation, considering that it takes about two minutes to walk down the road. A one-way ticket is 55p. There are also horse carts that do the same trip as the tram.

Pharmacies Robert's Pharmacy *(The Coombes; Tel 01503/272-250; 9am-5:30pm Mon, Tues, 9am-6:30pm Wed, Thurs, Fri, 9am-1pm Sat, closed Sun, open every day from Apr-Sep)* is easy to find, as it's located on the main street running through town.

Telephone City code: *01503*

Trains The nearest train station is in nearby **Looe.** From Plymouth, take the train to **Liskeard** and then catch the smaller branch line through the countryside to Looe. From there, it's a short bus ride to Polperro, or take a cab (£5-7). Trains leave from **London Paddington** for **Plymouth** *(3 hours; one way £44)*.

Bus Lines Out of the City The trip from **Plymouth** to **Polperro** *(one way £3.15)* takes two hours and is quite an interesting little journey. Call **Hambly's Coach Service** *(Tel 01503/220-660)* for information. At one point, trees hanging over the road enshroud the bus and whack its sides, which is unnerving and beautiful at the same time. The bus even goes onto a ferry at one point to cross from Devon to Torpoint, considered the "gateway to Cornwall."

Alternatively, grab a **cab** from Polperro to Plymouth *(Tel 01503/272-448, Mobile 07970/902-659 or 01503/272-851),* which costs between £30-35.

Bike/Moped Rental If you're up for a little exercise, you can rent a bike from **Looe Mountain Bike Hire** *(Tel 01503/263-871 or 262-877)* and ride the six or so miles to Polperro to spend the afternoon. In Polperro, you don't need a bike, as everything is within easy walking distance.

Postal The **post office** *(Fore St., Tel 01503/272-225)* is also a small store selling stationary, greeting cards, maps, books, gifts, and even fishing tackle and bait.

ST. IVES

St. Ives is known for lots of things, but primary among them is its reputation and history as an artistic community. Many of England's most famous writers and artists have congregated here since the 19th century to live along the magnificent beaches and rugged coastline of this Cornish town. "We are here," wrote American painter James Whistler, "to paint ships and seas and skies." The artistic legacy of St. Ives is apparent today with its many art galleries tucked away in the narrow streets of the old part of town. The rest of the town's center is stuffed with clothes stores, coffee shops, and pasty stalls.

But it's not all about the art—it's also about the surf. Most of the action in St. Ives revolves around the harbor and Porthmeor beach—a big, beautiful beach that is popular with both resident and visiting young surfers. The people of St. Ives are very low key and relaxed, which isn't surprising when you consider most of them are either artists or surfers. Another big draw, also on the outdoor tip, is for the coastal walk from St. Ives to Zenmor [see *great outdoors,* below].

For news on the local arts scene and details of galleries and exhibitions in the area, pick up a copy of the free publication *Cornwall Arts* from the TIC.

bar, club, and live music scene

St. Ives isn't brimming with nighttime activity, which is surprising, considering what a summer attraction it is. Maybe the surfers are too worn out after a day of hanging ten to get too wild at night....The few bars there are more than passable, though—laid back and inviting.

The dark and low beamed **Sloop** *(harbor front, corner of Fish St. and The Wharf; Tel 01736/796-584; open 11am-11pm daily, food served noon-3pm/6-8:45pm)* is a traditional English pub that attracts a young, somewhat rough crowd. If you find it too suffocating inside, there are benches and tables outside overlooking the harbor where you can take your drink and breathe in some fresh air. You're not likely to meet up with locals here though, because people tend to sit at tables and drink with their friends rather than mill about talking.

A laid-back traditional English style pub, **The Queen's Tavern** *(High St.; Tel 01736/796-468; accepts all major credit cards)* offers different types of music every night, a bar, and a full menu of decent pub grub. Local folk gather here for a game of pool with their mates or to have a pint and watch their favorite sport on the big screen TV.

Isobar *(Tregenna Place; Tel 01736/796-042 or 799-199; nights open 10pm-2am Wed, Fri, Sat, till 1am Thur; No credit cards)* is St. Ives's main nightspot. Conveniently close to the Backpackers hostel, it is decked out in wood and features a foosball table. It is a nice place during the day for lunch or a coffee. During both the day and in the evenings, tapas are served in Isobar's casual setting. At night, the two dance floors open up and the DJs deliver garage, house, and drum 'n' bass. On Wednesdays all drinks are £1. The crowd here is primarily backpackers, who flock here because it's really the only place in town to dance and hang out in a club environment.

arts scene

Managed by the Tate Gallery in London, **The Tate** *(Porthmeor Beach; Tel 01736/796-226, Fax 01736/794-480; 10:30am-5:30pm Tues-Sun and Mon in July and August; information@tate.org.uk, www.tate.org.uk; £3.90 adults; there is a joint Hepworth/Tate same-day ticket for £6, £3.30 students)* has a completely different feel from its city counterpart. This gallery is light, bright, and very modern, a funky architectural gem overlooking the beach. The glass, circular exterior of the building blends well with the airy interior design. The gallery mainly showcases Cornish artists active in the early 20th-century, like Alfred Wallis, Tony Lattimer, and Wilhelmina Barns-Graham. The works of Wallis, a completely self-taught painter from St. Ives who started painting in 1922 after his wife died, are particularly notable. A central figure in the St. Ives school, Wallis painted in a simplistic style that critics have described as "primitive" and "naive." On the second floor of the Tate, there are also vibrant hanging canvases by Wilhelmina Barns-Graham (including *June Painting, Ultramarine,* and *Yellow, 1996*) and photographs by Diane Comely on the walls as you walk upstairs.

Accompanying the works of local artists are extracts from books and poems written by Cornish writers who worked and lived in the same community and time period. The exhibit makes it clear that the writers and artists of the St. Ives School were instrumental in fueling each other's work.

festivals/cool annual events

The **St. Ives September Festival** *(Tel 01736/796-888; September 8-22)* is the largest in the West Country. Lots of international names come to participate in the classical, jazz, folk, comedy, and poetry events. There are also exhibitions of paintings, pottery, and crafts, in addition to talks on art and literature. Since St. Ives is the artists' haven of southern England, there are also "Open Days" where you can visit the galleries of local artists for free. These are particularly fun if you prefer the brush to the board (surfboard that is).

In June, the harbor is the focal point of the **St. Ives Regatta & Biathlon** *(Tel 01736/796-297),* which includes dinghy and gig racing, water polo, swimming competitions and, of course, partying on the beach MTV spring break–style. That is, of course, without the bikini-clad Yanks. The five-day event ends with the Sailing Club Regatta Day.

After your visit to the Tate, there is a charming coffee shop on the top floor where you can enjoy fantastic views over the beach and town.

The other famous art gallery in town is the **Barbara Hepworth Museum & Sculpture Garden** (*Barnoon Hill; Tel 01736/796-226, Fax 01736/794-480; 10:30am-5:30pm Tues-Sun and Mondays in July and August; £3.50 adults, £1.80 students; there is a joint Hepworth/Tate same-day ticket for £6, £3.30 students*). Hepworth was a contemporary of Henry Moore, and her sculpture shares a similar bronze organic look. The museum is in a small house that contains the studios where she worked and a lush sculpture garden upstairs.

Across from the Backpackers lodge is the **Royal Cinema** (*Lower Stennack; Tel 01736/796-843; £4.50 adults*) showing mainstream Hollywood flicks.

great outdoors

If you're a surfer, St. Ives is an awesome place to add to your résumé. The beaches are huge and plentiful. They also swarm with people from all over the world—especially in summer—making for an international bonding experience. The main surfing beach is **Porthmeor,** but **Porthgwidden** and **Porthminster** (which you'll pass on the train on the way in) are also popular.

The **St. Ives International Backpackers** [see *crashing,* below] will arrange surfing lessons and expeditions for you. Alternatively, contact one of the schools directly:

St. Ives Surf Center (*Porthmeor Beach; Tel 01736/793-366; £18 per lesson*); **Shore Surf School** (*3 Dracaena Ave., Hayle; Tel 01736/755-556; la@shoresurf.fsnet.co.uk, www.shoresurf.com; lessons £20 including equipment, student discounts*) is in nearby **Hayle.** It has a free minibus service, so it may be willing to pick you up. It can also arrange accommodation for you in Hayle.

There is a beautiful **coastal walk** between St. Ives and Zennor, about six miles away. People come to this part of Cornwall especially for this walk, which skims the edge of the ragged, heart-stopping coastline. The **Old Chapel** backpackers' lodge is a good place to crash, literally, once you're in Zennor [see *crashing,* below].

eats

The harbor and Fore St. are good places to go when you need some sustenance.

▶▶CHEAP

As usual in Cornwall, there are plenty of ice cream and pasty stalls on the harbor, but make a beeline for **The Bayview Café** (*The Wharf; Tel 01736/794-925; 9am-5pm daily, takeout 9am-midnight daily; meals £5-7; MC, V accepted on £10 or more*). Here they serve up delicious cheap pizzas in three sizes and with a variety of toppings—very *un*-Cornish. Get one to go and eat it on a bench on the pier.

breaking scones

If their regional dishes are anything to go by, the Cornish are not health nuts. The most famous—and artery clogging—Cornish delicacy is cream tea. This is something you must try if you're in Cornwall for the first time. Along with the requisite pot of tea, you'll be served two piping hot scones, a little bowl of strawberry jam, and another heaping bowl of clotted cream so thoroughly whipped you can stand a spoon up in it. The idea is to dollop these condiments on the scone with great gusto. It's rich—*very* rich—but delicious. Just don't make it a habit or you might not be able to squeeze into your jeans after a week or so. A far less decadent local dish is the Cornish pasty, which traditionally consists of red meat, onions, and turnip stuffing. There are a variety of other pasties made in Cornwall now, including ones with vegetarian and sweet fillings. To quench your thirst there's mead, a fermented drink served with honey to sweeten it. The seafood in these parts, particularly the crab, is also pretty damn good.

Granny Pasties *(9 Fore St.; Tel 01736/793-470; 9am-5:30pm daily; coffee drinks average £1; pasties average £2; MC, V accepted on purchases of £10 or more)* is great for a morning coffee, a sweet, or a savory pasty. Don't forget to pick up a copy of the paper at the newsstand next door to read while you're having your coffee and pasty. There's also a good selection of jams, chutneys, and marmalades to take home. Or, watch the pasties being made through the window at **Pengenna Pasties** on the High St.

Cobblestones *(The Warren; Tel 01736/797-800; 10am-10pm daily; under £5; No credit cards)* offers sea views as well as snacks and full meals at value prices. Vegetarian options are available, and homemade soups, cakes, and puddings are a specialty.

There is a **supermarket** next door to the Backpackers' lodge, open till 11pm daily.

▶▶**DO-ABLE**

A sleek cafe, **Joseph's** *(39A Fore St.; Tel 01736/796-514; 10am-4:30pm/6:30-10pm daily)* is out of place in casual St. Ives. The restaurant is lovely, though, with views of the water. The menu includes fresh pasta, local fish, and seafood, as well as lighter meals for lunch like jacket potatoes and salads. There are also wines to choose from, and a range of desserts and pastries.

The highlight at **Annie's Restaurant** *(3 Chapel St.; Tel 01736/793-215; noon-3pm/5:30pm-late daily; entrees £8.75 and up; AE, MC, V)* is dishes prepared using fresh local produce, fish, and shellfish. Seafood possibilities at this smart little bistro depend on the catch of the day, but other possibilities include "Sweet Chilli Chicken" and "Tournedos Rossini."

If you've had enough of cream teas and want to spice things up a bit, **The Mex** *(3 Gabriel St.; Tel 01736/797-658 or 01736/796-711; 5:30pm-late; AE, MC, V)* offers the kind of lively atmosphere and menu you might find at a tex-mex bistro in the States. It's as authentic as tacos and burritos get in England, and vegetarian options are available.

crashing

Most of the better B&B's are clustered on Bunker Hill *(off Fore St., right before the harbor)*, an attractive side street that is quiet, but still near the action. The Warren is another street with a bunch of B&B's, although these aren't quite as smart. For a town that attracts a ton of young people in the summer there is a definite shortage of cheap accommodation. In fact, the one resident hostel only opened fairly recently. The visitor information center will help you book for a fee [see *need to know,* below].

▶▶**CHEAP**

Housed in what used to be a Wesleyan Chapel School, **St. Ives International Backpackers** or "The Gallery" *(Lower Stennack, town center; Tel/Fax 01736/799-444; mostly 8-bed dorm rooms, some doubles and twins; st.ivesbackpackers@dial.pipex.com, www.backpackers.co.uk/st-ives; £8-9 per person in all rooms, £12 in July & August)* is a huge, multilevel hostel. This fact certainly accounts for the building's chilly interior. You may need to keep your sweater on indoors, but the exceptional friendliness of the staff and residents will warm the cockles of your heart. The many amenities of the huge common room include couches, a coffee bar, and a small e-mail hut [see *need to know,* below]. The owner, Ray, also owns the Newquay International Backpackers and is an amazingly hospitable host. He is closely involved in the running of both places and will happily take you on drives up or down the coast if you express an interest in a particular place. He will also help in any other way to make your time in the area more enjoyable. In short, if you're looking to meet people and have fun, stay here.

If you don't feel like making the trek back to St. Ives after walking the southwest coastal path [see *city sports,* above], or if you are looking for a midway pit stop before going on to Land's End, **The Old Chapel Backpackers** *(Zennor; Tel/Fax 01736/798-307; six rooms sleeping 32, one family room; £10 for dorm beds, £30 family room)* is a great place to stay. You'll relish an evening in this small farming village, with its resident 11th-century church and local pub, that's situated just half a mile from the path (don't worry, there are signs to help you find it). Yes, even miniature villages in England off the beaten track have local drinking holes. There is also a cafe restaurant in this hostel with scrumptious homemade cakes.

The Hollies Hotel *(4 Talland Rd.; Tel 01736/796-605; john@ hollieshotel.freeserve.co.uk; en suite, TV; £16 and up; £20 and up Jun-Sep; No* *credit cards)* is a quaint brownstone hotel close to Porthminster Beach and the town center. Run by a local family, it offers a quiet, family atmosphere.

▶▶**DO-ABLE**

A 5-minute walk from the train station, **Harbour Lights** *(Court Cocking, Fore St.; Tel 01736/795-525; £20 single with shared bathroom; £22 single en suite; £20 double with shared bathroom; No credit cards)* is close to the center of town, and breakfast is included.

Also located near the city center, the **Horizon Guest House** *(Carthew Terrace; Tel 01736/798-069; some rooms en suite; £18-22 depending on season; No credit cards)* has the added bonus that the proprietress will arrange for a taxi to pick you up at the train station if you're too bogged down with bags to make the not-so-long walk. Breakfast is also included.

For holistic enthusiasts, the **Whitesands Lodge** *(Sennen, Tel/Fax 01736/871-776; guest house has one single, one twin, one double, one double en suite, one family en suite, also backpackers dorms with self catering facilities; £4 camping, £10 dorm, £15.50 single, £29 double, £35 en suite double, £49.50 en suite quad; all major credit cards)* is a converted granite farmhouse that has been split into a backpackers hostel and a B&B. It also has a colorful restaurant and bar serving divine cream teas and veggie, vegan, and whole food. There's a TV and video lounge with a log fire, pool table, laundry, a place to rent and store surfboards and bikes, garden area, and tent space. The staff offers surf lessons at the gorgeous Sennen Cove white sand beach and tours of nearby standing stones, ancient settlements, and sacred wells. In the winter, the lodge offers spiritual workshops on holistic topics like meditation, light work, and healing.

▶▶**SPLURGE**

The Regent Hotel *(Fern Lea Terrace, next to the bus station; Tel 01736/796-195, Fax 01736/794-641; info@RegentHotel.com; all doubles and twins en suite, two singles share a shower and toilet; £29.50-33.50 per person; all major credit cards)* has color TVs, radio alarm clocks, and hair dryers in all the rooms. Along with these small luxuries, most of the rooms have one additional big luxury: a magnificent view over the beach and water.

WITHIN 30 MINUTES

If you have a car, a wonderful driving route is along the coast from St. Ives around the bottom of Cornwall, past Land's End, and up to Penzance. Between these two spots you'll not only pass sensational coastal scenery, but also you'll discover some historical and regional treasures: Near St. Ives, you'll pass through the moorland of West Penwith, which still has stone walls and stone formations. Some of these are more than 4,000 years old and date back to the Stone and Bronze ages. There are also ruins from old tin mines in the area.

Tiny **Sennen** village is an intimate place to stay if you're enjoying this part of Cornwall [see *crashing,* above]. As it is only 1-1/5 miles from Land's End, the most western point of Britain, it can serve as a superb base for exploring the surrounding coastal paths and smugglers coves.

From Sennen, you can either walk to Land's End or drive and park in the £3 lot. The theme park you have to walk through to get to the edge of the cliffs is completely incompatible with the rugged beauty that confronts you on the other side, with the wild waves crashing against the rocks on both sides.

Around the point and up the coast is **Porthcurno,** home of the **Minack Theatre** *(at the seaward end of the valley go up the winding hill and the theater is on your left; Tel 01736/810-181; open for day visits 9:30am-5:30pm Apr-Sept, 10am-4pm Oct-March, closed during the afternoon when there is a matinee; www.minack.com; £2.50 adults, student concession between November and March; ticket prices for performances £5.50-6.50 adults; V, MC).* It's impossible to imagine a more extraordinary position for an open-air theater than sitting here precariously on the cliffs looking out over spectacular coastline. Even its history is unbelievable: A woman named Rowenda Cade built the theater with her own hands—literally. Rowenda wasn't rich or famous in any way; she just wanted a theater on this spot, and so she built one. She'd be delighted to know that each summer the theater sponsors a festival of productions, including visits from London's Royal Shakespeare Company. If you're in town during the summer, it would be worth your while to get tickets.

About 10 miles up the coast from Porthcurno is **Mousehole** (pronounced "mowzel"), another cute fishing village where you'll have to employ expert driving maneuvers on the tiny, tight roads. This toy town is a perfect example of a traditional Cornish fishing port. The houses here were built tiny on purpose to better retain heat, and each house has a "coffin hole" in the ceiling because the staircases were too narrow to accommodate a coffin.

After you've become really claustrophobic in Mousehole, make a brief stop in **Newlyn,** just about 2 miles up the coast, for Jelbert's ice cream (said to be the best in Cornwall) and to get a look at one of the busiest harbors in Britain. There is not a huge amount to do in Penzance, the next town over, so skip over to **Marazion,** another 5 miles up the coast, where you must have a look at **St. Michael's Mount,** *(Tel 01736/710-507, 10:30am-4:45pm Mon-Fri, call for weekend hours (they vary); guided tours, £4.50, available Mon, Wed, Fri—call for times; V),* the sister monastery to Mont St. Michel off the coast of Normandy. At low tide you can walk to St. Michael's Mount on the boardwalk. However, at high tide the island is completely cut off from the mainland and you'll need to take a ferry over. Ferries run all day from 10:30am till dusk, at a cost of £1 each way; they leave from the landing stages at the shore.

need to know

Currency Exchange Barclays is located on the main drag *(High St.; Tel 01736/362-261; open 9:30am-4:30pm Mon-Tues and Thur-Fri, 10am-4:30pm Wed).*

Tourist Info The Guildhall *(Street-an-Pol; Tel 01736/796-297, Fax 01736/798-309; open 9:30am-6pm Mon-Sat, 10am-1pm Sun, closed*

Sat-Sun in winter) books accommodations for 10 percent of the first night's bill.

Pharmacies For all that ails you, get to **Leddra Chemists** *(7 Fore St.; Tel 01736/795-432).*

Telephone City code: *01736*

Trains St. Ives is accessible from Plymouth and Penzance via the short branch line **St. Erth** (about 10 minutes between St. Erth and St. Ives, between 5 and 6 hours between London Paddington and St. Erth) run by **Virgin Trains** *(Tel 0345/222-333; www.virgintrains.co.uk).* Trains run roughly every 90 minutes, starting at 5:55am; the last train is at 5:49pm. The fare is £10.30 one way. Call 0345/484-950 for National Railway info. The train station is near Porthminster Beach; it's just a five-minute walk north to the center of town.

Bus Lines Out of the City **National Express** *(Tel 0990/808-080)* operates several buses a day to St. Ives from London Victoria Coach Station (about 7 hours). There are also **Western National** buses to Newquay, Plymouth, and Penzance. The bus station is located very near the train station up the hill. You can easily walk to the center of town from here.

Bike/Moped Rental Bikes or **surfboards** can be hired at **Windansea Surf Shop** *(25 Fore St.; Tel 01736/794-830; open daily 9:30am-9:30pm; £5 per day for surfboard or wetsuit, £5 deposit).*

Postal Send that hang ten postcard from the St. Ives **post office** *(1 Tregenna Place; Tel 01736/795-004; open 9am-5:30pm Mon-Fri, 9am-1pm Sat).*

Internet See *wired,* above.

rock

Across the **Camel Estuary,** a small coastal inlet, from Padstow is the little village of **Rock.** Rock is a bit like Salcombe in the county of Devon, in that quaint, little-boats-bobbing-in-the-harbor sort of way. Rock is more sparse in terms of shops (two), restaurants (four), and hotels (four). You can see all you need to see in Rock in one day, or even in an afternoon trip from Padstow. But if you're looking for some serious R&R, it's an ideal place to stick around for a night or two.

Pick up the informative *and* free newspaper *Coast Lines & Countryside News* for detailed information on guided walks, camping sites, local news, features, and important numbers in the North Cornwall region.

bar scene

Located on the waterfront street, **The Rock Inn Bar & Bistro** *(Tel 01208/863-498; 11am-11pm daily)* serves beer on tap in a casual, friendly environment overlooking the water. Outdoor tables provide a perfect spot during the day to gaze at the idyllic boats sailing on the estuary.

great outdoors

If you're keen to take up a new watersport, Rock is an ideal place to learn, as the water is calm, and there is a multitude of sports to try. The **Camel School of Seamanship** *(The Pontoon; Tel 01208/862-881, Fax 01208/862-974; hours vary, usually 9:30am-dusk in summer; camel sailing@btclick.com)* will teach you a new sport or rent equipment to you. The school offers windsurfing lessons *(£24 per person for a 2-hour session)*, novice and advanced power boating courses or lessons by the hour, and sailing on dinghy boats. Or try shore-based courses in activities like learning to be a skipper. If you want to rent equipment, there are canoe trips *(£10 per person for 2-hour trips, £15 per person for 3-hour trips)*, or sail boats *(£15 per hour for a wayfarer, £80 for six hours, £10 per hour for a topper)*. Inquire about the **Multi-Activity Day** *(Fridays only)*, which allows you to try out a variety of the above-mentioned activities for £45.

Mackerel fishing, wreck, and reef trips leave the Rock Pontoon daily from the **Fishing Hut** *(Rock Pontoon; Tel 01208/863-975; £25 per person per day, £6 mackerel trips; all fishing tackle supplied)*. For sailing on a Drascombe Lugger or a Cornish Shrimper, both bareboat and skippered charters, contact **Allan Green** *(Floating Pontoon; Tel 01208/841-246, Mobile 07977/870-603; £29 and up bareboat, £38 skippered charters; about a 2-hour sail; No credit cards)*.

There's some wonderful walking here too, if you're a land lover. If you follow the town's waterfront street southwest past the parking lot, you'll come across some grassy dunes crisscrossed with narrow walking paths. After passing a few small stretches of beach, you'll eventually get to **Polzeath Beach,** one of the largest surfing beaches in England. (You'll see a sign on the path telling you that Polzeath Beach is below.) The landscape is undeveloped and overgrown, with fields of pink flowers, in season, scattered between the dunes.

Adjoining the **St. Enodoc Hotel** [see *crashing*, below] are the two awesomely positioned 18-hole courses of the **St. Enodoc Golf Club** *(Tel 01208/863-216 or 862-402; 8:30am-dusk; 18 holes £35 weekdays, £40 weekends; Play all day for £50)*. The main course, which is the posh one, is called **Church** course and is rated one of the top 50 golf courses

in the UK. In order to play there, you have to have a handicap of at least 24 and a certificate to prove it. Call ahead to book but no more than four days in advance. The **Holy World** course is a slightly shorter course and here anyone can play (no minimum handicap required). You also don't need to book in advance (£15 for a round, £25 for the day). You can rent golf clubs from the St. Enodoc club shop.

eaTs

▶▶**CHEAP**

For affordable pub food in a laid-back atmosphere, go to **The Rock Inn Bar & Bistro** *(Rock Rd.; Tel 01208/863-498; food served noon-2:30pm/7-10pm; lunch £5).* A favorite with locals for its unpretentious food: veggie burgers, salads, and the like. Daily specials are written up on a chalkboard.

Stop in at the **Soft Rock Café** *(Ferry Point; Tel 01208/863-841; Open daily Easter-Autumn, weekends only off season; sandwiches £2 and up, salads £5 and up)* for cream tea, a cheap sandwich, or a seafood salad.

Di's Dairy and Pantry *(Rock Road; Tel 01208/863-531, Fax 01208/869-035; 8am-8pm Mon-Sat, 8:30am-6pm Sun, in season (before Sept 15); 8am-5:30pm Mon-Sat, 8:30am-4:30pm Sun, off season (after Sept 15); sandwiches £1-2.50 and up, depending upon filling)* offers the freshest deli food you'll find anywhere, from vegetables to cheeses and fresh-cut bacon. Get a sandwich to go.

▶▶**SPLURGE**

The St. Enodoc Hotel's [see *crashing,* below] restaurant, the **Porthilly Bar and Grill** *(Tel 01208/863-394; £6 start, £12-16 mains; V, AE, DIN, Access, Switch),* is a modern country eatery, serving stylish Pacific Rim cuisine on colorful plates. The split-level restaurant spills onto the terrace for some alfresco dining with panoramic views of the water.

crashing

Your crashing options are limited in Rock, but the Padstow TIC will help you book accommodations [see *need to know,* below] for a fee.

▶▶**CHEAP**

A 5- to 10-minute walk from the main street, **Silvermead** *(Rock Wade-bridge; Tel 01208/862-425, Fax 01208/862-919; Barbara@silver mead. freeserve.co.uk; single from £18.50 not en suite, £24 per person for en suite double)* is an above-average B&B in an attractive house with a large garden and offers a good value.

▶▶**DO-ABLE**

A basic hotel overlooking the water, **Roskarnon House Hotel** *(Main Street; Tel 01208/862-329, Fax 01208/862-785; £25-37.50 per person, £93-115 per person for three days; dinner, bed, and breakfast, most rooms en suite)* has a lovely terrace in the garden where cream teas are served in the afternoon.

▶▶**SPLURGE**

The wonderfully sophisticated **St. Enodoc Hotel** *(Rock Wadebridge; Tel 01208/863-394, Fax 01208/863-970; enodoc@aol.com, www.enodoc*

hotel.co.uk; £50-95 single, £70-145 double/twin, £95-195 suite, all bed-rooms en suite, depending on season; package rates for three nights during the week or on weekends and weekly rates; V, AE, DIN, Access, Switch) with its rustic appeal, is located opposite the Silvermead B&B. It has great estuary views from all the rooms and a superb downstairs area and terrace. The library in the lounge is stocked with books by Cornish authors. Athletic types will appreciate the heated outdoor swimming pool, the gym, the sauna, the squash court, and the billiards room. The St. Enodoc was also the only seaside recipient of the Good Hotel Guide Cesar award in 2000.

WITHIN 30 MINUTES

The two towns of **Boscastle** and **Tintagel** are tourist havens, but worth a quick visit en route to or from Rock. If you're traveling by bus, you'll pass through them if you're coming from Bude or another northwest point. The main attraction in Tintagel is **Tintagel Castle,** rumored to be the birthplace of King Arthur. The magic of the place is attributed both to the Knights of the Round Table legend and the aesthetics of the castle itself, which is located on a finger of land projecting into the sea. This location puts half of it on the mainland and half over a narrow neck of land between two inlets. Boscastle is a fishing village with a narrow, cliff hanging harbor entrance and a small quay.

NEED TO KNOW

Tourist Info The **TIC** in Padstow caters to Rock visitors as well. It is located immediately opposite the ferry landing at **The Red Brick Building** (North Quay, Padstow; Tel 01841/533-449, Fax 01841/532-356; 10am-5pm daily; padstowtic@visit.org.uk) and is surprisingly well stocked for such a small town. It has a huge range of books on places in the area, as well as pamphlets and lists of places to stay. The staff of the TIC will help you book accommodations in advance for a fee of £3.00, or on the day for £2.00.

Trains and Bus Lines out of the City Unfortunately, there are no train stations in this part of Cornwall, so you'll have to rely on the very unreliable bus system if you don't have a car.

　　Buses in this area are now privatized, so often only one or two buses a day will be going to your chosen destination—it is advisable to arrive well ahead of the posted departure time. If you do miss your bus, your best option would be to take an alternative route to the closest point to your destination and catch a cab from there.

　　Also keep in mind that there's a nature reserve around Padstow and Rock, so motorized transportation has to make its way around this protected area, adding even more traveling time. If you're coming from southern Cornwall towards Rock, you'll save time by getting off at Padstow and taking the ferry across the estuary. Buses from Padstow to Rock also require a change at Wadebridge. It's about a 15-mile trip.

　　Western National buses operate from Padstow (Tel 01208/798-98 or 01752/402-060) but you can also call **National Express** (Tel

01872/404-04 or 01209/719-988) for info. Timetables change seasonally and are available at the TIC, but they are also pasted onto the
bus stops.

The nearest train station is about 14 miles away at **Bodmin
Parkway** *(Tel 0345/484-950, 24 hours a day for information at the
local phone rate);* you can get a bus connection from there.

Boat Ferries *(Tel 01841/532-239; £1.60 round-trip)* operate regularly
between Rock and Padstow, going back and forth across the Camel
Estuary all day long, except Sundays in winter. At night, the **water
taxis** *(Tel 01208/862-815 daytime, 01208/862-217 evening; £3 one
way, £4 return trip)* replace the ferries. A taxi trip across the estuary
costs about £3 one way and £4 for a round trip. Both ferries and water
taxis leave from the harbor ferry steps, or lower beach at low tide.

padstow

Padstow can be summed up in one word: glorious! This beautiful little
village sits on the **Camel Estuary** across the water from another gorgeous
and smaller village: **Rock.** Although every second building in Padstow is
a B&B and there are enough pasties made here to sink the *Titanic,* the
charm of this place has not been lost to commercialism, perhaps due to
the unadorned stretches of beach it is sandwiched between.

The streets are typical Cornish village streets: narrow, windy, cobblestoned, and lined on both sides with diminutive cottages too breathtaking for words. People here clearly take pride in how their homes look
from the outside, as the window boxes are bursting with colorful plants—
that is, when the flowers aren't already growing directly out of the stones.
Padstow is more upmarket than **St. Ives,** and definitely more upmarket
than **Newquay.** As a result, accommodations and dining are not cheap.
Try to visit when it's warm, but not in the middle of summer, as everyone
in the UK seemingly descends on these parts.

Pick up the free *Coast Lines & Countryside News* for detailed information on guided walks, camping sites, news, features, and important
numbers in the North Cornwall region.

bar, live music, and club scenes

Perched right on the harbor, the pub on the ground floor of **The Old
Custom House** *(South Quay; Tel 01841/532-359)* is the perfect spot to
sit and watch the boats that come in and out, as well as the passing parade
of tourists on the streets.

arts scene

Since Padstow is a small town, there isn't a burgeoning arts scene. The
one gallery, **The Picture House** *(North Quay; Tel 01841/533-888; pic-
turehs1@aol.com),* sells the kind of art usually found in tourist traps:

padstow

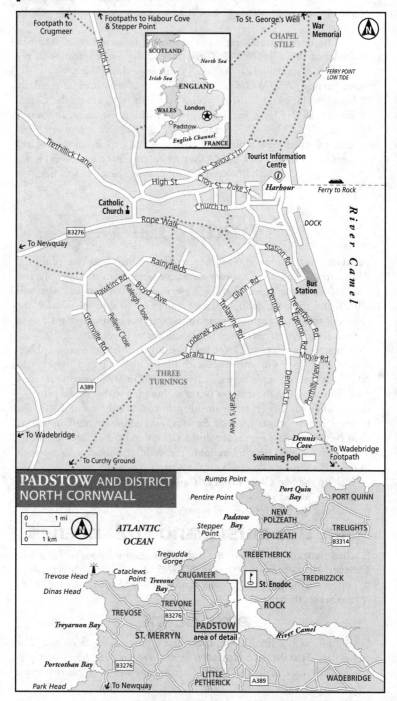

cheerful watercolors of striped deck chairs, families in bathing suits, very happy fish, and the like.

The only cinema in town, **The Cinedrone** *(Lanadwell St.; Tel 01841/532-344; £4.50)*, screens mainstream Hollywood movies.

city sports

A lovely footpath meanders along the coast of Cornwall and runs through the center of Padstow. You can pick it up by heading to the harbor, and taking the path either to the right or the left. The wider, flatter coastal walk to the left leads you onto cliffs that loom over huge beaches. There are many paths leading down to the sand, where you can either swim or tan. To the right of the harbor is the **Camel Trail,** a 17-mile walk or bicycle trek that stretches around the peninsula toward the town of **Wade-bridge** (about 6 miles) and ultimately to **Bodmin** (roughly 14 miles). Part of the trail goes over the old railway bridge, but trains don't operate in this part of Cornwall anymore.

stuff

▶▶GOODIES
Feast your eyes on the window display in **Gwyneth's** *(Market Strand)*, the sweet shop to end all sweet shops. Come for the long list of ice cream flavors, pots of fudge, and sticky strings of licorice. Employees and customers have left wacky little poems and notes on all the walls and the door in tribute to the culinary wonders of the shop.

▶▶SKIN
For all your holistic needs, **Harmony** *(4-6 Broad St.; Tel 01841/533-378; 11am-4pm Wed-Sun; No credit cards)* has natural soaps and bath balls and offers massage.

eats

▶▶CHEAP
You will not find a larger selection of fudge, butter cookies, ice cream, and pasties in such small square footage. The best of Padstow's pasty shops though, are **Pasty Presto** *(2 Mill Square)* and the **Chough Bakery** *(West Quay)*. Pasty Presto is one of the only pasty sellers to make pasties with vegetarian fillings, and the only one to make sweet ones (try

wired

www.cornwall-online.co.uk/ northcornwall provides a good overview of what you'll find in Cornwall. It gives a rundown of each town: the history, the major attractions, and the local places to eat, sleep, and play.

the outstanding chocolate and banana for £1.65). Chough Bakery also sells chunky, homemade breads.

Walkers *(West Quay; Tel 01841/532-915; noon-6:30pm; takeout £2.50; No credit cards)* is the place to go for takeout fish and chips. For pizza, try **Rojano's** *(9 Mill Square; Tel 01841/532-796; 10:30am-10:30pm; £1.95-4.95 a slice; V, MC)*. They deliver!

▶▶**DO-ABLE**

Well-known British TV chef Rick Stein not only lives in Padstow; he also owns three restaurants and runs a cooking school there. **The Middle Street Café** *(Middle St.; Tel 01841/532-700, deli Tel 01841/532-221; noon-2:30pm/7-9:30pm Mon-Sat; £6 lunch, £10 dinner; all major credit cards except AE and DIN)* is the newest, most casual, and most affordable of the three. The main seafood restaurant has a deli next door where you can take a piece of culinary heaven home. Hidden inside the fudge from Stein's deli, a message awaits on a small slip of paper: "Would you believe that there is a fudge so good that strong men weep if deprived of it and otherwise scrupulous people creep through dark-ened rooms at dead of night to steal another morsel?" Just taste any dish here and you'll believe that about any of Rick Stein's food, not just the fudge.

crashing

Since Padstow is more upscale than your average Cornish town, there aren't any hostels in this area. There are heaps upon heaps of B&B's, though, ranging from £16 up per night. However, most of the cheaper ones are quite a walk uphill from the town center, hence their cheapness. The TIC will gladly book your accommodation for you, for a £2 fee [see *need to know,* below]. If you'd prefer to pound the pavement yourself, it will give you an extensive list of names to work with.

▶▶**DO-ABLE**

Janet Dawe *(50 Church St.; Tel/Fax 01841/532-121, mobile 07790/333-443; two doubles at £50 per room both en suite, Cash or trav-elers checks only)* has a 2-room B&B in a terrific house. Room 1 is very spacious with a big bathroom and has an excellent view of the church and trees next door. (Room 2 is nice too, but if you have a choice, go for Room 1.) You'll also get a delicious breakfast in Janet's kitchen, and with her charm and warmth, you'll feel like a personal houseguest.

If you just want to crash, and fast, the **London Inn** *(Lanadwell St.; Tel 01841/532-554; standard rooms share WC and shower, suites have pri-vate bathrooms; £18.50 standard, £22.50 suite; No credit cards)* is three minutes on foot from the center of town and the quay.

Tarka's Rest *(Sandy Lane, Trevone Bay; Tel 01841/520-007; fox@tarkasrest.freeserve.co.uk; en suite, TV in deluxe; £22 per person stan-dard, £27 per person deluxe)* is a quiet but friendly B&B right on Trevone Bay, just 150 yards from the beach. There's fresh air inside and out, thanks to the prop's no smoking policy. It's just 2 1/2 miles north of Padstow off

> ## only here
>
> Every year on **May Day,** the celebrated 'Obby 'Oss dances around town. The man who dresses as the 'Obby 'Oss wears a fearsome head mask that drapes into a body covering costume made of sailcloth. A circular wooden hoop about six feet in diameter shapes the costume's structure. 'Obby 'Oss dances and swirls through town accompanied by a "Teazer" who leads the procession with a "Teazer's Club" (a black leather pad colorfully painted and mounted on the end of a wooden rod). Other figures in the procession include people dressed in white with ribbons and sprays of cowslips and bluebells, musicians and drummers, dancers, and followers who sing the traditional "May Song."
>
> The celebration is a pagan folk ritual. 'Obby 'Oss is a rainmaker, fertility symbol, deterrent to the possible landing of the French centuries ago, or just a welcome to the summer. Whichever theory people prefer to believe, masses of them come to watch—40,000 during the year 2000.

the B3276 Newquay Road. Another quiet retreat, **Woodlands Close** *(Treator Padstow; Tel 01841/533-109; John@Stock65.freeserve.co.uk; £17 and up, one single, one double, one twin, all en suite)* offers a secluded bungalow with lovely gardens.

▶▶**SPLURGE**

Rick Stein's **The Middle Street Café** *(Middle St.; Tel 01841/532-700; rooms £65, £75, £85 per person, all en suite; all major credit cards except AE and DIN)* also has a beautiful B&B upstairs. The three rooms are rich in mahogany wood and beautiful decorative touches such as graceful chairs, rich cream bed throws, and lovely soaps in the bathroom.

need to know

Currency Exchange There are branches of **Barclays, Lloyds, Midland,** and **HSBC.** ATMs are located outside the Midland and Barclays, and inside Lloyds.

Tourist Info This tourist information center caters to Rock visitors as well, because Rock is too tiny to have one of its own. The center is located immediately opposite the ramp off the ferry at **The Red Brick Building** *(North Quay; Tel 01841/533-449, Fax 01841/532-356; 10am-5pm daily; padstowtic@visit.org.uk)* and is surprisingly well- stocked for such a small town. They have a huge range of books on places in the area, as well as pamphlets and lists of places to stay. The staff of the TIC will help you book accommodations in advance for a fee of £3, or on the same day for £2.

Public Transportation Everything in Padstow is within walking distance. **Ferries** *(goes back and forth all day except Sundays in winter; £1.60 round-trip)* operate regularly between Rock and Padstow across the Camel Estuary. At night, the **water taxis** *(Tel 01208/862-815 daytime, 01208/862-217 evening)* replace the ferries. A taxi trip across the estuary costs about £3 one way and £4 for a return trip.

Health and Emergency Police, fire, ambulance, and coastguard: *999* **Padstow Police Station** *(New St;. Tel 01841/532-514);* **Padstow Medical Center** *(Tel 01841/532-346).*

Pharmacies For your miscellaneous needs, head to **Taylors Chemist** *(8 The Market; Tel 01841/532-327).*

Telephone: City code: *01841*

Trains and Bus Lines Out of the City See **Rock,** above, for train and bus information.

Bike/Moped Rental A sublime trail is the Padstow-Wadebridge path (5-miles long) on the Camel Trail [see *city sports,* above]. You can rent bikes at **Padstow Cycle Hire** *(South Quay; Tel 01841/533-533, Mobile 07977/593-704; 9am-5pm daily, 5-9:30pm July and August; emmamurphy@padstowcyclehire.freeserve.co.uk; £6-8 for mountain bikes, tandems, or trailer bikes).*

Postal The **post office** *(Duke St.; Tel 01841/532-297)* sells a range of greetings cards, gifts, and wrapping paper. It is staffed with about four people who can handle all your postal needs.

central england

central england

you may be surprised to learn that the most popular tourist destination for North Americans in the UK (after London, of course) isn't birth-of-the-Beatles Liverpool, but birth-of-the-bard Shakespeare Country. **Stratford-Upon-Avon** is Britain's biggest tourist trap, but don't let that scare you away from the entire area. Just cruise through Stratford on your way to **Nottingham,** which is far less commercial and has far better places to hang out. It's famous for Robin Hood and **Sherwood Forest,** but that's old news—today Nottingham's ultrahip party scene attracts cool Brits from all over the country.

There are plenty of good party scenes in Central England's bigger cities, too: **Birmingham** and **Leicester** can easily satisfy your club cravings. Yet the overall vibe of the region is still about history, romanticism, and folklore. You've seen that Hollywood image in movies like *Shakespeare in Love, Robin Hood: Prince of Thieves,* and *National Lampoon's European Vacation.* That can acually be a good thing. The area is full of quaint little towns that can be fun to visit; Nottingham's nightlife is great, but so are its cobblestoned streets. And despite the throngs of tourists, you can catch Shakespearean performances in Stratford-upon-Avon's world-renowned theaters. Or you may want to get in some hiking in the sheep-grazing, thatched-roof rural areas of the **Cotswolds.** If you're looking to get away from it all, Central England is a great place to do it.

The region stretches from the mountainous valleys of the English-Welsh border in the west to the **North Sea** in the east. It is made up of smaller areas that consist of different counties that end with the postfix *shire.* In what's known as the Heart of England, there's **Staffordshire** in the north, which is mostly made up of a loose confederation of towns known as **Stoke-on-Trent; Shropshire** in the west, the home of the Tudor town **Shrewsbury; Gloucestershire** and the Cotswolds in the south; and **Warwickshire** in the middle, containing the Shakespearean Stratford-upon-Avon. **Leicestershire** in the east, and **Lincolnshire, Derbyshire,** and **Nottinghamshire** in the northeast are referred to as The East Midlands. When you drop the suffix "shire," you've got the names of the major cities of the Midlands.

The most industrial, big-city heart of Central England is, of course, the country's second largest city, **Birmingham,** which is in the process of being "spruced up." Birmingham and Leicester, which were once rather lackluster and drab, are continually being refurbished, with public funds

TRAVEL TIMES

Times by train unless otherwise indicated
*By road.

	Birmingham	Stratford-upon-Avon	Leicester	Derby	Nottingham
Birmingham	-	:50	:55	:45	1:15
Stratford-upon-Avon	:50	-	2:00	2:10	2:35
Leicester	:55	2:00	-	:35	:30
Derby	:45	2:10	:35	-	:30
Nottingham	1:15	2:35	:30	:30	-
Shrewsbury	1:00	2:15 / 2:35	2:20	1:50 / 2:40	2:15 / 2:45
Lincoln	2:05 / 3:20	4:00 / 4:25	1:35	1:20 / 1:50	:45 / 1:05
Warwick	:35	:25	2:05	1:35 / 2:10	2:15 / 2:35
Chipping Campden	1:00*	:20*	1:10*	1:35*	1:40*
Moreton-In-Marsh	1:45	2:15 / 2:35	2:50 / 3:35	2:30 / 3:00	3:00 / 3:50
Stow-On-The-Wold	1:05	:30*	1:20*	1:45*	1:50*
Lower Slaughter	1:10*	:35*	1:25*	1:50	1:55*

Shrewsbury	Loncoln	Warwick	Chipping Campden	Moreton-in-Marsh	Stow-On-The-Wold	Lower Slaughter	London
1:00	2:05 3:20	:35	1:00	1:45	1:05*	1:10*	1:40 2:05
2:15 2:35	4:00 4:25	:25	:20*	2:15 3:25	:30*	:35*	2:30
2:20	1:35	2:05	1:10*	2:50 3:25	1:20*	1:25*	1:30
1:50 2:40	1:20 1:50	1:35 2:10	1:35*	2:30 3:00	1:45	1:50	1:40 2:40
2:15 2:45	:45 1:05	2:15 2:35	1:40	3:00 3:50	1:50*	1:55*	1:40 2:05
-	4:15 5:15	1:50 2:20	1:45*	2:50 3:50	1:50*	1:50*	3:30
4:15 5:15	-	3:20	1:45*	4:50 5:50	1:50*	1:50*	2:20 3:00
1:50 2:20	3:20*	-	:30*	1:30 2:40	:40*	:45*	2:00
1:45*	1:45*	:30*	-	:10*	:15*	:20*	2:00*
2:50 3:50	4:50 5:40	1:30 2:40	:10*	-	:05*	:10*	1:20 1:10
1:50*	1:50*	:40*	:15*	:05*	-	:05*	1:50*
1:50*	1:50*	:45*	:20*	:10*	:05*	-	1:50*

building up the arts and historical sites, and creating inner-city parkland. Visitors are discovering the charms that make it worthwhile to penetrate the urban sprawl. And what these two cities have to offer you is an amazing nightlife.

In the Midlands, refer to **69 Magazine** for excellent advice on where to spend the evening, as it details club nights in Derby, Leicester, Nottingham, and Birmingham. The downside is that you may have trouble finding it in Derby, unless you've picked it up in bars or cafes in Leicester. The free **What's On Midlands** guide doesn't have descriptions of places to chill, but it is a good source of information for cultural attractions, concerts, and performances, as is the black & white **City Lights.**

GETTING AROUND THE REGION

Central England is easily accessible from London, Manchester, Cardiff, and Edinburgh via an intricate network of railway lines, and by National Express buses. Birmingham also has a major international airport. A quick tour of the region's spots is quite easy using public transportation. But you might want to consider renting a car in the Cotswolds, where bus service will work, but requires quite a lot of planning.

▶▶SUGGESTED ROUTES

A good, quick, circuitous tour from London would be to take few days to hit Stratford-upon-Avon first, then Birmingham, followed by Leicester, Nottingham, and Lincoln, and then head back to London.

If you're looking for more time in the outdoors, extend your visit into the Cotswolds. When you stop in Stratford-upon-Avon, take the local Badgerline bus to your pick of Cotswold towns along its route (Moreton-in-Marsh and Chipping Campden are really great R&R stops).

birmingham

Long before Duran Duran put it on the map, Birmingham was a favorite target of the Nazi *Luftwaffe*. They bombed it so many times that the repeated efforts to patch up the holes turned Britain's second-largest city into one gigantic blob of concrete. The City Centre is an ugly jumble of vehicle-free pavilions, empty piazzas, traffic-jammed highways, and a large underground network of pedestrian tunnels. Sporadic splotches of grass have been planted as a weak attempt to break up the brutal monotony, but an overall feeling of ugliness remains.

So why go there? It's a blast! You'll be surprised at how much fun it is to party in this city of over a million people. Not only does Birmingham claim to have more pubs and bars per square mile than any place on earth, it also has a completely unpretentious and racially diverse population that is mercifully free of the airs and tension you find in cities such as London. It's not that people here are woefully unhip, it's just that they don't put it in your face. Four universities keep the city fresh and are the reason behind occasional ultra-dope venues you wouldn't want to miss. It's not as trendy as the smaller nearby city of Leicester, but in some ways it's better because it has the edge of being "up-and-coming."

Brummies—the locals—represent a range of tastes from designer-label fanatics to shabby-looking vagrants. The city's vibrant racial mix is particularly refreshing if you've been traveling around England and visiting way too many all-white towns. It feels as multicultural as London, with a lot of immigrants, many of them Russian or Indian, and refugees seeking religious asylum.

Still, Brummies you encounter on the street aren't necessarily as friendly as the ones you hang out with in the bars and clubs. If you're

five things to talk to a local about

1. **Directions:** In this metropolis of concrete, asking how to get somewhere is the perfect ice-breaker.
2. **National music festivals:** The national pastime for people under 30 is attending hard house, drum 'n' bass, and trance music festivals with infamous DJs, such as the annual English countryside musicfest Gatecrasher *(www.efestivals.co.uk/gatecrasher/)*, usually held in Sheffield. Brummies seem to be especially fond of the event.
3. **The City of Brighton:** The consensus seems to be that the coastal city of Brighton is the place to party, and young Brummies may be able to offer you advice on where to go and where not to go in the beachside town (it's best reached by rail through London for a weekend).
4. **Vinyl:** There are quite a few vinyl shops in Birmingham, indicating that spinning is a major activity.
5. **Restaurants:** Fine dining is a specialty of the city; find out where the best local eats are.

holding a map and looking lost, chances are no one's going to stop and offer you help. And if you're female, don't be surprised if strange men leer at you and call out, "Hey, beautiful," every few minutes. Don't take it too personally—that's just life in the big city. Save your energy for pubbing and clubbing at night and exploring the rich variety of neighborhoods by day. And if you have any energy left over, you may want to check out the city's first-rate symphony, ballet company, art galleries, and museums.

Several publications tell you where to find the parties, what's on exhibit at which gallery, and who's performing at what theater. The fabulous *69 Magazine* and *City Lights* will assist you in making critical hanging out decisions. Also pick up a copy of *What's On Birmingham* at the main tourist information center, properly known as the Birmingham Convention and Visitor Bureau [see *need to know,* below]. The BCVB also has a free 95-page magazine-style guide called *Birmingham* that lists hotels, restaurants, historic buildings, nearby sights, and pretty much anything else you need to know at a glance.

neighborhoods

Birmingham's main shopping district is the **City Centre,** which also has most of the city's cultural atractions as well as two hot areas for nightlife:

birmingham 297

Brindley Place, a broad plaza on the southwestern end of the center, and **Broad Street,** a wide main thoroughfare running southwest from the Town Hall. After dark these areas are packed with bar-hoppers looking to pull (English slang for "pick up"). During the day, you might see small groups of individuals discreetly smoking weed on the street—an activity that is quite popular in Central England. The City Centre is bounded on the west and north by the Canal, and on the east by **James Watt Queensway** and **Moor Street Queensway,** which leads to New Street Station, the main rail terminus on the southeastern edge of the center. Dead center of the City Centre is the St. Philip's Cathedral, and, five blocks to the southwest, the Town Hall. North of the City Centre is **Old Snow Hill,** which sports a small train station as well as office buildings. To the northeast is Aston University and the surrounding student area; surprisingly, there aren't that many trendy bars packed with students in this neighborhood. Southeast of the city center, three blocks beyond the New Street Station, is the central bus depot, Digbeth Coach Station, which marks the beginning of a dodgy area called **Digbeth.** It's a bit scary to walk around here alone after dark, but it is home to the cool **Sanctuary** night club [see *club scene,* below], as well as the **Medicine Bar** [see *bar scene,* below].

Like any proper big city, Birmingham has both a Chinatown and a gay village. The **Chinese Quarter,** between **Smallbrook Queensway** and **Ladywell Walk** (reachable via bus 126 to Ladywell Walk) is minuscule; it takes up about a city block, with just a couple of shops and restaurants in buildings with Chinese-style facades. Unless you've never been to any Chinatown in any city, just skip it. Right next door is the **Gay Village,** in the area between **Shirlock Street** and **Queensway,** with **Bromsgrove, Kent** and **Hurst** streets as the main avenues. It's bigger than the Chinese Quarter, thankfully; the main shops and bars are along Hurst Street. It really comes alive at night, with house music pumping from—and big crowds packing into—all the clubs.

A duller but better-known neighborhood is the **Jewellery Quarter,** the area between **Fredrick Street** and **Great Hampton Street,** reachable via bus 101 and 101a from **Livery** or **New Street.** From the City Centre, it's a 10-minute walk northwest up Newhall or Fredrick, both of which are lined with inconsequential brick and white office buildings. When you come to the traffic circle with a clock tower, you're in the heart of this district, which includes more than 100 jewelry shops. Aside from bargains in diamonds, the only thing arguably worth seeing in the Quarter is the **Museum of the Jewellery Quarter** [see *culture zoo,* below].

About 2 miles southwest of the City Centre is **Edgbaston** (reachable via bus 128 from City Centre), home to the **Birmingham Botanical Gardens Glasshouses,** [see *culture zoo,* below] as well as the University of Birmingham, a sociable place to hang out. Other than the university, the neighborhood is mainly a quiet, nondescript residential area, but it has tons of small hotels and B&Bs along the main drag, **Hagley Road.**

So if you haven't made hotel reservations, just hop on a bus and check into any of the accommodations lining the street.

A particularly whacked-out area to visit is **Wolverhampton,** northwest of City Centre (reachable via bus 128 or the train). Technically, it's not part of Birmingham, but most young Brummies have adopted the college neighborhood as their own, anyhow. Ask any young hipster where the party is and you're likely to hear: "Have you been to Wolverhampton yet?" University of Wolverhampton students fill the bars; pubs packed with students line the streets; and the predominance of Italian eateries makes it feel a bit like Little Italy—or at least *The Sopranos.*

hanging out

If you're looking to meet young-adult Brummies, the University of Birmingham in Edgbaston, southwest of the City Centre, is a great place to chill. Their Student Union, on the campus, has an outdoor seating area—a perfect place to drink a pint (or ten) of lager and chat up attractive students. Considering Birmingham's large student population, you may wonder at first why you don't see more of them running around in the City Centre by day. But after you've seen this lovely campus you'll know why. There's no reason to leave unless they're looking for some serious partying, and for that they'll venture downtown—but only after dark.

One good nighttime hang in the City Centre (some parts are definitely livelier than others) is Broad Street, which leads southwest to Edgbaston from the City Centre. It's packed with bar-hoppers hanging out inside the many pubs and clubs. While some of the commercial pubs on this street, such as the Walkabout, may not appeal to you, they are at least fantastically social places.

down and out

Birmingham's a great city because you won't have to dish out big quid to enjoy its attractions. Amazing art galleries and museums that are free include The Barber Institute of Fine Arts, Birmingham Museum & Art Gallery, and the Ikon Gallery. Pubs are great places to check out the different Brummie scenes. Visit Coster Mongers to join in with the rocker crowd, and Sputnik to be amongst the trendy people. Of course, it's almost as much fun to chill out in the City Centre—people-watching is always free!

Rules of the game

Liquor laws in pubs appear to forbid any drinking after 11pm—but after the pub, it's onto the club, where you'll likely be able to down pints and sip cocktails till 2am, maybe later. Drinking is socially acceptable, and it's quite common to see youth and adults alike walking around with open booze in their hands. But Brummies are a bit tough on underage foreigners getting drunk in the pubs, especially during tourist season, which includes the entire summer. Expect to be asked for ID proving you're over 18—and always be prepared to show it. You'll see the occasional pot smoker, but everybody keeps their toking on the down low. And if you see folks rolling something up in papers at the local pub, don't assume it's marijuana—hand-rolled cigarettes are the latest trend.

In Birmingham, you should behave in the same way as you would back home; assuming that you visit the jail infrequently in your town, you shouldn't expect to see a British prison anytime in the near future. Even better, you can drink without the brown paper bag hiding your beer; coppers keep their focus on more serious crime. Overall, the police are people you can ask for directions. They'll be the least memorable part of your trip to the city—that is, unless you have bank-robbing or drug-dealing on your itinerary.

bar scene

Like any British university city, there's a profuse amount of drinking among the college-aged kids. Birmingham has a staggering mixture of pubs and bars, so you'll have your pick between traditional, retro, and hip.

Off the U of B campus, a traditional-style pub with dodgy music that's popular with University students is the **Old Varsity Tavern Public House** *(561 Bristol Rd.; Tel 0121/472-31-86; Noon-11pm Mon-Sat, noon-10:30pm Sun; V, MC)*, on the main highway leading south from Birmingham City Centre. As the third-largest pub in England, you can imagine how many wasted students it takes to pack the place to capacity.

Walkabout *(266 Broad St; Tel 0121/632-57-12; 11am-11pm daily)*, at the southeastern end of the City Centre, is another student hang, with lots of outdoor chill space and a perpetual U2 soundtrack.

A pub with a trendier feel goin' on is **Sputnik** *(Temple St.; Noon-3pm/5-11pm Mon-Fri, 6-11pm Sat)*. Located around the corner from the St. Philip's Cathedral, this bar has a "space walk" happy hour

birmingham

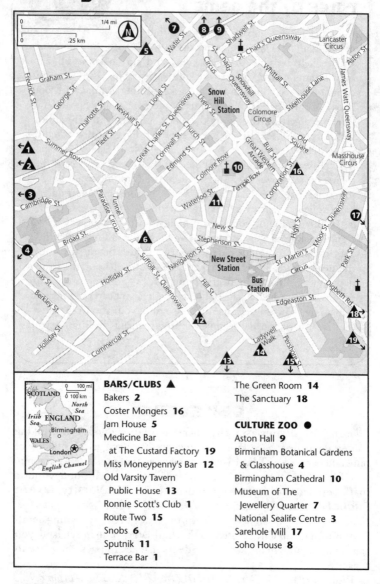

BARS/CLUBS ▲

Bakers **2**

Coster Mongers **16**

Jam House **5**

Medicine Bar
  at The Custard Factory **19**

Miss Moneypenny's Bar **12**

Old Varsity Tavern
  Public House **13**

Ronnie Scott's Club **1**

Route Two **15**

Snobs **6**

Sputnik **11**

Terrace Bar **1**

The Green Room **14**

The Sanctuary **18**

CULTURE ZOO ●

Aston Hall **9**

Birminham Botanical Gardens
  & Glasshouse **4**

Birmingham Cathedral **10**

Museum of The
  Jewellery Quarter **7**

National Sealife Centre **3**

Sarehole Mill **17**

Soho House **8**

between noon-2pm and 5-7pm Mon-Fri. If that doesn't entice you, then maybe this underground pub's stairway will: it's painted with trippy space aliens invading Earth. Unfortunately, there are no real Martians (that we know of) in this dimly-lit pub, but there are live DJs spinning hip music, and a relaxed, stylishly dressed twentysomething crowd drinking and shooting the shit.

Another downstairs pub, located at the entrance of the Priory Square shopping center, is **Coster Mongers** *(Dalton Way; Bus 74, 78, 79 to Ball St.; Noon-11pm Mon-Sat, 7pm-10:30pm Sun)*. Its stairway is covered with Guns 'N' Roses, Bon Jovi, and Cult posters. An army-pants wearing, industrial-looking mixed-aged crowd gathers here for loud indie/mainstream alternative/rock/'80s music spun by a DJ.

Don't let the bland exterior decor of **Miss Moneypenny's Bar** *(14-16 Suffolk St.; Tel 0121/633-77-70; glamourous@miss-mon eypennys.com; Bar 5:30-11pm Mon-Sat, club 9:30pm-2:30am Sat; V, MC)*, a 5-minute walk north of New Street Station in Queensway, fool you. It attracts a good-looking crowd, a deliberate strategy carried out with ads targeted at what is hopefully thought of as a glamorous, city-chic clientele. There are weekly DJ theme parties like '60s or Ibiza nights, but on most nights it's mainly an eclectic mixture of tunes.

LIVE MUSIC SCENE

Believe it or not, Birmingham is home to a high-brow live music scene. Jazz music tops the list: Expect to see world-renowned stars jamming at the city's infamous Ronnie Scott's Club. If you're in the mood for heavier metal, emmo(tion) music, or mainstream bands, no worries: Birmingham has two major venue arenas, the National Exhibition Centre (NEC) Arena, and the National Indoor Arena.

The star of Birmingham's live music venues is **Ronnie Scott's Club/Terrace Bar** *(Broad St.; Tel 0121/643-45-25; info@ronniescotts. demon.co.uk; www.ronnie-scotts.co.uk; table reservations and pre-booked tickets highly recommended; £5-18.50 cover; AE, V, MC, D)*. Outside there's a terrace (as the name promises) with a burrito stand, and inside there's a bar area to your left. If you take a right and go down the sexy red corridor, you'll end up in the very crowded club, with a stage towards the back. While you eat your fixed-price dinner (£19.95-23.95) of salmon roulade or braised lamb shank with prune, your ears will fill up with the vocals of old-school crooners like Tony Bennett, new-jack masters like Joshua Redman, world-renowned Jamaican artists, or perhaps some Brit Pop Mod. You're not required to eat dinner or even order a drink, but they can't guarantee you a table unless you do.

For live R&B, soul, dance and funk, check out the **Jam House** *(1 St. Paul's Sq.; Tel 0121/200-30-30; Noon-midnight Mon, Tue, noon-2am Wed-Fri, 6pm-2am Sat; info@thejamhouse.com, www.thejamhouse.com; Free Mon, Tue; £3 after 9pm Wed, Thur; £3 after 7pm Fri, Sat, £5 after 8pm, £7 after 10pm; AE, V, MC, DC)* just northeast of City Centre. It attracts a straight-laced, mixed-aged (though mostly older) kind of crowd, but don't think stodgy—these people come to get down and boogie. There's a "bucket menu" with burgers around £6, and main courses for about £13 (try the steamed coconut chicken).

If you want to catch the big-time music acts like Radiohead, Santana, etc., there's the **National Exhibition Centre [NEC] Arena** *(near Birmingham International Airport; Tel 0121/780-41-33; Show times and* *prices vary; www.ticketweb.co.uk, www.ticketmaster.co.uk; MC, V),* which can hold 12,000 fans, or the **National Indoor Arena** *(King Edward's Rd.; Tel 0121/780-44-44, credit card hotlines 0121/220-99-88 or 08705/321-321; www.ticketzone.co.uk; Show times and prices vary; MC, V),* a 5-minutes walk west of Town Hall, just across Canal.

club scene

There are so, so, so many places to party in Birmingham—each good on a different night—that it's impossible to list them all. But here's a selection of places chosen for their reputation, popularity, range of music, and highly-reviewed parties:

There's nothing dodgy to say about the **Medicine Bar** at the **Custard Factory** *(Gibb St., Digbeth; Bus 37; Tel 0121/693-63-33; £3-4 cover; No credit cards),* off Digbeth High Street, an artists' building complex complete with a central pond—it's just something you've gotta check out. The Medicine Bar hosts a rotation of killer once-a-month parties. The last Friday of every month, *Overproof* hits you with highly infectious Ska, Reggae, and a bit of Dub—a total change from the "mind-elevating" trance so common in club land. If you want a party with style, try to be in town for *Procreation,* held on the first Saturday of every month, so you can get your groove on to the deep house dished from the decks. To make a weekend out of it, stick around for *Real,* held on the first Sunday of the month. It's DJed by the hosts of a radio show on Real FM, and there's no admission charge.

Thankfully, **Snobs** *(29 Paradise Circus; Tel 0121/643-55-51; 10pm-3am Fri, Sat; £3-4 cover; www.snobs-nightclub.com),* next door to the Town Hall in the City Centre, doesn't live up to its name—the only thing elitist about this place is that it requires slick duds, as defined by your friendly bouncer fashion consultant. It occupies a corner of a building surrounded by a busy highway—not very exclusive-looking. The club's "big room" and "small room" pack a jumpin crowd of friendly young

boy meets girl

When you go out for a night on the town, it's common to see separate groups of girls and guys. In all, it's a bit reminiscent of elementary school. With this in mind, it's easy to predict how a young gentleman approaches a girl he's interested in. He'll come up to her with a friend, or perhaps, if he's really shy, get that friend to introduce them. To generalize, you might label The Approach as somewhat less aggressive than you're used to. This is quite surprising, considering all the men in the city who will give ladies a whistle as they walk by.

locals dancing and hanging out. *Freak Scene,* every other Friday, is a night of "alternative disco" and "female trouble"—'70s, glam, and '80s music. This party alternates with *UFO,* a night of Brit Pop, mod and soul music, with groovy big beats and disco in the small room. To make the party rotation more complex, every four weeks Friday becomes *Life is Easy:* A devoted crowd lines up for music for 1962 to Y2K in the big room and '60s, '70s, jazz, hip-hop, and funk in the small room. Saturdays alternate between *Melt* and *Loaded. Melt's* a night without a dress code, when the sloppily-dressed people show up to listen to indie and alternative music in the small room and '60s soul in the big room. *Loaded* has the same music, but the sounds played in the two rooms are reversed (so everybody gets their chance to feel important).

Satan's Paradise *(Moseley St.; Bus 50 to Digbeth from Moor St.; Tel 0121/440-66-33; £4-5 Fri)* offers up another cool Friday night party, *Fused.* It's a night of underground British garage and breakbeats. Resident DJs alternate on the decks as a young-adult crowd dances along in ritual worship. This party is truly what UK music is all about; an essential if you're keen on the scene or want to experience true Britishness.

Another seriously good place to spend your weekend nights is **The Sanctuary** *(78 Digbeth High St., Digbeth; Bus 37 from Corporation St.; Tel 0121/246-10-10; 9pm-2am Wed-Sat; Free after 1am).* Pass through a red hallway with chandeliers to venture into the club's four rooms, including the spacey Dragon Bar chill-out room, fully equipped with free Sony Playstations. The other three rooms are straight-up dance halls. Saturday's party, *Ramshackle (www.ramshackle.org.uk),* mixes up "Indie and Funky Shit" for the hipster crowd, and Thursday's *Club Blitz* pumps out the goth, rock, industrial, and punk. As for dress code, there's no pressure here to dress to impress.

A club that's hard to find, but may be worth the effort—depending on the day you go—is **Bakers** *(162 Broad St.; Tel 0121/633-38-39; 10pm-2am Wed, 10pm-2am Fri, Sat; Cover varies up to £10),* located in a shopping complex on Auchinleck Square, off the busy expressway of Broad Street. You know you're there when you see the crowd waiting to get in through the dark entranceway, lit mainly by blue-plasma screens on the ceiling. Friday night's *Horney* is hit or miss—depending on the DJ, you may be better off elsewhere, but not if Dave Pearce, a Radio 1 DJ and monthly resident, hits the decks. The hefty door fee and queue are *always* worth it to hear the string of UK guest DJs at Saturday's *Republica* party. Go even if you haven't heard of the DJs—trust us, they're known on the Birmingham scene.

And finally, there's the three-floor **Que Club** *(Corporation St.; Tel 0121/212-07-70; 9pm-6am Sat, sometimes Fri; £10-20; No credit cards),* a 10-minute walk east of Town Hall. This is another one not to miss for the best of British music. Well-known for crazy X-static all-night partying till dawn, the club has a nice underground rave quality. Depending on the party promoters, you may get an earful of hard house or a blissed-out helping of trance.

ARTS SCENE

▶▶VISUAL ARTS

If you're looking to enjoy a visit to a full-on art gallery—one with no uniformed staff following you around to see if you're going to stuff an oversized painting in your backpack—go to the remarkable little **Ikon Gallery** *(1 Oozells Sq.; Tel 0121/248-07-08; No admission charge)*, just off Brindleyplace. Expect installations that consist of video art using wall projections, along with other media.

▶▶PERFORMING ARTS

Birmingham has a really excellent theater scene, with everything from serious concert halls to comedy clubs. You can get half-priced tickets for most of the main venues on performance days by going to the Tourist Information Centre in the Town Hall after 11am, or calling the **Half-Price Ticket Information Line** *(Tel 0845/769-71-26)*. For students and/or people under the age of 24, there's a discount pass that allows you to save up to 50 percent off ticket sales throughout the city (as well as 10 percent off purchases at the city's Tower Records); it's called the **YES Pass** *(Tel 0121/622-12-34; Information also available at box offices; £6 1-year membership)*.

For quality drama, dance, live music, or indie film screenings, don't miss the **mac (Midlands Arts Centre)** *(Cannon Hill Park; Bus 1, 35, 45, 47, 62, 63 to Edgbaston Rd.; Tel 0121/440-38-38; Box office 9am-8:45pm daily, building 9am-11pm daily; Prices vary; www.birmingham arts.org.uk/mac;)*. Located in Edgbaston, opposite the County Cricket Ground, the mac houses three performance arenas, and often puts up free art exhibitions.

Since its completion in 1990, **Symphony Hall** *(International Convention Centre, Broad St.; Tel 0121/212-33-33; www.symphonyhall.co.uk/ symphony; Admission varies, £7.50 student & YES-Card stand-by tickets available from 1pm on performance days; AE, V, MC, DC)*, just west of Town Hall, has been hailed as an "acoustical gem". But you'd never guess by looking at it: The inside of the Hall looks more like a mall or bus station than the home to the City of Birmingham Symphony Orchestra. There's a glass ceiling, white walls, a beige tile floor, and multi-level balconies with glass railings next to rows of what look like seats from an airport waiting room.

Next door is the **Birmingham Repertory Theatre** *(Centenary Sq.; Tel 0121/236-44-55; Box office 9:30am-8pm Mon-Sat; Admission varies)*, just west of Town Hall, which appropriately looks much more like a theater than a bus station. It houses one of the top repertoire companies in England, with which some of the world's greatest actors have performed over the years, including Lord Olivier, Dame Edith Evans, and the sexy Kenneth Branagh. The widely known REP comprises the main house, which seats 900 theater-goers, and The Door, a more intimate 140-seat theater that often stages cosmopolitan, artsy works.

The **Birmingham Hippodrome Theatre** *(Hurst St.; Tel 0121/622-74-86; Box office 10am-8pm Mon-Sat)*, in the Gay Village, is home to the Birmingham Royal Ballet and visiting companies from around the world. It hosts a variety of events from the Welsh National Opera and musicals to dance.

National touring companies, many putting on productions from London's West End, perform at the **Alexandra Theatre** *(Hill St.; Tel 0870/670-75-33; Box office 8:30am-10pm Mon-Fri, 8:30am-9:30pm Sat, 10am-8pm Sun; www.tickets-direct.co.uk; Show times and prices vary; AE, V, MC)*, just southeast of Town Hall. It shows a lot of those childhood musicals you never thought you'd see performed again, like *Annie*. Past productions targeted at a more adult audience include *Elvis the Musical, Stand By Me,* and *Rent.*

Okay, so maybe a comedy club stretches the definition of "performing arts," but getting up on stage and bringing down the house every night is an art, right? The comedians doing live stand-up at **Glee Club** *(Arcadian Centre, Hurst St.; Tel 0121/693-22-48; Ticket and table reservations available; Thur-Sat; Admission varies, student discounts)* would say so. Both hot locals and star out-of-towners play here, to belly-laughing crowds.

gay scene

The best gay bars in Birmingham are in the Gay Village (where did you expect them to be?):

Partners *(Hurst St.; Tel 0121/622-47-10; 1pm-11pm daily)*, a community bar during the week, offers early-evening live cabaret, DJs, and occasional strippers on the weekends.

Boots Bar *(Wrentham St.; Tel 0121/622-14-14; 8pm-2am Wed-Sat, 3-11pm Sun; £2 cover before 10:30pm Wed-Fri, £3 after; £3 before 10:30pm, Sat, £4 after)* is your classic all-male cruise club, with two dark rooms throbbing with trance music.

The **Green Room** *(Hurst St., opposite the Hippodrome Theater; Tel 0121/605-43-43; Noon-11pm Mon-Wed, till 1am Thur, till 2:30am Fri; V, MC with £5 minimum charge)* is a relaxed cafe-bar that welcomes a friendly mixed crowd of gays, lesbians, transgenders, and straights. There are live bands on Thursdays; the rest of the time you can chill out to pre-recorded trip-hop mixes.

An older crowd hangs out at **The Jester** *(Horsefair, Holloway Circus; Tel 0121/643-01-55; Noon-11pm daily)*, a windowless cellar bar in Queensway. People sometimes get up and dance, especially on Friday and Saturday nights when the DJ comes in and plays cheesy dance music.

After an evening of bar hopping, keep things going at one of the Gay Village's super-duper clubs. A good first stop on your clubbing itinerary would be the 31-year-old **Nightingale** *(Essex House, Kent St.; Tel 0121/622-17-18; hours vary Tue, Wed, Fri-Sun; Free-£7 cover;nightin gale.club@virgin.net; www.nightingaleclub.co.uk; AE, V, MC, DC)*, which boasts of its "five bars, three levels, two discos, restaurant, cafe-bar, games room, and garden." Whew! But really, all you need to know is that it's a good place for meeting cute gays with English accents. The heavily advertised *Ultimate Karma* party moves in to "the Attic" (the third floor) on

birmingham gay and lesbian pride

When you see a crowd of straight-laced office workers and outlandish pink-wigged drag princesses mingling, and a hint of festivity in the air, it's probably **Birmingham Gay and Lesbian Pride** *(Birmingham Pride Media Centre, 72 Hurst St.; Tel 0121/ 244-80-80; www.birminghampride.com)*. This highly-acclaimed event, held every year during bank holiday weekend (usually the last Monday in May) appears to get better and better each year, as the celebration moves beyond the Gay Village boundaries and into the City Centre. Besides the plenitude of special events the gay clubs and bars offer, there's a street festival and the Mass Camp Parade, which attempts to compare itself to Sydney's Gay Mardi Gras. Although it doesn't draw hundreds of thousands of people as its role model does, it's definitely a Don't-Miss.

the second Friday of the month; look for flyers around town. Many of the parties seem to be the epitome of gay stereotypes: Tuesday's *Fabba than Abba* is a night of '70s and '80s music complete with a go-go boy; Wednesdays are karaoke disco. On the weekends, Top-40 dance and commercial house takes over the whole place.

Dress casual for a fun night at the popular **Route Two** *(139/147 Hurst St.; Tel 0121/622-33-66; 7pm-2am Mon-Sat, 7-10:30pm Sun; Free-£4; V, MC)*. While disco balls spin, fly boys dance to Cindy Lauper's "Girls Just Want to Have Fun." Mixed male and female clientele gather at the center bar, catch their breath in the table area, or scope things out from the standing-room-only balcony that overlooks the dance floor. There's also a separate back room with a typical English pub atmosphere. On Saturdays, this is where you'll see co-ed couples kissing.

Located away from the gay heartland, in what seems to be the middle of nowhere—an area that's practically deserted at night—sits **Subway City** *(27 Water St.; Bus 74, 78, 79 from Moor St. to Constitution Hill; Tel 0121/233-03-10; Hours vary Thur-Sat)*. This well-known, recently born gay club actually has a designated "straight" night on Fridays, with Brit pop and indie music, that draws a student crowd. Thursdays are packed to capacity with a crowd of mostly gay guys grinding to '70s and '80s tunes. Saturday is Subway City's big night, with a mixed lesbian and gay crowd in their twenties or thirties dancing to hot dance hits.

If all that clubbing starts to make you hungry, head to **Angels Café Bar** *(127-131 Hurst St.; Tel 0121/244-26-26; 11am-11pm daily)* for a next day brunch where you can gobble down a make-your-own sandwich for £2.50. There are also venue flyers for your next night of partying.

CULTURE ZOO

Birmingham's cultural sites range from multiple-visit-worthy to "you should pay *me* to visit this site." Get your share of childish fun at Cadbury World, the famous British chocolate factory's visitor center, and the National Sea Life Centre, a creative and intelligent aquarium. Decidedly more adult-oriented (and arguably much duller) are two historical houses, Soho House and Aston Hall. Art hounds have two impressive, well-funded museums to choose from. Learn everything you've ever wanted to know about stone cutting at The Museum of the Jewellery Quarter. There are also several offbeat tours of Birmingham worth considering, all arranged by the main Tourist Information Centre [see *need to know*, below], but you'll need to drop by in person to book ahead. Like most towns in Central England, Birmingham has a double-decker bus tour, plus a walking Graveyard Trail that explores the whereabouts of notable deceased Brummies.

Cadbury World *(Bournville Lane; Tel 0121/451-41-59, 24 hour info 0121/451-41-80; Bus 83, 84 and 85; Times vary, open daily mid Feb-Oct, days vary Nov-mid-Feb; Reservations strongly recommended; Admission varies):* Come live out your Willy Wonka fantasies here. On your visit, you (and about a million children) will learn about the history of chocolate, and get to ride on the "Cadabara" through an enchanted chocolate wonderland, as well as eat liquid chocolate served by tired-looking staff members. You don't get to see the actual workings of the factory, but that's probably for the best—it would just take the magic out of it to see hair-netted workers plopping chocolate on to an assembly line....

The **National Sealife Centre** *(Brindleyplace; Tel 0121/633-47-00; 10am-5pm daily; £7.50 adult, £5.95 student, www.sealife.co.uk):* Just west of Town Hall, this great attraction brings in as many adults as children. Relaxing music flows from the speakers as you follow the rampways past what seems like miles of sea creatures and plants. Hands down the coolest exhibit is the 360-degree glass tunnel that lets you walk through the shark tank (don't worry, the glass is *extremely* thick). The only downside is the hefty admission price.

Barber Institute of Fine Arts *(University of Birmingham; Tel 0121/414-73-33; Admission free):* Don't be put off by the stark stone and brick building that houses this Edgbaston institution—some English art critics consider this to be the finest small art museum in England. Its selection of paintings includes works by Beeline, Turner, Van Gogh, and Whistler; two gotta-sees are Simone Martini's *St. John the Evangelist,* and Monet's *Church at Varengeville.*

Birmingham Museum & Art Gallery *(Chamberlain Sq.; Tel 0121/303-28-34; No admission charge):* Though mainly known for its pre-Raphaelite paintings, the BMAC (as it's known to Brummies) also has exceptional 18th-century watercolors. Even if you skipped art history in college, you'll still enjoy a trip here. Easy to find, right next door to Town Hall.

The **Museum of the Jewellery Quarter** (*75-79 Vyse St.; Tel 0121/554-35-98; Bus 101, 101a to Warstone Lane or Fredrick St.; 10am-4pm Mon-Fri, 11am-5pm Sat; www.birmingham.gov.uk/html/ tourist info/jewel.html; £2.50 adult, £2 student; V, MC with £5 minimum charge):* Okay, so it sounds like someplace you were forced to visit on an 8th grade field trip, but this place is actually very recommendable—at least it's a nice change from all those fussy art museums you've been going to. It displays some wildly artistic work of jewelry school students from the Birmingham Institute of Art and Design. You'll get a 1-hour tour of an old-world jewelry-making factory—exactly how the owners left it when the factory shut its doors. The machinery, which your friendly guide will turn on during the tour, is authentic, running just as it did in another past

Soho House (*Soho Ave.; Tel 0121/554-91-22; Bus 70, 74, 78, 79 to Soho Rd.; Bus 74, 78, 79 or metro to Soho Benson Road; 10am-5pm Tue-Sat, noon-5pm Sun and bank holidays; www.birmingham.gov.uk/bmag; £2.50 adult, £2 student):* Birmingham has several "heritage" sites highly promoted as tourists attractions, but they really only appeal to older audiences and history nuts. The 18th-century home of pioneer Matthew Boulton, just off Soho Road, is one of those attractions. This house, which may have been the first centrally heated house in England, is a bit of a bore unless you're into looking at antique clocks and vases, plates and tableware—products made at Mr. Boulton's factory.

Sarehole Mill (*Cole Bank Rd.; Tel 0121/777-66-12; Bus 5 or 6 to Stratford, Metro to Hall Green Station; Open afternoons daily Apr-Oct; Free):* Another site you may want to put off seeing for another 20 years, this working watermill was the "childhood haunt" of J.R.R. Tolkien.

Aston Hall (*Trinity Rd.; Tel 0121/327-00-62; Bus 65, 104, 7, 11, 653 to Aston or the train to Aston or Witton Road metro stations; 2-5pm daily Easter to Oct; Free):* Built between 1618 and 1635 in "flamboyant Jacobean style," this beautiful "proud heritage site" is actually worth seeing. Its ceilings have elaborate plaster ornamentation, and there's an awesome oak staircase that bears scars from when the house was damaged by cannon-fire after King Charles I spent a night here during the English Civil War.

St. Philip's Cathedral (*Colmore Row; Tel 0121/236-43-33; 7am-7pm Mon-Fri, 9am-5pm Sat, Sun; No admission charge):* Smack in the middle of the City Centre is something no English city would be complete without—a church designated to be a cathedral. It's not that spectacular, though, especially if you've visited the grandiose cathedral in Lincoln.

Birmingham Botanical Gardens & Glasshouse (*Westbourne Rd; Tel 0121/454-18-60; Bus 10, 21, 22, 23, 29, 103 to Westbourne Road; 9am-7pm Mon-Fri, 9am-8pm Sat, Sun, May-Aug; Closes one hour earlier Sept-Apr; admin@bham-bot-gdns.demon.co.uk; www.bham-bot-gdns. demon.co.uk; £4.60 adult Mon-Sat, £4.30 Sun and bank holidays):* Birmingham has several nature preserves, and this one in Edgbaston is one of the nicest. Lovingly manicured lawns, walking trails cut through flora, landscaped shrubbery with views of peacock cages and fish ponds, and tunnels made from towering beds of flowers make this place a pleasure on a hot and sunny day.

The **Graveyard Trail** *(Tourist Info Center, Town Hall; Tel 0121/693-63-00 or 0121/643-25-14; Times and dates vary; £4.50 adult, £4 students):* This really excellent guided walk through various districts explores burial grounds including the spooky Birmingham catacombs.

modification

There are plenty of places to get an extra hole poked in your body, but the hippest shops are in the gay hood. You'll see ads in all the gay magazines for the **Needle Works** *(The Arcadian Centre, 84 Hurst St.; Tel 0121/622-73-46; 1-6pm Mon, till 8pm Thur-Sat; www.clonezone.co.uk).* You don't need to be any particular sexual orientation to get body pierced, though, or to purchase gold, surgical steel, colored, or gem-stone jewellery. After paying for your puncture wounds, you can complete your look with a new *coiffure* at the unisex **Funky Crop Shop** *(Tel 0121/622-23-02),* a hair salon at the same location.

The posh **Umberto Gianni** *(Brindley Place; Tel 0121/633-01-11; 10am-7pm Mon-Wed, 10am-8pm Thur, Fri, 8:30am-5pm Sat; V, MC),* just west of Town Hall, offers more services than you'd want to know about (like the "External Colonic Cleansing" for £75). Join the upper-class clientele for a manicure (£15 and up), eye lash and eyebrow treatment (£5 for plucking, £8.50 and up for tinting), waxing (£5 and up), or simply receive a massage—perhaps a 70-minute aroma-therapeutic body massage (£35).

stuff

Strangely enough, British are buying fewer CDs than in previous years, yet record sales are up and turntable sales have risen by almost 15 percent. Spinning vinyl is obviously the trend-setting way to go, and Birmingham has several LP shops around town. There are also plenty of places to shop for club gear and clothing, new and used, and skate gear.

▶▶TUNES

One great place to start your hunt for UK vinyl is in the Gay Village, at **Meat Beat Records** *(86 Hurst St.; Tel 0121/622-36-79; 10am-8pm daily).* **Highway 61** *(Fletcher's Walk; Tel 0121/212-14-21; 9:30am-5:30pm Mon-Sat; V, MC),* off Paradise Circus next door to the Town Hall in the City Centre, is also a popular choice. It has a big fat selection, with both underground UK dance and garage tracks and a good assortment of rock LPs.

Another option is **Swordfish Records** *(Temple St.; Tel 0121/633-48-59; 10am-6pm Mon-Sat; V, MC),* just east of Town Hall, which sells used LPs and CDs. Even if you're not interested in buying anything, go check out the amazing posters in the main entry.

▶▶BOUND

Finished that trashy novel you bought at the airport? Check out the funky bookstore **The Works** *(137 New St.; Tel 0121/643-30-92; 10am-6pm*

birmingham

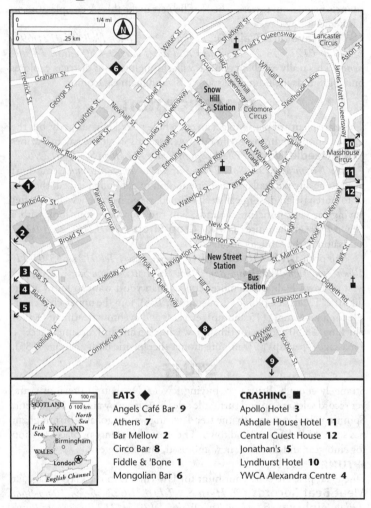

EATS ◆	CRASHING ■
Angels Café Bar 9	Apollo Hotel 3
Athens 7	Ashdale House Hotel 11
Bar Mellow 2	Central Guest House 12
Circo Bar 8	Jonathan's 5
Fiddle & 'Bone 1	Lyndhurst Hotel 10
Mongolian Bar 6	YWCA Alexandra Centre 4

Mon-Sat; MC, V), right next to the New Street train station, for a great novella to take with you up to the University of Birmingham campus.

▶▶GOT GOTH?

If you want to go home draped in the trappings of Birmingham's dark side, think about **Psiclone** *(189 Corporation St.; Tel 0121/212-27-00; 11am-6pm Mon-Sat; MC, V),* a 15-minute walk east of Town Hall, which promotes its stock as "Clothes for pure devils." We're talking rubber, latex, gloves, capes—a regular one-stop Goth headquarters.

▶▶SPARKLERS

Up To Date Jewellers *(297 Soho Rd.; Tel 0121/523-66-92; Tue-Sun*

10am-6pm) in Handsworth has a good range of Asian bracelets, pendants, and cool little pins with Yin and Yang symbols on them.

▶▶GEAR

It may be predictable, but at least **Miss Selfridge** *(79 High St.; Tel 0121/643-44-17; 10am-8pm daily; MC, V),* just north of New Street Station in the City Centre, is very British—and actually has some pretty slick girls' party togs.

 Cult Clothing *(29-30 Stephenson St.; Tel 01242/578-376; V, MC)* is your all-around streetwear, clubwear, and skatewear spot. They also sell some fresh rubber-soled sneakers.

eaTs

One good thing about big, ugly cities—they usually provide lots of good, cheap eats. Birmingham is no exception and the City Centre alone is riddled with popular spots, many of which double as style bars such as Circo Bar and Bar Mellow. Posing while noshing was never so easy.

▶▶CHEAP

One place where you can dine while chillin' is the **Circo Bar** *(6/8 Holloway Circus, City Centre; Tel 0121/643-14-00; Noon-1am Mon-Thur, till 2am Fri, Sat; £4-7 meals; AE, V, MC).* The days of the week sport different names, such as "Melange," "Bar Bedlam," "Polyrhythm" and "Different Drummer," a hint of how important background music is here.

 Also serving excellent late-night cuisine to a trendy 20s-30s crowd is **Bar Mellow** *(Broad St.; Tel 0121/643-51-00; 10am-7pm Mon, Tue, 10am-2am Wed-Sat, 11am-midnight Sun; £4-7 meals; AE, V, MC),* west of the city center.

 If your goal is shovelling as much food into your mouth as you possibly can in 2 hours for less than a "tenner," your destiny is the **Mongolian Bar** *(Ludgate Hill; Tel 0121/236-38-42; 6pm-midnight; £6-10 meals; AE, V, MC),* off of St. Paul's Square, northwest of City Centre. It specializes in stir-fry.

 For an authentic Balti dining experience, head to Ladypool Road— you should be able to smell the savory garlic-and-onion-based curries from a block away. One of the best places (and proud of it) is **I Am the King of Balti** *(230-232 Ladypool Rd.; Tel 0121/449-11-70; £3.40-6.90 dishes; V, MC),* which offers high-quality meat and vegetable dishes in superb rich sauces, as well as steaming *naan* of assorted flavors.

▶▶DO-ABLE

There's a cafe-bar with live folky-rock music nightly called the **Fiddle & 'Bone** *(4 Sheepcote St.; Tel 0121/200-22-23; 11am-11pm daily, noon-10:30pm Sun; £6-11 meals; V, MC with min. charge £5),* in Brindley Place just southwest of the City Centre. It serves up excellent pub food *(Noon-3pm/6-10pm Mon-Fri, noon-10pm Sat, Sun)* and also has a restaurant (same hours) with a more thorough menu. Brummies who enjoy cultured, city-sophisticated places often cringe when you mention this place, but the folks who come here seem to be having a damn good time.

wired

For good general city info, check out ***www. birmingham.gov.uk*** or the flashier ***www.go2birmingham.co.uk.*** **NetAdventure Cyber Café** *(68/70 Dalton St., City Centre; Tel 0121/693-66-55; 10am-10pm Mon-Sat, 10am-9pm Sun; £1 for 20 min. then £3 per hour)* and **Internet Exchange** *(Pallasades Shopping Centre, City Centre; Tel 0121/633-98-03; www.internet exchange.co.uk; minimum £1 charge first 10 minutes, then 3p-7p per minute for members, 10p a minute for non-members; No charge for membership; AE, V, MC with min. £5 charge)* offer Internet access as well as printing, faxing, and scanning. At the **Birmingham Central Library** *(Paradise Circus, City Centre; Tel 0121/303-45-11; www.birmingham.gov.uk/libraries; Adult Lending Library open 9am-8pm Mon-Fri, 9am-5pm Sat; Free;),* next door to the Town Hall in the City Centre, you will have to put your name down and wait in a queue—but it's all free of charge.

Follow the loud Greek music and the sound of braking plates to **Athens** *(31 Paradise Circus; Tel 0121/643-55-23; 6-11pm daily; V, MC),* next door to the Town Hall in the City Centre. Things often seem to be out of control, but in a good way, with patrons spilling out onto the street, dancing and shouting with what appear to be the wait staff. And Athens serves up good food—in fact, reservations are required on the weekends—so it's well worth enduring a little chaos.

The **Bucklemaker Restaurant and Bar** *(30 Mary Ann St., St. Paul's Sq.; Tel 0121/200-25-15, Fax 0121/236-98-87; Noon-2:30pm/ 5:30-10:30pm Mon-Fri, 7-10:30pm Sat; £3.50-6.95 starters, £7.95-14.50 main courses; www.thebucklemaker.co.uk; V, MC, AE),* set in the cellar of a one-time Georgian silversmith workshop, serves fresh fish and meat dishes, matched up with a variety of vegetables hand-picked for flavor and color. They also serve a variety of tapas (£3.25), ranging from fish cakes with red pepper and coriander confit to jellied eels.

▶▶**SPLURGE**

52 Degrees North *(Arcadian, Hurst St.; Tel 0121/622-52-50, Fax 0121/622-52-69; www.fiftytwodegreesnorth.co.uk; Noon-1am Mon-Wed, till 2am Thur-Sat, till 10:30pm Sun; £3.50-8 starters, £9.50-16.50 main courses, £12.95 two-course prix fixe menu, £15.95 three-course prix fixe menu; V, MC, AE)* is a groovy restaurant-lounge-bar set in a glass tower around the corner from the Hippodrome. Start with the won-ton fish-cake with prawns, tuna, and wasabi and move on to the filet of salmon layered with puree of roasted tomato and red pepper served with a pesto and nut crumb topping. If you're still hungry after all that, treat yourself to passion fruit brûlée or baked raspberry cheesecake.

crashing

There are tons of B&Bs, guest houses, and hotels in Birmingham. Many of them were built to accommodate the swarm of business people that come for the city's giant conventions, which leaves loads of affordable places to crash in when conventions aren't in town, and even when they are. Nevertheless, it's best to book ahead if you're on a budget. The Tourist Information Center will help you book for free [see *need to know,* below].

▶▶CHEAP

Birmingham may not have a YHA youth hostel, but it does have the **YWCA Alexandra Centre** *(27 Norfolk Rd.; Tel 0121/454-81-34; £10 single, £15 refundable deposit; No credit cards),* reachable via bus 128 to Norfolk Road off of Hagley Road. You'll get your own spacious, simple, and sunny room for only ten quid(!)—that's 50 percent cheaper than the cost of some urban YHA hotels! You'll also get to meet Brummies under 30 (a lot of locals live at the Y), watch television in the lounge, and fix your own cuisine in clean, self-service kitchens. The single-sex bathrooms have showers and private bathtubs, and are sparkling clean, thanks to the grandmotherly house cleaner who'll get on your case about wiping your feet after bathing so you won't stain the well-maintained, freshly polished and waxed wood floor. If you're still not convinced that this is the place for you, then you should know that the YWCA is only a short bus ride east of the City Centre (and buses run very frequently), there's no curfew to ruin the fun, and no lockout, so you can sleep til 3pm without any annoyances. Make a reservation now.

There are quite a few B&B options in Birmingham, located just outside the City Centre—if you walk east from the Centre down Hagley Road, you'll see a profuse amount of places to crash. They list their prices on billboards facing the street; some (seemingly marginal places) are as low as £12.

The **Central Guest House** *(1637 Coventry Rd.; Tel 0121/706-77-57; Bus 900 from Moor St.; £20-25 single, £40-45 double; mmou826384@ aol.com; V, MC)* in South Yardley, a 10-minute walk east of Town Hall, offers clean and safe bed and breakfast accommodation with television and free tea- and coffee-making pots in each room. Atmosphere is best described as safe, friendly, and functional.

The spacious Victorian **Ashdale House Hotel** *(39 Broad St.; Tel 0121/706-35-98; £22 single, £28 single with private bath, £38 double, £44 double with private bath; V, MC),* in Acock's Green about 4 miles southeast of the City Centre, is one of Birmingham's best B&Bs. The rooms are cozy and well-maintained, ranging from small to medium in size. Rooms with a bath have a shower stall and good shelf space, but don't despair if you choose to share—the corridor baths are clean and tidy. Breakfasts feature vegetarian choices, and organic produce for everybody. It's a good idea to book well ahead for this one.

For an affordable hotel stay, there's the spic-and-span **Awentsbury Hotel** *(21 Serpentine Rd.; Tel 0121/472-12-58; Bus 54Y; £32 single, £42 single with private bath, £46 double, £54 double with private bath, breakfast included; V, MC)* in Selly Park. The smallish bedrooms come with your very own tea- and coffeemakers and thin but reasonably comfortable mattresses—they aren't stylish, but they're acceptable in every other way. The bathrooms are minuscule but do the job, and if sharing, you'll rarely have to wait to use one since there are quite a few.

▶▶DO-ABLE

A reasonably priced hotel with private baths for all, the **Lyndhurst Hotel** *(135 Kingsbury Rd.; Tel 0121/373-56-95; £44 single, £56 double; AE, V, MC DC)*, in the Erdington/Aston University area, is a lovely Victorian house with a stone exterior. With 14 rooms that all have a TV, hairdryer, and electric kettle, this place does its best to make you comfortable, although most units are a bit small. You can lounge around the bar, the homey dining room, or the TV room.

Birmingham also has plenty of moderately priced chain hotels, which are perfectly comfortable even if they lack the character (e.g. lace doilies) you might get at a B&B. Closest to New Street station is the **Comfort Inn** *(Station St.; Tel 0121/643-11-34; £60, £75 twins/doubles, breakfast included; Private baths; V, MC, AE)*. The **Travel Inn** *(230 Broad St.; Tel 0121/644-52-66; £50 double; V, MC)* and the **Ibis Hotel** *(Arcadian Centre, Ladywell Walk; Tel 0121/622-60-10; £42 double Mon-Fri, £35 weekend; V, MC, AE, DC)* are both centrally located.

▶▶SPLURGE

A 5-minute drive or bus trip west of the City Centre in Edgbaston, where the streets are crammed with hotels, is the modern **Apollo Hotel** *(Hagley Rd.; Tel 0121/455-02-71; £75 single, £85 double, with private bath; AE, V, MC, DC)*. Rooms are a bit cramped but filled with such amenities as trouser presses and beverage makers, plus extra mattresses on the twin or double beds. Bathrooms are small but tidily organized, with super-clean shower stalls.

Looking for a little more frill for your buck? In a classic 19th-century country house 5 miles northwest of New Street Station is **Jonathan's** *(16-24 Wolverhampton Rd.; Tel 0121/429-37-57; bus 126, £88 single, £110 double, with private bath; bookings@jonathans.co.uk; AE, V, MC, DC)*. The suite-like rooms, tavern, and restaurants are all floor-to-ceiling with Victorian antiques. Bathrooms feature thick towels, a tub and shower combination, and your very own hair dryer.

within 30 minutes

Wonder what it was like a century before the Nazis bombed the hell out of the city? Travel to the South Staffordshire coal fields to visit the **Black Country Living Museum** *(Tipton Rd.; Tel 0121/557-96-43; Bus 126 to Dudley; 10am-5pm daily, Mar-Oct; 10am-4pm Wed-Sun, Nov-Feb; £7.95 adult, £4.75 child; info@bclm.co.uk; www.bclm.co.uk)*. It's a bit like an elementary school field trip—or coal-mining version of the Renaissance Fair—

but Brummies seem to love recommending this museum to tourists of all ages. (Revenge?) People dress in period costumes from the 1850s and recreate what it was like to work and live in the "Black Country"—a name for the countryside during the Industrial Revolution. On your visit, an electric tramway will take you to a thick, underground coal seam. Trolleys move through a reconstructed industrial village with a schoolhouse, anchor forge, rolling mill, and working replica of a 1712 steam engine. The Black Country Living Museum provides an insight into the truly hard times of the not-too-distant past. I'd never make the cut at Disney World.

need to know

Currency Exchange Reputable banks such as **Barclays** *(Tel 0121/480-54-00),* **National Westminster** *(Tel 0845/604-26-04),* **HSBC** *(Tel 0121/252-62-00),* and **Lloyd's** *(Tel 0121/233-12-55)* can be found easily throughout the city but also share quarters with **American Express** [see *American Express,* below] and **Thomas Cook** *(within Midland Bank, 130 New St.; Tel 0121/ 643-50-57; 8:30am-5pm Mon-Fri, 9:30am-3:30pm Sat),* just east of Town Hall, also have offices.

Travel Info The **Birmingham Convention & Visitor Bureau (BCVB) Ticket Shop and Information Office** *(2 City Arcade, City Centre; Tel 0121/643-25-14; 9:30am-5:30pm Mon-Sat)* is a 5-minute walk east of Town Hall, right next to the New Street train station. They offer free hotel booking service and loads of maps and guides. Check out the city web site: ***www.birmingham.org.uk.***

Public Transportation The local bus and rail hotline is **Centro** *(Tel 0121/200-27-00).* A West Midlands day saver pass costs £2.50 and is economical, as single trips cost £.90. A day pass for all buses and metro is also available for £3. Maps are available in all the stations. Exact change required on buses, except on the Centrebus 77, which circles the City Centre and is free. Taxis queue at various spots in the city centre, the rail station, and the NEC. Travelers can also ring up mini-cab companies such as **BB's** *(Tel 0121/693-33-33);* **Beaufort Cars** *(Tel 0121/784-44-44);* and **Birmingham Radio Cars** *(Tel 0121/624-222).*

American Express Cash those checks from home at the local **Amex** *(8 Cherry St.; Tel 0121/644-55-33; 8:30-5:30 Mon-Fri, 9am-5pm Sat),* a 10-minute walk east of Town Hall in the City Centre. There's another branch in Birmingham International Airport, which offers card and traveler cheque services from 5am-midnight.

Health and Emergency The Birmingham area has a toll-free hospital information hotline *(0800/665-544).* The **City Hospital** *(Dudley Rd.; Tel 0121/554-38-01)* is in Winston Green just north of Broad Street, 2 miles southwest of the City Centre via bus 82, 87, or 88 from the Corporation Street station.

Pharmacies Boots *(66 High St.; Tel 0121/212-13-30; 8am-6pm Mon-Wed, Fri, Sat, till 6:30pm Thur, 11am-5pm Sun)* is a 5-minute walk east of Town Hall.

Telephone The Birmingham city code is *121*.

Airports The major international carriers fly transatlantic flights directly to **Birmingham International Airport** *(Tel 0121/767-77-98 or 77-99; www.bhx.co.uk)*, 8 miles southeast of the city center. **Flightlink** *(Tel 0990/757-747)* is a national service that provides bus service to all airports in Britain, including BHX.

Direct air services between Birmingham and London is practically non-existent. Many air carriers maintain shuttles between London airports and Manchester, a 1.5 hour trip from Birmingham via ground transport. It's definitely more practical and economical to take a bus or train from London.

Trains InterCity offers express train service every half hour (Mon-Fri) between London's Euston station and Birmingham, a 90-minute trip. Regular train service is also available from London's Euston station. Trains depart every 2 hours for Birmingham, arriving at **New Street Station, (New St.; Tel 0345/484-950)** below the Pallasades Shopping Centre in the middle of the City Centre. The International Airport station links the city to the national rail network. Trains leave Manchester's Piccadilly station nearly every half hour for Birmingham, a 90-minute trip.

Bus Lines out of the City **National Express** buses arrive at the main bus station *(Digbeth Hight St.; Tel 0990/808-080)* a 15-minute walk southeast of Town Hall.

Bike Rental On Your Bike *(10 Priory Queen's Way; Tel 0121/627-15-90; 9am-6pm Mon-Fri, noon-5pm Sat, 11am-3pm Sun; £10-15 per day; V, MC)*, is next to the Moor Street train station, a 15-minute walk east of Town Hall.

Laundry Laundry facilities are scattered throughout the city but one popular with travelers is **Clean and Care** *(758 Alum Rock Rd., B8; Tel 0121/327-12-44; 8am-8pm daily; £2 wash, £1 dry)* a mile east of the City Centre.

Postal The central post office *(Corporation St.; 9pm-5:30pm Mon-Fri, 9am-5pm Sat, closed Sun)* is just east of Town Hall.

Internet See *wired*, above.

everywhere else

stratford-upon-avon

Here's the thing about Stratford-upon Avon: It may have been a hip, happening town when William Shakespeare was born there, but today it's a major tourist trap that requires great patience even for a day trip—and it's definitely nowhere you'd want to spend an entire weekend if you're looking to party. To say it is infested with tourists is almost an understatement. Busloads of Seinfeld-esque Florida grandmothers—along with their Japanese, Canadian, and German counterparts—are dropped off at the Tourist Information Center area and make their way up into the city center for daily invasions (the word "swarms" comes to mind). On the other hand, if Shakespeare nostalgia turns you on beyond belief, Stratford can actually be the starting point of a romantic weekend, especially if you beef it up a bit with trips to nearby Warwick Castle and the Cotswolds, with their picture-postcard, thatched-roofed houses.

Although Stratford's attractive for its Elizabethan essence, it couldn't really be described as peaceful. There's an outlandish and unpleasant amount of traffic in the town center. Walking is the only feasible way to see the sights without getting a migraine, and even then, navigating around cars as well as people will surely give you a headache if it's sunny out and you don't quite know where you're going.

For an all-encompassing walking tour, start at the Tourist Info Center [see *need to know,* below] on **Bridge Foot,** where the Avon forks on the eastern edge of the old center of town, and walk south down **Waterside.** The Bancroft Gardens, near the **Royal Shakespeare Theatre** [see *culture zoo,* below], are packed with families listening to music from the bandstand. Swans will eat bread out of your hand, and you can swim in the muddy water of the Avon. Turn west on **Old Town** to visit Hall's Croft, the former residence of Shakespeare's daughter, and go north onto **Church Street.** At the corner of Chapel and Church is Nash's House and New Place, where Shakespeare's granddaughter lived. Walk

stratford-upon-avon

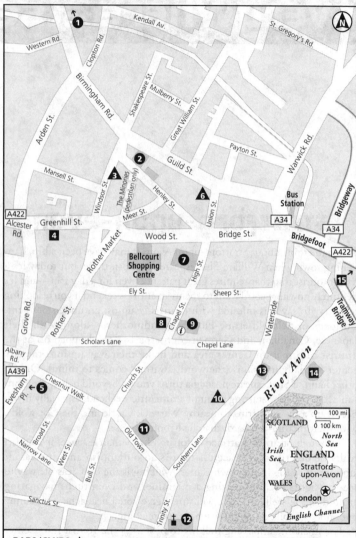

BARS/CLUBS ▲
Cask and Bottle **6**
Picture House Bar **3**
The Dirty Duck **10**

CULTURE ZOO ●
Ann Hathaway's
  Cottage **5**
Hall's Croft **11**

Harvard House **7**
Mary Arden's House **1**
Nash's House **9**
New Place **9**
Shakespeare's Birthplace **2**
Shakespeare's Tomb **12**
Swan Theatre **13**
The Shakespeare
  Countryside Museum **1**

CRASHING ■
Sequoia House **14**
Stratford-upon-Avon
  Backpackers Hostel **4**
Stratheden Hotel **8**
YHA **15**

down **Chapel Street,** which turns into **High Street.** On your left is Harvard House; go inside for a free taste of what the entrance of Tudor houses were like. Traveling north now up the High Street, turn west on **Wood Street,** to **Market Place.** Walk up the Minories pedestrian road to get to the Shakespeare Centre on **Henley Street.** To conclude the culture blitz visit Shakespeare's birthplace [see *culture zoo,* below], which is pretty much the last of the town center's attractions. Return to the tourist info center via **Bridge Street** and Bridge Foot, to get to Cox's Yard, a small complex that contains, among other things, an equally small art gallery, a sizeable pub, and a restaurant. Afterwards, head east across **Clopton Bridge** or **Tramway Bridge** to get to Rose's Boathouse, where you can cheaply canoe on the river. Alternatively, you could walk down **Riverside Walk,** a pathway extending from the canal to a "butterfly jungle" and cricket ground. The best thing about following this route is that it can be done in 1 day—which is more than enough time to spend on a taste of the Bard's hometown—perhaps as a day trip from London.

And that just about sums up Stratford-upon-Avon, folks. There's really nothing else to do. No trendy cafes for hanging out and people-watching. No clubs worth raving at. No streets you'd necessarily want to linger on, no distinctive neighborhoods, no shops you'd want to be seen in. Literally everything that goes on in town is listed at the Tourist Information Center [see *need to know,* below], which gives you a pretty clear idea of the total lack of a party scene in this landlocked town. Occasionally you may see a local smoking a joint on the street, or a group of young locals dressed up to go to a pub. But make no mistake about it, this town belongs to tourists—mostly middle-aged folks, families, or senior citizens—so your chances of making fast friends here are just about zero.

But if you do decide to hang around for a bit, take in a local theater production (after all, that's the whole point of Bard-World, and the productions here really are wonderful), then hop on a bus the next day and visit the Cotswolds [see below]. Buses depart daily for towns with honey-colored stone buildings and acres of pastures. **Warwick Castle** [see below] can be reached quickly by train also, and would be an excellent escape for a Stratford-upon-Avon/Cotswold weekend.

bar and live music scene

In a town where even the pubs require reservations for dining, you know somehow you're not going to find a trend-setting bar with icy martinis served 'till midnight (which is late for pubs in England anyway).

The closest joints with such status include the **Cask and Bottle** *(7/9 Union St.; Tel 01789/267-881; 11am-11pm daily; MC, V)* a 5-minute walk west of Bridge Foot, where local DJs spin, and the **Picture House Bar** *(Windsor Place; Tel 01789/415-500; 6-10:30pm Mon-Thur, Sun, 2-10:30pm Fri, Sat; V, MC),* a 5-minute walk west of Bridge Foot, which hosts an acoustic jam on Tuesdays at 7:30pm.

If you want to be seen with the aging movers and shakers of Stratford, head for the **Black Swan** *(Waterside; Tel 01789/297-312;*

11am-11pm Mon-Sat, noon-10:30pm Sun; V, MC in grill room only), aka the Dirty Duck. Take a look at the wall of famous patrons (most of whom you've probably never heard of) before heading to the front lounge and bar for some conversation about the region. The Dirty Duck offers a traditional English grill. In summer weather, enjoy a refreshing glass of fizzy lemonade (Sprite, basically) in the garden that overlooks the Avon.

arts scene

Aside from the obvious theatre scene, there are actually a few places in town to catch some art that doesn't involve Shakespeare.

▶▶VISUAL ARTS

While there aren't a ton of art galleries in Stratford, there is **The Art Gallery at Cox's Yard** *(Bridge Foot; Tel 01789/404-600; info@CoxsYard.co.uk; www.CoxsYard.co.uk, 10am-4pm daily, closed between exhibitions; Free).* It's a tiny second floor exhibition space, with one-artist shows of different media. Past exhibitions have included minimalist work from a Chinese brush painter and a surprising collection of objects embroidered with natural elements like wild bird feathers.

▶▶PERFORMING ARTS

What, you're gonna come here and *not* see some Shakespeare? The world-renowned **Royal Shakespeare Company** or **RSC** *(Waterside; Tel 01789/403-403 or 01789/403-404; Box office 9:30am-8pm Mon-Sat; 9:30am-6pm when there is no performance; £5-40, £7 student stand-by tickets; MC, V)* performs classic plays by the Bard and his contemporaries. Productions take place at three local theaters:

The **Royal Shakespeare Theatre** is the major, famous showcase for the RSC. It seats 1,500 on three floors of seats: the Stalls (most expensive), Circle (mid-priced), and Balcony (cheapest). The glamorous performances here are predictably thrilling.

Catching a production at the smaller and more personal **Swan Theatre** next door can be just as fun. The two levels above the ground floor that surround the stage on three sides offer extremely cozy seating, but try to get a seat on the ground floor, which is level with the performance area. The actors running up and down the aisles next to you gets you right into the action.

On an even more interactive level, there's **The Other Place,** located across the street just 300 yards from its counterparts. It's an experimental workshop theater without a permanent stage or seating plan. In a recent production of *Julius Caesar,* the actors performed the entire play while maneuvering around a standing audience.

If you think of blockbuster films as art, then you won't be too disappointed to catch a show at The **Stratford Picture House** *(Windsor St.; Tel 01789/415-511 or 01789/415-500; Show times vary; £4.50 adults, £3.80 students before 6pm Mon-Fri; www.picturehouse cinemas.co.uk; V, MC).* It's puzzling that the Arts Council of England would support such a commercial cinema, but to be fair, there are classic black and white and more arty and indie films shown several times a week.

CULTURE ZOO

Needless to say, Stratford's cultural scene—and cash cow—is all about one Shakespeare sight after another. (Now, if they had an actual Shakespeare sighting, that might be interesting. But alas, sightings are reserved for Elvis and other allegedly dead celebrities.

Shakespeare Houses *(Tel 01789/204-016; info@shakespeare.org.uk; Combined tickets for three in-town attractions £8.50 adults, £7.50 students, all five attractions £12 adults, £11 students;):* Stratford's five biggest attractions are collectively known as the Shakespeare Houses. They are coordinated as part of a unified system, with passes for any three the most practical way to go. Do all five and you'll qualify as a true stalker!

Shakespeare's Birthplace *(Henley St.; Tel 01789/704-016; 9am-5pm Mon-Sat, 10am-4pm Sun, Oct 20-Mar 10; AE, V, MC):* Naturally the top dog among the Shakespeare Houses, this one's a 5-minute walk west of Bridge Foot. A Tudor house that is preserved as a national shrine, it marks where Shakespeare was born on April 23, 1564, to a leather worker and his wife. 600,000 admirers a year pass into the house through the visitors' center, which contains displays of Stratford in the 16th century and the theater in London where the Bard's plays were performed. The house itself is, of course, stuffed with Shakespeare memorabilia. The room where Shakespeare was supposedly born is open to visitors. It's been

QUICK TIX FOR RSC

Most published sources say that you'll usually need to reserve Royal Shakespeare Company tickets well in advance. There is supposedly a limited number of tickets, including student-priced ones, available on the day of a performance. Yet, on a recent test visit, one customer easily obtained an excellent ticket for a performance at the Swan at the box office less than 5 minutes before show time. Interestingly, there was a large range of seats free to choose from. Perhaps this was a fluke, but it was May—usually the start of tourist season. It is foreseeable, however, that on a different night, the RSC theater would be packed with Japanese and American tour groups who have booked their tickets months in advance. Bottom line: If you're traveling off-season, don't be afraid to take your chances; if not, stay a jump ahead of the teeming masses and reserve.

noticeably re-vamped, with colorful curtains over the four-poster bed and fanciful walls. You can also nose around the oak-beam living room, fully-equipped 16th-century kitchen, and garden.

Nash's House and New Place *(Chapel St.; Tel 01789/214-016; 9:30am-5pm Mon-Sat, 10am-5pm Sun, Mar 20-Oct 19; 10am-4pm Mon-Sat, Oct 20-Mar 19; £3.50 adults, £3 students; V, AE, MC):* The house where Shakespeare died, on his 52nd birthday, was torn down in the 1700's, but you can see its foundation and grounds, which are called *New Place* (we're not sure why). There is no charge to enter the grounds, which consist of a lawn full of manicured bushes, as well as a mulberry tree which grew from a cutting of an original mulberry tree that Shakespeare himself planted. Nash's House was the early 17th-century home of Shakespeare's granddaughter. The upstairs contains exhibits on the history of the town through the 18th century, including prehistoric Roman and Anglo-Saxon artefacts. Downstairs there's period furniture in the entrance hall and living room, and a small kitchen with items from the 19th century. This is the most tedious of the Five Houses, and when it comes down to it, it really has little to do with Shakespeare's legacy.

Hall's Croft *(Old Town; Tel 01789/214-016; 9:30am-5pm Mon-Sat, 10am-5pm Sun, Mar 20-Oct 19; 10am-4pm Mon-Sat, Oct 20-Mar 19; £3.50 adults, £3 students; V, AE, MC):* Located a 5-minute walk southwest of Bridge Foot, this is yet another example of opportunistic entrepreneurs making a quick quid from Shakespeare-related tourism— Hall's Croft lures tourists into a half-timbered house where Shakespeare's daughter *might* have lived. (What's next, tours of the outhouse supposedly used once by Shakespeare's grandmother?) Shakespeare's granddaughter's husband happened to be a physician, so there are exhibits illustrating the theory and practice of medicine during the period in the consulting room where Dr. Hall treated his patients. After you exit the house, you may want to walk through—or pass on by—the lackluster plant and flower garden.

Mary Arden's House and the Shakespeare Countryside Museum *(Wilmcote; Tel 01789/214-016; 9:30am-5pm Mon-Sat, 10am-5pm Sun, Mar 20-October 10; 10am-4pm Mon-Sat, 10:30-4pm Sun, Oct 20-Mar 19; £5, £4.50 student; V, AE, MC):* Three miles south of Stratford on the eastern side of the Avon is a Tudor farmstead that was the alleged home of Shakespeare's mother. A good choice for history buffs, Anglophiles, and families, this site contains an extensive collection of farming implements, country furniture, domestic utensils, and the like. Attractions include falconry demonstrations, oxen, and prize-winning livestock. If you leave the Shakespeare Countryside Museum with an urge to learn more about traditional farm life, drop by the nearby Glebe Farm, and picture yourself in the exciting role of a late Victorian-era farmer.

Anne Hathaway's Cottage *(Cottage Lane; Tel 01789/214-016; 9am-4pm Mon-Sat, 9:30am-5pm Sun, Mar 20-Oct 19; 9:30am-4pm Mon-Sat, 10am-4pm Sun, Oct 20-Mar 19; £4 adult, £3.70 student; AE, V, MC):* If you're up for a 1-mile hike west of town to Shottery, you can see the home

Anne Hathaway lived in before becoming Shakespeare's wife. The house's original furnishings include utensils that the Bard may have possibly eaten with, if and when his bride-to-be lovingly prepared him hearty dinners. Outside this charming thatched-roofed house is a garden overflowing with flowers and home-grown herbs—it's a beautiful setting, Shakespeare or no Shakespeare.

Shakespeare's Tomb at Holy Trinity Church *(Old Town; Tel 01789/266-316; 8:30am-6pm Mon-Tue, Thur-Sat, 2-5pm Sun, closed for funerals; No admission charge):* Shakespeare once wrote "Curst be he who moves my bones." Apparently his message came through: he's never been relocated from his original resting spot, a 5-minute walk southwest of Bridge Foot, where he was buried in 1616 in the chancel of Holy Trinity. Copies of his baptism and death certificates are on display inside the church. You can also see the graves of his widow, daughter, Thomas Nash, and Dr. Hall—the people who, we're told, lived in the houses you may have just visited.

Harvard House *(High St.; Tel 01789/204-507; 10am-4:30pm Tue-Sat, 10:30am-4:30pm Sun, May 27-Sep 10; Free):* Believe it or not, there are some non-Shakespeare attractions in Stratford. A 5-minute walk west of Bridge Foot is the former home of Katherine Rogers, mother of John Harvard, the founder of Harvard University. As one of the few freebies in this tourism-milking town, it should be first on your cultcha to-do list. The house, a good example of a 16th-century country cottage, is actually quite interesting if you've never seen the interior of an authentic Tudor house. Inside, wooden beams divide rooms, and there's heavy period furniture crammed into little rooms. Videos and displays informatively tell you how to make pewter and mold it into shape. Harvard alum should feel ultra-welcome here, as a sign invites them to contribute their signature to the visitors' book.

Swan Theatre [see *performing arts,* above]: This performance hall itself is a worthwhile attraction, even if you're not planning on catching a show here. There's a gallery full of portraits of famous actors and scenes from Shakespeare's plays by 18th- and 19th-century artists. Perhaps more interesting for theater fanatics are the guided tours for which the theater operates as a base. You'll get to check out where RSC actors perform on a more intricate level, and tour the backstage area.

STUFF

Shakespeare souvenirs aren't the only game in town. Cool clothes and New Age stuff aren't unusual in a big city, but are a welcome break from the Bard here in Stratford.

▶▶DUDS

A surprisingly trendy (for the area) clothing store is **Hub** *(27 Rother St.; Tel 01789/299-377; 10am-5:30pm Mon-Fri, 10am-6pm Sat, noon-5pm Sun; MC, V),* a 5-minute walk west of Bridge Foot. Retro-style bags, hippie shoes, city-sophisticated clothes and glamorous accessories—they've got it all. Men and women shop at this unisex store while bopping their heads to the funky music blasting through the sound system.

▶▶NEW AGE

A yin-yang sign is prominently placed over the door of nearby **Naquiba** *(7 Union St.; Tel 01248/263-766; 10am-5:30pm Mon-Fri, 9:30am-6pm Sat, 11am-5pm Sun; AE, V, MC),* a 5-minute walk west of Bridge Foot. This spiritual shop caters to women, selling pretty, flowing clothing, incense, creatively decorated picture frames, and purses. You've probably been to dozens of stores like this one before, full of pretty things that you don't really need....

EATS

Where there are tons of tourist, there also are tons of places to eat. Most of them are in the city center, from small bakery side cafes to larger chain restaurants.

▶▶CHEAP

For traditional fish 'n' chips, try **Barnaby's** *(25 Sheep St.; Tel 01789/261-485; £4.60 fish & chips to stay, £3.80 takeout; No credit cards),* right across from the Royal Shakespeare Theater.

There are more than a few cheap Indian takeout places in town: The **Lalbagh Balti Restaurant** *(3 Greenhill St.; Tel 01789/293-563; 6pm-12:30am Sun-Thur, 6pm-2am Fri, Sat)* and **Raj Tandoori Balti** *(7 Greenhill St.; Tel 01789/267-067; 6pm-12:30am Sun-Thur, 6pm-1:30am Fri, Sat),* two of the best, both offer curries starting around £5.

▶▶DO-ABLE

An Indian restaurant with a Greek name, **Thespians** *(26 Sheep St.; Tel 01789/267-187; 5:30-11:30pm daily; £6.75-9.95 meals; MC, V),* a 2-minute walk west of Bridge Foot, dishes out take-away or eat-in food. The Chicken Shahi Kurma (in sweet sauce) is a winner, and so is the Jinga Masala, shrimp in creamy sauce. It's typically a theater-going crowd.

A Greek restaurant with a Greek name, **The Greek Connection** *(1 Shakespeare St.; Tel 01789/292-214; Noon-2:30pm daily, summer; 5:30pm-late year-round; £10-25 meals; V, MC, DC),* a 5-minute walk northwest of Bridge Foot, occupies a 19th-century Methodist church. There's a festive aura as tourists eat moussaka while live music plays and dancers perform traditional Greek steps. Expect a basic evening here to cost you at least a "tenner" each; add a little red wine and a couple appetizers, and you'd better double that.

crashing

Like everything else in this town, the accommodation options don't encourage you to stick around. That is, unless you've got money to burn.

▶▶CHEAP

The **YHA Stratford-upon-Avon** *(Wellesbourne Rd, Alveston; Tel 01789/297-093; Bus 18; £14.90 per person for members, £1 student discount, dorms with shared bath; stratford@yha.org.uk; AE, V, MC)* is a bit ridiculous for the individual traveller, as it's mighty pricey for dormitory accommodation, and will cost you around £6 in taxi fare from the train station or tourist info center if you don't want to hoof it 2.5 miles or wait for a bus that never seems to come. Since the buses stop running at an early hour, you're doomed to evenings watching TV in the lounge with a very mixed-aged crowd, perhaps containing both senior citizens and children, if you don't want to spring for cabfare. On the positive side, the place has had a recent refurbishment, the bunks are adequately comfortable, there's Internet service and a nice sunny dining room. But the more pleasant aspects don't make up for the moment when you realize that for these prices, with transport costs, you could have stayed in a cozy B&B in the town center.

The clearly wiser choice is the homey **Stratford-upon-Avon Backpackers** *(33 Greenhill St.; Tel 01789/263-838; www.hostels.co.uk; £11-12 per person dorms with shared bath; stratford@hostels.demon.co.uk; V, MC),* a 5-minute walk west of Bridge Foot. The friendly staff encourages long stays by putting up a notice board with job listings around town, but even if you're only planning on staying one night, you should fully enjoy this place. It has comfy bunk beds, laundry facilities, a pool table, and a TV room where you'll meet like-minded shoestring American and Australian travelers. This is definitely the most economical, convenient, and social place for the independent traveler. Reservations are recommended in the summer.

▶▶DO-ABLE

For some of the most comfortable accommodations in town for a price that won't send you away screaming, check out the **Sequoia House** *(51/53 Shipston Rd.; Tel 01789/268-852; £69-89 double with private bath, breakfast included; www.stratford-upon-avon.sequoia.htm; info@sequoia hotel.co.uk; AE, V, MC, DC),* a 10-minute walk south of Bridge Foot east of the Avon. All rooms are non-smoking and contain a telephone, television, hairdryer, tea and coffee maker, and some bedrooms even have Victorian brass beds. You can join the mostly middle-aged guests and their families in the lounge, where you'll find a bar and a Victorian fireplace.

The **Stratheden Hotel** *(5 Chapel St.; Tel 01789/297-119; £41 single, £32-35 per person double with private bath; AE, V, MC),* a 5-minute walk southwest of Bridge Foot, was built in 1673, and they don't let you forget it. Everything about this place screams antique, from the slanted, beamed ceilings in the top-floor rooms to the family heirlooms displayed in the entryway. Rooms have comfy beds and small bathrooms just big enough for a shower stall and a set of medium sized-towels.

need to know

Currency Exchange To change your dough, try **American Express** *(Tourist Information Centre, Bridge Foot; Tel 01789/415-856; 9am-5:30pm Mon-Sat, 11am-5pm Sun)* or **Thomas Cook** *(Midland Bank, 13 Chapel St.; Tel 01789/294-688; 9am-5pm Mon-Fri, 9:30am-12:30pm Sat),* a 5-minute walk west of Bridge Foot.

Travel Info The **Tourist Information Center** *(Bridge Foot; Tel 01789/293-127; 9am-5:30pm Mon-Sat, 11am-5pm Sun)* is a 5-minute walk southeast of the train station.

Public Transportation The center of Stratford is entirely walkable, but taxis for reaching the YHA hostel and outlying attractions can be found on Rother Street, 5 minutes west of Bridge Foot.

Trains The **train station** *(Alcester; Tel 0121/200-2700)* is a 5-minute walk west of Bridge Foot. There are several direct trains daily to London Paddington (2-1/2 hours, £17.50). **Warwickshire Traveline** *(Tel 01926/414-140)* also has rail and bus info for the region.

Bus Lines Out of Town National Express buses from London connect to Stratford daily, arriving at the **main station** *(Riverside; Tel 0990/808-080)*, a 5-minute walk southwest of Bridge Foot on the west bank of the Avon. **Stagecoach Midland Red** *(Tel 01788/535-555)* runs to Warwick, Coventry, Birmingham, and Oxford. The useful Cotswold Shuttle offers service three times daily (except Sun) to Broadway, Moreton-in-Marsh, Stow-on-the-Wold, and Bourton-on-the-Water. There's also weekday service to Chipping Campden.

Health and Emergency The **Stratford-upon-Avon Hospital** *(Arden St; Tel 01789/205-831)* is a 5-minute walk west of Bridge Foot. ßEmergency: *999.*

Pharmacies Boots *(11 Bridge St.; Tel 01789/292-173)* is a 5-minute walk west of Bridge Foot.

Bike Rental Touring bikes, roadsters, and mountain bikes are available at **Clarkes Cycles** *(Guild St.; Tel 01789/205-057; 10am-9pm Mon-Fri, noon-6pm Sat, Sun; from £6 per day, £25 per week)*, a 5-minute walk west of Bridge Foot.

Laundry Sparklean Launderette Services *(74 Bull St., Old Town; Tel 01789/269-075; 8:30am-9pm daily; £2.50 wash, £1 dry)* is a 5-minute walk southwest of Bridge Foot.

LEICESTER

Leicester's a small city, but don't let anyone tell you it's worth only a spare afternoon—it's good for at least a weekend, especially during the school term, when the party season is going strong. Students make up around 12 percent (36,000) of the total population (300,000), so there's definitely a youth vibe in the air. The profusion of chic clubs, cafes, cafe-bars, bars, and pubs provides prime chilling possibilities till the wee hours.

Leicester (big points for pronouncing it LES-ter) has a concentrated City Centre—where the city's Roman and medieval roots are visible—that takes up an oblong area encircled by the A594, a major highway. The city also is wonderfully mixed in terms of ethnicity: Leicester is the heart of the UK's Asian community. Indian, Chinese, and Caribbean culture flavor every aspect of life in the city, from food and music to commerce, clothing, and accents. The lively mix makes the party scene here way more fun than in a lot of the lily-white industrial towns in Central England.

One really cool thing about the small-town scale of Leicester is that people are super-friendly. Young people walking the streets are eager to help lost-looking visitors; they'll likely walk you to your destination and take great interest in where you're from. And the ethnic diversity seems to add to the sociability, because most of the neighborhoods are truly integrated. In Leicester's Asian Quarter [see *neighborhoods,* below], where white people are actually a minority, you may run into a strict Muslim, devout Sikh, religious Catholic, or Hassidic Jew. The city council's website is not only in English, but in Bengali, Gujarati, Punjabi, and Urdu as well.

Leicester's people also represent all interests and lifestyles. Young businessmen in the requisite black suits, blue shirts, and multicolored ties share the sidewalks with gothed-out or grunged-up teens and crunchy pot smokers. Keep your eyes open and you'll see weed toked on the streets, but on the QT of course. Of course, the clubs have the usual X-ers.

And they all seem to live to party. Local venues are all the rage with residents, as the clubs have special rave nights with massive crowds. There's live music at **De Montfort Hall** and smaller shows at **The Charlotte** and the **Spread Eagle** [see *live music scene,* below, for both]. Buy tickets for local venues at **5HQ** *(Tel 0116/262-7475)* and **Rockaboom** [see *stuff,* below]. And, as always, check out the ultra-hip *69 Magazine, City Lights,* and the *What's On Midlands* guide, available all around the City Centre.

neighborhoods

The **City Centre** is bordered on the southeast by the main train station and on the west by the **River Soar.** Despite its wide streets and office buildings, Leicester shows its age around the edges at places like **Abbey Park and Grounds** [see *culture zoo,* below].

Most of the nightlife is based in the old center, as are the city's main attractions. At the middle of it all is **Town Hall Square,** 7 blocks northwest of the train station, halfway to the River Soar. There are numerous shopping promenades and nifty courtyard niches too, such as **St. Martin's Square** and its adjoining "lanes" area, which has bounded back from its former life as a derelict zone in the 1980s. If you ask locals where to bar-hop after dark, they'll recommend **Granby** and **High Streets** in a heartbeat. The area around the **Clock Tower** in the City Centre is crawling with vivacious crowds headed for some serious partying at the commercial clubs and cafe-bars along **Church Gate** and **Silver Street** off of High Street. Most of the clubs are clustered in a vast, empty industrial area in the north part of the city center.

Leicester has a thriving **Asian Quarter,** a district surrounding **Belgrave Road,** a 5-minute walk north of the town square. You'll feel like you're in India, especially as you walk around the heart of the quarter, also known as **The Golden Mile.** Asian Brits come from all over the country to dine and buy savories, sweets, beaded bracelets, saris, and Hindi music. The quarter's two best-known restaurant-bakery shops are **Bobbys** and

Leicester

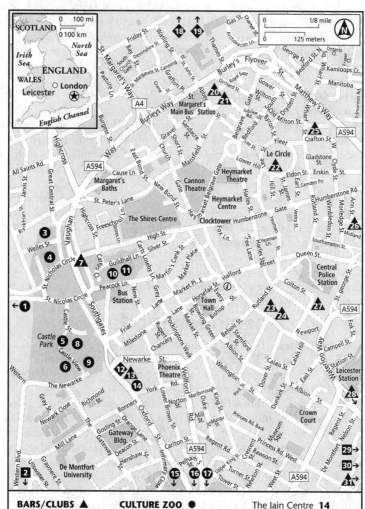

BARS/CLUBS ▲
Club City **22**
Du Monfort Hall **31**
Junction 21 **26**
Leicester University
  Student Union **28**
Mosquito Coast **7**
Oxygen **20**
r/bar **24**
Spread Eagle **27**
Starlite 2001 **25**
The Charlotte **13**
The Fan Club **21**
Turkey Café **23**

CULTURE ZOO ●
Castle View **6**
Castle Yard **5**
Ecohouse **1**
Guildhall **10**
Guru Nanak Sikh Museum **3**
Jewry Wall & Museum **4**
Leicester Infirmary
  Museum **15**
National Space
  Science Centre **17**
Newarke Houses Museum **9**
St. Mary's Church **8**
The Cathedral **11**

The Jain Centre **14**
The Leicester Gas
  Museum **16**

EATS ◆
Bobby's **19**
Castle Rock Café **12**
Sharmilee **18**

CRASHING ■
Belmont House Hotel **30**
International
  Youth House **2**
Spindle Lodge Hotel **29**

Sharmilee [see *eats,* below], which compete for customers. The **Asian Quarter** is sprinkled with several Indian nightclubs, as well as the Mumbai Blues pub, where you can eat curried grub while listening to Indian pop classics played live.

Don't let a dodgy first impression scare you away from the intersection of **Oxford** and **Newarke Streets,** where signs welcome you to the seemingly dingy "Old Town" area of **Castle Park** [see *culture zoo,* below]. Things brighten up as you walk a bit north into the **Castle Yard.** This tranquil area, which used to be used for executions, contains wildflower gardens next to the ruins of the moat and gate of a fortress. The remains are beautiful, and there are actually some interesting sites to visit.

hanging out

Hanging out happens—as in most small British cities—in pubs, with conversing, smoking, and hoisting central to any discussion or social exchange. Places like the **Spread Eagle** [see *live music scene,* below] are ideal for this. More stylish hanging is much-encouraged by the new generation of cafe-bars, like **r/bar** [see *bar scene,* below]. On sunny days, though, there's a fresh-air alternative, the **Abbey Park and Grounds,** about 1.5 miles north from Castle Park, which is home to the ruins of Leicester Abbey. Locals now use the land, which was once the richest Augustine monastery in England, for socializing, springtime picnics, jogging, and sunbathing.

bar scene

Pubs are, of course, the mainstay of Leicester's bar scene, but cafe-bars are catching up fast.

Typical popular city center taverns include the **Pump and Tap** *(Braunstone Gate, Duns Lane; Tel 0116/254-03-24; 5-11pm Mon-Fri,*

wired

Cyber Café @ The Ark *(2-4 St. Martins Sq.; Tel 0116/233-96-60, Fax 0116/253-93-03; 10am-10pm Mon-Sat; £1.50 for first half hour computer time, £2.50 per half hour after that)* has six PCs and one Mac, and plenty of plants. The Ark has been open since December 1994, and has an organic vegetarian restaurant upstairs, where they use locally-produced ingredients to prepare really good food. Downstairs there's a shop and environmental information center, with a couple of touch-screen Macs giving information about resident nonprofit Environ's work in the community, and all sorts of stuff, from books to compost bins.

noon-11pm Sat, noon-10:30pm Sun) and **The Orange Tree** *(99 High St., Tel 0116/223-52-56).* Stop by either to sample Leicestershire's three home-brews: Everards, Ruddles, and Hoskins.

Topping the A-list of cafe-bars is **r/bar** *(78a Granby St.; Tel 0116/255-94-49; Noon-11pm Mon-Sat, Sun till 10:30pm; V, MC, DIN),* just south-east of the town square. DJs spin Thursday through Sunday, and occasionally on Tuesdays, adding a cool groove to this bar-turned-Italian-Chinese-Indian eatery. The r/bar is proud to host "Leicester's own" DJ Johnny Frisco, spinning chill-out music on Sundays. Monday's main attraction is a variety of £1 shooters, including the popular Cocaine—a mixture of Galliano and tequila gold. There's also a summer courtyard and reasonably priced food—most main courses, like big juicy ham-burgers, are less than £5.

For a touch of glamour, head to **The Turkey Café** *(Granby St.; Tel 0116/251-1717; 10am-midnight Mon, Fri, Sat, 10am-11pm Tue-Thur, 10am-10:30pm Sun),* just southeast of the town square. If the sign outside reading "booze" fails to entice you, then maybe the food will. You can dine or drink upstairs in a mellow turquoise-walled dining room or on the ground floor, a great street-level people-watching spot. Or chill with the promised booze in the downstairs lounge bar, while soaking in the pumped-up sounds of everything from Groove Armada to Frank Sinatra.

Revolution *(New Walk, Tel 0116/255-96-33; Noon-midnight Mon-Wed, noon-1am Thur, noon-1:30am Fri,Sat, 2-10:30pm Sun; V, MC)* boasts over 70 different varieties of vodka, including chili, licorice, and

hints for cheap drinking

So you want to get trashed in Leicester but don't want to waste a fortune? Here's a hint: For a cheap vodka drink, order a vodka with soda and lime. Soda's just a term for seltzer, and lime, in this case, is that sweet, concen-trated syrup. When mixed with water or soda, you've got a limeade cocktail that costs about £1.90. For reasons known only to them, most bars charge more, usually at least 50p, for an official cocktail, but seem to consider this one kid stuff. When you multiply 50p by six or so, depending on your capacity, you'll soon realize you're squeezing the maximum juice out of those quids. In addition, although ordering tap water at the bar is taboo—it's considered really cheap—you can easily get away with it as a naïve American (the English figure that the damn Yanks just don't know any better). And downing water between those vodkas could be wise indeed—otherwise that kid stuff will sneak up on you fast.

just about every imaginable fruit. Buy four shots and your fifth one is free—not that you'll remember it. By that point, you'll probably be sprawled across the couches around the huge fireplace. The restaurant upstairs is also recommended, especially if you're planning on taking advantage of the shot special afterwards (gotta pad that tummy!).

The **Fat Cat Cafe Bar** *(41 Belvoir St., Tel 0116/255-36-10; 10am-11pm Mon-Thur, 10am-2am Fri, Sat, 10am-10:30pm Sun)* looks like a small bar from the outside, but walk in and you'll be taken aback at how spacious it really is. There's a big restaurant area at the back of the bar, and in the summer you can sit outside in their courtyard garden, which comes complete with outdoor heaters. The Fat Cat is part of a popular British chain, so don't be surprised if you see others in your travels. It's also open for coffee in the morning to help you recover from the night before.

No longer the newest bar in town, but still one of the coolest, **Marz Bar** *(34 Belvoir St., Tel 0116/275-68-00; 10am-11pm Mon-Sat, noon-10:30pm Sun)* situated opposite the Fat Cat, has one bar on the ground floor and another downstairs. The downstairs one has a low ceiling and can get quite smoky. The upstairs bar gets packed on Thursday, Friday, and Saturday nights when the DJ moves in.

LIVE MUSIC SCENE

Indie bands make Leicester's live music scene not just cool, but credible. Visiting acts, from drum 'n' bass DJs to Norwegian bands, play at **The Charlotte** *(8 Oxford St.; Tel 0116/255-39-56;11am-11pm daily)*. This purple building on the corner of Newarke Street in the southeast part of the center is a popular haunt of University of Leicester students.

The **Spread Eagle** *(2 Church Gate; Tel 0116/262-48-65; Noon-midnight Mon-Thur, noon-2am Fri,Sat, noon-10:30pm Sun; Cover free-£3.50)*, 2 blocks north of the town square, has that rank smoke and beer aroma of a traditional pub, but offers a lot more. In the crowd, you'll spot patchouli-smelling punkers, indie rock chicks, alternative guys wearing phat hats and young teenagers sipping Coke and trying to look older. The bands do their thing upstairs; downstairs, sexy barmen serve up pints while the regulars play pool.

De Montfort Hall *(Granville Rd.; Tel 0116/233-31-11; www.demontforthall.co.uk; Box office 10am-6pm Mon-Sat, 10:30-6pm Wed, 10:30am-8pm show days; Prices vary)* a major venue concert hall with the tidy look of a museum, is where you'll catch Nick Cave if he rolls through. There's limited seating at stage level and on the balcony, but you can always squeeze your way up to the stage in the standing area. It's a 20-minute walk southeast of the City Centre.

CLUB SCENE

Several local promoters take charge of Leicester's party scene. **Praha7** *(www.praha7.co.uk)* claims to be "a futuristic version of Andy Warhol's Exploding Plastic Inevitable." They not only throw wicked rave-type events, but also back a notorious band *(theband@praha7.co.uk)*, whose members consider themselves "half band-half DJ." They mix pre-programmed PC tracks and breakbeats to great effect.

Starlite 2001 *(Wharf St. South; Tel 0116/262-00-77;10pm-2am Thur-Sat; £4-10 cover)*, a five-minute walk northeast of the town square, isn't a club itself but a place that promoters rent out to throw fabulous trance/acid/techno parties. Starlite's best-known party is *Peek (Tel 0797/092-23-56 or 0777/340-45-42; info@peek.org.uk; www.peek.org.uk)*. The website will tell you when it's on next, and show you cool photos of ravers in action under the lights and lasers.

Junction 21 *(13 Midland St.; Tel 0116/251-93-33, 07989/440-617; 10pm-2am Thur-Sat; £6-10 cover)*, is located on a desolate road in that vast empty industrial area of Leicester just northeast of the city center near the big St. George's roundabout known as Club Land. You can't miss it—just look for the flashy leopard-print paint job. Thursday's *Jigsaw* is quite insane with special guests on the decks, including hyped-up E-static Gatecrasher contributors, and Friday's trance and house mayhem is consistently uplifting. Make sure you check out who's spinning before you decide to commit your Saturday to raving here, though—it's hit or miss.

Also in Club Land is **Club City** *(Lee Circle; Tel 0116/253-88-37; 10pm-6am Thur-Sat; £8 cover; No credit cards)*, where you should let nothing stop you from enjoying an ecstatic Friday night of mood-elevating trance in the house of the *Forbidden*. Saturday's *Adrenaline* is the highlight of the week, with funky club kids letting it all out to trance and pumping hard house. Club City hosts the old-skool and trance *Unification* parties, which take place on occasional Saturdays. If you're a naughty raver, it's just about mandatory to attend.

The first Monday of every month at **The Fan Club** *(40 Abbey St.; Tel 0116/242-57-65; 10pm-2am Mon-Sat, occasionally Sun; £1.50-2 cover Mon-Thur, £4-5 before 11pm; No credit cards)* is *Spellbound,* a gothic, rock, mainstream alternative, and '80s night. Tuesdays it's *Wired,* with a student clientele favoring Mod 'dos listening to Britpop, big beat, and retro music. Wednesday's *Up the Junction* attracts a similar following with music from the '60s and early '70s, mostly Motown. Thursdays are truly *Twisted,* with a 10pm to 11pm "Trash Hour" of rock music you naïvely thought you'd never hear again. Continuing with this "flash from the past" theme that this club existence thrives on is Friday's *Atomic,* a night of '70s, and '80s pop. Saturday's *Intro* features indie rock from the '80s to the present.

Next to the Fan Club is **Oxygen** *(46 Abbey St; Tel 0116/251-32-15; www.oxygennightclub.co.uk; 9:30pm-2am Wed-Sat; Free-£4 cover)*, where you'll fit right in if you crimp your hair and put on light pink lipstick. DJ Dilly plays the "bestest" rock and pop from the '80s. On Thursdays, go with the urge: let the 69p tequila shots lure you in for this indie night for students. If you think Lori Petty was sexy in Tank Girl, try Friday's alternative rock night *Riot Riot,* which advertises £1.30 beers before 11pm. Saturday's a bit simpler, just referred to as a party night.

A fabulous weekly party worth mentioning on its own is *Goodbye Cruel World* at **Mosquito Coast** *(27 St. Nichols Place; Tel 01164/254-99-66; 10pm-3am; £8 cover; goodbyecw@aol.com)*. It enforces its up-and-up reputation with selective door policies and chic clientele. They present only top-notch DJs in the main room, and live cabaret drag acts in the second room, which is funky and disco-crazy. (Mosiquito Coast is pretty boring the rest of the week.)

The **University of Leicester Student's Union** *(University Rd.; Tel 0116/223-11-11; 10pm-2am Thur; www.leicester.ac.uk/su)*, a 20-minute walk southeast of Town Hall Square, is also, as you'd expect, a great place to party on the cheap just about any time, with decent dance space, music that's all over the map, and a welcoming student crowd.

▶▶PRE-CLUB PARTY

You may want to join the clubbers that sometimes meet on Saturdays for pre-venue partying at **The 39 Steps** *(16 Silver Walk, St. Martin's Sq.; Tel 0116/262-29-22; 8pm-11pm Sat; No cover)*, 2 blocks west of the town square.

ARTS SCENE

For a smallish city, Leicester has a surprisingly vibrant art scene. Local galleries exhibit innovative stuff, and theaters present avant-garde originals as well as Londin hits.

▶▶VISUAL ARTS SCENE

The **City Gallery** *(90 Granby St.; Tel 0116/254-0595; 11am-6pm Tue-Fri, 10am-5pm Sat, closed Sun, Mon, Bank holidays; Free)*, on the street running off the main square to the east, has three exhibition halls filled with challenging modern work. Past exhibits included "Handbag," which aimed at gaining insight into the desire to penetrate the hidden interiors of purses in attempts to identify their owner. Another, "Surface and Repetition," displayed textured paintings of objects—and some body parts—in hieroglyphic style.

▶▶PERFORMING ARTS SCENE

One of Leicester's top performing arts venues is the **Haymarket Theatre** *(Belgrave Gate; Tel 0116/253-9797; Box office 10am-8pm; Admission varies)*, 15 minutes north of Town Hall Square, a regional stage where you can catch everything from top West End productions to avant-garde Indian theatrics.

Another mainstay is the **Phoenix Arts Centre** *(Newarke St.; Tel 0116/255-4854; Box office 10am-8pm; Admission varies)*, five minutes southwest of Town Hall Square, that hosts dance, music and theater productions from around the world. Local musicians, dancers, and actors also entertain here, and you can catch an occasional film as well. For an online directory of Leicester's musical artists, bands, studios, venues, music shops, and more, check out *www.leicestermusic.co.uk.*

GAY SCENE

East Midland gays agree: The cosmopolitan city of Leicester offers plenty of diversions outside of the totally straight domain. Though not as grand as Birmingham's Pride Festival, Leicester's **Gay Mardi Gras** is still worth attending. The festival, held in Abbey Park, has support from the city council, and usually takes place in July (though that's never absolutely certain). Check out local mags like *69 Magazine,* for updates.

For more serious cruising, head to the south side of Abbey Park. If you aren't in the mood to pull a stranger (or even if you are) you'll definitely enjoy spending an evening at **The Dover Castle** *(34 Dover St.; Tel 0116/222-8826; 11am-11pm daily),* on the street that joins Granby east of Town Hall Square which has a cultlike following. The clientele is a young and old collection of shiny, happy people mixing under the disco lights. The pub's already boisterous ambience really gets going during the thrice-weekly live cabaret drag shows.

Another gay pub with a movin' dance floor is **The Pineapple Inn** *(27 Burleys Way; Tel 0116/262/3384; Noon-4pm/7pm-midnight Mon-Wed, noon-3pm/7pm-1am Thur, noon-4pm/7pm- 2am Fri, Sat, noon-3pm/7pm-10:30pm Sun; No credit cards),* on the ring road a 20-minute walk north of Town Hall Square. Although there are some lesbians, the clientele mostly consists of men cruising for men. The music is whatever they feel like playing at the time, though it's mainly disco and house. Shake, shake, shake your booty.

University of Leicester Student's Union [see *club scene,* above] has a party every Thursday that caters to lesbians and gays and promises a young, hip crowd, not just a cruise scene.

CULTUrE ZOO

Leicester has a historical area that's actually worth visiting: Castle Park. There are so many attractions here, it's doubtful you'll be able to visit them all. The Roman Emperor Hadrian first began fortifying Leicester, and the Danes later built up the massive castle, which then became the base of the earls of Leicester. On the top of your itinerary in the park should be the Newarke Houses Museum, with two former residences restored to their Victorian mint condition—a fascinating taste of daily life in the days of yore.

Newarke Houses Museum *(The Newarke; Tel 0116/247-3222; 10am-5pm Mon-Sat, 2pm-5pm Sun Apr-Oct; 10am-4:30pm Mon-Sat, 1:30pm-4:30pm Sun Nov-Mar; Free):* The upstairs may bore you with its needlecraft tidbits and the history of Leicestershire's role in the Anglo-Boer War, but on ground floor you'll get to cruise through a 19th-century street scene with fake storefronts, like a shoemaker's shop complete with a mannequin cobbler. Take a peek at the wildflower garden that's enclosed by the remains of an ancient castle.

Castle Yard *(The Newarke; Tel 0116/299-88-88; Free):* Around the bend from the Newarke Houses Museum is Castle View, a cobblestoned road whose ruined archway was part of a fortified south entrance to the castle enclosure. Beyond it lies the ruins of a 14th-century gatehouse, and to the left of the gate is a tranquil garden area with trees and ivy, and what used to be the castle moat. At the top of Castle View lies Castle Yard, a tranquil retreat surrounding the imposing Norman-era Great Hall. Though the hall's not open to visitors, it's worth seeing even just from the outside, especially when you realize that its brick façade hides its true age well—records put its foundation date at 1150.

St. Mary's Church *(The Newarke; Tel 0116/262-52-94; 7:30am-5pm; Free):* Located just across from the Great Hall is this little chapel, said to have been where Geoffrey Chaucer married in the 1360s. Cool, dark, and very atmospheric, it's worth looking into and lingering around in.

Jewry Wall and Museum*(St. Nicholas Cir.; Tel 0116/247-30-21; 10am-5:30pm Mon-Sat, 2-5:30pm Sun; Free):* A 10-minute walk west of Town Hall Square (just west of the castle grounds area by the riverbank), are the ruins of the largest Roman civic building site in Britain. The museum's exhibits give information on Leicestershire's history from pre-historic times to the 15th century. Site highlight: a female Saxon skeleton.

Guru Nanak Sikh Museum (Sikh Temple) *(Holy Bones; Tel 0116/262-86-06; Open to devotees daily, to the public 1pm-4pm Thur; Free):* Just beyond the Jewry Wall is this museum on the site of a former hosiery factory, dedicated to the Sikh religion, with displays on the history of Sikhism and religious sacrifice. A nice switch from Gothic cathedrals.

Jain Centre *(Oxford St.; Tel 0116/254-30-91):* Another Castle Park temple, this one is one of the few churches of this ancient Indian religious sect in the west, featuring beautiful hand-carved ceilings, pillars, and domes, stained glass windows, mirrored walls, and shrines. The Jainists are devout believers in human harmony, honesty, and respect for all living things (but ironically, their belief in purity extends to the practice of not allowing women to attend services during that special time of the month). Visitors are welcome in the entrance lobby, or may arrange a more thorough visit by appointment.

Guildhall *(Guildhall Lane; Tel 0116/253-25-69; 10am-5:30pm Mon-Sat, 2pm-5:30pm Sun; Free):* Five minutes northwest of the current Town Hall Square stands the city's original town hall. An impressive sight, it was built between the 14th and 16th centuries and contains one of Britain's oldest libraries, as well as splendid civic murals and a mayor's parlor. Those interested in criminal deviance (and who's not, really?) will appreciate the 19th-century prison cells.

St. Martin's Cathedral *(St. Martin's East; Tel 0116/262-52-94; 9am-4:30pm daily; Free):* Next door to Guildhall, this Castle Park church was one of the city's six parish churches, according to records from 1086, and was enlarged during 14th and 16th centuries. When walking by you might catch organ music drifting through its gray stone the walls. As for the inside of the cathedral, though, you'll definitely see bigger and elsewhere.

Leicester Abbey *(Abbey Park, Abbey Park Rd.; Tel 0116/222-10-00; Dawn-dusk daily; Free):* The ruins of these monks' quarters, originally built in 1132, lie 1.5 miles north of the city center in a vast park. They make for a great afternoon outing—and the price is right.

The Leicester Gas Museum *(195 Aylestone Rd.; Tel 0116/250-31-90; Bus 37, Noon-4:30pm Tue-Thur; Free):* This is the place to go if you have the burning urge to smell gas-operated machinary. The museum gives guests insight into the story of gas, past and present, and contains equipment used to make gas. Huffers take note: Don't let the brochure's mention of gas-sniffing opportunities fool you; there's no chance of getting high.

National Space Science Centre *(Exploration Dr., off of Corporation Rd.; Tel 0116/253-08-11; Bus L54; 9:30am-4pm Tue-Sun; £7.50 admission; info@nssc.co.uk; www.nssc.co.uk; MC, V):* With a price tag of £46.5 million, the mission of this complex is to attempt to explain our universe and how "the final frontier" affects our future. Attracting a diverse group of people, but really aimed at families, the center's exhibits include a 41-meter-high rocket tower, an audience-participation weather forecasting studio, a satellite control room, and a state-of-the-art planetarium, where the audience journeys onto comets and tunnels through black holes. The Space Connections Trail attempts to answer questions of the Earth's origin and eventual destruction, but not in a morose way, of course—wouldn't want to scare those kiddies.

Blue Badge Guides *(Tickets at Tourist Information Centre; Various locations; Free-£2.50):* These public guided walks in and around Leicester, prebooked or paid to the guide directly, can be surprisingly interesting. There's a big variety of offbeat themes: Examine the life of the tragically disfigured Joseph Carey Merrick on the Elephant Man tour, or see the haunts of the nasty Richard III, the king who, if you recall, murdered princes by locking them in a tower.

modification

For body alterations, these sister stores are the artists of choice in Leicester: **Inkhouse Tattooz** *(47 Silver Arcade, Silver St.; Tel 0116/251-35-48; 10am-6pm Mon-Sat),* just west of the town square, a tattoo parlor aimed at a mainstream/alternative clientele, and **The Kazbah** *(13 Malcolm Ave.; Tel 0116/253-05-43; 11am-7pm Mon-Sat),* which has both male and female piercers, and claims to have the largest selection of body jewellery in the Midlands.

stuff

There's no shortage of standard shopping centers in town—the Silver Arcade, Shires, and Haymarket—but you'll probably want to pass on those and check out some of Leicester's hipper little shops.

▶▶BAZAAR

You'll find novel things at **Leicester's Markets** *(Market St.; Tel 0116/252-67-76; Mon-Sat 6am-6pm; Free),* a block west of the town square. The Markets encompass over 400 stalls selling anything from bazaar-style clothing and fake gold jewelry to produce and fresh cod.

▶▶**TUNES**

For the best range of sounds go to **5HQ** *(Charles St.; Tel 0116/262-74-75; 10am-6pm Mon-Sat)*, a block east of the town square, a record shop that also sells venue tickets and specializes in British dance music. A better second-hand selection is available at **Rockaboom** *(St. Martin's Sq.; 9am-5:30pm Mon-Sat; AE, V, MC)*, five minutes northwest of Town Hall Square, which sells a good variety of new and used LPs, CDs, and vinyl. It's also a good place to pick up flyers.

▶▶**SKATE**

When it comes to Leicester skate shops, you're either in one camp or the other: **Casino Skates** *(64 Silver Arcade, Tel 0116/251-63-62; 10am-5:30pm Mon-Sat; www.casinoskates.com; V, MC, AE)* is, according to many, the only *true* skate shop in Leicester. It's owned and operated by—you guessed it—skaters. **Rollersnakes** *(East Broad St., Tel 0116/251-61-67; 10am-6pm Mon-Fri, 9:30am-6pm Sat; V, MC, AE)* is more of an all-around extreme sports store, with a larger selection that includes snowboarding and in-line skate gear. Both stores sell a wide range of apparel; you'll just have to decide which camp you identify more with.

EATS

In Leicester there are great options for soaking up the worldliness of this small city at much-loved Indian eateries. Then again, you can always just cheap-out on good old student grub.

▶▶**CHEAP**

The **Castle Rock Café** *(4 Oxford St.; Tel 0116/255-42-00; 10am-6pm most days; £1.50-£5 entrées)*, located next to the Charlotte, caters mostly to students. This no-thrills, pre-night-out place serves English food at student prices, like baked potatoes with beans and home-made vegetable soup.

In the Asian Quarter, you can't go wrong with the two competing Indian restaurants located across Belgrave Street from each other. Both offer affordable home-cooked vegetarian food, pastries, and savories from the region of Gujarat, Northwest India. In the upstairs restaurant of **Sharmilee** *(71-73 Belgrave Rd.; Tel 0116/261-05-03; 11am-11pm daily; £4-10 meals; No credit cards)*, a 20-minute walk north of Town Hall Square, the *masala dhosa*, a thin crispy pancake with potatoes and onions, is especially rapturous. If you're on the go, try the Mohanthal sweet pastry from the ground-floor bakery.

Sharmilee's competitor, **Bobby's** *(154-156 Belgrave Rd.; Tel 0116/266-01-06; 11am-11pm daily; £4-10 meals; No credit cards)*, a 20-minute walk north of Town Hall Square, has decor that's not as nice, but the food's just as scrumptious.

The newly opened **Shimla Pinks** *(65-69 London Rd., Tel 0116/247-14-71; Noon-2:30pm/6-10:45pm Mon-Thur, noon-2:30pm/6pm-11:15pm Fri, Sat, closed Sun; V, MC, AE, DC)* is part of a nationwide chain with a reputation for great food at great prices. The all-you-can-eat lunch buffet (£6.95) is a particularly good value. The bright and cheery decor can be

food of the golden mile

While in the Asian Quarter, it's a crime to miss the chance to eat what a lot of people say is the best Indian food in the world—including India. The best place to sample the authentic cuisine is the Golden Mile. Order *dhosa* and *samosa*—spicy, triangular fried pastries stuffed with vegetables—which should be washed down with a *falooda*, a rose-flavored ice-cream milkshake, or *lassi*, a sweet or salty yogurt smoothie-type drink that counteracts the most fiery of curries. For dessert, eat *kulfi*, Indian ice cream, or *gulabjamun*, spongy balls of fried dough soaked in saffron-flavored sugar syrup—it's not for the faint-hearted, but it's perfect for the sweet-toothed.

a bit much, especially after a hard night of drinking, but once you start eating you'll hardly notice it.

▶▶DO-ABLE

Altoco *(3 St. Martin's Sq.; Tel 0116/253-39-77; Noon-2:30pm/6-11pm Mon-Sat; V, MC, AE, DC),* formerly Joe Rigatoni's, serves excellent pizzas (£6-£8) and pasta dishes (£6-£10) in a lively atmosphere. The mostly Italian waitstaff is attentive and efficient.

Jones Bistro *(93 Queens Rd., Tel 0116/270-88-30)* is the sort of neighborhood place you dream about, with a very friendly waitstaff and an excellent menu of traditional English food with modern twists, including lots of veggie options. Try the Yorkshire pudding filled with broccoli and cheese and drizzled with a roasted baby onion gravy (£7.95) or the fresh spinach wild rice and potato patties fried in bread crumbs with red cabbage and cranberries (£7.95). They also serve top-quality steaks (£15.95) and a daily assortment of fresh fish.

▶▶SPLURGE

Not your run-of-the-mill curry house, **The Tiffin** *(1 De Montfort St.; Tel 0116/247-04-20; £19 avg. dinner; V, MC),* just around the corner from Shimla Pink, is widely considered the best Indian restaurant in town. Lots of gourmets from the U.S. make this restaurant their first stop when they come home to Leicester, so you know you're in good hands. There can be long waits even if you book ahead; the waiters are apologetic, but there's really nothing they can do—it's the price of popularity.

crashing

A scarcity of cheap crashes is one drawback to this otherwise highly affordable town. But the International Youth House is a good bet and the

Spindle Lodge Hotel is reasonable on weeknights. The Tourist Information Center [see *need to know,* below] can help you book a room.

▶▶**CHEAP**

The **International Youth House** *(Upperton Rd., Bede Island; Tel 0116/255-15-54; £11 under 26, £13 adult; infoshop@youthhouse.ntlmid lands.com; www.youthhouse.ntl-midlands.com)* just off Narborough, a quarter-mile southwest of the city center, is a unique kind of hostel, run by a youth organization promoting social welfare (they offer free pregnancy testing on Tuesdays and Thursdays!) The rooms are clean but small, and some overlook the city's muddy river. Although it looks a bit like a day care center from the outside, it's close to the city center, safe, and makes patrons feel welcome. Beware the 1:30am curfew.

Three miles from the center of town, **Dodgy Dick's Backpackers Hostel** *(157 Wanlip Lane, off A6; Tel 0116/267-31-07; Bus 61 to Haymarket every 20 mins.; 6:30am-10:30pm reception; £9 first night, £7.50 each additional night, £45/week, shared shower, breakfast included; No credit cards)* is a small place with a sort of hanging-with-the-boys feel. Besides the bunks, there is a double room and a triple room, and if you have a tent, Dick is glad to let you crash on his lawn. Despite his questionable name, Dodgy Dick says he has never had a complaint, except for one woman guest who was so shocked by walking in on a group of lads watching football on the telly in their underwear one hot day that she filed a complaint with the tourist board.

The **Scotia Hotel** *(10 Westcotes Dr.; Tel 0116/254-92-00; £21 singles, £27 singles with bath, doubles with bath £42, full English or à la carte breakfast included; V, MC)* offers 11 rooms in an original Victorian building. This family-run B&B is just off Narborough Road, a few minutes' walk from the center.

▶▶**DO-ABLE**

The **Spindle Lodge Hotel** *(2 West Walk; Tel 0116/233-88-01; £27.50-45 single, £50-59, some with private bath; V, MC),* 15 minutes southeast of Town Hall Square near the train station, is a supremely comfortable guest house. While it's not the fanciest hotel and has only 13 bedrooms, it did get three stars from the English tourist board. The price includes breakfast, and it's accessible to city attractions.

For more hotel-like accommodations, try **The Gables Hotel** *(368 London Rd.; Tel 0116/270-69-69; £45 singles with private bath, £56 doubles with private bath; AE, V, MC, DIN),* a privately owned spot situated in a building that looks more like a large house, a half-mile southeast of the City Centre. All rooms have TVs and coffeemakers, and the hotel houses the Cavalier Restaurant, a white-tablecloth sort of place with £15 fixed-priced dinners. There's also a very homey lounge bar with an eclectic collection of cushy floral-print sofas.

▶▶**SPLURGE**

Appealing but pricey, the **Belmont House Hotel** *(De Montfort St.; Tel 0116/254-47-73; £85 single with private bath Sun-Thur, £45 single with private bath Fri, Sat, £93 double with private bath Sun-Thur, £70 double* *with private bath Fri, Sat; AE, V, MC, DIN)* is located about a half-mile southeast of the city center. Each of the 70 rooms comes with free breakfast, a TV, direct-dial phone, coffeemaker, hairdryer, and desk. The hotel's actually a member of Best Western, but they don't really like to emphasize that fact. It's actually not a bad deal on the weekends, when the discount kicks in.

WITHIN 30 MINUTES

Although now in ruins, the **Ashby de la Zouch Castle** *(South St., Ashby de la Zouch; Tel 01530/560-090; Arriva buses 118, 218; 10am-6pm Apr-Sept daily; 10am-5pm Oct daily; 10am-4pm Wed-Sun Nov-Mar; £2.60 adults, £3 concessions)* is still spectacular. It makes for a great afternoon getaway if you have access to wheels or don't mind taking the bus. Built by Lord Hastings between 1473 and 1483, Sir Walter Scott wrote about it in *Ivanhoe,* and Mary Queen of Scots was imprisoned there. The castle's 80-foot tower provides panoramic countryside views, so get to climbing.

NEED TO KNOW

Currency Exchange There are exchange facilities at banks throughout the city, at **Thomas Cook** *(31 Gallowtree Gate; Tel 0116/251-15-95; 10am-5:30pm Mon, 9am-5:30pm Tue-Sat),* and at **American Express** [see *american express,* below].

Travel Info The **TIC** *(5-7 Every St.; Tel 0116/299-88-88; 9am-5:30pm Mon-Wed, Fri, 10am-5:30pm Thur, 9am-5pm Sat),* right on Town Hall Square, will help you find a room—not just in Leicester, but wherever you're headed—and load you up with info on events and attractions.

Public Transportation Leicestershire Busline *(Tel 0870/608-26-08)* serves the whole county as well as the city. Or buy from the driver a one-day **Explorer pass** valid throughout Leicestershire on Arriva buses (£5 adults). For taxis call **Skyline Taxis** *(Tel 0116/222-07-77)* or **Highfield's Taxis** *(Tel 0116/262-4004).*

American Express Cash those checks at Amex *(1 Horsefair St.; Tel 0116/251-48-09; 9am-5:30pm Mon -Sat, 9:30-5:30 Wed),* a block northwest of Town Hall Square.

Health and Emergency Emergency: *999.* **Leicester Royal Infirmary** *(Infirmary Sq.; Tel 0116/254-14-14)* is 10-minute walk south of Town Hall Square.

Pharmacies For your legal pharmaceutical needs, try **Pearl Chemist** *(185-187 Evington Rd.; Tel 0116/273-82-65; 9am-7pm Mon-Fri, till 6:30pm Thur, 9am-6pm Sat)*

Trains Trains to Leicester's **main station** *(London Rd., 0345/484-950),* a 10-minute walk southeast of Town Hall Square, depart from London's St. King's Cross-St. Pancras station throughout the day, an hour journey. There are also hourly trains between Birmingham and Cambridge or Norwich via Leicester.

Bus Lines Out of the City From London's Victoria Station, there are usually eight **National Express** buses a day to Leicester, stopping at the St. Margaret's St. Station *(Gravel St.; Tel 0990/808-080),* a 10-minute walk northwest of Town Hall Center, off Burleys Way. Though the bus trip takes nearly twice as long as it does by train, it's much cheaper.

Laundry The Launderette *(106 Narborough Rd.; Tel 0116/254-63-78; 8:30am-8pm daily; £2 wash, £1 dry)* is a 20-minute walk southwest of Town Hall Square.

Postal The main **Post Office** *(Bishop St.; 9pm-5:30pm Mon-Fri, 9am-5pm Sat, closed Sun)* is on Town Hall Square.

derby

Mundane architecture, bland shopping centers, seen-it-all-before museums, and commercialized pubs characterize the town of Derby (pronounced DAR-by). What the town does have to offer is comfortable accommodations, decent restaurants, and a passable small-scale city nightlife. In other words, Derby is a place to crash for a night when you're on the road, a place to stop for lunch or dinner, or a desperate booty-call when you absolutely must go to a club to try and pull, as the British so cutely call picking up a partner for the night. But you really wouldn't want to use Derby as a base for exploring the picturesque Peak District, the region's biggest mountain preserve, 15 miles to the north. You'd be better off using towns in South Yorkshire and Staffordshire—after all, if you're in the Peak District, you're more than likely going for astonishing natural beauty, not tepid nightlife.

The people of Derby are not discernibly different from anyone else in Central England: There are skateboarders, grunge-looking kids, young to middle-aged mothers pushing babies in old-fashioned prams, teens sporting Reebok outfits, and your typical late-night drunk chip eaters. But, unlike other East Midland towns, Derby's not plagued by tourists. If you visit Derby, you'll feel quite special; friendly locals may well take notice of you. If you're looking for a chat or advice on where to play, head to the nearest fish-and-chip shop. There aren't many here, so chances are good there's going to be a queue—a perfect opportunity to chat with locals.

As always, refer to *69 Magazine* for club night details. But be warned: You may have trouble finding it, unless you've already picked it up in bar-cafes in Leicester. The *What's On Midlands* and *City Lights* magazines list clubs, theaters, and cultural attractions, but they don't go into as much detail as *69* does.

Derby's "city" center, where you'll be hanging out, is defined by highway-sized roads semi-circling the town. To the southeast, there is quite a large market area (see *to market,* below). But you'll want to shop on **Sadler Gate** and **the Strand.** There are two surprisingly cool shops on Sadler Gate—one sells phat club clothes and the other, well, the word bizarre doesn't begin to describe it [see *stuff,* below]. Sadler Gate also has

derby

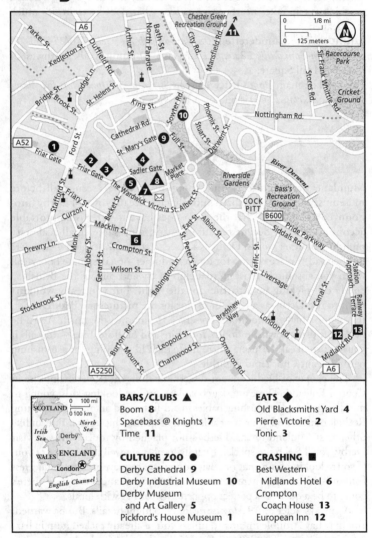

BARS/CLUBS ▲
Boom **8**
Spacebass @ Knights **7**
Time **11**

CULTURE ZOO ●
Derby Cathedral **9**
Derby Industrial Museum **10**
Derby Museum
  and Art Gallery **5**
Pickford's House Museum **1**

EATS ◆
Old Blacksmiths Yard **4**
Pierre Victoire **2**
Tonic **3**

CRASHING ■
Best Western
  Midlands Hotel **6**
Crompton
  Coach House **13**
European Inn **12**

a restaurant area adjoining, called Old Blacksmiths Yard [see *eats,* below], offering Mexican, Greek, and Continental eats. There are numerous commercial pubs sprawled throughout the town center, and the city has a well-known gay club on **Curzon Street,** an easterly road leading away from the center. These spots are pretty much it, as far as places to chill and meet folks. Fortunately, the area is easily walkable. There are no distinct neighborhoods, and subsequently, no real need for public transport.

bar and live music scene

Gossips *(Gower St.; Tel 01332/332-942, Fax 01332/371-772; leeholl@ gossips.fsnet.co.uk; £2 cover Mon-Wed, free Fri, Sat)* is a fun, if a bit tacky, bar just off Greenlane. On Mondays there are live bands—they're generally local and unheard of, but you never know. Tuesday there's a salsa class from 7:30 to 8:15pm followed by a solid night of salsa disco dancing. Wednesday is the boldly and aptly named *Titty Twister,* a "gentleman's evening" with strippers, lap dancers, and bar dancers. Fridays are party nights with different themes each week, like *Tequila Night, Vicar and Tart night, Phone Chat-Up,* and *Medieval.* Saturday is *Spin the Wheel,* when you literally spin the big wheel to see what drink special you get to take advantage of—your choices are usually 70p shots, £1 pints, £1.20 Hooch, £1 Red Stripe, £1 Black Russians, and £1 vodka shots. The music is mainly chart hits from the '60s to the '80s, and the local dancing crowd is boisterous, to say the least.

The **Late Bar** *(Willow Row; Tel 01332/202-048; www.derby.ac.uk/udsu; 7:30pm-2am Mon-Sat)* is owned by the University of Derby Students Union (UDSU), and is basically one big room with a DJ spinning garage, drum 'n' bass, or indie. Next to the DJ booth is a single bar, and there are a few tables and chairs scattered about. The mood here is inebriated and naturally laid-back. It's the best place to get a drink in the wee hours if you don't feel like being in a nightclub.

Also run by the UDSU, the **Riverside Bar** *(Mill St.; Tel 01332/367-699; www.derby.ac.uk/udsu)* is the most popular student venue in the city. It's reasonably spacious with plenty of entertainment like pool tables, games machines, karaoke and quiz nights. The prices are cheap, but you need a UDSU card (make friends with a UD student beforehand) to get in. Good traditional food like burgers, roast chicken, and lasagnas is provided for no more than £3.

The **Victoria Inn** *(Midland Place; Tel 01332/740-091; thevic@ mindless.com, www.derby65.freeserve.co.uk/v-cont.htm; 2-11pm daily, doors open for live acts at 7:30pm; £2-10 cover)* just a few steps from the rail station, is the place to go for punk, ska, and indie shows.

The **Flower Pot** *(King St.; Tel 01332/834-438 or 0115/912-90-00 for credit card booking; £5-12 cover; www.rawpromo.co.uk)* presents big-name British folk and rock performers—such as Al Stewart, Steve Harley, and Nine Below Zero—that Americans have never heard of. Check out their well-laid-out Web site for descriptions of the artists and schedules of upcoming gigs.

club scene

Clubbers can't be choosers when it comes to Derby's nightlife. But smaller-scale parties can sometimes be as much fun as the megaparties of Birmingham, as Time and Knights clearly show.

Try to hit **Time** *(Mansfield Rd.; Tel 01332/345-860; 9:30pm-4am Fri, Sat; £2-12 cover),* across the river to the east of the town center off of

Phoenix Street, on Saturday night for *Progress (Tel 01332/600-700)*, an exalted 8-year-old party fueled by banging house and garage that will leave you begging for more. On Fridays, students are lured into the club in droves by 99p drink specials all night long with DJs playing dance anthems. Thursdays are strictly students only.

Locals describe **Boom** *(6 Sadler Gate; Tel 01332/200-910; Usually 9pm-3am Wed-Sun; Free-£4 cover; No credit cards)* as, "adequate." Wednesday is trance; Thursday is salsa and dance; Fridays and Saturdays have an endless supply of chart house music spun by resident DJs. But Boom is *the* place to be on Sundays, as they have a late booze license and are open and serving until a whopping 3am (unheard of for a Sunday night in the UK).

If you're lucky enough to be in Derby the last Friday of any month for *Spacebass* at **Knights** *(St. James St.; Tel 07977/718-227; 9:30pm-2:30am last Fri of the month; £5 before midnight, £7 after)*, 5 minutes southeast of Sadler Gate, you really should check it out. A wicked crew takes over for this late evening feast of deep British house, hip-hop, soul, and R&B, with a dress code of no sneakers or hoodies. It has that element of trendy ambience that Derby lacks most days of the week.

A really confusing-to-describe venue is **Union 1 & Union 2** *(University of Derby Student Union, Willow Rd.; Tel 01332/202-048; free-£4 cover; www.derby.ac.uk; No credit cards)* just west of the town center. While Unions 1 & 2 are both located in the Student Union, they are two separate clubs with different entrances. Union 2 has a late bar *(8:30pm-2am Mon-Thur, 7:30pm-2am Fri, Sat)* considered it's own entity, and a club area *(8:30pm-2am Tue, Fri, Sat)*. There's no particular pattern to the music at either. Fridays and Saturdays at Union 1 *(10pm-2am Fri, Sat)* and Union 2 both seem to consistently play commercial dance, while Union 2's bar is more likely to play a vibrant set of '60s, '70s, and '80s music. Rather surprisingly, the two clubs attract a mixed-age clientele, not just students, which makes for a more open, funky, laid-back vibe.

arts scene

▶▶PERFORMING ARTS SCENE

It seems that every town, no matter how small, has a place for big-time shows. Derby's got the **Assembly Rooms** *(Market Place; Tel 01332/255-800; Times and prices vary)* just north of Sadler Gate, where you can see everything from cover bands to quartets, and African to contemporary Irish Music.

If you're looking for more drama than the Derby streets provide, there's the **Guildhall Theatre** *(Market Place; Tel 01332/255-800; Show times and prices vary)*, on the same street as the Assembly Rooms. In a small auditorium with floral-patterned ceiling frescoes, you can watch small-scale touring theatrical companies strut whatever stuff they've got.

More well-known in the East Midlands is the **Derby Playhouse** *(Theatre Walk, Eagle Centre; Tel 01332/363-275; Show times and prices* *vary)*, in the Eagle Market. Past performances have included poetry-while-you-eat as well as contemporary tragedies (and no, we're not talking about the performance quality).

gay scene

Derby doesn't have a booming gay scene, but it does have a couple of well-known cruise spots for men: the bus station [see *need to know*, below] and the Fish Market, aka "Fish Cottage," off Victoria street just south of the city center. You might be able to pick up a Brit, in fact, by asking him what the term "cottaging" means.

A highly recommended gay club called **Curzons** *(Curzon St.; Tel 01332/363-739; 10pm-3am Thur-Sat, 9pm-midnight Sun; Free-£3 cover; No credit cards)*, a block west of Sadler Gate, plays '70s to '90s music on Tuesdays and commercial music on Thursdays. Friday is cabaret night with drag shows, and on Saturday you can groove to commercial garage and disco house. Sunday is *Camp Night* with free supper. Promoters rent out the club once a month either on Mondays or Thursdays for *D-votion*, a night of gay vampirism *(9:30pm-2am)*. This Goth party plays music suitable for fetishists with a melange of tastes ranging from retro-Goth to house and trance. Call ahead to see when the next night of darkness is taking place.

The last Thursday of every month at **Union 2** [see *club scene*, above] is also very popular with gays, lesbians, and bis, as well as straights. It not only attracts a crowd of mixed preferences, but mixed ages, so you can find that sugar daddy you've been looking for (kidding!).

culture zoo

Derby has a few museums that attempt to preserve the town and the 'shire's history. With the exception of the Derby Museum and Art Gallery, the cultural sights are rather disappointing, though. The Derby City Council puts out a pamphlet thrillingly called "Exhibitions Programme," with a calendar of events at the first three attractions listed below (you'll find it at the Tourist Information Center and at hotels). Alternatively, there's the net: *www.derby.gov/museums.*

Derby Industrial Museum *(Silk Mill Lane, Tel 01332/255-308; www.derby.gov.uk/museums; 11am-5pm Mon, 10am-5pm Tue-Sat, 2-5pm Sun & bank holidays; Free):* On the sight of the world's first modern factory (or so they'll tell you here) is this museum, with Rolls Royce–made airplane engine parts and machinery from the industries of Derbyshire. It's all of more interest to engineers and assembly line workers than to most folks, though you might enjoy pretending to drive the electric train. Can you say "skippable"?

Derby Museum and Art Gallery *(The Strand; Tel 01332/716-659; 10am-5pm Tue-Sat, 2-5pm Sun & bank holidays; Free):* Housed around the corner from the Industrial Museum, west of Sadler Gate, is this far more fascinating collection of artefacts dug up in Derbyshire, some dating back to Neolithic times. There's a series of badly sharpened knives that haven't cut steak for 6,000 years and the remains of a Viking sword, as well as some beads that came off of the same Viking's necklace.

Pickford's House Museum *(41 Friar Gate; Tel 01332/255-308; www.derby.gov.uk/museums; 11am-5pm Mon, 10am-5pm Tue-Sat, 2-5pm Sun; Free):* Dating back to 1770, this Georgian-era family home, a block west of Sadler Gate, recreates the feel of olden-days domestic life with rooms decorated entirely in period furniture. The more modern bomb shelter is novel, as is a rotating exhibit of historical fashions. Past exhibitions have included "Fabulous Frocks," a showcase of evening dresses and accessories from the past half century, and, we kid you not, "Derby's Embroidery Pioneers." The best part of the museum may be the 1930s bathroom that you can actually use.

Derby Cathedral *(Iron Gate; Tel 01332/341-201; 8:30am-6pm; £1.50 tower admission, Cathedral free):* This place calls itself a cathedral to get more attention from tourists, but it's clearly just a large church with delusions of grandeur. The walls are lined with plaques and the nave is full of ordinary wooden pews. That's pretty much it, except, of course, for the beautiful, glimmering iron and gold gate surrounding the altar. But that actually turns out, on further inspection, to be simply painted blue and gold.

modification

Salamander's *(40 Sadler Gate; Tel 01332/296-436; 9am-5:30pm Mon-Sat; Body piercing hours 11am-5pm Mon-Sat; AE, V, MC, DC)* is probably the strangest shop in the East Midlands. In the cafe on the first floor you can dine on toasted cheese sandwiches—aka "toasties"—for just 99p, or order takeout. On the ground floor you can buy wind chimes and a new outfit to go with your newly pierced tongue(£25), nose ring(£15) or eyebrow stud(£15). And you thought Wal-mart had it all!

STUFF

You'll probably want to join the teens and young adults loitering around Sadler Gate's small amount of brand-named coffee shops (you know which ones I'm talking about). The road contains a hybrid of independently owned and commercial chain shops, creating decent shopping for young and old alike.

▶▶DUDS

The gold star goes to **Redhaze** *(1/2 Sadler Gate; Tel 01332/200-202; 10am-5:30pm Mon-Sat; AE, V, MC, DC),* a fashion store that's too hip for the town it resides in. This is the place to go when you're in dire need of unique florescent-yellow two-piece outfits, clear plastic blow-up backpacks, and other outlandish narcissistic British clubwear that you can take back home as a souvenir. The store is multi-leveled, and if you need assistance, shop-hands will help out, as well as take an interest in where you come from.

Another place to go for unbridled hipness is **Peak Performance** *(22 Sadler Gate; Tel 01332/293-694),* a skate shop that sells big pants, big shirts, shoes, and decks (skateboards, not turntables) from top designers

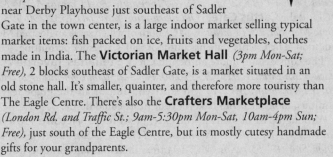

TO MARKET

Every town in the East Midlands must have a market, and Derby has three worth browsing around in. The **Eagle Centre Market** *(Morledge Rd.; No phone; 9am-5:30pm Mon, Tue, Thur-Sat; Free)*, in the area near Derby Playhouse just southeast of Sadler Gate in the town center, is a large indoor market selling typical market items: fish packed on ice, fruits and vegetables, clothes made in India. The **Victorian Market Hall** *(3pm Mon-Sat; Free)*, 2 blocks southeast of Sadler Gate, is a market situated in an old stone hall. It's smaller, quainter, and therefore more touristy than The Eagle Centre. There's also the **Crafters Marketplace** *(London Rd. and Traffic St.; 9am-5:30pm Mon-Sat, 10am-4pm Sun; Free)*, just south of the Eagle Centre, but its mostly cutesy handmade gifts for your grandparents.

like Blueprint, Volcon, Addicts, and DC. The staff is very friendly, and they really know their skating.

▶▶TUNES

The town's cool record shop, **BPM** *(The Strand; Tel 01332/382-038; 10am-6pm Mon-Sat; AE, V, MC, DC)*, around the corner west of Sadler Gate, sells LPs and CDs, new and used. Be on the lookout for posters on the walls advertising upcoming shows and parties.

   Reveal Records *(37 Main Centre; Tel 01332/349-242; www.reveal records.com, Sales@revealrecords.com)* specializes in moldy old vinyl, particularly of the rock variety (okay, so it's really not moldy).

EATS

Your best option for a convenient and tasty feed is to plot a course for Old Blacksmiths Yard, a brick courtyard off Sadler Gate surrounded by several passable ethnic restaurants.

▶▶CHEAP

To satisfy that Thai craving, head to the **Chai Yo Restaurant** *(8 Bold Lane; Tel 01332/360-207; Noon-2:30pm/6-11pm daily; £4-8 meals; AE, V, MC, DC)*, just north of Strand a minute's walk west of Sadler Gate. It's atmospherically strewn with candles, and has (fake) flowers on each table and in the window boxes. The tasty variety of lunch specials—including a bunch of veggie options—are served with fried or steamed rice. Non-vegetarian options include some great curries and a renowned stir-fried duck. Set dinner menus for parties of two or more offer the same kinds of stir-fries plus more complex curries, pungent soups, and tangy salads.

Tonic *(Friar Gate; Tel 01332/347-444; Noon-3pm/5-11pm daily; Meals £4-8; AE, MC, V)*, a block west of Sadler Gate, is the perfect spot for a drawn-out late-afternoon lunch. A restaurant and bar with French doors that open onto a plaza seating area, Tonic attracts a sizeable crowd during off-peak hours on a sunny day. Try one of the scrumptious French bread sandwiches, like the spiced Cajun chicken baguette, or the extra-large Caesar salad.

▶▶DO-ABLE

Two other decent spots on Old Blacksmith's Yard are **Amigos** *(Old Blacksmiths Yard; Tel 01332/521-234; 7-11pm daily; £5-11 meals; AE, V, MC, DC)* and the **Cactus Café,** *(Old Blacksmiths Yard; Tel 01332/290-993; 6-10pm Mon-Sat; £5-11 meals; V, MC)*, both of which serve anglocized Mexican food. The Cactus Café has outdoor tables, weather permitting.

The considerably more authentic Greek **Stelianas Taverna** *(Old Blacksmiths Yard; Tel 01332/385-200; Noon-2:30pm/6pm-midnight Mon-Sat; £4-10 meals; MC, V)* will stuff you full of all the grape leaves, hummus, moussaka, and baklava your heart could desire.

Although part of a chain, the charming **Pierre Victoire** *(18 Friar Gate; Tel 01332/370-470; Noon-3pm/6-11pm Mon-Sat, 12:30-3:30pm/6-10pm Sun; £7-15 meals; MC, V)* offers delicious and unique (for the region) French food. The restaurant's full vegetarian menu includes main courses such as sweet potato and French bean pasties. The three-course lunch specials (£5.95 and up) include enough food to satiate your appetite for the rest of the day.

crashing

The few available rooms in town are are within easy walking distance of the center of town, mostly clustered within a 5-minutes walk to the south on the way to the London Road. There aren't any huge bargains or hostels, though. The Tourist Information Center can help you book accommodations [see *need to know,* below].

▶▶CHEAP

For a high-quality, low-cost night's rest, bed down at the **Crompton Coach House** *(45 Crompton Street; Tel 01332/365-735; £15 per person; No credit cards)*, 4 blocks southwest of Sadler Gate. You can choose from a single, double or a larger family room. All are refurbished and bright and thankfully lack the cheesy floral decor you usually get in a B&B. There are TVs and tea and coffee makers in all rooms, plus sinks in rooms that don't have private baths. Reservations are recommended.

If the Crompton is full, check across the street at **Chuckles Guest House** *(48 Crompton St.; Tel 01332/367-193; ianfraser@chucklesguestgoue. freeserve.co.uk; £19 single, £34 double, £49 double with private bath; No credit cards)*, which really isn't as bad as it sounds. The rooms in this cheap B&B have all the same amenities as the Crompton. Bonus enthusiasm points are given for the wildly Technicolor decor—it may not exactly aid sleep, but the owners proudly show it off in their print advertisements.

If you're still looking for a place to stay on Crompton street, the **Wayfarer** *(27 Crompton; Tel 01332/348-350; £18 single, £32 double, breakfast included; Shared baths; No credit cards)* offers cheap, no-frills accommodation in a small, single-family house.

▶▶**DO-ABLE**

If you need more of a comfort fix, try the **European Inn** *(Midland Rd.; Tel 01332/292-000; £46.50 single, double, or family room with private bath; AE, V, MC, DC)*, on a street adjoining London Road 3 blocks southeast of Sadler Gate. The Inn charges by bedroom, not per person, so if you're traveling with a couple of friends you can make a stay pretty economical. All 88 rooms have standard hotel facilities including a television, telephone, hair dryer, and free tea and coffee.

When you want to stay somewhere with that familiar commercial hotel feeling, try the **Best Western Midlands Hotel** *(Midland Rd.; Tel 01332/345-894; £49 single, double, and double occupancy suite, Sat, Sun; £77.50 single, £84 double with private bath, Mon-Fri; www.midland-derby.co.uk; AE, V, MC)* on the same street as the European Inn. You won't get a whole lot of character, but you'll at least be guaranteed a certain level of quality and classy reception-area decor. The Best Western practically shares its grounds with the train station—very convenient if you don't want to schlep your luggage anymore.

need to know

Currency Exchange Thomas Cook *(1 Saint Peters St.; Tel 01332/294-044; 9am-5pm Mon-Fri, 9:30am-3:30pm Sat)* is within the Midland Bank, 2 blocks southeast of Sadler Gate.

Travel Info For accommodation advice, town information, theater tickets, and National Express bus tickets, go to the **Tourist Information Centre** *(Market Place; Tel 01332/255-802; 9:30am-5:30pm Mon-Fri, 9:30am-5pm Sat, 10:30am-2:30pm Sun; tourism@derby.gov.uk; www.derby.gov.uk/tourism)*, in the Assembly Rooms on the northwest corner of the square opposite Sadler Gate.

Health and Emergency Emergency: *999*. The **Derbyshire Royal Infirmary** *(London Rd.; Tel 01332/347-141)* is 4 blocks south of Sadler Gate.

Pharmacies Boots *(15 Victoria St.; Tel 01332/347-295; 8:30am-8pm Mon-Fri, 8:30am-5:30pm Sat)* is 2 blocks south of Sadler Gate.

Trains Derby is easy to reach from Nottingham, Birmingham, and London with daily connections via train *(Tel 0345/484-950)* arriving at the main station a mile south of the town center.

Bus Lines Out of Town National Express daily connections to Nottingham, Birmingham, and London arrive at the main station *(Morledge St.; Tel 0990/808-080)*. For other regional connections, use **Derbyshire Busline** *(Tel 01332/292-200)*.

Laundry The **Friargate Launderette** *(67 Friargate; Tel 01332/340-709; 8:30am-9pm daily)* is 2 blocks west of the town center.

Postal The **Post Office** *(Victoria St.; Tel 0345/223-341; 9pm-5:30pm Mon-Fri, 9am-5pm Sat, closed Sun)* is just across from Green Lane in the town center.

nottingham

Though it's most famous for the whole Robin Hood scene in Sherwood Forest, Nottingham has become one of the up-and-coming party capitals in the East Midlands. The city's roots are as deep as any in England—older than Norman/Saxon conflicts—but today its personality is an appealing hybrid of old and new. The Lace Market, built in the 19th century when Nottingham was an industrial city based on knitting (and the lace capital of the world), is still a vital part of the city center, but today it houses bars, clubs, cafes, restaurants, and theaters rather than sweat shops cranking out lace for traders and entrepreneurs.

Long before the bars and the lace, Nottingham was an important 11th-century fortress, mostly because it was situated on the Trent River, an important waterway. You can visit castles, caves, and museums with artifacts from a thousand years of local history [see *culture zoo,* below], but that's not what makes the place so charming. What's really great is that those old, narrow streets and ghost-filled half-timbered buildings haven't been torn down or made into cheesy tourist attractions; they're actually being used for modern businesses, even if most of the profits come from parties rather than products.

That hybrid mode is characteristic of this city: Even though it's home to Nottingham Trent University, the party scene goes above and beyond that of a typical university town. **Media** [see *club scene,* below] draws around-the-block queues equal to those at London's Fabric. Bar-clubs, which are a bit too large to be called bars, but not as grandiose as clubs, dish out funky grooves and beats too. So if you're burning out on hitting one brightly lit, horribly decorated pub after another, these new hybrids offer a level up. And at cafe-bars, you can drink cocktails while eating increasingly sophisticated cafe cuisine in a dimly lit atmosphere with chill music flowing through the speakers. In fact, if you've gotten Pub Overload during your English travels, you can totally recover here.

With streets named Marion's Way and Friar Lane, you might expect to be overrun with horrific Robin Hood attraction crap, but the cheese is completely avoidable. Nottingham is a prosperous small city, as its folklore attracts tourists and creates a sizeable income for the town. But, like other towns in Central England, there are a few homeless people and needy buskers on the street. In fact, it's common to see young people chatting it up with the homeless, providing them with food and emotional support. The majority of city residents seem genuinely concerned about the welfare of others, making for a very welcoming vibe.

nottingham

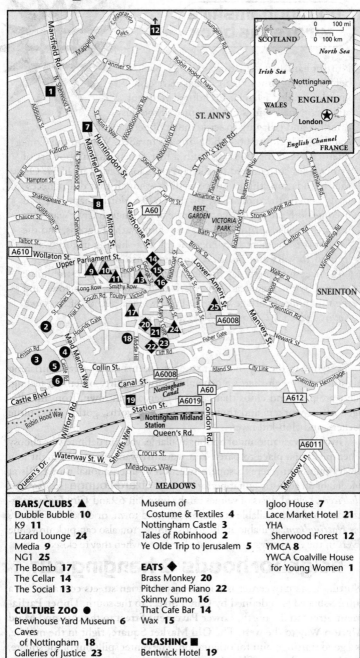

BARS/CLUBS ▲
Dubble Bubble **10**
K9 **11**
Lizard Lounge **24**
Media **9**
NG1 **25**
The Bomb **17**
The Cellar **14**
The Social **13**

CULTURE ZOO ●
Brewhouse Yard Museum **6**
Caves
  of Nottingham **18**
Galleries of Justice **23**

Museum of
  Costume & Textiles **4**
Nottingham Castle **3**
Tales of Robinhood **2**
Ye Olde Trip to Jerusalem **5**

EATS ◆
Brass Monkey **20**
Pitcher and Piano **22**
Skinny Sumo **16**
That Cafe Bar **14**
Wax **15**

CRASHING ■
Bentwick Hotel **19**

Igloo House **7**
Lace Market Hotel **21**
YHA
  Sherwood Forest **12**
YMCA **8**
YWCA Coalville House
  for Young Women **1**

nottinghamshire wrote the book

Nottinghamshire's history extends back before Saxon times when it was part of a kingdom called Mercia. It endured frequent attacks by the Vikings but they proved too busy drinking and pillaging to settle much of permanent standing. Then, in 1066, the Normans invaded. William the Conqueror arrived in 1068 and built a fort, where the supporters of Prince John surrendered to Richard the Lionhearted in 1194. On that foundation, things grew steadily—though that didn't necessarily benefit the monarchy: By the 1640s, Nottinghamshire had become both the birthplace and grave of the English Civil War. This little region also sprung America's forefathers, the Pilgrims, and the Separatist Movement they engendered. But shaping history wasn't limited to wars and politics; Nottinghamshire aslo was a major influence on modern day literature. It contains the ancestral home of Lord Byron, Newstead Abbey [see *within 30 minutes,* below], and the tiny miner's cottage where D.H. Lawrence, author of *Sons and Lovers* and *Lady Chatterley's Lover,* was born.

Everyone in the city, not just students, seems to enjoy its flourishing nightlife. Although there's a general twenty- to thirtysomething feeling, there are pubs and clubs that cater to everyone in town, from middle-aged office-workers and their elders to gays, goths, gothic gays, indie rockers, and club-kid ravers.

Given the vast amount of options available, you can definitely be choosy when picking a place to party. You wouldn't want to waste a night in a dreary pub when there's a superb selection of international trance DJs at Media, or an acoustic guitar performance at **Lizard Lounge** [see *bar and club scene,* below]. Lists of venues can be found in *69* and *City Lights* magazines, which are available at cafe-bars around town, or check out *What's on Nottingham,* available at the tourist office. You also can pick up venue flyers in the entryways to many cafe-bars even when they're closed.

neighborhoods & hanging out

Nottingham's city center is a maze of pedestrian streets contained in a square-shaped area defined by **Canal Street** to the south, **Upper Parliament Street** to the north, **Lower Pavement Street** to the east, and **Maid Marion Way** to the west. The **Old Market Square,** right in the middle, is a good starting point for orientation. The center spills out of the square, and includes the site of **Nottingham Castle** [see *culture zoo,* below] in the west; Victoria Market, the main bus station, and shopping center [see *stuff*, below] in the north; and Nottingham Midland Train Station, south of the Nottingham Canal.

The **Hockley** district is located in the City Centre west of the Old Market Square, and is centered on **Carlton Street,** which turns into **Goosegate.** By night, it's a fantastically fun hooch area where you can roam the streets as drunk as you please and not be bothered by police (most of the time). It's all very Greenwich Village-esque, attracting an assortment of punk and goth twentysomethings. The trendy, hip neighborhood has lots of small shops that sell retro clothes and the standard assortment of hippie and New Age supplies, from incense to costume jewelry. Along with cafe-bars, the area sports numerous small shops peddling jewelry, incense and retro-style clothing.

Nottingham's gay neighborhood—the "Pink Triangle"—is in the eastern part of the city center. It's literally a traffic triangle formed by the junction of **Lower Parliament Street** and **Southwell Road,** and is surrounded by several gay bars, pubs, and clubs on streets leading immediately from it [see *gay scene,* below].

The Lace Market is located in the southern part of the City Centre, along **High Pavement.** You'll know you're there when you see the throngs of senior-citizen tourists seeking that perfect shawl.

Nottingham's student ghetto is north of **Upper Parliament Street,** along **Talbot Street** and the Nottingham Trent University campus. Students mostly stick to the bars and pubs on Talbot Street. The eastern corner of Talbot and **Goldsmith** streets, which has a cluster of pubs, often smells of weed, and, speaking of odors, late-night public urination on university buildings is common among both genders.

The city center is entirely walkable, but if you need to get across town, you might want to catch a bus. They run frequently during the

sin and scrooby don't mix

It was in the tiny village of Scrooby, Nottinghamshire, where the Pilgrim leader William Browser was born in 1566. Browser and his Separatist followers seemingly escaped to Holland on the now black and murky River Ryton. The town's notable history is made more interesting by the fact that the corpse of one John Spencer dangled over the town's turnpike for over 60 years, as a reminder to derelicts of the harsh penalties of wrongdoing.

day, and at night a bus service runs to surrounding suburbs [see *need to know,* below].

bar scene

Most of Nottingham's pubs, which are packed with students, offer drink specials during the university semester. The outdoor courtyard at the corner of Talbot and Goldsmith streets—pub central—is typically jammed with students drinking at picnic tables. But if you're not in the pub mood, visit the chic bar-clubs for excellent music and a trendy young crowd.

Saturday is the hot night at the small, trendy, **Lizard Lounge** *(St. Mary's Gate, Lace Market; Tel 0115/952-32-64; 10/10:30pm to 2am Mon-Sat, till 3am Sun; AE, V, MC, DC).* If you can get past the door personnel (dress designer-y and be blasé), you'll hear R&B and British retro kitsch pop. The Lizard plays a variety of music other nights, making it less of an authentic "scene" than bars that stick to one style.

The first floor of **The Social** *(23 Pelham St., Hockley; Tel 0115/950-50-78; Downstairs: noon-11pm Mon, Tue, till midnight Wed, till 12:30am Thur, till 1:30am Fri, Sat; upstairs opens between 6-8pm; £3 Sat upstairs; www.thesocial.co.uk; V, MC minimum £10 charge),* just east of the Old Market Square, is usually jam-packed with a surprisingly non-hoochy (hooch=person looking to get laid) group of patrons. Later in the evening, move upstairs and show it off on the small dance floor.

club scene

The clubs in Nottingham have a rep throughout Central England. The parties, which are comparable to the best of the much bigger cities, attract world-class DJs, and the crowds are often as hip as you'd find in London or New York.

Solid bass vibrates the entire building containing **Dubble-Bubble** *(17 Greyhound St.; Tel 0115/952-00-21; www.dubbub.co.uk; Thur-Sat, fortnightly Sun; £2-6),* in a city center alleyway. You'll have fun dancing on this cozy club's two floors any night of the week with your trendy, alternative-style, New York-esque fellow-clubbers. Next door, the same owners opened the stylish K9 bar—the perfect place for a pre-venue cup of English tea.

wired

The best internet cafe in town, mouses down, is the drably named **Nottingham Internet Cafe** *(111-117 Alfreton Rd.; Tel 0115/978-81-11; 9am-6pm Mon-Fri, 10am-11pm Sat; £1.50 for 30 minutes),* which has 14 computers at which college kids linger, travelers e-mail, and teens play games.

Renaissance is the reason why you came to Nottingham, right? Held at **Media** *(Queen St.; Tel 0115/910-11-01; 9:30pm-2am Tue-Thur, 9pm-3am Fri, 9pm-3/6am Sat; £2-8 Tue-Fri, £10-12 Sat; www.media nottingham.com; MC, V, AE, DC),* just north of Old Market Square, this party is truly massive and merits thorough ranting and raving. Every week it attracts a different lineup of world-class DJs. Past events include a 6-hour Deep Dish marathon with confetti falling from the sky, and all-night feasts from Seb Fontaine, Boy George, Gordon Kaye, Nick Warren, and Eric Morillo. The list goes on. *Kiss Kiss* is Nottingham Trent University's student party, *Airport* on Wednesdays is similar, and Friday's *Mono* has quite a rep for its weekly presentations of funky house vocals. The club itself is a sight to behold. In the main arena, large white ramps that extend from the dance floor, wind around the DJs turntables, and make their way upstairs to a red-lit balcony with a bar. Action from the main arena is projected in the chill-out room, which has video games and TVs built into the walls. On the top floor, florescent lights sporting the Media logo circle a small dance floor while impoverished clubbers drink at blue-lit bars. The dark basement below the Main Arena is the perfect place to chill when the night hits you too hard.

For a more intimate club experience, try **The Bomb** *(45 Bridlesmith Gate; Tel 0115/950-66-67; 10pm-3am Tue-Thur, till 5am Fri, Sat; £2-6 Tue-Thur, £7-10 Fri-Sat),* just south of the Old Market Square in City Centre. Florescent-lit white walls, low white ceilings, and dim lighting add to the club's cozy atmosphere, whose general musical style is house, breakbeats, and drum 'n' bass. Girls and guys dressed in everything from funky flared-pants to clubwear to casual duds mingle together, sipping cocktails in a chill-out room while others linger at the bar smoothly chatting each other up. Tuesday is student night—the rest of the week is très chic. Wednesday's *Free Range* is an open deck session for up-and-coming DJs. Once a month it's *Drumfunk* breakbeat funk *(www.in-sight2000.com).* On Saturdays, *Drop the Bomb,* the "In-front" and "Out-back" rooms usually get the action going with one floor dedicated to house and the other to soul, jazz, and funk. Past guests have included Groove Armada and Derrick Carter.

arts scene

▶▶VISUAL ARTS SCENE

The galleries in Nottingham are well-stocked for a place this size, most notably the edgy Angel Row Gallery. Even movies go postmodern here, at the Broadway Cinema.

The **Angel Row Gallery** *(Nottingham Central Library, Building 3 Angel Row, City Centre; Tel 0115/915-28-69; Free),* in the City Centre, exhibits British and American contemporary artists. Past shows have displayed art made from discarded objects and installations dealing with genetically modified food and microwave cooking. There are also coffee bar readings, slide shows, and "meet the artist" nights. The shows here are highly recommended—it's best to check with the gallery or in *What's on Nottingham* or *City Lights* for details on current happenings.

The **Djanogly Art Gallery** (*University of Nottingham Arts Centre, University Park; Tel 0115/951-31-92; Bus 12, 13 to University Boulevard, 11am-5pm Mon-Sat, 2-5pm Sun and bank holidays; www.nottingham. ac.uk/artscentre; Free*), has a wide range of art on permanent exhibition dating from the last several centuries to the present. Temporary exhibits include mixed and single media works by intriguing, well-known local artists. Like Angel Row, Djanogly offers chances to talk with artists about their work.

Nottingham's showcase for art films is **Broadway Cinema** (*14/18 Broad St.; Tel 0115/952-66-11; Times and prices vary; AE, V, MC, DC*), just west of the Old Market Square. With an eclectic program of current and past fringe film, this place has done such inspired events as the screening of silent films with live musical accompaniment.

▶▶PERFORMING ARTS SCENE

Every city in central England seems to have a token university theater—Nottingham has the **Djanogly Recital Hall** (*University of Nottingham Arts Centre, University Park; Tel 0115/951-47-64; www.nottingham.ac.uk/artscentre; 10am-2pm Mon-Fri; Bus 12 or 13 to University Blvd; Prices vary*). The hall offers a variety of musical performances ranging from the University Philharmonic to a series of jazz performances, and such gems as "Troubadour Love Songs Aiming to Prevent Stylised Medieval Images of Women as Objects of Distant Desire." Get yer tickets early, kids, this one's gonna sell out quick!

Girls, are you looking for some high-cheese erotic excitement? If so, you might get lucky enough to catch the Chippendale Dancers at the Royal Centre's **Royal Concert Hall** (*South Sherwood St.; Tel 0115/989-55-55; 9am-8pm Mon-Sat; enquiry@royalcentre-nottingham.co.uk; www. royalcentre-nottingham.co.uk; V, MC, AE, DC*) on Theatre Square, just north of the city center. You can also see more serious performers like the Polish Opera. The Centre also houses the **Theatre Royal,** where productions vary from dance to Shakespeare. Tickets are available for both at the Royal Concert Hall box office.

For more theatrics, check what's playing at the **Nottingham Play-house** (*Wellington Circus; Tel 0115/941-94-19; www.nottinghamplay house.co.uk; various times and prices*), three blocks northwest of Old Market Square. Productions of adult dramas and more kid-friendly plays like *The Secret Garden* run about 2 to 3 weeks.

Alternatively, the **Lace Market Theatre** (*Lace Market; Tel 0115/950-72-01; times and prices vary*) has a thing for dramatic plays on heavy literary and psychological topics.

To hear classical music or big-time concerts, your best bet is **Nottingham Arena** (*National Ice Centre; Tel 0115/950-19-38; www.nottingham-arena.co.uk; Times and prices vary*), just east of City Centre, the city's major arena. Tickets are available at the Royal Concert Hall Box Office.

gay scene

Nottingham's gay area, centered around the Pink Triangle, is small and friendly. The close-knit community enjoys its bars and pubs, although sometimes they can be quite empty.

On the triangle, gay house music penetrates the walls of **Jacey's Bar** *(Lower Heathcote St.; Tel 0115/941-48-86; 6-11pm daily)*, a fairly nondescript but nevertheless popular area watering hole.

Booming house music can also be heard in the **Admiral Duncan** *(74 Lower Parliament St.; Tel 0115/924-02-13; 6-11pm daily)*, which has a dark, small club atmosphere and dance floor.

One pub listed in the gay pages but not in the gay area—and definitely not identifying itself as a gay bar—is the three-story **Criterion** *(217 Mansfield Rd.; Tel 0115/924-02-13; 5-11pm Mon, Tue, 4-11pm Wed, Thu; Noon-11pm Fri, 1-11pm Sat, 1-3:30pm Sun; No credit cards)*, just north of the city center. It's known for attracting a mixed gay and straight clientele of various ages. They play clubbish music, but the atmosphere is very pub-like—if you don't want to shake that thang, you can also play pool or foosball.

Many Nottingham gays and lesbians are ecstatic that the large, exquisitely designed **NG1** *(76/80 Lower Parliament St.; Tel 0115/958-84-40; 10pm-2:30am Wed, Thur, Fri, till 3am, Sat till 4am; £3 mandatory membership, then free-£5 cover; V, MC)*, in the heart of the Pink Triangle, has opened to fill the town's void of gay clubs. Some folks say it's too grandiose, frivolous, and image-oriented, but you can't argue with the crowds that come to groove on its two dance floors and bask in the chill atmosphere. It really *is* a shame that no one running the place focuses on the music, which is mainly commercial house and dance anthems.

culture zoo

You wouldn't be surprised that a city rich in Robin Hood folklore would have worthwhile cultural attractions, would you? Well, in case there's still some doubt in your mind, consider the Nottingham Castle Museum & Art Gallery's incredible grounds and history. Or the oldest inn in England, or at least so claim the proprietors of Ye Olde Trip to Jerusalem. And if those are just way too conventional, there are still the dank cavities of the Caves of Nottingham.

Nottingham Castle Museum & Art Gallery *(Castle Rd.; Tel 0115/915-37-00; 10am-5pm daily, Mar-Oct, 10am-5pm Sat-Thur, Nov-Feb; £2 adult, £1 student, Sat, Sun; Free weekdays)*: Rightfully perched at the top of your cultural to-do list, this ancient pile two blocks west of the Old Market Square sits on a hill overlooking the city. Built in 1679 on the remains of a Norman castle by the Duke of Newcastle, it was restored in 1878, and the grounds opened as a museum. The museum's exhibits may be miss-able if you bore easily, but the view from the building is fantastic.

Mortimer's Hole *(Tours available at the Castle Museum; Tel 0115/915-37-00; 2 & 3pm Mon-Fri, with additional summer hours)*: A

festivals and events

During the month of May the annual **NOTT Dance Festival** *(Wellington Circus; Tel 0115/912-34-00; nottdance@dance4.co.uk, www.dance4.co.uk; Prices vary)* in the City Centre at the Nottingham Playhouse [see *performing art scene,* above] hosts performances by internationally acclaimed contemporary dance companies. Dance 4 at the same venue also manages **Dance Blitz** *(Wellington Circus; Tel 0115/912-34-00; blitz@dance4.co.uk, www.dance4.co.uk; £1-5 per workshop),* a late July/early August series of daily workshops teaching steps from street jazz to flamenco and traditional Malaysian dance—booking recommended.

castle option you really shouldn't miss, this tour covers a remnant of the original Norman castle. King Edward III supposedly led a band of noblemen through this secret subterranean passage to sneak up on and kill Roger Mortimer.

Ye Olde Trip to Jerusalem *(1 Brewhouse Yard, Castle Rd.; Tel 0115/947-31-71; 11am-11pm Mon-Sat, noon-10:30pm Sun):* A candidate for the oldest inn in England, dating back to 1189, this amazing pub is reachable via the Mortimer's Hole passage. You needn't take the tour to get here though—it still functions as a stand-alone inn, which is free to visit.

Brewhouse Yard Museum *(Castle Rd.; Tel 0115/915-36-00; 10am-4pm daily, closed Nov-Feb; Free Mon-Fri, £1.50 weekends and bank holidays):* Five 15th-century cottages at the foot of the castle make up this museum, presenting a panorama of early Nottingham life through a series of furnished rooms and shops. If beset by elementary-school field-trip flashbacks, follow the roped path to the exit sign. If not, stay to investigate the creepy cellars cut into the rock the castle stands on.

The **Caves of Nottingham** *(Drury Walk, Broad Marsh Shopping Centre; Tel 0115/924-14-24; 10am-4:15pm last admission Mon-Sat, 11am-4pm Sun; £3.25 adult, £2.25 student):* After putting on a hard-hat, walk underground to view the hand-carved sandstone caves just south of City Centre dating from the 13th century. A tour explains each exhibit and gives a good history of the 'shire.

Museum of Costume and Textiles *(51 Castle St.; Tel 0115/915-35-00; 10am-4pm Wed-Sun; Free):* The gorgeous pieces in this amazing collection of 17th-century garments were frowned upon as gewgaws and frivolity by the disapproving puritans of the time. Thankfully they survived those closed-minded prudes and are here today for you to gape at in this neat little museum just southwest of Old Market Square.

Galleries of Justice *(High Pavement; Tel 0115/952-05-58, 0115/952-05-55; 10am-4pm Tue-Sun; www.galleriesofjustice.org.uk;*

£7.95 adult, £6.35 student): Right in the Lace Market area, this place will allow you, for a substantial price, to be witness to a Victorian courtroom trial, crack a forensics case, and learn about English law—a fairly cool chance to play Sherlock.

modification

You might mistake **Surreal Hair** *(8 Byard Lane; Tel 0115/958-23-56; 10am-6pm Tue, Thur, 9am-7pm Wed, Fri, 9am-5pm Sat; AE, V, MC, DC),* just south of Old Market Square, for a cozy card shop, because the front entrance walls are covered with postcards and offbeat greeting cards for sale. But beyond lies a trendy salon that charges £12 and up just for a blow-dry. For a discount, you can put your hair in the hands of a trainee on Thursdays. From 5:30pm onwards, you can score a cut and blow-dry for £8, half a head of highlights for £16, a full head of highlights for £21, and bleaching or tinting for £16.

28 Men's Hair Salon *(Goosegate, Hockley; Tel 0115/958-66-28; 9:30am-6pm Mon-Fri, 9:30am-5pm Sat; No credit cards),* just east of the Old Market Square, is no dingy barber shop. Wacky lights hang from the ceiling of this small shop, and targets are painted around the coat hooks. Cuts are £11, a wash & cut's £13; Monday to Thursday, students get cuts for £9.

STUFF

Nottingham has all the Robin Hood memorabilia you'd expect—and, unfortunately, more—but it's easily avoided in the small, hip shops around town.

▶▶TUNES

Funkey Monkey *(Goosegate, Hockley; Tel 0115/956-11-81; 11am-5:30pm Mon-Sat; AE, V, MC, DC),* just east of the Old Market Square, is a small, independently owned record shop selling a variety of imports, LPs, and CDs.

There's also a branch of the super-cool London-based shop **Selectadisc** *(21 Market St.; Tel 0115/947-54-20; 9am-6pm Mon-Sat)* here, which sells new and used CDs and vinyl.

▶▶DUDS

The unique little **Bug Clubwear** *(5 Heathcoat St., Hockley; Tel 0115/941-02-56; 11am-6pm Mon-Sat; info@bug-clubwear.co.uk; www. bug-clubwear.co.uk; V, MC),* just east of the Old Market Square, sells strange-looking, astonishingly creative, space-age clothing. The store's signature outfits are made from a specialised rubber fabric with glow in the dark features, ultra-violet effects, and glitter.

For clothes to fit your alternative lifestyle, go to **Void** *(40 Carlton St., Hockley; Tel 0115/952-00-39; 10am-5:30pm Mon-Sat; enquires@void clothing.co.uk; www.void-clothing.co.uk; AE, V, MC, DC),* just east of the Old Market Square. They have black lace-up shirts and frilly Victorian-inspired dresses for the Goth at heart. The vinyl and rubber dominatrix outfits in the back area of the shop are a favorite among fetishists. Anything you see can also be purchased online (in case you don't want anyone to see you carrying that whip...).

The very stylie **Daphne's Hand Bag** *(63 Mansfield Rd.; Tel 0115/924-05-50)* sells vintage and '70s retro rags, as well as cool-and-kitschy novelty toys. Pop your head into the no-name shop next door too—they hand-make clothes from scraps and remnants of the clothes that were too broken to sell at Daphne's.

▶▶BOUND
Mushroom Books *(10-12 Heathecote St.; Tel 0115/958-25-08)* is Nottingham's choice for alternative lit: vegan cookbooks, anarchism, political tracts—they've got it all.

▶▶HOW BAZAAR
The **Nottingham Market** *(Victoria Centre; Tel 0115/915-69-70; 9am-4pm Mon-Sat; Free)* is accessible through the Victoria Shopping Centre just northeast of the Old Market Square. As your typical English market, it contains items ranging from electronics to cheese. Vegetarians beware—the separate meat and seafood section is redolent with crabmeat smells (crabs sell like crazy for about £1.30 each).

eats

When it comes to food, Nottingham prizes itself on not only having trendy restaurants, but eateries that cater to every taste, especially vegetarian.

▶▶CHEAP
For vegetarians, **V1** *(7 Hounds Gate, City Centre; Tel 0115/941-51-21; 8:30am-6pm Mon-Sat, noon-4pm Sun; £3-5 meals; V, MC)*, is an excellent alternative fast-food restaurant. Instead of artery-clogging Big Macs, you can choose between the BBQ Bean Burger, the Tikka Burger, and the Chili-Flavored Burger, all served on wholemeal or white bread. The V2 value meal consists of a burger, fries, and a drink for a mere £3.50.

Nottingham's best-named cafe-bar is surely the **Brass Monkey** *(11 High Pavement; Tel 0115/840-41-01; 10am-11pm Mon-Sat, 4-11pm; £3-5 meals; V)*, in the Lace Market. Although chances are slim that you'll run into Ad-Rock, you should still enjoy sitting in orange plastic chairs and sipping cocktails while munching on toasties at tables situated next to the open window facing the street. The sweets counter rocks, too.

The locals talk much about **Skinny Sumo** *(11/13 Carlton St., Hockley; Tel 0115/952-01-88; Noon-3pm/6-11pm Mon-Fri, 10am-11pm Sat; £3-7 meals; V, MC)*, a bright Japanese sushi bar/restaurant, either because they haven't heard of sushi before, or the place is just damn good. The tempura and main course noodle dishes are recommended by nearly every local magazine in the Midlands. For a meal worth stuffing yourself sick on, try starting with the miso soup, then sampling the Hot Platter consisting of sweet potato and prawn tempura, chicken yakitori and veggie spring rolls. Or try a creamed salmon croquette before devouring fried banana & vanilla ice cream—a great combo.

▶▶DO-ABLE
Though it's part of an un-hip pub chain, Nottingham's **Pitcher and Piano** *(High Pavement; Tel 0115/958-608; Noon-11pm Mon-Fri, 11am-11pm Sat,*

noon-10:30pm Sun; AE, V, MC), in the Lace Market, is worth visiting for its location—right in an old church. Feast on the gammon with eggs and chips (£7) or the vegetarian Mexican nachos (£6) while drinking pints of cider and peering at the religious icons on the stained glass window.

That Cafe Bar *(43 Broad St., Hockley; Tel 0115/952-61-16; Noon-midnight Mon-Sat; £5-11 meals; AE, V, MC, DC),* just east of the Old Market Square, is a lovely dimly-lit restaurant with a colorful interior and strange metal artwork on the walls. It serves up delicious dishes inspired by the best eats around the planet. The most popular meals include the extraordinary jerk chicken and teriyaki steak. After chowing down, head downstairs to **The Cellar** *(8pm-11pm Mon-Sat).* Fridays down here alternate between Freestyle and "Smoove" music: The former consists of deep house, jazz beats, and funky grooves; the latter is an evening of jazzy chilled beats with Latino breaks. Saturdays are either *Freaky Chic,* funky underground sounds, or *Phat Beats,* with a resident DJ.

For a sandwich fix, go next door to **Wax** *(Broad St., Hockley; Tel 0115/959-00-07; Noon-11pm Mon-Fri, 11am-11pm Sat; £3-8 meals; AE, V, MC, DC).* Try the Breakfast Baguette, a delish egg and bacon sandwich, in the AM, and the sirloin steak with tomato and mushrooms later in the day. The food isn't actually that exceptional—it's the cocktails (around £3.50) that people really come for. And it's a good place to load up before hitting the Cellar.

▶▶**SPLURGE**

Join the beautiful crowd at **Sonny's** *(3 Carleton St.; Tel 0115/947-30-41; 11:30am-3:30pm Mon-Thur, noon-3:30pm Sat, noon-2pm Sun, 7-10:30pm Sun-Thur, 7-11pm Fri, Sat; £8-13 entrées; V, MC, AE),* where the word is fusion. Grilled amngo duck with sesame oil, rack of lamb with butter beans and au jus, and fruit salad with soft cheeses, lime, and ginger await you.

crashing

Your quid definitely doesn't stretch as far in Nottingham as it does in other central England towns, but there are some good cheap options if you don't mind dorms, shared baths, or staying above a pub.

▶▶**CHEAP**

The oddly named **Igloo House** *(110 Mansfield Rd.; Tel 0115/947-52-50; Bus 90 to Mansfield Rd.; £10 per person with shared bath; www.igloo hostel.co.uk; No credit cards)* youth hostel, a 10-minute walk north of the City Centre, offers dormitory accommodation for 36 guests in four colorful rooms with metal bunk beds. It's pretty bare-bones and there is a 3am curfew, but the staff is remarkably friendly and throws in free coffee, tea, and milk in the self-service kitchen. The TV room and the small front lawn are always filled with lounging travelers.

Your YHA member option, **YHA Sherwood Forest** *(Forest Corner, Edwinstowe; Tel 01623/825-794, YHA Booking Bureau 01629/581-061; sherwood@yha.org.uk; Bus 133, 136 to Edwinstowe Village's Royal Oak Pub; £10.85 members, £12.85 non-members with shared bath, £3.20 for breakfast;*

AE, V, MC), is out of the way, some 20 miles from Nottingham in Sherwood Forest (reachable via bus). And there's a 10am-5pm lockout and 11pm curfew...*but* it's a romantic, folklorey place to crash, with laundry facilities and a self-service kitchen. The beds themselves are just the standard-issue dorm ones, but the surroundings go a long way to make up for that.

It'll remind you of a co-ed college dorm, but the **YMCA** *(4 Shakespeare St.; Tel 0115/956-76-00; £17 single with breakfast and shared bath; V, MC, before 10pm)* is cheap, clean, conveniently located just three blocks north of Old Market Square, and has a self-service kitchen.

YWCA Coalville House Hostel for Young Women *(22 Coalville St.; Tel 0115/941-88-39; £14 per person with shared bath; No credit cards),* just north of the City Centre, may be called a hostel, but its rooms are just a step up from dorms. The YWCA offers several short-term single rooms for women travelers, mostly Nottingham locals. Reservations aren't taken far in advance but it's always worth a shot.

The **Bentwick Hotel** *(Station St.; Tel 0115/958-02-85; bentwick hotel@bentwick.demon.co.uk; £19.50 per person, £23.50 per person with private bath, £10 deposit up-front per person per night; V, MC),* just south of the City Centre, would definitely not be mistaken for something other than a no-frills room above a bar. But the six double rooms, two quads, and one family room (accommodating seven) do at least come with TV and coffee makers, and it's just minutes from the train station.

▶▶SPLURGE:

Located across from the Galleries of Justice in a very classy brick building, the **Lace Market Hotel** *(29 High Pavement, Lace Market; Tel 0115/852-32-32; £69-89 single, £79-99 double with private bath; AE, V, MC, D)* has meticulously kept-up rooms, as well as an elegant bar and restaurant with an upper-class clientele.

WITHIN 30 MINUTES

Sherwood Forest *(B6034, Edwinstowe; 01623/823-202, 24-hour line 01623/824-317, Visitor's Centre 01623/824-490; Park dawn-dusk daily; Visitor Centre 10:30am-5pm daily, Apr-Oct;, 10:30am-4:30pm daily, Nov-Mar; Free entry, small parking fee),* 20 miles north of Nottinghamshire reachable via bus 33, was the infamous hangout of Robin Hood and his merry men, Friar Tuck and Little John. Once extending to the city of Nottingham itself, Sherwood Forest now contains 450 acres of protected oak and silver birch trees. Near the Sherwood Forest Visitor's Centre lies the Major Oak, which was Robin Hood gang's chill-out hiding tree. Interestingly, analysis of the tree's bark reveals that it wasn't even around in the 13th century; yet, a historical document marks Robin Hood's birth date to be in 1160...hmmm. If you're really into this stuff, you might want to partake in the "medieval merriment" of the Robin Hood Festival, which takes place during late July and early August. The Visitor's Centre here has detailed hiking and trial guides, too—even if men in tights don't do a thing for you, you can enjoy the gorgeous woodlands.

Newstead Abbey *(Mansfield Rd. [A60], Linby; Tel 01623/455-900; Train or bus 157, 747, 737 from Victoria Shopping Centre; £4 adult, £2 student; Noon-5pm daily, Apr-Sep; No credit cards)*, 12 miles north of Nottingham, is the former house and grounds of Lord Byron. You can tour the mansion or just stroll the gardens. In the 19th century, the mansion was given a neo-Gothic restoration. Byron mementoes, including first editions and manuscripts, are displayed inside. The grounds cover a whopping 300 acres complete with waterfalls, rose gardens, and a Japanese water garden.

need to know

Currency Exchange All major British banks and American Express [see below] can be found in the City Centre.

Travel Info City Information Centre *(1/4 Smithy Row; Tel 0115/915-53-30; 8:30am-5pm Mon-Fri, 10am-4pm Sun, Easter-Oct; 8:30am-5pm Mon-Fri, 9am-5pm Sat, Oct-Easter; tourist.information@nottingham-city.gov.uk; www.nottinghamcity.gov.uk; www.profilenottingham.co.uk)* is a 5-minute walk north from the main bus station.

Public Transportation Nottingham City Transport *(Tel 0115/950-36-65, Nottinghamshire hotline 0115/924-00-00)* buses cover the city but it's usually faster and always cheaper to walk. A Nottinghamshire Public Transport Map is available from the TIC (see above). The last Nottingham City Nightbus leaves Queen Street, just north of Old Market Square, at 3:15am.

American Express Cash checks at Amex *(Bridlesmith Gate; Tel 0115/924-16-66, 0273/696-933; 9am-5:30pm Mon-Fri, 9:30am-5:30pm Wed, 9am-5pm Sat)*, just south of Old Market Square.

Health and Emergency Police: *0115/967-09-99.* **Queen's Medical Centre,** University Hospital NHS Trust *(Derby Rd.; Tel 0115/924-99-24)* is 3 miles west of the city center via bus 12 or 13 bus from Friar Lane, which adjoins Old Market Square.

Pharmacies Boots the Chemist *(2 Broad Marsh Centre; Tel 0115/950-73-81; 8am-6pm Mon, Tue, Thur-Sat, 8:30am-7pm Wed, 10:30am-4:30pm Sun; V, MC, DC)* has branches throughout the city.

Telephones The Nottingham city code is *115.*

Airports The small **East Midlands Airport** *(Tel 01332/852-852)* is about a 25-minute ride from town. **National Express** *(Tel 0990/808-080)* runs buses to and from.

Trains There are around seven trains a day from London's St. Pancras Station; trains from Birmingham run more frequently. For schedules and information, call **National Rail** *(Tel 0345/484-950)*. The **train station** here is on Station Street.

Bus Lines Out of the City The **National Express** station *(Broad Marsh; Tel 0990/808-080)* has daily links to London via route 450. The bus station here is on the square directly off Canal Street.

Bike Rental Bunneys Bikes *(97 Carrington St.; Tel 0115/947-27-13; 9am-6pm Mon-Fri, 9am-5pm Sat, 11am-3pm Sun; £8.50 mountain* bike, *£6.00 cycle per day; AE, V, MC, DC),* a 5-minute walk south of the city center, has negotiable rates for long-term rentals, but a stiff £100 cash or credit deposit is mandatory.

Laundry Wash 'n' Dry *(81 Alfreton Rd.; Tel 0115/960-98-09; 8:30am-8pm daily; £2 wash, £1 dry)* is a 15-minute walk northwest of Old Market Square via Derby Street.

Postal The **Post Office** *(Queen St.; Tel 0115/947-46-26; 9:30am-5:30pm Mon-Sat),* is just north of Old Market Square.

Internet See *wired,* above.

shrewsbury

Located near the Welsh border, Shrewsbury—the town that spawned Charles Darwin—is a pleasant, Elizabethan-type place for a stroll. You won't find much of a party scene here, but there are a few cool places to check out after the sun sets.

While there are a few choice pubs, the party scene isn't raving. It consists of young adults socializing with their friends in an atmosphere of small town mellowness. Shrewsbury's mainly a well-manicured family-oriented town that breeds affluent, well-educated people. You won't find shabby-looking nackers (English slang for low-class youth dressed head to foot in sport logo wear) here in England's version of Pleasantville. Younger and middle-aged men alike wear polo shirts or clean T-shirts with trousers, or a neatly-ironed pair of jeans. And the women—mostly middle-aged soccer moms—look as if they bought out the GAP's entire collection of khaki pants, cotton tops, and sunglasses.

But Shrewsbury wasn't always a page out of the GAP catalog. Like most British towns, it was home to a series of invaders—euphemistically called "settlers"—from Saxons to Romans and finally to Normans, who built up its massive castle. Later, the town became a major player in the wool trade, and tidy little Tudor and Jacobean townhouses were built around town. Shrewsbury is known throughout the UK for those houses, which define its personality.

The locals are friendly as long as you maintain the appearance of respectability. If you look lost and you're not drinking or toking on the street, it's likely that a resident will ask if you need directions.

It you're looking for event information, the Tourist Information Center's your best bet. If you want to find the gay scene, pick up the free 'zine *Zone* and the *Pink Paper* at the **Peach Tree Restaurant** [see *eats,* below].

neighborhoods

A good place to start your town tour is in the city center at **Butcher Row,** which is lined with gorgeous, crooked three-story Tudor buildings. From here, walk down narrow **Fish Street,** past more fairy-tale Tudor buildings to the church, where you'll find the steep Bear Steps. Walk down the stairs to busy **High Street** and you'll be on **The Square** at the heart of the old center, with its **Old Market Hall,** a redolent rectangular stone building dating back to 1596 that's held up by a series of columns and arches. Stop for an al fresco snack at one of the several cafes and eateries or grab a sandwich and sit with the business people and "scrubby-bubs" eating on benches.

Head northwest via High Street to Pride Hill, the town's brick pedestrian shopping street, lined with a mixture of brick and Tudor buildings. You'll see major UK chain stores, such as Virgin Records and Boots and chain haircutters Tony and Guy as you walk up to **Castle Street.** Pay your respects to a bearded statue of Darwin at the town's academic-looking library. If you keep walking northwest, you'll pass more timbered houses and, after crossing the River Severn, you'll arrive at the red sandstone **Shrewsbury Castle** [see *culture zoo,* below], the train station, and a H.M. (Her Majesty's) Prison. As you cross the **River Severn** via the **Welsh Bridge,** you'll be welcomed to the less touristy, less affluent part of town by a dodgy-looking tattoo parlor. You wouldn't want to get lost here after dark, but it's not really dangerous—it just lacks the happy-face facade that makes the old center seem more welcoming.

The old center is entirely walkable but if you want to get to the Abbey, Cineworld movie complex, or the YHA, all located to the east across the Severn, you can catch a bus at the small station on the corner of Raven Meadows and Meadow Place [see *need to know,* below]. It costs less than 50p.

bar, club, and live music scene

On weeknights when nothing seems to be going on, everybody heads to **Abbey Forgate,** a small hub of nightlife across the river to the east of the old center. People go there to find good house music, and many of them end up hanging out at the **Peach Tree Restaurant** [see *eats,* below].

The blue fluorescent lights outside the **Bar Severn** (*Welsh Bridge; Tel 01743/264-041; Bar: 5pm-11pm Mon-Fri, noon-11pm Sat, noon-10:30pm Sun; Club: 10pm-2:30am Tue-Sat, no admission after midnight;*

wired

Some good Shrewsbury web sites include: *www.virtual-shrews bury.co.uk* and *www.go2.co.uk.*

Surf the net or use the fax machine at **Castle's Gate Public Library** (*Castle's Gate; 9:30am-5:30pm Mon & Wed, 9:30am-7pm Tue & Fri, 9:30am-4pm Sat; £2/internet hour, £1/Word hour, £1 and up faxing; £.50 fax receipt for 10 sheets; No credit cards*), a 5-minute walk west of The Square.

shrewsbury

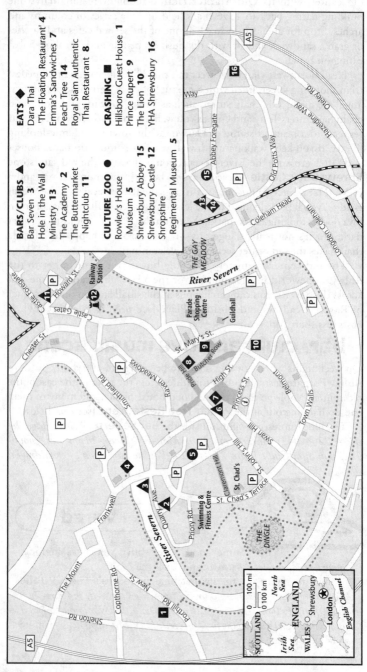

BARS/CLUBS ▲
Bar Seven **3**
Hole in the Wall **6**
Ministry **13**
The Academy **2**
The Buttermarket
Nightclub **11**

CULTURE ZOO ●
Rowley's House
Museum **5**
Shrewsbury Abbey **15**
Shrewsbury Castle **12**
Shropshire
Regimental Museum **5**

EATS ◆
Dara Thai
'The Floating Restaurant' **4**
Emma's Sandwiches **7**
Peach Tree **14**
Royal Siam Authentic
Thai Restaurant **8**

CRASHING ■
Hillsboro Guest House **1**
Prince Rupert **9**
The Lion **10**
YHA Shrewsbury **16**

Club: £2-5) create a Day-glo effect against the evening sky. On a nice day, drink a pint outside the open French doors on the steps overlooking the River Severn. The chattering in the large pub area gets noisier and more flamboyant as the night goes on. If you're still good to go after last call, head around back to **The Academy,** the club section of this pub-club, part of a large chain. There's nothing special about its dance floor and booming chart anthem music, but it is a raucous good time. They play disco music on Tuesday's '70s night, and every Friday and Saturday resident DJs attract a large crowd of young drunk locals.

Disco lights and loud music might draw you to the **Hole in the Wall** *(Shoplatch; Tel 01743/264-971; 11am-11pm Mon-Sat, noon-10:30pm Sun),* just north of The Square. If that doesn't do it for you, note that girls get free beer, cider, and wine coolers 8:30-10:30pm on Mondays after dropping a quid for a glass—this special attracts lots of well-dressed girls and not-so-well-dressed men looking for some action. Wednesday also has drink specials, for both sexes: £1 cover and £1 drinks from 8pm to closing. Thursday's '70s and '80s music attracts a retro-loving crowd. On the weekends, dance club music is played by DJs. As with any real pub, the Hole in the Wall serves up typical bar food, like yummy Cajun chicken baguettes for £3.25, and £4 main dishes that come with chips and salad or a Brit fave, mushy peas, which are exactly that.

For a club that feels like you're in an actual discotheque, not a pub with some lights strung up and the stereo turned all the way up, go to **The But-termarket Nightclub** *(Howard St.; Tel 01743/241-455; 9:30-2am Fri-Sat, no admission after midnight, various times Thursday).* Just a five-minute walk northeast of The Square, it aims for a crowd that's at least in their mid-20s, which is nice if you've had enough of teenage hoochy girls in their too-tight pants. Thursdays are the *Jazz and Roots Club,* which hosts actual bands from the past—on some rare occasions even good ones like the Wailers—live. Friday's the night you'll likely be here, though—the club's been known to occasionally host famous British DJs, though non-famous DJs are more usual, playing house and other dance tracks. Saturdays the crowd's a bit older, with 25 about the youngest age, and the music runs to garage, house, and '70s and '80s tunes. Local bands from the present day sometimes play here on Sundays—it's best to call ahead and check.

arts scene

For live stand-up comedy, theater, dance, concerts, art films and any other kind of performance, look into the **Shrewsbury Music Hall** *(The Square; Box office: Tel 01743/281-281; prices vary; mail@musichall. co.uk; www.musichall.co.uk; V, MC).* It shares its space with the Tourist Information Centre, but the rest of the building is dedicated to the arts. Past performances on the center stage include comedies like *The Rise and Fall of Little Voice* and *Australian Pink Floyd.*

If photography is your thing, pop into the small, free **Photographic Gallery** in the same building. The gallery showcases local artists working in a variety of styles—color, black and white, and digital.

the gay scene

The gay community here isn't terribly out and seems to prefer a quieter middle-class existence, just as the rest of the town does. But queer Shrewsbury lets its hair down in the gay hangouts around the little street of Abbey Forgate, just east across the River Severn from the old center.

Gay or straight, if you're walking down Abbey Forgate on a Monday evening, pumping house music may pull you into the **Peach Tree Restaurant** [see *eats* below]. The cafe-bar owner is the publisher of *What's Up Birmingham,* so as you'd guess, he's wired into the cool crowd—and they all seem to hang out here. We saw slim guys wearing tight cruising clothes, and cute straight girls and lesbians both with cropped hair.

Next door is **Ministry Bar and Night Club** *(Abbey Forgate; Tel 01743/353-357; 9:30pm-2am Mon, Tue, Thu-Sat; £4-5; No credit cards),* which attracts a similar following. DJs dish out different uplifting beats on different days. Saturday everyone seems to take the night's name, *Let Yourself Go,* literally, as the large fashionable gay crowd grooves to music from the '60s to the present.

culture zoo

This town's history as a military outpost and a vital trade link translate into some rich, impressive fortifications, churches, and museums. Set aside a half-day to visit Shrewsbury Abbey, Castle and Rowley's House Museum.

Shrewsbury Abbey *(Abbey Forgate; Tel 01743/232-723; 10:30am-3pm daily Nov 1-Easter, 9:30am-5:30pm daily Good Fri-Oct 31; Free):* Five minutes east of The Square and across the Severn, this eerie morbidly beautiful Benedictine monastery dates back to 1083. Inside this massive stone church you'll see an elaborate golden alter, headstones from the graveyard and 14th-century effigies. The somber mood of the interior, the redolent reddish exterior and the age of the structure all combine to create an overpowering feeling of spiritual strength.

Shrewsbury Castle and the Shropshire Regimental Museum *(Castle Gates; Tel 01743/358-516; Grounds open: 9am-5pm Mon-Sat, 10am-4:30pm Sun; Museum hours: 10am-4:30pm Thu-Sat Feb 3-Mar 18, Tue-Sat Mar 21-Apr 22, Tue-Sun & Bank holiday Mon Apr 23-Oct 1; Museum: £2 adults, grounds: No admission charge):* This red sandstone fortress, built in 1083 to secure the Welsh border, has undergone dozens of structural changes over the centuries. Its great hall houses the Shropshire Regimental Museum, home to a vast collection of military paraphernalia representing some 300 years of British history. Highlights include a lock of Napoleon's hair, an American flag seized during the burning of the White House in the War of 1812, and early Norman weaponry.

Rowley's House Museum *(Barker St.; Tel 01743/361-196; 10am-5pm Tue-Sat Oct 2-Easter, 10am-4pm daily Easter-Oct 1; free; museums@ shrewsbury-atcham.gov.uk):* Just north of The Square in a Tudor-style building that was once a sixteenth-century warehouse—and an adjoining

where's darwin?

You'd think a small town like Shrewsbury would focus its tourism on its most notorious homeboy, Charles Darwin. After all, Stratford-upon-Avon has milked the Shakespeare thing just about dry. Yet, aside from a small monument, Shrewsbury makes almost nothing of its associations with the father of the theory of natural selection. They've entirely missed the chance at creating yet another cheesy attraction to rob you of your hard-earned vacation savings. Which leaves one wondering: How can you learn something of the man when visiting this town? Well, if you're a true fan and want to pay homage to him, you can always walk by **Darwin House** *(The Mount; 01743/840-416)*, the building where the great one was born. It's a mere 10-minute walk west of The Square near the motorway. These days it's a government tax office, not officially open to the public as an attraction, but if you call Carmen Garrett at the above number, you might just be able to wheedle yourself a glimpse at the inside. There's nothing much to see here, apart from some surrounding apartment buildings, but if you try, you may be able to imagine the great biologist ambling down the surrounding streets, deep in thought, wandering vaguely toward a pub. And, if enough people continually walk by with their guide-books in hand, maybe this town will decide to acknowledge its neglected hero with a museum—or at very least a tacky curio shop.

seventeenth-century brick and stone mansion—is this impressive museum. Its exhibitions cover local history from prehistoric through Roman archaeology, geology, natural history, and costumes. The museum is especially proud of its display of artifacts from the nearby one-time Roman town now called Wroxeter, including a perfectly intact silver mirror from the third century.

CITY SPORTS

Shrewsbury isn't an outdoor adventure seeker's kind of town, but if you want a quick workout or dip in the pool, head to **Quarry Swimming and Fitness Centre** *(Priory Rd; Tel 01743/236-583; 10am-6pm Mon-Fri; Noon-6pm Sat-Sun; £4-8 entrance; www.shropshire-cc.gov.uk)*. The center has a pool with a flume and diving boards, and a sauna, spa, and gym.

EATS

As in most of the UK, ethnic eats are your best bet for bargain meals—and an escape from heavy, bland Brit food. Thai is a particularly good choice in Shewsbury, with several scenic options.

▶▶CHEAP

The Floating Thai Restaurant *(Welsh Bridge; Tel 01743/243-123; 11am-10pm daily; Meals £3-8; MC, V)* looks a bit like an elongated trailer home with a moat: It's a white, narrow, one-story building with a covered porch, surrounded by water. It's a charming location, though, expecially at night. You can't help but notice its bright yellow lights if you're walking over the Welsh Bridge. When you've arrived, choose from a variety of Kashmir specialties done, for the most part, with zest and flare. The chicken curry with *dhal* (lentils) is a great choice.

For more excellent Thai food, dine at the **Royal Siam Authentic Thai Restaurant** *(Butcher Rd.; Tel 01743/353-117; 6pm-10:30pm Mon-Sat, noon-2:30pm Fri-Sat; Meals £1.50-6; V, MC),* just north of The Square. You'll smell the good eats as you round the corner onto Butcher Road. This place is pretty affordable if you keep it simple. Scrumptious Thai egg-fried rice is a steal, and the spicy squid with warm salad and Thai herb dressing is a seafood lover's fave.

If you're looking for something simple and tasty for lunch, head to the most popular sandwich joint in town, and wait in a line with young-looking office types at **Emma's Sandwiches** *(Shoplatch; 01743/236-611; 8:30am-3pm Mon-Sat; Sandwiches £1.10-2; No credit cards)* just north of The Square. The fillings are creatively vegetarian: Try the banana and sugar or cheese and beetroot sandwich served on wholemeal, white, grain braid, or a baguette (it's good, trust us!). It's a take-out shop, so head to The Square to devour your strange but tasty treat.

The **Peach Tree** *(21 Abbey Foregate; Tel 01743/355-055; Cafe-bar 10am-10:30pm, restaurant 6pm-10pm Tue-Sat; Meals £2.95-14.95; www.thepeachtree.co.uk; V, MC, AE),* just east of The Square, is Shrewsbury's hippest eatery. You can order from the full menu at the ground floor cafe-bar or from the evening a la carte menu upstairs. Brunch is served daily until 6pm and gives you a variety of traditional English breakfast options, a choice of designer coffees and teas, and seven baguette sandwich combinations. The Sweet Gypsy Toast combo is fried eggs and toast with grilled smoked bacon. If you're not in the mood for breakfast, there's also a variety of crisp salads, Italian-style pastas, grilled meat main courses, and vegetarian sandwiches. The fanciful a la carte menu includes delicately done lamb, steak, fish and deer meat, as well as vegetarian eggplant 'steaks,' salade Nicoise and pasta. Great food and a swanky clientele—this place can't be beat.

crashing

Shrewsbury's not the cheapest place in the UK to crash, but there is a YHA very handy to the old center and Hillsboro Guest House is a scenic, and fairly economic option.

▶▶CHEAP

For dorm accommodation, your only option is the **YHA Shrewsbury** *(The Woodlands, Abbey Forgate; Tel 01743/360-179; VMA booking line: Tel 01629/581-061; £9 adult members, £1 off with student card; shrews* *bury@yha.org; V, MC cards*) is just five minutes east of The Square. This quaint Victorian house sits off the main road on an dark driveway. Inside you'll find 4 10-bed rooms, a dining room, self-service kitchen, and a TV lounge—all the basic YHA facilities. The staff is friendly, but won't let you check in after 11pm—and make sure you're back by then, as the curfew's strictly enforced. The lockout is between 10am and 5pm, and the evening meal (£4-5) is served at 7pm.

▶▶**DO-ABLE**

Affordable B&B accommodation can be had at the **Hillsboro Guest House** *(1 Port Hill Gardens; Tel 01743/231-033; £17.50-20 per person, some rooms with private bath; No credit cards)*. Although it's located in a residential section out on the west end of Shrewsbury, you can get to the city center in 10 minutes by cutting through a nearby park called The Quarry. The guest house is cozy and rooms are comfortable, and you're entitled to free tea and coffee facilities and, of course, breakfast.

▶▶**SPLURGE**

With Charles Dickens on the roster of past guests, you'll be in good company at **The Lion** *(Wyle Cop; Tel 01743/353-107; £90 doubles with no breakfast, or £42 per person per night bed & breakfast, private bath; AE, V, MC, DIN)*, on a big hill in town above English Bridge, east of The Square. The rooms are larger than they were when Chuck stayed here, and loaded with patterned chintz, modern amenities, and good, firm mattresses. The bathrooms are small and compact, with a tub and shower combination.

The **Prince Rupert** *(Butcher Row; Tel 01743/499-955; £95 doubles, with private bath; AE, V, MC, DIN)*, just north of The Square, is one of the most historic structures in this very historic town. In the 17th century, this half-timbered building was home to Bohemian-born Prince Rupert, nephew to Charles I. Nowadays, most of the rooms are conservatively modern and somewhat bland, but breakfast comes free with them on weekends.

need to know

Currency Exchange The **American Express** *(27 Claremont Street; Tel 01743/357-204; 9am-5:30pm Mon-Fri)* is just northwest of The Square.

Travel Info Pick up town information and a map at the **Shrewsbury Tourist Information Centre** *(The Square; Tel 01743/281-200; 10am-6pm Mon-Sat and 10am-4pm Sun May 1-Sep 30, 10am-5pm Mon-Sat & Easter Sun 10am-4pm Oct 1-Apr 30; www.shrewsburytourism.co.uk)*, a five-minute walk southwest of the train station. Not only do they have extensive information about every lodging in town, they can also book a room for you at no charge.

Health and Emergency The **Royal Shrewsbury Hospital** *(Mytton Oak Road; Tel 01743/261-000)* is west if The Square, best reachable via bus 13 from Raven Meadows bus station or the Welsh Bridge west of The Square. The local **police station** *(Tel 01743/232-888)* is but a a few minutes' walk towards the riverside from the center of town, near the bus station on Raven Meadows Rd.

Pharmacies The local **Boots the Chemist** *(7/9 Pride Hill; Tel 01743/351-311; 9am-5:30pm Mon-Sat; V, MC)* is just north of The Square.

Trains On weekdays, trains depart hourly from London's Euston station to Birmingham or Wolverhampton, where you'll need to change to the Shrewsbury **National Rail** station *(Castle St; Tel 0345/484-950)* a five-minute walk northeast of The Square. Travel time is three hours.

Bus Lines Out of Town Three buses leave London's Victoria Station daily and will take you directly to the Shrewsbury **National Express** station *(Raven Meadows; Tel 0990/808-080)*, across the street from the train station, in five hours. You can also get buses from Shrewsbury to Telford and Birmingham, as well as nearby Ironbridge Gorge. As one of Mid-England's western border towns, Shrewsbury provides easy access to Wales via rail and bus.

Bike Rental Dave Mellor Cycles *(9A New St.; Tel 01743/366-662; 9am-6pm Mon-Sat; £12/day, £50 deposit required)* is the place for wheels.

Laundry The **Shrewsbury Laundramatic** *(Long Row; Tel 01743/355-571; 7:30am-6pm daily)* is 20-minute walk north of The Square off the Ditherington Way.

Postal The **General Post Office** *(St. Mary's St and Pride Hill; 9pm-5:30pm Mon-Fri, 9am-5pm Sat, closed Sun)* is just north of The Square.

Internet See *wired*, above.

LINCOLN

Lincoln lacks cool venues for clubbers, but it makes up for the handicap with its profound beauty. On a late summer evening, the yellow-lit stone of the ancient Lincoln Castle walls and the magnificent Lincoln Cathedral look radiant against the turquoise sky. The town is worth visiting just to see the magnificent 11th-century cathedral, but you'll find plenty of other great places to see, including Tudor homes and narrow cobble-stoned streets. Lincoln's a lot less of a party town than Nottingham—or even remote parts of Wales—despite a student crowd from the University of Lincolnshire. On a weeknight you'll pass only a few adults roaming the streets after an evening of drinking at one of the town's commercialized chain pubs. They'll probably come up to you for a friendly chat, as the people of Lincoln are quite sociable (and the streets are not exactly crowded with company).

The entire nightlife scene revolves around High Street, the main road in the city center. The area consists of large pubs, some commercial, such as the Walkabout, Edward's, O'Neills, and Yates, and a few others, such as the Reef Bar, which are not chains but seem equally as massive and generic.

If you want to get a feel of true Lincolners, keep your eyes peeled when walking up High Street, day or night. Near the archway in the wall surrounding town center, sights of teenagers rolling cigarettes among other things may surprise you. At night, you'll spot homeless panhandlers on the town's main pedestrian road. It's almost as though they're hidden from view of the well-off community.

To city dwellers, Lincoln's teenagers may seem to lack style. Girls might wear high-healed boots and boot-legged pants, along with an uncoordinated fleece "jumper" (Brit for sweater). Not the kind of outfits you'd see in New York. The skateboarders dress better, though their idea of style seems to be khakis and polo shirts rather than wild 'board wear.

For local museum, gallery, and historical site information, pick up the free ***Look at That Guide*** available at the Tourist Information Center [see *need to know,* below]. If you're looking for nightlife, look for venue posters on archways or signposts about town.

neighborhoods

Walking is the best way to get around town, especially since the city center is practically traffic-free. Start at **High Street,** which is lined with the same stores (Dixon's electronics, Boots, C&A) found on every British High Street. This main, seen-it-before pedestrian road turns to cobblestones and narrows, running into **Steep Hill. St. Mary's Street,** where the Tourist Information Center and train station are, lies just south of the Witham River, which divides the old center of town into north and south halves. High Street crosses the river as the main link. It's easy to distinguish between the tourists and the locals: the locals don't pant while walking up this lane. The road changes names again to **Bail Gate.** If you're not in the mood to join senior citizens gazing in the windows of crafts shops, steer clear of **Gordon Road,** which is loaded with oh-so-quaint stores selling picture frames and fake floral arrangements.

hanging out

There are no noticeable 'hoods in Lincoln. It's a *very* small place—which means there's no underground rave scene or even a great place to hang out. A few skateboarders, mostly teens, 'board and do wheelies on their bikes on a stepped plaza just across the canal from the Waterside Shopping Centre, but that's about it.

bar scene

Lincoln's nightlife is a bit drab, but at least people aren't afraid to embrace the traditional commercial and non-commercial pubs and music with gusto.

The subterranean pub **Cornhill Vaults** *(Cornhill Exchange, Tel 01522/535-113; 11am-around 11pm Mon-Sat, 8-10:30pm Sun; No credit cards),* just south of the Castle by the river, was once a Roman wine cellar. But the glory of Rome is long gone, and now it's just a plain old pub, with

LINCOLN

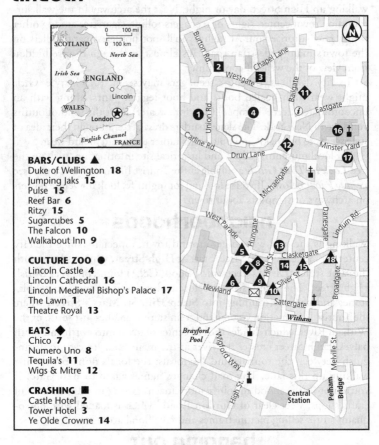

BARS/CLUBS ▲
Duke of Wellington **18**
Jumping Jaks **15**
Pulse **15**
Reef Bar **6**
Ritzy **15**
Sugarcubes **5**
The Falcon **10**
Walkabout Inn **9**

CULTURE ZOO ●
Lincoln Castle **4**
Lincoln Cathedral **16**
Lincoln Medieval Bishop's Palace **17**
The Lawn **1**
Theatre Royal **13**

EATS ◆
Chico **7**
Numero Uno **8**
Tequila's **11**
Wigs & Mitre **12**

CRASHING ■
Castle Hotel **2**
Tower Hotel **3**
Ye Olde Crowne **14**

niches and cubbyholes decorated with brewery papherna. On weekends, it fills with a mixed clientele and a dense fog of smoke.

If you're up for some Karaoke, take the stage Wednesday nights at **Cheltenham Arms** *(Guildhall St.; Tel 01522/512-135; 11am-11pm Mon-Sat, till 10:30pm Sun; No credit cards),* just west of High Street. It attracts clientele of various ages, folks that like to mingle on its large wooden floor or dance on the small stage. Nothing too exciting.

Even though it's open late (a definite plus in this sleepy town), **Badgers** *(King's Arms Yard; Tel 01522/524-620; 7pm-2am daily; £1-2 Thur-Sat; No credit cards),* just off High Street, lacks a certain element of "cool." The Badgers experience includes a bad quality speaker blasting Britney Spears, those cheap flickering multi-colored disco lights that seem to be all the rage in British pubs, and more karaoke (this time Sundays).

The Falcon *(Saltergate; No phone; 11am-11pm Mon-Sat),* just south of the Castle by the river, *can* be defined as cool, attracting an alternative-ish crowd in their 20s. Different colored lights shine on the walls to create "sections." The pub goes with cheesy music like many others in Lincoln, never straying too far from classic rock and pop.

The **Reef Bar** *(Mint St.; No phone; 11am-11pm daily),* just west of High Street, is dead during the week but perks up on Saturday when DJs spin old-skool and trance. The decor's nothing to write home about: ground floor's wood, the walls are blue, and there's a center bar and square tables with plain '70s-looking yellow seats for your rear. There's also a pool table for all you sharks and hustlers.

LIVE MUSIC SCENE

The best place to see hot local live bands is the **Duke of Wellington** *(37 Broadgate; Tel 01522/527-069; Noon-11pm daily, till 10:30 Sun; around £2 upstairs entry fee to see bands; No credit cards),* east of High Street just south of the Cathedral. The bands play upstairs, usually on Fridays, to an appreciative crowd of locals. Between sets, amuse yourself downstairs with a game of pool.

The infamous commercial Australian chain the **Walkabout Inn** *(233/237 High St.; Tel 01522/538-663; Noon-11pm daily, till 10:30pm Sun; www.walkaboutin.com; V, MC)* has spread through the UK like the bubonic plague. Normally not worth mentioning, this location gets our okay because it's usually packed with locals. It's a comfortable drinking place with brown leather chairs overlooking the street. Pop rock tunes on the stereo attract a young crowd, as do the live bands that play chart rock covers on Tuesdays, Thursdays, and Sundays.

CLUB SCENE

Just for the record, this isn't a hand-picked list of the best chill places to party in Lincoln—it's all they've got, period.

The liveliest club in town would have to be **Sugarcubes** *(1 West Parade; No phone; 10pm-2am Fri, 9pm-2am Sat, as well as Tue & Thur during the university semester; £3-5 cover; www.sugarcubesnightclub.co.uk).* Located in a two-story building on the corner of Hungate & West Parade in the town center, this club is not part of a huge commercial complex and subsequently offers a "homely" (British for home-like) quality. On Fridays, mainstream alternative and trashy rock make your head throb (in a good way, of course). Friday nights are the club's most active promo nights for new album and film releases and they often give away merchandise and samplers and hold competitions. Saturdays alternate between *Dubwiser,* a feast of drum 'n' bass, UK garage, hip-hop, and breakbeats, *Tonked,* a night of "deep chunky solid" house grooves, and *Cupidity (www.cupidity. org.uk; sistorm@cupidity.org.uk), a night* of funky house and underground distributed by DJs Simon Storm and Sass. The schedule changes a bit during the university term so call ahead or look for flyers.

You'll be greeted by suits at the door of **Jumpin' Jaks/Ritzy/Pulse** club complex *(Silver St.; Tel 01522/522-314; 10pm-2am Wed, 9:30pm-2am Thur, 8:30pm-2am Fri, Sat; 7-10:30pm Sun; Free),* at Clasketgate just downhill from the **Castle** [see *culture zoo,* below]. With a rep as a meat market, the complex targets a crowd in their '20s and older, although teenage girls manage to sneak in somehow. Often you can walk freely between Ritzy and Pulse *(www.pulselincoln.co.uk),* where you'll hear acid jazz and the like. Jumpin' Jaks often has cover bands and nights with cheesy themes such as *Value For Money (VFM)* and worse, *Dueling Pianos,* advertised to be a concept from America (How embarrassing for us Yanks). To save a pound or two, pick up a free club loyalty card, available from the club card desk in the entrance of Ritzy or in the cloakroom at Jaks. It'll get you different nightly cover discounts good for one or two of the complex's clubs.

After warming up at The **Walkabout Inn** [see *live music,* above], cross the street to **Barracuda Nightclub** *(280/281 High St.; Tel 01522/525-828; 10pm-2am; Cover £1-4).* Or get *Loaded* on Saturday night's party of indie anthems, Brit pop, 'block-rockin' beats and retro grooves. Tuesday's *The Twilight Zone* is for all you mainstream alternative rock lovers—think Courtney Love and the Beastie Boys. This is a great night to meet local students. Pints and bottles are only £1.30 before 11pm.

ARTS SCENE

▶▶PERFORMING ARTS SCENE
The **Theatre Royal,** located just south of the Castle between Butchery Row and Flaxengate, does manage to entertain audiences, although its exterior is so ugly it's almost off-putting. It's located in the left-hand corner of a brick building and looks more like a cinema. However, the Lincoln Shakespeare Company tours here regularly, and the Lincoln Mystery Plays, another respected traveling company, occasionally does shows here too.

GAY SCENE

Lincoln's gay scene is practically invisible to visitors. The town does have a gay information line that takes calls two days a week: **Lincoln Lesbian & Gay Switchboard** *(Tel 01522/535-553; 7pm-10pm Thur, Sun)*— they can tell you what (little) is going on. As for cruising and hanging out, though, you'd be way better off in Birmingham.

CULTURE ZOO

Once you've seen the magnificent Lincoln Cathedral and Lincoln Medieval Bishop's Palace, nothing else in town can really compare.

Lincoln Cathedral *(Minster Yard; Tel 01522/544-544; 7:15am-8pm Mon-Sat, 7:15am-6pm Sun, June-Aug, 7:15am-5pm Sun Sept-May; £3.50 adults, £3 concessions between 9am-6pm daily, June-Aug, 10am-4:15pm Mon-Sat, 12:30-2:45pm Sun, Sept-May; Free entrance to west end of Cathedral, free roof and ground tours):* Towering above the town center, this is the one place you *must* visit when here. A honey-colored, 11th-century monument (with a really confusing pricing scheme), it features soaring Gothic architecture and a play of light that goes way beyond the word incredible. If you don't want to pay admission, you can see the chandeliers, grandiose archways, and spiked pipes of the organ from the entryway. Or, attend a service or an organ recital (times and dates posted on an entranceway wall) to feel the magnitude.

Lincoln Medieval Bishop's Palace *(Minster Yard; Tel 01522/527-468; 10am-6pm daily, Apr-Sept; 10am-5pm Oct; 10am-4pm Sat, Sun, Nov-Mar; Open during the Christmas Market; £1.90 adults, £1.40 concessions):* To the south of the Cathedral lies the remains of the Bishop's Palace. The grounds contain a small vineyard and Alnwick Tower, which you can climb, but it's not very exciting compared to the Cathedral. The palace ruins are quite beautiful, however, made from the same honey-colored stone as the town's star attraction.

Lincoln Castle *(Castle Hill; Tel 01522/511-068; 9:30am-5:30pm Mon-Sat, 11am-5:30pm Sun, summer; 9:30am-4pm Mon-Sat, 11am-4pm Sun, winter; £2 adults, £1.20 concessions):* If you missed seeing an original edition of the *Magna Carta* at London's British Museum, you have another chance here. One of four surviving copies of that infamous document you read so much about in your 10th-grade European History class makes its home here. It's contained in a temperature-controlled, glass-topped compartment in a room echoing with a recording of the charter spoken in Latin. It's a sobering sight, especially if you paid attention in class. If not, they provide information about how the *Magna Carta* laid the foundation for much of the American justice system. The castle grounds also has a prison complex containing its own chapel, complete with a very scary, hairy, werewolf-looking priest mannequin.

The Lawn *(Union Rd.; Tel 01522/873-705; 9am-5pm Mon-Fri, 10am-5pm Sat, Sun, Easter-Sept; 9am-4:30pm Mon-Fri, 10am-4pm Sat, Sun, Oct-Easter; Free):* To see more freaky-looking mannequins, plus a lot more, visit this spread, which faces the drawbridge of the castle's back entrance. The Lawn is on the grounds of Bedlam, the former insane asylum where the patients—portrayed now by mentally disturbed-looking (to say the least) mannequins dressed in period clothing—once chained up their wardens. The Lawn also offers a smattering of other attractions, including a garden, a squadron exhibit, a children's archaeology center, a pub, a fudge shop, a "ladies" shop, and an information center (whew!). Don't leave without walking through the Sir Joseph Banks Conservatory. This tropical house contains rain forest trees, birds and fish, and muggy, humid air that will make you feel like you're in Florida.

Usher Gallery *(Lindum Rd.; Tel 01522/527-980; 10am-5:30pm Mon-Sat, 2:30-5pm Sun; £2 adults, 50p students):* Though it's a might precious for some folks, this collection of Dutch masters, porcelain, and the effects of Alfred Tennyson, one of Lincoln's proud sons, is at least indubitably English.

Brayford Waterside Cruises *(River Witham embankment; Tel 01522/881-200, The Belle 07970/942-801; Historic cruises leave on the hour 11am-3pm, Ghost cruises 8pm Thu June-Sept; £3-6):* This service, based on the River Witham embankment a 5-minutes walk south of the Castle, runs historical canal cruises that last 30-35 minutes on *The*

Belle, a survivor of the Dunkirk evacuation of the British during WWII. They also do the Lincoln Ghost Cruise, which is good for a laugh and takes up only an hour of your time.

modification

For corporeal art including hair extensions and body paint, try **Blue Banana** *(Exchange Arcade, Sincil St.; Tel 01522/521-886; 9am-5:30pm Mon-Sat, Piercing & tattoos 10am-5pm Mon-Sat; www.bodypiercing.uk.com; V, MC)*, just south of High Street on the riverfront. The front shop area is full of trinkets that attract pre-teen girls. The tattoo parlor is in the back, lined with a large selection of sample tattoos to pick from. The store offers £15 piercing for practically every body part—skin, eyebrow, or tragus (whatever that is). Your lip, navel, or nipple will cost £20. Prices don't include jewelry.

stuff

Lincoln's token market, **Cornhill Market,** just south of High Street on the riverfront at Sincil Street, is a small yet rather appealing place to buy inexpensive imported Asian clothes, cheaply made bags, candy, plants and so on.

eats

Unlike in most British towns, where the only good cheap eats are Indian or Chinese food, in Lincoln you can actually get traditional English on the cheap—and in classy surroundings at that—at places such as the Wig & Mitre. Plus, this town actually *delivers,* so you can kick back in your room and order up a pizza and eat in your underwear.

▶▶CHEAP

At the end of an art graffiti-covered archway, with slogans along the lines of *Viva Mexico,* is the tastefully decorated **Tequila's** *(77 Bailgate; Tel*

wired

Sun Café *(St. Mary's St.; Tel 01522/579-067; Opens 9-10:30am, closes about 6pm Mon-Wed, 9pm Thur, later on Fri; £2.50 per 1/2 hour, £3.75 per 3/4hour, £5 per hr; webmaster@sun-cafe.u-net.com; www.suncafe.u-net.com),* just south of the Witham River and east of High Street, has a few computers. Adequate food includes baked potatoes and sandwiches at £1.25 and up. **Trayer's** *(The Glory Hole; Tel 01522/511-156; 10am-5:30pm Mon-Fri, 9am-5pm Sat, 11am-4pm Sun; £4 per hour or £3.75 per hour including coffee),* just off High Street in the town center, is an odd little place selling coffee and a small section of used books.

01522/529-991; 6pm-midnight daily; £6.50-12 meals; MC, V, DC). This is Brit-Mex at its finest, served in a dim, candle-lit space with Latino beats flowing from the speaker system. Some tasty menu items include bacon and tomato quesadillas (the cheapest main course), spicy chimichangas, and camarones (prawn) fajitas. And, of course, there's a great selection of tequila.

The **Wig & Mitre** (29 Steep Hill; Tel 01522/535-190; 8am-11pm Mon-Sat, till 10:30pm Sun; £4-12 meals; AE, V, MC, DC), built into a 14th-century masonry house, has our vote for Best Pub Food. Located on the aptly-named Steep Hill leading up to the Castle, it's loaded with Olde English atmosphere. The main restaurant has oak timbers and Victorian armchairs, and you can eat at the downstairs bar as well. Main courses and tasty sandwiches are suprisingly cheap—maybe that's why it's such a popular place.

For delivery to your room try one of two Corporation Street takeout joints: For pizza, pasta, salad, and baked potatoes it's **Numero Uno** (Tel 01522/533-336; £3-10). For something with more spice try **Chico** (Tel 01522/540-444 £3.50-11), which offers a complete Mexican menu.

crashing

There are some reasonably cheap crashes around the center of town, but for the best deals in Lincoln be prepared for bunk beds and schlepping a mile out of the hub to the YHA Lincoln. The Tourist Information Center can help you find rooms [see *need to know,* below].

▶▶**CHEAP**

To save some quid, stay at Lincoln's youth hostel, **YHA Lincoln** (77 South Park; Tel 01522/522-076 or YHA general booking 01629/581-061; Easter-October only, lockout 10am-5pm, curfew 11pm; Members: £9.80 adults, £8.80 students; lincoln@yha.org.uk). Located in a brick house a mile south of the town center, it offers nothing out of the ordinary, just your standard bunk-bed dormitory accommodation in rooms of 2-10 beds.

For cheap accommodation in the town center, check into the pub-and-guesthouses, such as **Ye Olde Crowne** (Clasketgate; Tel 01522/542-896; £18.80 single, £37.60 double; AE, V, MC), located across the road from the Theatre Royal, between Butchery Row and Flaxengate. Despite the unattractive decor and parking-lot view, the rooms, some with private baths, are tidy and chain-esque with matching bedspreads and modern TV sets.

▶▶**DO-ABLE**

The **Newport Guest House** (26/28 Newport; Tel 01522/528-590; £28 single, £40 double with private bath, £32 twin with shared bath; info@newportguesthouse.co.uk; www.newportguesthouse.co.uk; No credit cards), is a comfy B&B located in a brick townhouse just a 5-minute walk north of the town center. Newly refurbished, all rooms are comfortable with television and tea and coffee making facilities.

A very bourgeois, ivy-covered brick building houses the **Tower Hotel** (38 Westgate; Tel 01522/529-999; £47 single, £65 double, £70 suite with private bath; AE, V, MC, DC), just below the Castle and to the north. The comfortable, floral-motif rooms all have telephones, TVs, and coffeemakers. The hotel also has its own not-too-ugly restaurant and pub.

▶▶**SPLURGE**

If you're looking for classy accommodations, try the **Castle Hotel** *(Westgate; Tel 01522/538-801; £62 single, £79-89 double, £128 one- to two-person suite; Includes full English breakfast; V, MC, DC),* just below the Castle and to the north. Most bedrooms, called "lodges," are in a brick and stonewalled building with red doors, white windowsills, and a charming Spanish-style tiled roof. A cozy reception area is near the entrance to the hotel, which is across a small parking lot where guests park their Jags. You can dine in style at the Castle's restaurant, Knights, which suprisingly has a vegetarian and vegan menu. Prices range from £8.95 for a chicken and bacon salad to £15.95 for Dover sole.

need to know

Currency Exchange Post offices on Bailgate and Cornhill, just south of the Castle, will change money, as well as **Thomas Cook** *(Midland Bank, 221 High St.; Tel 01522/511-486; 9am-5pm Mon-Fri, 9:30am-3:30 Sat).*

Travel Information Machines throughout town dispense maps with details of local attractions and eats for £1. Accommodation, sites, and Lincoln brochures are available at the **Tourist Information Centre** *(9 Castle Hill; Tel 01522/873-213; 9:30am-5:30pm Mon-Thur, till 5pm Fri, 10am-5pm Sat, Sun),* just down from the Castle on Cornhill, a 2-minute walk west from the bus main station.

Public Transportation The center of Lincoln is totally walkable, but the best way to reach an out-of-the-way hostel is by pooling for a **Freephone Taxi** *(Tel 0800/332-211).*

Health and Emergency Lincoln County Hospital *(Greetwell Rd.; Tel 01522/512-512)* is a 5-minute walk east of the town center.

Pharmacies Boots the Chemist *(311/312 High St.; Tel 01522/524-303; 11am-5pm daily; V, MC, DC)* is right in the town center.

Trains Trains from London's King's Cross Station serve Lincoln daily, a 2-hour journey, which usually requires a transfer at Newarke or Peterborough, pulling into Lincoln's main station *(St. Mary's St.; Tel 0345/484-950),* just south of the Witham River, east of High Street.

Bus Lines Out of Town The **City Bus Station** *(St. Mary's St.; Tel 01522/553-135)* is opposite the train station just south of the Witham River, east of High Street. **National Express** *(Tel 08705/808-080)* bus 448 leaves London's Victoria Coach Station daily for the 3-hour journey to Lincoln.

Laundry Fresh as a Daisy *(Birchwood Shopping Centre, Jasmin Rd.; Tel 01522/691-071; 8:30am-9pm daily; £2 wash, £1 dry)* is in a shopping center 10 minutes southwest of the center via city bus SB6.

Postal Lincoln Post Office *(Cornhill; Tel 0345/223-341; 9pm-5:30pm Mon-Fri, 9am-5pm Sat, closed Sun)* is just south of the castle.

Internet see *wired,* above

warwick castle

Horror fans will think they've died and gone to Goth heaven (or is that hell?) at Warwick Castle, 8 miles northeast of Stratford-upon-Avon. The castle's Ghost Tower is said to be haunted by the pampered Sir Faulke Greville, who spent £20,000, a huge amount of money in the early 1600s, to convert the castle into a luxurious mansion. Some 20 years later he was stabbed to death by an angry servant; but after sinking all that cash into the place, it seems even death couldn't get him to part with it—it's said he walks the halls at night. You can also tour the dungeon's Torture Chamber where cheeky or wayward subjects were straightened out with hot irons, among other nice little toys. The newly opened "Death or Glory" attraction contains more than a thousand pieces of armor spanning the last millennium. The exhibit shows visitors how soldiers lived—and mostly died—on the battlefield.

Long before the existing castle was built, other forts and palaces sat on that prime real estate perched high above the **River Avon.** The first significant structure was built by Ethelfleda, the daughter of Albert the Great, way back in 914. In 1068, William the Conqueror ordered a motte-and-baily castle built, a Norman fave consisting of a tower (the motte) at one end of a built-up circular mound (the baily), of which just the mound remains today.

Throughout the year, but mainly in summer, the castle hosts a variety of festivals, orchestral performances, and tournaments with a lot of medieval jousting and people dressed in period costumes. If you're missing your homeland around Independence Day, just crash the Grand Summer Spectacular and pretend it's for the USA—it takes place close to the 4th of July.

need to know

Contact Info Tel *01926/406-600;* Online *www.warwick-castle.co.uk.*

Hours/Days Open Warwick Castle is open 10am-6pm daily, Apr-Oct; 10am-5pm daily, Nov-Mar.

Cost Admission to the castle is £9.50 for adults.

Directions/Transportation Warwick Castle is a 15-20 minute bus trip from Stratford-upon-Avon; **Stagecoach** buses *(Tel 01788/535-555)* depart hourly from Market Place. The castle is also easily accessible by train from Stratford; a combined rail and entry package is even available through **Chiltern Railways** *(Tel 08705/165-165).*

Eats Fanshaw's Restaurant *(22 Market Place, Tel 01926/410-590; 6-10:30pm Mon-Sat; £8-£16.50 main courses; V, MC, AE),* in the heart of Warwick, occupies a late Victorian building whose dull brick facade brightened up by flowered window boxes. Inside, there are only 32 seats in the flouncy dining room that's accented in pink and white, filled with fresh flowers, and lined with mirrors. A well-trained staff serves a menu of the classics: sirloin steak; filet of beef, Wellington style, with a red wine and shallot sauce; breast of pheasant with a shiitake and oyster mushroom brandy sauce; and sautéed lamb kidneys with Dijon sauce in a puff pastry "pillow." Especially elegant, usually offered during game season, is a brace of quail with a hazelnut and apricot stuffing.

Findon's Restaurant *(7 Old Sq., Tel 01926/411-755; Noon-2pm/7-9:30pm Mon-Sat; £5 set lunches, £15.95 set dinners; V, MC, AE, DC)* offers equally elegant dishes like sauté of pigeon breast with red wine and celery; fresh cod with lemon and prawn butter and deep-fried parsley; and filet of sea bass with a fumet of lime. Consider grabbing lunch here—a two-course "plat du jour" includes a soup of the day followed by entrees like venison sausages with mustard sauce and fresh vegetables (they have vegetarian options too), all for only £5. It's a great deal considering that's about what you'd pay for a mediocre lunch in a local pub.

Crashing Since the town of Warwick itself is nothing to write home about, it's best to crash back in Stratford [see above].

The Cotswolds

So the first thing you're wondering is probably, "What the hell is a Cotswold?" *Wold* is the name for the barren plateaus that, along with grassy hills and dramatic ravines, make up this little region—apparently it translates to "God's high open land" in Old English. The residents of the Cotswolds got rich off the wool trade and spent their sheep-gotten wealth building the gorgeous honey-brown stone houses and extravagant (for little villages, anyway) churches that are a big tourist attraction today. Actually, pretty much everything in the Cotswolds is a tourist attraction (and you should know by now what that means: nothing is going to come cheap here). There are a few reasonably-priced spots to lay your head, but for the most part you're looking at fairly pricey B&Bs or hotels—the Cotswolds are definitely not geared toward the backpacker crowd. There's also a distinct lack of cultural attractions, but trees and birds—and charming little stone cottages—are the big show in these parts. Oh, and of *course* you're not expecting any nightlife here, right?

Travelers from all over flock here to drive through the stunning landscape and ancient villages. The Cotswolds are all about antique shops, tour bus coaches, and a sickening amount of preppy, Polo-shirted, khaki-pant-wearing American tourists driving rented Mercedes and Land Rovers. Each town has a High Street that is lined with inns of cream-colored stone and shop buildings dating back to the 18th and 19th centuries.

Wait—where are you going? We haven't gotten to the good part yet! You can escape the hoards by choosing to hike or bike it, if you have the energy and time, on the Cotswold Way [see *great outdoors,* below]. This way you get all the good stuff (the stunning landscapes) while only having to spend minimal time dealing with the annoying stuff (the other people).

The most worthwhile Cotswold villages are: **Moreton-in-Marsh, Lower Slaughter, Stow-on-the-Wold,** and **Chipping Campden.**

Moreton-in-Marsh is a 13-century planned market town that lies on the crossroads of the Fosse Way, an ancient Roman road. It is, of course, beautiful, though it gets boring quick when the moody English sky clouds over. Use Moreton-in-Marsh as a hub for your Cotswold explorations—it's easily accessible by train and offers a variety of accommodations (fairly pricey, though).

Landmarks include the **Curfew Tower,** whose clock and bell date back to the 17th century, the not-so-old **Redesdale Hall,** circa 1887, and **St. David's Church** on Church Street, with its 18th-century graveyard. The **Tuesday Market** (in the parking area around Redesdale Hall), is said to be the largest open-air market in the Cotswolds. Items from cheese to underwear to Indian spices are sold to the vast throngs of shoppers, many of whom are on traveling bus tours. On the opposite end of High Street, next to the inn on the right-hand side of the road, there lies a duck pond, which manages to completely tie up traffic every time a mother duck and her babies cross the road looking for handouts. (It's a sad day in the town when one of the brood becomes road kill). There aren't any distinguishable neighborhoods or hangouts other than those natural ones, nor is there any published guide to events here other than pamphlets at the Cotswold District Council Offices [see *need to know,* below]. When you arrive via the train station, the main streets, High Street, the London Road and Redesdale Place, are all a 5-minute walk west.

Okay, so it's plagued by Antique Roadshow–heads on antiquing sprees, but Stow-on-the-Wold is still worth a stop for its history. Just about 7 miles southwest of Moreton, it also lies smack in the middle of the Fosse Way. Kings have passed through here, including Edward VI, son of Henry VII, and they've bestowed their approval on the town, as plaques and monuments attest. That, plus the town's clear status as a pleasure for the eye, make it textbook, stereotypically English. When you leave the main square, you'll walk through some of the narrowest alleys in Britain. The town's Market Square is where most of the locals hang out (because there isn't really another option). In the middle of the Square stands a 14th-century cross, which was supposedly placed here to inspire merchants to be honest, plus the stocks where those who weren't (honest, that is) were once jeered at and bombarded with rotten eggs by the townspeople. The last battle of the English Civil War took place nearby in Stow, during which Cromwell, the future "Lord Protector," incarcerated 1,500 Royalist troops in the open air because the jail wouldn't hold them. But you can just look at the pretty buildings and forget all that nastiness....

If you're looking for a town with architecture you'll remember till you're 80 years-old, visit Lower Slaughter, about 5 miles southwest of Stow. The town that you'll likely tell your grandchildren about (when you get to the talkative stage of old age) holds the motherlode of that honey-colored masonry we were talking about, and is home to flocks of wandering ducks begging for food scraps, surrounded by gentle quintessentially English vistas of rural life. It's probably the most famous of the Cotswold villages. The best known site is the still functioning Old Mill, designed during the 19th-century for grinding flour. Its massive water wheel still powers it today. On your visit, you can join your fellow tourists licking ice cream cones while staring at the attraction.

In the other direction, about 7 miles north of Moreton, is the town of Chipping Campden. It's enchanting in a precious kind of way, with small shops and inns occupying the rows of old, burnished stone buildings along High Street and the landmark 15th-century tower of the Church of St. James, smack dab in the center of town. Chipping Campden is a reasonable base for seeing the local sites on foot: It stands at the beginning of the Cotswold Way [see *great outdoors,* below].

great outdoors

If you'd like to get off the main roads along the Cotswolds and see hidden countryside that's not visible from a bus window, the **Cotswold Way** is the way to go. This 104-mile path, staked out in 1968, cuts across the Cotswolds' country lanes, riverside towpaths, and fields of rolling hills, winding goat paths, and meadows of grazing sheep.

The Cotswold Way begins in **Chipping Campden** and goes all the way to **Bath** [see **wiltshire & somerset region,** above]. Very few hikers go the whole route, except hardcore backpackers who can make it in 6 to 8 days. Most hikers, especially beginners, just do the first section of the hike, which can be done in one day—it's easier, and it takes in the most evocative of the Cotswold scenery and the more beautiful of the region's villages. The route is clearly signposted with bright yellow signs at almost any intersection. You can get on and off at dozens of points, depending on your stamina and interest. Because of uncertain weather conditions, the trail is best walked from June to September. We prefer the late spring, when wildflowers cover the fields.

So is it worth it? Yes indeed. The Way gives you a sense of England in the Middle Ages as no other does. The panoramas are spectacular. And mercifully, you're never far from at least one of the Cotswolds' pubs, where you can refuel your tired bod with some brew and grub. In most cases, it is only a quarter-mile walk from the trail into one of dozens of villages. Camping is possible along the route, but only in designated camp sites (a great map of them, along with every other pertinent detail of the route from Chipping Campden as far as Winchcombe, is the ***Outdoor Leisure Map 45,*** put out by Ordnance Survey, the British government map office, available for £5.95 in any bookshop and many hotels in Chipping Campden).

Any of the local tourist offices en route [see *need to know,* below] can supply you with tons of data on the Way, ranging from Cotswold Way ordnance maps to specialized walking tours. The English Ramblers' Association publishes the best of these, ***The Cotswold Way Handbook and Accommodations List*** (£2). The best place to call for specific information is the know-it-all Cotswold Voluntary Warden Service *(Tel 0145/242-56-75).* The staff here has been over every inch of the trail and can offer sound advice.

If you don't take the whole Way, there are some shorter options for getting out into nature on foot. In Lower Slaughter, you'll avoid the exhaust from tourists' cars by following the foot path referred to as **Warden's Way,** which runs along the edge of the town's River Eye, the one that powers the mill. Heading 1 mile from Upper Slaughter on the trail, you'll see an amplitude of birds, including Canadian Geese (mind the duck poop) and mute swans. If you're an ornithology buff, you can spot native grey wagtails and coots. You'll happen upon old footbridges, trees arched over ancient millponds, endless enchanting little stone cottages, and sheep grazing in meadows.

eats

▶▶MORETON-IN-MARSH
The Moreton-in-Marsh town supermarket, **Budgens of Moreton** *(High St., Moreton-in-Marsh; Tel 01608/651-854; 8am-10pm Mon-Sat, 10am-4pm Sun; £3-5; V, MC),* a 5-minute walk west of the train station, is a good choice if you want to have a picnic in the children's park across the street, or if you want to make some sandwiches for a hike through the 'wolds. Great cheddar cheeses and fresh bread or scones are the way to go here.

If you'd rather have the cooking done for you, the **Bell Inn** *(High St., Moreton-in-Marsh; Tel 01608/651-688; 10am-11pm Mon-Sat, 10am-10:30pm Sun; £3.95 meals; AE, V, MC)* serves a "Trio of faggots, mash, and vegetables" for cheap (by Cotswolds standards, anyway) on picnic tables in the driveway/courtyard or indoors.

For traditional English cuisine, go to **Mermaid Fish Bar** *(High St., Moreton-in-Marsh; Tel 01608/651-391; 11:30am-2pm Mon-Sat, 4:30pm-11pm Sun; £3.50 meals; V, MC).* It's the only definitive fish and chips takeaway in town. Plan on spending £1 for chips and £2.50 for cod. Ketchup's 65 pence extra.

Tasty Indian dishes are whipped up at the **Hassan Balti** *(High St., Moreton-in-Marsh; Tel 01608/650-798; Noon-2pm daily, 6-11:30pm Mon-Thu, Sun, 5:30pm-midnight Fri, Sat; £4.15-6 meals; No credit cards).* It's an eat-in or take-away restaurant popular with tourists and locals alike. The chicken tikka and Tandoori chicken are the favorites, though the prawn curry also has its fans.

▶▶CHIPPING CAMPDEN
For a quick bite, there's always the local bakery, **Leopold & Son** *(High St., Chipping Campden; No phone; 7am-6pm daily),* which happens to be a Cotswolds chain with beautifully decorated pink cakes in the window. They also offer traditional English cuisine—fish and chips.

Two Chipping Campden hotels, the **Cotswold House Hotel** and the **Kings Arms Hotel** [see *crashing,* below, for both], offer decent pub grub as well as three-course dinner affairs.

▶▶STOW-ON-THE-WOLD
The Market Square in Stow-on-the-Wold is packed with pubs and outdoor cafes. They all offer fairly good eats, and best of all, you can people-watch without being branded as nosy by gossipy locals. A popular one is

the **White Hart** *(Market Sq., Stow-on-the-Wold; No phone; 11am-11pm daily; £10.85 meals; MC, V).*

A few of the hotels in Stow-on-the-Wold also offer full sit-down meals: The **Old Farmhouse Hotel** [see *crashing,* below] serves dinner from 7-9pm daily, with a table d'hôte menu that changes daily, and the **Stow Lodge Hotel** *(The Square, Stow-on-the-Wold; Tel 01451/830-485, Fax 01451/831-671; Dinner served 7-9pm daily; £11-18 dinners; www.stowlodge.com; V, MC, DC)* serves à la carte dinners featuring poached salmon steak, grilled local trout, various steaks, and roast duckling in a choice of sauces.

▶▶**LOWER SLAUGHTER**
Lower Slaughter Manor [see *crashing,* below] serves the best English produce cooked in the modern French style. A three-course prix fixe dinner costs £45, and you can choose from about six different dishes—including fresh fish, beef, lamb, chicken, duck, and vegetables—for each course. They also have an extensive wine list, with emphasis on French and New York vintages.

crashing

We've already warned you: Finding a place to sleep in these parts is going to cost you. Skimp on hostels on some other leg of your trip so you can afford to live it up here, where you don't have much choice.

▶▶**STOW-ON-THE-WOLD**
Typical dormitory accommodation is offered by the **YHA Stow-on-the-Wold** *(The Square, Stow-on-the-Wold; Tel 01451/830-497; Reception open 5pm-11pm; £10.85 members),* one of the few cheapies around these parts. Rooms have four, six, and eight beds; all the dorms are same-sex. It's conveniently located in the town centre, across from the market square. The downside is the 10am-5pm lockout. You probably won't mind the 11pm curfew, however, being that there's no nightlife in Stow-on-the-Wold.

Stow-on-the-Wold has several pleasant and affordable B&Bs like **The Gate Lodge** *(Stow Hill, Stow-on-the-Wold; Tel 01451/832-103; £40 doubles with private bath; No credit cards).* True to its name, this B&B is in a former gate lodge to a manor built in 1910. It offers basic accommodation and private parking a half mile south the town center.

While you're in the countryside, take the opportunity to stay at a charming converted 16th-century farmhouse. The **Old Farmhouse Hotel** *(Lower Swell, Stow-on-the-Wold; Tel 01451/830-232; £50 double, £70 double, en suite, £10 extra for single occupancy; oldfarm@globalnet.co.uk; V, MC)* is a small, intimate, and popular hotel that's been completely refurbished. The original fireplaces blaze with log fires, each bedroom has a comfortable bed, and most have a small bath with a shower stall and rack of medium-sized towels. Reservations are a good idea.

Also one and a half miles from town is the adorable **Little Broom** *(Maugersbury, Stow-on-the-Wold; Tel 01451/830-510; £50 en suite, £55-60 apartment-style doubles, deposit required with reservation; No credit cards).* It's pricier, but you get television and free tea and coffee in each room and, most importantly, an outdoor swimming pool. For more privacy, the B&B has a self-contained building with two double bedrooms—one with a kitchen and laundry facilities, and the other with its own patio.

▶▶MORETON-IN-MARSH

The cozy **Blue Cedar House** *(Stow Rd., Moreton-in-Marsh; Tel 01608/650-299; £21 single, £42 double ; No credit cards)* is one of the best B&B values in Central England. The four clean, homey bedrooms have TVs, radio alarm clocks, tea and coffee makers, and a sink and/or shower; some rooms have a private bath. The comfy beds and soft duvets will send you deep into slumberland, and cots are available for extra guests. Your hosts are good-hearted and eager to help you choose the best Cotswold sights. It's a short 10-minute walk southwest of the train station.

The **Warwick House B&B** *(London Rd., Moreton-in-Marsh; Tel 01608/650-773; £40 double, £35 after first night; No credit cards)*, a 5-minute walk east of the train station, is the most inexpensive B&B in the town center. The proprietors will pick you up from the station, just give them a ring.

The rather dingy front hallway at the **Redesdale Arms Hotel** *(High St., Moreton-in-Marsh; Tel 01608/650-308; £35 single, £45.50 double, £60 four-person family room with private bath; AE, MC, V)*, a 5-minute walk west of the train station, doesn't do this nice hotel justice. All bedrooms are comfortable, equipped with satellite TV, free tea- and coffee-making facilities, and compact-but-clean bathrooms with shower stalls. There's private parking, and uniformed waiters serve in the restaurant—and if the weather's nice, you can eat outside in the back courtyard.

The 17th-century **White Hart Hotel** *(High St., Moreton-in-Marsh; Tel 01608/650-731; Singles with private bath from £52, doubles from £68; MC, V)*, a 5-minute walk west of the train station, caters mainly to those upper-middle-class American tourists. The smallish rooms are haphazardly decorated with a few antiques mixed with modern furniture, but the bathrooms have a tub and shower combination and a set of good-sized towels. Thankfully, breakfast is included in the hefty price.

▶▶LOWER SLAUGHTER

The **Lower Slaughter Manor** *(Off the A429, Lower Slaughter; Tel 01451/820-456; £135-325 single, £150-375 double, including breakfast; V, MC, AE, Delta, Switch)* sounds like the setting for a horror flick, but looks more like some remarkable English home you would see in a Jane Austen movie adaptation. It's pricey, but there are benefits if you can swing it: (1) you probably won't have many opportunities to stay in an authentic English manor, (2) you'll feel like a movie star, and (3) it has an indoor heated pool and tennis courts. The hotel doesn't get many young guests—but neither does any place in the Cotswolds.

▶▶CHIPPING CAMPDEN

The B&Bs in Chipping Campden are some of the less-outrageously priced in the Cotswolds, but they still ain't cheap. Your best options are **Sparrings** *(Leysbourne, Chipping Campden; Tel 01386/840-505; £27* *single, £46.50 double, private baths)* or **Marnic House** *(Broad Campden, Chipping Campden; Tel 01386/840-014, fax 01386/840-441; £25 single, £44 double).* Slightly more expensive is the **Kings Arms Hotel** *(The Square, Chipping Campden; Tel 01386/840-256; £55 single; £75 double; AE, V, MC),* which dates back to the late 1600s. It's recently renovated and has its own garden that provides the fresh vegetables that are used in its meals. All of the meticulous rooms are en suite, with bath and shower combos. Breakfast is traditional English food of course, but it's mighty tasty, especially if you're craving a greasy hangover cure after a night of drinking in the hotel bar.

need to know

Tourist Information There are good tourist info centers in **Chipping Campden** *(Noel Court, High St.Campden; Tel 01386/814-206, 10am-6pm daily)*, **Moreton-in-Marsh** *(High St.; Tel 01608/650-881; Mon-Fri 9am-5pm)* and **Stow-on-the-Wold** *(Hollis House, The Square; Tel 01451/831-082; 9:30am-5:30pm Mon-Sat, 10:30am-4:30pm Sun, Easter-Oct; 9:30am-4:30pm Mon-Sat, Nov-mid-Feb; 9:30am-5pm Mon-Sat, mid-Feb-Easter)*. None, however, will make hotel reservations for you.

Trains and Buses The easiest way to break into the Cotswolds from London is to hop on a train from Paddington Station, which will put you in Moreton-in-Marsh in 1-1/2 to 2 hours. Call **National Rail Enquires** *(Tel 0345/484-950)* for information on schedules and fares. You can also bus it from Paddington, on **National Express** *(Tel 0990/808-080)*. To get to Chipping Campden (also often spelled Chipping Camden, but it's the same place), Stow-on-the-Wold, or Lower Slaughter from here by bus, your choices are **Badgerline** *(Tel 01225/464-446)* and **Stagecoach Cheltenham District** *(Tel 01242/522-021)*. Buses leave about five times a day.

Bike Rental Country Lanes Cycle Centre *(Train Station; Tel 01608/650-065; 9:30am-5:00pm daily, Easter-Nov; £14 per day; www.countrylane.co.uk)* in Moreton-in-Marsh will set you up for touring these fairytale hills and dales.

If you're in Chipping Campden, try **Cotswold Country Cycles** *(Longlands Farm Cottage, located 2 miles from Chipping Campden; Tel 01386/438-706; Apr-Sept; £10 full day, £7 half-day, £60 weekly; ian&julia@cotswoldcountrycycles.com; www.cotswoldcountrycycles.com)*.

Postal Chipping Campden Main Post Office *(High St.; Tel 01386/840-235)* will mail your postcards.

Internet If you need an e-mail fix, your only option is the **public library** (next to Noels Arms Hotel across from Town Hall) in Chipping Campden.

the
northwest
and the peak
district

the northwest and the peak district

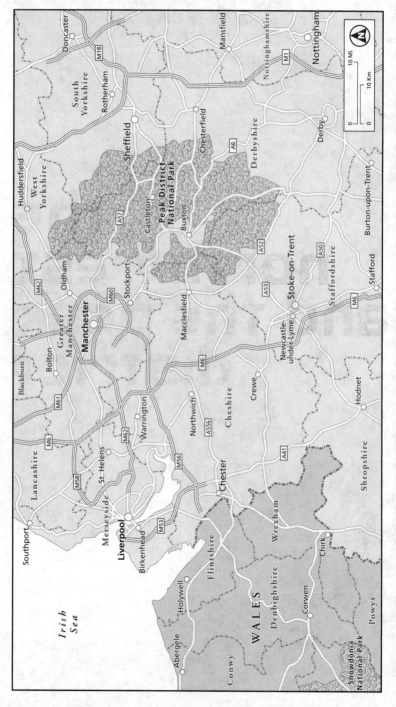

England's Northwest got a bad rep during the Industrial Revolution as the place to go for smog and exploited workers. But these days, after serious slumps in the once booming economy, some of the old mojo seems to be back, minus the sooty skies and the scary Victorian pin factories. A Northern town today has a quality which you could even accuse of being very un-British: it's upbeat. Renovations are everywhere, and shiny new buildings gleam in the sunlight. The vibe is all about renewal and rebirth, and if you still can't find a job, there are plenty of new places where you can get pissed in style and complain about it. No matter how attractive the changes are, though, Northerners aren't as quick to make their turf as tourist-friendly as the folks in Yorkshire or the Lake District. This can make them seem harsh sometimes when they're only being direct. Their friendliness seems infused with a working-class no-bullshit approach. There's still enough grit around to keep things real, and plenty of youthful vitality to fuel a kicking nightlife.

It's been years since the birth of the **Manchester** sound and since then, every stripe of techno, house, rap, and electronica has found its way into Mancunion's (as they are called) hearts. Club kids, hipsters, and music afficanados from all over Europe and the UK flock here for the legendary all-night madness, the huge student population and the thriving gay community supplying fresh energy to the scene. A little to the south and west, perched on the Irish Sea, is **Liverpool,** the home of...well, you know. Beatlemania is still big business here (as it seems to be everywhere, seeing how well *One* sold!), but the Fab Four are also the patron saints of an innovative music and club scene thriving around the world-class Cream (the club, not the band, you hippie). And if all that urban grit gets to be too much for you, the beauty of this region is that you can easily escape to the pastoral gritstone of the **Peak District National Park.**

Just to the south in Derbyshire, you can clear your mind of all that party-static, strolling leisurely (as one does in Britain, my dear) on the smooth, green, grassy hills. The only thing you won't see is a peak of any kind—the name refers to the Peac, the Celtic tribe that used to call this area home. The Northern section of the park, called Dark Peak, offers spectacular outdoor thrills. **Castleton** is an excellent base for exploring the Dark Peak, not to mention the crumbling and slightly spooky Peveril Castle and caverns, which will take you about as close to the underworld

all's well

Folks around here have taken dressing well to a whole new level: They actually dress their wells. Occurring at various times throughout the summer, primarily in the limestone villages of the central and southern Peak District, this ancient ritual involves decorating and blessing the village water supply. The well dressings themselves begin on flat wooden trays, with a layer of wet clay. After a design is drawn, it's colored by pressing thousands of flower petals into the clay. Other natural elements like berries, bark, and seeds can also be used in a pinch. The design varies, but often features a Biblical scene. This is ironic, considering that the whole tradition most likely began as a pagan fertility rite, honoring the well's water spirits and even crowning a Well Queen.

Although well dressing all but died out by the 1950's, today it's become a popular attraction for tourists. The wells are blessed with a short outdoor ceremony, often with accompaniment by a brass band, which kicks off a weeklong summer celebration. For information on possible well dressing festivals during your trip, contact any of the local tourist offices.

as you want to get in this lifetime (or the next, for that matter). You can also take a great hike along **Mam Tor,** the largest mountain in the park, really a steady grade that only reaches 1,040 feet. The nearby **Kinder Plateau** is actually a few feet higher (2068 ft.), allowing for some awesome views and wild sculpted outcroppings such as Stanage Edge. As the last train stop, heading north from London, rough-and-tumble **Matlock** gives you southern access to the park. If you start to feel your legs go out from under you (all those nights finally catching up, only yourself to blame) you might want to hop the cable car to the top of a mountain at the Heights of Abraham and atone for your sins.

In the southern White Peak area, the landscape loses some of its haunting depth, giving way to the bright cheeriness of limestone and emerald greens. With mostly grassy hills and sheep to keep them trim, this is the English countryside of lore. The village of **Bakewell** certainly meets the quaintness requirements, with homey teashops, grand 18th-century estates, and a postcard-perfect bridge. The Victorian resort town **Buxton** maintains its snooty legacy, offering high art, high class, elegant archirecture and exquisite gardens. Just remember to bring your silk parasol. Either town makes a fine base for exploring the area, before heading back to Manchester or London.

If you're a hard-core hiker, you'll want to hike at least part of the 110-mile long **Pennine Way** or the less difficult **Limestone Way.** Cycling is another great way to see the best of the Peak District—you can rent bicycles in Buxton, Bakewell, and Matlock, and pedal your way through England's pleasant land.

getting around

Both Manchester and Liverpool are well-connected by train and plane. Trains and buses also connect Manchester to Derbyshire's Peak District. Luckily, the bus system within Derbyshire isn't all that bad, although the buses are at times infrequent and travel gets harder as you move into the less populated Dark Peak areas in the north. If you're planning on doing a lot of travel in one day, consider buying a Derbyshire Explorer pass, which costs £5.25 and allows unlimited travel on most buses for that day. At £7.25, the Derbyshire Wayfarer pass allows travel on all trains as well as buses for just £2 more. You purchase the passes right on the bus, from the driver (how easy is that?). Trains reach to the south to Matlock and across the north from Sheffield to Manchester, also servicing Edale. Trains are also available from Manchester to Buxton. The complete *Peak District Timetable,* a comprehensive map of all transportation services available in the area, is available at most stations and tourist offices for 60p. An information line *(Tel 01298/230-98)* for the various bus service providers is available 7am-8pm.

suggested routes

If you're on a frantic two-day schedule, you can still manage to take the train from London to Manchester for a quick dip into the deep end of the pleasure pool. Then it's just a fast train northwest to Liverpool for a "Fab Four" T-shirt and a sip of sweet Cream.

Add a few more days and you can take in some of the Peak District National Park as well, although it takes six to eight days just to walk the Pennine Way for the full Peak experience.

Those on a five-day jaunt can take an early train from London to Manchester, see its attractions in the afternoon and club-hop well into the early morning. On the second day, get your hung-over hiney on the train from Manchester southeast to Edale (trip time: 50 minutes). From Edale, you can sweat out those nasty toxins with a scenic walk of three-and-a-half miles to Castleton. After an overnight there, walk southeast to Bakewell, which offers inexpensive food and accommodation. (It's also just a quick 36-mile bus trip back to Manchester, if you want to get back to the clubs). On the next day, a bus ride along A6 northwest will take you to high-class Buxton, which also has hourly train service back to Manchester. A train to Manchester early the next morning can be followed by a train to Liverpool for a final mop-up of the area before a return to London or wherever your final destination may be.

If you want to hit the park en route to Manchester from London, you can take the train to Matlock, continue along the Pennine Way to overnight in Bakewell, and than hike to Buxton, where you can catch a train to Manchester.

TRAVEL TIMES

Times by train unless
otherwise indicated
*By road.

	Manchester	Liverpool	Buxton	Bakewell	Matlock
Manchester	-	1:00	:55	1:45	2:30 2:50
Liverpool	1:00	-	2:10	2:50	3:15 3:55
Buxton	:55	2:10	-	2:20 2:40	3:10 4:00
Bakewell	1:45	2:50	2:20 2:40	-	4:30 5:40
Matlock	2:30 2:50	3:15 3:55	3:10 4:00	4:30 5:40	-
Castleton	:20	1:30 1:45	1:35	2:20 3:20	:35
Pennine Way	:50	2:05 3:15	1:30	2:20 3:20	:40*
Limestone Way	2:40 2:50	3:15 3:55	3:10 4:00	4:30 5:40	:05*
Heights of Abraham	3:20 3:00	3:20 4:00	4:30 3:55	:15* 5:35	:40*
Stanage Edge	:50*	1:30*	:20*	:15*	:25*

Castleton	Pennine Way	Limestone Way	Heights of Abraham	Stanage Edge	London
:20	:50	2:30 / 2:50	2:35 / 3:00	:50*	3:00 / 3:50
1:30 / 1:45	2:05 / 3:15	3:15 / 3:55	3:20 / 4:00	1:30*	2:00
1:35	1:30	3:10 / 4:00	3:20 / 3:55	:20*	3:45
2:20 / 3:20	2:45 / 4:10	4:30 / 5:40	4:30 / 5:35	:15*	3:55
:35	:40	:05	:40	:25*	2:40
-	:10*	:35*	:40*	:10*	3:10*
:10*	-	:45*	:40*	:10*	3:10
:35*	:40*	-	:40*	:25*	2:40
:40*	:40*	-	:30*	2:40	
:10*	:40*	:25*	:30*	-	2:55

manchester

There's enough stark grey industry—both active factories and long defunct ones—defining Manchester's skyline to make you wonder why the hell you'd want to visit the place. But persist past your shallow first impressions, fickle traveler, wander the streets of England's second-largest city, and behold as soot-blackened walls give way to color. The old industries have been replaced by newer, shinier technologies, the buildings are being scrubbed squeaky clean, and the interiors are re-done with the giddy enthusiasm of a kid who just discovered fingerpaints. The destruction caused by the infamous IRA bombing in 1996 has also, ironically, cleared the way for a complete renovation of the City Centre. Wherever you turn, something is under construction, cleaning up this "Cottonopolis."

Manchester got its start as a Roman fortress way back in 79 A.D., and the empire's handiwork can still be viewed at the ancient gate, (restored, like everything else), in **Castlefield** [see *culture zoo,* below]. But the city really came into its own beginning in the mid-17th century and mushroomed through the Industrial Revolution, fueled by the textile industry and that other new-fangled contraption, the railways. Since then, through many ups and downs, Manchester has kept its edge, and is now home to 2.5 million folks, arguably the most diverse city in the U.K.

In addition to the large Chinese and East Indian populations, Manchester is also the home of 250,000 students (now there's a Spring Break that could actually scare somebody!), and a thriving gay scene keeping things lively. Like the city itself, the people of Manchester (Mancunions or simply Mancs to you) can seem a little rough around the edges, but you'll do well to meet them head on and discover their very special brand of genuine warmth. They have more than enough ingenuity, energy and grit to tackle adversity and have a pint and a laugh or two along the way. To put it simply: Mancunions really know how to party.

But that shouldn't make you careless; mugging is still a serious problem here. Be especially careful at the cashpoints on Oxford and Wilmslow road in the southern quarter and those on the north side of Piccadilly Gardens, and don't brave Piccadilly Gardens at night. A little caution will greatly improve your enjoyment of this party capital.

Sure, it's been a while since Manchester landed on the pop/rock map with angst-miesters like Joy Division, Morrissey and badboy upstarts like Oasis, but the music scene is still kickin' and varied. Whether it's the new wannabe-melancholic bands or the fierce grooves of electronica spinning on turntables, or the Manchester version of hip-hop, there's something here for everyone. The club scene is raucous almost any night of the week, the vibe is not-at-all snobbish (as it can sometimes be in London), and after much imbibing, the crowds go nuts dancing. Hey, what more do you need?

For info on what's on and where it's happening, the *City Life* 'zine, available at newstands for £1.60, is a super resource, listing happenings for the month ahead as well as a venue guide with locations and phone numbers.

neighborhoods

The typical strapping young visitor can walk across Manchester's **City Centre,** just about a half-mile wide, in less than 45 minutes. **Town Hall** is smack in the middle, beside **Albert Square,** site of dozens of fun pubs and restaurants. A second cluster of pubs, clubs, and restaurants—plus

five things to talk to a local about

Mancunians love to talk about their city and the people in it, so anything revolving around this will keep a conversation going for hours. The following are some of the favorites:

1. The Lowry and how great it is, inside and out.
2. The Lowry and how great a waste of money it is, inside and out.
3. The Manchester United football team, and the related topic of soccer hooliganism, and how proud they are to contribute to it.
4. The metro, and how convenient it is that it doesn't stop running until midnight, right when the parties really start.
5. Manchester's reputation as the home of industry, the obvious lack of same today, and the trash it left behind.

12 hours in manchester

Only here for a short time? Start off at **Castlefield Urban Heritage Park** to get a handle on where Manchester's coming from [see *culture zoo,* below]. Then head on over to **The Lowry** for a better sense of where the city's heading [see *arts scene,* below]. Spend some time in the Northern Quarter with the fringe elements at **Affleck's Palace** [see *stuff,* below] on Oldham Street. Affleck's offers a little bit of everything from great shopping to tattoo artists to barbers to cafes—you can entertain yourself for an afternoon watching all the funky characters walking around. As your short day journeys into night, dive into the NQ's bar and club scene, or head on over to Canal Street to explore the gay clubs (whatever your sexual preference, you should know the gay clubs throw the best parties). Just remember to shake 'em if you've got 'em—that's what Manchester after dark is really all about.

theaters and concert halls—is clustered around **Bridgewater Hall** and the **Exhibition Centre** along the City Centre's southern edge, and a third cluster of pubs lies along **Deansgate** at the western edge.

The compact City Centre branches out into distinct neighborhoods: the alternative **Northern Quarter,** the student-centered **Southern Quarter, Castlefield** to the southwest, and **Chinatown** and the **Gay Village** to the southeast.

The **Northern Quarter,** or NQ, is actually at the northeastern edge of the City Centre, starting at **Picadilly Gardens.** In the past, it's been the site of the city's alternative scene. Major streets include **Oldham Street,** running northeast-southwest, and **Swan Street,** running northwest-southeast, which becomes **Great Ancoats Street.** Unfortunately, the NQ has become a little too popular for nightly carousing—it's not uncommon to find sportswear-clad punters facedown in garbage cans, trying their best to hold onto their dinner.

These days, you're better off in the **Southern Quarter,** where the student scene lives. The sprawling campus of the **University of Manchester** lies on either side of **Oxford Road** (the southern extension of **Oxford Street**), about a mile south of the City Centre's southern perimeter. A few blocks still further south is the **Rusholme District,** a low-income neighborhood known for its burgeoning avant-garde politics and its dense concentration of relatively inexpensive Indian and Pakistani restaurants. Its busiest thoroughfare is **Wilmslow Road,** which intersects with Oxford Road just south of the University.

On the southwestern perimeter of the City Centre is the **Castle-field** district, site of renovated Victorian warehouses and trendy restaurants and cafe-bars, as well as the **Castlefield Heritage Park,** with its ancient Roman excavations [see *culture zoo,* below]. The **Gay Village** is along **Canal Street,** which runs parallel and just to the south of the much bigger **Portland Street,** on the City Centre's southeastern edge. Portland Street is the main thoroughfare of **Chinatown.**

The buses in town will confuse the hell out of you—people who have lived here their whole lives still don't understand them. Instead of trying to make sense of it all, they just built the Metrorail, and we suggest you follow their lead and use it if at all possible. Manchester maintains two Metro lines, an east-west line and a north-south line, both of which travel above ground. As we said, the city is small so you can get by walking most of the time, but if you're hopping around from place to place, you can buy a daily ticket for £3 that's good for all trains during the day.

by foot

Start canal-side at the **Roman Gate** in Castlefield. The ancient Roman stronghold offers a jarring contrast to the cold steel of this center of industry. With the fort behind you, head right onto **Liverpool Road** and under the bridge to a left turn on **Deansgate,** where you'll pass by a bunch of trendy—not to mention pricey—shops and cafe-bars. Just past **Lincoln Square** (which is more of a pentagon, really), a right turn onto John Dalton Street takes you to the financial center and an eyeful of classic Edwardian architecture. At **Albert Square** hang a left onto **Cross Street** and up to the **Arndale Center,** where you'll find designer shops trying to elbow out old-world bazaars. A right onto **Market Street** turns into **Piccadilly Gardens** and the center of the city. Stop for some urban outdoor entertainment (aka panhandlers) and move on to **Oldham Street.** Now you're moving into the **Northern Quarter,** where the hardest partying happens at night. A right onto **Ancoats Street** then a quick right onto **Newton** and you're now heading southwest. Once Newton turns into **Portland Street, Chinatown** (and cheap food) will be on your right, and the **Gay Village** to the left. You'll eventually smack into **Oxford Street,** the beginnings of the **Southern Quarter,** where you'll find the more offbeat hotspots. The further out of town you head, the more ethnic the scenery becomes, as **Rusholme** fills your senses with the sights and smells of India.

wired

Manchester's all over the web. For an almost overwhelming amount of information on everything you didn't even realize you needed to know about Manchester, check out Virtual Manchester at *www.manchester.com.* For a hip guide to Manchester's youth scene, try *www.madforit.com,* which features cool shockwave animation. You can also try the city government's tourist site at *www.manchester.gov.uk.*

With all of Manchester having a mad on for technology, you'd think someone would jump all over the Internet craze, but as far as the world-wide web goes, they seem to be stuck in a postindustrial slump. There's one Internet cafe out in **Cyberia** *(10 Oxford Rd.; Tel 0161/237-97-53; 11am-11pm Mon-Sat, till 8pm Sun; Drinks £2.25; www.manchester.cyberiacafe.net)*—actually it's in the Southern Quarter—where you can get sloshed while you surf.

hanging out

If you want to kill some time, you'll most likely find yourself around **Piccadilly Gardens,** a bit of shaggy urban green space at the northeastern edge of the City Centre near Market Street. Street performers and the types who throw money at them are always milling about, and innocent bystanders run for cover as skaters attempt pedestrian bowling, using the smooth pavement as their lanes. At the corner of Oldham and Church Streets in the NQ, alternative shopping mecca **Affleck's Palace** [see *stuff,* below] attracts loafers and loiterers inside and out. Descend into Affleck's labyrinth and rub elbows with all of the hipper-than-thou set, from skate kids to moody goths to Morrissey look-alikes.

bar scene

Every neighborhood here has its own scene: Castlefield supplies the modern sophisticate with all the cafe-bars their trendy little heart desires. The Gay Village on Canal Street is where boys go to meet boys and girls go to meet girls [see *gay scene,* below], but it's also just a damned good time, whatever your orientation. The students' merry-go-round orbits around Oxford Street in the Southern Quarter. The Northern Quarter's Oldham Street is known for it's rough-and-tumble all-nighters. And the standard old-fashioned Brit pubs make their home in the City Centre.

Castlefield was hit by the waterfront renewal scheme that ran through industrial England, with places all decked out in vibrant colors as revolt against the formerly predominant gray. With its aluminum interior and exposed brickwork, the Spanish-themed **Barça** *(Arches 8-9, Catalan Square; Tel 0161/839-70-99; Noon-11pm Mon-Thur, till midnight Fri, Sat,*

Food till 11pm; MC) evokes the city's industrial past, but is brightened up by its primary color scheme, outdoor balcony, and sandstone parapet. Inside you'll find adventurous food and some interesting drink mixes like the Brave Bull, a tequila and Kahlua mix, or more mellow champagne cocktails. Drinks cost about £2.10.

Also in Castlefield, **The Box** *(380 Deansgate; Tel 0161/819-59-11)* is the place for sports, with the entire wall behind the bar dominated by a movie-size screen. On match days, punters practically kick the ball into your drink. Music videos flash across the screen the rest of the time, along with anything else the manager feels like showing. The restaurant on the balcony above also serves food into the night.

Peveril of the Peak *(127 Great Bridgewater St.; 11:30am-2:30pm/5-11pm daily; No credit cards)* may look like a place that would draw Queen Victoria, but most of the punters look more like Prince William. A 15-minute walk south from Piccadilly Gardens, the bustling pub lures a young crowd with its pool table, jukebox, and summer beer garden (beers are £1.70). Stop in on Tuesday nights for live music.

One of Manchester's grand old alehouses, **The Marble Arch** *(73 Rochdale Rd.; Tel 016/832-59-14; 11:30am-11pm Mon-Fri, noon-11pm Sat; No credit cards)* is just a five-minute walk north of Piccadilly Gardens in the NQ. It's the place to go not only for the brew, but for a friendly game of pool or to hit up the pinball machines. The food is decent too, with pub grub going for £4-6, and in summer there's a small beer garden out back.

A microbrewery with Victorian style, **The Lass O'Gowrie** *(36 Charles St.; Tel 0161/273-69-32; 11am-11pm daily; No credit cards)* is a favorite student hangout—they come here to watch a match on the big-screen TV, crank on the slot machine or the jukebox, and...oh yeah, drink. A 10-minute walk southwest of the center of town, the pub offers a small menu of steak and chips for £2-4, among other items, but it's the brew that's the star.

Rules of the game

Rule number one is to steer clear of the bobbies in general, and anyone in riot gear in particular. (This actually serves as a good rule for life in general...) Though there are surveillance cameras everywhere in the city, Manchester can still be a rough place, so watch your back. For safety's sake, it's also a good idea to get along to wherever you're going, or at least reach the well-lit Piccadilly Gardens, before midnight. The metro stops running about midnight, so you have to depend on taxis in the early-morning hours.

manchester

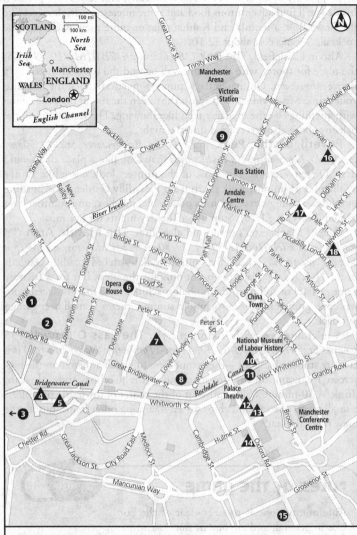

BARS/CLUBS ▲
Band on the Wall **16**
Barça **4**
Elemental **12**
Jilly's Rockworld **13**
Manto **10**
Planet K **17**
The Box **5**
The G-Mex **7**

The Music Box **14**
The Roadhouse **18**

CULTURE ZOO ●
Bridgewater Hall **8**
Chetham's Library **9**
Granada Studios **1**
Greater Manchester
  Opera House **6**

Greater Manchester
  Palace Theatre **11**
Manchester Museum **15**
Museum of Science
  and Industry **2**
The Lowry **3**

LIVE MUSIC SCENE

Live music in Manchester is as varied as it comes, from rock to hip-hop and acid jazz. Follow your tastes or try something new; wherever you end up, it's almost guaranteed the crowd will be fun (we can't make any promises about the quality of the music though...).

Though the name sounds like a contradiction, **Dry Bar** *(28-30 Old Oldham St.; Tel 0161/236-98-40; 11am-3am Mon-Sat, 11am-10:30pm Sun; MC, V)* is a chic rendezvous, especially around midnight. Launched by new wave band New Order and their label, Factory Records, this big bar with an ultra-modern industrial steel look draws a hip young media crowd. Live acts ranging from hip-hop to acid jazz play every weekend and sometimes on weekdays, too. The food is a bit incongruous with the atmosphere—it's Jamaican all the way, with truly authentic jerk chicken. It's just a five-minute walk north into the NQ from the City Centre.

Known all over the north as the only place worth mentioning if you're into rock, **Jilly's Rockworld** *(65 Oxford St.; Tel 0161/236-99-71; 9pm-2am Thur,Sat, till 7am Fri; Cover varies, usually £3-4)* is fueled by the bohemian lust for guitar, bass, and drums. With three rooms, each playing different music, this Southern Quarter hotspot continues to provide the city known for the electronica revolution with a dose of pure rock, from punk and grunge to goth, metal, and indie rock. With barely room to breathe any night of the week, this bar is proof that rock 'n' roll will never die.

Some of the best local beats find their way to **The Roadhouse** *(8 Newton St.; Tel 0161/237-97-89; Hours vary; Cover £3-4)*, featuring music with real soul, from jazz to funk and the occasional Saturday night of Brit pop. Just east of Picadilly Gardens, it began as a blues club, but the owners boast that the Roadhouse was the launchpad for bands like the Verve, the Lemonheads, and Blink 182, who blasted their way to fame, fortune, and heavy MTV rotation.

The derelict facade of the Victorian building may scare off the faint of heart, but once inside **Star & Garter** *(18-20 Fairfield St.; Tel 0161/273-67-26; Mon-Sat 11am-11pm, Sun noon-10:30pm; Cover £3; No credit cards)*, you'll find a surprisingly mellow rustic charm, especially considering it's *the* place to hear punk bands in Manchester. A five-minute walk east of the town center, it attracts strictly a college crowd who like to spend the night banging their heads to some seriously antisocial metal.

Devoted to bringing hip-hop and jazz to the forefront of the Manchester music scene, **Band on the Wall** *(25 Swan St.; Tel 0161/832-66-25)* seems to be doing its job—the crowds here get bigger every weekend. It's located in the Northern Quarter, off Oldham Street.

If you want to get in on the student scene, you gotta head to the source. The **Manchester University Students Union** *(Oxford Rd.; Tel 0161/275-29-30; 9am-11pm daily; Ticket price varies; No credit cards)* offers a range of performances, from jazz to rock to classical. There's drinking on the grounds at the Solem Bar, where pub grub, running about £3-5, is also dished out.

club scene

The Renaissance of music in the north is slowly moving away from Manchester, and the clubs are suffering as a result. Oldham Street in the Northern Quarter isn't cutting-edge anymore; after 11pm, you'll find more people interested in getting pissed and fighting than in the music. Most of the innovation in music is happening on Oxford Street in the Southern Quarter, with University of Manchester students out to create a bigger and better party.

As the top of the trend for clubs right now, the Northern Quarter's **Planet K** *(46-50 Oldham Street; Tel 0161/839-99-41; 10pm-2am daily; Cover varies)* manages to produce quality music, even if a lot of the crowd is more concerned with drinking and how they look than with what the DJ is spinning. A theme night that pops up on Wednesdays called *Loaded* is just that—packed with a wide range of music from Motown to Mogwai. The second Saturday of each month brings the original electronica revolutionaries: Fat City. These clever DJs were throwing the best parties in the city back when most of today's clubbers were still raging at Chuck E. Cheese, and they still carry on with the best of them.

Manchester club-hoppers get started on Friday nights at **South** *(4A South King St.; Tel 0161/831-77-56; 10pm-3am Fri,Sat; Cover £5; No credit cards)*. A 10-minute walk north of Piccadilly Gardens in the NQ, this small industrial club caters to the coolest of the cool, with '60s and '70s music on Friday and red-hot house on Saturday. Beers go for £2.50-3.

Designed for the perfect party, **Elemental** *(45-47 Oxford St.; Tel 0161/236-72-27; 8pm-2am daily; Cover varies)* in the Southern Quarter is a haven for hedonists on Fridays with the ever-popular *Angel Deelite*. They cover all the bases, with old-school disco during the week and drum 'n' bass on weekends. The modern decor is all glass and shiny metal—even the barstools are made of aluminum. No one's sitting down though—the red-eyed crowd spends most of the night on the dance floor.

Underground music nights at **The Music Box** *(65 Oxford St.; Tel 0191/236-99-71; 8pm-2am; Cover varies)*, also in the Southern Quarter, attract the best of England's DJs, with funk so loud it'll make your bones

boy meets girl

Cruisers should stick to the clubs, where people are not only expecting to get picked up, but quite looking forward to it. A tip? Fake an accent. Just don't attempt a Manchester accent—those wily Mancunians aren't so easily fooled.

shake. *Electric Chair,* a packed celebration of eclectic beats with a crowd just as mixed, happens the last Saturday of the month, when the Music Box stays open until 4am.

A 10-minute walk south of Piccadilly Gardens, the aptly named **Generation X** *(11-13 New Wakefield St.; Tel 0161/236-48-99; 11am-midnight Mon-Thur, 11am-2am Fri,Sat; Cover £2-5; MC, V)* is one of the more fashionable bars in Manchester. DJs play a variety of tunes, mostly house music plus drum 'n' bass or soulful soul. Contemporary art from local painters provides the decor, and the mellow lighting conspires with the potent drinks to make everyone look beautiful.

In contrast to some of the holes-in-the-wall that pass for clubs, **Bar 38** *(10 Canal St.; Tel 0161/236-60-05; 10am-2am Mon-Sat; Tapas menu £3-5, No cover; No credit cards)* is known for its award-winning design, with artwork displayed on the bright orange glow of its walls. Weekend DJs play house and disco for a crowd of young polysexual hothouse flowers, and a live funk band steams things up on occasional Thursdays. Just a 2-minute walk west of the center in the Gay Village, it also offers a tasty tapas menu and beers for £2-3.

The Attic *(50 New Wakefield; Tel 0161/236-60-71; 10:30pm-3am Thur-Sat; Cover usually £5; No credit cards),* just southwest of the town center, offers the best of both worlds. The downstairs pub, the Thirsty Scholar, is a chill-space for sweet eye candy. Ascend into The Attic for pure funk/soul chaos, with a college crowd that just keeps dancing.

ARTS SCENE

The new center of the arts in Manchester is the Lowry, on the reborn waterfront at Salford Quays. But almost anywhere you go, you're likely to find an all-in-one arts experience. Many performance halls also showcase art galleries, restaurants, cinemas and even bars, providing the ultimate night out.

▶▶VISUAL ARTS

Located in the Salfrod Quays a mile east of Castlefield, **The Lowry** *(Broadway, Salford; Tel 0191/876-20-00; 9:30am-midnight daily; Free admission)* is one of the most talked-about attractions in town. Its ultra-modern structure, with glass and metallic surfaces designed to reflect the surrounding docklands, may inspire mixed emotions among the locals, but the exhibits inside generate unanimous raves. Intended as an artistic microcosm, it offers more than just galleries—including everything from highbrow theater, ballet, and opera, to audience-friendly jazz, comedy, and cabaret. A restaurant and shops feed visitors literally while feeding the whole enterprise financially.

Beyond the romantic Edwardian facade of **Whitworth Art Gallery** *(56 Whitworth St. West; Tel 0161/950-97-77 or 0161/950-59-00; 10am-5pm Mon-Sat, 2pm-5pm Sun, showtimes 8pm; Free)* in the Southern Quarter, you'll find everything from local paintings to nationally recognized antique wallpaper. Where else can you stare contemplatively at the wallpaper and not have someone nudging you to snap out of it? Even if

down and out

When the quid run dry, there's always the museum. Pick a museum, any museum—but the **Museum of Science and Industry** is your best bet. **The Lowry** is actually worth the admission cost, and you can easily spend the whole day there. In addition to some medieval atmosphere that's almost too authentic, **Chetham's Library and School of Music** also offers free lunchtime concerts for anyone willing to fill their ears with amateur musical experiments. Much of what goes on in the **Castlefield Urban Heritage Park** is absolutely free, and a great way to get to know Manchester, especially if the sun's making one of its rare guest appearances [see *culture zoo*, below, for all].

art isn't your thing, the building itself, with its red Ruabon brick facade, modernist open-plan interiors and Mezzanine floors, is worth a visit.

A tributary off the mainstream, the **Cornerhouse Arts Centre** *(70 Oxford St.; Tel 0161/228-24-63; Cafe 11am-8:30pm daily, galleries 11am-6pm Tues-Sat, 2pm-6pm Sun; Admission free)* is the place to taste the spice of the local arts scene. Anything new and innovative that wanders into town finds its way to this complex southeast of the City Centre. Contemporary paintings, photographs, and sculptures are complemented by international and indie film showings, along with a restaurant [see *eats*, below] and a huge bar offering the occasional live bands.

Run by artists, the **Castlefield Gallery** *(5 Campfield Ave.; Tel 0161/832-80-34; 10:30am-5pm, Tues-Fri, noon-5pm Sat-Sun; Free)* off Deansgate offers exhibitions and education featuring contemporary works, which are, of course, for sale.

▶▶**PERFORMING ARTS**

The Greater Manchester Opera House *(Quay St.; Tel 0161/242-25-09; Tickets £15-£30; V, MC, AE)* offers all the good stuff out of London's West End, as well as any musician popular enough to draw a huge crowd. Located just west of the Town Hall, it's no different than what you'd see in any larger city, but if you're into Victorian theaters, this one, dating back to 1912, is no disappointment.

The Greater Manchester Palace Theatre *(Oxford St.; Tel 0161/242-25-03; Tickets £15-330; V, MC, AE)* in the Southern Quarter is primarily home to the larger touring productions in dance, drama and opera, which you'd think they'd show at the Opera House...go figure.

The massive, modern structure of the **Bridgewater Hall** *(Lower Mosely St.; Tel 0161/907-90-00; 10am-8pm Mon-Sat, noon-6pm Sun;*

Tickets £7-30; Main courses £5- £15; AE, MC, V) is designed to look like a ship and is set on huge springs for better acoustics(!). The Bridge-water offers an earful of musical artistry, with everything from the best of contemporary jazz to the British Philharmonic. It's also home to the internationally acclaimed Hallé Orchestra, dating from 1857, and of the Manchester Camerata, one of the best chamber orchestras in England. Mediterranean cuisine is served at the on-site Charles Hallé Restaurant.

A complex of small theaters, the **Green Room Theatre** *(54-56 Whitworth St. West, Tel 0161/950-57-77 info, 0161/950-59-00 box office; MC, V)* in the Southern Quarter attracts all the best of the local theater scene. The shows are often wild and experimental, so if you're into the abstract, find your way here. The in-house restaurant is great for a quick bite [see *eats,* below].

Instead of pushing travelers on their way, ex-railway station **G-Mex** *(Windmill St.; Tel 0161/834-27-00 info, 0161/832-90-00 box office; www.g-mex.co.uk)* now serves as an entertainment destination. It's just off Deansgate, not far from the Opera House. In addition to attracting all the top touring concerts in the U.K., the G-Mex also hosts sporting events and exhibitions.

gay scene

The gay community in Manchester, made famous by the BBC television show *Queer as Folk* (not smurfy like the American version), offers the liveliest scene outside of London. Although Canal Street, just south of Picadilly Gardens, is becoming better known as the Gay Village, it's still welcoming to straights as well, and is one of the best party neighborhoods in the city for *everybody.* Rough pubs and packed clubs give way to trendy cafe-bars, with more style per square inch than anywhere else in Manchester. Restaurants by day turn into bars by night, all of them packed with a mixed crowd.

Outrageous garb and flashy lights are the ingredients for fun at **Manto** *(46 Canal St.; Tel 0161/236-26-67; 11am-midnight Mon-Thur, 11am-1am Fri, Sat, 6am-2:30am Sun; Cover £5; AE, MC, V)* in the heart of the Gay Village, to the northeast of Princess Street, a five-minute walk from the center. Open into the later hours of the night/earlier hours of the morning, it's known as *the* place for cruising, as well as the place to go to get the latest on Manchester's gay happenings. The purple interior show-cases all the action, with both a dance floor and the chi-chi Sarasota restaurant upstairs, and a lounge area downstairs. Be sure to show up for the *Breakfast Club* in the early hours of Sunday morning, which is quickly becoming a Manchester tradition.

More mixed and mellow, **Via Fossa** *(28-30 Canal St.; Tel 0161/236-65-23; 11am-midnight Sun-Wed, till 2am Thur-Sat, food till 10pm; £2.20 drinks, £4-6.50 entrées; MC, V)* offers classic style, with Gothic church pews and plenty of nooks and crannies to hide away in intimacy. The restaurant serves original fare bordering on the gourmet. At night, relaxation is replaced with more energy and a distinct focus on drinking, but at a comfortable pace.

Not far from Oxford Road in the Southern Quarter, **Paradise Factory** *(112-116 Princess St.; Tel 0161/273-54-22; 10pm-2am Sun-Thur, till 3am Fri, Sat; Cover £3, includes one drink)* offers three floors of dancing and a lounge area. Internet kiosks are also available for clubbers so dissatisfied with the possibilities on the dance floor that they'd rather cruise online.

Down the road from Paradise Factory, the cavernous **Cruz 101** *(101 Princess St.; Tel 0161/237-15-54; 10:30pm-2am Mon, Wed-Sat; Cover £2-5)*, is a members-only club, but don't worry—they offer memberships at the door. There's lots of dancing to '70s and '80s tunes—Monday is the night to come for cruising.

The only club in Manchester that caters specifically to lesbians, the Southern Quarter's **Follies** *(6 Whitworth St.; Tel 0161/236-81-49; 10pm-3am daily)* is more quiet and comfortable than fast and furious. It's perfect for a conversation at the bar or a slow dance with the grrrl of your choice...if you're lucky.

Just to prove that being queer in Manchester is about more than cruising the bars, **Queer Up North** *(48 Princess St.; Tel 0161/228-19-98, Fax 0161/226-77-32)* sponsors one of the world's largest international lesbian and gay arts festivals every two years; the next one's due in 2002.

Two blocks northwest of Canal Street, **Clone Zone** *(36-38 Sackville St.; Tel 0161/236-13-98; 11am-10pm Mon-Thur, 11am-11pm Fri, Sat; 1pm-7pm Sun; AE, MC, V)* is Manchester's gay bookstore; they also sell videos, cards, and other gifts. You can pick up any of the local gay publications here, including the monthly *Gay Times* and weekly *Boyz. City Life*, available at most newsagents, also has a gay and lesbian section.

festivals and events

The **Manchester Food and Drink Festival** *(First week of Oct; Tel 0161/294-19-44)* is perfect for any kind of glutton, with specials and promos citywide. For the more focused glutton, the **N4 Alternative Beer Venues Tour** *(End of May; www.manchester. gov.uk)* highlights everything good about being a fan of fine and oddball ales. Another big event is the **Manchester Arts Festival** *(Last week of July, first week of Aug; Central Library, St. Peters Square; Tel 0161/234-19-64, Fax 0161/236-79-52; mcrfest@libraries. manchester. gov.uk, www.the-manchester-festival.org.uk)*, which celebrates the best that the city's arts scene has to offer in comedy, theater, music, fashion, and even multimedia.

CULTURE ZOO

Like most English cities, Manchester is a city steeped with history, but unlike many of them, it's definitely not stuck in the past. Taking in the local museums and historical sites gives you a sense of the scrappy Mancunians, riding the waves of conquest and technological revolution, changing with the times, but always holding tight to their charm.

Castlefied Urban Heritage Park *(Castlefield Centre, 101 Liverpool Rd.; Tel 0161/834-40-26, Fax 0161/839-87-47; 10am-5pm daily; www.castlefield.org.uk):* The historic center of the city is in Castlefield, where the Romans established their fortress in 79 A.D. This is the place to compare and contrast Manchester throughout the centuries, with the restored Roman fort alongside the Bridgewater Canal, the world's first industrial canal, and its first railway station, now the Museum of Science and Industry. Speaking of which...

Museum of Science and Industry *(Liverpool Rd.; Tel 0161/832-18-30; 10am-5pm daily; Admission £4):* Where else but Manchester would there be a museum devoted to the wonders of the Industrial Revolution? It's actually quite a kick, with hands-on displays and huge working machines clunking away. Once you've seen it with your own eyes, you'll really believe that Manchester is where the modern world was born. Take notes, there may be a pop quiz later.

Chetham's Library and School of Music *(Long Millgate; Tel 0161/834-79-61; 9:30am-12:30pm/1:30pm-4:30pm Mon-Fri; Free):* The oldest public library in the English-speaking world, this Medieval building in the Northern Quarter, dating from 1421, is astounding even to non-bookworms. Legend says that John Dee, the warden of the Collegiate Church in the 1490s, included black magic among his extracurriculars. Check out the large oak desk in the study—the round burn mark on the corner is said to be the devil's hoofprint. You can also head to the Reading Room to gaze upon the detailed woodcarving on Chetham's coat of arms and imagine Karl Marx spouting off on how to change the world—it happened here in the 1840s.

Manchester Cathedral *(Victoria St.; Tel 0161/833-22-20; 8am-6pm daily; Free):* This cathedral may seem small compared to some of the others in England, and maybe it's not as showy as the ones at York or Durham, but it does have some of the best medieval woodwork in all of England. If you're into that sort of thing, take a gander and see if you can find the depiction of rabbits cooking huntsmen. It's at the northern end of the City Centre, at the end of Deansgate.

Manchester Museum *(University of Manchester, Oxford Rd.; Tel 0161/275-26-34; 10am-5pm Mon-Sat; Free):* With displays about the wonders of nature and tributes to once-world-dominating cultures that are now long gone, this run-of-the mill museum in the Southern Quarter is an interesting and cheap way to spend a rainy day. Check out the collection of Egyptian mummies and other spoils brought home from around the world by those plundering British imperialists.

The Pumphouse People's History Museum *(Castlefield, Left Bank, Bridge St.; Tel 0161/275-26-34; 10am-5pm Mon-Sat; Free):* For those with a radical bent, the Pumphouse tells you what was *really* going on with England's unsung working class, from Victorian cotton workers to Yorkshire coal miners. Started as an archive of Britain's Communist party, it remains one of Manchester's most controversial attractions, with exhibits on events like the government's 1819 Peterloo Massacre of union activists. Fight the Power!

The Jewish Museum *(190 Cheetham Hill Rd.; Tel 0161/834-98-79; 10:30am-4pm Mon-Thur, 10:30am-5pm Sun, closed Jewish holidays; Adults £3.25, Students £2.50):* Originally a synagogue built in 1874, this is one of only two museums in England that give you the story on the Jewish community. The recorded voices of immigrants tell you what it was like to be Jewish in Manchester before World War II. It's on Cheetham Hill at the north end of the City Centre.

Granada Studios *(Water St.; Tel 0161/832-49-99; 9:45am-5:30pm Tues-Sun, June-Sept; 9:45am-5:30pm Wed-Sun, Oct-May; £15):* Located in Castlefield, Granada is the studio behind England's popular long-running soap, *Coronation Street,* and some more highbrow productions, like *A Tale of Two Cities,* that have been exported to the U.S. through PBS. The studio tour, which lasts about 45 minutes, recreates live television and movie sets with total accuracy, with a visit to Coronation Street itself as a highlight. Advance reservations are a good idea, as this is one of Manchester's most popular attractions.

modification

The Midlands punk scene has probably done more to popularize body modification—piercings, tattoos, etc.—than any other subculture in the world. The Manchester telephone directory lists literally dozens of tattoo artists, many of whom stay busy day in and day out. The most celebrated is Mr. Rambo Ramsbottom, owner of **Rambo of Manchester** *(42 Shude Hill; Tel 0161/839-00-90; 11am-4pm daily; No credit cards),* a few hundred yards north of the cathedral. He counts the ornamented bodies of Spice Girls, Manchester United soccer players, and every member of the Australian rugby team among his masterpieces. Tattoos begin at £20, but go up into the thousands—this is true art. Tribal patterns and Celtic designs are a specialty.

For a less drastic makeover that won't risk anything more than your hair follicles, head to Affleck's Palace and into **Under Your Hat** *(Affleck's Palace, 52 Church St.; Tel 0161/832-16-92; 10am-5:30pm Mon-Fri, 10am-6pm Sat),* which offers cuts and specializes in all types of extensions and waves. Rock star wannabes can spend as much as £60 to get the works, but you can get a simple trim for far less.

city sports

Thanks to the pollution and congestion of downtown Manchester, most hyperactive sports junkies head to the outskirts for bike riding and jogging. One of the best recreation spots is **Platfelds Park,** on the northern outskirts of town, accessible via Bus 43 from the City Centre. Jog, bicycle, and, weather permitting, soak up some rays. (Sun? In Manchester?) To rent a cyle, you'll have to travel a few miles northwest of the City Centre, to the leafy suburb of Macclesfield, and **Bollington Cycle Hire** [see *need to know,* below].

STUFF

If that cash is burning a hole in your pocket, Manchester offers just about anything you could want to buy. Most shopping is near the City Centre. The chichi boutiques are on St. Ann's Square and King Street, off Deansgate, while the big chain stores are on the mostly all-pedestrian Market Street, which funnels into Picadilly. But you should really head to Picadilly and Oldham Streets in the North Quarter, where there are bargains to be had. All the club kids go for the one-stop shopping at alternative shrine Affleck's Palace, on the corner of Oldham and Church Streets. No relation to Ben, this shopping mecca provides four floors of consumer bliss, with 50 of the most widely varied shops in town.

▶▶DUDS

Fashionistas should head for St. Ann's Square and King Street. **Flannel's** *(68-78 Vicar Lane and 7-11 Cross Arcade; Tel 0161/834-94-42; 9am-5:30pm Mon-Sat, noon-5pm Sun)* offers two locations in the area, with clothes a bit more cutting-edge than the lumberjack staple the name suggests. Whether you're into DKNY, CK, D&G, or some other acronym, you'll find it here.

▶▶CLUBGEAR

Outrageous is the word at **The Strawberry Patch** *(Affleck's Palace, 52 Church St.; Tel. 0161/839-11-10; 10am-5:30pm Mon-Fri, 10am-6pm Sat)* the venue for reflective clothing, platform shoes, studded necklaces,

fashion

Manchester is probably one of the only places in the country where all kinds mix together, so fashion ranges from suit-wearing punks to skate-boarding hippies. There is a strong punk crowd, so chains, spikes, blue hair and black head-to-toe are common, but you'll often catch punks hanging out with cutting-edge fashion divas decked out in London's finest. Attitude is everything: even if you're a little dog, just act like a big dog and you'll fit right in.

and everything you'll need to make someone's worst-dressed list. From black body paint to glow sticks, the Strawberry Patch brings you club couture at its fruity best.

▶▶TUNES

If you're looking for a vinyl fix, you're in luck—the **Vinyl Exchange** *(18 Oldham St.; Tel 0161/228-11-22; 10am-6pm Mon-Sat, noon-5pm Sun)* in the NQ is the largest secondhand CD and record store in England. Typical radioheads will get lost amidst the 25,000 selections in stock, searching for those long-lost beats they can't live without. You can also find secondhand music stalls near Picadilly Station, along Church Street. If you prefer brand-spanking new to used, there's always the enormous and shiny **Virgin Megastore** *(52-56 Market St.; Tel 0161/833-11-11 9am-6pm Mon-Sat, 9am-7pm Thur, 11am-5pm Sun)*, but really, don't you get enough of megastores back home?

▶▶BOUND

Frontline Books *(255 Wilmslow Rd.; Tel 0161/249-02-02, Fax 0161/249-02-03; Noon-7pm Tue-Fri, 10am-5pm Sat, 1pm-5pm Sun)*, which bills itself as "Manchester's only radical bookstore," is chock full of edgy stuff and alternative mags. It's in Rusholme, south of the Southern Quarter.

▶▶USED AND BRUISED

Want to go retro? Head for **American Graffiti** *(Affleck's Palace, 52 Church St.; No phone; 10am-5:30pm Mon-Fri, 10am-6pm Sat)* named after the 1970s movie classic. Golden oldies range from £2 for a beaded hippie-chick necklace to £20 for a vintage RAF bomber jacket from WWII.

▶▶FOOT FETISH

Isel 4 Life *(Affleck's Palace, 52 Church St.; Tel 0161/834-10-77; 10am-5:30pm Mon-Fri, 10am-6pm Sat)* does for your feet what the Strawberry Patch does for your body. The inventory ranges from brand-name designer shoes to hiking boots-a-go-go. Some of the wilder creations are simply not suitable for the unsuspecting middlebrow public. You have been warned.

EATS

If you're spending a lot of time in the North, Manchester will be your only chance for relief from English pub food, so take advantage of it while you can. Dining options are as diverse as the city itself, with Turkish, Arabic, Mediterranean, Chinese...you get the idea. Of course, if you're into fish & chips or kidney pies, there are plenty of places for that, too (mmm, kidneys...). Many of the cheaper places are in the Southern Quarter near the university; students and cheap food go together like bangers and mash.

▶▶CHEAP

Finally, a dish that's not mooing at you! **The Eighth Day Vegetarian Café** *(107-111 Oxford Rd.; Tel 0161/273-18-50; 9am-7pm Mon-Sat; £5 per entrée; www.eighth-day.co.uk; V)* in the Southern Quarter serves veggie

TO MARKET

Arndale Center is the main marketplace, with a shiny new interior. Designer shops on one end clash with penny bazaars and cheap food on the other. The **Arndale Market** *(Market St.; Tel 0161/234-73-57; 8am-4pm Mon-Sat)* in the City Centre is one of the largest bazaars around, with over 100 stalls selling everything from roots to boots.

and vegan fare that might as well have been cooked up in heaven. The menu ranges from salads and spinach quiches to Mediterranean special-ties like tabouleh and houmous, with baklava for dessert.

With a preponderance of young actors and models among its clien-tele, the **Green Room Theater Café** *(54-56 Whitworth St. West; Tel 0161/950-57-77; 11am to 11pm daily; £3.50-5 main courses; MC, V)*, is the place to watch your figure—and everyone else's. The attached theater [see *arts scene,* above] adds to the stylish high-drama ambience. No wor-ries about Mad Cow disease here; the chefs don't even stock red meat. The menu is dominated by succulent pastas, fresh seafood, and vege-tarian options, along with a selection of homemade soups and open-faced sandwiches.

The eclectic menu at the **Corner House Café** *(70 Oxford St.; Tel 0161/228-76-21; 10am-8:30pm daily; £3.50-4.50 main courses; MC, V)*, located in the Cornerhouse Arts Centre [see *arts scene,* above] is as young as today—nothing too exciting, but no disappointments either. Select from an array of freshly made soups, salads, and pastas. With the attached galleries, theaters, and bar, it's a popular choice for starting an evening out.

A fierce Little India exists along Winslow Road in Rusholme. Choices are everywhere: the streets are lined with colorful shops and cheap restau-rants. Dodge the hawking shop owners yelling for a sale and duck into the exceptional **Tandoori Kitchen** *(131-133 Winslow Rd.; Tel 0161/224-23-29; Noon-2:30pm/5pm-midnight Mon-Fri, Noon-midnight Sat, 1pm-11pm Sun)*. They offer Indian, Persian, and Iranian cuisine. Try the podina lamb or Khoresteh Lapeh Spinach.

▶▶DO-ABLE

Rustic and traditional, **Belle Pasta** *(Deansgate and St. Mary's St.; Tel 0161/832-43-32; 11am-midnight daily; £4-10 main courses; AE, MC, V* is an Italian restaurant designed for mere mortals, not gods and goddesses. Good, cheap Italian eats, from pasta dishes to an endless selection of

manchester

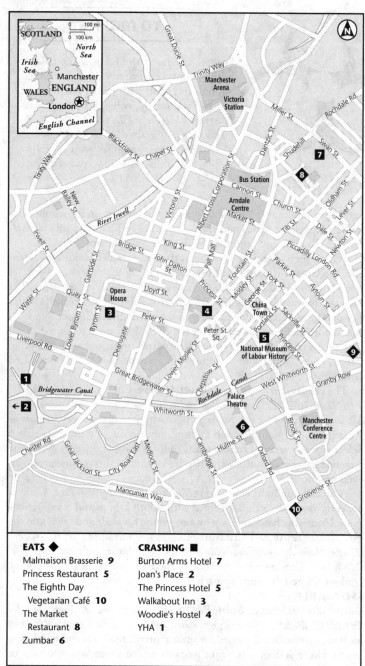

EATS ◆

Malmaison Brasserie **9**
Princess Restaurant **5**
The Eighth Day
  Vegetarian Café **10**
The Market
  Restaurant **8**
Zumbar **6**

CRASHING ■

Burton Arms Hotel **7**
Joan's Place **2**
The Princess Hotel **5**
Walkabout Inn **3**
Woodie's Hostel **4**
YHA **1**

pizzas, are happily devoured by crowds of students. If you're feeling a little more swank, try the seafood of the day.

For Mediterranean delights, it's **Dimitri's** *(1 Campfield Arcade; Tel 0161/839-33-19; 11am-11pm Mon-Sat, Sun noon-10:30pm; Reservations recommended; £3-6 entrées; AE, MC, V)* all the way. Italian and Spanish fare, including a tapas menu, are available, but go for the Greek delicacies Dimitri's serves up nightly, which include some of the best veggie dishes in Manchester. On weekends, you can sit at the bar with a savory Greek coffee and listen to a live jazz band. Located in the City Centre, Dimitri's is so popular you should call at least a day ahead to get a table.

Yang Sing *(34 Princess St.; Tel 0161/236-22-00; Noon-midnight daily; £3-9 main courses; AE, MC, V)*, off Portland Street in Chinatown, serves the best Cantonese food in Manchester. A young, sophisticated crowd eats up the authentic, traditional cuisine, which ranges from delectable lobster with black bean sauce that's worth celebrating to Chinese greens that are a meal in themselves. Call in advance for the city's best Peking duck.

The inarticulate, mostly indifferent service keeps **Pearl City** *(33 George St.; Tel 0161/228-76-83; Noon-midnight daily; £4-6.50 main courses; AE, MC, V)*, from really competing with Yang Sing to be the best Cantonese restaurant in Manchester. Also in Chinatown, it's just a few blocks off Portland Street, via Nicholas Street. If you can get the aloof waiters to warm up to you, you'll be treated to some authentic and unusual Cantonese dishes with the freshest of ingredients. The roast duckling is superb.

Although it's been described as a mainly Arabic cafe-bar, exotic food from just about *anywhere* is available at **Zumbar** *(14 Oxford Rd.; Tel 0161/236-84-38; Noon-11:30pm daily; £5-10 per entrée; V, MC)* in the Southern Quarter. Zumbar means "to buzz," and as the name suggests, you'll get an eclectic, exciting meal and a helping of contagious energy. Vegetarian options are plentiful—try a vegan burger served up with potato wedges.

If you can't stomach the spice, head over to the restaurant at the **Princess Hotel** *(101 Portland St.; Tel 0161/236-51-22; 9am-9:30pm daily; £5-8.50 per entrée; V, MC)* near the Picadilly Gardens, where traditional English food is all they know. They do it well.

▶▶**SPLURGE**
Decorated in a vaguely Mediterranean style, **Café Istanbul** *(79 Bridge St.; Tel 0161/833-99-42; Noon-3pm/5-11pm daily; £8.50-12 main courses; MC, V)* evokes an old Marlene Dietrich flick you'd catch on the late, late show, and it offers the best Turkish cuisine in Manchester. The young, well-traveled crowd that comes to this savory spot off Deansgate in search of exotic flavor is never disappointed. The selection of *meze* (starters) alone is worth the trek here, but the lamb kebabs and grilled seafood are equally tantalizing. The wine list is extensive and reasonable.

With 25 years of service under its belt, **The Market Restaurant** *(104 High St.; Tel 0161/834-37-43; 6pm-9:30pm Wed-Sat; £9.96-15.95* *main courses; V, MC, AE, DC),* proves that experience pays off. Set in a 19th-century industrial building, the Market offers a constantly rotating menu that varies from earthy British standards to Cajun to Far Eastern. For the traditional British dining experience, try roast filet of lamb with "bubble and squeak" (that's potatoes and cabbage to yanks), with rhubarb crumble ice cream for dessert. Cheers! It's quite a trek, northeast of the City Centre; while you can take Metrolink to Victoria or Picadilly Station and hoof it from there, it's probably best to take a cab.

crashing

Manchester knows how to suck money from your pocket as quickly as any big city. Thank God for hostels—these cheap little digs will save you dough so you can spend it on the more important things, like getting into the clubs. If you're having trouble finding a bed, the tourist office [see *need to know,* below] can help you out.

▶▶**CHEAP**

Right at groundzero of the parties in the NQ, **Woodie's Hostel** *(19 Blossom St., off Ancoats; Tel 0161/228-34-56; £11 per person, shared bath; www.woodiesuk.freeserve.co.uk)* offers all the comforts a backpacker could need. With a large common room and plenty of people who are always willing to party, there's also a good chance you'll make some friends at no extra charge. It's also convenient to transportation, not far from Victoria and Picadilly Stations.

A little southeast of Castlefield in a neighborhood with potential, the **YHA** *(Potato Wharf; Tel 0161/839-99-60; £17.40 per person, private baths; No credit cards)* provides brand-new rooms, all with private baths. It's a little impersonal and less efficient than other hostels, but a cheap night's stay just the same.

Another kind hostel, **Joan's Place** *(41-43 Great Stone Rd.; Tel 0161/834-20-39; £8-10 mixed dorm, £14 single, £25 double, £36 triple, shared baths; No credit cards)* is a metro stop out of town, an eight-minute ride to Old Tafford Station. It's right next to the Manchester United Football grounds; you can't miss it. The proprietor will fill your ears for hours with a wealth of information on the history and bright future of Manchester—who needs a museum when you've got Joan?

If Joan's Place is full up, try nearby **Peppers** *(17 Great Stone Rd., Stretford; Tel 0161/848-97-70; £10 per person 4-bed dorm, £14 single, £20 double, £25 triple, shared baths; continental breakfast extra; pepper59@hot mail.com; No credit cards).*

A few more cheap and reliable options include the **International Backpackers Hostel** *(64 Cromwell Rd.; Tel 0161/865-92-96; £11 dorm beds, £15 singles, £30 doubles with private bath; No credit cards),* six minutes on the Metrolink to Stretford near the Manchester United football stadium; **Green Gables Guest House** *(152 Barlow Moor Rd.; Tel 0161/445-53-65, Fax 0161/445-53-63; £30-£40 doubles);* or the **University of Manchester** housing *(The Precinct Centre, Oxford Rd.; Tel 0161/275-28-88),* available only in the summer months, call for details.

▶▶DO-ABLE

For a few extra bucks, and a slightly longer walk into the Northern Quarter, the **Burton Arms Hotel** *(31 Swan St.; Tel 0161/834-34-55; £22 single, £40 double, en suite available, TV; No credit cards)* will give you a bed with your very own four walls. It's a short stumbling distance to the old-world pub on the ground floor, and the bend-over-backwards friendly proprietors will leave you well rested for your next day of partying.

Other options close to the City Centre are along Liverpool Road: **The Commercial Hotel** *(125 Liverpool Rd.; Tel 0161/834-35-04, Fax 0161/835-27-25; £25 single, £35 double, private baths, £3.50 breakfast; No credit cards)* is just a 10-minute walk from the train station. The hotel formerly known as the Oxnoble, **The Ox** *(71 Liverpool Rd.; Tel 0161/839-77-40, Fax 0161/839-77-60; £44.95 double, £59.95 triple, private baths, £5 breakfast, david@theox.co.uk, www.theox.co.uk; V, MC)* is just a few minutes walk from the Deansgate metro stop.

Close to Victoria Station and just a quick cab away from Picadilly, the **Cornerhouse Hotel** *(Gravel Lane, Greengate; Tel 0161/833-02-72; £12 single, £18 en suite single, £30 double)* is also a 5-10 minute walk from the City Centre. **The Grafton Hotel** *(56-58 Grafton St.; Tel 0161/273-30-92, Fax 0161/274-36-93; £22.50 single, £27.50 en suite single, £37.50-£47.50 double, £52.50 triple, £67.50 quad; No credit cards)* is about a mile from the City Centre, accessible by taxi or bus lines 40 and 49. **The Rembrandt** *(33 Sackville St.; Tel 0161/236-13-11, Fax 0161/236-42-57; £35-45 single, £40-50 double, £45-55 triple, £50-60 quad; rembrandthotel@aol.com, www.therembrandthotel.co.uk; V, MC, AE)* is in the Gay Village, a 10-minute walk from Picadilly Station.

▶▶SPLURGE

An Australian bar and disco that also rents out rooms, the **Walkabout Inn** *(13 Quay St.; Tel 0161/817-48-00; £39.95 flat rate, en suite, breakfast £6.70; V, MC)* is conveniently located off Deansgate, near the **G Mex** [see *arts scene*, above]. Go into the bar and head down the side stairs to the reception area in the basement. Clubbing goes on Thursday through Saturday, so if you're looking for a good night's sleep, ask for a room on the fourth floor. (And if you're not, of course, you should head on down and see if you can keep up with the Aussies.) Each room offers a private bathroom, which is always a plus.

need to know

Currency Exchange Your best bet for changing cash is department store **Marks & Spencer** *(7 Market St.; Tel 0161/831-73-41, Fax 0161/246-11-61; 9am-4pm Mon-Wed, 9am-8pm Thur, 9am-6:30pm, 8:30am-6:30pm Sat, 11am-5pm Sun),* northwest of Picadilly Gardens. With no commission, a decent exchange rate, and hours all week long, this place beats the bank hands down.

Tourist Information The **Manchester Visitor Information Center** *(Town Hall Extension, Lloyd St.; Tel 0161/234-31-57; 10am-5:30pm Mon-Sat, 11am-4pm Sun; www.manchester.gov.uk/visitorcentre)* in the

Town Hall maintains a large pool of information on all things Mancunian, so feel free to dive right in. They'll also help you find a bed to rest your weary, hungover head.

Public Transportation Metrolink *(Tel 0161/205-20-00)* trams run every six minutes most days, every 15 minutes on Sundays. Both east-west and north-south lines originate at **Piccadilly Railway Station,** on the southeastern perimeter of the City Centre, before linking with **Piccadilly Gardens Station** *(Market St.; Tel 0161/228-78-11),* a short ride to the northwest. From there, one line (the **Altrincham** line) heads north, while the other (the **Bury** line) runs south, connecting the far-flung suburbs with the city's inner core. The subway costs £2 per ride; you can also buy a daily ticket for £3 that's good for all trains during the day. An all-day **Wayfarer bus pass** costs £6.60, but you're better off sticking to the metro if you can. Tickets are available from the bus driver. Fares range from £1-3, depending on how far you travel. Timetables, bus routes, and fare information are available at **The Kiosk** information booth in the Picadilly Gardens bus station. When the metro and trams stop running at midnight, most kids use the **night buses.** You can also call **Centre Cars** *(Tel 0161/723-13-02)* or **New Link Private Hire** *(Tel 0161/445-33-99).*

American Express You'll find your friendly **Amex** *(10 Saint Mary's Gate, Tel 0161/833-73-03; 9am-5pm daily)* in the City Centre.

Health and Emergency Emergency: *999.* **Manchester Royal Infirmary and Royal Eye Hospital** *(Oxford Rd., adjacent to Nelson St.; Tel 0161/276-12-34),* near the University of Manchester, offers medical attention.

Pharmacies Get to **Cameocord** *(7 Oxford St.; Tel 0161/236-14-45, 8am-midnight daily)* in the Southern Quarter to fill that prescription.

Airports The **international airport** *(Tel 0161/489-80-00 or 0161/489-30-00)* is 15 miles south of the City Centre, just a train or taxi ride away. The **Airport Link** train connects the airport to the **Piccadilly Railway Station** *(Market St.; Tel 0345/484-950).* Trains leave every 15 minutes, 5:15-10:10pm, with the whole trip taking about 25 minutes. Buses 44 and 105 also run between the airport and Picadilly Gardens, but the ride takes 55 minutes. If you'd rather just give up and call a cab, try **Airtax** *(Tel 0161/499-90-00).*

Trains Trains run from **Piccadilly Station** *(Market St.; Tel 0345/484-950).* Direct lines are available to Edinburgh, Liverpool, and Windermere.

Bus Lines Out of Town **National Express** *(Tel 0161/228-78-11 or 0990/808-080)* runs frequent buses from **Chorlton Street station** in the City Centre. You can also catch a bus from London to Manchester at **Victoria Coach Station.**

Laundry There's really nowhere convenient to wash your duds in the City Centre, so if you're feeling grubby, head over to the Student Center at the **University of Manchester** *(Oxford Rd., first floor of the Student Union; Tel 0161/275-29-30).*

Bike Rental There aren't any cycle rental places in the center of Manchester, and with all of the traffic and carbon monoxide about, cycling in the City Centre isn't really recommended anyway. But if you're willing to trek to the northern suburb of Macclesfield, **Bollington Cycle Hire** *(Grimshaw Lane, Bollington, call for directions before you go; Tel 01625/572-681, Fax 01625/574-160; 10:30am-6pm Mon-Fri, Jul 6-Aug 31; Noon-6pm Sat, 10:30am-6pm Sun, Easter-Nov)* can hook you up.

Postal Get those cards and letters moving at the **Whitworth post office** *(48-50 Whitworth St.; Tel 0845/722-33-44; 9am-5:30pm Mon-Fri, till 1pm Sat),* located in the Southern Quarter.

Internet See *wired,* above.

liverpool

Wherever you go in this city the Fab Four are still playing—they're standard on every dang jukebox. There are Beatles tours, Beatles historical sights, Beatles gift shops, etc, etc. There seems to be no successful therapy for Liverpool's Beatlemania [see *the fab tour,* below], and everyone here simply loves them, although some locals are getting pretty annoyed with tourists who keep asking how they can get to Penny Lane.

You'd never guess it from the city's marketing machine, but Liverpool actually predates the Beatles. Norsemen lived here along the River Mersey on the northwestern coast of England as early as the year 1000, and King John put the place on the map by chartering the city's seaport (hence the wafting fishy-smell from time-to-time) in 1207. Liverpool fast became the most important commercial seaport in the country, and remained so up into World War II, when the now-chic Albert Dock served as headquarters for Allied Troops in the Battle of the Atlantic. Some time after that, four spirited young lads picked up their instruments and...oops. (See how seductive those fellas can be?)

Today Liverpool does its best to present itself as a world-class city, with museums, galleries, cafes, clubs, and two cathedrals to brag about [see *culture zoo,* below]. Another post-industrial city trying to scrub the soot off its buildings, Liverpool is sailing on a second wind after some serious renovation. The once gray Albert Dock has been decorated with chic cafes, bars, restaurants, and shops, even as a new **Maritime Museum** celebrates the seaport's history [see *culture zoo,* below]. This reborn Quayside area has inspired other development as well, so construction still runs rampant in all parts of the city.

WIRED

There's a city website at *www.visitliverpool.com,* but it's confusing and hard to follow; you'll probably be better off at *www.merseyworld.com* or *www.liverpoolguide.co.uk,* which are more helpful. For info on everything Beatles-related, there's *http://beatle-city.merseyworld.com.*

As far as technological advancement goes, Liverpool is still waiting in line, but they do have one Internet cafe in town: **Planet Electra** *(36 London Rd.; Tel 0151/708-03-03; 9am-11pm daily; www.planetelectra.com; £1.50 per hour).* Located at the juncture of Lime Street and London Road, one block north of Lime Street Station, the Planet offers a few computers and excellent food.

Liverpool takes great pride in its reputation as Music City, and while local clubs live in the engulfing shadow of the Beatles, they can bump and grind with the best of 'em. DJ mavericks like Fatboy Slim have made **Cream** [see *club scene,* below] world-famous as ground-zero of Northern England's techno explosion. Students from the local John Moores and Liverpool universities fuel the fire, and it's not extinguished till 3am, pretty unusual in asleep-by-eleven England.

The people here call themselves Scousers (although Liverpudlians does have a nice ring to it). Just ask anyone from the rival city Manchester, and they'll tell you that Scousers have a serious inferiority complex. This might explain why they tend to keep to themselves—you may have a hard time getting anyone in Liverpool to talk to you at all. Or maybe it's just that it's a large urban area with its share of crime, so locals don't let strangers in too easily. But that attitude definitely changes when you find yourself in the middle of an impromptu block party in the Artistic Quarter. Something about walking back and forth from pub to club makes people quite talkative. Go figure. So take the time, make the effort, and get to know some locals, and you'll discover that what Manchester mistakes for self-pity is actually a brand of wry self-deprecating Liverpudlian humor. Even back when the Beatles were more popular than Jesus, Scousers knew themselves well enough to know they weren't all that. Yeah, yeah, yeah.

L:Scene magazine and the free *City XBlag,* available at most clubs and pubs, provide info on the club scene, and the afternoon newspaper, *Liverpool Echo* is hawked at news kiosks for 30p.

neighborhoods

With lots of winding streets that sometimes change names and direction, Liverpool can confuse the hell out of you. The **City Centre** is roughly

five things to talk to a local about

1. **Home of the Beatles:** That will either cause a local to rant about how great they are or want to kill yet another tourist asking a stupid question about the Fab Four. Either way, you still got them to talk to you.
2. **Football:** This *is* England, you know; the Liverpool vs. Everton game is a particularly loaded subject. Someone decided it would be wise to build their stadiums within view of each other, and the two teams have been rivals ever since.
3. How confusing this city is, how long they have lived there and, hey **where the hell am I, anyway?**
4. **Construction:** Will it ever end, and if it does, will it improve anything?
5. **This place gets a bad rap:** The locals want to change that. It's deserving of a better reputation than it has, so give a local a chance.

defined by **Albert Dock** on the banks of the River Mersey in the west, and **Lime Street Station** in the east. Neighborhoods are also only roughly defined, and sometimes seem to run together. **Great George Street,** which leads into **Renshaw Street,** divides the town from north to south. **Hanover Street,** which becomes **Ranelagh Street,** splits the town from east to west. A quick tour may be helpful to orient yourself. Start at Albert Dock, the site of a tourist office and many of the city's new bars and tourist attractions, including the **Tate Gallery** [see *culture zoo,* below], and **The Beatles Story** [see *the fab tour,* below]. From here, you can walk anywhere in the City Centre within about a half-hour.

First, head north onto **The Strand,** which is the main street running up the west end to **Water Street.** From Water Street, head in an easterly direction until you reach **John Street** and the Cavern Quarter. Just off John Street is **Mathew Street,** ground zero of Liverpool's continuing Beatles explosion. From Albert to Mathew is just a 10-minute walk.

From Albert Dock you can also take Hanover Street to **Duke Street,** heading in a southeasterly direction to reach the **Cathedral Church of Christ** (a 15-minute walk), or head north on **Berry Street,** leading into Renshaw Street. The Roman Catholic **Metropolitan Cathedral** is another half-mile south down **Hope Street** [see *culture zoo,* below for both].

That's all fine and good, you say, but where do I get a drink in this town? No problem: walk east from Albert Dock onto Hanover Street and continue in a southeast direction onto **Bold Street.** This is known as the **Artistic or University Quarter,** home to the best pubs and clubs. The intersection of Bold Street, **Fleet Street** (both east-west), and **Concert Street** (north-south) is known as **Concert Square.**

hanging out

The **Cavern Quarter** is a popular hangout area, not really for young Scousers (they've long ago seen everything here), but for young visitors to the city, especially those with an appreciation of John, Paul, George, and Ringo. Currently, come nightfall, the sounds of music on Mathew Street are replaced by drunken jock-types, known as "slappers," moving from club to pub and back again. The pubs and clubs in the Artistic Quarter are a bit more sophisticated, frequented by students, boho hipsters, and those who love them.

bar scene

Seems like every industrial city in Northern England was visited by the same urban renewal guru, whose mantra was "Build the cafe-bars, and they will come." These stylie little cosmopolitan joints are everywhere, with their slick, colorful decor and their overpriced drinks. But the food is tasty, and so are the patrons, so put on your game face and go for it.

See the moneymakers living the high life at the **Blue Bar** *(17 Edward-Pavilion; Tel 0151/709-70-97; Noon-midnight Mon-Thur, till 2am Fri, Sat, food served noon-2:30pm/6-10pm)* on Albert Dock, where you can expect everyone to be dressed to the hilt, the better to fit in with the angular, ultramodern surroundings. Draws include a selection of high-brow beers, wines, and cocktails (around £2.50), Cuban and Dominican cigars, and the chance to catch a peek at the elite (expect attitude). Until 9pm, the upstairs is devoted to serving up fantastic California fusion cuisine, along with international tapas and just-so desserts (£6.25-11 per entrée). Face it, everything looks good from a balcony seat.

You can never go wrong with an innovator, as long as it keeps up. In

fashion

Fashion? In Liverpool? You won't find anything ultra-trendy or high society here—even the club-goers are a little more laid-back. T-shirts and jeans are the norm. During the day, most people wear dark and lifeless clothes to try to blend in with the soot of the buildings. Come to think of it, they may actually be covered with soot....

the fab tour

Beatlemania lives in Liverpool, and it's not going away anytime soon. **The Beatles Story** *(Britannia Vaults; Tel 0151/709-19-63; 10am-6pm daily; £6.95)* on Albert Dock offers an interesting and entertaining history of the Fab Four. There's even a yellow submarine with live fish swimming by the portholes, but it still may not be worth the pricey admission, especially if you're already familiar with John, Paul, George, and Ringo. **Cavern City Tours** *(Central Building, 41 North John St; Tel 0151/236-90-91; £8.50)* offers the 2-hour *Magical Mystery Tour,* leaving from Albert Dock at 2:20pm and Clayton Square at 2:30pm. It takes you around to everything made famous by those rock'n' roll insects, including their birthplaces and former homes. The **McCartney House** *(20 Fortlin Rd., Allerton 16; Tel 0870/900-02-56 info, 0151/708-85-74 booking; Noon-5pm Wed-Sat, Mar31-Oct; Sat only, Nov-Dec; £5 adult, £2.60 child),* where Paul spent his childhood, was named a historic site by the National Trust, and has been restored to its original 1950s condition, right down to the patterns on the ugly sofa and the shabby wallpaper. For hard-core Beatlemaniacs only, it's hardly Graceland (but then, there's only *one* Elvis).

Into the Beatles but not enough to spend a quid? Take a walk down Mathew Street where you can browse around the **John Lennon Gallery and Beatles Shop** *(Mathew St.; Tel 0151/236-00-09; 10am-5pm Mon-Sat, 11am-4pm Sun; Free).* Containing a gallery full of Lennon's artwork, and sadly only a few rare Beatles tunes, this may be the only place you can sample something Beatles-related without a fee.

Had enough of the Beatles tourist-machine? Hungry for some real Beatles history? Check out the **Jacaranda Club** *(20-23 Slater St.; Tel*

the Artistic Quarter, the **Baa Bar** *(43 Fleet St.; Tel 0151/707-06-10 or 0151/708-68-10; 11am-11pm Mon-Thur, till midnight Fri, Sat, Noon-10:30pm Sun)* was Liverpool's first designer bar, serving as the model for all of the others to come. It's the main launch pad for ravers intent on heading off to **Cream** [see *club scene,* below] as the night wears on. Exposed beams and welded metal furniture give Baa Bar style creds, but the cheap booze and music, ranging from jazz to soul to pounding house, are what keep 'em coming back.

A couple of blocks northeast of Baa Bar, **XS** *(80A Bold St.; Tel 0151/709-48-88; 11am-2am daily;)* lives up to its name, taking style over the top. Minimalist design with simple shapes and colors offers a contrast to the atmosphere of overindulgence the name suggests. With pints priced at £1.50, drinking to excess quickly becomes the rule, not

0151/708-94-24; Noon-2am Mon-Sat, noon-10:30pm Sun) in the Artistic Quarter, where the lads played before they made it big. Once owned by the group's original manager, Allan Williams, it's not a tourist trap like the Cavern Club, but remains pretty much what it was all those years ago. Still adorning the walls are funky murals painted by Stu Sutcliffe (the Beatle who left the group before they made it big) with a little help from his friend, John Lennon. Check out the eerie red and yellow eye above the stage.

Looking for the inspirations for John and Paul's lyrics? **Strawberry Field** is now a Salvation Army children's home. John Lennon and Yoko Ono were among its most generous benefactors. Head east down Menlove Avenue from the City Centre if you're interested in staring past the iron gates; you won't be allowed inside. Meanwhile, Smithdown Place, at the end of **Penny Lane,** is now a busy intersection, packed with taxis and buses. The only thing that will be "in your ears and in your eyes" is carbon monoxide. The statue of **Eleanor Rigby,** sitting on a bench on Stanley Street near Mathew Street, may be more worthy of your time. She's dedicated to "all the lonely people," who sometimes leave her flowers.

Over 100,000 not-so-lonely people attend the **International Beatles Festival** during the last week of August, where bands with names like Lenny Pane and Wings Over Liverpool cover Lennon and McCartney tunes. Contact Cavern CityTours [see above] for details.

the exception. Even the bartenders have been known to become victims of their own wares...

Undergrads tend to flock wherever the drink is cheap and the food is greasy, so **Qube** (67 Wood St.; No phone; 8am-10pm Mon-Sat), despite being a bit of a dive—or perhaps because of it—has also become a students' haven. This little venue in the Artistic Quarter at the end of Back Colquitt Street acts as a pre-clubbing meeting ground.

LIVE MUSIC SCENE

As the club where John, Paul, George, and Ringo got their start, the **Cavern Club** (8-10 MathewSt.; Tel 0151/236-19-62; 11am-midnight Sun-Tue, till 2am Wed-Sat; £3cover) bills itself as "the most famous club in the world." Truth is, the original club actually closed in 1973 to meet

Liverpool

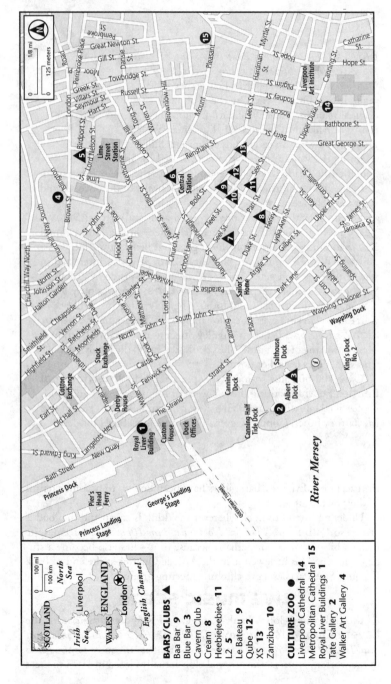

BARS/CLUBS ▲

Baa Bar **9**
Blue Bar **3**
Cavern Club **6**
Heebiejeebies **11**
L2 **5**
Le Bateau **9**
Qube **12**
XS **13**
Zanzibar **10**

CULTURE ZOO ●

Liverpool Cathedral **14**
Metropolitan Cathedral **15**
Royal Liver Buildings **1**
Tate Gallery **2**
Walker Art Gallery **4**

rules of the game

As with anywhere else in England, drugs are illegal, so don't get caught with them and try not to make it obvious that you're under the influence. As for being drunk in the streets, you can be pretty obnoxious to a bobbie before he gets out of his riot van and cuffs you—but don't take that as a challenge.

an ignoble end as the most famous parking lot in the world. The new club, opened in 1984, is an exact replica of the original and is actually next door to the aforementioned parking lot, so observe a moment of silence as you cross that asphalt. The Beatles' mojo lives on in the new club—the place has since made a cottage industry out of their legacy, sponsoring all kinds of Beatles-related tours and events [see *the fab tour,* above]. The staff is the friendliest you'll find in any bar in the city. The club also sports a Wall of Fame which names all the bands who played there in the good ol' days, but it's not exactly on the music forefront any more. Stop by late in the afternoon for a beer and a chat, between sound checks of course, with whichever live band they have playing that night. If you like what you hear, it may be worth coming back for the show.

Instead of always following the whims of popular science, the bookers at the **L2** *(11-13 Hotham St.; Tel 0151/707-99-77; 9.30pm-2am Fri,Sat, occasional weeknights; £5 cover)* stick to high-quality sounds, so you're guaranteed a good show. If you want to be a part of the "I saw them when..." club, wiggle your way over to this largest of the small clubs, across from the Lime Street Station off Lord Nelson Street, because, as the Fab Four have proven, up-and-coming bands don't stay up-and-coming for long.

club scene

All the clubs host a number of nights ranging from Oasis-esque pop bands to heavy techno. For music that will get you moving, shake it on down to the Artistic Quarter (right around Bold and Seel streets), where students search for beats to accompany the light bubbly that passes for beer around here.

Club anthems rule the night at the world-famous **Cream** *(Wolstenholme Sq.; Tel 0151/709-16-93; 10pm-4am daily; £13 cover),* the epicenter of Liverpool's youthquake, where Fatboy Slim and the rest of the DJ elite occasionally hang their hats. If you actually want to get inside the enormous warehouse club, near the corner of Parr and Slater Streets, make your attempt before the other bars close. Infamous for its crowds, cheap beer, and wall-to-wall students, this top-of-the-line club feels more like a huge college party with a great sound system. Dance, trance, and hard house pump up the main room on weekends, with indie rock and 60s stuff in the annex. Infamous for the reputed steady supply of illicit drugs that

As long as the bobbies stay in their riot vans, everything should be OK. Although riot vans are around on weekend nights, they're eerily absent during the day. Makes you wonder exactly *where* they go, doesn't it?

somehow find their way into the club, Cream pulls an all-nighter the first Friday of every month that attracts ravers from all over the UK.

Be sure to catch the grooves at the **Zanzibar Club** *(43 Seel St.; Tel 0151/17-08-96-10; 9:30pm-3am; £4cover)*, one of the top spots in the north. One look at the pulsating crowd and you can see why. Hip-hop nights called *No Fakin'* on the weekends range from mainstream to underground to jiggy to oldskool. During the week, Zanzibar has more of an indie-rock feel, hosting live bands like Dirty Rotten Scoundrels, the Maybes, and the Mighty Saguaro. It's not a bad little venue, though someone should tell them watered-down beer doesn't cut it in England.

Get down early if you want to get down at *Liquidation,* Liverpool's most popular Saturday night out, unless waiting in line is your idea of a good time. That's when students pack it in at **Le Bateau** *(62 Duke St.; Tel 0151/709-65-08; 9pm-3am Fri, Sat; £4 cover)*, a spiffy two-level club at the western end of the Artistic Quarter. Thursday night's *Voodoo* is an equally packed might, adding a touch of techno to the Liverpudlian scene. Plans to build a proper stage downstairs and the hope of more live performances will likely draw an even bigger crowd. Do yourself a favor and check it out.

Smooth groove is the thing at University Quarter hotspot **Hee-biejeebie's** *(80-82 Seel St.; No phone; 10pm-2am; £5 cover, £1 beer)*. The first in a wave of jazz clubs to hit Liverpool, their serious jazz-fascist attitude has given way to an interdisciplinary groove—a jazz/indie/beat fusion thing. Monday's *Monte Carlo* night delivers French pop, Northern Soul, sixties psychedelia, and tons of students. Jazz meets trip-hop on the weekends, with a variety of local and touring bands the rest of the week. If you're a beer aficionado, pass over the cheap beer promotions and their basically undrinkable muck (of course, after the first few you won't taste anything anyway...).

arts scene

▶▶VISUAL ARTS

Inside an elaborate traditional 18th-century structure in the Artistic Quarter, the **Bluecoat Arts Center** *(School Lane; Tel 0151/709-52-97; 10am-5:30pm Mon-Sat; Free)* is anything but traditional, exhibiting postmodern work by local artists, many of them students. It also hosts occasional events and lectures.

►►PERFORMING ARTS

Living on the love of the common people, the **Everyman Theatre** *(5-9 Hope St.; Tel 0151/709-47-76; £10-£12 tickets; www.everyman.mersey world.com; V, MC, AE),* near the Cathedral Church, houses small local productions that are worth checking out, along with an occasional show from national touring companies. Productions include off-kilter adaptations of Brit classics like *Alice's Boogie Wonderland* and Dickens's *Hard Times,* as well as edgier avant-garde stuff that wins awards. But the real show is in the smoky basement lounge's Everyman Bistro, where the deep actor-types get their first taste of public adulation ("You've got real star-quality, baby!").

Adjacent to the Everyman, **Unity Theatre** *(1 Hope St.; Tel 0151/709-49-88; Avg £7 per ticket; V, MC)* provides a state-of-the-art venue where new performers and playwrights often get their start. The Unity sometimes mounts productions from unknowns, hoping they won't stay unknown for long.

gay scene

Gay nightlife in Liverpool isn't as frenetic it is in Manchester or Leeds, but there's a certain scruffy appeal to the hard parties at some of the post-industrial city's gay bars. Many of them make their home near the Moorfields Railway Station, off Dale Street in the Cavern Quarter.

On a weeknight, queer Victorian pub **Masquerade** *(10 Cumberland St.; Tel 0151/236-77-86; 11am-11pm Mon-Sat, noon-10:30pmSun; No cover)* is the most consistently crowded and animated of the gay bars off Dale Street. Come to the street-level bar to drink, talk, and watch the occasional cabaret *artistes,* whose acts are presented after 11pm every Friday and Saturday. Head for the basement-level dance floor to boogie down with the queer 'Pudlians.

The street level **G-Bar** *(1-3 EberleSt.; Tel 0151/258-12-30; 10pm-2am Wed-Sun; £3-5 cover)* is a pseudo-Gothic piece of kitsch that only a true raver can fully appreciate. The cellar has a floor where crowds of gay and sexually ambiguous fans dance dance dance, while the relaxed "love lounge" offers a place to chill and catch up on the latest drama.

Set close to Moorfield railway station, **The Lisbon** *(36 Victoria St.; Tel 0151/286-54-66; 11am-11pm Mon-Sat, noon-10:30pm Sun; No cover)* offers a more relaxing groove, with a tastier blend of men than you'll find at some of the seedier gay dives nearby.

Near the Paradise Street bus depot off Hanover Street, gay dance emporium **The Escape** *(41-45 Paradise St.; No phone; 10pm-2am Tue, Thu-Sat; £3-5 cover)* competes with G-Bar for the devotion of Liverpool's gay men and, to a lesser extent, women.

CULTURE ZOO

Yes, there is more to Liverpool than the Beatles. The cultural attractions are standard—churches and art galleries and couple local-interest museums—but worth a look none the less.

only here

In the center of the city, just off Albert Dock, lives **Superlambanana,** a 15-foot bright-yellow statue with the head and front legs of a lamb and the posterior of a banana. Superlambanana inspires both disgust and laughter in the locals, and remains a mystery to most tourists, who probably mistake it for the Beatles' Yellow Submarine. According to its creators, students from local John Moores University, the sculpture is meant to illustrate the potential dangers of genetic tampering. But no matter how you analyze it, the damn thing still looks like a sheep with a banana in its butt. Baa!

Cathedral Church of Christ *(St. James Mount; Tel 0151/709-62-71; 8am-6pm daily; Admission free, donations welcomed):* Begun in 1904 but not completed until 1974, the Gothic-style Church of Christ is the largest cathedral in England, its 331-foot tower visible as far away as North Wales. Whether you take in the tower's spectacular views or simply sit and contemplate the church's airy enclosed space, it's definitely a great way to spend an hour or two. It's on the southeastern side of town, not far from the Liverpool Art Institute.

Roman Catholic Metropolitan Cathedral of Christ the King *(Mount Pleasant; Tel 0151/709-92-22; 8am-6pm daily; Admission free, donations welcomed):* While the Metropolitan Cathedral can't compete with its Anglican neighbor a half-mile down Hope Street, it offers its own quiet grace. The highlight of this space-age cathedral, completed in 1967, is its 2,000-ton, multi-colored lantern, which has to be the largest kaleidoscope/disco-ball in the world.

Walker Art Gallery *(William Brown St.; Tel 0151/478-41-99; 10am-5pm Mon-Sat, noon-5pm Sun; £3 adults, £1.50 students; www.nmgm.org.uk;):* Although British artists like pre-Raphaelites Ford Madox Browne and W. R. Yeames have the strongest presence here, the Walker has managed to wrestle up some of the top names in art over the centuries, from Rembrandt to Monet, Seurat to Degas, making it one of the most impressive galleries in Europe. It's just north of Lime Street Station.

Tate Gallery *(Albert Dock; Tel 0151/702-74-00; 10am-6pm Tue-Sun; Free admission; www.tate.org.uk):* This gallery on Albert Dock will blow all of your accepted norms right out of the water with its exquisite and stimulating displays of modern art. The Tate specializes in 20th-century art, with special exhibits from artists like Joan Miró and Rachel Whiteread.

Merseyside Maritime Museum *(Albert Dock; Tel 0151/478-44-99; 10am-5pm daily; £3adults, £1.50students):* For a historic spin through the waterfront, from transatlantic slave trade to the World War II Battle of the Atlantic, check out the Maritime Museum on Albert Dock. Restored buildings, floating exhibits, and hands-on displays make it all seem real.

The Royal Liver Buildings *(Mann Island, Quayside):* Made famous by John Lennon in *Yellow Submarine,* the Liver Buildings at Quayside, north of Albert Dock, stand on their own as the most beautiful architecture in the city. Built in 1911, they're distinguished by two clock towers, which at 25 feet in diameter have Big Ben beat as the largest striking clocks in England. Local folklore says that if the copper "Liver Birds" that stand on the towers ever fall, Liverpool will crumble into the sea.

modification

To liberate the beauty you always knew you could be, head to **Tony and Guy's Salon** *(46 Button St.; Tel 0151/227-34-24; 9am-9pm Mon-Fri, 9am-5:30pm Sat; £23-30; MC, V)* off Church Street in the Artistic Quarter. This high-class salon caters to men and women, with some of the best cutters in England. It's pricey but you'll end up looking gorgeous.

If decorating your dermis sounds like a better idea, try **Ritchie's Tattoos** *(24 Newington St.; Tel 0151/709-14-22; 11:30am-5pm Tue-Fri, 11:30am-3pm Sat; £25 and up; No credit cards)* at the corner of Newington and Renshaw streets in the Artistic Quarter. Open for more than 8 years, Richie's is a safe spot to get inked in style; bring in your own custom design for Richie to work on personally.

great outdoors

It doesn't get much wetter than the **Liverpool Water Sports Centre** *(110 Mariners Wharf; £10 membership, lessons £7.25 per hour; No credit cards),* a half-mile south of Albert Dock, where you can take lessons in canoeing, sailing, and windsurfing. You need to book your day on the

down and out

The **Eight Pass,** a 1-year membership to the **NMGM (National Museums and Galleries on Merseyside),** will get you into almost any of Liverpool's museums, including the **Walker Art Gallery, Maritime Museum** [see *culture zoo,* above], Museum of Liverpool Life, Liverpool Museum, Lady Lever Art Gallery and Sudley House, as often as you like. It's just £3 for adults, £1.50 for students, and can be purchased at any participating museum. So go ahead and soak up a little culture.

dock about a week in advance. And make sure to pack a change of clothes—that Liverpool air is nothing short of frigid when you have a wet tush.

STUFF

There are plenty of Beatles souvenirs to be had [see *the fab tour,* above], but shopping isn't much of a pastime in Liverpool. Still, you should be able to find any last-minute items you forgot to cram into your duffel. Most stores are located in the City Centre.

▶▶**MALL RATS**

On the east side of the City Centre, three-floor mega-store **George Harry Lee** *(Basnett St; Tel 0151/709-14-35; 9am-5:30pm Tue-Sat; MC, V)* sells just about anything from best-selling books to designer clothing, shoes, and jewelry.

▶▶**BOUND**

Get your literary fix at **W.H.Smith** *(Church St.; Tel 0151/709-14-35; 9am-5:30pm Mon-Wed, 9am-6pm Thur-Sat, 1-5pm Sun)* in the city's center. They offer CDs, DVDs, and video games, as well as those bundles of paper covered with print.

EATS

Following the lead of the swanky cafe-bars, new designer restaurants are emerging everyday while many old-time restaurants find themselves on the receiving end of a facelift. The City Centre provides a number of choices ranging from traditional English and French fare to ethnic eats like Thai and Latin American.

▶▶**CHEAP**

The Hub Café Bar *(9 Berry St.; Tel 0151/707-94-95; 10am-6pm daily; £2-4 main courses; MC, V)* in the City Centre attracts veggie and vegan devotees with freshly prepared food that tastes great without resorting to the horrors of butter or cheese. Friendly and welcoming—unless you happen to be a bloodthirsty carnivore—the Hub serves health-conscious dishes against a modern cafe backdrop with whimsical furniture crafted from old bike parts.

Advertising itself as a sports bar, **De Coubertin's** *(43 North John St.; Tel 0151/284-19-96; 10am-11pm Sun-Thur, till 2am Fri, Sat; £5 per entrée),* just south of Mathew Street, almost feels like a diner, offering what it claims is American food, but with lots of puddings, and chips in place of fries. The attempt at imitation is, well, almost cute. With 20

TO MARKET

The **Heritage Market** *(Stanley Dock; Tel 0906/608-68-86; Sun mornings),* on the waterfront, is a bargain hunter's dream, with over 500 stalls.

large-screen TVs and tacky sports memorabilia on display, they're able to capture America's sports obsession a little more accurately than its food.

Right in the center of Liverpool, **Casa Italia** *(40 Stanley St.; Tel 0151/227-57-74; Noon-10pm Mon-Sat; £5-6 main courses; AE,MC, V)* feels more like a back-street trattoria in Rome. Some of the Italian dishes have lost a bit of flavor in the migration north, and the pizza, while good, is pretty standard, but Casa Italia remains popular among young Liverpudlians and visitors alike.

The perfect place to feed that post-clubbing case of the munchies, **Twenty Four Seven** *(47 Paradise St.; Tel 0151/708-82-47; All hours; under £5)* offers breakfast, lunch, or dinner at any hour, most likely because the wired staff is so confused about what time of day it actually is. Besides, what's the point in refusing to cook an English breakfast at 4am anyway? It's off Hanover Street in the Artistic Quarter, not far from **The Escape** [see *gay scene*, above].

▶▶**DO-ABLE**
Romance is in the air at the **Life Café** *(1a Bold St.; Tel 0151/707-23-33; 9am-7pm daily; £4-8.50 per entree; MC)* in the Artistic Quarter. Housed in an elaborate 18th-century building, the circular dining room features a domed ceiling, impressive balcony seating area, funky orange and blue decor, and the second largest glitterball in the world. (If you've been to the **Metropolitan Cathedral** [see *culture zoo*, above], you may be wondering if Scousers have a giant glitterball fetish. Hmmm...). Who could ask for anything more? Food perhaps? No worries—the varied menu ranges from Brit standbys like bangers and mash to burgers to more exotic fare, such as yellow-bean prawn chicken. A number of vegetarian options are also available, a rarity in this empire of meat and potatoes. A wide variety of tasty liquors and wines add to the festivities. With all that, repeat visits are highly likely.

Offering the best value on Albert Dock, **Est Est Est** *(Unit 6, Edward Pavilion, Albert Dock; Tel 0151/708-69-69; Noon-10pm Mon-Thur, noon-1pm Fri, Sat; £5-10 main courses; MC, V)* is a bustling pizza and pasta joint with a rustic, old-world-Italian look. All the sensuous flavors of the Mediterranean are here, with the emphasis on hearty ingredients over delicate seasonings.

Large wooden tables make the possibility of eating with strangers likely, but everyone is so friendly at **Modo Bar and Grill** *(23-25 Fleet St.; Tel 0151/709-65-24; Noon-7:30pm daily; £5-8 per item; MC, AE)* that no one is a stranger for long. Almost everything in this Artistic Quarter eatery is kabob-style, except the hot chocolate fudge cake, which wouldn't really make it on a skewer, but nevertheless shouldn't be missed. An extensive vegetarian menu is also available—how about some skewered tofu?

Off Mathew Street in the Cavern Quarter, **Metz Café** *(Baker House, Rainford Gardens; Tel 0151/227-22-82; Noon-midnight daily; £4-9 main courses; MC, V),* is a soft, candlelit bistro with freshly made soups, wellstuffed sandwiches, and other fare prepared with a light touch.

liverpool

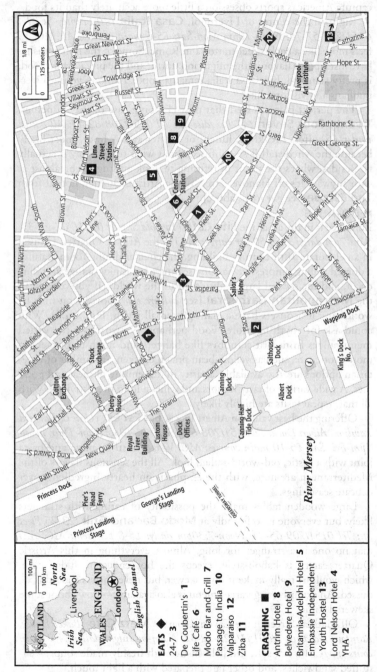

EATS ◆
24-7 **3**
De Coubertin's **1**
Life Café **6**
Modo Bar and Grill **7**
Passage to India **10**
Valparaiso **12**
Ziba **11**

CRASHING ■
Antrim Hotel **8**
Belvedere Hotel **9**
Britannia-Adelphi Hotel **5**
Embassie Independent
Youth Hostel **13**
Lord Nelson Hotel **4**
YHA **2**

The **Passage to India** *(76 Bold Street; Tel 0150/709-64-41; Noon-2pm/5:30pm-midnight Sun-Thur, till 2:30am Fri, Sat; £5.50-11.55 per entrée; V)* in the Artistic Quarter will take you as close to India as Liverpool can get. Try the lamb, chicken, prawns, fish—anything tandoori will satisfy your need for spice and keep your eyes watering for hours. Takeout is also available for those late-night curry cravings on the weekend.

▶▶SPLURGE

With its soft lighting and virtual rainforest, **Valparaiso** *(4 Hardman St.; Tel 0151/708-60-36; Noon-10pm daily; £9-15 entrées; www.valparaiso.merseyworld.com; AE, MC, V)*, just north of the Liverpool Art Institute, successfully offers elegant surroundings and gourmet food with a Chilean flair. After the paella Valparaiso, you may have the sudden urge to abandon the UK for good and head off to Latin America.

Style and innovation are the focus at nearby **Ziba** *(15-19 Berry St.; Tel 0151/708-88-70; Noon-midnight Mon-Sat, noon-4pm Sun; £6-10 per entrée)* which serves up food high in fashion, like lobster terrine or marmalade brûlée, without sacrificing substance. The minimalist decor is just as stylish, with blond wood accents and chairs in leather and chrome.

Near the Everyman and Unity theatres [see *arts scene,* above], **Becher's Brook** *(29A Hope St.; Tel 0151/707-00-05; Noon-10pm Mon-Sat; £10-20 main courses; AE, MC, V)* is a cozy nest popular with theater-goers drawn to its classic but imaginative cuisine, which includes both British and modern international dishes. Treats include roast codfish in a vanilla broth accompanied by an oyster beignet and caviar sabayon. This culinary show takes place in a restored Georgian-era townhouse just a 10-minute walk south from the City Centre.

crashing

Liverpool accommodations aren't the most luxurious in the UK (or the cleanest, for that matter), but they are cheap. Your best bets are the hostels, and there's always room at the YHA, although it's quite a way from the City Centre. The tourist office at Queens Square Center [see *need to know,* below] can help you reserve a room.

▶▶CHEAP

A short walk south from Albert Dock and the Tate Gallery, the **YHA** *(25 Tabley St.; Tel 0151/709-88-88; £13.10 per person, private baths; V, MC,AE)* is brand new and avoids the institutional feel of some hostels; it's more like a budget hotel. The only downfall is its location near the docks, about a half-mile south of the City Centre. But you're not afraid of a little walk, are you?

Though it's a bit cramped, the **Embassie Independent Youth Hostel** *(1 Falkner Sq.; Tel 0151/707-10-89; Bar open 11am-11pm Mon-Sat, noon-10:30pm Sun; £11.50 per person; No credit cards)* in town is a bit more upscale. Right around the corner from the Anglican Cathedral, it also has location on its side: just a 15-minute walk from Lime Street Station, and two blocks down from the bus stop at the corner of Catharine and Canning Streets. The fun crowd that stays here makes the close quarters and shared bathrooms bearable. The brass chandeliers and oak bar in the recently renovated dining and bar area are classy—do you care?—but you pay a bit more for the extravagance.

The **YWCA** *(1 Rodney St.; Tel 0151/709-77-91; £12 single; No credit cards)*, in the east of town near the Metropolitan Cathedral, fills up quickly, so reserve well in advance. They accept men as well as women.

If the hostels are all full, try **Selhal** *(1 Rodney St.; Tel 151/709-77-91; £12 per person, No credit cards)* in the City Centre, just a 10-minute walk from Lime Street Station. And there's always the **University of Liverpool** *(Oxford St.; Tel 151/794-32-98; July-Sept; £15.50 per person)* in a pinch. They sometimes rent out rooms in the late summer months.

▶▶DO-ABLE

A faded B&B decorated with leftovers and salvaged furniture, the **Belvedere Hotel** *(83 Mount Pleasant; Tel 0151/709-23-56; £18.50 per person, shared bath; V, MC)*, just a few blocks north of the Anglican Cathedral, gives you little more than a lumpy bed to rest your head—but it'll make up for that with a huge breakfast.

Perfectly located for the tired traveler, the **Lord NelsonHotel** *(Lord Nelson St.; Tel 0151/707-13-21; £23-38 per person, en suite; V, MC)* is adjacent to Lime Street Station in the City Centre. Basic or designer accommodation is available, depending on how much you want to pay. But no matter which price bracket you're in, the beds are cooomfy.

Run by a very friendly family, the **Antrim Hotel** *(73 Mount Pleasant; Tel 0151/709-52-39; £32 single, £46 double w/private bath; V, MC)* is another City Centre gem, just north of the cathedral. The extra cash may be worth it for your own bathroom and a very comfortable, very clean room to come home to after a long night out.

The **Alpin House Hotel** *(35 Clarendon Rd.; Tel 0151/427-50-47, Fax 151/280-98-41; £26-27 Single, £38-45 double, private bath available; No credit cards)* is a little farther out—about 5 miles from the city, in the suburbs—but is easily accessible by train.

▶▶SPLURGE

Built in the early 1900s with the mission of becoming the most luxurious hotel in the country, the **Britannia-Aldelphi Hotel** *(Ranelagh Place; Tel 0151/708-07-43; £45 single, £60 double, private baths; www.britannia-hotels.co.uk; MC, V, AE)* has lost none of its grandeur. It's decked out in white marble from top to bottom, breaking only for minor flecks of gold, so it's easy to feel like royalty while staying here. The staff is rather trusting of guests, so you may be able to cram a few more people than normal into a room and split the cost. It's conveniently located southwest from Lime Street Station, just down the street from the Central Station.

The **Feather Hotel** *(117 Mount Pleasant; Tel 0151/709-96-55, Fax0151/709-38-38; feathershotel@feathers.uk.com, www.feathershotel.uk.com; £54.95 single, £74.95 double, private baths, breakfast included; V, MC, AE)* is a 10-minute walk from the train station, as is the **Campanile Hotel** *(Chaloner St.; Tel 0151/709-81-04; Fax 0151/709-87-25; £40.95 double/family room, private baths; V, MC,AE)*.

If you really want to live like a Beatle, try the **Atlantic Tower Thistle** *(Chapel; Tel 0151/227-44-44; Fax 0151/236-39-73; liverpool@thistle.co.uk, www.thistlehotels.com; £70 and up doubles, private baths; V, MC, AE)* in the center of the city. Just remember, you don't have the McCartney millions to fall back on.

need to know

Currency Exchange The most convenient place to change money is the **post office** [see below], which takes a minimum 1.5 percent commission but offers competitive rates.

Tourist Information Information on all things Liverpudlian can be found at the **Tourist InformationCentre** *(Atlantic Pavilion, Albert Dock; Tel 0151/708-88-54; 9am-5:30pm Mon-Sat, 10:30am-4:30pm Sun)*, the **Merseyside Welcome Center** *(Clayton Sq., Tel 0151/708-88-38; 9am-5:30pm Mon-Sat, 10:30am-4:30pm Sun)*, and **Queen's Square Center** *(Tel 0845/601-11-25; 9am-5:30pm Mon-Sat, 10:30am-4:30pm Sun; askme@visitliverpool.com)*.The Queen's Square Center can be helpful in arranging accommodations as well.

Public Transportation Even though the city is small enough to be traveled by foot, its **Smartbuses** are helpful, since the drivers know where they're going. Smartbuses 4 and 1 run every 20 minutes 7:05am-6:25pm and every 30 minutes 7:10pm-10:35pm. They travel a circular route within the City Centre or to the docks. There's also the underground **Mersey Rail** system that will take you around the city as well as out of it. **MerseyCabs** *(Tel 0151/207-22-22, or 0151/298-22-22)* are also useful, especially late at night, when the buses and trains aren't running. Call **MerseyTravel** *(Tel 0151/236-76-76)* for information.

American Express For your "green card" needs, drop by American Express *(54 Lord St.; Tel 0151/208-74-74; 9am-5pm daily)*.

Health and Emergency Emergency: *999;* **Police** *(St. Anne's St., northeast of the City Centre; Tel 0151/777-40-30)*. **Royal Liverpool University Hospital** *(Prescott St.; Tel 0151/706-20-00)*, northeast of the City Centre, offers medical attention.

Pharmacies For all things pharmaceutical, try **Moss Chemists** *(68/70 London Rd.; Tel 0151/709-52-71; 7am-11pm daily)*, off Lime Street, north of the station.

Airports The **Liverpool Airport** *(Tel 0151/288-40-00)* is about 7 miles southeast of the City Centre. Shuttle buses operated by **Merseytravel** *(Tel 0105/236-76-76)* depart from the City Centre at Lime Street, Queen Square Bus Station, and Paradise Street Bus Station. The service operates 5:15am-12:15am (just past midnight) and costs £2 one-way.

Bus and Train Lines Out of the City Buses operated by **National Express** *(Tel 0990/808-080, www.nationalexpress.co.uk)* and trains operated by **British Rail** *(Tel 0345/484-950)* leave from Lime Street Station and will take you almost anywhere in the country.

Boats Mersey Ferries, which offer trips across the river for both commuters and tourists. Ferries depart from **Pier Head Ferry Terminal** and run a commuter route (basically a straight shot) 7:45am-9:15am and during the evening rush hour. They also run a cruise route (10am-3pm Mon-Fri, 10am-6pm Sat, Sun) which takes 50 minutes and has a commentary. Call **MerseyTravel** *(Tel 0151/236-76-76)* for information.

Bike Rental Head down to the **Liverpool Cycling Center** *(9-13 Berry St.; Tel 0151/708-88-19; 10am-6pm daily; £8 per day; AE, MC, V)* in the City Centre for all of your cycling needs. It's attached to the Hub Café, where you can grab a bite to eat as well [see *eats,* above].

Laundry Spiff up your duds at **Liver Launderette** *(Princess Rd.; Tel 0151/475-23-76; 8am-8pm daily),* off Parliament Street.

Postal Mail your "I Love Ringo" postcards from the City Centre's **post office** *(St. John's Centre, Houghton Way; Tel 0151/707-10-05; 8am-5pm Mon-Sat, 9am-5pm Sun).*

everywhere else

buxton

People come to Buxton for the water. It started with the Romans and continued with medieval pilgrims, Elizabethan queens, and eventually England's elite—all of them looking for relaxation, rejuvenation, and a good long soak in a hot tub. The mineral springs flowing from St. Ann's Well at a constant 85 degrees Fahrenheit may have established this cosmopolitan little town as a spa and resort, but along the way it's built itself into an oasis of sophistication in the midst of the rough-and-tumble Midlands.

With all of the gray stone buildings in the Peak District, the extravagance of Buxton's grand architecture is definitely eye-candy. Hoping to remake Buxton as a world-class spa that could rival Bath, the 18th-century Duke of Devonshire initiated the town's golden age by bankrolling a series of large-scale constructions, the Crescent with its 164-foot dome being the most notable. Later additions, like the Edwardian **Buxton Opera House,** fit right in, and today high-class visitors (like you, baby) arrive from all over the world to join in the celebration of high art at the annual opera festival.

Unmistakable class drips from Buxton's buildings like mineral water and seems to have leaked into its residents as well. You may find yourself diving into discussions of high-minded philosophy with the bartender, the bus driver, or the bellhop. But for all their sophistication, they still know how to have a good time—stepping one foot into the **Old Sun Inn** [see *bar, club, and live music scene,* below] will prove that.

Though the mineral baths have been closed for decades, Buxton is still a spa at heart—it's all about relaxation. So take in a performance at the Opera House, enjoy a good meal at any of the excellent restaurants, or stretch out on the well-manicured grass in Pavilion Gardens. At 1,000 feet above sea level, Buxton is the second highest town in England, so it's no exaggeration to say that the air is more rarified up here. Take a deep breath, and enjoy it.

buxton

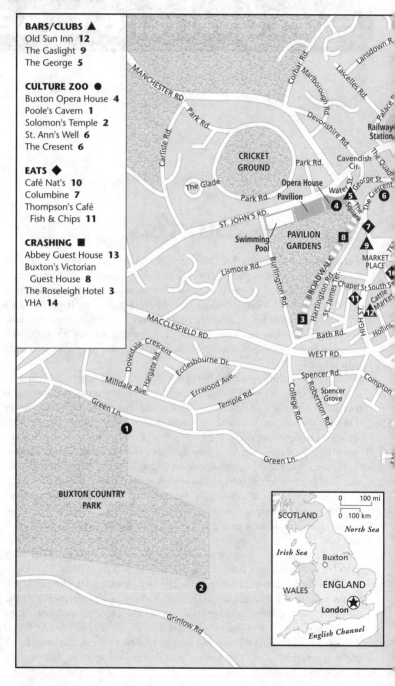

BARS/CLUBS ▲
Old Sun Inn **12**
The Gaslight **9**
The George **5**

CULTURE ZOO ●
Buxton Opera House **4**
Poole's Cavern **1**
Solomon's Temple **2**
St. Ann's Well **6**
The Cresent **6**

EATS ◆
Café Nat's **10**
Columbine **7**
Thompson's Café
 Fish & Chips **11**

CRASHING ■
Abbey Guest House **13**
Buxton's Victorian
 Guest House **8**
The Roseleigh Hotel **3**
YHA **14**

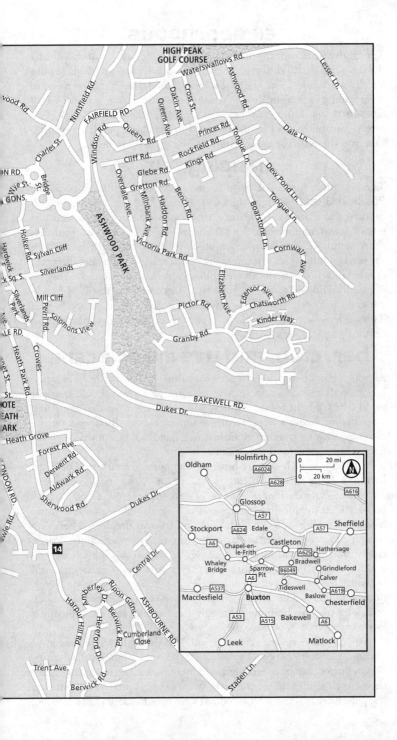

HIGH PEAK
GOLF COURSE

Waterswallows Rd.
Ashwood Rd.
Cross St.
Lesser Ln.
vood Rd.
Nunsfield Rd.
FAIRFIELD RD.
Dakin Ave.
Queens Ave.
Dale Ln.
Charles St.
Windsor Rd.
Queens Rd.
Princes Rd.
Tongue Ln.
ON RD.
Bridge St.
Wye St.
GDNS.
Cliff Rd.
Rockfield Rd.
Kings Rd.
Dew Pond Ln.
Glebe Rd.
Gretton Rd.
Tongue Ln.
Holker Rd.
Sylvan Cliff
Overdale Ave.
Milnbank Ave.
Haddon Rd.
Bench Rd.
Boarstone Ln.
Cornwall Ave.
Hardwick
Silverlands
ASHWOOD PARK
Victoria Park Rd.
k Sq. S.
Silverlands Park
Mill Cliff
Pevril Rd.
Solomons View
Pictor Rd.
Elizabeth Ave.
Ednsor Ave.
Chatsworth Rd.
AVE.
ALE RD.
Heath Park Rd.
Crowes
Granby Rd.
Kinder Way
er St.
St.
OTE
EATH
ARK
BAKEWELL RD.
Heath Grove
Dukes Dr.
Forest Ave.
Derwent Rd.
ONDON RD.
Aldwark Rd.
Sherwood Rd.
Dukes Dr.
ale R
14
Central Dr.
 berley Dr.
Ripon Gdns.
Berwick Rd.
ASHBOURNE RD.
Harbour Hill Rd.
Amberley Dr.
Hereford Dr.
Cumberland Close
Trent Ave.
Berwick Rd.
Staden Ln.

Holmfirth
Oldham
A6024
A628
A616
Glossop
A57
Stockport
A624
Edale
A57
Sheffield
A6
Chapel-en-le-Frith
Castleton
Hathersage
Whaley Bridge
Sparrow Pit
Bradwell
Grindleford
Calver
B6049
A6
Tideswell
Macclesfield
A537
Buxton
Baslow
Chesterfield
A619
A53
A515
Bakewell
A6
Leek
Matlock

0   20 mi
0   20 km
N

neighborhoods

The **High Street,** running north to south, is Buxton's main drag, splitting the town in half. All the major shops, the marketplace, and the best pubs are all found along "The High." **St. John's Road** divides the town east to west, leading to **Station Road,** the site of the train station, naturally. **The Crescent** [see *culture zoo,* below]is located at the north end of High Street, just south of St. John's. No need to fret about public transportation; you can walk the entire length of Buxton in 45 minutes.

hanging out

The best place for a walk or to lounge about on a summer day is the **Pavilion Gardens,** site of the Opera House. Laid out in the early 19th century, this 23-acre conservatory has Victorian landscaping, beautifully tended lawns, and a pond that's home to a pair of swans and countless other waterfowl. There's also a hothouse with exotic tropical plants. When the sun is shining, kids run across the lawns, dragging kites and their parents behind them, and locals and tourists alike lounge about, soaking up the health-and-wellness vibe. Kick back and enjoy the smells of freshly cut grass and even fresher air—the living is easy and admission is free. The gardens lie just around the corner from the tourist information center along St. John's Road.

bar, club, and live music scene

Although Buxton may take the prize for culture in Derbyshire, its nightlife is not overly refined. In fact, there are some places you should outright avoid (the Gaslight for one) unless you absolutely need that last drink after 11pm. Possibly because of the Opera House, Buxton is on the touring circuit for larger more mainstream bands, and the town also hosts a small but kickin' local music scene.

Housed in a 19th-century building, the intimate and cozy **Old Sun Inn** *(33 High St., Tel 01298/234-52; 11am-11pm Mon-Sat, noon-10:30pm Sun, food served till 8pm; £2.25-£8.50 per entrée, £1.50 pints; V)* is every inch the idealized image of the English pub—a maze of little rooms, each with dark wood interior and its own fireplace. There's no shortage of people eager to partake of the extensive selection of beer, decent pub grub, and intelligent conversation that you'll get here. The building's age validates the authentic pub experience—a passageway still leads to an area reserved for horse parking. You half expect a shaggy, burlap-clothed peddler with a tin mug full of stout and a partially eaten turkey leg to come bounding through the door and lead the crowd in a slurred version of "God Save the Queen."

A quick walk north and across the road, **The Gaslight** *(Eagle Parade; No phone; 10pm-4am Thur-Sat; £4 cover, £2.25 pints; No credit cards)* is the only club in Buxton, but it's essentially a local meat market, where residents get to choose their tenderloin for the night (what's that we heard about Buxton being the height of class?). Music doesn't seem to be much of a consideration;

old disco tunes and some 1980s remixes are the norm. The only thing the Gaslight has going for it are its hours—they're open until 4am, after all the other bars have closed. It's the only place in town to get an early morning drink, but really, didn't you get enough ale at the Old Sun?

For a more modern bar experience, try **The George** *(The Sq.; Tel 01298/247-11; 11am-11pm Mon-Sat, noon-10:30pm Sun, food served noon-6pm; No credit cards),* located behind the Crescent. Essentially just a large rectangle lined with tables, the George offers the best of the local music scene. It's the home of the *Roots Section,* a music marathon featuring local bands and some very laid-back grooves. If the music inspires you, there's plenty of room to shake yourself into a frenzy. If frenzies aren't your thing, there's also enough seating room to talk over your drinks or just coolly nod your head to the beat. During the daytime hours, excellent vegetarian cuisine is served.

ARTS SCENE

Just east of the Crescent on Pavilion Gardens, the **Buxton Opera House** *(St. John's Rd.; Tel 01298/721-90; 10am-8pm Mon-Sat for booking; Ticket prices vary; www.buxton-opera.co.uk; V, MC, AE)* opened in 1903 as Buxton's theater for high art, from opera to ballet to classical music. That's what it remains today, though it got a big face-lift restoration in the 1970s. Each summer's annual **Buxton Festival** [see *festivals and events,* below] pushes high culture to the max, drawing diva-worshippers from all over the world. If you figure the Opera House is only for highbrow snobs who know the difference between an alto and a mezzo-soprano, you're wrong. Following in the grand tradition of Benny Hill and Mr. Bean, they commonly host works like the bump-and-grind sequel *The Full Monty, Part II,* and recently offered a screening of the grungy heroin-laced classic *Trainspotting.* The Opera House is also one of the foremost examples of Edwardian architecture in England, and it's probably worth it to check out any performance, highbrow or lowbrow, just to see it from the inside.

CULTURE ZOO

Buxton is that rarity in England, a town that's actually devoted itself not only to keeping up its glorious old buildings, but also to putting them to use. A walk through town gives you a hint of what it must have been like in the old days, when the elite flocked here looking for a nice warm bath.

St. Ann's Well *(The Crescent; No phone; Always open; Free):* A constant stream of warm mineral water flows from the mouth of a bronze lion at St. Ann's Well near the Crescent. It's currently the bestselling mineral water in England, so people fill up gallon jugs to take home, and you'll have to wait in line to get a taste. (You can also buy Buxton original mineral water packaged up all pretty from any store in town.) This spring was probably visited by pilgrims as early as the Middle Ages and had become a spa by Elizabethan times, when it was visited by Mary Queen of Scots, who despite being imprisoned, really seemed to get around.

festivals and events

The **Buxton Festival** *(Second week of July; Tel 01298/721-90 box office, Tel 01298/703-95 information; www. buxtonfestival.co.uk)* draws opera lovers from all over the country to performances at the **Opera House** [see *arts scene,* above]. If sopranos wailing in Italian is too highbrow for you, there's also the **Buxton Festival Fringe** *(July 6-22, 2001; Tel 01298/705-62 or 01298/251-04),* at about the same time, when the entire town takes advantage of the influx of people to put on a great show. Street performances range from jugglers to traditional English dancers. Be sure to check out the Morris Men—it may be your only chance to see grown men in funny Olde English garb dancing in the street with bells and other odd instruments.

Then again, if you just can't get enough of grown men in funny clothes, you can stick around for the *Pirates of Penzance* at the **Gilbert and Sullivan Festival** *(Late July-early August; Call the Opera House for details).* Wear your ruffly shirt and see if you can blend in.

The Crescent *(Houses the Tourist Information Office; Tel 01298/251-06; 9am-5pm daily):* Constructed over the river alongside St. Ann's Well, the Crescent is the most impressive structure in town, and the de facto cultural center of Buxton. A quick tour of the building will give you a sense of the faded grandeur of this spa town. Commissioned by the Fifth Duke of Devonshire in 1780, it includes the pump house, which supplied the bathhouse with fresh water while it was still in use, a ballroom, and an assembly hall, as well as shops on the ground floor. Today, the tourist office is located in the old bath house, and the pump house is used for local craft fairs and artist exhibitions. The circular stables above and to the west now house the Devonshire Royal Hospital.

Solomon's Temple *(1 mile southeast of town, 20-minute walk from Poole's Cave; No phone; Always open; Free):* Situated atop a burial ground from Neolithic times, Solomon's Temple offers stunning views of the entire Peak District. Climb the spiral staircase inside and take a look. Constructed as a folly (which seems to be the English way of saying "just for the hell of it") in 1895, it may remind you of the Tower of Pisa, without the wacky tilt. It's about 1.25 miles south of the city center.

Poole's Cavern *(Green Lane; Tel 01629/269-78; 10am-5pm daily Mar-Oct; £3.50; No credit cards):* About a mile south of town, this cave was once inhabited by Stone Agers, and excavations have also revealed Bronze Age and Roman Era artifacts. The caverns are all electrically lit, so you can gape at the dangling stalactites to your heart's content—just watch your head. The caves are located on the edge of the Buxton Country Park, which seems a bit more inviting, especially if you haven't eaten lunch. Picnic, anyone?

EATS

Buxton offers a full spectrum of excellent eats, from the best fish & chips in Derbyshire to high romance by candlelight. At many of the restaurants, you get great views of Pavilion Gardens with your meal.

▶▶CHEAP

Not far from the Old Sun Inn, **Thompson's Café Fish & Chips** *(9 High St.; Tel 01298/225-96; 11am-9pm daily; 50p-£2.50 per item; No credit cards)* offers some of the best takeout in Derbyshire, with a perfect ratio of crunchy batter to moist fish. Dressed in blue and white, they even manage to pull off a seaside theme while being completely landlocked.

Located north of High Street, off South Street, **Café Nat's** *(9-11 Market St.; Tel 01298/239-69; 10am-8:30pm daily; £4.25-8.95 per entrée)* offers an innovative mix of freshly prepared vegetarian and nouveau cuisine, and some of the most satisfying meals in town. The dining area is dominated by large fluffy couches, which encourage strangers to become friends and share a meal. If you're interested in taking a piece of Nat's home with you, go right ahead. Everything—silverware, couches, wall-hangings—is for sale. Just ask.

▶▶DO-ABLE

Charming Victorian architecture, dim lighting, and soft music set the mood at **Columbine** *(7 Hallbank; Tel 01298/787-52; 7pm-10pm Mon-Sat, lunches during summer; £7.95-11.50 per entrée; V, MC, AE)*, just south of the Crescent. Top quality traditional French and English cuisine is served in a bistro setting, with dishes like grilled tuna steak and chicken stuffed with sautéed mushrooms. It's all fresh, flavorful, unpretentious, and reasonably priced. Top off your meal with a romantic midnight stroll through town.

crashing

Buxton is one of the most popular summer vacation spots for visitors from all over England, so it's stocked with B&Bs. In addition to the lone hostel, it shouldn't be a problem finding a room for about £15 along South Avenue, or for about £20 along Broadwalk. Unfortunately, the tourist office isn't much help booking accommodations; if you're looking for a bed in Buxton, you're on your own.

▶▶CHEAP

Situated in unspoiled woodland, the **YHA** *(Harper Hill Rd.; Tel 01298/222-87; Reception 5pm-11pm Fri, Sat Feb-Mar, Mon-Sat Apr-Oct, Thur-Mon Nov-Dec; £8.10, shared bath, membership required)* is about a mile's walk south, downhill from the city center. Take High Street, which becomes Ashbourne Road. This converted Victorian house offers typical

YHA accommodations, with institution-style dorm furniture and interior. It also has a sweet view of the stone bridges crossing the dales.

A lot of the cheaper B&Bs are grouped together along Compton Road in the south of town: **Griff Guest House** (2 Compton Rd., Tel 01298/236-28), **Compton House** (4 Compton Rd., Tel 01298/269-26), and **Templeton Guest House** (13 Compton Rd., Tel 01298/252-75) all offer bed and breakfast for around £15 or £16 per person.

▶▶DO-ABLE

For slightly more comfortable accommodation, try the **Abbey Guest House** (43 South Ave.; Tel 01298/264-19; £14.50 single, £23 double, shared bath; No credit cards), located just off Market Street. The proprietors are friendly and accommodating—they'll even cook up a vegetarian breakfast at your request. They also provide a modest evening meal, though with all the good restaurants in town, you should go out for something more exciting.

The more expensive B&Bs are along Broadwalk, southeast of the Crescent. The young, knowledgeable proprietors of the tastefully decorated **Roseleigh Hotel** (19 Broadwalk; Tel 01298/249-04; £22 single or en suite double; enquires@roseleighhotel.co.uk, www.roseleighhotel.co.uk; No credit cards) can talk all day about Buxton, Derbyshire, and even more exotic areas like Egypt and Turkey if you care to ask.

On the other end of Broadwalk, the beautiful **Victorian Guest House** (3a Broadwalk; Tel 01298/787-59; £25 per person en suite; No credit cards), which dates back to the 1870s, is decorated with authentic antiques. Many of the rooms have themes: The Egyptian Room is worth checking out, and the dining room has an Asian motif, complete with a huge dragon mural.

▶▶SPLURGE

Lee Wood Hotel (The Park, 13 Manchester Rd.; Tel 800/528-12-34 in the U.S. and Canada, Tel/Fax 01298/230-02 in the U.K.; £95-116 doubles, breakfast included; leewoodhotel@btinternet.com; www.bestwestern.co.uk; V, MC, AE, DC) is the most sophisticated hotel in town. A 15-minute walk north of the town center, it overlooks Buxton's most popular cricket ground. Built in Victorian times and renovated in the 1990s, its comfortable bedrooms are tastefully decorated, and bathrooms are outfitted with a shower/tub combination.

need to know

Currency Exchange The **post office** [see below] will exchange your old money for new, taking 1.5 percent commission, with a £3 minimum.

Tourist Information The **Tourist Information Center** (The Crescent; Tel 01298/251-06; 9am-5pm daily) is housed in the town's old bathhouse, the **Crescent**. In addition to offering information on area attractions and accommodations, it provides a glimpse into the spa town's history, with an adjacent room dedicated to the bathhouse itself.

Health and Emergency Emergency: 999. Police: Silverland; Tel

01298/721-00. The nearest hospital is **Macclesfield District General Hospital** *(Victoria Rd., Macclesfield; Tel 01625/421-000),* 13 miles east toward Manchester, via Roads A53, A54, A537 and A523.

Pharmacies Scarsdale Pharmacy *(Market St.; Tel 01298/234-88; 9am-1pm/1:30pm-6pm Mon-Sat; V, MC)* will fill your prescriptions.

Trains Trains depart for Manchester from **Station Road** every hour during the day. Check at the tourist office for schedule and fare information.

Bus Lines Out of the City Half a dozen **bus lines** run daily to and from Manchester. Buses stop at Market Square. Call **Travel Line** *(Tel 01298/230-98)* for information.

Bike Rental Bikes are available at **Mark Anthony Cycles** *(115 Spring Gardens; Tel 01298/721-14; Fax 01298/732-12; £12 per day, £30 per 3 days, £40 per week; info@www.mark-anthony.co.uk, www.mark-anthony.co.uk; MC, V).* Each rental includes a helmet, pump, repair kit, tool kit, and area map for no extra charge.

Laundry Five Ways Launderette *(London and Greet Sts.; Tel 01298/720-18; 8am-6pm daily; £2 wash; 70p dry)* provides a cafe next door so that you can munch on lunch while your laundry spins.

Postal The **post office** *(12a High Street; Tel 0345/223-344; 9am-1:15pm/2pm-5:30pm Mon-Fri, 9am-12:30pm Sat)* will satisfy all your postal needs.

bakewell

Although it dates back to the Saxon era, it took a tart to put Bakewell on the map (no, nothing to do with the Royal Family). It's home to the nationally acclaimed Bakewell Pudding, a delicious pastry covered with strawberry jam and an egg-yolk spread (trust us, it's better than it sounds). Stumbled upon quite fortuitously by a 19th-century cook, this unconventional dessert quickly put the town on the gourmet food circuit. But Bakewell has something else going for it: location, location, location. Within the borders of the Peak National Park, it attracts hundreds of tourists every day.

Bakewell is a quaint English village right out of a Miramax movie. You'll be eating up small-town charm with a spoon (just leave room for Pudding). The five-arched Bakewell Bridge stretching across the River Wye is a postcard waiting to happen, and the cobblestoned streets are lined with cafes, pubs, restaurants, and shops, all in well-preserved 17th-century granite buildings. Unfortunately, the streets are frequently lined with people as well, which can really kill the mood.

One way to avoid the masses is to hike around during the day. A reasonably soft hike through Monsal Dale offers some spectacular views, with greens even Kermit would love. Nearby Chatsworth House is the

bakewell

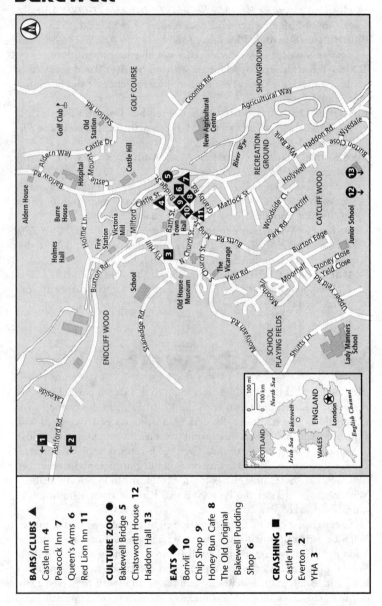

BARS/CLUBS ▲
Castle Inn **4**
Peacock Inn **7**
Queen's Arms **6**
Red Lion Inn **11**

CULTURE ZOO ●
Bakewell Bridge **5**
Chatsworth House **12**
Haddon Hall **13**

EATS ◆
Borivili **10**
Chip Shop **9**
Honey Bun Cafe **8**
The Old Original
Bakewell Pudding
Shop **6**

CRASHING ■
Castle Inn **1**
Everton **2**
YHA **3**

greatest collection of excessive knickknacks in the North, and hosts some beautiful gardens. Drop back in to enjoy Bakewell's many charms at night. The town undergoes a major metamorphosis sometime around 9pm, when the camera-toting mums and dads retire for the evening and the young emerge like ants swarming to a pile of sugar.

neighborhoods

Bakewell swirls around the traffic circle in its center, the crossroads of town where everything comes together. **Buxton Street,** which winds along the **River Wye,** comes in from the north and ends up at the round-about in the center of town; it's called **Matlock Street** as it runs south from there. The two intersect with **Bath Street** and **Bridge Street** to form the town square. You can walk Bakewell from end to end in about 15 minutes, so no public transportation is necessary.

At the roundabout, you can take the first exit and go along **King Street,** where you'll find an array of shops selling antiques. If you continue up King Street you'll run in to **All Saints Parish,** also known as **Bakewell Church** [see *culture zoo,* below].

bar and live music scene

If you're looking for cosmopolitan, look somewhere else. Located around the central square, Bakewell's traditional English pubs are brimming with cheerful country punters and a large selection of quality ales, but there's nothing trendy about them. The crowd can range from stuffy, old-money suits to fresh-out-of-school youngsters looking for the cheapest and fastest way to get drunk. There's really only one scene here, and it involves drinking. A lot. If people want some live music or clubbing action, most head over to Sheffield, about 15 miles to the northwest.

Tucked behind the TIC is a traditional English pub dressed up in American garb. Walking into the **Queen's Arms** *(1 Bridge St.; Tel 01629/814-586; 11am-3pm/7pm-11pm Mon-Fri, 11am-11pm Sat, Sun, food served till 9pm; £3.25 pub grub, £1.50 drinks; V, MC)* is like walking into a temple dedicated to American pop stars. Cultural icons enshrined

festivals and events

Around the first weekend in August, the agricultural extravaganza called the **Bakewell Show** *(Contact Clare Fletcher, Tel 01629/812-736, Fax 01629/813-597; info@bakewell-show.demon.co.uk, www.bakewellshow.demon.co.uk)* draws farmers from all over the north to talk and trade livestock. Bored with sheep, restless Bakewell youth have found an alternative use for farm equipment. Participants push each other from pub to pub in wheelbarrows, drinking a pint at every stop. The winner of these wheelbarrow races is the first to toss his freshly eaten tart in the River Wye. For those of us who prefer to not to analyze the recent contents of the stomach, live music and festival booths line the streets as well.

on the walls include Marilyn Monroe, Billie Holiday, Ronald Reagan, and Monica Lewinsky, thrown in for a chuckle. One of the liveliest places in Bakewell, most likely due to its £1.50 pints and spirits, the place gets packed with the young and thirsty after 9pm, when the top of the pops starts blaring from the jukebox. Some decent pub grub, including jacket potatoes and sandwiches, is also served.

With its exposed stone walls, open fireplace, and pool table, the **Castle Inn** (*Castle St.; Tel 01629/812-103; 11am-11pm Mon-Sat, noon-10:30pm Sun, food served noon-9pm daily; £4.95 pub grub, £12.95 per entrée; V*), just north of the bridge on the west bank, offers refuge to Bakewell locals trying to escape the rush of tourists. It also offers a more relaxed night out, and some familiar '60s rock. After about 10pm, the crowd gets younger and friendlier, and conversation really gets going. Local bands occasionally set up shop for the night here, and that's about the extent of Bakewell's music scene. Bar meals are served whenever the bar is open and the cook hasn't had too much too drink.

Yet another traditional pub, the **Red Lion Inn** (*The Square; Tel 01629/812-054; 11am-11pm Mon-Sat, noon-10:30pm Sun, food served until 9pm; £4.80 pub grub, £1.80 drinks; V*), right on the town square, is full of comfortable booths and intimate nooks and crannies. It's divided into two rooms, one dominated by the music of everything from the Beatles to Finley Quay, and the other for watching the customers in bar number one. After perusing the deep selection of lagers and ales, including local brews like Castle Eden and Pedigree, you'll find just the thing to ease the pains of hiking through hills and dales all day.

Cozier and less crowded, the **Peacock Inn** (*Market St.; Tel 01629/812-994; 11am-11pm, Mon-Sat, noon-10:30pm Sun, food served until 9pm; £6.50 per entrée; No credit cards*) is a little rougher around the edges than some of the other pubs in town, attracting more locals than tourists. Deep and dark, it's a great place to have a slow pint and sink deeply into the velvety cushions of the carved cherry-wood chairs. Unfortunately, the selection of drafts is rather limited and kinda pricey, from £2 upward. The music is strictly for ambience, not dancing. It's just south of the Bridge on the west bank.

CULTUPE ZOO

If you're turned on by historical architecture, a walk around town will put you right in the middle of the 16th century. More historic sites are a short trek away, just a few miles out of town.

Bakewell Bridge (*Bridge St.*): One of the most striking examples of the architecture of the 1500s is the bridge over the River Wye. Its five arches provide the perfect photo op.

Bakewell Church (*King St.*): This Norman church, just west of the central square, dates back to the 12th century, although the spire was added in 1340. The churchyard is even older, as evidenced by two 9th-century Saxon crosses and some ancient coffins with magnificent carvings.

It gives you a good sense of Bakewell's pre-pudding history, and is definitely worth a look if you want to get in touch with your inner Celt.

Chatsworth House *(Chatsworth; Tel 01246/582-204; 11am-5pm daily, Mar 15-Oct 29; Bus, V, 210 in summer; £6.75 adult, £5.50 student; www.chatsworth-house.co.uk; V, MC):* Still home to the Duke of Devonshire and his family, Chatsworth House dates back to 1686. Mary Queen of Scots was held prisoner here under orders of Queen Elizabeth I, and Queen Victoria was entertained here some 200 years later. The British upper crust has always believed that more is better, and Chatsworth House follows that tenet. Impressive murals and ceiling paintings adorn the entrance hall, and the house beyond is packed full of art treasures, not to mention the obligatory don't-touch red ropes and all the stuffy dignity of the former British Empire. If it all gets to be a bit much, the grounds, with one of the most celebrated gardens in Europe, are more enjoyable, with footpaths, sculptures, and a hedgerow maze that must have provided hours of fun in the days before DirecTV.

Haddon Hall *(A6; Tel 01629/812-855; 10:30am-5pm daily, Apr-Sept; 10:30am-4:30pm Mon-Thur, Oct; Bus 61, 171, 172, 179, 181, 210, 404, 411, 473, R61, TP to Haddon Hall; £5.50 Adult, £4.75 Students; No credit cards):* About 2 miles south of Bakewell, Haddon Hall is a 14th-century manor abandoned for hundreds of years before being returned to its former glory by a painstaking renovation begun in the early 1920s. While it can't match the grandeur of Chatsworth House, it offers a glimpse of well-to-do country life hundreds of years ago.

great outdoors

A short bus ride from the square or 3-mile walk through rolling hills and pastures will get you to **Monsal Head,** where the River Wye makes a sharp turn south before carving its way through a limestone ridge. After stopping to enjoy the view, you can take a bus back into Bakewell (Bus 173, 4) or continue along the **Monsal Trail.** This easy yet satisfying hike follows old railway lines though Monsal Dale, moving over an old Victorian viaduct that provides incredible views of the surrounding countryside—deep greens crisscrossed by ancient stone walls. Following the River Wye, the trail continues for about 6 miles, almost all the way to Buxton. If you're heading there anyway, it's certainly the most gratifying way to go.

stuff

Shopping in Bakewell is more about soaking up the local color than making any actual purchases. Most of the cuter-than-cute little shops are around the square and along Matlock Street.

▶▶BOUND

To dance with the Celtic fringe, head over to the **Bakewell Bookshop** *(Matlock St.; Tel 01629/812-818; 9:30am-5:30pm Mon-Sat, 12:30pm-5:30pm Sun; www.bakewellbookshop.co.uk; V, MC).* With lilting Celtic chords bouncing off the walls, this little New Age gem has the most extensive selection of guidebooks and maps for the area, as well as entire sections devoted to all things Celtic and the betterment of your soul.

▶▶CRAFTS

For gifts that may actually return home in your duffel intact, try the hand-stitched wonders at the **Wye Needlecraft Shop** *(2 Royal Oak Place, off Matlock St.; Tel 01629/815-198; 9:30am-5:30pm Mon-Sat, noon-5pm Sun; clive@wye.co.uk, www.angus.co.uk/wye; V, MC),* just below the roundabout on Matlock Street.

▶▶BAZAAR

A market is held along **Matlock Street** every Monday selling a wide variety of food and clothing, along with crafts and other items. This is one of the oldest markets in England, first held in 1300 and still going strong.

eats

With a teashop on every street and around every corner, you almost feel like you're being forced into trying a Bakewell Pudding. Ironically, but not surprisingly, many of the locals have had their fill of the strawberry tarts, but that doesn't stop them from raving about the finery of their famous dessert. When ordering, be careful to ask for a Bakewell *Pudding,* not a Bakewell *Tart.* For some reason, the locals are sensitive about the name, and ordering the wrong way may cost you more than the £5.50 they charge for a Bakewell Pudding.

Fortunately, man does not live on pudding alone (nor does woman), and the town has a decent selection of good food, with traditional English fare available at low prices in any of the pubs [see *bar and live music scene,* above]. If you're hoping for something exotic, East Indian is as far as you're going to get. There are a few takeouts, but stick with the cafes, which, despite their repetitive menus, serve cheap and tasty food.

▶▶CHEAP

Whether you're avoiding the rain or just hoping to relax awhile, the **Honey Bun Café** *(Water St.; Tel 01629/815-150; 10am-5pm daily; £2.50-4.50 per entrée; No credit cards),* situated just east of the main square, is an ideal home away from home. So what if the pudding ain't great—there are good, home-cooked soups and sandwiches, as well as more innovative desserts and pastries. The cheerful decor and welcoming atmosphere make you feel like you're sitting in the owner's kitchen.

We're pretty sure it's been written into law that every English town has to have a good fish & chips takeout. Located just off the main square, the **Chip Shop** *(Water St.; Tel 01629/813-658; 11am-3pm/5pm-10pm Mon-Sat; £2 per item; No credit cards)* is great for a white-paper-wrapped meal on the go. Grab a quick bite here to nibble on as you wander in and out of the quaint and tidy shops lining this cobblestoned snake of a street.

▶▶DO-ABLE

The best place for pudding? Situated in the main square, **The Old Original Bakewell Pudding Shop** *(The Square; Tel 01629/812-193; 9am-9pm daily May-Oct; 9am-6pm daily Nov-Apr; £7 per entrée, Bakewell*

Pudding £5.50; V, MC) claims to have the old original recipe, if you can believe it. Dining in this well-preserved 17th-century stone structure, you can actually imagine you're biting into that very first revolutionary dessert. The shop also provides excellent meals, served by a waiter dressed in the traditional getup of a housemaid of that era. They'll also ship authentic Bakewell Pudding anywhere in the world.

Beat the cold with a little spice-induced body heat at **Borivli** *(4 Portland Sq.; Tel 01629/815-489; 6pm-midnight daily; £4.95-8.95 per entrée; V)*. Hidden in the small, pedestrian cobblestoned Portland Square off Station Road, it offers some of the best Indian cuisine in northern England. From the ubiquitous curry and rice to Samosas and vegetarian dishes, this taste of East Asia is as authentic as it gets, with no English influence whatsoever. Outdoor seating is available in good weather.

crashing

The buses stop running at midnight, so it's a good idea to stay in the center of town if you're going to be out carousing. On the other hand, the number of tourists that come into the area drive the prices up, so looking for a B&B on the outskirts of town may prove more comfortable for your wallet. Although you may have to deal with a bathroom down the hall and a shower on another floor, a home-cooked breakfast makes up for the impossibility of stumbling to the loo in your underwear at 4am. The TIC books rooms at no extra cost and will always try to find you something, even at 3 in the afternoon on a holiday weekend.

▶▶CHEAP

There's an institutional feeling to the **YHA Hostel** *(Fly Hill; Tel 01629/812-313; Reception 5pm-10pm Mon-Sat; £9 dorm; bakewell@yha.org.uk; V, MC)*, but if all you're looking for is a bed to rest your bones, it serves its purpose. The employees are outrageously friendly and helpful, and will happily dump truckloads of information on you. Meals are served by arrangement but, unless you feel like reliving high school cafeteria food, we suggest not arranging them. It's located just northeast of the town square, off Church Street.

About 2 miles south of Bakewell, **Haddon Park Farm** *(A6, Tel 01629/814-854; Bus 61, 171, 172, 179, 181, 210, 404, 411, 473, R61, TP to Haddon Hall; £22 per person double with bath; No credit cards)* is set on a hilltop overlooking Bakewell and the Wye Valley. It's a real working farm, so you can expect breakfast to be fresh.

▶▶DO-ABLE

South of the town center, **Everton** *(Haddon Rd; Tel 01629/813-725; £22 single, £32 double, en suite available; V)* is a Victorian house offering a warm welcome and a lovely English garden. The rooms are moderately sized and most even have a bathroom in the room. A classically decorated dining room and full English breakfast complete the package.

Located in the beautiful area of Monsal Head [see *great outdoors*, above], about a 10-minute bus ride from the town center, the **Cliff House** *(Monsal Head; Tel 01629/640-376; Bus 4, 173 to Monsal Head;*

£29 single, £32 double, £35 triple, en suite; MC) is a great place to spend the night if you want a head start on the Monsal Trail. It's also a very cozy inn. A natural therapy center located on the premises offers services including reflexology, herbology, massage, and aromatherapy, although booking ahead is necessary.

▶▶SPLURGE

Just feet from the Bakewell Bridge, the **Castle Inn** *(Castle St.; Tel 01629/812-103; £39.50 single or double, en suite available; V)* is a creaky old hotel offering both luxury and comfort. While you pay for the convenience, the inn's charm and well-preserved 16th-century architecture are worth the price.

need to know

Currency Exchange You can always get the lowest exchange rate from the banks, but they normally charge a minimum commission of at least £3. The two banks in town are **HSBC** *(Bridge St.; 9am-5pm Mon-Fri)* and **Natwest** *(Bridge St.; 9am-5pm Mon-Fri).*

Tourist Information Information on the park and nearby attractions is available at the **Bakewell Information Centre** *(Old Market Hall, Bridge St.; Tel 01629/813-227; 9:30am-5:30pm daily Mar-Oct; 9:30am-5pm daily Nov-Feb).* They can also book accommodations for you.

Health and Emergency Emergency: 999; Police: *Granby Rd.; Tel 01629/812-594.* The nearest hospital, **Whitworth Hospital** *(Bakewell Rd.; Tel 01629/57911)* is in Matlock, 8 miles southeast via Roads A6 and A615.

Pharmacies Boots the Chemist *(Granby Rd.; Tel 01629/812-043; 9am-5pm Mon-Sat, 11am-4pm Sun)* will have you popping pills in no time.

Buses Bus services through Bakewell from Matlock and Buxton include **Stagecoach** *(Tel 01298/23098)* and **Trent** *(Tel 01773/712-265).* Most buses stop near the square; information and schedules are available at the tourist office. You can also call the national **Travel Line** *(Tel 0870/60-82-26-08).*

Bike Rental Bikes are available at **Bakewell Cycle Shop** *(Buxton Rd.; Tel 01629/813-155)* near Bakewell Station.

Laundry Bakewell Laundrama *(Water St.; 7:30am-7pm daily; £2 wash, 50p dry; No credit cards)* is tucked away on a corner off the main square.

Postal Mail things at the **Bakewell Post Office,** *(Granby Rd.; 8:30am-6pm Mon-Fri, 8:30am-3pm Sat).* That's what it's for.

matlock

As the last stop on the train heading north from London, Matlock is the closest you can get to the Peak District National Park, without actually crossing its borders, and marks one end of the popular Limestone Way. Its proximity to the park, with its wonders both natural (the nearby Heights of Abraham) and supernatural (Nine Ladies and Arbor Lowe stone circles), is really all Matlock has going for it. Historically, it's known mainly for its 19th-century hydrotherapy spa, built by entrepreneur John Smedley just 2 miles south in what's known today as Matlock-Bath. He hoped that people would flock to Matlock the way that they did to Bath and Buxton, for the water and fresh air. Unfortunately, it didn't work out quite as he planned, and Matlock today remains for the most part an unremarkable little town. Crown Square in the town center, the most likely place to hang out, is often deserted.

Matlock sits alongside the River Derwent. The surrounding landscape is dominated by picturesque, green rolling hills, 18th-century stone buildings, and the forbidding **Riber Castle** [see *only here,* below], which isn't quite as old as it looks. The tightly knit community is devoted to the beauty of the surrounding countryside as well as what some people call traditional family values. As one local graybeard put it, "If anyone gets too kinky, they drift off eventually to London, like that Billy Elliot."

If there's a cultural quirk in Matlock, it's the extraordinary number of pubs, maybe more than 25 in all—remarkable for such a small town. Still, this isn't the place to kick up your heels and let your debauched inner child run wild and free—most of the drinking here is done quietly. Most pubs lie over the bridge, off Dale Road, about a ten-minute walk from the town center. There's also one club in town, but unless you're in the mood to hang out with the underaged or just feel like giggling at English small-townies, it's not worth visiting. Most of the locals who've seen the inside of a nightclub at all managed to do so on a trip to Derby or London.

neighborhoods

The town winds along neighboring cliffs in the shape of an *S,* and is segregated horizontally by the **River Derwent.** The **A6** runs in a north-south direction dividing the town; it changes names as it runs through town, so is commonly referred to as "the main road." Other major roads running off the main traffic circle at **Crown Square** include **Bakewell Road** (east-west), **Snitterson Road** (east-west), and **Dale Road** (north-south). The bridge just southeast of Crown Square crosses the river. Matlock occupies just 1 square mile, so you can easily walk it in a half-hour.

bar scene

Most of the pubs worth mentioning are located along Dale Road, southeast of Crown Square and across the River Derwent. It's clear from the facades of these little pubs that they've seen plenty of time go by, but whatever wild stories they may hold within their walls seem to be long forgotten.

The Underground *(77 Dale Road; 11am-11pm Mon-Sat, noon-10:30pm Sun; Cover £5 women, £10 men; V, MC)* stands proudly on the corner near Crown Square. Appearances are deceiving, however, as this bar loses any hint of stuffiness as soon as you walk through the door. It's

MATLOCK

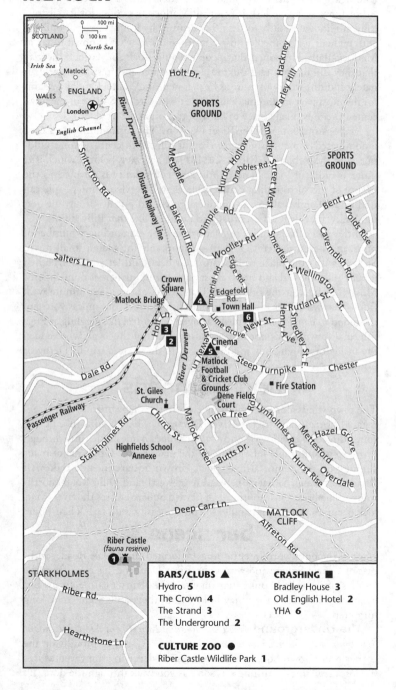

SCOTLAND

North Sea

Irish Sea

Matlock

WALES

ENGLAND

London

English Channel

Holt Dr.

SPORTS GROUND

SPORTS GROUND

Hackney

Farley Hill

Snitterton Rd.

River Derwent

Disused Railway Line

Megdale

Bakewell Rd.

Hurds Hollow

Smedley Street West

Drabbles Rd.

Dimple Rd.

Bent Ln.

Wolds Rise

Salters Ln.

Woolley Rd.

Edge Rd.

Imperial Rd.

Smedley St.

Wellington St.

Cavendish Rd.

Crown Square

Matlock Bridge

Holt Ln.

Causeway Ln.

Edgefold Rd.

Town Hall

New St.

Rutland St.

Henry Ave.

Smedley St. E.

Lime Grove

Chester

Dale Rd.

River Derwent

Cinema

Matlock Football & Cricket Club Grounds

Steep Turnpike

Fire Station

Passenger Railway

St. Giles Church

Starkholmes Rd.

Church St.

Matlock Green

Dene Fields Court

Lime Tree Rd.

Lynholmes Rd.

Mettesford

Hazel Grove

Overdale

Hurst Rise

Highfields School Annexe

Butts Dr.

Deep Carr Ln.

MATLOCK CLIFF

Alfreton Rd.

Riber Castle (fauna reserve)

STARKHOLMES

Riber Rd.

Hearthstone Ln.

BARS/CLUBS ▲
Hydro **5**
The Crown **4**
The Strand **3**
The Underground **2**

CRASHING ■
Bradley House **3**
Old English Hotel **2**
YHA **6**

CULTURE ZOO ●
Riber Castle Wildlife Park **1**

filled with young punters, doing their best to perpetuate the myth of the heavy English drinker. (Myth? Who says it's a myth?) Sandwiches go for about £4.50 and are served till 9pm. If all of those cheap drinks go to your head, the hotel upstairs is a convenient place to crash for the night [see *crashing*, below].

Just down the road, the small and smoky **Boat House Inn** *(110 Dale Rd.; Tel 01629/583-776; Noon-11pm daily; AE, MC, V)* has become a hangout for local youth, probably because of the loud jukebox, pool table, and other games. It also offers one of the best food values in town, including dishes for vegetarians. Everything is washed down with Hardys & Hansons ales, and the average beer costs around £2.

Continue south along Dale Road until it makes a bend and becomes Derby Road; then turn off onto Starkholmes Road and head north to reach the venerable 18th-century **White Lion Inn** [see *eats*, below], which draws drinkers of all ages. Continuing north on Starkholmes Road, you'll reach **Duke William** *(Starkholmes Rd.; Tel 01629/582-585; Noon-11pm daily; MC, V)*. It draws a big, often young crowd with its warm, mellow atmosphere, traditional oak interiors, and old coal fireplace that's kept burning through most of the year. Beers cost about £2, and Sunday meals are the hottest ticket in town, for carnivores anyway, offering all-you-can-eat old English pork or beef roasts for just £6. Other dishes range from £4-10.

Just about the only late-night bar in town is, unfortunately, a chain. **The Crown** *(Crown Square; Tel 01629/580-991; 11am-11pm Mon-Sat, noon-10:30pm Sun; V, MC)* is the English version of TGI Friday's—there's one in almost every town in England. Nothing to rave about, these cookie-cutter "old-fashioned" pubs offer cheap beer and standard English bar food into the later hours of the evening, with entrées going for £4.50-7.55, so as the night wears on and the other places in town close, just about everyone ends up here. Elderly couples in tweed hobnob with young punks in ripped black T-shirts and spiked collars, who are undoubtedly considering catching the first available train to London. So sit back, down a pint or two, and enjoy the show. It's right on Crown Square.

club scene

Matlock's pathetic—and thankfully only—attempt at a club is located just off Crown Square. Evidently named in honor of the town's former hydrotherapy spa, **Hydro** *(Causeway Lane; Tel 01629/760-100; 10pm-2am Fri,Sat; £5 women, £10 men, open bar; No credit cards)* caters to a very young crowd before 9pm, so you're better off avoiding it. After 10pm, they open the bars and the DJs begin Matlock's version of a dance-hall, with two floors of music—'60s through '90s dance mixes on the top deck and a local DJ down below. Decidedly untrendy, Hydro is really more of a modest bar with big speakers than an upscale club.

great outdoors

After a night at the pubs, you might prefer to head out of town and stare at some rocks. The crags and mysterious pagan stone circles nearby are perfect for some serious staring. (Back in the day, pagans could have taught the kids in Matlock a thing or two about partying.)

About 11 miles east of the town center on Snitterton Road, you'll find the **Nine Ladies Stone Circle** on Stanton Moor. No one knows who assembled this circle or why. Legends say nine witches were transformed to stone for dancing on the Sabbath, but that probably tells us more about how medieval Christians felt about their pagan neighbors than how these stones really got here. Today, there are still rumors of full moon rituals involving drum circles and primitive dancing around bonfires. Unfortunately, only four of the gray ladies are still around to work up a good pagan groove.

About 220 yards (that's roughly two football fields) southeast of the dancing stones, you'll see **Robin Hood's Stride,** a series of craggy grit-stone rocks perched 16 yards apart on a ridge between Harthill Moor and the Alport-Winster Road. Its name is derived from the idea that Robin used the crags as stepping stones, although this legend is probably derived from ancient stories of a pagan hunting god known as the Green Man. (Maybe he was on his way to a pagan love-in with the gray ladies of the circle.)

About 10 miles west of Matlock, between the village of Middleton and Road A515, **Arbor Low** is called "the Stonehenge of the North." With a diameter of 250 feet and 47 total reclining stones, it's larger and more impressive than the Nine Ladies. This particular circle is notable because the stones were placed lying down, although some suggest they originally stood upright (They've fallen and they can't get up!). There are no footpaths to Arbor Low, so after the 10-mile hike from Matlock, you might want to join them in a lie-down. If 10 miles seems like just a good warm-up and you're ready for more, you should consider hiking the length of the Limestone Way [see below].

eats

The best places to grab some grub in Matlock are the pubs. There are a few other options, but nothing that'll knock your socks off.

The Strand *(Dale Rd.; Tel 01629/584-444; 10am-2pm, 7pm-10pm Mon-Sat; £9.95 two-course entrée; No Credit Cards)* is Matlock's tiny bite of sophistication, with elaborate cherry wood interior, two-person tables, and live jazz whenever they can find someone to play. It's more of a romantic and elegant place for dinner than a smoky, seductive jazz club, so leave your black beret and bongos at home.

Some come to the **White Lion Inn** *(195 Starkholmes Rd.; Tel 01629/582-511; 1am-11pm daily, summer; Noon-3pm/5-11pm daily, off-season; Main courses £8-14, beer £1.70-2.20; AE, MC,V)* for the beer, others for the reasonably priced French and international cuisine. Try the

Gressingham duck with caramelized pineapple or the chicken *cordon bleu*. For dessert, why not a baked chocolate ganache with kumquats? An Old World ambience is created by tin advertisements of long-gone candy companies. It's south of the town center, across the river.

In the town center, the **Lemon Tree Restaurant** *(Main Rd.; Tel 01629/581-652; Noon-2pm/7-11pm Mon-Sat; Main courses £9-12, beer £1.80-2.40; MC, V)* offers a light bistro fare, with a modern, mellow atmosphere and classical music played in the background. It's popular with hikers passing through Matlock on their way to tour the park.

crashing

Accommodations in Matlock are simple, but homey. The tourist office offers assistance with reservations.

▶▶CHEAP

Housed in a 19th-century building about 200 yards east of Crown Square, the **Matlock YHA** *(40 Bank Rd.; Tel 01629/582-983; Reception 1pm-11pm; £10.85 adult, £9.85 student, shared bath, breakfast £3.20; Membership required; V, MC)* has many interesting twists and turns and an almost overly helpful staff. Rooms are pretty standard, filled with dorm-like furniture and tiny plastic rectangular showers stuck into closets. The dining room is a little less cafeteria-like than you might expect and for a few quid, and the breakfast isn't bad. One drawback to YHA living is the strict 11pm lockout policy. They fill up quick, so show up early to grab a room.

▶▶DO-ABLE

Above the Underground pub, the **Old English Hotel** *(77 Dale Rd., Tel 01629/55028; £32 single, £39.50 double; V)* provides standard rooms right in the town center off the A6. From the Tudor exterior to the musk and oak smell inside, it's every inch an old English inn. The full English breakfast, charming rooms, convenient location, and lively in-house bar downstairs will make your overnight in Matlock a little more worthwhile.

If the smell of old English musk is too much for you, the **Bradley House** *(14 Dale Rd.; Tel 01629/582-677; £18 single, £29 double; No Credit Cards)* is right across the main road. This small, friendly B&B provides comfortable rooms at a reasonable rate, with a huge English breakfast. For an additional £5, the proprietors will even pack you a lunch before you head on your way.

If these are all full, try stately **Victoria House** *(65 Wellington St.; Tel 01629/55862; £20 per person, shared bath, TV, breakfast included; amsmatlock@hotmail.com)*, which offers a panoramic view of the area, and vegetarian meals by request.

▶▶SPLURGE

In nearby Matlock-Bath, the **Hodgkinson's Hotel** *(South Parade, Matlock-Bath; Tel 01629/582-170; Fax 01629/ 584-891; £40 single, £50-70 double, baths en suite, TV, breakfast included; enquiries@hodgkinsons* *hotel.co.uk; V, MC, AE)* is a beautifully kept Victorian inn built in the 1700s. There are some cool caves behind the inn that were used as a brewery cellar in the mid-1800s, and a terraced garden high above the hotel, where you can catch spectacular view.

within 30 minutes

Local tourist attraction the **Heights of Abraham** is just 2 miles south of Matlock. The highlight is a cable-car ride up to the top of some craggy peaks, which offer stunning views of the surrounding dales [see below].

need to know

Currency Exchange Your best bet in this mini-town will be the **HSBC Bank** *(5 Dale Rd.; Tel 01629/774-200; 9:30am-3:30pm, Mon-Fri)* or the **post office.** You can get better rates at the bank, but the post office is open later and charges less commission for a minimum of £2.

Tourist Information Center Matlock Tourist Information Centre *(Crown Square; Tel 01629/583-388; 9:30am-5pm daily Mar-Oct, 10am-4pm daily Nov-Mar)* is located right off the main traffic circle before the bridge over River Derwent. Be prepared to be loaded down with paper, as the employees seem overly enthusiastic about giving out publications.

Health and Emergency Emergency: *999.* ***Whitworth Hospital** (330 Bakewell Rd.; Tel 01629/57911),* about a 1.5 miles out of town on the A6, offers medical attention. The **police station** *(Bank Rd.; Tel 01629/583-388)* is just east of Crown Square.

Pharmacies For all of your pill-popping or beautifying needs, head to the town **Chemist** *(12 Bank St.; Tel 01629/57924; 9am-6pm Mon-Sat).*

Trains and Buses Matlock and Matlock-Bath accommodate lots of tourists heading for the park, so it's relatively easy to move on to other areas of the Peak District from here. **Stagecoach** *(Tel 01298/23098)* and **Trent** *(Tel 01773/712-265)* are among the bus lines that run dozens of buses through Matlock daily. The main bus and train stations are located on Bakewell Road, up a steep hill off Matlock Bridge. Timetable information is available at the tourist office.

Bike Rental Bicycles can be rented through **Stanley Fearn Cycles** *(19 Bakewell Rd.; Tel 01629/582-089; 9am-6:30pm Mon-Wed,Fri; 9am-5:30pm Sat, closed Thur,Sun; £17 per day; MC, V).*

Laundry In an effort to make dirty clothes more appealing, Laundromats are sometimes given the cuter name of "launderette," as with the **Matlock Launderette** *(First Parade; Tel 01629/582-094; £1.50 wash, 50p dry),* but you still have to do your laundry yourself.

Postal Someone must have discovered how well chocolate goes with the taste of stamp adhesive, because at the **Matlock Branch Post Office** *(14 Bank St.; Tel 01629/582-011; 9am-5pm daily)* you can get stamps, send your letter, and grab a candy bar all in one shot.

CASTLETON

As you approach Castleton, Mam Tor dominates your vision and your imagination. It seems to be both a grassy hill and a majestic mountain, sounding a call that hikers and mountain bikers find hard to ignore. At the other extreme, the otherworldly Peak Cavern at the town's edge beckons you down into the underworld. Come to Castleton to commune with the sublime landscape, but don't miss out on the tiny village itself, which seems to have changed little since the 17th century.

The village was founded in 1080, along with Peveril Castle, which William the Conqueror offered as a gift to one of his sons. Traces of history remain throughout town, from the Norman arch across the nave of the old church to the town ditch (much cooler than it sounds), a defensive earthwork built around the village in Norman times. The presence of semiprecious Blue John stone in Peak Cavern established Castleton as a mining town in the 1600s, although evidence suggests that the Romans first mined it some thousand years earlier. The locals seem comfortable with the trappings of the ancient world that surround them—if possible, the contrast makes them seem even more down-to-earth. Anywhere you go, expect to be treated as a visiting family member rather than a tourist. You'll find some of the most comfortable and, though we hate to say it, *quaint* bed and breakfasts in England here. As for the nightlife, while the town pubs host thirsty hikers fresh from Mam Tor, the entire town is generally in bed by 11pm.

The village's gritstone buildings fit entirely within a half-mile of road shaped in a backwards *Z*, which can be walked in a matter of minutes. Old cottages, the church, and the youth hostel surround the village square, and most of the pubs, restaurants, and shops are along the main road, **Castleton Road,** which becomes **How Lane, Cross Street,** and finally **A625** (it's easier just to refer to "the main road"). Considering its tiny size, Castleton does an excellent job of accommodating tourists, offering all a backpacker could need, with outdoor equipment shops and lots of helpful information at the tourist office.

bar scene

Even in tiny little Castleton, you can find people out to get pissed—that means "drop-dead drunk" to us Yanks—so if that's what you have in mind, you won't be disappointed. There are only slight differences between the pubs, the most significant being the kind of beer they serve. All of them are located along the main road and offer accommodation and full meal service in addition to the usual libations. That makes downing a pint in Castleton feel a lot like hanging in a buddy's living room. Don't be surprised to find yourself talking with your fellow barmates as if you've all lived here your whole life. Pubs are open 11am to

castleton

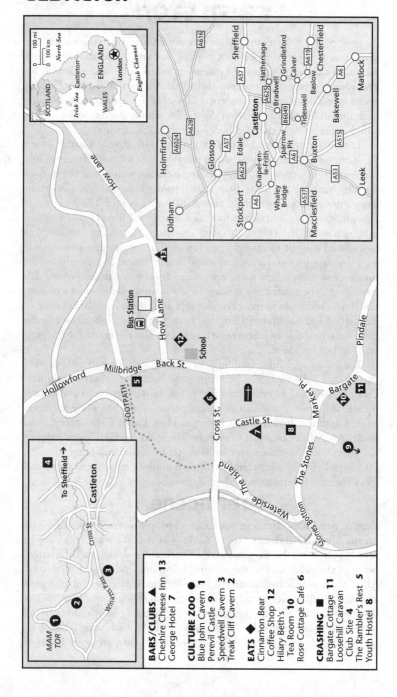

BARS/CLUBS ▲
Cheshire Cheese Inn **13**
George Hotel **7**

CULTURE ZOO ●
Blue John Cavern **1**
Perevil Castle **9**
Speedwell Cavern **3**
Treak Cliff Cavern **2**

EATS ◆
Cinnamon Bear
Coffee Shop **12**
Hilary Beth's
Tea Room **10**
Rose Cottage Café **6**

CRASHING ■
Bargate Cottage **11**
Loosehill Caravan
Club Site **4**
The Rambler's Rest **5**
Youth Hostel **8**

11pm, with the exception of Sundays, when law requires more limited hours: noon to 10:30pm.

You won't find massive crowds at the **Chesire Cheese Inn** *(How Lane; Tel 01433/620-330; 11am-11pm Mon-Sat, noon-10:30pm Sun, food till 9pm; £3.95-11.95 per entree; V, MC)*. What you will find is people out to get enough drink in them to relieve the pain from hiking all day. This place is also your best bet for a meal after 5pm, but don't expect gourmet fare—we're talking fish & chips and shepherd's pie. A seat at the bar guarantees you some good conversation, especially after 8pm when the place starts to fill up with cargo pants-clad hikers.

Just off the west end of the main road, the **George Hotel** *(Castle St.; Tel 01433/620-238; £7.50-15.95 per entree; V, MC)* has an interior dressed in old-world-style English extravagance. Although it's slightly more expensive, they offer a number of fine ales. The beer's a bit heavier, and the crowd's a bit more mellow as a result, but they're every bit as friendly, and the staff even more prone to conversation. Food is again typical English fare—just keep telling yourself: "The deep-fat-fryer is my friend."

culture zoo

Not only is Castleton in the shadow of **Mam Tor** [see *great outdoors,* below], it's home to a spectacular ruin of a castle with an even more spectacular view.

Peveril Castle *(Off Castle St.; Tel 01433/620-613; 10am-6pm daily, Apr-Sept; till 5pm, Oct; till 4pm Nov-Mar; £2.20 adults, £1.70 students; V, MC):* Climb the breathtakingly steep and thankfully short hill to Peveril Castle, and you'll be rewarded with some jawdropping views of the Peak Cavern Gorge. The view is the main reason to visit this ancient keep, among the oldest castles in England. Awarded by William the Conqueror to his illegitimate son William Peveril in 1080, the fortress eventually fell into disuse in the 17th century. Today only ruins remain, although you can still see Roman tiles and a well-preserved tower that dates back to 1176. Sit still for a moment, and you'll realize that Peveril is no longer under the control of that bastard William—thousands of tiny black flies are the new conquerors. Easy come, easy go.

great outdoors

Standing at 1,040 feet, **Mam Tor** may seem more like a hill than a mountain—until you try to cross it. It's actually a vast expanse of deteriorating rock—alternating layers of shale and sandstone that crumble down into the valley below—which has given it the nickname "Shivering Mountain." The view from the top is worth the steep climb—the green dales open up before you, and on a clear day, you'll never see a deeper sky. You can also see the crumbled fortifications of an Iron Age fort—the foundations of hut circles and ancient artifacts on the site indicate it once held a village as well, but its story has been lost to the erosion of time. To begin your tor trek, start at the car park off Hollowford Lane, at the northern edge of town, and follow the footpath marked with signs to Edale. This path will take you over the ridge to an area known as Hollins Cross. Your descent will lead you into Edale and the beginning of the Pennine Way [see below]. Crossing from Castleton to Edale is just over 2 miles. If you need equipment or advice on making the hike, the friendly folks at **The Old Barn** *(Market Place, Castleton; Tel 01433/620-528; 10am-5pm daily)* are happy to provide both.

If you love the feeling of mud splattering up from your spokes, you'll be happy to hear that Mam Tor has also become a popular, albeit treacherous, destination for mountain bikers. Some possible routes include the old Mam Tor Road, past the Blue John Cavern, and the much steeper Winnats Pass. While bikes aren't available for rent in town, you can get one at the Derwent Reservoir nearby [see *need to know,* below].

There are sights to be seen underground as well. For a brief visit to the Underworld, check out **Peak Cavern** *(Off A625; Tel 01433/620-285; 10am-5pm daily Apr-Oct; Sat,Sun only, Nov-Mar, last tour 4pm; £5; No credit cards),* which the 16th-century locals fondly referred to as the "Devil's Arse." If the scatological nickname alone doesn't scare you off, you'll get a long look at an immense natural cavern with an underground stream, known as "The Styx." Village maidens once performed here for Queen Victoria, who evidently wasn't afraid of the devil or any of his body parts. Peak Cavern is located directly beneath Peveril Castle; from the top of the town square, make a right and walk westward.

If you don't mind ducking a bit, you can glide through the network of underground rivers of the **Speedwell Cavern** *(Off A625; Tel 01433/620-512; Bus 403, 203, 260; 9:30am-5pm daily summer; till 4pm winter; £4.75 adult, £3.75 student; V, MC)* by boat, ending at the Bottomless Pit, an underground lake that at one point swallowed over 40 thousand tons of waste rock from the mine without changing the level of the water. Swimming is not recommended. Speedwell Cavern is uphill from Castleton, at the foot of Winnats Pass.

The most spectacular displays of the Blue John stone can be found, appropriately enough, in the **Blue John Cavern** *(Off A625; Tel 01433/620-638; Bus 403, 203, 260; 9:30am-5:30pm daily summer; 9:30am-dusk daily winter; £4.50 adult, £3.50 student; No credit cards),* the first mine in the area. The high ceilings are lined with veins of the colorful mineral in blue, yellow, white, and red. There's also abandoned mining equipment on display. Blue John Cavern is also up the hillside from Castleton; continue up Winnats Pass and turn down the old Mam Tor Road.

Further up the old Mam Tor Road, the **Treak Cliff Cavern** *(Off A625; Tel 01433/620-571; Bus 403, 203, 260; 9:30am-5:30pm daily Mar-Oct, till 4pm Nov-Feb; £4.75 adult, £3.75 student; www.bluejohn stone.com; V,MC)* is still mined for Blue John today, although current activity is hidden from view. This cavern has more stalactites and stalagmites than visible in Blue John, but it is still striking in areas such as the Dream Cave, where it seems as if the walls are melting.

eats

The pubs are the best places for a meal after 5pm [see *bar scene,* above], but don't wait too long—they only serve food until 9pm. If you're looking for a light lunch, step into any of the teahouses, which might as well be your grandmother's kitchen. They're all on the main square.

▶▶**CHEAP**

If you love that spicy ground-up bark, the **Cinnamon Bear Coffee Shop** (*Back St.; Tel 01433/621-385; 10am-5pm daily; £1.50- £7.25 per entrée; No credit cards*) is *the* place to go for high tea. It lives up to its name, providing a number of desserts with cinnamon as the key ingredient. The cinnamon-spiced bread pudding beats out a scone any day. Hot and cold lunches are also served, and this is one of the only places in town where "vegetarian" isn't a foreign word.

If you feel deserving of a meal like Grandma used to make before the doctor put her on that low-cholesterol diet, head for the **Rose Cottage Café** (*Cross St.; Tel 01433/620-472; 10am-5pm Sat-Thur; £2.25-6.00 per entrée; No credit cards*). Ignore doctor's warnings and load up on bangers and mash (sausage and mashed potatoes) and cream teas (tea served with a crumpet and whipped cream as thick as ice cream). It's easy to fool yourself into thinking that you are actually on holiday at your grandmother's house—the only things missing are the plastic covers on the chairs and a big red-lipstick kiss mark on your cheek.

If you get caught in one of the all-too-frequent rainstorms, ultra-cozy **Hilary Beth's Tea Room** (*Market Place; Tel 01433/620-397; 10am-about 6pm daily; 60p-£3.25 per snack; No credit cards*) is the perfect place to recover from a good soaking. Enjoy their hot teas, homemade desserts, and fresh scones, and take as long as you like to finish up. Hilary Beth doesn't seem to mind.

crashing

For a village that has let time pass it by, Castleton has managed to stay on top of quality accommodations. There are a number of very attractive and friendly B&Bs in town, as well as some hotels that are better known for their pubs. One word of warning: Castleton's buildings were designed during a time when people were a little shorter, so when in doubt, duck. If you happen to arrive during the evening meal hours, you have a good chance of finding a place to stay by going door-to-door—most of the locals run B&Bs. The tourist office can also help you find a place.

▶▶**CHEAP**

No building in town looks a day under 200 years old, and the **YHA** (*Castle St.; Tel 01433/620-235; Reception 7am-11pm, Feb-Dec; £10.50 per bed, £3.50 breakfast; castleton@yha.org.uk, www.yha.org.uk; V,MC*) is no exception. Marking the end of the Limestone Way [see below] (or the beginning, depending on which way you're going), this is a great place to meet other travelers. The common room is filled with publications, including hiking guides and histories of the Peak District. Stocked with regulation YHA-issued furniture, the sleeping quarters are nothing spectacular.

If you don't mind roughing it, one way to fully appreciate the sublime landscape surrounding Castleton is to camp out. Approximately 1 mile east of Castleton, the **Loosehill Caravan Club Site** *(Castleton Rd., Tel 01433/630-636; £3-£6 per site; No credit cards)* provides a piece of land to rest your head, with no angry farmers yelling at you to get lost.

▶▶**DO-ABLE**

Out on the east side of town, which amounts to all of a five-minute walk, the luxurious **Bargate Cottage** *(Market Place; Tel 01433/620-201; £21.50 per person, en suite; No credit cards)* was built in 1650 and refurbished in 1988. Fortunately, the proprietors have maintained the rugged simplicity of the original building, while adding all of today's modern amenities. They also offer a full English breakfast.

Across the street is the warm **Rambler's Rest** *(Mill Bridge, Back St.; Tel 01433/620-125; £22 single, £35 double, en suite available; No credit cards).* It's housed in a 17th-century structure with stone floors and exposed beam ceilings, making staying in this ancient English village feel all the more authentic. The welcome you receive on arrival makes up for the slight chill of the stone floors. The tiny dining room, with the original fireplace still intact, encourages lively conversation over breakfast.

On the Hope end of the main road, **Kelsey's Swiss House Hotel** *(Castleton Rd., Tel 01433/621-098; Doubles and twins £50, triples £70, breakfast included; swisshousehotel@castleton8wj.fsnet.co.uk; V, MC)* offers pleasant rooms with private baths. They also have a restaurant that serves a Mediterranean-style menu.

need to know

Currency Exchange There's nowhere to exchange currency in Castleton, so stock up on cash before you arrive.

Tourist Information The **Tourist Information Center** *(Castle Rd.; Tel 01433/620-679; 10am-5:30pm Mon-Fri, 9:30am-5:30pm Sat, Sun)* is loaded with maps and guides for walks in and around the area.

Health and Emergency Emergency: *999.* The nearest **police station** is in Bakewell *(Granby Rd.; Tel 01629/812-594).* The nearest hospital, **Claremont Hospital** *(401 Sandygate Rd.; Tel 0114/263-0330)* is in Sheffield, about 14 miles east.

Pharmacies There are **no pharmacies** in town, so you'll have to go cold turkey till you reach the next stop.

Bus Lines Out of Town Buses stop along the main road; service is provided by **Stagecoach** *(Tel 01246/311-007).* There is no train service to Castleton.

Bike Rental The nearest place to rent a bike is in the nearby village of Bamford, about 8 miles east. **Fairholmes Cycle Hire** *(Derwent Reservoir; Tel 01433/651-261; 9:30am-5:30pm daily; Closed Sat-Mon Nov-Mar; £7.50 per 3 hrs., £20 deposit; MC, V)* is near the Derwent dam; take road A625.

Postal Send your postcards from the edge of Mam Tor at the **post office** *(How Lane; 7am-1pm/2pm-5:30pm Mon-Fri, 7am-12:30pm Wed; 7:30am-12:30pm Sat,Sun).*

pennine way

To touch the wildest, remotest parts of England, crossing open moorlands and grazing fields, woodlands and river banks—places you would otherwise never see—hike the Pennine Way. Britain's best-known national trail, first laid out in April 1965, is a challenge to even the experienced long-distance walker, stretching a distance of 268 miles from start to finish. The trail begins just north of **Castleton** in the small village of **Edale** in Derbyshire and runs to **Kirk Yetholm** across the border in Scotland, cutting through three gorgeous national parks along the way: the **Peak District National Park,** the **Yorkshire Dales National Park** [see **Yorkshire,** below], and the **Northumberland National Park** [see **Northumbria,** below]. There are 535 access points to the trail, which means that you never have to walk more than two or three hours before cutting off for supplies, food, or accommodations. There are 110 pubs stretched along the trail. This is England, after all; what's the point of hiking without a pub to crash in at the end of the day?

Most visitors settle for only a day walk of 2 miles or so, although there are also thousands of long-distance walkers every year who spend as little as six to eight days or as long as two weeks traveling the full length of the Way. Be prepared for long periods of wet and rather chilly weather, even during the summer months. All provisions for hiking or walking, such as rainwear or hiking gear, should be purchased in a big city such as Manchester before heading to Edale to begin the walk.

The trail starts at the **Nag's Head Pub** [see *need to know,* below,] the only pub in the valley of Edale, heading up **Grindsbrook** onto **Kinder Scout** and across the highest section of the Kinder plateau. If you aren't out to hike the entire way, this hike makes a satisfying climb in itself.

If you're in it for the long haul, the path continues north and east along the **Alport River** and through some extremely desolate moorlands. Unfortunately, the path here suffered from erosion to the point where it needed to be paved. After the town of **Crowden,** the path takes you up to **Black Hill.** With heavy humidity, this is the most miserable remaining stretch of the Way. The path divides and continues to Stanage Edge [see below] and the end of the Peak District.

After Stanage, the Way takes you into the **Yorkshire Dales National Park.** Sights along the way include the impressive limestone amphitheater **Malham Cove.** After leaving the Dales, the Way joins with a section of Hadrian's Wall [see below], built by the Romans to fend off possible invasions from the "barbarians" to the north (better-known as the Scottish and Irish to you and me). It then continues north through

Northumberland National Park. The end of the line is at **Kirk Yetholm,** just over the Scottish border.

need to know

Tourist Info The Way is marked with the **National Trail acorn symbol** at infrequent intervals, so a good guidebook is not only helpful, it's essential. The *National Trail Guide: Pennine Way South (Edale to Bowes)* and *National Trail Guide: Pennine Way North (Bowes to Kirk Yetholm)* by Tony Hopkins (Aurum Press, £9.99 each) include Ordinance Survey Maps. Both are available through John Needham at the **Rambler's Association/Pennine Way Association** *(23 Woodland Crescent, Hilton Park, Prestwich Manchester M25 9WQ; www.ramblers.org.uk)* which also offers an accommodation and camping guide for £1.50. You can also purchase maps and information in Edale at the **National Park Information Centre** *(Tel 01433/670-207; 9am-1pm/ 2-5:30pm daily, Easter-Oct),* a five-minute walk from the train station, on the main road. Call for information in advance, but it's best to visit personally as well.

Directions and Transportation The Peninne Way begins behind the **Nag's Head Pub** *(Grindsbrook Booth; Tel 01443/670-291; 11am-11pm Mon-Sat, noon-10pm Sun)* in the village of Edale, which is linked to public transportation, including hourly **train service** from Manchester's **Piccadilly Station.** You can also begin your hike by crossing **Mam Tor** from Castleton.

Crashing Accommodations along the trail range from around 150 B&B houses to nearly 50 camping sites, along with 17 hostels and a dozen "bunk-barns." Listing all of these accommodations would fill another book—it's best to write for a comprehensive guide. You can obtain limited accommodation and service guides free from most tourist information centers along the way. The best and most comprehensive guide is available through the Rambler's Association for just £1.50, including postage. If you want to go the hostel route, bookings can be made through the **Pennine Way Booking Bureau** *(P.O. Box 67, Matlock, Derbyshire DE4 3YX; Tel 01629/581-061).* Youth hostels are evenly spaced within a day's hike, which can range from seven to 30 miles. For the most rugged accommodations, book into one of the camping barns (called bunk barns), rented by private farms who offer sleeping platforms and running water (cold only). You'll get a toilet at these bare-bones places but not much more. Rates are generally from £4 a night. If you'd like to sleep in barns along the route, make arrangements through **YHA Camping Barns** *(16 Shawbridge St., Clitheroe BB7 1LZ; Tel 01200/428-366).* They can also provide directions.

THe LIMESTONE WAY

Instead of taking the Pennine Way, you can opt for the far less daunting challenge of the Limestone Way, which cuts across the most scenic part of the **Peak District National Park.** This walk begins in **Matlock** and continues north until it reaches **Castleton** (or begins in Castleton and ends in Matlock, if you're traveling south). The entire 26-mile trail can be walked in about 10 hours. Bakewell, which lies between Castleton and Matlock, is a good place to break up the hike, with plentiful food, lodgings, and bus transportation to neighboring cities, including seven daily buses to Manchester [see above].

Beginners might want to take just the southern part of the trail, which starts in Matlock and heads northwest to Bakewell. This gentler part of the trail centers in the southeast around the White Peak, which is split with limestone dales carved by water, including **Dovedale, Bradford Dale,** and **Lathkill Dale.** This is some of the loveliest countryside in the Midlands, with rolling farmland, ancient dry-stone walls, and spiderweb footpaths. Along the way, you may notice a lot of birds—most are concentrated at Water-cum Jolly Dale (only the English could come up with names like this).

The northern part of the Limestone Way, between Bakewell and Castleton, is rougher and more suitable for hardcore backpackers. The north of the trail, formed around the Dark Peak, is hard gritstone, with wild heather moors and turbulent rivers. The terrain includes conifer woodland, moorland, and tussocky sheep pastures. This leg of the Way has its fair share of wildlife as well, including grouse and white hares.

need To Know

Directions/Transportation Tourist offices in both Matlock *(Crown Sq.; Tel 01629/583-388; 9:30am-5pm daily, Mar-Oct; 10am-4pm daily Nov-Mar)* and Castleton *(Castle Rd.; Tel 01433/620-679; 10am-5:30pm Mon- Fri, 9:30am-5:30pm Sat,Sun)* can provide maps and information on traveling the Way. But the real experts are in Edale, just north of Castleton, at the **Peak District National Park Information Centre** *(Castle St.; Tel 01433/620-679; 10am-1pm/2-5:30pm daily, Easter-Oct; Till 5pm Nov-Easter).*

Rental Equipment rental along the Limestone Way is limited. Some is available in Castleton at **The Old Barn** *(Market Place; Tel 01433/620-528; 10am-5pm daily).* However, it's a good idea to get all of your hiking equipment and other provisions in a bigger city, such as Manchester, before you set out.

heights of abraham

About 2 miles south of Matlock is **Matlock-Bath** and the Heights of Abraham. At one time, these peaks offered nothing more than some breathtaking views of the **River Derwent** gorge below. Then someone decided there was money to be made, and built a cable car up to the top. Voila! Instant tourist attraction that's fun for the whole family. Today the 60-acre **Heights of Abraham Country Park and Caverns** *(Tel 01629/582-365; Fax 01629/580-279; www.heights-of-abraham.co.uk; £6.50; V, MC, AE)* is one of the most popular destinations in the Derbyshire Dales. The cable car runs from the village of Matlock-Bath over the trees and deep limestone gorge up to the summit, where you're rewarded with the greatest possible vista of the Derbyshire Dales.

Along with the price of your cable-car trip you receive admission to the two cavern exhibits near the summit. In one, the **Great Rutland Cavern-Nestus Mine,** you can see the harsh life of a 17th-century lead miner. In the **Grand Masson Cavern,** there's a video presentation showing how volcanoes and ice shaped the surrounding geology. After that you'll be taken on a guided walk underground into the passages of the cavern.

eats

At the summit you'll find the **Heights of Abraham Coffee Shop, Bar & Restaurant** *(Matlock-Bath; Tel 01629/582-365; 10am-5pm Sat, Sun only, Feb-Mar; 10am-5pm daily Apr-Oct; AE,MC,V)* serving very routine British food. It's more fun to pack provisions for a picnic at one of the many tables set up in the park.

need to know

Hours/Days Open The park and caverns are open 10am to 5pm, Saturday and Sunday, from February through March; and 10am to 5pm daily, April through October. The best time for a visit is the summer, when clearer weather means the views are less likely to be obscured by clouds.

Directions/Transportation The Heights of Abraham lie on the A6 at Matlock-Bath, 2 miles south of Matlock and 18 miles north of the city of Derby. If you're driving, the attraction is sign-posted from M1 at junction 28. Matlock-Bath is also accessible from Derby by frequent trains throughout the day. The trip time is 45 minutes, with a one-way ticket costing £5 per person. The train delivers you practically to the grounds of the park.

Stanage Edge

Located just north of the tiny village of Hathersage, about 6 miles from Castleton, Stanage is the largest and most impressive of the area's grit-stone edges, a harsh gray cliff-side jutting up from the calm purple moors. Visible from miles down the Hope Valley, the Edge is approximately 3.5 miles long, with the northern tip at Stanage End and the southern point near the Cowper Stone. At an elevation that varies between 1,300 and 1,500 feet, Stanage is often snowbound in winter. The rock face itself averages between 50 and 65 feet, but achieves a maximum height of 82 feet at High Neb, near the north end.

There are currently 800 recorded climbs along the Edge, answering to colorful and descriptive names like Marble Wall, Crow Chin, Goliath's Groove, the Tower, the Unconquerables, Mississippi Buttress, and Robin Hood's Cave. Unfortunately, the area's popularity has caused a great deal of erosion: heather no longer sneaks between fissures in the rocks, so many of the most well-known climbs have been smoothed away. But the Edge endures: there are still hundreds of climbs left to be discovered and conquered.

crashing

There are many places available in Castleton [see **Castleton,** above], but if you want to be right in the middle of the action, the **YHA hostel** *(Castleton Rd., Hathersage; Tel 01433/650-493; 5pm-11pm Mon-Sat, Apr-Oct; £9.80 dorm)* is just west of the center of Hathersage. There are also camping barns available about 1 mile north of Hathersage and 2 miles south of Stanage Edge. The **Old Stables** and the **Old Shippon** *(Thorpe Farm, off the A625; Tel 01433/650-659; £6 dorm)* provide a dormitory setting with heating, showers, drying facilities, toilets, and well-equipped kitchens. They're located just off the A625, which in this area is called the A6127, on the way to Hope and Castleton.

need to know

Directions/Transportation Take a **bus** east from Castleton (lines 174, 175, 257, 272, 279, 673, V) to Hathersage. From Hathersage, continue on Bus 257 to Hook's Car, where you will be a quarter-mile from the southern end of Stanage Edge. Call **Travel Line** *(Tel 01298/23098)* for schedule information.

Rental Outside *(Main Rd., Hathersage; Tel 01433/651-936; 9:30am-5:30pm Mon-Fri, 9am-6pm Sat,Sun)* has all the equipment, lessons, and advice you'll need to make your climb.

yorkshire

yorkshire

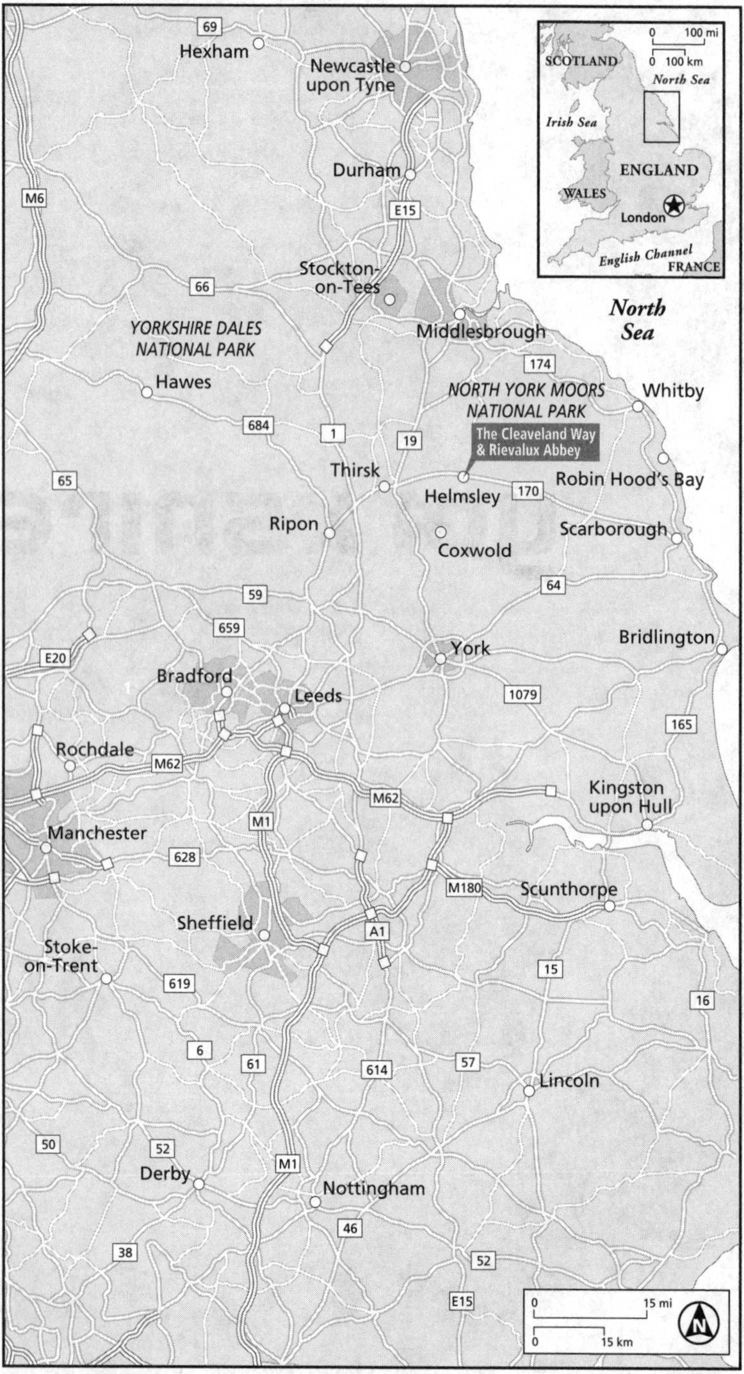

69
Hexham
Newcastle upon Tyne
Durham
M6
E15
Stockton-on-Tees
66
Middlesbrough
YORKSHIRE DALES NATIONAL PARK
Hawes
174
NORTH YORK MOORS NATIONAL PARK
Whitby
684
1
19
The Cleaveland Way & Rievalux Abbey
65
Thirsk
Helmsley
170
Robin Hood's Bay
Ripon
Coxwold
Scarborough
59
64
659
Bridlington
York
E20
Bradford
Leeds
1079
165
Rochdale
M62
M62
Kingston upon Hull
M1
Manchester
628
M180
Scunthorpe
Sheffield
A1
Stoke-on-Trent
619
15
16
6
61
614
57
Lincoln
50
52
M1
Derby
Nottingham
46
38
52
E15
0 15 mi
0 15 km
N
SCOTLAND
0 100 mi
0 100 km
North Sea
Irish Sea
ENGLAND
WALES
London
English Channel
FRANCE
North Sea

for those who actually read *Jane Eyre* and *Wuthering Heights* in lit class, the mere mention of Yorkshire conjures up images of doomed lovers meeting along the desolate moors, the bitter wind howling off the North Sea chilling them to the bone. That was the Brontë sisters' idea of a perfect setting for their signature star-crossed-lovers motif. But even if *Wuthering Heights* is just an old Kate Bush song you only vaguely remember, you'll undoubtedly be happy to know that Yorkshire isn't all gloomy romanticism and ancient history. The modern day vampires in **Whitby,** the town where Bram Stoker wrote *Dracula,* aren't the only ones who don't sleep till dawn; the clubs in **Leeds** rock all night long. The university town has a huge rep for being a 24-7 party spot, and clubbers as well as DJs come all the way from London to check it out.

On the opposite end of the scale, the city of **York** banks mostly on its ancient past to attract visitors, from the excavation of Jorvik, a primitive Viking village which has been reconstructed beneath the streets of the modern city (tours are open to the public) to York Minster, one of the greatest cathedrals in Europe. Everyone from the Romans to the Vikings to the Normans left their fingerprints all over the city's medieval walls, which are still standing. But York also has a modern side. Chic boutiques and hip cafe-bars are crammed along the cobblestoned streets in the busy city center, giving the city an almost-cosmopolitan feel.

Reaching from Manchester and the Lake District up to the northeastern coast, Yorkshire's landscape is quite varied: The rolling hills and deep green dales and wolds of the **Yorkshire Dales National Park** give way to the moors in the North—lonely, treeless flatlands that blossom with purple heather in the late summer. Yorkshire also claims a bit of coast line, but don't even think about catching rays here—these beaches are definitely more Brontë than *Baywatch.* They're made for searching through the fog, wrapped in a wool sweater and rainjacket. The air's brisk, even in the summertime. A few days wandering the **North York Moors National Park** is the best way to achieve the full Brontë (not likely to be confused with the full Monty, of course); hard-core backpackers will want to hike the **Cleveland Way** that skirts the edges of the park before heading down the coast.

TraVel TIMes

Times by train unless
otherwise indicated
*By road.

	Leeds	York
Leeds	-	:35
York	:35	-
Whitby	3:10	3:10
The Cleveland Way	1:15*	:40*
Yorkshire Dales	1:30*	1:20*
North York Moors National Park	1:10*	:45*

geTTIng around The regIon

Transportation around both the Yorkshire Dales and Moors is difficult at best. The easiest way to see this area is to base yourself in York, the region's transportation hub, then day trip it outward. Both York and Leeds are served by frequent trains from London. The **Yorkshire Coastliner** *(Tel 01653/692-556 or 0113/244-89-76) runs a bus service from Leeds to York and along the coast.* July-September, the **Moorsbus** *(Tel 0870/608-26-08 or 01439/770-657; www.moorsbus.net)* services North Yorkshire Dales National Park; it runs Sundays only May-October. Rail service is sporadic; call **National Rail Enquiry** *(Tel 0345/484-950)* for info.

ROUTES

If you have only one or two days in Yorkshire, and you don't want to spend them in York, head straight for the party town of Leeds. It's an easy train ride from London and can easily eat up a couple of days and sleepless nights as well.

	Whitby	The Cleveland Way	Yorkshire Dales	North York Moors National Park	London
	3:10	1:15*	1:30*	1:10*	2:20
	3:10	:40*	1:20*	:45*	2:10
	-	:50*	1:50*	1:00*	5:05 5:40
	:50*	-	1:10*	:05*	4:15*
	1:50*	1:10*	-	1:10*	4:40*
	1:00*	:05*	1:10*	-	4:10*

If you have a few more days, check out York, then head for the North Yorkshire Moors National Park and east to the coastal town of Whitby, where an active vampire subculture still thrives (see www.vein-europe. demon.co.uk) and you can visit the fictional birthplace of Dracula as well as a 12th-century abbey. After that, you'll probably be more than ready to say goodbye to the vampires and hello to the zillions of sheep in the nearby Esk Valley and the little village of Danby.

With another day or two, you can explore the market town of Helmsley in the west, as well as the ruins of 12th-century Rievaulx Abbey. Spend your last day in the Yorkshire Dales, using Skipton, the southernmost town of the Dales—with some of the best rail links in the area—as a base. From either Helmsley or Skipton, you're just a quick bus ride back to York.

Leeds

Leeds is well on its way to becoming England's first city that never sleeps. The days when pubs closed early and factory workers staggered home to get up before dawn to turn a few more cranks in the cogs of the Industrial Revolution are long gone. In 21st-century Leeds, clubs stay open until 3 or even 4am—*and* 5 or 6am on weekends—pretty much unheard of in the north of Europe. These relaxed licensing hours have jump-started an electric club scene that's giving the old sods in Manchester a run for their money. Club nights don't get any more outlandish than the come-as-you-aren't *Speed Queen*'s polysexual marathon [see *gay scene,* below], and little boho hideaways like **Soul Kitchen** groove all night long [see *bar scene,* below].

This city that once was known as the grimy horror of the north is now becoming a hip hotspot, and the tarnished Victorian cityscape that was almost destroyed by smelly, sooty factories is now being restored to its original beauty. Although Leeds has medieval origins as a marketplace for weavers, in the 19th century the city became known as the quintessential northern textile town, thanks to lots of pastureland and sheep, and rivers and canals to get the finished goods to market. Post-Industrial Revolution, Leeds was the poster child for capitalism run amok, with problems including depopulation of surrounding farms, overpopulation of the City Centre, and squalid living conditions for factory workers. Since the 1950s, the theme in Leeds has been urban renewal. Some £400 million and a lot of elbow grease have pushed the City Centre into the modern era. Instead of tearing everything down and constructing some hideous modern plasticene and fiberglass blemish on its site, Leeds's 700,000

fIVe ThInGs To TaLk To a LoCaL abOut

Apartments: Even though they are finally building housing within the city, no one can live there since it's too damn expensive.

Construction: You can't go anywhere that they aren't rebuilding something, and they do it really loud.

Drinking: The fact that you aren't doing enough, and would you like another?

Leeds, the new London: With cafe-bars popping up on every corner, the city peeps seem to be grooving to the cosmopolitan lifestyle.

The character of the city: Most everyone who lives here loves it, and has a thousand reasons why. Ask them.

inhabitants have converting old warehouses, long-abandoned office buildings, and storefronts to restaurants, clubs, and shops.

Immigration to Leeds has created a kind of multi-culti stew, with West Indians, Bangladeshis, Pakistanis, and East Africans taking the place once reserved for Scots and Irishmen in "colorful" British neighborhoods. Expect lots of blue-collar panache, and a wry skepticism that is both friendly and unpretentious. Today the city is warm, welcoming, funny, and loaded with options to "help a bloke become a mate."

Several monthly publications can help you navigate this party, including the *Leeds Guide,* which sells for £1.50 at newsstands around town, and *Alive,* a free bar rag available at both news stands and pubs. The pocket-sized *Little Book of Leeds* is available for £3 at bookstores and newspaper kiosks as well.

neighborhoods

Virtually everything you'll want to see is in the **City Centre,** the neighborhood encircled by "City Loop Road," an interconnected ring of densely trafficked roads that includes **The Calls,** the **East Parade, New York Road,** and **St.Peter's Street.** Traffic on the Loop moves clockwise only, and although buses and cabs navigate freely around the **City Centre,** access by private cars is somewhat restricted. Most local residents leave their cars in parking lots outside the Loop, then walk anywhere within the City Centre (never more than about 20 minutes).

Main arteries within the Loop include **The Headrow** (which becomes **Eastgate** at its eastern end and, you guessed it, **Westgate** at its western end) and **Boar Lane** (east-west streets) and **Briggate, Vicar Lane,** and **Park Row** (all north-south streets.)

You'll also want to check out the **University District,** site of both the University of Leeds and the somewhat smaller Leeds Metropolitan University.

Leeds

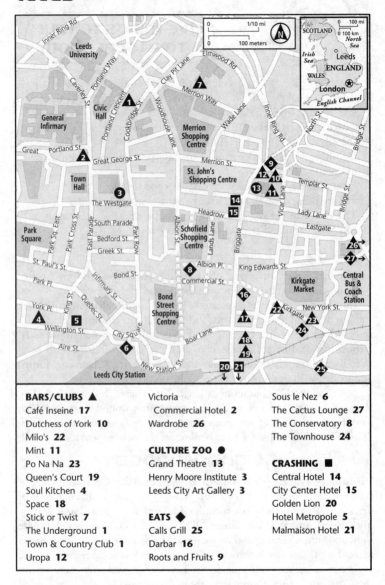

BARS/CLUBS ▲

Café Inseine **17**

Dutchess of York **10**

Milo's **22**

Mint **11**

Po Na Na **23**

Queen's Court **19**

Soul Kitchen **4**

Space **18**

Stick or Twist **7**

The Underground **1**

Town & Country Club **1**

Uropa **12**

Victoria

  Commercial Hotel **2**

Wardrobe **26**

CULTURE ZOO ●

Grand Theatre **13**

Henry Moore Institute **3**

Leeds City Art Gallery **3**

EATS ◆

Calls Grill **25**

Darbar **16**

Roots and Fruits **9**

Sous le Nez **6**

The Cactus Lounge **27**

The Conservatory **8**

The Townhouse **24**

CRASHING ■

Central Hotel **14**

City Center Hotel **15**

Golden Lion **20**

Hotel Metropole **5**

Malmaison Hotel **21**

Both are headquartered about 3.2 kilometers (2 miles) northwest of the City Centre on either side of **Woodhouse Lane,** a street that changes its name to **Headingley Lane** to the north and **Albion Street** to the south. Remember that Bus No. 1 is your friend: It makes frequent north-south runs between the University section in the city's northwest to the City Centre and on to the railway station [see *need to know,* below].

12 hours in Leeds

Start your day out by taking in some of the architecture. Most of the impressive buildings have been turned into shopping centers, but the beauty of the **Corn Exchange** and **Victorian Quarter** is apparent even amidst the capitalist feeding frenzy. Once all of the Edwardian buildings start to look alike, stop for lunch and a talk with the Japanese koi in the fishpond at the Conservatory [see *eats,* above]. Then take in the afternoon street performers along **Briggate** and **Albion Place,** or head over to the **Leeds City Market** to pore over the junk on sale, and buy some candy for a pence a piece. Your evening's entertainment takes off in the **Corn Exchange Quarter.** Both the Townhouse and Café Inseine can provide you with an early start on your evening libations, as well as some imaginative pub grub. Then hit one of the city's nightspots—the Warehouse offers the big bang of Leeds's club scene, while the Mint Club provides a more intimate buzz.

The city's industrial zones are south of town. Working-class neighborhoods to the northeast of the city, including **Chapeltown** and **Harehills,** are crammed with back-to-back terraced housing that recalls the dingy Leeds of the Industrial Revolution.

hanging out

All the cool kids hang at the **Corn Exchange,** on the northwest corner of Boar Lane and Vicar Lane in the City Centre. Once used as a mercantile exchange, this circular 19th-century building is loaded with shops, bars, clubs, and restaurants. You'll also find plenty of party pals in the **Victorian Quarter,** the neighborhood near the junction of the Headrow and New Briggate, where multiple Victorian-era arcades have been transformed and much-renovated with new shops, new bars, and new nightclubs. If you're looking for the student scene, try the **University of Leeds Student Union** *(Woodhouse Lane, Tel 0113/243-17-51),* where there's a pub, restaurant, and bookstore, not to mention the highest concentration of students in Northern England.

bar scene

Searching for a good stiff drink? You won't be disappointed in Leeds. Whether you're hoping to dive solo into a crisp pint of ale or dreaming of a sly tango with the bloke or bird of your choice, you'll find plenty of

down and out

Sit in a cafebar like **Soul Kitchen** [see *bar scene,* below] buy a cup of coffee or a pint, and watch the circus of human nature. The scenes consist of every type of person you could imagine, and some you can't. If you can't even afford the pint, head to **Leeds Market** [see *stuff,* above] to haggle with the junk dealers—always an intriguing look inside the workings of the human mind.

opportunities. If it's eye candy you're after, fashionable twentysomethings regularly strut through the flashy bars of the Corn Exchange as if they've come right off the catwalk. As the center of Leeds's new club culture [see *club scene,* below], this Quarter is all about noise and movement, which is a blast if you're in the mood, but maddening if you're looking to chill. Luckily, there are plenty of hip little bars where you can do just that.

Slightly off-center from its Corn Exchange neighbors, **Milo** *(Call Lane; Tel 0113/245-71-01; 11am-midnight daily; £2 pints)* calms the hearts of pre-club beasts with its cool blue and peach interiors, while soulful DJs make Fridays and Saturdays sizzle. People pack in around the small downstairs bar—luckily there's an overflow space upstairs for catching your breath. There are plans to serve a hip Indian-influenced menu in the future, which will only make the best bar experience in Leeds even better.

Stuffed with comfy couches, **Café Inseine** *(13 Duncan St.; Tel 0113/242-24-36; noon-midnight daily, food until 8pm; £3.95-5 per entrée)* is another welcome oasis in the *Temptation Island* atmosphere of the Corn Exchange. Fridays the music is cool and smooth, with sax-and-bongo style jazz. Saturdays crank up the volume a notch with deep house music, but everyone keeps their cool—there are no swaggering, drink-spilling lunks to kill the buzz.

Dirt-cheap drinks draw crowds of people to **Stick or Twist** *(Merrion Way; Tel 0113/234-97-48; 11am-11pm daily; £1.30 bottles),* in the City Centre. It's a favorite first stop for folks who want to get buzzed early and for cheap—which is just about anybody in Leeds, but students in particular. This chain bar is short on atmosphere—there isn't even any music—but long on business sense. They've found their niche and they fill it well.

In total contrast, the bar at the **Victoria Hotel** *(Great George Street; Tel 0113/245-13-86; 11am-11pm daily, food until 6pm),* near the Town Hall in the City Centre, has atmosphere to spare, with dark wood interiors, etched-glass mirrors, and antique globe lamps. At this homey *olde Englishe* alehouse, the drinks are proper, the pace is leisurely, and the clientele are authentic Yorkshire characters. If you're hungry, the steak-and-ale pie is a real find for £4.95. The friendly staff will even regale you with creepy ghost stories.

Often overlooked because of its location between King and Queen Streets in the heart of the financial district, **Soul Kitchen** (11 York Place; Tel 0113/242-12-02; noon-11pm daily) hosts always-intellectual crowds of young, white-collar professionals mixed with professional club kids on their way to *Speed Queen* [see *gay scene,* below]. Sexy electronica heats up this groovy little hideaway on Friday and Saturday nights. The vaguely aquatic decor is boho all the way, with lots of pink and bubbles. True to its name, the Kitchen also serves great food [see *eats,* below].

LIVE MUSIC SCENE

There's enough rap and funk pounding through Leeds to make you wonder if James Brown is really an Englishman. Live performance seems to be giving way to the DJ-driven club scene; three of the city's live music venues, including the legendary Duchess of York, have closed in the past year, each making like the Terminator, saying "I'll be back." Let's hope they're right.

Set in a converted railway arch not far from Leeds City Station, the **Cockpit** *(Swinegate, the Arches; Tel 0113/244-15-73, Fax 0113/243-48-49; doors open at 7pm, closing times vary; Cover £3-5)* keeps things real, with a reputation as Leeds's premiere music venue. All the big acts coming through town end up here, with names like the Stone Roses, Happy Mondays, and Spacehog tossed around quite a bit. Indie and alternative music is the mainstay, but there's a bit of hip-hop and world beat thrown in for good measure. When there's no band, the Cockpit is still hopping with an eclectic series of club nights, including Thursday's *Poptastic* [see *gay scene,* below].

Another prominent live music venue is **The Josephs Well** *(Chorley Lane, Tel 0113/203-18-61, Fax 0113/203-1862; www.josephswell.co.uk, at_the_well@hotmail.com),* just off Clarendon Road on the west side of town.

One of the liveliest spots in town is **The Wardrobe** *(5 St. Peter's Building, St. Peter's Square, Tel 0113/383-88-00; V, MC),* across the street from the West Yorkshire Playhouse and the Leeds College of Music. Wednesday nights feature high-quality jazz acts; Friday nights you can come early and take a salsa lesson before dancing the rest of the night away to an 8- to 12-piece samba band. "Root Down" Saturdays are dedicated to funk, with live bands playing downstairs. Upstairs is a cafe where students from the college often perform during the day "for soup and chips," so any time you stop by you're likely to find some kind of performance going on,

RULES OF THE GAME

Leeds abides by the unwritten rules to partying, and you're expected to know them too. People will leave you alone, if you leave them alone. No matter how invincible you feel, drunken absurdity in public will get your butt thrown in *gaol*. Leeds just isn't much fun from behind bars.

whether it be a jazz quartet, a classical trio, or a poetry reading. The management is really into supporting young artists, and has even started a record label for developing young talent.

club scene

The club culture in Leeds is really taking off, to the point where it not only competes with Manchester but is even drawing DJ-artistes from London. Leeds offers a little bit of everything, from pissed-up students sloshing around on stained carpets to a sleek underground refuge for serious music-lovers, and a glitterboy drag celebration that never ends. New clubs are born almost monthly and the old warhorses are having a hard time keeping up. You might want to arrive early, between 10 and 11pm, to make sure you'll get in, but don't plan on leaving early—most places are still hopping well past 3am.

The revelry never ends at **The Warehouse** *(19-21 Somers St.; Tel 0113/246-10-35; 10pm-4am Fri-Sat; Cover varies, usually around £10),* near Park Square off Westgate. This mammoth basement club is Leeds's undisputed party central, with a crowd that's young, vivacious, and in a word, *hot.* A long, sleepless weekend begins on Thursday with *Tequila,* where you never know what you'll see next, from slamming competitions to go-go dancers to karaoke that's way hipper than you'd think. Friday's devoted to live performances, then Saturday slides into Sunday with the gaudy glitz of *Speed Queen* [see *gay scene,* below]. The dynamic music mix bumps along from house to techno, with a blend of funk and soul to keep you guessing. If you're out for a good time, you'll end up at the Warehouse at least one of your nights in Leeds—be sure to get there early if you want to get in at all.

For an evening that's more intimate but just as wild, check out electronica's underground prince Dave Beer spinning drum and bass basics Saturday nights at **The Mint Club** *(8 Harrison Street; Tel 0113/244-31-68; until 4am Fri-Sat; cover varies; £2.50 per drink),* in the City Centre off Briggate Street. The small room makes for a sexy little groove, and it doesn't take long to work yourself into a lather. If you feel like the walls are closing in, the Evian water garden out back is the perfect place to refresh and re-hydrate. Because this place is so tiny, getting in can be a challenge—be smart and dress to impress (no jeans or sneakers). With music as serious as this, you'd be a fool to pass Mint by. It's worth the wait.

fIVE-0

The cops know what goes on, but they don't want to see it. Thankfully, crime is pretty low in this city, so the cops are really not visible in the party areas, which makes for an anything-goes policy. Don't forget, however, that certain magical plants are not exactly legal here.

A tropical paradise in the midst of Yorkshire's electronica chill, **Po Na Na** *(Unit 2 Waterloo House Assembly Street; Tel 0113/243-32-47; www.ponana.co.uk; 9pm-2am Mon-Sat; Pavement bar open from 2pm in summer, cover varies)* specializes in hot salsa, with a funk/soul twist. Tuesdays offer pure salsa—there are even lessons from 8-9pm—and things get progressively funkier as the week goes on. Located not far from Leeds City Market, the place has the look and style of a grand Mediterranean manse, filled up with undulating twentysomething bodies.

One of the biggest clubs in Leeds, **Club Uropa** *(54 New Briggate; Tel 0113/242-22-24; open Wed-Sun, hours vary; cover varies)* offers none of the continental sophistication the name promises. The DJs spin out a credible spread of dizzying house, but hordes of pissed-up students cram the soggy-carpeted dance floor. It must have something to do with the 50p per pint special. The first Sunday of each month, *Sundissential* offers a marathon of these same sticky-footed students dancing till they drop, which happens none too soon. It's really not worth the trek northwest of Great George Street unless you're feeling especially rowdy.

Leeds's newest addition, **The Space** *(Hirst's Yard, behind Strand on Duncan Street; Tel 0113/246-10-30; open Thur-Sun, hours vary; cover £10 Fri, Sat)* has potential, and already attracts the cream of London's DJs. The music's thumping, with the newest underground danceables in jungle, garage, trance, and a kicky fusion of all of the above. Space-age lights throwing bursts of color into the crowd provide quite a trip, even without the benefit of illegal substances. The problem is that many of the kids on the dance floor aren't motivated so much by the astonishing visuals or unheralded groove as they are feeling their way to their favorite high or the nearest piece of boo-tay. Currently, the queues go round the block, but the novelty may soon wear off. It's in the Corn Exchange Quarter, not far from the Leeds City Station.

arts scene

Culture? In Leeds? Today there's enough art and culture here to give Leeds some class. It has England's largest collection of 20th-century art outside London. It's also worth checking the local theatres to see if there's anything worth catching while you're in town. All of the venues are located in the City Centre.

▶▶**VISUAL ARTS**

Showcasing student work, the **Leeds Metropolitan University Gallery** *(Woodhouse Lane; Tel 0113/283-26-00; 10am-4pm Mon-Fri, 10am-3:30pm Sat; Free)* could definitely be called experimental. In addition to traditional visual arts exhibits, it often offers a peek into studios where you can see artists in the midst of creation—drawing, painting, or sculpting. It's just down the street from the City Gallery, heading north on Portland Way.

▶▶**PERFORMING ARTS**

While its 19th-century façade is impressive, the productions at **The Grand Theatre and Opera House** *(New Briggate; Tel 0113/222-62-22; ticket* *costs vary)* are nothing extraordinary, just old reliables like Shakespeare and *West Side Story*—which is really just Shakespeare with switchblades. Also the home of Leeds's opera company, it's located in the City Centre, at the corner of New Briggate and Lady Lane.

A teensy bit more adventurous, when **The West Yorkshire Playhouse** *(Quarry Hill Mount; Tel 0113/213-77-00; ticket costs vary)* talks about staging the classics, it most likely means Bertholt Brecht, not Shakespeare. With two stages, it also offers crowd-pleasers like *Singin' in the Rain* and Noël Coward's *Blithe Spirit.* How's that for edgy? (Not very.) The Playhouse Bar in the foyer offers a casual atmosphere for drinks before the show, or even dinner, from soups and salads to full home-cooked meals. It's located on Quarry Hill, at the junction of March Lane and Ring Road.

gay scene

Leed's doesn't have a big gay Mardi Gras like Manchester's Canal Street, but it's home to a visible and surprisingly integrated gay and lesbian community. There's only one all-gay club, but many of the others host gay nights, which have a good mix of men and women, both gay and straight. The drag-happy *Speed Queen* is one of the most popular parties in the city, no matter what your orientation. Women-only nights are few and far between, you'll just have to keep your ear to the ground.

A little west of the Leeds City Station and north of the Corn Exchange, **Queen's Court** *(Lower Briggate; Tel 0113/245-94-49; noon-2am Mon-Thu, noon-4am Fri-Sat, noon-10:30pm Sun; Cover varies, usually around £5)* is all-gay, all the time—with that name, it almost has to be. The friendly downstairs bar offers cheap, hearty food (meals around £5, served 4:30-7pm), while the dance-pop in the disco upstairs makes shaking your moneymaker inevitable. The outdoor courtyard is heaven on balmy summer evenings, and the glass wall at the front of the bar is perfect for ogling tasty passersby. Grab a window seat and feast your eyes.

Just down the street and over the train tracks, where Briggate becomes New Bridge, the **Bridge Inn** *(1-5 Bridge End; Tel 0113/244-47-34; 11pm-2am daily; Cover £3; MC, V)* offers the more traditional gay pub experience. Featuring cabaret, karaoke, and disco standards, it's more popular with locals than tourists. The place gets more and more clubby as the night wears on (and on and on—it's just received a late license).

Nearby **Blayds Bar** *(Lower Briggate; Tel 0113/244-55-90; 4-11:30pm Mon-Sat, 1-10:30pm Sun)* has an all-pine interior and a quieter atmosphere, well suited for conversation with the object of your affection. Wednesday night's *The Woman in Me* is very popular with local lesbians. **Velvet** *(Hirst's Yard, behind Norman; Tel 0113/242-50-79; noon-11pm Mon-Sat, noon-10:30pm Sun)* attracts a hip mixed crowd. Food is served upstairs (entrees are around £10, because, darling, you don't get style for free!), with balcony dining available so you can scope while you scarf. Cool jazz Monday through Thursday gives way to disco on weekends, when, judging by the proliferation of sequined headdresses and feather boas, it seems to be a popular first stop for costumed clubbers on their way to *Speed Queen.*

Hedonism reigns supreme at Saturday night's *Speed Queen (10pm-4am Fri-Sat; Cover £10),* where drag queens run wild and free, with the emphasis on *wild.* Hosted by the **Warehouse** [see *club scene,* above], it's Leeds's hottest gay party—actually, it's Leeds's hottest party *period.* Flamboyant, over-the-top outfits are not only tolerated, but required—if you look too dull, you won't get in. Whether you're into feathers and sequins, leather and chrome, or Day-Glo bodypaint, think big and colorful. The DJs have to work up a sweat just to keep up with the kitsch couture, but they rise to the challenge. Pounding speed garage and house mix it up downstairs while upstairs the divas take over with some free, funky soul. The crowd is very mixed—about half gay and half straight, with equal helpings of men and women.

Many of the other clubs in town offer gay nights of their own. *Poptastic (11pm-2:30am Thu; Cover £3.50)* at the **Cockpit** [see *live music scene,* above] spins indie favorites for queer kids not remotely interested in the disco dolly lifestyle. New rooms are devoted to dance and chart hits as well. The crowd is young, friendly, and has shagging on the brain, as evidenced by the "shag tags" offered at the door. These ready-to-wear numbers make hooking up easier. If someone fancies your shape, not to mention your gender, they give your number to the attendant, who flashes it up on a video screen larger than life. Wouldn't it be easier to just say hello?

CULTURE ZOO

Leeds isn't a national historical treasure like York, but it's no cultural wasteland either. They've got a 16th-century manse and their own version of high-brow history: a museum dedicated to weaponry. Hit someone over the head with it, that's a criminal act; put it in a museum, and it's high culture.

Temple Newsam House *(Temple Newsam Road, off Selby Road, 6.4 kilometers [4 miles] from Leeds City Centre off A63A; take Bus 27 from Leeds; Tel 0113/264-73-21; 10am-5pm Tues-Sat, 1-5pm Sun, summer; 10am-4pm Tues-Sat, noon-4pm Sun, winter; Adults £2, Students £1):* Today it shelters the largely lackluster overflow from the Leeds City Art Gallery, but a grand Tudor and Jacobean mansion was once the birthplace of the ill-fated husband of Mary Queen of Scots, Lord Darnley, back in 1545. Think of him as Sonny and her as Cher. The highlight of the art show here is the stunning collection of silver pieces and Chippendale antiques (furniture, not strippers). The 1,200-acre grounds make for a great picnic.

Royal Armouries Museum *(Armouries Dr.; Tel 0113/220-19-99; 10:30am to 5:30pm daily, Mar 4-Nov 8; 10:30am-4:30pm Mon-Fri; 10:30am-5:30pm Sat-Sun Nov 8-Mar 4; Adults £7.95, Students £6.95):* After a visit here, you'll never question that the Brits knew how to kick ass first and take names later—There's enough devious and savage weaponry here to fill the bloodlust quota of any Schwarzenegger movie. Once a working arsenal for medieval kings, it's the new home of the Tower of London's Royal Armouries, which outgrew the actual tower long ago. Shoot a crossbow like Robin Hood, direct operations on a mock battlefield, or just marvel at how cunning and cruel the medieval

festivals and events

Think you can stay up all night for three days straight, partying with bands like Beck, Foo Fighters, Pulp, Elastica, Rage Against the Machine, and Blink 182? Test your concert/bash endurance at the **Reading Leeds Festival 2001** *(End of August; Tel 09003/404-906 or 020/89-63-09-40; 10am-6pm; www.reading festival.com),* put on by the cities of Reading and Leeds. After the stage has gone dark, campsite fires keep the party burning well into the morning hours, appropriate in up-all-night Leeds.

On the other hand, there's always the calmer, more Boho **Leeds International Film Festival** *(October; Tel 0113/247-83-98; www.leeds.gov.uk/liff).* It's a visual feast for aspiring Spielbergs and Tarantinos, showcasing national and international films, including world premieres.

bastards could be. The exhibition is installed along a 13-acre dockland site just a 15-minute walk west from the City Centre.

Spread out over three floors, **Leeds City Art Gallery** *(The Headrow; Tel 0113/247-82-47; 10am-5pm Mon-Tue, Thu-Sat, 10am-8pm Wed, 1-5pm Sun; free)* offers England's best collection of 20th-century art outside of London. Located at the corner of East Parade and Headrow in the heart of town, it's an art groupie's dream come true, with French postimpressionist paintings, contemporary British sculpture, prints, and watercolors all well represented. Featured artists include Britain's two greatest sculptors, Barbara Hepworth and Henry Moore.

Just next-door and a short walk across a glass bridge, the **Henry Moore Institute** *(74 The Headrow; Tel 0113/234-31-58; 10am-5:30pm Mon-Tue, Thu-Sun, 10am-9pm Wed; Free)* is the largest sculpture gallery in Europe. This may be due in no small part to the monumental nature of the artist's work. Yorkshireman Moore is remembered as the greatest British sculptor of the last century, with his masterpiece *Reclining Woman* on display here. Judging by his other works, he was also fond of dogs. Rotating exhibits from other modern sculptors are often featured as well.

CITY SPORTS

Leeds isn't the nature capital of England, to say the least, but it does have a huge park where you can walk, ride a bike, and see some trees at the same time.

About five or so kilometers (three miles) northeast of the City Centre on Otley Road, **Roundhay Park** is one of the biggest city parks outside of London. Leeds itself is too big, and too congested, for bicycling, but here you can pedal to your heart's content [see *need to know,* below]. If you're in the mood for a lazy afternoon of boating, a kiosk within the park *(Tel 0113/265-18-04; May-mid-Oct only)* also rents rowboats.

modification

There's no shortage of tattoo parlors and body piercers in Leeds, from the type that tend to service drunken longshoremen to the slightly hipper joints that cater to young hipsters.

If you want to turn that new tat in your mind's-eye into a reality, the artists at **Kaleidoscope Tattoo Design** *(96 Kirkgate; Tel 0113/244-55-02; noon-8pm Tues-Sat)*, near the Leeds City Market, has the steadiest hands in the city, and is extremely clean—always a bonus. Along those same lines, the folks at **Leeds Piercing Studios** *(4-8 Call Lane; Tel 0113/242-04-13; 10:30am-5pm Mon-Sat; £10-35 per piercing; call for appointment)*, near the Corn Exchange, will poke holes in you wherever you want.

stuff

It doesn't really matter if you're a high-fashion diva or more of a lunatic-fringe type, if you've got money in your wallet, someone in Leeds is eager to take it. Luckily you'll most likely get some pretty cool stuff in return. The hipsters shop at the **Corn Exchange** *(Call Lane; Tel 0113/234-03-63; 9am-5:30pm Mon-Sat, 10:30am-5pm Sun)*, a clubber's paradise, with circular floors of independent shops hawking clubgear and vinyl. Sophisticates cruise the stores a little ways north at **Victoria Quarter** *(Briggate; Tel 0113/245-53-33; 10am-6pm daily)*, where the chi-chi boutiques and upscale fashions could make even a dyed-in-the-wool communist drool.

▶▶USED AND BRUISED

You could spend all day in **Blue Rinse** *(11 Call Lane, 97 Kirkgate; Tel 0498/587-815 or 587-822; 10am-5:30pm daily)*—it's so big it winds around a corner and takes up two addresses. Just outside the Corn Exchange, this secondhand sanctuary sells everything from ancient go-go boots to leather pants worn onstage by rock stars (let's hope they've cleaned).

▶▶CLUBWEAR

With colors bright enough to damage your retinas, **Plastique** *(At the Corn Exchange, Call Lane; Tel 0113/244-99-42; 9am-5:30pm Mon-Sat, 10:30am-5pm Sun)* has the clubwear formula perfected.

▶▶BOUND

England's answer to Barnes and Noble, **Waterstones** *(96 Albion St.; Tel 0113/244-45-88; 8:30am-8pm Mon-Fri, 8:30am-6pm Sat, 11am-5pm Sun)* in the City Centre not only stocks just about every book ever published, it'll offer you a cup of coffee and a comfy sofa to sit on while you're browsing. If your interests are more on the fringe, **Forbidden Planet** *(The Headrow, Tel 0113/242-63-25; 9:30am-5:30pm; AE, MC, V)* has a wide and wacky selection of comics, specialty books, videos, toys, and other playthings.

▶▶TUNES

From esoteric vinyl treasures to Top-of-the-Pops CDs, **Trax** *(At the Corn Exchange, Call Lane; Tel 0780/115-10-97; 9am-5:30pm Mon-Sat, 10:30am-5pm Sun)* will be your first, last, and everything music stop in the city, with nothing over £10. If you can't find that obscure album you've been dreaming about, ask Carl. He knows where it is.

▶▶**HOW BAZAAR**

If you can't find it inside the **Leeds City Market** *(Kirkgate, access to other levels on Vicar Lane; 8am-5:30pm Mon-Sat, until 1pm Wed)*, it's most likely available in the open-air stalls outside. Located northwest of the Leeds City Station, this bizarre bazaar offers food, furniture, and everything in between (sweets, vegetables, cheeses, spices, fabric, clothes, etc.), all waiting to be bought and sold on the cheap.

EaTS

A new night-friendly City Centre has emerged from the last few years of renovations, with a number of excellent restaurants and oh-so-cosmopolitan cafe-bars. The bars around the Corn Exchange tend to be more hip, and offer more imaginative food as well as atmosphere.

▶▶**CHEAP**

Take two flights downstairs to swank basement bar **The Conservatory** *(Albion Place; Tel 0113/205-19-11; 11am-11pm daily; £4.25 per item, £2.25 spirits; V)* in the City Centre for crafty lunches and dinners, a step beyond typical pub grub. The bar itself is one-step-beyond as well, with comfortable wing-backed chairs, a large fishpond populated by colorful Japanese koi, and life-size wooden sirens guarding the bar. The place gets its name from the eclectic mix of strange and special hardcover books covering the walls—they're worth a browse if you've got the time.

Located behind the Corn Exchange, **The Townhouse** *(Assembly Street; Tel 0113/219-40-00; 10-2am Mon-Sat, food until midnight, noon-10:30pm Sun; £5.50 per entrée, V)* caters to daytime shoppers and nighttime punters. The downstairs bar is vast and open, with minimal decor, but the inventive menu makes up for the lack of decorative creativity. It offers the same traditional English fare you'll see in most pubs (let's just say there's cabbage is involved), but also pushes the gastric envelope with more audacious selections like spinach and ricotta pancakes and grilled shark.

With simple Mediterranean interior design and a menu to match, **Roots and Fruits** *(The Grand Arcade; Tel 0113/243-37-37; 10am-7:30pm Mon-Sat; £4.45 per item)* is Leeds's prime vegetarian restaurant. Main courses include sweet pepper lasagna, chili burritos, and Mediterranean kabobs, all good enough to coax even the staunchest Englishman away from his roast beef. It's off Briggate, north of Headrow.

Another good choice for veggie fare is **Strawberry Fields** *(159 Woodhouse Lane; Tel 0113/243-15-15; noon-2pm/6-11pm Mon-Fri, 6-11pm Sat, last orders at 10pm; entrees around £6)*, a sweet little bistro in the University Quarter that's always full of students. The menu can be limited, but it's all healthy, and vegetarians will have a field day with dishes like eggplant and red pepper enchiladas in a sour cream sauce.

▶▶**DO-ABLE**

First impressions can be wrong, and **Darbar** *(16-17 Kirkgate; Tel 0113/246-03-81; 11:30am-2:30pm/6pm-midnight; £4-8.50 per item)* is a prime example. You'd never guess that you were on your way to the best Indian restaurant in town from the run-down stairwell out front. But once you get down the stairs and in the door, you're in a different world: The posh decor evokes a Far Eastern palace, with authentic Pakistani draperies and chairs. The food is just as authentic, with a good balance of vegetarian and non-vegetarian options; try the chicken in ginger.

Named one of the top Mexican restaurants in the country, **The Cactus Lounge** *(3 St. Peter's Square; Tel 0113/243-65-53; 11:30am-3pm/5pm until late, £5-8.25 per entrée)* gets everything right, from the two-tone desert paint job and furnishings to a wide range of Southwestern dishes, each with the perfect balance of spices. Order up taco salads, fajitas, and burritos big enough for two, or a number of vegetarian options. The Corn Exchange Quarter location is also choice, next door to both the **Warehouse** [see *club scene,* above] and **West Yorkshire Playhouse** [see *arts scene,* above], so reservations are a good idea. It's the perfect place for a post-theatre and/or pre-clubbing salsa experience.

A hopping hidden-away nightspot, **Soul Kitchen** [see *bar scene,* above] serves food for the body as well as the soul *(noon-2:30pm/5:30-8:30pm Mon-Sat, 3-6pm Sunday; £5-8),* making for a funky daytime repast. The menu is as eclectic as it is delicious, with eggs Florentine, lemon chicken salad, and kicky kebobs.

With its rustic brick-and-stripped-pine interior, **Calls Grill** *(36-38 The Calls; Tel 0113/245-38-70; noon-2:30pm/5:30pm-11pm Mon-Sat, 5:30-11pm Sun; £14.95 full three-course meal; V, MC)* is a stylish steakhouse located behind the Corn Exchange, offering a view of the canal. The steaks and chips are choice, but the menu covers a wide range, and even has some tasty vegetarian options. As for dessert, the fondue (£4 per person) is a meal in itself, with rich chocolate and honey sauce and loads of fresh fruit and marshmallows for dipping. Get there early to take advantage of the "Beat the Clock" special. From 5:30-7:30pm, whatever time the waitress clocks your arrival will be the cost of any two-course meal. So if you walk in at 6pm, your meal will only be £6—you can't beat that.

▶▶**SPLURGE**

Don't let the pretentious French name fool you—snobbery is kept to a minimum at **Sous le Nez En Ville** *(Quebec House Basement, Quebec St. Tel 0113/244-01-08; noon-2:30pm/6-10pm Mon-Thurs, noon-2:30pm/6-11pm Fri-Sat, closed Sundays and bank holidays; entrees £12; V, MC, AE),* a basement restaurant that manages to be bright and charming despite its lack of windows. The wine list is excellent, and the menu is even better, with with an elegant mix of French and English fare. The restaurant is known for its fish, which is served the right way—grilled with lemon, not hidden under crunchy batter. It's located in the heart of the financial district, between the City Square and East Parade.

crashing

Many of Leeds's hotels cater to business types who stay in the city weekdays and go home to the countryside on weekends. As a result, rates can be outrageously high Monday-Thursday, but are often drastically reduced Friday-Sunday. Even the elite hotels become affordable on the weekends, which is when you want to be here anyway. The tourist office [see *need to know*, below} can help you make reservations.

▶▶**CHEAP**

In the University Quarter, **Mr. and Mrs. D. Hood** *(17 Cottage Rd., Headingly; Tel 0113/275-55-75; £18 single, £36 double; Bus 93 or 96 from Infirmary St.; No credit cards)* rent out affordable rooms. Home-cooked breakfasts feature homemade bread, marmalade, and coffee talk with Mr. and Mrs. D. Hood themselves.

The **Holme Leigh Guest House** *(19 Pinfold Lane, Halton; Tel 0113/260-78-89; singles £23, doubles £35; Bus 40 from Boar Lane to Temple Walk; No credit cards)* offers comfortable accommodations in a Victorian house on a quiet street.

At **Fairbairn House** *(71-75 Clarendon Rd., Tel 0113/233-69-13, Fax 0113/233-69-14; singles from £25; No credit cards)*, a sprawling Victorian in the City Centre, there are TVs in every room—surprising, since the house is owned by the University of Leeds. Doesn't anybody read anymore?

In a pinch, you can try the **University of Leeds** *(Tel 0113/233-61-00; singles with shared bath £15, singles with bath and breakfast £34; V, MC)*, which offers rooms when students are away for summer or holiday. They're dorm rooms—need we say more?

▶▶**DO-ABLE**

The **City Centre Hotel** *(51a New Briggate; Tel 0113/242-90-19; private baths available; £25 single, £40 double; V, MC)* will have a bed almost any day of the week. It offers simple accommodation in an older building just a few minutes walk from shopping, nightclubs, and just about everything worthwhile in Leeds.

Right next door, the **Central Hotel** *(47 New Briggate; Tel 0113/294-14-56, Fax 0113/294-15-51; private baths available, breakfast included; £26 single, £42 double; V, MC)* provides standard accommodation and a breakfast in the attached cafe downstairs. There are plenty of signs to lead you through the winding, maze-like hallways to your breakfast in the morning, and the bathrooms when you need them.

wired

Get online at **The Mouse House** *(3 Wellfield Place, Headingley; Tel 0113/274-25-33; 10:30am-8pm Mon-Fri, 10:30am-7:30pm Sat, 11am-6pm Sun; themouse.house@virgin.net; £3 half hour. £5 hour)*, in the University Quarter. There's no food, but there are iMacs for checking your email, as well as a 20% student discount.

Some other reasonable accommodations include the **Avalon Guest House** *(132 Woodsley Rd; Tel 0113/243-25-45, Fax 0113/242-06-49; Bus 57 or 58 from the train station; private baths available, £25-40 single, £35-50 double, breakfast included; V, MC)*, an easy bus ride from the train station; **Fairbairn House** *(71-75 Clarendon Rd.; Tel 0113/233-69-13, Fax 0113/233-69-14; www.leeds.ac.uk/nuffield.fairbairn; £25-£39.50 single, £45.50-51.50 double, private baths available, breakfast included; V, MC)*, just 10 minutes from the City Centre; the **Glengarth Hotel** *(162 Woodsley Rd; Tel 0113/245-79-40, Fax 0113/216-80-33; www.smoothound.co.uk/a13930.html; £25-40 single, £40-50 double, £60-70 triple, private baths availaabe; V, MC)*, about a mile out from the train station, and the **Manxdene Hotel** *(154 Woodsley Rd; Tel 0113/243-25-86; £25 single, £38 double, shared bath, breakfast included; No credit cards)* just down the street from the Glengarth; and the **Aragon Hotel** *(250 Stainbeck Lane; Tel 0113/275-93-06, Fax 0113/275-93-06; Bus 5, 8 or 40; aragon@onmail.co.uk, www.aragonhotel.co.uk; £43.90 single, £53.90-59.90 double, £64.90 triple, private baths available, breakfast included; V, MC, AE)*, in the gardens four kilometers (two-and-a-half miles) from the City Centre.

▶▶SPLURGE

One of Leeds's oldest hotels, **The Golden Lion Hotel** *(2 Lower Brig-gate; Tel 0113/243-64-54; info@goldenlion-hotel-leeds.com, www.peel hotel.com; £99 single, £110 double, £30 per person weekends, private bath available, breakfast included; V, MC)* has recently been refurbished, restoring this City Centre treasure to its Victorian grandeur while adding modern touches like satellite TV. The atmosphere is bright and friendly, and the attentive staff will treat you like royalty.

With a modern design and commitment to high-quality service, the sleek **Malmaison Hotel** *(Sovereign Quay; Tel 0113/398-10-00; leeds@malmaison.com, www.malmaison.com; £79 single, £105 double, £40.50 per person weekends, private bath available, £8.50 breakfast; V, MC, AE)* in the City Centre will put you up in style. With dark wood paneled rooms, a French brasserie and high-tech fitness rooms, style feels pretty good. You can convince yourself it's worth the extra pence just to pretend you're one of England's elite, right?

need to know

Currency Exchange For the best rates, take it to the banks and ATMs. Just off the City Centre, **HSBC** *(Park Row; 9am-3:30pm Mon-Sat; 2% commission, £3 minimum)*, **Lloyds** *(Park Row; 9am-3:30pm Mon-Sat; 2% commission, £3 minimum)*, and **Barclays** *(Park Row; 9am-3:30pm Mon-Sat; 2% commission, £3 minimum)* are all in a row.

Tourist Information The **Gateway Yorkshire Regional Travel & Tourist Information Centre** *(Leeds City Station; Tel 0113/242-52-42; 9:30am-6pm Mon-Sat, 10am-4pm Sun)* has a metric ton of info on transportation, accommodation, dining, shopping, and entertain-ment. It can also help you book places to stay.

Public Transportation Almost everything worth seeing is within walking distance of the City Centre. However, both long-haul and local municipal buses are headquartered at **The Leeds City Station** *(St. Peter's Street; Tel 0113/245-76-76)*. You can buy a bus ticket from the driver of any bus; fares range from £1 to £1.90. Remember that many of your transportation needs can be solved by taking Bus No. 1, which makes north-south runs between the University section in the city's northwest to the City Centre and on to the railway station. You won't have much luck hailing a cab; you're better off calling for a late-night ride. Try **Telecabs** *(Tel 0113/263-04-04)*, **City Cabs** *(Tel 0113/246-99-99)*, or **Streamline** *(Tel 0113/244-33-22)*.

Health and Emergency Emergency: *(Tel 999)*; Police: *(Tel 0845/606-06-06)*. For medical attention, the **Leeds General Infirmary** *(Tel 0113/243-27-99)* is close to the City Centre, at the junction of Caverly and Portland Streets.

Pharmacies Get your meds and make-up at **Boots the Chemists** *(Leeds Station Concourse; Tel 0113/242-17-13; 7am-midnight Mon-Fri; 8:30am-midnight Sat; 9am-midnight Sun)*.

Airport The **Leeds Bradford Airport** *(Tel 0113/250-96-96)* is about 13 kilometers (8 miles) northwest of the City Centre on Road A658. Although there is bus service *(Airlink 757; Tel 0113/245-76-76; £1.50 adult fare)*, it is sporadic and infrequent. A £10-12 taxi ride will take you right where you want to go, from the airport to the city.

Bus Lines Out of the City Daily bus service to London and elsewhere is provided by **National Express** *(Tel 0990/808-080)* at the Leeds City Station [see *public transportation* above], at the south end of town off The Arcade.

Trains Leeds is a significant hub for train service in this part of the country. Trains come and go from **Leeds City Station,** off the City Square, with hourly service to and from London's King Cross station (the trip takes about two hours). Other destinations include York, Manchester, Liverpool, Newcastle, and Edinburgh. For information, call **Metroline** *(Tel 0113/245-76-76)*.

Laundry A **Laundrette** *(Hyde Park Corner, near Headingly; 10am-7pm Mon-Sat; £1.60 wash, 50p dry)* is available in the University Quarter.

Postal Get your postal needs satisfied at the **Leeds Branch Office** *(City Square; Tel 0113/237-28-49; 9am-5:30pm Mon-Sat)*.

Internet See *Wired*, above. count.

everywhere else

york

On the banks of the River Ouse, York looks like a Hollywood movie set of a quaint English town, complete with a Gothic cathedral, foggy, lamplit cobblestoned streets, and friendly but slightly eccentric residents whose most commonly uttered phrase is, "Lovely." There are two colleges in town—the University of York and St. John's College—but the student scene is disappointingly polite, unlike the raucous punky student capital of Manchester or the earthy, blue-collar scene in nearby Leeds. But don't give up: The "Mickelgate Run" pub crawl is nothing short of legendary, and the hip new bars near York Minster are also really fun.

York is, in a word, a tourist town. That doesn't mean it's not cosmopolitan, or is not actually a very "lovely" place to visit. You could spend a few days here without getting bored. Just don't expect a modern, urban edge. What's most interesting about York, actually, is it's past.

Harsh ghosts walk these same cobblestone streets: the Romans, Vikings, Normans, and Britons all had their time here, and their influence and presence can still be felt today. Medieval walls, towers, and dungeons still stand, memories of a time when this city was an island of relative civilization in a country torn with strife and barbarism. The shadow of the Industrial Revolution passed York by in favor of other cities like Manchester, Newscastle, and Leeds, which explains how the architecture is so well preserved, and why so many of the buildings, including great York Minster, are relatively soot-free.

neighborhoods

The original York was built where the **River Ouse** and much smaller **River Foss** meet. Today, the Ouse bisects the city, and is crossed by three bridges: **Lendal Bridge** is the northernmost, **Ouse Bridge** is in the middle, and **Skeldergate Bridge** is the southernmost. Most of the historical sites are within the city's medieval walls (the thicker dark line on the map), a small-scale radius that takes no more than 15 minutes to walk

york

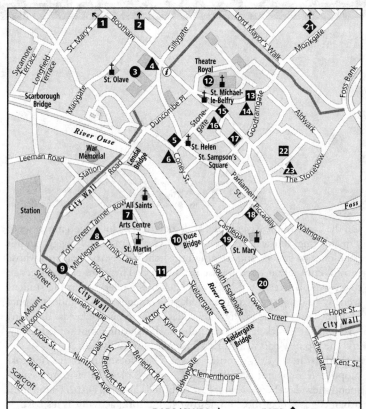

0   100 mi

0   100 km

SCOTLAND

North Sea

Irish Sea

York

ENGLAND

WALES

London

English Channel

BARS/CLUBS ▲

DeGray Rooms **4**
Fibber's **23**
Lendal Cellars **6**
Micklegate **8**
Old White Swan **14**
Oscar's **17**
Slug & Lettuce **16**

CULTURE ZOO ●

Clifford's Tower & York
  Castle Museum **20**
Ghost Walk **10**
York City WAlls **9**
York Minister **12**
Yorkshire Museum **3**

EATS ◆

Ask **5**
El Piano **15**
Francois **19**
Gert & Henry's **18**
Oscar's **17**
The Cloisters **21**

CRASHING ■

Aldwark
  Guest House **22**
Dean Court Hotel **13**
The Beckett **2**
York Backpacker's
  Hostel **7**
York YHA **1**
York Youth Hostel **11**

across. The streets are cobblestoned and narrow. They have so many nooks and crannies, which the locals call "snickleways," that it would take forever to thoroughly explore them all.

The historic zone is shaped roughly like a triangle whose corners are the **Minster** in the northwest, the **Museum Gardens** in the northeast, and the **Jorvik Viking Center** in the south. Within that triangle, primary north-south arteries include **High Petergate** and **Low Petergate,** mostly pedestrian zones lined with upscale shops; and **Coney Street** and **Parliament Street,** broader avenues lined with souvenir shops and workaday stores selling CDs and electronics. East-west streets include **Duncombe** and **Church Streets.** One street worth checking out is **The Shambles,** a very narrow lane intersecting Low Petergate. Once the city's meat-butchering center, it dates back to the Norman Conquest, and shows off York's medieval origins better than any other street in town.

The city filled with throngs of shoppers and tourists by day becomes a playground for the barhopping crowd at night. The newer, trendier bars are near **Swinegate,** while other possibilities are along **Goodramgate,** both just south of the Minster on the east side of the River Ouse. Over the Ouse Bridge on the west bank, **Micklegate** has most of the local hangouts, some of which get a little rough after a few too many pints have washed away some of that famous local politeness.

by foot

Visible from any part of town, the **York Minster** is the obvious starting point for a tour of York. Once you're able to tear yourself away, take a right onto **Goodramgate,** and take notice of all the bars you'll be spending time in later in the day. As the road narrows, it becomes known as **The Shambles.** This pedestrian cobblestone area will take you back to the 17th century with its tiny streets, just two arm-lengths wide, and soot-stained stone buildings. You'll either feel gigantic or claustrophobic. A right onto **Pavement Street** will put you smack in the middle of the **Newgate Market** along **Parliament** and **Piccadilly Streets.** Continuing down Piccadilly Street will lead you past St. Mary's Square and **Clifford's Tower** on the right. After a quick climb up the tower to stare at the city, continue on to the end of Piccadilly at the city walls. Heading right again will take you along a shorter span of the walls; crossing the two bridges to the left will give you a longer tour. Either way, you'll get some spectacular views of the city and surrounding countryside.

hanging out

In fair weather, locals and visitors alike hang out in the **Museum Gardens** or **Dean's Park** [see *great outdoors,* below]. But more often than not, the damp chill off the moors drives people indoors to any of the city's numerous pubs. Why did you think there were so many of them?

bar scene

They say there are 365 pubs in York, one for every day of the year. Anyone who's tried to count has most likely gotten too plastered to finish, so the number is dubious, but there are definitely plenty of places to go for a good time—Swinegate, Goodramgate, and Micklegate are all decent sites for a pub crawl. Established hours of 11am-11pm Monday-Saturday and noon-10:30pm on Sunday apply pretty much everywhere, except at the Plaza, which has a late license.

Despite its stomach-turning name, the **Slug and Lettuce** *(The Courtyard, Back Swinegate; Tel 01904/679-900; 11am-11pm Mon-Sat, noon-10:30pm Sun, pub grub till 9pm; No credit cards)* is a really modern bar with slick trappings. The cool and calm exposed gray stone interior is enlivened by splashes of color, a glass dome, and Ikea-style furniture. You'll find the people in this bar tend to follow the lead of their surroundings: young, beautiful, and slickly clad.

An intoxicating warmth pervades **Lendal Cellars** *(26 Lendal; Tel 01904/623-121; 11am-11pm Mon-Sat, noon-10:30pm Sun; £2.50 pint; No credit cards),* just off Swinegate. As the name implies, this bar's located in a cellar, which seems like the right place to offer a range of high-quality wines and beers. You're even welcome to have a taste before you order. The place can get pretty wild, but it's easy enough to duck unnoticed into a cozy couch-lined corner with some friends.

Combining modern comfort with continental style, **Oscar's Wine Bar and Bistro** [see *eats,* below] is packed with hungry shoppers by day

down and out

The people in this city are so welcoming that if you're wandering around one of the parks in the rain and happen to stumble on a game of cricket, you'll be asked to join in. They'll even teach you to play, you ignorant Yank. For a vivid memory of England, there's nothing better than getting laughed at by a bunch of British kids. So, who cares? You've got better things to do; the **York Minster** and **York-shire Museum** [see *culture zoo,* above, for both] don't charge admission, and will even keep you dry.

fIVE-0

The stumbling shuffle and meaningless jabbering common to post-pub wanderers really seem to amuse the local law enforcement. Really—they're not out to get you here. They'll be happy to help you out if you're lost, and even happier if you're lost, loud, and drunk (hey, even cops need a little entertainment).

and heavy drinkers by night. The exposed brick walls of the beer garden offer plenty of old-world charm, and outdoor heating lamps take the chill off the night air. The beer is cheap, which means the crowd is young and energetic. If you've been told you're too loud, Oscars is the place to go—*everyone* else here is loud.

The crowd is older and much mellower at the legendary **Old White Swan** *(80 Goodramgate; Tel 01904/540-911; 11am-11pm Mon-Sat, noon-10:30pm Sun, food until 7pm; £3.50 per item; £2 pints)*, which dates back to the 17th century, when it also housed an inn and a pigsty. Luckily, it's been cleaned up a bit since then—a recent renovation incorporated medieval features like the hayloft and massive fireplace to maintain the Swan's earthy charm. It's a good place for easy conversation or watching a football match surrounded by 50 or so of your newest friends.

The single late bar in town, the new **Plaza** *(St. Leonard's Place; Tel 01904/642-761; 11am-11pm Mon-Sat, noon-10:30pm Sun, open till 2am Thur-Sat; complimentary tapas; drinks £2.50)*, is housed in the posh 17th-century DeGrey Rooms above the tourist information center. As the grand ballroom with its original Victorian chandelier fills up with smooth jazz, you may feel as refined as the now-forgotten 17th-century duke who commissioned the building. Just leave the tuxedos and ball gowns at home; khakis will do just fine.

West of the River Ouse, Micklegate street once greeted visitors with the decapitated heads of traitors; today the "Micklegate Run" is almost as intimidating. It's a rite of passage among York's young turks, but few succeed in the given task of downing a pint in every pub along the way. If you feel up to it, you're welcome to head on over—just don't do anything stupid. Local pub crawlers tend to tolerate less foolishness from foreigners than they do from themselves.

On a typical Saturday night, Micklegate Runners overrun **Harry's Bar** *(127a Micklegate; Tel 01904/622-293; 11am-11pm Mon-Sat, noon-10:30pm Sun; drinks £2.50)*. Every last bit of space in this place is occupied—the dance floor is typically used more for schmoozing than moving. Never mind that no one's dancing, club music will still be blasting your ears. No, you're not hallucinating, colorful fish are swimming along the ceiling—it's part of the decor. Beer is on the pricey side (£2.50 for a bottle of Bud!? Well, it *is* imported), because somebody's got to pay for those ceiling fish.

rules of the game

During the day, the snickleways in the city center are overrun by shoppers and residents. It gets so congested that this small city feels bigger than it actually is. At night, the streets are empty except for the punters wandering in zigzags from pub to pub. Drinking in the street isn't allowed, but being publicly drunk is pretty commonplace. As long as you're discreet, being or appearing to be under the influence won't really get you into trouble.

You won't see flying fish at **Walker's Bar** *(47 Micklegate; Tel 01904/628-501; 11am-11pm Mon-Sat, noon-10:30pm Sun);* people don't come for the decor. It's the beer, stupid. Departing from the usual Guinness and Bass, Walker's offers a nice selection of the liquid ambrosia, with Theakston's bitter, XB, and Old Peculier among the notables. The staff is friendly, and the pub grub is typical—straight from the deep-fat fryer.

Just off Micklegate, **Brubaker's** *(22-26 Blossom St.; Tel 01904/612-159; 11am-11pm Mon-Sat, noon-10:30pm Sun; drinks £2.50)* doesn't serve the best beer in York, nor does it serve any food. So what's the appeal? Maybe it's the thumping dance music or the large video screens, which offer a bit of stimulation for the senses. Whatever the cause, expect to queue up to order drinks—the place is always packed.

LIVE MUSIC SCENE

Outside of opera, live music is rare in this self-conciously high-class city. Some of the pubs will sponsor a jam session now and then, but **Fibber's** *(Stonebow House; Tel 01904/651-250; music starts 8pm nightly)* is really all that's going in York when it comes to live bands. It's a little out of the way, just east of the Shambles. This always hoppin' bar features primarily local boys trying to make good, although occasionally a struggling tour band will stop by for a gig. The furnishings consist of an anomalous red phone booth and old fliers and contracts from some of the featured acts on the walls—some of the bigger names are Everything but the Girl and Travis. A tip: if you're looking for some food to wash down that pint of Tetley's or Guinness, try the nachos. They're a meal in themselves, with plenty left over to share with your mates.

CLUB SCENE

There's not much club action in York, especially compared to the pleasure palaces of Manchester, Liverpool, and Leeds. For the authentic Yorkshire experience, you might be better off sticking to the pubs. But if you just don't feel like yourself without thumping bass rattling your bones, try

The Gallery *(12 Clifford St.; Tel 01904/647-947; 10pm-2am Mon-Thu, 9:30pm-2am Fri-Sat; Cover £5-10)* just north of Clifford's Tower, voted best dance club in the area by people who queue up to get in. There's a kitschy heaven-and-hell theme to the place, which is all clouds and cherubs upstairs, all fire and brimstone downstairs. Music ranges from '70s and '80s stuff to the usual chart hits—not exactly heavenly. The cover varies, and can get pretty pricey, but the six bars and two dance floors give you a good chance to get your groove on.

arts scene

York is all about trying to be high-brow, so don't bother looking for a cutting-edge arts scene here. Their idea of avante garde is disco at the Opera House.

▶▶VISUAL ARTS

See the world through a photographer's lens at **Impressions Gallery** *(19 Castlegate; Tel 01904/654-724, Fax 01904/651-509; 9:30am-5:30pm Mon-Sat; www.impressions-gallery.com; free admission),* north of Clifford's Tower. Arresting images from British and international artists are featured. Magazines, books, and cards are on sale, and there's also a cafe to complete the boho ambience.

South of the Minster, the cosmopolitan **Adze Gallery** *(24A Goodramgate; Tel 01904/674-348; 11am-5pm Tue-Fri, 11am-4pm Sat-Sun; free admission)* exhibits paintings, sculptures, prints, and ceramics in an open setting, with none of the trappings of snobbery.

Just southwest of the Minster, **Pyramid Gallery** *(43 Stonegate; Tel 01904/641-187; 10am-5:30pm Mon-Sat, 11am-4:30pm Sun; free admission),* features works in wood, glass, and ceramics, as well as paintings. Artwork and handcrafted jewelry are sold in the shop downstairs.

▶▶PERFORMING ARTS

York's **Theatre Royal** *(St. Leonard's Place; Tel 01904/623-568 box office or 01904/610-041 for info, Fax 1904/611-534; showtimes and ticket prices vary)* near Swinegate stages a wide range of productions, from old Broadway revivals like *A Funny Thing Happened on the Way to the Forum...* to edgier fare like *Rumblefish.*

boy meets girl

Whereas catcalls are uncommon, invading personal space in any way turns the cold English stare into a look of affection. There's an old Yorkshire saying: "Stand within kissing reach of an Englishman, and he probably will."

If you prefer your drama flickering on a screen, the **City Screen Cinema** *(Coney St.; Tel 01904/612-940; showtimes and ticket prices vary)*, northeast of the Lendal Bridge, has three of them. There's also a restaurant and Internet cafe on-site.

If you're looking for high art, be advised that the **York Grand Opera House** *(Cumberland St.; Tel 01904/671-818; showtimes and ticket prices vary)*, just south of the Ouse Bridge on the east bank, doesn't take the word "opera" in its name too seriously. Recently, it's hosted such spectacles as *Abbamania* and *Bee Gees Fever*. Disco, opera—maybe they're not that different after all.

CULTURE ZOO

York's culture is rich, if you define culture as historical attractions. There are plenty to choose from, including some Disney-style recreations of what life in York was like way-back-when. If time is limited, skip those; a walk around the city's ancient walls offers the best illustration of its history. Even if you're already a bit burnt-out on looking at ancient buildings, you'll probably really be amazed by York Minster, one of the few cathedrals that lives up to the hype.

York Minster *(4 Deangate, St. William's College; Tel 01904/557-216; 7am-8:30pm summer, 7am-6pm winter; no admission charge):* Without a doubt, this is one of the greatest cathedrals in Europe. Dating back to 1220, it took over 300 years to complete, and the painstaking craftsmanship is evident in every ornate detail, from the three Gothic towers reaching for the sky to the hundred stained-glass windows coloring the sunlight in deep blues, ruby reds, forest greens, and honey ambers. If the climb up the staircase of the central tower doesn't take your breath away,

only here

Situated right on the east bank of the river south of the Ouse Bridge, the **King's Arms Pub** *(King's Staith; Tel 01904/659-435; 11am-11pm Mon-Sat, noon-10:30pm Sun)* not only offers a boisterous good time, it's a living timeline of the River Ouse. The weathered brickwork inside is striped with lines and dates, each representing a different time the pub was flooded, and demonstrating exactly how high the water got. Instead of giving it all up, the owners have marked the wall each time, creating a bona-fide tourist attraction. Apparently, they took that Monty Python song seriously. "Always look on the bright side of life... "

festivals and events

Despite their rep for the world's most bland and boring cuisine, the English throw themselves into food and drink with gusto. At the **York Festival of Food and Drink** *(last week of September; Tel 01904/554-425; www.yorkfestivaloffoodanddrink.com)* you can sample a variety of Brit food, from traditional English peasant dishes (are you ready for yet another steak and kidney pie?) to the latest concoctions from elite celebrity chefs. There are also musical performances, open-air markets, and even discussions of food science from the local brain trust. And of course, the local restaurants and bars bring out all their best. Or you could just nibble on a few snacks and move on to something slightly more interesting: *The Ale Trail* is highly recommended. Cheers!

its view of the Yorkshire dales will. One look and you'll know what all the fuss is about—if you see only one cathedral in England, this should be it.

York City Walls *(Contact the tourist office at 01904/621-756 for info; 8am-dusk; free):* Walking along these ancient walls, originally built by the Romans and reconstructed time and again over the centuries, is like walking through York's history. One Roman tower remains intact, and 14th-century stone figures are still on duty, ready to scare the bejeezus out of approaching attackers. The walls run the entire perimeter of the original city; you can walk them all in about two hours.

Clifford's Tower *(Clifford Street, Tel 01904/646-940; 10am-6pm Apr-Oct, until 4pm daily Nov-Mar, £1.80 adult, £1.40 student admission):* Built by William the Conqueror to show everyone just how big a man he really was (Hmm, what would Freud say?), this 13th-century stone tower just north of the Skeldergate Bridge is named for Roger Clifford, who was hanged here in 1322. There's no real need to go inside; it's more of a shambles than it seems from the outside—just make sure you go up to the top for the great view of the city.

Yorkshire Museum *(Museum Gardens; Tel 01904/629-745; 10am-5pm daily; admission £3.75 adult, £2.40 student):* Some of the richest archaeological finds in Europe, from Jurassic-era fossils to Viking swords and elaborate 15th-century jewels, are encased in glass here. Unfortunately, much of it is indecipherable to the average joe; if you're feeling less than average, you may be better off admiring the gardens outside.

York Ghost Walk *(King's Arms Pub, Ouse Bridge; Tel 01759/373-090; 8pm nightly; £3 adults):* With all of the medieval tortures, executions, and garden-variety bloodshed in its long history, York comes with more than its fair share of spooks. Pack the Scooby snacks and head out to the **King's Arms** [see *only here,* below] for the creepy nighttime tour in search of all the wailing lost souls. With authentic backdrops and expert storytelling, it makes a quirky pre-pub-crawl adventure.

York Castle Museum *(The Eye of York; Tel 01904/653-611; 9:30-5pm daily Easter-Nov; 9:30-4:30pm off-season; £4.95 adult, £3.50 child admission):* If you can't imagine life in York hundreds of years ago simply by walking the streets of this very Victorian town, this museum will do it for you. Housed in two 18th-century prison buildings north of the Skeldergate Bridge, its exhibits offer a re-creation of times past—the highlight is an authentic Victorian cobblestone street. Workshops demonstrate the local crafts and skills, from blacksmithing to leatherwork. While the effort involved is impressive, it's really for the imagination-impaired and Victorian fanatics only.

Jorvik Viking Centre *(Coppergate; Tel 01904/643-211; 9am-5:30pm daily Apr-Oct; 9am-3:30pm Sun-Fri, 9am-4:30pm Sat Nov-Mar; £5.35; No credit cards):* No, it's not a *real* 10th centurey Norse village, it just looks like one. This hyper-accurate re-creation is built on the site of a recently excavated Norse village, and appears just as it was in 948, pretty much. Jump in a Disneyland-style "time car," tour the Vikings' homes, and watch the Normans sack the city, as they did in 1067. The presentation may be strictly Disney, but all of the Viking artifacts on display are real.

city sports

On the west bank of the River Ouse near the Skeldergate Bridge, **Rowntree Park** *(Terry Ave.; Tel 01904/613-161 ext 3399 for facilities; 8am-dusk daily; free)* offers 20 acres of open space, as well as tennis courts and bowling greens. There's also a basketball court if you're itching to shoot some hoops. Unfortunately, if you want to see if the Yorkies got game, you'll have to bring your own ball.

great outdoors

There are plenty of places in this medieval city to take a breath of fresh air and a gander at some greenery. The **Museum Gardens** *(Museum St.; Tel 01904/629-745; 8am-dusk daily; free),* named for the Yorkshire Museum [see *culture zoo,* above] on the grounds, extend from the back of the Exhibition Center to the east bank of the River Ouse. In addition to the ruins of the 11th-century St. Mary's Abbey, once the stage for the city's medieval mystery plays, you may come across some restless peacocks. Don't chase them—you really don't want to be on the receiving end of a pissed-off peacock. **Dean's Park** *(8am-dusk daily; free),* between the Minster and the city wall, is another choice early-afternoon chill spot.

stuff

There are plenty of places in York where your inner consumer can run wild and free. Even if there's no room in your backpack for any new acquisitions, you can have a good time peering in storefront windows and roaming the little boutiques inside the city walls, not to mention the old world swap meet at the Newgate Market [see *to market,* below]. Be warned that every winding street and snickleway will be crammed with tourists. Unforunatley, your only other options are power-shopping at designer stores near Swinegate, and the big name chains like Marks & Spencer, the Body Shop, and the Disney Store are near Parliament Street, at St. Sampsons Square and Coppergate.

▶▶SCENTS

Established in 1880, **Burgins Perfumery** *(2 Coney St.; Tel 01904/623-137; customer—service@burginsperfumery.co.uk or www.burginsperfumery. co.uk; 9am-5:30pm Mon-Sat; AE, V, MC)* is the sort of little specialty shop that just doesn't exist anymore. With literally hundreds of perfumes and colognes in stock for women and men alike, it's a veritable olfactory extravaganza. Open up those nasal passages and sniff yourself into a frenzy; it's an experience you won't enjoy again any time soon. It's next to Betty's Tearoom on St. Helen's Square.

▶▶SWEETS

It's hard to know if the chocolate pigs available at the **Chocolate Store** *(33 Goodramgate; Tel 01904/679-672; 9:15am-5:30pm daily)* are meant as an ironic comment on gluttony, but ultimately, who cares? They've got just about anything you can think of made of chocolate—pigs, mice, cars, airplanes—as well as a good selection of old-time sweets like Coke bottles and flying saucers. It's just a minute's walk from York Minster on Goodramgate, so stop by on your way out. You'll hate yourself if you don't.

▶▶TUNES

There's reputed to be some good vinyl-browsing in Micklegate, but if you need your music fix now, head to Coney Street and **Virgin Megastore** *(15 Coney St.; Tel 01904/611-101; 9am-6pm Tue-Sat; 8am-6pm Mon, 11am-5pm Sun; V, MC, AE).* Sure, it's a chain, but at least it's a *British* chain.

fashion

Judging by the wardrobe of the local populace, York doesn't seem to be making much of a statement. There aren't even any of the scantily clad women that are typical in other northern cities after 9pm. Since just about anyone can get into the bars, which don't even employ bouncers, fashion trends are left up to the local college students, who basically stick to unisex trainers and jeans. Not exactly hot stuff.

▸▸BOUND

Along with comfortable chairs, **Waterstone's** *(9-10 Ousegate; Tel 01904/610-044; 9am-5:30pm Mon, Wed-Fri; 9:30am-5:30pm Tue; 9am-6pm Sat, 11am-5pm Sun; MC, V)* offers a good selection of titles from kid's stuff and travelogues to art history and gay and lesbian lit. Used books are often available at the tables of the **Newgate Market** [see *to market*, below].

▸▸USED AND BRUISED

For antique duds that are used but not the least bit bruised, head to **Priestleys Vintage Clothing** *(11 Grape Lane; Tel 01904/631-565; noon-5pm Mon-Fri, 10am-fpm Sat; No credit cards)*, near Swinegate for some great finds—dresses, suits, sweaters, purses, and even swimsuits dating from the 1930s to the 1970s. It's not exactly a thrift shop—everything's in great condition, and prices can get a little high, but it's worth a look if you're a fashionista with a sense of history.

EATS

No matter how large your appetite or how small your wallet, York offers a good range of restaurants, so you can afford to be choosy.

▸▸CHEAP

Just southwest of the Minster, **Oscar's Wine Bar and Bistro** *(8 Little Stonegate; Tel 01904/652-002; 11am-11pm daily; £2-9.95 per entrée, £1.50 drinks, £3.50 lunch special including drink; V)* is a rambunctious bar by night with great quick meals by day. The beer garden is charming in any kind of weather, thanks to outdoor heaters. Indoors the candle-lit oak surroundings are as cozy as it gets, and the gourmet meals, from burgers to more daring bistro fare, will warm you from the inside out. Take advantage of the lunch special—you won't get as tasty a meal for so few quid. The glass of wine that comes with it is an additional bonus.

TO MARKET

Get up early in the morning to snag the good stuff at the daily outdoor **Newgate Market** *(Tel 01904/551-355; 8am-4pm daily)*, bordered by the Shambles and Parliament and Church Streets. Everything you need—but couldn't bear to buy at one of the crowded, touristy shops in town—is on sale at its covered stalls: fresh fruits, vegetables, flowers, and plants, specialty cheeses, Italian breads and cakes, dishes, fabric, hats, and even used books. Bring cash.

If you want to know what traditional English fare should *really* taste like, pull up a stool next to one of the locals at **Gert & Henry's** *(4 Jubbergate; Tel 01904/621-445; 10am-10pm daily; everything about £5.50; No credit cards)* just north of Clifford's Tower, and munch on some Yorkshire Pudding. Down-home puddings and flaky scones are the rule here, so if you're looking for low-cholesterol, look elsewhere. Be prepared to eat large quantities of red meat covered in a sauce so thick and creamy you might mistake it for the beef itself.

Located inside a church (did the name give it away?), **Cloisters** *(The Spurriergate Center, St. Michael's Church; Tel 01904/629-393; £1.50 per item; No credit cards)* combines a fair trade store on the second floor with a cafeteria offering home-cooked meals. Aside from the ecclesiastical surroundings, the decorations are few. Food is cooked by members of the congregation, and all profits are donated to the church. Eat. Shop. Pray. Now that's convenience.

▶▶DO-ABLE

People don't mind queuing up to get into **Betty's Cafe and Tea Rooms** *(6 St. Helen's Sq.; Tel 01904/659-142, Fax 01904/627-050; 9am-9pm Mon-Fri, 8:30am-9pm Sat)*, a quick walk southwest of the Minster, known as *the* place in York for high tea. With an enormous dining area lined with stained-glass windows, it's every inch the elegant English teahouse. A myriad of gourmet tea and coffee choices from exotic locales like South Africa and the Galapagos Islands are featured. You can either get the traditional high tea (£9.15)—pot of tea, sandwich, sultana scone, and York's curd tart—or the cream tea (£5.15)—pot of tea and two sultana scones served with butter, fruit preserves, and heavy cream.

Named for the musical instrument in the middle of the dining room, **El Piano** *(15-17 Grape Lane; Tel 01904/610-676; opening times vary; V, MC)* near Swinegate is a pleasant vegetarian cafe with a Latin theme and international flavor. The rotating menu offers vegan and all-organic dishes, and there are even vegan desserts. For £1.95 you can get something called "Dead on a Plate," which can be anything from a Spanish omelette to a chimichanga; "Dead in a Bowl," generally a pasta dish, costs £2.95. For £14.50, you get a huge platter of savory appetizers, salad, bread, and olives—enough for two or three people. There is also famously good fresh-ground coffee, served in large jugs that hold enough for two or three cups (£1.85). The place is open late, and sometimes there's even someone playing that piano.

Ask *(Blake Street; Tel 01904/637-254; noon-11pm; £5.50 per entrée)* has successfully remodeled the interior of the historic Grand Assembly building near Swinegate while maintaining its 18th-century grace. Marble surfaces, paired Corinthian columns, ornate ceilings and glittering chandeliers will make you feel like you're dining in a more cultivated era. The menu offers reasonably good Italian fare, with rich pastas and pizzas, as well as seafood.

Put the myth of the haughty French waiter to rest at **François** *(28 Castlegate; Tel 01904/612-744; noon-2pm/5:30-10pm daily; £9.95 per* *entrée; V, MC),* north of Clifford's Tower. Waiters here will not only understand your order, whether it's steak filet in mushroom sauce or ham with crushed garlic potatoes, they'll serve it to you with a smile in a bright, friendly setting. The brick-and-stone entrance and stained glass accented windows all add to the casual elegance.

▶▶SPLURGE

If traditional English fare has you feeling earthbound, take to the air at **Kites** *(13 Grape Lane; Tel 01904/641-750; noon-2pm/6:30-10:30pm; entrees £10.50-14.50, reservations recommended; V, MC, AE, DC)* near Swinegate. The atmosphere in this upstairs bistro is simple and unpretentious, but the real draw is the dynamic menu, which ranges from medieval English dishes to authentic Thai favorites to vegetarian fondue. It's just a five-minute walk from the Minster near Stonegate.

crashing

One of the few advantages of visiting a popular tourist stop is that there are plenty of places to stay. With three youth hostels and almost every building in the city doused in history, you have a good chance of spending the night in a room that not only has character, but a dramatic story all its own. Rates get cheaper outside the city walls, and if you can manage a bit of a walk, the rooms are just as good. The tourist office [see *need to know,* below] can book reservations for you, but they charge a £4 fee; you're better off to book directly.

▶▶CHEAP

Housed in an 18th-century Georgian manse, the **York Backpackers Hostel** *(88-90 Micklegate; Tel 01904/627-720; shared bath; £9 per person; www.yorkbackpackers.mcmail.com; No credit cards)* offers an authentic medieval York experience. There are wood-paneled rooms, a sweeping staircase, rococo ceilings, and even secret passageways that have unfortunately been covered over. The more modern features include a TV/video lounge, Internet terminals, and laundry facilities. The atmospheric Dungeon Bar in the former kitchen is good for a pint. The convenient city center location inside the city walls is close to most city attractions; just five minutes' walk from the bus and train station, and a brief drunken crawl from all the pubs in Micklegate.

Despite being housed in an old Rowntree mansion, **York YHA** *(Water End, Clifton; Tel 01904/653-147; shared bath; £15.05 per person; V, MC)* manages to make a historic estate feel like a dorm. It's a beautiful ten-minute walk northwest along the River Ouse from the city center.

Bunkbeds are standard at the **York Youth Hostel** *(11-13 Bishophill Senior; Tel 01904/625-914; shared bath; £10-12 per person dorm, £14-16 private room; V),* but this minus is balanced out by the plus of a large private bar in-house. With its convenient location within the city walls, not far from the Ouse Bridge, this old house makes a great temporary home.

There are two cheap B&Bs on the riverbank between the Museum Gardens and the train tracks (not as sketchy as it sounds): The **Abbey**

Guest House *(14 Earlsborough Terrace, Tel 01904/627-782; rooms from £18/person; No credit cards)* and the **Riverside Walk Hotel** *(9 Earlsborough Terrace, Tel 01904/620-769; rooms with bath from £24/person)* both offer comfortable rooms at unbeatable prices.

▶▶**DO-ABLE**

Warm and clean, **The Beckett** *(58 Bootham Crescent; Tel 01904/644-728; £23 per person, en suite; V)* will set you up with a large room in an elegant Victorian townhouse northwest of the Minster. With quilts on the beds and country decor, you might expect to find a doorway leading out to the barn. (No such luck.)

Just minutes from Swinegate's most popular bars, **Aldwark Guest House** *(30 Saint Saviourgate; Tel 01904/627-781; en suite; £20 per person; No credit cards)* provides an easy walk home after the pub run slows to a crawl, and a comfortable bed for nursing your hangover the next morning.

If these are full, try the **Abbey Guest House** *(14 Earlsborough Terr; Tel 01904/627-782, Fax 01904/671-743; abbey@rsummers.cix.co.uk, or www.cix.co.uk/~ munin/sworld/abbey.htm; en suite available; £23 single, £53 double; V, MC)* in the city center, just a five-minute walk from the train station. Other options outside the city center include the **Avenue Guest House** *(6 the Avenue; Tel 01904/620-575; allen@avenuegh.fsnet.co.uk, www.avenuegh.fsnet.co.uk; £15-18 double, £17-22 double with private bath; No credit cards)*, just a 10-minute walk from the center of the city; and the **Cornmill Lodge** *(120 Haxby Rd; Tel 01904/620-566, Fax 01904/620-566; cornmilllyork@aol.com, or www.smokefree.co.uk/cornmill.htm; £20-26 per person, private baths; V, MC)*, accessible by Buses 1, 2, and 3 from the train station; or the **Foss Bank Guest House** *(16 Huntingdon Rd; Tel 01904/635-548; £22-24 single, £20-25 double, private bath available; No credit cards)*, a 10-minute walk from the city center.

▶▶**SPLURGE**

Built in 1850 to house the clergy, **Dean Court Hotel** *(Duncombe Place; Tel 01904/625-082; £47.50-80 per person, en suite, TV; www.deanscourt york.co.uk; V, MC, AE)* takes the cake for best location in the city, situated right below the towers of York Minster. With four-poster beds and washed-out color schemes, rooms are decked out in full Victorian fashion. Many have bay windows and balconies perfect for Minster watching.

need to know

Currency Exchange Change your dollars at **Marks and Spencer Department Store** *(9 The Pavement; Tel 01904/643-377; Tue-Sat 8:30am-5:15pm, Mon 9:30am-5:15p, Sun 11am-4:15pm; no commission, no minimum)*, on St. Sampson's Square.

Tourist Information The **Tourist Information Center** *(DeGrey Rooms, St. Leonard's Place; Tel 01904/639-986; Mon-Sat 9am-6pm, Sun 10am-4pm summer)* offers info on local attractions, including the free *What's On in York*. It'll also book accommodations for you for a fee of £4.

www.york-tourism.co.uk; www.thisisyork. co.uk; www.york.gov.uk:
These tourist web sites are pretty comprehensive, and can be particularly helpful in finding accommodation.

The **Gateway Internet Café** *(26 Swinegate; Tel 01904/674-557; 10am-8pm Mon-Sat, noon-4pm Sun; www.ymn.net/gateway; £5 per hour)* serves fresh juices, coffee, and herbal teas so that you can stay healthy as you absorb the UV rays from the computer screens.

Public Transportation York is really a pedestrian's city, so small that buses are unnecessary—vehicles aren't even allowed in the city center. All of the public transportation is going to and from the city. For information about the green and yellow city buses heading into the suburbs, call the **York Travel Info Line** *(Tel 01904/551-400; 6am-10pm Mon-Sat, 8am-1pm Sun)*. The primary bus stop in the city is at the city's railway station [see below], a ten-minute walk southwest of the Minster.

American Express For all the services that come along with a "green card," go to the **American Express Office** *(6 Stonegate Road; Tel 01904/611-727; 9am-5pm daily)*

Health and Emergency Emergency: *999*. Police: *Fulford Road; Tel 01904/631-321*. **York District Hospital** *(Wiggington Road; Tel 01904/631-313)* offers medical attention.

Pharmacies Pharmaceuticals are available at **Monkgate Clinic** *(31 Monkgate; Tel 01904/674-557; 7am-10pm daily)*.

Airport The closest airport is found in Manchester, and you can hop on a train heading there from Station Road [see below] just about every 20 minutes.

Trains Trains to and from London leave every half hour. York's train station is off **Station Road** *(Tel 0345/484-950)*, a ten-minute walk southwest of the Minster, just over the Lendal Bridge on the west bank. The **York Travel Info Line** *(Tel 01904/551-400; 6am-10pm Mon-Sat, 8am-1pm Sun)* also offers information on train services in York.

Bus Lines Out of the City Buses out of the city leave across from the **Tourist Information Center** [see above] on St. Leonard's Place. **National Express** runs buses to and from Leeds, Newcastle, and London. **The York Travel Hotline** *(Tel 01904/551-400; 6am-10pm Mon-Sat, 8am-1pm Sun)* offers information on bus services in York.

Bike Rental In season, you can rent city bikes from **York Cycleworks,** *(14-16 Lawrence Street; Tel 01904/626-664, Fax 01904/612-356; 9am-6pm Mon-Sat; £10 per day, £30 per 5 days, £45 per week; www.*

york-cycleworks.co.uk, martyn.miller1@virgin.net), just outside the city walls near walmgate bar.

Laundry You can spiff up your duds at the **Washeteria** *(Bishop Thorp Road; Tel 01904/656-145; 9am-5pm Mon-Wed, Fri-Sat, 10am-1pm Sun, closed Thu),* below the Skeldergate Bridge at the southern end of the city.

Postal Mail clever postcards to your mates from the **York Branch post office** *(22 Lendal; Tel 01904/617-285; 8:30am-5:30pm Mon and Tue, 9am-5:30pm Wed-Sat).*

whitby

At first glance, Whitby seems like nothing more than a stolid English fishing village resting at the mouth of the River Esk. Rugged cliffs protect gorgeous beaches, and equally rugged old fishermen haul in nets filled with the catch of the day, as fishermen have done since the town was founded by the Romans. But sometimes when darkness descends upon Whitby, creatures of the night cavort like groovy vampires, reclaiming the town as their own—Bram Stoker wrote *Dracula* here in 1897, and it's become something of a pilgrimage site for thirsty bloodsuckers ever since. The little town is a major setting in the novel, with a climactic moment taking place amid the ruins of Whitby Abbey, which towers ominously above the cliffs to this day. Don't be surprised to see pale Goth-girl princesses and their cloaked consorts here, especially at night. Clothed in black and wearing gobs of black eyeliner and lipstick, they scramble up the walls of the ruined abbey, wander along the Whitby Dracula Trail, cackle through the Dracula Experience museum [see *only here,* below, for both], and frolic morbidly at the local pubs. Some people really know how to have a good time.

If blood-sucking just isn't your thing (what are you, *sick*?), Whitby offers little to enjoy beyond the harsh seaside scenery and monuments to old-time explorer Captain Cook, who really can't compete with Vlad the Impaler—the real-life inspiration for Dracula—when it comes to lurid sex appeal. There's also the aforementioned ruined abbey, which is impressive mainly because of its historical significance in the early days of English Christianity. Most people stop in town as they make their way along the Cleveland Way or head into Moors National Park. Stopping is fine, but staying over for the nightlife, undead or otherwise, isn't really recommended. The pubs are pretty much meat markets, something even the lusty Count would find tacky. Unless you're a dark prince or Goth contessa, you're better off moving on to your next destination.

neighborhoods

The River Esk, which flows northward into the sea, divides Whitby into Old and New Towns. The **Old Town,** site of **Whitby Abbey, St. Mary's Church,** and the old Market Place, lies on the east side of the river.

whitby

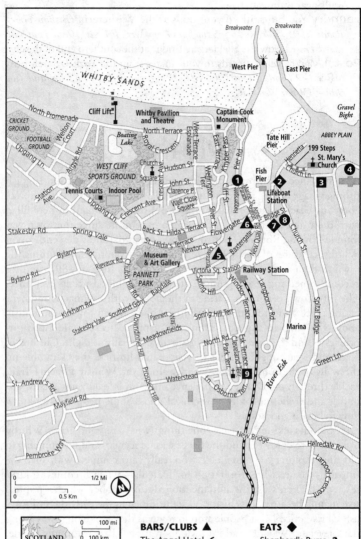

BARS/CLUBS ▲
The Angel Hotel **6**
The George Hotel **5**

CULTURE ZOO ●
Captain Cook's
  Memorial Museum **8**
Dracula Museum **1**
Whitby Abbey **4**

EATS ◆
Shepherd's Purse **2**
The Dolphin Hotel **7**

CRASHING ■
New Bridge View
  B & B **9**
YHA **3**

only here

Grab your crucifix and garlic-clove necklace and head over to the **Dracula Experience** *(9 Marine Parade; Tel 01947/601-923 or 01723/501-016; 10am-5pm daily, Easter-Oct; 10am-10pm daily Jul-Sep; noon-5pm Sat-Sun, Nov-Easter; £1.95),* in the Old Town, just north of the bridge. Dedicated to the story of Bram Stroker's *Dracula*, it's more of an experience than a museum, telling the story of the Transylvanian count with the help of animation, lighting, and sound effects, and even live actors. With a Halloween funhouse atmosphere, it's not for the nervous or lactose-intolerant (it's way too cheesy). Things can and will jump out at you—in other words, when you least expect it, expect it....

You can also stroll along the **Whitby Dracula Trail,** which takes you around town to various spots mentioned in the novel, as well as historical sites related to Captain Cook, who, as far as we know, never met either Dracula or Bram Stoker. A leaflet detailing the walk can be obtained at the Tourist Information Center for 30p [see *need to know,* below]. For more undead fun, you can also check out the town's various Goth events [see *festivals and events,* below].

Connected to it by two bridges (the New and the Old Bridges, built in 1980 and 1908, respectively) is the **New Town,** on the river's west bank, considered the town center. The New Town isn't all that new: many of the buildings date back to the 1600s.

Day-trippers flood the Old Town, which is where you'll find all of the old world pubs. An all-pedestrian shopping road, **Church Street** runs along the sea, parallel to the base of the cliffs that support the abbey. Modern-day commerce passes through New Town, whose main street is **Baxtergate,** a busy east-west street lined with shops. Intersecting with Baxter Street are two other pedestrian streets, **Skinner Street** and **Flowergate.** Whitby is very walkable; covering both New and Old Towns takes just 20 minutes.

hanging out

In fair weather, people stroll along the town's refreshingly uncommericalized **West Pier,** which juts seaward from the west side of the River Esk.

bar scene

However attractive they may look from the outside, most pubs around here should be avoided like the plague. Unless you're a grumpy fisherman or an alienated post-teenager, there's not much fun to be had. If you *are* an alienated post-teenager, this is a perfect place to wallow in your angst. All of the bars in town are open during "law hours" *(11am-11pm Mon-Sat, noon-10:30pm Sun).*

One exception to the fishermen-and-vampire scene is the **George Hotel** *(Baxtergate; Tel 01947/602-565; 11am-11pm Mon-Sat, noon-10:30pm Sun; £2 bitters),* in the New Town. With amiable music and friendly people, it's a bright, warm spot to down a cold beer. Another non-Goth possibility is the **Dolphin Hotel** [see *eats,* below] which shifts from restaurant to pub at 9pm.

CULTURE ZOO

Aside from vampires [see *only here* and *festivals and events,* below], Whitby's cultural heritage scene revolves around noble seaman Captain Cook and Saxon ruins.

Whitby Abbey *(Abbey Lane; Tel 01947/603-568; 10am-6pm daily Easter-Sep; 10am-4pm daily Sep-Easter; £1.80):* These are the stone ruins that you keep noticing on the eastern cliff above the River Esk. They carry some heavy baggage, as both the cradle of Christianity in England and the birthplace of English literature (no, really). St. Hilda was the abbess here, and Caedmon, the first identifiable English-language poet, was a monk here in the 7th century. Only the abbey's skeleton remains today, but you can still gaze up at the Gothic nave and lancets that capture the morning sunlight on the east side of the building, and clamor about the old 13th-century choir.

St. Mary's Church *(Church St.; Tel 01947/603-421):* We're not quite sure why, but walking the 199 steps up the eastern cliff from the end of Church Street to this church seems to be a popular pastime in Whitby. It's also notable because Bram Stoker used it as the setting for Dracula's seduction of Lucy in his novel. Walking through the indisputably creepy graveyard, you can see why. A paved path also leads to the 7th-century Saxon Caedmon's Cross and a view of Whitby Harbor.

Captain Cook's Memorial Museum *(Grape Lane; Tel 01947/601-900; 10am-5pm daily Apr-Oct; www.cookmuseumwhitby.co.uk; £2.80 adult admission):* As you might have guessed from the name, this is where you come to find out about the life and times of 18th-century explorer and native son James Cook, who discovered and charted Australia, New Zealand, and numerous Polynesian islands, explored the Alaskan coast, and in doing so produced the first coherent map of the Pacific Ocean. You can marvel at the house where Cook lived as a seaman's apprentice, still filled with lots of old furniture. Also take a look at his old maps and documents, as well as models of his three ships, *Endeavor, Discovery,* and *Resolution.* It's in the Old Town, just south of the New Bridge.

Whitby Museum *(Pannett Park; Tel 01947/602-908; 9:30am-5:30pm Mon-Sat, 2-5pm Sun May-Sep; 10am-1pm Tue, 10am-4pm Wed-Sat, 2-4pm Sun Oct-Apr; £2):* This place, set on the city's west side, hasn't changed much since the Edwardian era. Highlights include a

festivals and events

Pack your coffin and sharpen your fangs! **Whitby Gothic Weekends** *(Top Mum Promotions; Tel 0151/678-1252; whitby02 @whitby02.demon.co.uk, whitby.darkwave.org)* happen every April and November, and the **Whitby Dracula Society** *(P.O. Box 51, North Yorkshire, YO21 1YS; whitbydraculasociety@yahoo.com, www.ninemuses.demon.co.uk/wds/index.htm),* founded in 1994, sponsors similar zombie love-ins each October and May. These events, an eerie fusion of Lollapolooza Festivals and Star Trek conventions with a creepy twist, draw the tragically hip, alienated, and despairing from all over Europe for club nights, Goth band performances, and sideshow acts like the Blood Brothers, Nightmare, and Circus of Horrors. Most events take place in the local hotels, and cost around £20 (£13 for registered vamps). The WDS also hosts smaller events throughout the year, including *Lost Souls* dance nights and the unspeakable "Goth Karaoke." If you're a bona-fide bloodsucker, or just want to look like one, this is your chance for immortality.

fossil collection, whalebones, and more Captain Cook memorabilia (we're expecting the Captain Cook Happy Meal any day now).

eats

There are a few good places in town to ease the grumbling in your stomach, mostly with breaded seafood, as catch-of-the-day has been Whitby's bread-and-butter for centuries. Unfortunately, there's nothing terribly imaginative. For quick and cheap, go with take-away fish and chips.

Near the tourist office in the New Town, **Trencher's** *(New Quay Rd.; Tel 01947/603-212; Closed Nov-Mar; hours vary)* offers the best fish and chips in town in a bright pub setting. Across the bridge in the Old Town is the **Shepherd's Purse** *(95 Church Street; Tel 01947/820-228; 10am-9:30pm daily; £6 per item),* a cafe and whole foods store offering vegetarian, vegan, and organic fare. It doubles as a B&B [see *crashing,* below].

You can't get better value for your money than at the **Dolphin Hotel** *(Bridge Street; Tel 01947/602-197; noon-9pm daily; £9.95 per entrée),* just over the bridge on the eastern side. A London-trained chef roasts up splendid English fare at the restaurant's carvery. The cozy restaurant turns into a lively pub at night, so dine early (unless you like loud punters with your meal).

crashing

If you're willing to take the hike to the top of the steps, the YHA is your best. Otherwise, there are plenty of B&B proprietors willing to share their homes with you. The Tourist Information Center [see *need to know*, below] can help you out.

Housed in a converted brick stable house right next to the Whitby Abbey, the **Whitby YHA** *(East Cliff; Tel 01947/825-146; 5pm-11pm daily Apr-Oct, Fri-Sat Nov-Mar; shared bath; £9 per person; V, MC)* comes complete with gorgeous views of the harbor. Doubles, 4-, 6-, and 10-bedrooms are available, in addition to a 22-bed bunkhouse, plus there's a self-catering kitchen. The moderate accommodations are nothing to write home about—*rustic* is the word—but it's worth staying here for the view alone.

Mrs. Swales of the **New Bridge View B&B** *(34 Esk Terrace; Tel 01947/605-037; shared bath; £13.50 per person, doubles only; No credit cards)*, a ways south of the town center on the west side, is happy to open her door to you for a night or two. The rooms are comfortable and extremely clean, and she'll cook up a superb breakfast in the morning.

Above its popular vegetarian restaurant, **Shepherd's Purse** *(95 Church Street; Tel 01947/820-228; £16/person; vegetarian breakfast included)* also offers pleasant rooms for a night's stay.

Reasonably priced rooms with sea views can be found at both the **New Albany Hotel** *(3 Royal Crescent, Tel 01947/603-711; £23/person; breakfast included)* and **Ashford Guest House** *(8 Royal Crescent; Tel 01947/602-138; from £18/person)*.

need to know

Currency Exchange When it comes to changing money, the **post office** [see below] takes the prize, with 1% commission (minimum £2.50) and rates just slightly higher than you'll find at a bank.

Tourist Information The **Tourist Information Center** *(Langborne Road; Tel 01947/602-674; 9:30am-6pm daily May-Sep, 10am-12:30pm/1pm-4:30pm daily Oct-Apr)* offers guides to the Whitby Dracula Trail [see *only here*, above], as well as all of the other attractions in town. It can also help you book accommodations.

Health & Emergency Emergency: *(Tel 999)*; **Police:** *(Spring Hill; Tel 01947/603-443)*; **Whitby Hospital** *(Tel 01947/604-851)* is also on Spring Hill, just south of the town center.

Pharmacy The local prescription-filler is **Boots the Chemist** *(64-66 Baxtergate; Tel 01947/602-219; 9am-5:30pm Mon-Sat)*. After hours, check the store window for the late chemist on duty.

Trains and Bus Lines Out of the City Buses and trains out of Whitby are available at the **train station** *(Langborne Rd.; Tel 01947/602-146; 9am-5pm daily summer, closed Sun winter)* in the town center. The travel information center in the station offers information and schedules for both buses and trains. There is one bus per day from Whitby to London; the trip is direct and takes about seven hours. By train, you'll have to switch at Middlesborough or Scarborough for service to London.

Bike Rental You can hook up with a pair of wheels at **Dr. Crank's Bike Shack** *(20 Skinner St.; Tel 01947/606-661; 9:30am-5pm, closed Wed; £9 per day; MC, V).*

Laundry Spiff up that dusty old cape at the **Laundrette** *(Church Street; Tel 01947/603-957; 8:30am-5pm Mon-Sat, until 1pm Wed; £2 per wash, £1.20 per dry; £4.15 service wash).*

Postal Letters come and go through the **post office** *(Endeavor Wharf; Tel 01947/602-327; 8:30am-5:30pm Mon-Wed and Sat, until 7pm Thur-Fri),* southeast of the town center.

The Cleveland Way

Walking the 176-kilometer (109-mile) Cleveland Way National Trail offers the most immediate experience of the pale beauty of North Yorkshire. The Way follows a route around the edge of the North York Moors National Park and skirts along the coast, where you'll find Emily Brontë's eponymous wuthering heights: dramatic cliff-sides towering over tumultuous seascapes. (Yorkshire is sort of Brontëshire, in case you haven't figured that out already.) There's also a feast of historical sites along the trail with ruins of castles and abbeys. Be sure to check out the 850-year-old **Rievaulx Abbey,** just northwest of the town of Helmsley [see **North Yorkshire Moors National Park,** below], and **Whitby Abbey** [see **Whitby,** above].

Much of the trail is easy walking, although it becomes more strenuous crossing over the Cleveland Hills at the northern edge of the park. But there's certainly no need to walk the entire trail. It's divided into dozens of smaller sections, so you can easily take a short half-day walk at many points along the way. Each section of the trail is detailed in the *Waymark Guides,* produced by folks who know every inch of the trail. You can pick up the folks for 40p at the Helmsley tourist office [see *need to know,* below], or any other tourist office in the region. If you have only a day and want to walk the best of the trail, make it the Cliffside Walk, stretching for 32 kilometers (20 miles) along the jagged coastline between the towns of Whitby and Scarborough. Some of the cliffs rise to some 198 meters (650 feet), particularly at the village of Boulby, the highest point on the eastern seaboard of England. Take particular care when walking near to cliff edges, since erosion is not uncommon. A walk along the steep slopes can be broken up with stopovers in the tiny fishing villages where tightly knit houses cling to the cliff's edge.

If you're up to the whole 109-mile marathon, the best place to begin this trail is in Helmsley, 43.2 kilometers (27 miles) north of York. This western section of the trail is the largest concentration of moors in the country, covered in summertime by bright purple heather. Hundreds of lookout points along the way offer views of the Vale of York. The trail then climbs through the Cleveland Hills, passing through the tiny villages of Osmotherly and Kildale, before reaching the trail's northern-most point at the tiny coastal town of Saltburn-by-the-Sea.

The eastern section of the Cleveland Way takes in the most rugged coastline in Britain, 80 kilometers (50 miles) from Saltburn-by-the-Sea, heading south through Whitby. The Way reaches its end at the little sea-fronting town of Filey. If you still haven't worn all the blisters off your feet, you can continue south from Scarborough on the 127-kilometer (79-mile) Wolds Way. This hike is long, but not particularly strenuous if you break it up into do-able chunks. The thing is, you have to be willing to spend quite a few days doing it, especially if you take it relatively easy and just walk about 10 miles a day. Free advice: Check out the web site *www.woldsway.gov.uk* and talk to some other people who've done it before you go.

crashing

Literally hundreds of accommodations are available along the Way, most of them inexpensive. **The Cleveland Way Project** *(The Old Vicarage, Bondgate, Helmsley, Y062 5BP; Tel 01439/770-657; Fax 01439/770-691; www.northyorkmoor/npa.gov.uk)* offers an annual *Cleveland Way Information and Accommodation Guide*. Copies are available for 50p at the tourist office in Helmsley [see below]. Another way to book lodgings is through the various tourist offices. This is the easiest and simplest way, although they usually charge a small booking fee.

The **Helmsley Youth Hostel** *(Carlton Lane; Tel 01439/770-433; shared bath; £10 per person dorm bed; £6.25 for those 17 and under)* will put you up and provide information about other youth hostels along the route. Most of them charge in the area of £10 per person for a dorm bed (£6.35 if you're 17 or under), and provide dinner for about £4.50 and breakfast the following morning for around £3. Youth hostels are located along the Way at Osmotherly, Whitby, Robin Hood's Bay, Scar-borough, and Filey.

need to know

Travel Info At the **Helmsley Tourist Office** *(Town Hall, Market Place; Tel 01439/770-173, Fax 01439/770-433; 9:30am-6pm daily Mar-Sep; 9:30am-5:30pm daily Oct; 10am-4pm Fri-Sun Nov-Feb)* you can pur-chase maps of the trail and the *National Trail Guide: Cleveland Way* issued by Aurum Press, which contains an Ordnance Survey strip map.

Directions/Transportation Any of the tourist offices in the area dis-tribute timetables for bus connections in the moors throughout the entire North York National Park. If you plot carefully, you can plan to break from the trail at any point and arrange for a bus out of the park back to York or wherever you're heading. *Moors Connections*, a trans-port guide, is distributed free at tourist offices along the way. You can download transport connections on the web ***www.countrygoer.org/ny moors/cleveway/cwaymap.htm or www.countrygoer.org/nymoors/ northeng.html.***

Helmsley has good rail links to most northeastern cities, including York, Malton, Thirsk, Middlesborough, Great Ayton, Whitby, Scarborough, and Filey.

The network of **Moorsbuses** services the western parts of the Cleveland Way such as Sutton Bank, Osmotherley, Carelton Bank, and Clay Bank. In the east along the seacoast, with its many towns, transportation hookups are fairly easy, especially bus services back to York.

Rentals Purchase any supplies or gear you'll need in York before heading to Helmsley. Even if you're hiking in the summer, the weather in North Yorkshire can change dramatically in a matter of minutes, usually for the worse, so do like the Boy Scouts and be prepared.

yorkshire dales

To see what England looked like before the Industrial Revolution, look no further than the rolling farmland of the Yorkshire Dales National Park. You go to the dales for sleepy villages, bustling market towns, and castle ruins, as well as the chance to enjoy a little nature and the English country life. The nature part involves windswept fells, lush green valleys, heather-covered meadows, and lonely moors, white limestone cliffs, cascading waterfalls, and deep caves. Ordinarily, the park's wildlife population easily outnumbers its 19,000 human residents, but when you consider the 8.5 million tourists who descend on the park each year, the situation starts to look more cramped, to say the least. You might think you'll never escape the teeming hordes, but the area is so big that once you start hiking away from the crowd, you may think it's just you and the sky.

The Yorkshire Dales are accesible from the market towns of Settle, Skipton, Ilkey, and Harrogate, north of the city of York. Most of the southern dales such as Ribblesdale, Airedale, Malhamdale, Wharfdale, and Nidderdale run north to south, roughly parallel to one another. The northern dales such as Wensleydale, Swaledale, and Teesdale generally run from west to east. If you have specific questions about the park before heading here, you can contact **Yorkshire Dales National Park Authority Headquarters** [see *need to know,* below], which is located deep in the heart of the park. If you're not a world-class hiker and want only a few hours along the trails, any regional tourist office offers pamphlets that outline 4- to 5-mile walks. They also sell *Yorkshire Dales Cycleway* for (£2.50), which maps out six routes suitable for cyclists, each stretching for about 20 miles across beautiful countryside.

It's best to visit the park in the summer months. During the rest of the year, the weather can get pretty ugly—not to mention *cold.* If you have only a day or two, many of the park's must-see sites are easy day trips from York and Leeds. If you have time to stay overnight in the park, the small village of Skipton, about 40 miles east of York and 25 miles northeast of

Leeds, makes a good base [see *crashing,* below]. It's also the best place to rent bicycles [see *need to know,* below] and pick up provisions; for supplies, try **George Fisher** *(1 Coach Street; Tel 01756/794-305; 9am-5:30pm Mon-Sat, 10am-4pm Sun; V, MC, AE).* Unfortunately, the tourist office in Skipton has closed, a victim of poor cash flow, but 10 miles north, in the village of Grassington, you'll find a **National Park Information Centre** [see *need to know,* below].

Malham, 11 miles northwest of Skipton, is another popular place to spend the night. The National Park Information Centre [see *need to know,* below] in town is a good place to pick up information, maps, and advice. Malham also offers some of the most extraordinary natural rock formations in England and the only lake in the park. Surrounded by harsh limestone scenery, **Malham Tarn** seems like the answer in one of those "One of these things is not like the others" games on *Sesame Street.* If you dip your toe into the chilly water, you'll realize that the lake bed is actually flat limestone slate. The natural limestone amphitheater **Malham Cove,** about a two-hour walk from the village, is 250 feet of sheer glacier-carved rock face. Only 45 feet separate it from **Gordale Scar**, a deep chasm between two limestone cliffs. An 8-mile circular hike covering all three sites takes about five hours.

The small village of **Clapham**, 20 miles northwest of Skipton, offers the best vantage point for exploring the **Three Peaks.** Formed from millstone grit, these spectacular dark fells—Wherside, Pen-y-Ghent, and Ingleborough (the tallest of the three at 2,373 feet)—dominate the western terrain. They're one of the most popular destinations in the park, especially with cave groupies, who explore the caverns formed by the streams and rivers running off the fells. If you get off on caves, welcome to Valhalla: The entire park is honeycombed with dozens of them. New cave systems are explored every year, uncovering a vast subterranean world of stalactites, stalagmites, underground rivers, and chambers the size of large cathedrals.

The most significant historical sight in the park is near Ripon, about 30 miles northeast of Skipton. Set in landscaped gardens, **Fountains Abbey** *(Ripon; Tel 01765/608-888; 10am-7pm daily Apr-Sept; until 5pm Oct-Mar; Admission £4.30)* is yet another medieval ruin, but it's the most complete ruin in England, with a tower standing at its original height and window frames still holding stained-glass that date back to 1132A.D.. Check out the nearby water gardens and Fountains Hall, a stately home dating to the end of the 16th century.

One of the most famous waterfalls in the park is the 69-foot **Hardraw Force,** just outside the sleepy town of Hawes, 30 miles north of Skipton. Unfortunately, to get there you have to pass through the dimly lit Green Dragon pub, which charges a 60p entrance fee. The easy path out the back of the pub leads through a gate into a wide rocky gorge and grassy riverbank, where you can see the cascading water. For even more spray in your face, take Bus 156/157 from Hawes to **Aysgarth,** just 10 miles east. You'll find a mile-long walk along the River Ure, where whitewater tumbles down broad limestone steps.

eats

In Skipton, head to **Hemingway's Tearoom** *(Craven Court; Tel 01756/798-035; 10am-5pm Mon-Sat; £2-5; MC, V)* for a quick bite. It's in the shopping center along High Street, the town's main drag. The meals are light, but the renowned fudge cake is anything but. There's live music—a guy playing the piano—on Wednesday nights.

For veggie fare, try **Herbs** *(10 High Street; Tel 01756/790-619; 9:30am-4:45pm Mon, Weds-Sat, closed Tue and Sun; £2-5; AE, MC,V)*. The vegetarian and whole food cuisine includes the freshest salads in town. Soothing background music and cool green and white decor add to the health-and-wellness vibe. The health-food store on the first floor is probably the best place in town to stock up on good-for-you snacks before heading into the park.

crashing

There are literally hundreds of accommodations in the park, with hostels, B&Bs, converted barns, and old inns among the options. All national park centers [see above] distribute a free booklet called *Yorkshire Dales Accommodation Guide* which lists them all. If you don't mind roughing it, pick up a list called *Dales Barns*. Calling these facilities "rustic" would be an understatement, but they're cheap: bunkhouse dorm beds are £5-7.50 a night. Most have kitchens where you can cook up your own meals, as well as showers, but few have hot water. Talk about communing with English country life! **Grange Farm Barn** *(Tel 01756/760-259; £6.50, under 18, £5.50)*, **Airton Quaker Hostel** *(Tel 01729/830-263; £5.50, under 16 £3)*, and **Barden Bunk Farm** *(Tel 01756/720-330; £5)* are all a few miles, from Skipton.

In Skipton, decent accommodations are available at **The Woolly Sheep** *(38 Sheep Street; Tel 01756/700-966; en suite, TV; £45 per person double including breakfast; AE, MC, V)*. The 400-year-old pub downstairs has a summer beer garden that's popular with hikers. Beer ranges from £1.70-2.10 a pint. Bar food will set you back £3 for a snack or £8 for a complete fill-up.

Another possibility is the venerable **Red Lion** *(27 High Street; Tel 01756/790-718; en suite, TV, breakfast included; £35 double, £45 triple; MC, V)*, right in the town center. The downstairs pub is cozy, with an open fireplace and meals from £3-6.

One of the most convenient hostels is in Malham: the 85-bed **John Dower Memorial Hostel** *(Malham Tarn; Tel 01729/830-321; £11 dorm, under 18 £7.50)*, which offers storage lockers and reasonably comfortable beds.

need to know

Travel Info Located in the park, **Yorkshire Dales National Park Authority Headquarters** *(Yorebridge House, Bainbridge, Leyburn, North Yorkshire DL8 3EE; Tel 01756/752-748; 10am-5pm daily*

Apr-Oct, 10am-4pm Sat-Sun Oct-Apr) can set you up with all kinds of info. Grassington's **National Park Information Centre** *(Hebden Road, Wharfdale; Tel 01756/752-774; 10am-5pm daily Apr-Oct, 10am-4pm Sat-Sun Oct-Apr)* and Malham's **National Park Information Centre** *(Malhamdale; Tel 01729/830-363; 10am-5pm daily Apr-Oct, 10am-4pm Sat-Sun Oct-Apr)* are also handy resources.

Directions/Transportation Trains run from Leeds' City Railway Station to Skipton; for rail schedules into Skipton or Ripon, call **National Rail Enquiry** *(Tel 0345/484-950)*. If you're depending on buses to get around the Dales, ask one of the tourist offices in the area for a copy of *Dales Connection,* a timetable giving all details about public transport. It's important to get whatever information you can before arriving in Skipton. The tourist office here has gone bankrupt, and there are literally hundreds of people seeking information who are out of luck.

Bike Rental The best place for bike rentals in Skipton is **Burgess Cycles** *(Water Street; Tel 01756/794-386; 9am-5:30pm Mon-Wed, Fri-Sat, closed Thu, Sun; £12 per day; MC, V).*

north york moors national park

Once one of the world's great forests, the area that's now North York Moors National Park was altered forever by the introduction of grazing sheep. Today you'll see deep secret valleys and ridge upon ridge of vast, barren moorland sprawling out to the jagged northern coastline, as well as craggy ruins of medieval abbeys and castles.

Twenty-five miles north of the city of York, the parkland stretches east to the North Sea and west to the Cleveland Hills [see **Cleveland Way,** above]. It's bounded by the Vale of Pickering in the south, and the Teeside Plains in the north. The best time to visit is late summer and early autumn, when the moors are covered with blossoms of purple heather. As you hike the park, you'll come upon dozens of sleepy hamlets and little farming villages, where, except for modern conveniences, locals still live the traditional English country farm life.

There's no single, obvious route through the moors; trails and tracks crisscross in all directions. Get a good map and plot your own trail. The park headquarters is in the little village of **Helmsley,** which offers park access from the east, and the most convenient travel from the City of York—it's easily reachable by bus.

A good day tripo into the park is a hike through the **Esk Valley,** which stretches from the coastal town of Whitby [see **Whitby,** above] 15 miles inland to the little town of Danby. Hiking the Esk Valley you'll cross old stone trods where hearty wayfarers have journeyed since before the Roman conquest. Highlights of the valley include the ruins of 14th-century Danby Castle, which is indistinguishable from the farmhouse that's grown up around it, and Duck Bridge, in use since 1396 and still standing. At the end of the valley you reach the village of Danby. Follow summer hikers to the **National Park Moors Centre** [see *need to know,* below] on the eastern outskirts of town. This is the best place to go for books, maps, and endless printed material about the park. The Centre's also not a bad place to hang out and take a breather. The picnic tables set up along the front garden offer nice views of the valley below. There's also a tearoom if you didn't bring your own eats.

From Danby the trail continues for 2 miles west to the village of Castleton. At that point you can follow a signpost south leading over the top of the moors toward Hutton-le-Hole, 13 miles south of Danby. Before you get to Hutton-le-Hole you'll come to Ralph Cross, 5 miles south of Danby and the highest point along the trail.

For sheer beauty, the stuff old-fashioned English calendars are made of, no village in the moors surpasses Hutton-le-Hole, with a babbling brook, friendly sheep, and tiny cottages that look like dollhouses. The village's **Ryedale Folk Museum** *(Tel 01751/417-367; www.ryedale folkmuseum.co.uk/; 10am-5:30pm daily, mid-Apr-Oct; £3)* offers dozens of historic buildings and a medieval kiln. The museum is also the site of a **National Park Information Centre** [see *need to know,* below], where you can pick up leaflets detailing the best of the local hikes.

The second-most appealing area of the park is centered around the market town of Helmsley, an ideal base for the western moors, just 27 miles north of York. From Helmsley you can stroll one of the most romantic walks in the park leading to the 12th-century **Rievaulx Abbey** *(off B1257; Tel 01439/798-228; 10am-6pm daily Apr-Sept, until 5 pm Oct, 10am-1pm/2-4pm Nov-Mar, Admission £3,40)*. This beautiful monastic ruin, situated in a narrow valley, is a short 1.5-mile walk along a signposted pathway out of Helmsley. The River Rye winds about the valley a bit, creating a horseshoe where the abbey sits surrounded by woodland. The original Cistercian monastery was built in 1132. It was the richest in England, gathering its wealth from trading the wool of those same friendly sheep. The 124-foot-long refectory where the monks dined has 50-foot ceilings and lancet windows that are still intact. With pointed arches three stories high, and flying buttresses supporting its vaulted roof, Rievaulx is quite a sight, even in ruins.

EATS

A favorite of hikers along the trail is the **Stonehouse Bakery & Tea Shop** *(3 Briar Hill; Tel 01287/660-006; 9am-4:30pm Mon-Sat)* in Danby, which serves herbal teas, honey straight from the bee, and the world's greatest peanut brittle.

In Helmsley, join the locals for a pint at the **Black Swan** *(Market Place; Tel and Fax 01439/770-174; noon-2pm/6:30-10pm daily; meals from £5),* at the edge of the square. Originally a 16th-century coaching inn, this paneled bar, serving local brew and pub-grub lunches, is the best place to huddle around an open fireplace when the cold North Sea winds blow in.

crashing

Along the coast, you can stay in Whitby [see **Whitby,** above]. Inland, Helmsley is the best place to overnight. You can stay at the **Helmsley Youth Hostel** *(Carlton Lane; Tel 01439/770-433; shared bath; £10 per person dorm bed; £6.25 for those 17 and under),* with simple beds that are clean, decent, and comfortable.

need to know

Travel Info The **National Park Moors Centre** *(Danby Lodge; Tel 01287/660-654; 10am-5pm daily mid-Apr-Oct, 11am-4pm Sat-Sun off-season)* is the place to go for info. The *North York Moors Visitor* (50p) is the most practical guide of the moors, listing everything from special events to accommodations. Find out about more local hikes at the **National Park Information Centre** *(Hutton-le-Hole, Ryedale Folk Museum; Tel 01751/417-367; 10am-5:30pm daily mid-Apr-Oct).*

Directions/Transportation Access from the park is available from Helmsley, 27 miles north of the City of York via Road B1363. There are three buses running every day except Sunday; it's a 90-minute trip. Alternatively, you can approach the park from the coast, and the seaside town of Whitby [see **Whitby,** above]. Whitby can be reached from York via Road A169.

Bike Rental Rent some wheels for your venture into the park at **Dr. Crank's Bike Shack** [see **Whitby,** above],

THE LAKE DISTRICT

THE LAKE DISTRICT

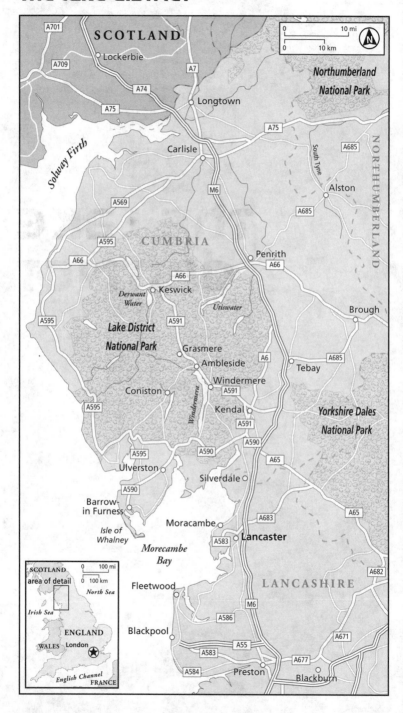

SCOTLAND

A701

A709

Lockerbie

A74

A7

Longtown

A75

Solway Firth

Carlisle

M6

A569

CUMBRIA

A595

A66

Derwent Water

Keswick

A66

Lake District National Park

A595

A591

Utiswater

Grasmere

Ambleside

Windermere

A6

Coniston

Windermere

A591

Kendal

A591

A590

Ulverston

A595

A590

Silverdale

Barrow-in Furness

A590

Isle of Whalney

Moracambe

Morecambe Bay

A583

Lancaster

Fleetwood

M6

A586

Blackpool

A583

A55

Preston

A584

A677

Blackburn

LANCASHIRE

Northumberland National Park

A75

A685

South Tyne

Alston

A685

Penrith

A66

Brough

A685

Tebay

Yorkshire Dales National Park

A65

A683

A65

A682

A671

N   O   R   T   H   U   M   B   E   R   L   A   N   D

0   10 mi

0   10 km

SCOTLAND

area of detail

0   100 mi

0   100 km

North Sea

Irish Sea

ENGLAND

WALES   London

English Channel   FRANCE

While there's no youth-driven party scene like you'll find in the big cities, the Lake District offers quite a rush—one that has nothing to do with electronica beats or mass quantities of alcohol; it comes from the landscape itself. People come to the Lake District on the northwestern coast to refresh their souls. Just 35 miles wide, it's a peninsula bound by the Morecambe Bay and the Irish Sea to the west and the Pennine Mountains to the east—some of the most inspiring scenery in all of England. In fact, it inspired William Wordsworth, grand poobah of the Romantic poets, to write some of his best works.

Today, it's one of the most popular destinations in the country. On holidays and summer weekends, Lake Country is crowded with people trying to get away from it all. Unfortunately, they bring it all with them. But if you avoid the highly trafficked regions in the southeast and seek out the more remote spots, you can still find Wordsworth's summer country. Follow his lead and wander lonely as a cloud—climb the rolling hills and craggy mountains, ramble through secluded valleys and daffodil-covered meadows, and soak in lakes as clear and smooth as glass. Get off on fresh air and blue sky; you may start to feel like a poet yourself. If you're up for a week of rambling, the 77-mile **Cumbria Way** will take you through the heart of the Lakeland. The Cumbria Way begins in **Ulverston,** 24 miles south of **Ambleside,** and continues north to **Coniston.** Most travelers walk it in five to seven days. Coniston and **Glenridding** both offer first-class hiking and mountain-climbing, and attract rock groupies from all over the UK. If your mother was a mountain goat, you won't want to miss tiny Glenridding, and a difficult and daring hike to the top of the razor-sharp **Helvellyn** mountain range.

The less-scenic, but more risky, 189-mile **Cumbria Coastal Way** is really a series of trails that take you along the less-frequented western seascapes.

In addition to the Lake District National Park, the region is dotted with charming little towns. **Grasmere,** once Wordsworth's home, offers much of the countryside that inspired him, while nearby mountain resort Ambleside offers lakeside frolic as well as a wild pub or two. **Ulverston, Keswick,** and **Penrith** offer more sublime scenery, as well as their own peculiar attractions, including the world's largest pencil and a Laurel and Hardy Museum (they had to do something to compete with Wordsworth's star-power).

travel times

Times by train unless
otherwise indicated
*By road.

	Ulverston	Coniston	Ambleside	Grasmere
Ulverston	-	:20*	:35*	:35*
Coniston	:20*	-	:15*	:15*
Ambleside	:35*	:15*	-	:10*
Grasmere	:35*	:15*	:10*	-
Keswick	1:00*	:35*	:30*	:20*
Glenridding	:45*	:25*	:20*	:20*
Penrith	1:00*	:50*	:35*	:35*
Cumbria Coastal Way	2:00*	1:05*	1:10*	1:00*
Cumbria Way	:05*	:25*	:40*	:40*

	Keswick	Glenridding	Penrith	Cumbria Coastal Way	Cumbria Way	London
	1:00*	:45*	1:00*	2:00*	:05*	4:40*
	:35*	:25*	:50*	1:05*	:25*	4:45*
	:30*	:20*	:35*	1:10*	:40*	4:40*
	:20*	:20*	:35*	1:00*	:40*	4:45*
	-	:25*	:25*	:45*	1:05*	5:05*
	:25*	-	:20*	1:05*	:50*	4:50*
	:25*	:20*	-	1:05*	1:05*	4:45*
	:45*	1:05*	1:05*	-	1:10	*5:35*
	1:05*	:50*	1:05*	1:10*	-	4:45*

getting around the region

The Lake District is a dyed-in-the-wool backpacker's dream. If you have the time, you can best experience the lake country on foot. If you're not hiking or driving, you'll be taking the bus. **Stagecoach Cumberland** *(Tel 01946/632-22)* serves more than two dozen of the most popular tourist towns. Pick up a bus schedule at any tourist center in the region. Trains link London to the lakes through the town of Kendal, 70 miles north of Manchester.

▶▶ROUTES

The geography of the Lake District, a maze of mountains, lakes, and streams, defies establishing a clear-cut path (is it any wonder that Wordsworth did so much wandering?). Where you go depends on what you want to do: exploring windswept fells, hiking the Cumbria Way, walking along the coast, or boating on legendary lakes like Windermere.

If you have just 2 days to spend, you'll want to spend them west of Kendal. Take the bus from Kendal over to Lake Windermere. The nearby village of Ambleside, with its pub crawl, and Grasmere, where you can pay your respects to dear old Wordsworth, make good places to overnight. If you're feeling boisterous, go for Ambleside; for a more contemplative stay, pick Grasmere, which also makes a good base for exploring the Lakeland scenery to the south.

For more extreme hiking and rock climbing go farther north, to Keswick, 14 miles west of the Ullswater, or Penrith, 30 miles north of Kendal. Use either town as a sort of base camp for your excellent outdoor adventure.

ULVERSTON

Tourists flock to Windermere, but Ulverston, at the start of the Cumbria Way, is actually a better gateway to the Lake District. Walk the winding cobblestoned streets, and check out the outdoor market that's remained pretty much the same since it began in the 13th century. Take snapshots of the lighthouse monument and grand Coronation Hall. Shake hands with the official town crier, who wanders about in full medieval regalia. Take a breath, note the refreshing absence of tourists, and stroll along the canal that joins **Lake Windermere** and **Morecambe Bay,** watching birds skim the water. At first glance, Ulverston seems like any other picturesque English town, proud of its accomplishments (the shortest, widest and deepest canal in the world) and local sons (Sir John Barrow and Stan Laurel).

To most people passing through, Ulverston may seem like just another series of photo ops, but there's something about the town that can only be described as quirky. Like the Laurel and Hardy Museum, which elevates a pie in the face to high art, or the nearby Buddhist Temple which looks like it belongs in Thailand instead of merry olde England. Obviously, this isn't your typical little English town but do us all a favor, and don't give the secret away.

neighborhoods

The town center is, not surprisingly, called **Market Square;** it's formed by the junction of **Market Street** (an east-west thoroughfare that's partially reserved for pedestrians) and **Queen Street** (a north-south thoroughfare). A cross at its center memorializes the dead soldiers of former

ulverston

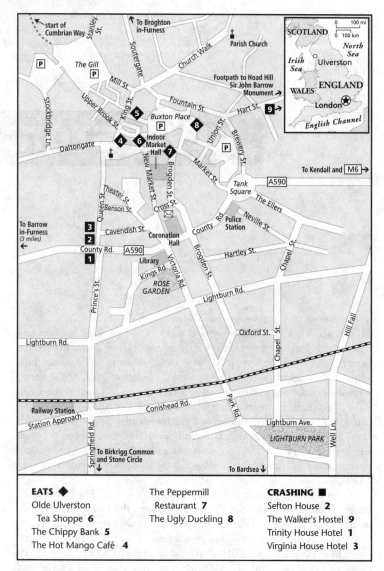

EATS ◆

Olde Ulverston
  Tea Shoppe **6**
The Chippy Bank **5**
The Hot Mango Café **4**

The Peppermill
  Restaurant **7**
The Ugly Duckling **8**

CRASHING ■

Sefton House **2**
The Walker's Hostel **9**
Trinity House Hotel **1**
Virginia House Hotel **3**

British wars. The town is very walkable—it takes only about 10 minutes to cover it all.

bar scene

Although there are a number of pubs in the area, they're all typically English and frequented primarily by graybeard locals, perfect for a relaxing drink. We think the best of the bunch is the oh-so-English **Rose &**

Crown Pub *(King St.; Tel 01229/583-094; 11am-11pm Mon-Sat, noon-10:30pm Sun; MC)*, at the on the Market Square. You'll find great ales (£1.70 pints) as well as backcountry English conversation from the aforementioned graybeards.

CULTURE ZOO

Slapstick or stuffy? These are the choices in Ulverston.

The Laurel and Hardy Museum *(4c Upper Brook St.; Tel 01229/582-292; 10am-5pm daily; £2 adult)*: Stan Laurel, one half of the legendary silent-screen comedy team, was born and raised in Ulverston. In case you're not up on your black-and-white movies, he's the slender fella who trailed chaos in his wake, which inevitably led to his living-large pal smacking him around and saying "This is another fine mess you've gotten us into!" This museum keeps the dynamic duo's memory alive and well, complete with gift shop and a screening room that shows clips of their films. In the town center, near Queen Street, it's worth a laugh on a rainy day—just watch out for falling pianos.

Sir John Barrow Monument *(Hoad Hill; Always open; Free)*: Resembling a lighthouse, this monument memorializes Ulverston's favorite son, Sir John Barrow, a bigwig in the British Navy who promoted arctic exploration and shook hands with Lord Nelson before he headed

OM

Spiritual enlightenment can come in the most unlikely places. Established more than 20 years ago at Conishead Priory, the **Manjushri Mahayana Buddhist Center** *(Conishead Priory; Tel 01229/584-029; www.manjushri.org.uk)*, located just south of the Lake District National Park, is one of the few serious oddities you'll come across in the English countryside. From the outside, it looks like any other stone English manor house, all stone parapets and arched gables, surrounded by 70 acres of woodlands. But explore a little further, and you'll see the peaked roofs of the Kadampa Temple and realize that you're leaving the England you've come to know. Inside, figures of the Buddha laugh at the riddles of the universe while cymbals echo, monks chant and pray, and students scrutinize sacred images while looking vaguely stoned. The monks offer frequent classes in Buddhist teachings, and if you've decided that the way of the Buddha is the way to go, you can make arrangements to stay for free for one week in exchange for 35 hours of work. Such is the path to enlightenment. Good luck!

off to the pivotal Battle of Trafalgar in 1805. The lighthouse offers a sweet view of Morecambe Bay, but other than the photo-op, there's not much to recommend it, unless of course, Sir John Barrow is one of your childhood heroes.

STUFF

What shopping exists is on Market Square and the all-pedestrian Market Street.

▶▶CRAFTS

The Tinner's Rabbit, *(48 Market St.; Tel 01229/588-808; 9:30am-5pm Mon-Sat; MC, V)* sells books, artworks, and crafts from local artisans. Pewter, copper, and wood-carvings seem to be the media of choice.

▶▶NEW AGE

Hang onto your crystals; the New Age has reached Ulverston. **Appleseed's** *(59 Market St.; Tel 01229/583-394; 9am-5pm Mon, Tue, Thur, and Sat,; 9am-3pm Wed; MC, V)* sells New Age gifts and crafts, as well as health supplements and organic foods.

EATS

Ulverston will surprise you with its culinary options, ranging from fish and chip take-aways to romantic little hideaways. There are some great restaurants in town as long as you eat dinner at English dinnertime—get in before 7pm or you'll be trawling for pub grub again. All of the restaurants listed are near the town center.

▶▶CHEAP

The Chippy Bank *(7 King St.; Tel 01229/585-907; noon-9pm daily; £1.50 per item, No credit cards)* is slightly more expensive than the typical fish and chips place, but it's worth a splurge. They offer just the right amount of crunchy batter, which enhances rather than overpowers the fresh, flaky white fish.

If soup and sandwiches suit your fancy, **The Olde Ulverston Tea Shoppe** *(2 Lower Brook St.; Tel 01229/580-280; 50p-£3.25 per item;*

TO MARKET

Known as the best in the region, the **Ulverston Market** *(Market St.; 9am-4:30pm Thur and Sat)* is an old-world affair, dating back to the 13th century. It feels more like a flea market than anything else, but with that quaint English twist. Vendors sell everything under the sun, from specialty foods and locally made delicacies to organic produce.

9am-4pm Mon-Sat; No credit cards) offers homemade breads to accompany both. Don't forget to leave room for the scrumptious selection of tearoom desserts.

California fusion comes to Ulverston at **The Hot Mango Cafe** *(King St.; Tel 01229/584-866; 9am-5pm Tue-Sat, closed Mon; £3.25-£5.00 per item; No credit cards).* If you're looking for a respite from the artery-clogging eats you've been gulping down, this is the place, with healthy veggie options like cucumber and sprout sandwiches (they taste good, really!). They also make the best cappuccino in town.

▶▶DO-ABLE

With traditional English and French influences, the menu at **The Peppermill Restaurant** *(64 Market St.; Tel 01229/587-64; noon-3pm/6-9pm meals, snacks all day; £6.25 per entrée; No credit cards)* offers what you've come to expect in England: Everything is served in large portions and covered in heavy meat sauce. It's warm and friendly, a nice place to linger over a meal. The price is right, and the summer berry pudding is awsome.

▶▶SPLURGE

Decked out in dark and musty wood and lit mostly by firelight, **The Ugly Duckling** *(Buxton Place; Tel 01229/581-573; hours vary; £9.95-£11.50 per entrée; V),* offers high romance along with traditional English fare. The food is standard, but the old-world atmosphere makes all the difference in the world, especially if you've got a swan of your own to share dessert with.

crashing

Overnight visitors are a rarity in this tiny coastal town, so most accommodations are slightly more expensive than you might expect. Your best bet is the independent hostel on the outskirts of town, where the hospitality alone is worth more than the price of a bed to rest in. Accommodations can also be booked through the tourist office [see *need to know,* below].

▶▶CHEAP

About a 15-minute walk from the center of town along Hoad Lane, and just a mile from the coast, **The Walkers' Hostel** *(Oubas Hill; Tel 01229/585-588; £10 per person; Shared bath; £6 evening meal; www.walkershostel.freeserve.co.uk; No credit cards)* is well-situated to take advantage of all that Ulverston has to offer. With soft music in the background, the sunshine-yellow common room offers plenty of warmth even on the rainiest of English mornings, and the comfortable bunk beds will ensure your night is well spent. The proprietors are avid walkers and will fill you up with info on everything from town history to local happenings. They're even happy to show you around.

The 18th-century **Church Walk House** *(Church Walk; Tel 01229/582-211; £22.50 per person; No credit cards)* is decorated like it was still the 18th century, and there's a morning breakfast included in the price. There are only five rooms, though, so call in advance if you are interested.

You can also try the **Rock House** *(1 Alexander Rd.; Tel 01229/586-879; opens in Mar; £20 single, £40 double; en suite, breakfast included; www.smoothound.co.uk/a09664.html; No credit cards)*, near the town center.

▶▶**DO-ABLE**

Built in the 1750s, the modest **Virginia House Hotel** *(24 Queen St.; Tel 01229/584-844; £25 single, £50 double, private baths; No credit cards)* shines as a result of its proprietors who make you feel right at home. This married couple has all the info you'll need on the Lake District, although they can't always agree on the details—such is married life.

Located in an old grey Georgian home, **Sefton House** *(34 Queen St.; Tel 01229/582-190; £27.50 single, £40 double, private baths; No credit cards)* is a classic English bed and breakfast. The rooms are cozy and relatively private, and the olde-style dining room is perfect for the traditional English breakfast, which is included.

▶▶**SPLURGE**

With more luxury than you can shake a stick at, the town center's **Trinity House Hotel** *(Princes St.; Tel 01229/587-639, Fax 01129/588-552; £32.50 per person; en suite, breakfast included; V, MC, AE)* is a bit pricey, but worth splurging. Formerly a church and men's residence, this hotel has modernized with old-world elegance in mind. The spacious rooms have huge French windows and warm, working fireplaces to take the chill off in the morning. It's in the town center, a short walk from the train station.

need to know

Currency Exchange The best place to change money is at the **post office** [see *postal,* below]. They offer decent rates (1.5 percent commission, £2 minimum) and convenient hours. There's also a 24-hour ATM located outside of the HSBC bank on Market Street.

Tourist Information The **Tourist Information Center** *(Coronation Hall, County Square; Tel 01229/587-120; ulvtic@telinco.co.uk; 9am-5pm Mon-Sat)* offers info on local walks and Ulverston's popular market.

Laundry Suds up your duds at the **Laundrette** *(Lightburn Rd.; No telephone; 6:30am-7pm daily; £1.60 wash, 55p dry)* just south of Market Square.

Health and Emergency Emergency: *999.* The nearest hospital, **Furness General Hospital** (Dalton Lane, Barrow-in-Furness; Tel 01229/870-870), is in Barrow-in-Furness, about 10 miles south via Road A590.

Pharmacies Boots the Chemist *(Market St.; Tel 01229/582-049; 9am-5:30pm Mon-Sat)* is the place to go for your meds. Late hours *(till 6:30pm Mon-Sat, 9am-noon Sun)* are available at chemists throughout town on a rotating basis; check the postings in the window to see which one is open.

Trains The train station is on Springfield Road; it's just a 5-minute walk south from the town center. Trains are operated by **Northern Western Rail** *(Tel 0345/484-950)*. Information and schedules are also available at the tourist office.

Bus Lines Out of the City Stagecoach Cumberland *(Tel 0870/082-608)* operates buses in and out of Ulverston. The main bus stop is on Victoria Road, 2 minutes south from the town center. Schedules and information are available at the tourist office.

Postal The **Post Office** *(County Square; Tel 01229/581-131; 9am-5pm Mon-Fri, 9am-noon Sat)* is the place to go for mailings or currency exchange.

Yewdale Road, Tilberthwaite Avenue ... the main this town's

CONISTON

The rugged peaks surrounding Coniston are a sharp contrast to the rolling
hills throughout the Lake District. These rugged beauty of these craggy
faces beguiles nature freaks. Hikers can't turn away from the views, and
climbers can't wait to get on the rock. The most prominent of these faces,
known as the Old Man, offers a challenge that most find hard to resist. If
climbing sounds like way too much effort, Coniston Water at the foot of
the village offers some of the best boating in the area. Don't miss the
steam-powered love boat operated by the National Trust.

The village itself is tiny and consists of small Victorian streets lined
with whitewashed stone and slate cottages. You can easily master its geography in about 5 minutes. Two main roads cut through town: **Yewdale
Road,** splitting the town from east to west, and **Tilberthwaite Avenue,**
crisscrossing it from north to south. These highways come together at the
unnamed town center, which isn't much of a hangout—it's just a handful
of gift shops, some food markets, and a few lackluster clothing stores. To
the east across the lake is Brantwood House, where John Ruskin lived. A
mile to the north, the copper mine that kept the town bustling in the
19th century has long since closed, and Coniston has become a place
where families and tourists come to get away from it all. There's no
nightlife to speak of—there's hardly a day life either—but that's not why
you came here anyway. What are you waiting for? Go climb a rock!

bar scene

There's no youth scene to speak of in Coniston, either—as one local said,
"When the kids finish school, they drift off somewhere else." But this is
still England, and that means there are pubs, perfect for quenching your
thirst after a day of roaming the mountainside.

The liveliest place in town is the **Black Bull Inn** *(1 Yewdale Rd.; Tel
015394/413-35; 11am-11pm Mon-Sat; noon-10:30pm Sun; MC, V, DC),*

a 400-year-old coaching inn just east of the town center, in the shadow of the Old Man. After an invigorating walk, duck in here for a home-brewed pint (beers range from £1.90-2.40) or some pub grub [see *eats,* below].

Log fires take the chill off cool evenings at the **Traditional Walker Inn** *(Brow Hill; Tel 015394/412-48; 11am-11pm Mon-Sat; noon-10:30pm Sun; MC, V, AE, DC),* located in the Coniston Sun Hotel, just southeast of the town center. Beers range from £1.75-2.

CULTURE ZOO

Brantwood *(Tel 015394/413-96; 11am-5:30pm daily, mid-Mar-mid-Nov; 11am-4:30pm Wed-Sun, mid-Nov-mid-Mar; closed Christmas Day and Boxing Day; £4 adults, £2.80 students, £2 nature walk):* Philosopher, artist, and naturalist John Ruskin was one of the greatest thinkers of the Victorian Age. His love of the rugged wildness led him to Coniston, where he lived on this 250-acre estate on the lake. Today, Brantwood displays some of Ruskin's paintings and memorabilia, and offers some inspiring nature trails as well. The estate is across Coniston Water from the center of town; transport is available on the **Steam Yacht Gondola** [see below] or through **Coniston Launch** [see *great outdoors,* below].

John Ruskin Museum *(Yewdale Rd.; Tel 015394/411-64; 10am-5:30pm daily, Easter-Oct; closed Nov-Easter; £3):* Ruskin's mementos, letters, and mineral collection are on display at this museum in the center of town.

National Trust Steamboat Gondola *(Coniston Pier; Tel 015394/638-56; 10:30am, noon, 2pm, 3:30pm, last return from Brantwood is at 4:40pm, Mar-Nov):* If you've always thought canoeing was missing a certain element of luxury, this Victorian yacht cruise is for you. Dating back to 1859, the steamship comes complete with gold trim and an ornate carved bow. It may feel more *Pirates of the Caribbean* than *The Love Boat,* but it gets you across the lake, and hey—a cruise is a cruise.

great outdoors

If climbing is your thing, **the Old Man** is waiting. Coniston's largest peak offers a rise of 2,634 feet then forms a grand ridge that drops in a series of steep, grassy slopes, about 656 feet at a time. Another likely peak for a good climb, **Dow Crag,** lies to the west. It offers some breathtaking cliffs, with sheer drops of 492 feet. There are also some low-level walks for acrophobics: The **Duddon Valley** east of the Coniston Fells is a good candidate. For hiking advice and route suggestions, try the ultra-helpful tourist office [see *need to know,* below].

The one-stop shop for outdoor fun, **Summitreks** *(Yewdale Rd.; Tel 015394/410-89; 9am-6pm daily; kayaks £5 per hour, £10 half-day, £14 full day; mountain bikes £5 per hour, £10 half-day, £13 full day; £20 deposit required; V, MC)* rents and sells everything from basics like compasses and maps, to mountain bikes, canoes, and kayaks. They also offer guided adventures and courses in hiking, biking, and water sports. If you're feeling extreme, they even offer cliff-jumping excursions.

Speaking of extreme, you might want to try paragliding: a cross between hang-gliding and parachuting in which you leap off a mountain peak and float gently down into the countryside below you. **Lakeland Leisure Paragliding** (*Coppermines Valley; Tel 015394/418-25 or 0370/393-193; £49 per flight; £125 2-day course, £205 4-day certification; paragliding@Lakeland-leisure.com; No credit cards*) will show you the ropes. Unless you're a certified paraglider, you'll need to take the leap accompanied by a licensed instructor, just to make sure you don't kill yourself. Sure it's risky—not to mention pricey—but you'll have another story of your misspent youth to tell your grandchildren.

If you're here to get back to nature, but prefer not to risk life and limb, **Coniston Launch** (*Pier Cottage; Tel 015394/362-16; 10:30am-4:30pm Mar-Nov, till 5:30pm in summer; limited winter service, 10:45am-varies with demand; £3.60/person 50-minute cruise, £5.80 90-minute cruise; No credit cards*) offers multiple lake cruises daily, and **Spoon Hall Holiday Caravans and Pony Trekking** (*Spoon Hall, Tel 015394/413-91; 10am-5pm daily; £12/person/hour, £17/person/90 minutes; advance reservations required; No credit cards*) will set you up with the horse of your dreams.

EATS

Dining options in Coniston are extremely limited, although they do offer some of the best ice cream in all of England. (Who said you can't make a meal out of ice cream?) You can find plenty of sandwiches and lunchy snacks, but your best bet for dinner is to eat at one of the pubs.

▶▶CHEAP

Right across from the tourist office, the **Coniston Dairy, Tearoom, and Picnic Box** (*Yewdale Road; No phone; 8am-6pm daily; £1.75-£3.25 per item; No credit cards*) will fill your lunch basket with home-baked food. If you're looking for bangers and mash or a soup and sandwich, this is the closest to Mom's that you'll get for a while. But the ice cream is the real attraction—rich, smooth, and creamy.

Just a bit down the road, the **Meadowmore Bakery Café** (*Tilberthwaite Ave.; Tel 051394/416-38; 6am-6pm Mon-Thur, 6am-9pm Fri-Sun; £1.45-£5.25 per item; No credit cards*) sells postcards, Hello Kitty pencil sharpeners, and miniature versions of the copper mines, all on the same counter. Oh, and cheap sandwiches, too, as well as fresh baked goods. It's not Grandma's cooking, but it fills the void in your stomach, and you may even end up with a cool souvenir. After the meal you can even ride off on a rented mountain bike [see *need to know*, below].

▶▶DO-ABLE

Your best bet at the **Black Bull Inn** (*[see pub scene, above]; entrees £3-10*) is the locally caught Esthwaite trout, which always tastes better with some of the local brew: Coniston Bird or Coniston Blacksmith. Cumberland grills or game pie duck are other options.

TO MARKET

If you'd rather play chef yourself, groceries are available at the **Coniston Co-op** *(3 Yewdale Rd.; Tel 015394/412-47; 9am-9pm Mon-Sat, 10am-8pm Sun; MC, V)* at the center of town.

Try the Lake District lamb at the **Traditional Walker Inn** *([see pub scene, above]; entrees £8-10)*. The portions at this pub are generous.

crashing

There are two comfortable youth hostels on the outskirts of the village, the perfect places to collapse in a heap after a hard day of hiking. The tourist office will try to help you out with reservations [see *need to know*, below].

▶▶CHEAP

Settled into the foothills, the **Holly How Youth Hostel** *(Far End; Tel 015394/413-23; reception 5-11pm daily; Fri-Sun only, Jan-Mar, May, June, and Nov; closed Dec; £9.80 per person; Shared bath; V, MC)* is busy with backpackers coming and going along the Cumbria Way, so don't expect peace and quiet—just expect to make some friends. Close to excellent hiking and lakeside trails, it's also surrounded by well-kept gardens.

Wake up face-to-face with the Old Man at the **Coniston Coppermine's Youth Hostel** *(Off the A593 in town; Tel 015394/412-61; Reception 5-11pm daily; Tue-Sat only, Apr, May, Sep, and Oct; group rentals only, Nov-Mar; £9.00 per person; Shared bath; V, MC)*, nestled in a perfect nook between the mountains. The white stone building itself is pretty plain, but nothing beats sleeping at the bottom of the fells, ready for a pleasant hike or challenging climb. It's only a mile out of Coniston village; head northeast along the dirt road between the Black Bull Pub and the Co-op for a steady climb directly to the hostel.

▶▶DO-ABLE

The **Beech Tree Guest House** *(Yewdale Rd.; Tel 015394/417-17; £18 per person; En suite available; No credit cards)* offers a dash of 18th-century luxury with its slice of small-town life, complete with whitewashed slate walls, trailing ivy, and a dining room that makes you feel like the food should have been cooked over an open fire.

With only three private rooms available, the cozy **Orchard Cottage** *(18 Yewdale Rd.; Tel 015394/413-73; £19 per person; En suite; No credit cards)* is so welcoming that you may feel like you've been adopted by a generous Coniston family.

need to know

Currency Exchange You can change money at the **Coniston Post Office** [see *postal,* below]. They take a 1.5 percent commission, £2 minimum.

Tourist Information The folks at the **Coniston Tourist Information Center** *(Ruskin Ave.; Tel 015394/415-333; 9:30am-5:30pm daily, Easter-Oct; 10:30am-3:30pm Sat, Sun, Nov-Apr),* at the center of town, are used to catering to outdoor fanatics. They offer information and advice on making the most of your stay, including suggested hikes and trails.

Health and Emergency Emergency: *999.* There is no police station in town; police matters should be directed to the **Kendal police station** *(Tel 01539/722-611).* The nearest hospital is in Kendal as well: **Kendal Westmoreland Hospital** *(Burton Rd., Kendal; Tel 015394/732-288).*

Bus Lines Out of the City Stagecoach Cumberland *(Tel 08706/082-608)* operates two buses to and from Windermere (line 505). The **National Trust** *(Tel 015394/355-99; Apr-Oct)* also operates free service five times a day between Coniston village and Coniston Water, as well as Hawkshead. Schedules and information are available at the tourist office [see above].

Bike Rental Mountain bikes are available at **Summitrek** [see *great outdoors,* above]. **Meadowdore Bakery Café** [see *eats,* above] will also rent you a set of wheels.

Postal Postal services and currency exchange are available at the **Coniston Post Office** *(Yewdale Rd.; 9am-12:30pm/1:30-5:30pm Mon-Fri, 9am-12:30pm Wed, Sat)* in the center of town.

ambleside

Built into the steep hills at the northern end of **Lake Windermere,** Ambleside has become one of the Lake District's tourist magnets. It's not only a common stopover for long-distance hikers tackling the Cumbria Way, but it also provides access to inviting trails leading over waterfalls, up mountains, and around the slender lake. Wilderness is the featured attraction here; whatever your activity of choice—hiking, rock-climbing, mountain-biking, sailing, or windsurfing—the best thing to do in Ambleside is to get outside and go and go, until you either drop from exhaustion or achieve that transcendental consciousness Wordsworth wrote about in all those poems.

Cosmopolitan isn't the word for Ambleside, but *quaint* definitely is. The town itself is nothing if not picturesque: the aged green slate buildings ringing the town square seem like part of the hills themselves. Quarried nearby, that same slate was once the town's livelihood, until tourism came along. There's a new consumer haven on Cross Street, trying its best to fit in with the same slate green walls, but it's clearly intended for tourists, and might as well house a Gap. You'll also find some less generic spots, including a New Age crystal boutique and a football museum. And the proliferation of good restaurants in town, from quality takeaways to fancy dinner houses, makes eating and drinking more of a pleasure than a simple necessity.

Did someone say *drinking?* Unlike its tranquil neighbors, Ambleside is one of the few villages in the district that offers a good measure of secular relief from all of that wilderness solitude—in a word, *pubs.* Ambleside's bars light up at nightfall along Lake Road; there also are a few places hidden away in winding alleyways. The clientele is mixed, from graybeard locals to backpackers fresh from the hills to energetic students from nearby St. Martin's College. If you've been missing your evening pub crawl, this is as good a place as any to get back into form. Things get loud and lively, just the way you like it, and stay that way until closing. So work up a thirst all day long, and quench it after the sun sets. That's the Ambleside experience.

neighborhoods

The main street of Ambleside is actually an urbanized version of the A591, which in the town center is a north-south thoroughfare known as **Rydal Road** in its northern stretches and **Lake Road** on its southern stretches. Where they meet, at a wide point, is **Market Square,** the geographical center of the town. Funneling into Market Square are **Cheapside** and **North Road.** North Road leads into the oldest neighborhoods of Ambleside, with antique stone-sided cottages, some dating from the 1500s. The oldest house in town, built in the 1500s, is a privately owned cottage marked only as "Howhead" on a street named **Chapel Hill,** which runs into North Road. The entire village can be walked in less than 10 minutes, but choose your steps wisely: it can be uphill all the way, depending on which way you're going

bar scene

The drinking life of this little mountain town is lively, to say the least. Most bars do everything from broadcasting football games to providing high-quality ales and the best music—and they cater to all kinds of crowds. Your best bet is to wander up and down the streets and see what's going on. Start at the bottom of Lake Street and head uphill—it will be a lot easier to stumble downhill when you're ready to head back to your room. None of the pubs in town have a late license and therefore operate during the "law hours" (11am-11pm Mon-Sat, noon-10:30pm Sun). For this reason, things start early—between 8 and 9pm—and then accelerate rapidly until closing.

Named for everyone's favorite PM (no, not Margaret Thatcher), Winston's bar at **The Churchill** *(Lake Rd.; Tel 015394/331-92; 11am-11pm Mon-Sat, noon-10:30pm Sun; Food until 6pm)* hosts an energetic crowd of

ambleside

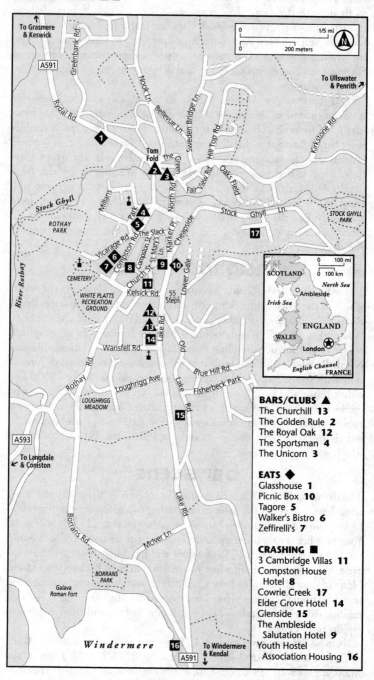

BARS/CLUBS ▲
The Churchill **13**
The Golden Rule **2**
The Royal Oak **12**
The Sportsman **4**
The Unicorn **3**

EATS ◆
Glasshouse **1**
Picnic Box **10**
Tagore **5**
Walker's Bistro **6**
Zeffirelli's **7**

CRASHING ■
3 Cambridge Villas **11**
Compston House
  Hotel **8**
Cowrie Creek **17**
Elder Grove Hotel **14**
Glenside **15**
The Ambleside
  Salutation Hotel **9**
Youth Hostel
  Association Housing **16**

students and younger locals in an oh-so-British brownstone setting. Things get loud and lively, with the latest pop hits blasting from the jukebox. They also sporadically feature local garage bands, but *never* when there's a big football match. As long as you like to drink and don't mind occasional conversational glitches, Winston's will serve you well as bar number one for the night.

Royal though it may be, **The Royal Oak** *(Market St.; Tel 015394/333-82; 11am-11pm Mon-Sat, noon-10:30pm Sun)* on the same side of the street (now named Market Street) as The Churchill, isn't quite the hotspot that The Churchill is. The front bar has quiz and gambling machines, and a pool table that gets dragged out in the winter. It's popular with older locals, none of them terribly chatty, who often use the entrance in the back.

Continuing on Lake Road, you'll reach **The Ambleside Salutation Hotel** [see *crashing*, below], which operates with an air of subdued class, both in the genteel hotel lounge and more boisterous pub, the Stock Ghyll Tavern. Unless you're interested in sipping white wine spritzers with the tweed blazer set, the tavern is where the action is, with a mix of tourists and locals downing Scottish courage beers, a huge fireplace that's just calling out for an old-time drinking song, and plenty of noise, noise, noise!

You'll hear the loud and lively **Sportsman** *(Compston Rd.; Tel 015394/325-35; 11am-11pm Mon-Sat, noon-10:30pm Sun; Pizza until 11pm)* long before you see it—continue on up Lake Road until it meets Compston Road and join in the fun. In keeping with the name, the walls are decked out with rugby jerseys and glory-day photos of local and national teams. The big-screen TV is match-ready, and the pizza bar in the back makes this place every armchair goalie's dream come true (cheers and beers and pizza, oh my!). Loud disco also plays on the weekends.

If you can still see at this point, walk up Compston Road past the tourist office and make a left onto narrow North Street. Just past the **Rock Shop** [see *stuff*, below] on the left, is the **Unicorn** *(North Rd.; Tel 015394/332-16; 11am-11pm Mon-Sat, noon-10:30pm Sun; Meals to 9pm)*. The punters, a good mix of locals and tourists, are as friendly as the surroundings are cozy, and the pool table remains a big attraction even in the summer. The excellent bitter ales on hand are, well, bitter—but the company is sweet.

Just where North Road turns back onto Rydal Road, you'll find the **Golden Rule** *(Smithy Brow; Tel 015394/333-63; 11am-11pm Mon-Sat, noon-10:30pm Sun)*. Any way you look at it, the rule applies here, especially when it comes to the question of who's buying the drinks—chances are if you offer a round, you'll get one in return. There's no TV, no games, and no jukebox noise—it's all about spinning a good yarn over a fine pint of ale. By the time 11pm rolls around, you'll be so caught up in the spirit of things that you won't want to leave.

Arts Scene

You won't find radical or cutting-edge art in Ambleside, but feel-good portrayals of local lakeland panoramas abound. Two of the best art galleries in town are **Studio House Gallery** *(Market Place; Tel 015394/324-97, Fax 015394/345-82; 9:30am-5:30pm Mon-Sat, noon-5.30pm Sun)* and the **Hobbs Gallery** *(1 Church St.; Tel 015394/328-82; 2-5:30pm Mon-Fri, 10am-5:30pm Sat; hobbs.gallery@virgin.net)*.

If you need to escape to the movies, take yourself to **Zeffirelli's** [see *eats,* below], the very cool local dinner-and-a-movie spot. Expect mainstream Hollywood fare.

Culture Zoo

After a walk around and a look at a shop or two, you will have had the best of sight-seeing in Ambleside. The local museum seems more of interest to locals, which may be the whole point.

Armitt Museum *(Royal Rd.; Tel 015394/312-12; 10am-5pm daily; £2.50 adults, £1.80 students):* The only museum in town is a 5-minute walk north of Market Square. Opened in 1999, the Armitt focuses on the culture, sociology, geology, and artistic output of Ambleside and the Lake District. Most attention centers on the big-name authors of the area, William Wordsworth, Beatrix Potter, and John Ruskin.

Great Outdoors

All of the usual outdoor activities can be had in Ambleside, but the most popular is, naturally, ambling. The tourist office distributes free maps outlining every conceivable nearby trek [see *need to know,* below]. If you want a more hands-on experience, contact **R & L Adventures** *(Knotts Farm, Patterdale Rd., Windemere; Tel 015394/451-04; hours vary, so call ahead; £12/person, groups of 6-8 for half-day, £30 individuals; No credit cards)*. They'll provide you or a group with experienced guides and—if you need them—accommodations scattered across your route.

Ambleside has several sporting goods stores well-stocked with boots and climbing gear. **Rock + Run** *(3-4 Cheapside; Tel 015394/336-60; 9am-5:30pm Mon-Sat, 10am-5pm Sun; info@rockrun.com www.rockrun.com; MC, V)* and **The Climbers' Shop** *(Compston Rd.; Tel 015394/322-97; 9am-5:30pm Mon-Sat, 10am-5pm Sun; MC, V)*, both in the town center, are two of the best.

Stuff

Most of the local gift shops focus on cute souvenirs that won't stand the test of time or an airplane luggage compartment. But there are some unusual shops worth ducking into.

▶▶**CITY SPORTS**

Ambleside's town center boasts its own temple to sports fanaticism, **Homes of Football** *(100 Lake Rd.; Tel 015394/344-40; 9am-6pm* *daily; www.homesoffootball.co.uk; £1 adults downstairs gallery).* The walls of this memorabilia shop commemorate famous events in the soccer world, from the triumphs of Manchester United's game-winning goals to the tragic deaths caused by football hooliganism. A Playstation video console is available to practice your kicks—your choice of game is either English football or European football. In the downstairs gallery, frighteningly realistic papier mâché people re-create stadium events throughout the gallery. The centerpiece is a couple arguing about the weekend scores over breakfast—now that's the true spirit of English football.

▶▶ROCKS

If you believe in the healing power of crystals, all of your anxieties should disappear as you walk trough the cavern-like entrance to the **Rock Shop** *(North Rd.; Tel 015394/319-23; 9:30am-6pm daily; V, MC, AE),* across from the tourist office. All of the earth's geological diversity seems to be on display, from various shiny rocks (pick your own bag for £3) to 3-foot pieces of amethyst, amber, or malachite priced as high as £20,000.

EATS

Some things in life are certain: No matter where you are in England, if the food is deep-fried, you can eat for under £2. But Ambleside has a lot more to offer than grease. From the New York–style pizza to an all-in-one dinner and a movie, this is a town where there's something for everyone. Unless otherwise indicated, all of the venues are located near the center of town, on Lake or Compston Road.

▶▶CHEAP

As close to an authentic deli as you're going to get in the land of tea and crumpets, the **Picnic Box** *(Lake Rd.; Tel 051394/324-75; 9am-5:30pm daily; £1.00-£3.25 per item; No credit cards)* is one of the best takeaways in town. We're talking serious food, with tasty sandwiches and soups and plenty of healthy options as well.

Along the same lines, **Walker's Bistro** *(Coniston Rd.; Tel 051394/321-34; 11am-2:30pm; about £5.00 per item; No credit cards)* serves pizza that even a serious New Yorker would grudgingly admit is pretty good. Unfortunately, they're only open for lunch—as busy as they are, they really don't need to stay open for dinner to stay in business.

▶▶DO-ABLE

If Indian curry gets your mouth watering, **Tagore** *(Compston Rd.; Tel 051394/343-46; noon-2pm/5pm-midnight daily; £2.60 per vegetarian entrée, £4.75-£5.50 per entrée, £26.95 for two; No credit cards)* will seem like a little piece of Nirvana. You can choose from a number of ear-steaming spicy dishes, with meat and without. The stylish dining area incorporates authentic Indian fabrics into a modern design scheme.

Zeffirelli's *(Compston Rd.; Tel 015394/338-45; dinner 6-9:45pm daily; cinema times vary; £4adult movie ticket; £8.25-£13.50 per entrée; V, MC)* has brought dinner-and-a-movie to a whole new level. For just £15.95, you get a 3-course meal in a sophisticated setting and a seat in the attached theater without ever having to leave the building. This is no refreshment-stand, hot dog-and-pretzel place—the menu ranges from wood-fired whole-grain pizza to vegetarian entrées. The atmosphere is more downtown eatery than Cineplex, with delicate printed fabric screens on the walls and soft lighting above the tables. The only thing ordinary about this place is the choice of movies—everything is mainstream.

▶▶**SPLURGE**

Medieval meets postmodern at the **Glass House** *(Rydal Rd.; Tel 015394/321-37; noon-3pm/6-10pm daily, reservations recommended; £7.95-£13.25 per entrée; V).* It's about a quarter-mile out of town, north along Rydal Road, but well worth the hike. The architecture of this former 15th-century mill includes a moss-covered, full-scale replica of the original water wheel and exposed views of the mill's original cogs. The oak interiors and big, sunny windows make for elegant dining, with a menu to match. Spinach ricotta with pasta and deep-fried sage and smoked salmon with oyster beignets and eggplant sound good?

crashing

Because it's so close to Windermere, accommodations in Ambleside are plentiful but fill up quickly. Numerous B&Bs are spread about town, along with the hotels and hostel off the lake. Reservations can be booked through the Tourist Information Center as well [see *need to know*, below].

▶▶**CHEAP**

Located right on the shore of Lake Windermere, the **YHA** *(Watershead; Tel 015394/323-04, 01946/632-22 for shuttle bus; 24-hour reception Mar-Oct, daytime only Nov-Feb; £12.95 adult with shared bath; V, MC, AE)* offers a rustic, seaside experience in a converted hotel. A shuttle bus runs between Windermere station and the hostel. Unfortunately, it's very popular with groups and organized tours, especially during the school year, so it fills up quickly.

About halfway between the lake and the town, **Glenside Guest House** *(Old Lake Rd.; Tel 015394/326-35; £15 single, £30 double; Shared bath; No credit cards)* offers a comfy night's stay for just a little cash. This 18th-century farmhouse features simple decor and hiking routes right at your doorstep. It's also smoke-free, so if you've picked up the habit and want to quit, this is your chance to go cold turkey.

Located between Lake and Compston Roads, **3 Cambridge Villas** *(Church St.; Tel 015395/323-07; Bus 555; £16 per person, £20 per person en suite; Breakfast included; No credit cards)* features spacious rooms filled with Victorian knick-knacks. Just a 3-minute walk from the center of town, it's run by some serious outdoor enthusiasts who've done the pub crawl a time or two themselves and know all the best cures for a hangover.

▶▶**DO-ABLE**

If the walk out to the lake is a little too sobering, the places in town provide a more convenient location, close to the pub crawl, for a slightly higher price.

The selling point at the **Elder Grove Hotel** *(Lake Rd.; Tel 015394/325-04; £23 per person, private baths; V, MC)*, just off the town center, is its beautiful Victorian decor. Most of the bedrooms have four-poster beds dressed in rich Victorian colors.

Any place that is closer to a set of waterfalls than the town center has its priorities straight. Offset from the village a bit, **Cowrie Creek** *(5 Stockghyll Brow; Tel 015395/337-32, mobile 07967/246-489; £20 per person; En suite; www.cowrie.freeserve.co.uk; No credit cards)* is not overtly luxurious, but the sound of rushing water will lull you into the best sleep money can buy. To get there, veer right as you head north up Lake Road.

The **Compston House Hotel** *(Compston Rd.; Tel 015394/323-05; £25 single, £40 double, breakfast included; compston@globalnet.co.uk, www.compstonhouse.co.uk; V, MC)*, located right in the town center, is dressed up in go-Yanks American fanfare, with each of the en-suite rooms decorated in an English interpretation of one of the fifty states. Fortunately, the breakfast is still very English, offering more food than you can eat in this American life.

Set in a 500-year-old building next door to the Glass House, **Mill Cottage** *(Rydal Rd., Tel 015394/348-30; £23 per person winter, £25 per person summer, £28 per person Christmas; Private showers, breakfast included; No credit cards)* offers comfortable rooms and historic ambience. Breakfast includes bacon, sausage, eggs, beans, toast, coffee, and tea—the English works.

▶▶**SPLURGE**

Whitewashed stone walls aren't the only things that distinguish the elegant **Ambleside Salutation Hotel** *(Lake Rd.; Tel 015394/322-44; lounge 11am-9pm; £37 single, £50 double; V, MC, AE)* from its neighbors in the center of town. It has all the style and amenities of a large cosmopolitan hotel, complete with exquisite rooms and its own lounge and pub downstairs for late-night drinkers [see *bar scene,* above], which makes the long drunken walk home as short as possible.

need to know

Currency Exchange The banks along Compston Road near the tourist office all provide fair currency exchange—try **HSBC** *(Market Cross; Tel 015394/620-00; 9:30am-3:30pm daily)*.

Tourist Information Ambleside's **Tourist Information Center** *(Market Cross; Tel 015394/325-82, 015394/31576 for accommodation booking; 9am-5:30pm daily)* offers information on local sites and attractions, publications suggesting possible hikes and walks, and assistance in finding a place to stay. It's right at the center of town, near Compston Road.

Health & Emergency Emergency: *999.* The **Ambleside police station** does not provide 24-hour coverage; for information and assistance, call the **Kendal police station** *(Tel 01539/722-611).* The medical center, **Kendal Westmoreland Hospital** *(Burton Rd., Kendal; Tel 015394/732-288),* is in Kendal as well, to the southeast.

Pharmacies The pharmacist that keeps the best hours is **Boots the Chemist** *(8-9 Market Cross; Tel 015394/333-55; 9am-5pm Mon-Fri, 9am-noon Sat).* Late hours *(6:30pm Mon-Fri, 8-8:30am Sun)* are available at chemists throughout town on a rotating basis; check the postings in the window to see which one is open.

Bus Lines Out of the City Stagecoach Cumberland *(Tel 08706/082-608)* offers hourly bus service to and from Grasmere, Keswick, and Windermere (lines 555 and 557). Main bus stops are located off Lake Road; information and schedules are available at the tourist office [see above].

Rentals Bikes and boats are available in Ambleside from **Ghyllside Cycles** *(The Slack; Tel 015934/335-92; 9am-5pm daily; V, MC)* and **Biketreks** *(Compton Rd.; Tel 015934/315-05, 9am-5pm daily; V, MC, AE),* both right in the town center.

Laundry For a good sudsing, try the **Ambleside Launderette** *(Kelsick Rd.; Tel 015934/322-31; £1.90 wash, 50p dry)* on the town square. Be warned—you'll have to do the laundry yourself.

Postal Mail your postcard wisdom from the **Ambleside Post Office** *(Market Place; Tel 015394/322-67; 9am-5:30pm Mon-Fri, 9am-12:30pm Sat)* on the town square.

grasmere

Like many other havens in the Lake District, this tranquil village is a good place to get away from it all. And also like other spots in the area, Grasmere was once home to the daddy-o of England's Romantic poets, William Wordsworth. His life and work were all about achieving a kind of transcendence in the natural world, and the surrounding countryside is ideal for doing just that, with gurgling streams and falls, gentle, rolling hills and valleys, and deep woodlands. Wordsworth called Grasmere "the loveliest spot that man hath ever known." Maybe he was a bit prejudiced, but the scenery here is something to behold.

If you're a literary groupie, you can visit Wordsworth's former home, or his grave in the church cemetery. Taste some of the village's famous gingerbread or walk through the manicured gardens at the center of town; Grasmere's not the place to go wild. Either you've come here to pay your respects to daffodil-lover Wordsworth or the daffodils themselves. Fortunately, there's time and world enough to do both.

neighborhoods

You can walk across the whole village in about 5 minutes. The center of town is **Red Lion Square,** formed by the intersection of **Langdale Road** (running east-west) and **Broadgates** (running north-south), Grasmere's biggest streets.

by foot—following in wordsworth's footsteps

The inherent poetry of the landscape is evident in the names given to everything in lake country: hills become "fells," waterfalls are "gills," and ponds are "tarns." Keep the vocabulary of the wild in mind as you follow in Wordsworth's footsteps on this easy 4-mile walk from Grasmere to Easedale Tarn. You'll follow a gurgling brook past frothy gills and rocky fells, offering distant views of the tarn and valley below. Guides, maps, and leaflets for this and other walks are plentiful at the tourist information center [see *need to know*,].

Near the bus stop on Broadgate, you'll find the beginning of a street marked Easedale Tarn. After about ten minutes along this less-traveled road, you'll cross a stone bridge over Easedale Beck. The river remains on your right as the path moves on through the woods. As you pass through the first gate, Sourmilk Gill, named for its milky-white water, tumbles down the gully. The path continues along the side, but if you don't mind getting your feet wet, you can scramble up the middle of the falls. On a clear day, you can see the gray-blue water of Easedale Tarn resting placidly ahead of you in the lull between the crumbling fells. The tarn is about a ten-minute walk past the top of the gill.

Before returning to the village, you may want to circle the tarn. The path is easy and clearly marked. There are a couple of different routes back to Grasmere. You can, of course, retrace your steps along Easdale Beck. It's also possible to walk down Far Easdale toward the gill of the same name. After the falls, continue alongside the river until you reach an old barn, at which point the path veers away from the water through some fields. Once you've walked through Brimmer Head Farm, follow the signed path for Helm Crag; it leads to a cobbled road back to the village. If time allows, you can take the path through Lancrigg Woods, which is lined with tall trees that create a sheltering green canopy overhead. The path ends in the gardens of the Lancrigg Guest House, where a marked trail will take you back to the village.

hanging out

In inclement weather, residents and visitors tend to hang out in local pubs, two of which are recommended below. On warm summer days, the closest thing to a hangout is Red Lion Square. But really, what are you doing in town if the sun's shining? Go frolic amid all the natural beauty, young poet [see *by foot,* above].

grasmere

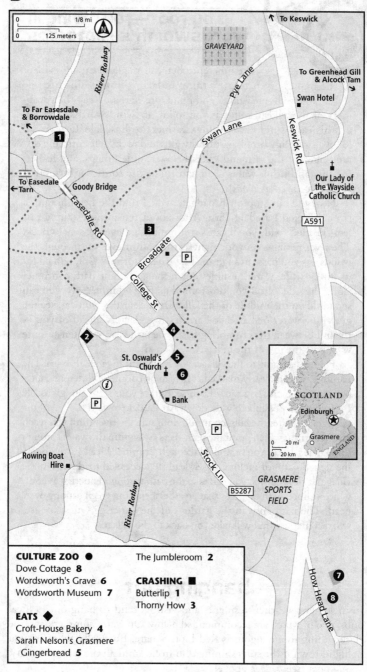

0 | 1/8 mi
0 | 125 meters

GRAVEYARD

To Keswick

To Greenhead Gill
& Alcock Tarn

Swan Hotel

River Rothay

Pye Lane

Swan Lane

Keswick Rd.

To Far Easesdale
& Borrowdale

1

To Easedale
Tarn

Goody Bridge

Easedale Rd.

Our Lady of
the Wayside
Catholic Church

A591

3

Broadgate

P

College St.

2

4

St. Oswald's
Church

5

6

SCOTLAND

Edinburgh

Grasmere

ENGLAND

0 | 20 mi
0 | 20 km

Bank

P

Rowing Boat
Hire

Stock Ln.

GRASMERE
SPORTS
FIELD

River Rothay

B5287

How Head Lane

7

8

CULTURE ZOO ●
Dove Cottage **8**
Wordsworth's Grave **6**
Wordsworth Museum **7**

EATS ◆
Croft-House Bakery **4**
Sarah Nelson's Grasmere
 Gingerbread **5**

The Jumbleroom **2**

CRASHING ■
Butterlip **1**
Thorny How **3**

bar scene

As you could guess, nightlife here is more about the stars in the black night sky than socializing. But there are always a few pubs available for a pint and a laugh.

The major gathering place for young and old alike is **The Dove & Olive Branch** *(Stock Lane; Tel 015394/355-92; 11am-11pm daily; MC, AE)*, at Red Lion Square in the landmark Hotel Wordsworth, which dates from the early 19th century. Most people drop in for a pint (£1.70-£2.20), but there's a pleasant-though-not-terribly-exciting menu as well, vaguely English like most pub grub (meals range from £3-£8). There's no music and no TV, so curl up next to the fire and and gab with the locals and walkers who happen by.

Much smaller and even quainter, **Tweedies** *(Langdale Rd.; Tel 015394/353-00; noon to 11pm daily; V, MC, AE, DC)* is just a 3-minute walk south of Red Lion Square. Even without the landmark pedigree of the Dove & Olive, it attracts a mixed crowd of various ages, from young and gorgeous London daytrippers to tweedy old men with walking sticks (hence the name). Punters listen to jukebox tunes and watch the latest match on TV. In summertime, you can also escape to the outdoor beer garden. Beers range from £1.70-£2.20, and you can pick up pub grub too.

CULTUre ZOO

Like most everything else in this neck o' the woods, Grasmere is all Wordsworth, all the time.

Dove Cottage/The Wordsworth Museum *(A591; Tel 015394/355-44; Bus 555, W1; 9:30am-5pm daily, Feb-Dec; www.wordsworth. co.uk; £4.80):* If you think ogling Wordsworth's personal items, faded original manuscripts, and articles of personal decor can give you startling insight into his psyche, then Dove Cottage, on the southern end of town,

festivals and events

Each summer on August 5, Grasmere celebrates St. Oswald's Day with the **Rushbearing Festival.** In ancient times, young girls of the village would parade into St. Oswald's Church bearing sweet-smelling rushes to purify the dirt floor and capture the warmth of the summer. Even though the floors are now paved, this vaguely pagan tradition continues today, with young flower children bearing crosses made of rushes and flowers. They're rewarded with a piece of Grasmere gingerbread. If you can pass for a gangly over-sized pre-teen, you might want to try to get in on the action.

is the place to do it. Wordsworth lived here for years with his sister and personal muse, Dorothy, who was no slouch when it came to writing either, as evidenced in her diaries. Guided tours are available, but you can also wander through this illustrated history of romanticism on your own—it's a good way to bask in their personal auras. They just don't make Romantics like they used to.

Wordsworth's Grave *(St. Oswald's Church, Stock Lane):* If you can't get enough of your favorite dead poet, he's buried along with his family in the cemetery behind St. Oswald's Church, a short walk east along Stock Lane. Wordsworth himself planted eight of the yew trees in the churchyard. Nothing more than a tombstone marks his passing, but wild lovers of words from all over the world have left him tributes, ranging from bouquets of daffodils to poems of their own.

Rydal Mount *(Off the A591; Tel 015394/330-02; 9:30am-5pm daily, Mar-Oct; 10am-4pm Wed-Mon, Nov-Feb; Buses 599, X8, X9, X72, X85, X95, and NE; £3.50):* Situated between Ambleside and Grasmere off Road A591, Rydal was Romantic poet William Wordsworth's home during the final years of his life, until his death in 1850. Still owned by his descendants, it features many of his mementos, books, and furniture—what isn't on display at Dove Cottage, anyway. Wordsworth himself landscaped the garden, which has been maintained according to his plan—go nuts in the tranquil greenness of it all.

EATS

People don't flock to Grasmere for gourmet dining, so there aren't many choices. But the cafes are excellent for an afternoon craving, and occasionally stay open for dinner. Full traditional meals are a little harder to come by.

▶▶CHEAP/DO-ABLE

With a Romantic's approach to food, **The Jumbleroom** *(Langdale Rd.; Tel 015394/351-88; 10am-5pm daily, 6.30pm-10pm or until the food runs out Thur-Sat; £4.25-£6.50 per entrée; V, MC),* just behind the Tourist Information Center, is a restaurant Wordsworth would have loved. The owners have lived in the area for generations, and you can taste the love that goes into their daily home-baked cafe-fare. Their "Food for the Sun" menu, served in the evenings, is traditional food with a gourmet twist. Specialties include "Soul Soup" (rich vegetarian broth with Spanish onions and gruyere cheese), Thai chicken salad, baked fennel and lemon pasta, and Moroccan lamb with coriander couscous. Reservations are recommended for dinner.

If you like your tearooms traditional, it doesn't get much more English than **Baldrey's Cafe** *(Easedale Rd.; Tel 015394/353-49; 8:30am-6pm daily; £2.25-£6.45 per item; No credit cards),* housed in a 19th-century cottage. In the dining room, made cozier by warm wallpaper and muted lighting, you'll find everything English, from scones to rarebit (spiced cheese melted over bread). Some selections from the rest of the world also manage to sneak in—but they're Anglicized as much as possible—hummus appears on the menu as "chick-pea pate."

Satisfy your sweet tooth at **Sarah Nelson's Grasmere Ginger-bread** *(Easedale Rd.; No phone; 9am-6pm daily; £1.00-£1.50 per item; No credit cards)*, known throughout the country for its secret recipe. Don't look for any restless cookie-men here; this gingerbread is a soft toffee infused with ground ginger, a taste sensation that's worth the long wait in line.

crashing

Because Grasmere is so popular with literature-happy tourists, the price of accommodation in town is ridiculous. The only lodging under £40 per person is at the two hostels, and finding a bed in either of them is difficult. Both are located within close proximity of the village. Although the tourist office is too small to book accommodations for you, the staff there can advise you about vacancies in the area [see *need to know,* below].

▶▶CHEAP

Imposing in its Victorian-age grey-stone grandeur, **Butterlip How** *(Easedale Rd.; Tel 015934/353-16; reception 7:30am-10pm daily; £11.90 per person; En suite; grasmere@yha.org.uk; V, MC, AE)* stands tall and proper on the northern edge of the village. Its rooms have been recently renovated and are arranged in suites, so they're best for large groups.

Just outside the village along the footpath to Easedale Tarn, **Thorney How** *(Easedale Rd.; Tel 015934/353-16; reception 7:30am-10pm daily; £9.80 per person; En suite; grasmere@yha.org.uk; V, MC, AE)* is a converted farmhouse with a more rustic atmosphere. Missing the high-class ambience you'll find at Butterlip but charming in its own way, it's also better for singles. You can't beat the rates.

▶▶DO-ABLE

If the hostels are full, the **Glenthorne Quaker Guest House** *(Easedale Rd.; Tel 015394/353-89; £24-£36 per person, £29-£40 per person en suite, £46 per person full board; Breakfast included; gthorn@globalnet.co.uk, come.to/glenthorne; V, MC)* is another possibility; it's just a few minutes from the train station and the center of town.

There are a few possibilities outside of town as well. To reach **Banerigg Guest House** *(Benerigg GH; Tel 015394/352-04; £26 per person, £24 per person after three nights; Most rooms en suite, breakfast included; No credit cards)* take Bus 555 from the train station. **Titter-ingdales Guesthouse** *(Pye Lane; Tel 015394/354-39; Feb-Nov only; £18.50 and under, single, £18.50-£25.50, double, depending upon room and season; Most rooms en suite, breakfast included; tittering dales@grasmere.net, www.grasmere.net; V, MC)* is 15 minutes from the center of Grasmere. It's also accessible via Bus 555 from the Windermere train station.

need to know

Currency Exchange The only place to exchange currency is at the **Tourist Information Center** [see below], which charges a minimum £3 commission.

Tourist Information Just east of Red Lion Square, the **Tourist Information Center** *(Red Bank Rd.; Tel 015394/352-45; 9am-5:30pm daily, Apr-Oct; 10am-4pm Sat, Sun, Nov-Mar)* offer tons of information, including leaflets on the plethora of nature walks available in the area. You can also hire guides here who will happily accompany you.

Health & Emergency Emergency: *999;* for information and assistance, call the **Kendal police station** *(Tel 01539/722-611).* The nearest hospital, **Westmoreland Hospital** *(Burton Rd., Kendal; Tel 015394/732-288)* is in Kendal as well, about 12 miles to the southeast.

Bus Lines Out of the City Stagecoach Cumberland *(Tel 08706/082-608)* runs hourly bus service to and from Windermere and Keswick (lines 555 and 557). Buses come and go off Broadgate Road; information and schedules can be found at the tourist office [see above].

Bike Rental Bikes can be rented through the **Forest Side Hotel** *(Keswick Rd.; Tel 015394/352-50; £10 per day, £50 deposit; MC, V),* off Broadgate.

KESWICK

Perched amid rolling green hills on the edge of the deep blue **Derwentwater lake,** Keswick (pronounced KES-ick) was one of the Romantic poets' favorite haunts. As you'd expect in the bucolic Lake District, the air seems pure here, and the landscape is invigorating. At the end of a long day of hiking, the sun settles into the silver mist in a fluid rainbow, and you feel that all is right with your universe. (Is this poetry thing getting to you yet?)

Keswick's population of 2,000 swells to up to three times that amount during the peak days of summer. There's nothing poetic about a relentless swarm of camera-toting tourists, but luckily the town has retained its rural character. Actually it hasn't changed all that much since its beginnings as a 13th-century marketplace, despite the introduction of mining into the local economy in the 16th century. But it makes a good base for exploring the northern lakes and the nearby stone circle at Castlerigg, and it offers its own attractions as well, including lakeside theater and some wonderfully weird museums. Where else can you see a stone piano, teapots shaped like purple monkeys, vehicular superstar Chitty Chitty Bang Bang, and the world's largest pencil? (Maybe the air *is* thinner up here.) *The Keswick Reminder,* published weekly, offers more details about local goings-on than you probably need to know.

neighborhoods

The town's most prominent street is **Main Street,** a northeast-to-southwest thoroughfare that widens midway along its length into **Market Square,** site of the village's tourist office and many predictable souvenir and gift shops. From Market Street, **St. John's Street** funnels traffic off to the southeast toward bigger highways and other parts of England. The entire town can be walked in less than 10 minutes.

bar scene

The pubs in Keswick function as de facto living rooms for many of their regular patrons. Quite a few are locals-only haunts where outsiders aren't exactly welcomed. Stick to the places near town.

Southeast of the Market Square toward the lake, **The Dog and Gun** *(Lake Rd.; No phone; 11am-11pm Mon-Sat, noon-10:30pm Sun)* feels likes an old hunting lodge, with beamed ceilings, an open fire, real ale, and fine food. You may notice the glint of coins here and there in the nooks and crannies of the stone walls. Following a local superstition, hikers will put a coin in a crevice the day before a hike. If the coin falls out, the walk should be cancelled. Superstition or barkeep's retirement fund? You be the judge.

One of the most appealing of the old-fashioned pubs, **The Pheasant Inn** [see *crashing,* below] is about a half-mile northwest of the town center. Lined with old, richly detailed paneling, it's the kind of pub you only see in England and serves some of the best beer and grub in town. A pint will put you back £1.50-£2. It also makes a great place to crash for the night.

Located in the courtyard of the King's Arms Hotel in the heart of town, **Casa's Bar** *(27 Main St.; Tel 017687/772-083; 7pm-11pm Mon-Thurs, 11am-11pm Fri-Sun)* is the center of Keswick's youth scene. The pub itself is done up in standard old pub decor, with dark wood and shiny brass. The attached pizzeria provides adequate Italian fare, but if you're here when the weather's nice, you'll be spending your evening circling the umbrella-covered tables in the courtyard outside. What was a stable yard 200 years ago has been transformed into a kicking-it beer garden, where the music from the jukebox is often overpowered by the whoops of over-enthusiastic punters getting as drunk as they can as fast as they can on £1.80 pints.

If you're young enough to appreciate life but old enough not to take it for granted, head to the Queenshead Free House, better known as **The Back Bar** *(Bell Close Car Park, Tel 017687/733-33; 11am-11pm daily, lunch served and dinner, 6-9pm; No credit cards).* Located where Bank Street and Heads Road meet near the center of town, this is the bar for the in-betweens, twentysomethings who came to Keswick in pursuit of natural beauty and decided to stay. Even though Top-40 crap is blasting in the background, punters here are more interested in conversation than a raging party. Jacket potatoes and soup are the pub grub of choice.

arts scene

Keswick is packed with artists as well as oddities [see *culture zoo,* below]. Along St. John Street you'll find numerous galleries exhibiting everything

KESWICK

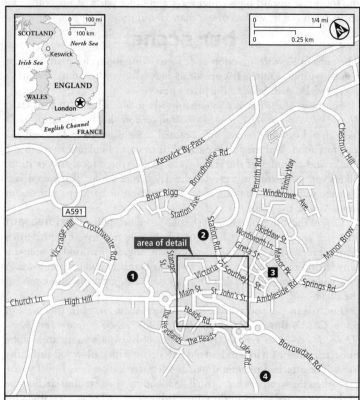

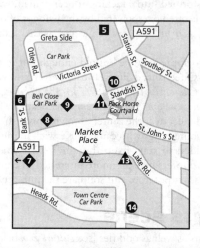

BARS/CLUBS ▲
Casa's Bar **12**
The Back Bar **11**
The Dog and Gun **13**

CULTURE ZOO ●
Cumberland Pencil
 Museum **1**
Keswick Museum
 and Art Gallery **2**
The Cars of the Stars
 Museum **10**
The Teapottery **14**
The Theatre by the Lake **4**

EATS ◆
Bryson's Craft Bakery **8**
Golden Hills **7**
The Lakeland Peddler
 Whole Food Cafe **9**

CRASHING ■
Bonshaw Guest House **3**
Swiss Court **6**
YHA **5**

from ceramics to landscape oil paintings to jewelry. With so much creativity, you start to wonder what's in the water around here.

▶▶**VISUAL ARTS**

One of the most sought-after art galleries lies just outside of town. The full-scale **Beckstone's Gallery** *(Greystokes Ghylll; Tel.01768/483-601; 10am-5:30pm daily, Mar-Oct; 10:30am-4:30pm Fri-Sun, Nov-Feb)* exhibits 300 paintings at all times; it's like visiting a museum of modern art. Although local lakescapes are featured, much of the work comes from Ireland and other parts of Europe as well.

The sweet smells of candles and potpourri fill the showrooms of **Fine Design** *(35 Lake Rd.; Tel 017687/730-34; 9:30am-5pm daily)*, near the center of town. Folk arts on display include handmade furniture, jewelry, and pottery.

▶▶**PERFORMING ARTS**

After a long day of hiking, an excellent night of entertainment can be had at the popular **Theatre by the Lake** *(Lake Rd.; Tel 017687/744-11; Restaurant and show hours vary; £5-£16 show tickets; www.theatrebythe lake.com)*. Lakeside near the end of Lake Road, Keswick's stone-house arts venue hosts everything from local comedy acts and stage plays to orchestra concerts and classic film screenings *(La Dolce Vita, The Philadelphia Story, This Is Spinal Tap)*. A restaurant and bar are also open on the premises during performances.

CULTURE ZOO

If you've ever wished you could lay eyes on Herbie the Lovebug or wanted a teapot in the shape of an armchair, this tiny town will fulfill your wildest desires.

Keswick Museum and Art Gallery *(Station Rd.; Tel 017687/732-63; 10am-4pm daily, Easter-Oct; £1 adults)*: As you enter this impressive Victorian structure on Fitz Park, east of the Market Square, you expect the usual dusty old history exhibits. They're here—from Wordsworth's

festivals and events

Hosted by a different beer company every year, the **Keswick Beer Festival** *(Keswick Rugby Club, 5 St. John St.; Tel 017687/754-14; First weekend in June; £11 2-day pass; www.chartcom.co.uk/keswick/beer/Default.htm)* brings in brew from all over the world, as well as the best of the English bitters. For a few quid, you get a bottomless souvenir mug that you can fill with beer, then stout, then bitter—then start the cycle all over again. Bands play, people drink, then people drink some more, and the party keeps going until everyone literally drops from drunkenness.

only here

Keswick is proud to be the home of the first pencil factory in England, the **Cumberland Pencil Museum** *(Southey Works, Greta Bridge; Tel 017687/736-26; 9am-4pm daily; £2.50; museum@pencils.co.uk, www.pencils.co.uk)*, and that achievement is commemorated here. In addition to detailing the history of writing implements, this inexplicably popular tourist attraction houses local artist exhibitions. You can also gawk at the world's largest pencil. All that's missing now is a gargantuan Scantron test (Choose "B").

letters to Roman-era artifacts and a scale model of the Lake District. But what stand out are the oddities—from a 500-year-old mummified cat to the bizarre collection of musical rocks, variously known as the stone dulcimer and the geological piano, which once entertained Queen Victoria.

The Cars of the Stars Museum *(Standish St.; Tel 017687/737-57; 10am-5pm daily, weekends only in Dec; www.carsofthestars.com; £3)*: Off Station Road, this garage of the silver screen houses displays ranging from *The Flintstones*'s foot-powered Stone Age sedan to the *Back to the Future* DeLorean, with a collection of James Bond's licensed-to-kill sports cars thrown in for good measure. But the biggest draw is kid vid superstar, Chitty Chitty Bang Bang, the Mary Poppins of automobiles.

The Teapottery *(Central Car Park Rd.; Tel 017687/739-83; 9am-5pm daily; free)*: When is a teapot not a teapot? When it's shaped like a toaster, a jukebox, or a cell phone. If you thought the English were serious about tea, this mini-museum and shop featuring the oddest-shaped and potentially most useless teapots you can imagine will make you reconsider. You can also get a glimpse of how the ceramic wonders are made, from the throwing of the clay to the glaze and painting. It's located near the center of town, where Bank Street and Head Road meet.

great outdoors

The ancient stone circle at **Castlerigg** is an ideal day hike from Keswick. It's just over a mile east of town. From the center of town, walk about a mile along the A591 to the A66. (If you prefer not to share the busy road with traffic, you can take Bus 73 along Penrith Road; the driver will tell you where to get off.) The circle is right along the side of the road, marked both by signs and the tourists scrambling out of their cars for a better look—you can practically drive right up to it. The stones are only about 6 feet high, but they offer a glorious view: tall jagged gray peaks to the north, and low, rolling green hills to the south. The terrain is so pristine that you can easily imagine yourself at a pagan ritual in 3,000 B.C., when the circle was supposedly assembled by local druids. Their purpose in doing so remains a mystery, but they might have had future postcards in mind. You never know.

Heading south along the Derwentwater, every village offers yet another postcard view. The village of **Borrowdale,** one of the beauty spots of the Lake District, is just 7 miles to the south. It's set against the backdrop of **Scafell Pike,** the highest in England at 3,210 feet and a climb for experienced hikers only. The green valleys outside Borrowdale are ideal for a more leisurely ramble.

The steep **Borrowdale Fells** rise dramatically over the little village of **Seatoller,** the southernmost settlement in the valley. It can be reached on Bus 77 or 79 from Keswick. The best route up the mountains is from another little village, Seathwaite, just a mile south, usually a 20-minute walk. **Seatoller Barn** *(Tel 017687/772-94; 10am-5pm daily, Easter-Nov)* dispenses maps and information about touring in the area.

For equipment, check out the **George Fisher** *(2 Barrowdale Rd.; Tel. 017687/721-78; 9am-5:30pm Mon-Sat, 10:30am-4:30pm Sun)* in Keswick. Everything from an emergency whistle to waterproof gear, tents, and even ski equipment and mountain gear are sold at this four-floor department store.

EATS

The food in Keswick won't impress you unless you've somehow become addicted to battered and deep fried everything. With a sharp eye, though, you can find a few tasty spots. Most restaurants are closed by 7pm, so eat early unless you want to grab something at one of the pubs.

▶▶CHEAP

Bryson's Craft Bakery *(38-42 Main St.; Tel 017687/722-57; 8:30am-6pm daily, Mar-Dec; £2.50 cream tea, £2.00-£3.25 sweets)* is the sweetest little teashop in the center of town, so sweet that the servers actually dress in green candy stripes. The take-away shop downstairs offers everything from sausage rolls to fudge. There's also a cutie tearoom upstairs, all deep glowing wood and black twisted iron. Try a Florentine—this concoction of nuts and dried fruit baked with toffee and Belgian chocolate will make your day.

For an atmosphere that's as light and healthy as the food, **The Lakeland Pedlar Whole Food Cafe** *(Henderson's Yard, Bell Close Car Park; Tel 017687/744-92; 9am-7pm daily; £3.50-£6.50 per entrée; lakeland.pedlar@btclick.com, www.lakelandpedlar.co.uk; No credit cards),* not far from the Back Bar, is your best bet. Everything on the menu, which includes Mediterranean and Mexican favorites and a selection of pizzas, is fresh, home-made, organic, free range, and meat-free. The breakfast burritos must be tasted to be believed. It's also populated by some real characters—don't be surprised to find the waiter howling out a song with his dog. The attached bike shop is affiliated with Keswick Mountain Bike Centre [see *need to know,* below].

▶▶DO-ABLE

Nearby on Main Street, some of the best Chinese food in the region can be found at **Golden Hills** (70 Main St.; Tel 017687/731-65; noon-1:45pm/5:30-11pm Mon-Sat, 5:30-11pm Sun; £5.50-£7.50 per item; V). The atmosphere consists of little more than a few red paper lanterns, but the quality of the food quickly makes decor irrelevant. The Pekinese and Cantonese menu offers the usual fried rice and pork dishes, but the Cantonese specialties really are special.

crashing

There are plenty of good places to stay in Keswick. Entire streets are devoted to B&Bs, most of which offer rooms for around £16 a night. Knocking on doors along Blencartha, Helvellyn, and Eskin Streets when you get into town is the quickest, and surprisingly, most efficient way to find a bed for the night. The Tourist Information Center [see *need to know,* below] also has limited listings and can help you find a bed if you go to the office in person.

▶▶CHEAP

Minutes from the town center and not far from Fritz Park, the **Keswick Youth Hostel** (Station Rd.; Tel 017687/724-84; 7:30am-11pm daily, reception, hostel access; £10.85 per person, shared bath; £3.20 breakfast; keswick@yha.org.uk; V, MC) is housed in a large boathouse right alongside the River Greta. The rooms are typical of a hostel, with dorm-style furniture and decor, but the porch that hangs out over the river is perfect for a little splashing around.

If you're a serious backpacker of the brought-your-own-tent variety, there's the **Camping and Caravanning Club Site** (Tel 017687/723-92; £10 membership required, £13.10 family membership available; £3.45-£3.80 per person per site, electricity £1.65-£2.40; V, MC, AE) in the center of town or **Castlerigg Hall Camping** (Tel 017687/724-37; Low season: £9 touring caravan, £8 motor home, £3 per person; High Season Apr 21-May 2, May 27-Sept 16, Oct 21-28: £11 touring caravan, £9.50 motor home, otherwise £3.70 per person; www.castlerigg.co.uk; No credit cards), right outside of town.

▶▶DO-ABLE

The **Bonshaw Bed and Breakfast** (20 Eskin Street; Tel 01768/773-084; £16.50 per person, en suite available; V, MC) is a comfortable house with eager-to-please proprietors. An electric water heater in each of the showers provides unlimited hot water, a luxury that seems like a necessity after walking along the rainy hillsides all day. It's not far, just east of the town center.

In addition to being one of Keswick's most popular pubs [see *bar, club, and live music scene,* above], **The Pheasant Inn** (High Hill; Tel. 01768/722-19; £20 per person, shared bath, breakfast included; No credit cards), about a half-mile northwest of the town center, is also a great place to crash at a reasonable price.

The charming red-brick **Swiss Court Guest House** *(25 Bank St.; Tel 017687/726-37; £22 per person, en suite with TV; V, MC)*, newly renovated and tastefully decorated, is possibly the most popular accommodation in town. Rooms are spacious and most offer excellent views of the mountains. Across the street from Back Bar, it also allows for a short stumble home.

Other lodging options in town include the **Bridgedale Guest House** *(101 Main St.; Tel 017687/739-14; £16 per person, £19.50-£23.50 per person en suite, breakfast included; No credit cards)*, right in the heart of town, and **Bluestones** *(7 Soutney St.; Tel 017687/742-37; £16.15 per person, £15 per person after three nights, £18.50 per person en suite (one room available), £20-£25 full board; Breakfast included; bluestone-keswick @cwcome.net; No credit cards)*, just 2 minutes from the town center.

need to know

Currency Exchange You can change money at any of the banks on Market Square—the rates vary little. Try **Barclays Bank** *(Market Square; Tel 017687/720-57; 9:30am-4:30pm Mon, Tues, Thur, and Fri, 10am-4:30pm Wed)*.

Tourist Information The **Tourist Information Centre** *(Moot Hall, Market Square; Tel 017687/726-45; 9am-5:30pm daily; keswicktic@lake-district.gov.uk)* offers local information, as well as limited accommodation listings.

Health and Emergency Emergency: *999;* **Police** *(Bank St.; Tel 017687/720-04)* are located in the town center. **Mary Hewetson Hospital** *(Crosthwaite Rd.; Tel 017687/720-12)*, in the northwestern part of town about a 10-minute walk from the center, offers medical attention.

Pharmacies J.N. Murray Ltd. *(15/17 Station St.; Tel 017687/720-49; 9am-5:30pm Mon-Sat)*, between the town center and Fitz Park, is the local chemist. The rotating schedule for late hours (till 6:30pm) is posted in the store window.

Bus Lines Out of Town Stagecoach Cumberland *(Tel 01946/632-22)* operates regular bus service from Windermere and Grasmere (line 555). Buses come and go off The Headlands more or less every hour between 9am and 7pm.

Bike Rental All of your cycling needs can be met at **Keswick Mountain Bike Centre** *(Mill Lane; Tel 017687/752-02, Fax 017687/751-35; 9am-5:30pm daily, closed Tue; £10 half-day, £13 full day, demo bikes £25 full day; david@keswickmtnbikes.demon.co.uk, www.keswick-bikes.co.uk; No credit cards)*, at the end of Mill Lane, off Main Street.

Laundry Spiff up your duds at the **Launderette** *(St. James Court, Main Street; Tel 01787/754-48; 9am-7:30pm daily; £1.60 wash, 50p dry, £4.40 service wash to 16 pounds)* near the center of town.

Postal The **post office** *(Market Square; Tel 01787/722-69; 8:30am-8pm Mon-Sat, 10:30am-4:30pm Sun)* is on the square.

glenridding

Squeezed into a square half-mile between the **Ullswater Lake** and the **Helvellyn Range,** Glenridding is really just a stopover for climbing fanatics who can't wait to get closer to the sky by getting onto the side of a mountain. If you get a charge out of climbing up a razor-sharp peak just to see how far you can see, it doesn't get much better. There's even a mellow lake for easing the inevitable aches and pains on the day after. Nightlife consists of a bunch of exhausted climbers sharing their literally tall tales about the day's climb along with a pint or two of stout. The town itself is tiny, with only 300 inhabitants, one road (the A592), slim accommodations, and not even a post office to call its own. Not into climbing? Skip this tiny mountain outpost.

bar scene

More than a few visitors have had serious summer camp flashbacks when they saw the plastic tablecloths covering picnic tables at **The Hiker's Bar** *(A592; Tel 017684/824-44; 11am-11pm daily; No credit cards).* The interior looks like a Catskills meshall, but don't let it ruin your evening—this is really the only place around to enjoy a good stout and share the trials of the day's hike with your mates. Pub grub snacks (£4.95-£6.25) are available any time.

great outdoors

The walk up the Helvellyn range is strenuous, with an elevation climb of 2,600 feet. Most people complete the circuit in about 6 hours. Starting from the National Park Information Office Car Park, follow the unpaved Greenside Road for about 2 miles before the path veers off into wooded areas. Before reaching the summit, the well-marked path will take you along Striding Edge, is an exposed ridge with unbeatable views of the glen below. Continue, with caution, past the waters of Red Tarn. Reaching the summit of 2,917 feet requires a scramble up the side of the exposed ridge. The top of this mountain is only a few feet wide, standing room only. The views of rose-colored hillsides and drop-away cliffs are well worth the effort.

Although the Helvellyn path is well marked, you should pick up a map along with a leaflet describing the trail. Both are available from the National Park Information Center [see *need to know,* below].

eats

Catering to outdoor maniacs intent on scaling Helvellyn's summit, **Karen's Lakeland Kitchen** *(A592; Tel 017684/823-92; 10:30am-5:30pm daily, Mar-Oct; Sat, Sun only, Nov-Feb; £3-£5.50 per entrée; No credit cards)* sells inventive vegetarian meals, with tofu and lasagna as the staples, and home-baked desserts. Sit down at one of the old sewing tables (there's even a pedal underfoot) and bite into a slice of American-style apple pie.

Next door, through the nook on the right side of the archway as you face the lake, is **Kilner's Coffeehouse** *(A592; Tel 017684/822-28; 10am-6pm daily; £2.25-£4.35 per item; £6 per hour for Internet use; No credit cards)*. Who would have thought tiny Glenridding would have a cybercafe? Of course, for what they charge to surf the web, you could probably buy your own laptop. The meals here are rather light, consisting of tea and various sandwiches, but the hearty soups are great.

crashing

The **Helvellyn YHA Hostel** *(Greenside; Tel 017684/822-69; reception open 5-11pm daily, Mon-Sat, Sept-Jun only; shared bath; £9.80 adult, £4.80 evening meal, £3.20 breakfast; helynellyn@yha.org.uk; V, MC)* is a stone house on a cliffside just a stone's throw from Helvellyn, overlooking the clear River Greta. People will tell you that it's just up the road, but it's really *up* the road, 2 miles from the center of town heading toward Helvellyn's crest. But you'll get a head start on your hike in the morning!

You may think campsites are for city-folk who're afraid of setting up a tent in the wild, but this camp is nothing more than an abandoned piece of farmland that's turning a profit. **Mrs. Lightfoot** *(Gillside Farm; Tel 017684/823-46; £3 per tent, £4 for caravans, £4 per person for bunkhouse)* will show you kindly to your little plot of land and send a chicken out to wake you in the morning. Toilet facilities are available, and groups of six or more can share a bunkhouse.

need to know

Currency Exchange There's really nowhere to change money in town. The nearest possibility is the post office in Patterdale [see below], which takes a commission of £3 or 1.5 percent.

Tourist Information Center The **Ullswater Tourist Information Center** *(Car Park, Glenridding; Tel 017684/824-14; 9am-5pm daily, Mar-Oct; Sat, Sun only, Nov-Feb)* is also a National Park Information Center, offering information and suggestions for getting the most out of your hike up Helvellyn.

Health and Emergency Emergency: *999.* The nearest **Police Station** *(Tel 01539/722-611)* is in Kendal, some 23 miles to the south. The nearest hospital is in Kendal as well: **Kendal Westmoreland Hospital** *(Burton Rd., Kendal; Tel 015394/732-288)*.

Bus Lines Out of the City Stagecoach Cumberland *(Tel 08706/082-608)* runs buses from Keswick (buses 73A, 491, 888, X4, X5, and X85), Penrith (buses 161 and 108), and Ambleside to Glenridding. Buses stop along the only road in town, on both sides of the street near the car park. For fare and schedule information, go to the tourist office [see above].

Boats Ferries are available to Pooley Bridge and Howtown from the southern tip of Ullswater. If you are heading northeast to Penrith, this is the best method of transportation, though it is somewhat expensive. Call **Ullswater Steamers** *(Tel 01764/822-29; £4.40 adult fare to Pooley*

Bridge, £2.40 to Howtown; www.ullswater-steamers.co.uk; No credit cards) for information.

Postal There are no postal services in town. The **Patterdale post office** *(A592; Tel 017684/822-20; 9am-5:30pm Mon-Fri, 9am-noon Sat)* is about 1 1/2 miles south along the A592.

penrith

Nestled between the northern edge of the **Lakelands** and the foot of the **Pennine Mountains,** the red sandstone town of Penrith has been many things in its day: regional capital, military fortress, farmland marketplace, and gateway to Cumbria. Today, with a population of 15,000, it's primarily a crossroads for people on their way somewhere else, whether heading deeper into Cumbria, down into the lakes, along the Pennine Way, or even on into Scotland. That makes the townspeople more comfortable with strangers, whatever their destinations.

Like many towns in England, Penrith is built on centuries of history, both remembered and forgotten. The red sandstone circle just outside town dates back to the Bronze Age, but earliest records of Penrith remember it as the capital of Cumbria and a strategic city in the Kingdom of Scotland. It was so strategic, in fact, that England seized it from the Scots in 1070 in one of their tag-you're-it military skirmishes. The architecture in town reflects this conflict: Many of the buildings have pele towers, with slit-like windows for firing arrows at enemy marauders. Nearby Penrith Castle is another reminder of the old border wars—it was once called the Castle of Kings, but today it stands in ruins.

It's no longer home to royalty, but this little market town has its own charms. Check the local newspaper, *The Cumberland & Westmorland Herald,* or the tourist office to see what's going on during your stay. Penrith's pub scene is classic Brit: cozy dark wood rooms filled with jolly locals raising their pints in a rousing, off-color, drinking song. Conversation flows as easily as the ale, so even if you're just passing through, raise your glass and your voice—in Penrith, no one minds if you sing off-key.

neighborhoods

The center of town is **Market Square,** which is formed by the junction of **King Street** (heading south), **Cornmarket** (heading west), and **Devonshire Street** (heading north). An 1861 gothic revival monument to a local aristocrat, Philip Musgrave of Edenhall, rises from the center of the Square, and St. Andrew's Church is on its east side. Everything worth seeing or doing is around the square, so you can hoof it all the way. It takes about 20 minutes to walk the entire town, so local bus service is limited. Buses depart from the Bus Station at Sandgate *(Tel 01768/892-727 for schedules and information).*

hanging out

When it starts to rain, locals and tourists alike take cover in the pubs, most of which are located on Great Dockray, a 2-minute walk west of Market Square. All the young hipsters hang at **The White Horse Pub** [see *bar scene,* below]. Its nearby competitors have a higher percentage of farmers from the outlying districts. Head for the town center lounge at the **George Hotel** [see *crashing,* below] for tea, scones, and all the local gossip.

bar, club, and live music scene

Penrith's best pubs are just west of Market Square, on Great Dockray. The pub crowd includes tourists, business travelers, and students from the local university, so choose your spot accordingly or you could end up at a bar full of traveling insurance salesman. Be ready to raise a microphone as well as a pint—karaoke has hit it big in Penrith, and almost every bar on Market Square hosts a night for amateur songsters.

Recently renovated, **The White Horse** *(Great Dockeray; Tel 01768/890-780; 11am-midnight Mon-Sat; noon-10:30pm Sun)* is a modern version of the Olde English Public House, with whitewash brightening up the traditional wood and brass. It's what passes for hip in Penrith, with a younger crowd than most of the other places in town. The featured entertainment is public humiliation, or as they euphemistically refer to it, karaoke. Every Thursday night, you can entertain your fellow punters by wailing tonelessly into a microphone. It's often quite painful for singer and audience alike, but that's the whole point, isn't it? You can get pub grub for about £3 and drinks are around £2.

For something a little easier on the ears, try the **General Wolfe** *(Little Dockray; Tel 01768/868-484; 11am-11pm Mon-Sat, noon-10:30pm Sun; No credit cards).* This rustic English pub is filled with alcoves perfect for spinning a good yarn with your mates while the football hooligans in the back room holler at the big screen TV. Other diversions include a jukebox filled with leftover Brit pop, a pool table, and a wide selection of quality beers and hand-drawn bitters (drinks around £2).

With cheap drinks and food served late, **The New Vic's** *(46 Castlegate; Tel 01768/862-467; 11am-11pm Mon-Sat, noon-10:30 Sun; No credit cards)* knows how to lure in the college crowd (£1.50 drinks). It's actually pretty homey for a chain bar, but the pub grub reveals its corporate origins. If there's one thing worse than pub grub, it's pub grub from a chain bar.

The only club in town, **Topper's** *(Southend Rd.; Tel 01768/863-923; 10pm-2am Fri; £6 cover),* has a hip marketing campaign going for it, but that's about it. There are two levels for dancing, but the tedious mix of old chart hits and dance anthems keeps the crowds thin and lifeless. Topper's is the only place in town open after 11pm, so it's quite a meat market in the wee hours, when the lonely and way-too-drunk stop in for one last chance to score. If this is the only game in town, it may not be worth playing.

penrith

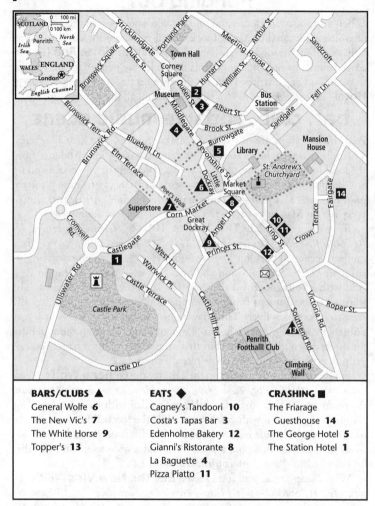

BARS/CLUBS ▲
General Wolfe **6**
The New Vic's **7**
The White Horse **9**
Topper's **13**

EATS ◆
Cagney's Tandoori **10**
Costa's Tapas Bar **3**
Edenholme Bakery **12**
Gianni's Ristorante **8**
La Baguette **4**
Pizza Piatto **11**

CRASHING ■
The Friarage
  Guesthouse **14**
The George Hotel **5**
The Station Hotel **1**

CULTURE ZOO

Cultural attractions in Penrith are meager, worth only a brief look before moving on to wherever your final destination may be.

Penrith Castle *(Along Ullswater Rd.; No phone; Gates close at dusk; Free):* Constructed in 1399 as a fortification against possible Scottish invasion, this castle crumbled into obsolescence when Scotland reluctantly joined Her Majesty's dominion. The ruins remain, a 15-minute walk west of Market Square, across the street from the railway station.

Acorn Bank Garden & Watermill *(Temple Sowerby; Tel 017683/618-93; 10am-5pm daily, Apr-Oct; £2.50 adults, £1.75 students):* If you get off on horticulture (and who doesn't?), this bloom bonanza is six miles southeast of town on Road A6. This is *not* an English showplace garden with elaborate flowerbeds and ornamental mazes grown out of shrubbery, but they do take pride in their huge beds of herbs and their expertise with daffodils (paging Wordsworth...).

Penrith Museum *(Robinson's School, Middlegate; Tel 01768/212-228; 9:30am-5pm, Mon-Sat, winter; 9:30am-6pm Mon-Sat, noon-6pm Sun, summer; Free):* Adjacent to the tourist office at the northern edge of town, this 17th-century building contains exhibits of paintings by local artists, exhibits about the geology and botany of the Lake District, and cultural overviews of the region. Good only on a rainy day....

great outdoors

Penrith's outdoor sites connect the little market town to its past, both ancient and medieval. If the mysterious wisdom of the ancient Celts makes your heart beat faster, pay a visit to **Long Meg and her Daughters,** the third-largest stone circle in England. Just outside of Penrith at the edge of the National Park, these red sandstone slabs are actually arranged in an ellipse, with the 12-foot pillar called Long Meg off to one side. Bronze Age carvings are also discernible on Meg's face, which is turned away from the circle. Scientists speculate that the circle may have been used to find the mid-winter sun. Legend has it that ill-mannered witch Meg and her squirrelly brood were dancing on the Sabbath, got caught, and were turned into stone as their punishment. Another legend claims that if anyone accurately counts the number of stones in the circle twice, the spell will be broken. Give it a try, there may be a movie deal in it for you if it works.

The **Penrith Beacon** is an hour's walk up steep Fell Lane and offers a view of the red sandstone buildings below and the Lakeland beyond. Built in 1719 at the northern edge of town, this monument tower commemorates the long chain of medieval light towers that at one time led down into the southern parts of England. When an invader was spotted, a tower would be lit, giving ample warning to the settlements below. This complex alarm system gives a whole new meaning to the phrase, "Don't break the chain."

stuff

Every market town has shopping. In this case, the covered Devonshire Arcade on the eastern edge of the market square offers chain stores and chi-chi boutiques. All of the odd-ball mom-and-pop businesses are a little farther south on either side of Castle Road at Angel Square and Little Dockray.

eats

There are lots of good affordable restaurants in Penrith with a diversity of choices you wouldn't expect in a small Northern town. Whether you're craving Italian, Spanish, or East Indian, you'll find it here.

▶▶CHEAP

Wholesome and affordable, the dishes at the **Edenholme Bakery** *(Lazonby; Tel 01768/898-437; 8:30am-5pm daily; 50p-£1.75 per item; No credit cards)* beat out burgers any day. Sweet flaky phyllo dough is wrapped around meat pockets or quiches for a hearty lunch. Sweet bread puddings, cakes, and of course, fresh bread are also available—making for a satisfying meal for just the change in your pocket. Unfortunately, it's an 8-mile trek from the city center, on the northern edge of town in Lazonby, off B6412.

La Baguette *(Middlegate; Tel 01768/728-985; 8:30am-4pm daily; £1.50 per item; No credit cards)* offers comparable fare, with deli-style sandwiches and soups, and it's right off the market square.

Run by Italians who actually speak Italian, **Pizza Piatto** *(21 King St.; Tel 01768/862-467; noon-midnight Sun-Thur, till 1am Fri, Sat; £2.20-£4.40 per pie; No credit cards)* serves the most authentic pizzas this side of Sicily. A standard pizza feeds about four people. It's just southeast of the market square.

▶▶DO-ABLE

Walking into **Costa's Tapas Bar** *(9 Queen St.; Tel 01768/895-550; noon-4pm/6-11pm daily; £4 tapas; No credit cards)* is like walking into Barcelona. Feast on authentic Spanish finger foods while you feast your eyes on the vibrant decor and wash it all down with some quality beer. It's just southeast of the market square.

Gianni's Ristorante *(11 Market Square; Tel 01768/891-791; noon-2pm/5:30-10pm Mon-Sat, happy hour 5:30-7pm; £5.30-£7 per entrée; MC)* offers casual dining with excellent Italian staples. It's the kind of family restaurant where the staff will drag out all the bells and whistles to embarrass the hell out of you on your birthday.

While curry houses can be found in most English towns, **Cagney's Tandoori** *(17-18 King St.; Tel 01768/867-721; noon-2pm/5-11:30pm daily; £5.25-£9.25 per entrée; AE)* far exceeds the norm. It's decked out from floor to ceiling in the fabric and art of India, with statues of Hindu gods and goddesses blessing your meal. Just about anything made with curry or masala will hit the spot.

▶▶SPLURGE

Passepartout *(51 Castlegate; Tel 01768/865-852; 7-10pm Tue-Sun; £10-£15; No credit cards)* offers all the makings of a romantic evening out. Candlelight gives the painted stone walls a warm glow, and the imaginative menu puts local ingredients to good use in dishes like pork loin in caraway-and-port-wine sauce on a bed of fennel. The desserts are daring as well—think butterscotch ice cream and oyster amaretto soufflé with chocolate sauce. (We still can't figure out how the oysters got in there, but trust us—it's tasty.)

crashing

It's tough to find inexpensive places to stay in Penrith. The best option is the independent hostel in town, the Corney House. There's also one seasonal guesthouse in town, the Friarage (available in the summer), but most places are pretty far out on the outskirts—difficult to get to unless you're willing to walk. The tourist office [see *need to know*, below] is happy to assist with reservations, both here and elsewhere along your route.

▶▶CHEAP

Just at the northeastern corner of the market square, the **Corney House** *(1 Corney Place; Tel 01768/867-627, Mobile 07808/836-159; £10 per person; Shared bath; No credit cards)* lives up to its name. It's decorated in sunshine yellow, and the oh-so-British proprietors seem to be walking on sunshine themselves. The accommodations, consisting of only one room with bunk beds, are basic, but comfortable and warm.

Tynedale Guest House *(4 King St.; Tel 01768/867-491; £17-£20 per person, twin, double, or family room; children under 15 half-price; Private baths available; Breakfast included; No credit cards)* offers comfortable rooms in a beautiful Victorian house. Located along the town's main entry road, it's known as a "pedal stop" because they get so many cyclists as overnight guests. They serve quite good food, and cater to vegetarians.

You can also try the **Victoria Guest House** *(3 King St.; Tel 01768/863-823; £19-£17-£20 per person, double; Breakfast included; No credit cards)*, owned by the same woman who runs the Tynedale Guest House next door. Even she says they're pretty much exactly the same.

The family-run **Blue Swallow Guest House** *(11 King St.; Tel/Fax 01768/866-335; £18 per person, double with bath, £19 in summer; £17 per person, twin without bath, £18 summer; Breakfast included; www.blueswallow.co.uk, blueswallows@lineone.net; No credit cards)* is also set in a lovely Victorian townhouse, just a few doors down from the Tynedale and Victoria guesthouses, in the heart of the guesthouse district.

▶▶DO-ABLE

The Friarage *(Friargate; Tel 01768/863-635; £15-£20 per person; No credit cards)* is a 13th-century guest house located just east of the market square, off Bridge Road. Forget that vow of poverty, you'll sleep in comfort here.

The Station Hotel *(Castlegate; Tel 01768/866-714; £25 per person; No credit cards)* is housed in a 19th-century building that hasn't changed much in the past hundred years. Its main selling point is its convenient location at the southwestern edge of the market square, right near the train station.

▶▶SPLURGE

Penrith's premiere accommodation, the **George Hotel** *(Devonshire St.; Tel 01768/862-696; £45 per person single, £35 per person double, en suite; V, MC, AE)* is an elegant coaching inn right in the center of town that goes back 300 years, at least—Bonnie Prince Charlie slept here in 1745. This is luxury done right: bright, airy, oak-paneled rooms and chic modern furnishings in light colors. A full breakfast is included with the price of your stay. Despite the swank surroundings, the George is so welcoming that you'll feel comfortable walking into the lobby in hiking boots with a pack strapped to your back.

need to know

Currency Exchange The **HSBC Bank** *(Market Square; 9am-3pm Mon-Fri, 9am-noon Sat)* takes a 1 percent commission with a £2.50 minimum.

Tourist Information Located on the eastern edge of the market square, the **Tourist Information Centre** *(Robinson School, Middlegate, Penrith; Tel 01768/867-466; 9:30am-5pm Mon-Sat, 9:30am-6pm daily, summer)* offers information and advice on the surrounding area. They also offer assistance booking accommodations.

Health and Emergency Emergency: *999*. **Police** *(Hunter Lane; Tel 01768/864-355)* are located about a 5-minute walk north of the town center. **Penrith Hospital** *(Bridge Lane; Tel 01768/245-300)*, about a 20-minute walk from the town center (follow posted signs), provides medical attention.

Pharmacy The local chemist is **Joseph Cowper** *(50 King St.; Tel 01768/862-063; 8:45am-5:30pm Mon-Sat)*, located just southeast of the market square.

Trains There is train service to London several times daily (approx. 4 hrs). The **train station** is just southwest of town, a 5-minute walk along Ullswater Road.

Bus Lines Out of the City **Stagecoach Cumberland** *(Tel 01946/632-22)* buses run to and from Carlisle, where connections to London are available on **National Express** *(Tel 0990/808-080)*. Buses arrive and depart hourly from Sandgate, east of the market square. Information and schedules are available from the local branch of National Express *(Tel 01768/892-727)*.

Laundry Go for the old fluff and fold at **Dollytab** *(Princess St.; Tel 01768/868-081; 7am-7pm daily; £2 wash, 50p dry, £4.90 service wash)*.

Postal Get your cards and letters to the **Post Office** *(Crowne Square; Tel 01768/862-708. 9am-5:30pm Mon-Fri, 9am-12:30pm Sat)*.

cumbria way

One of the great walks of England, the Cumbria Way heads north from Ulverston on the southern edge of the Lake District National Park and goes all the way to the capital of Cumbria, Carlisle, 70 miles to the north. In six days of walking, you can cut through some of the most romantic countryside in England. See the world through the poet William Wordsworth's eyes—gentle meadows filled with sheep, the golden daffodils of spring, rugged bracken-clad fells, and mirror-still lakes. You'll pass the ruins of ancient castles and pele towers, long-abandoned mineral mills, and pretty little time-lost villages.

Although you don't have to be an Olympic athlete to make the hike, you should be in decent shape. If you don't want to walk the entire 70 miles, buses are available at many of the towns along the way to get you back to relative civilization. It's best to plan out your hike, and make reservations for accommodation each night.

Begin in Ulverston, where you can pick up advice on the trail and maps at the local tourist office [see **Ulverston**]. If you arrive in the afternoon in Ulverston, it's best to overnight here and begin the trail early the next morning. On the second day, walk 15 miles north to Coniston, an ideal stopover with plentiful food and lodging [see **Coniston**]. You'll have excellent views of Coniston's Old Man and other nearby peaks. The last two hours you'll find easy ambling, skirting the shoreline of Coniston Water on the approach to the village itself. If you've seen enough, Coniston is a good place to break from the trail, as it has bus connections to other parts of the country.

Otherwise, on the third day you can head north from Coniston to Langdale, a distance of 11 miles, cutting through the heart of the Lake District and passing the beautiful Tarn Hows and crossing the River Brathay at Skelwith Bridge. Skelwith Bridge is 3 miles west of the village of Ambleside, which makes a good refueling stop with plenty of B&Bs and pubs [see **Ambleside**]. The Bridge also marks the beginning of Great Langdale, a valley created during the ice age and overshadowed by the towering Langdale Pikes, the most dramatic of the Lakeland fells. Lodging is available in the little village of Langthwaite.

On the fourth day you can hike the 9-mile route from Langthwaite to Rosthwaite, taking you to the head of Langdale Valley before crossing the Stake Pass and beginning a descent into Langstrath Dale. You pass through the little village of Borrowdale and Scafell Pike, the highest in England at 3,210 feet, before journeying on to Rosthwaite for an overnight stopover. The fifth day is one of the easiest legs of the trail, as the distance between Rosthwaite and the town of Keswick is only 8 miles. Follow the shores of Lake Derwentwater before arriving in Keswick for refueling [see **Keswick**]. The sixth day is more difficult, stretching 14-17 miles (depending on what trail you follow). The path circles around the back of the mountain of Skiddaw at 1,500 feet above sea level, just 6 miles from Keswick.

At this point on the trail there are two alternative routes. The shorter one goes up over Hike Peak; the longer one, taking an extra 3 miles, cuts through the valley and passes the park's most stunning waterfall, the Whitewater Dash. At some point 2 miles before you reach the village of Caldbeck, the two trails come together again. Overnight in Caldbeck.

The final stretch of the trail takes you from Caldbeck along a 14-mile stretch into Carlisle. At some point you'll leave the park and follow the River Caldew for an easy walk into Cumbria's capital, which has the most choices for food and lodging along the entire route [see **Carlisle**].

need to know

Transportation/Directions If you're feeling lazy or would like to do the Way in style, you can hire the **Sherpa Van** *(131a Heston Rd., Hounslow, Middlesex TW5 ORF; Tel 02085/694-101, Fax 02085/*

729-788; £5 per day; info@sherpavan.com, www.sherpavan.com) to bring your luggage to your hostel each morning, leaving those heavy backpacks for someone else to deal with. They can also help you book accommodations.

Detailed information guides and maps can be ordered in advance through the **Rambler's Association** *(23 Woodland Crescent Hilton Park Prestwich Manchester M25 9WQ; www.ramblers.org.uk). The Cumbria Way* (John Trevelyan, Dalesman Publishing, £4.95) and *Cumbria Way* (Anthony Burton, Aurum Press, £12.99) are two of the best.

Eats The best places to eat or pick up groceries along the way are in the larger villages [see *Ulverston, Coniston, Ambleside, Carlisle*]. All of these villages are tiny, and restaurants generally lie along each village's single main street.

Crashing commodation is plentiful along the Cumbria Way [see *Ulverston, Coniston, Ambleside, Carlisle*]. After passing through Langdale, you can stay in Longthwaite at the **Borrowdale Youth Hostel** *(Longthwaite; Tel 017687/772-57; reception open 1-11pm Fri-Sat only, Oct-Feb; £10.85 per person)* where you can spend the night in a cedar building just off the River Derwent. If you're interested in staying in one of the most remote hostels in England, make reservations early at the **Skiddaw House Youth Hostel** *(Tel 016974/783-25; Mar 21-Nov 1; £9.50 dorm),* at the summit of Skiddaw peak, just 6 miles hike from Keswick. Inaccessible by car, it can only be reached by foot.

northumbria

northumbria

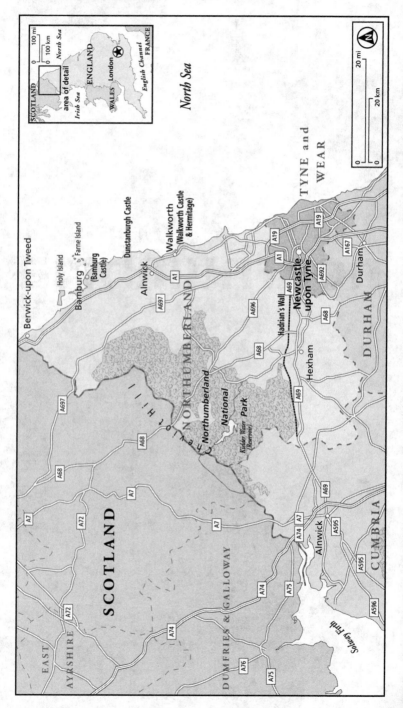

northumbria is home to *Newcastle Brown Ale*—called simply "broon" by locals who drink it like water—but there are far more castles than clubs in this part of England. You can avoid the castle obsession by taking a train directly from London to **Newcastle-Upon-Tyne,** a fun university town, but sooner or later your curiosity's going to get the best of you, and you'll end up—like everybody else—checking out these crumbling remains.

The most obvious site to see is **Hadrian's Wall,** a sort of ancient version of the Berlin Wall that stretched across the north of England to protect the Roman Empire—and many British monarchies, including the Elizabethans—from the "savages" up north (i.e., uppity Scots like Mel Gibson in *Braveheart*. Entire towns such as **Hexham** and **Carlisle** seem to exist primarily to host travelers who come to see the wall, so you can usually get a decent meal, and if you happen to run into a talkative local at just the right pub, you may even hear a few entertaining stories.

But Northumbria isn't all blood-and-broon; you can also do a major tranquility thing—walk along miles of deserted beaches, cycle through lush, green countryside, or visit colonies of gray seals and seabirds on the **Farne Islands.**

Speaking of islands, this definitely isn't Hawaii, but you can do a kind of cool island-hopping trip here. Just across the border from Scotland, **Berwick-Upon-Tweed** is a good place to start. From here, you can take a day trip out to the Farnes or **Holy Island,** which is linked to the mainland by a long causeway. On Holy Island, which once was a monastic center, visit the majestic **Lindisfarne Priory** and wander around the hermit's asylum. About 8 miles down the shore from the hermitage is **Bamburgh Castle.** The sands between here and Holy Island are passable, but before you take off to bike or hike it, you should get some advice from a local guide—the entire coastline is dotted with dangers ranging from quicksand to erosion.

Still not maxed out on nature and castles? Give yourself some sort of endurance award and travel on. There's more. Near **Alnwick,** you'll find the Brontë-esque **Dunstanburgh Castle,** and reasonable accommodations for the night if you're en route. In the tiny town of **Warkworth,** you can walk about a mile along the narrow river to a small boat that'll take you to a really cool hermitage carved into the side of a mountain—and a castle.

TRAVEL TIMES

Times by train unless
otherwise indicated
*By road.
**Involves boat crossing

	Newcastle-upon-Tyne	Carlisle	Durham	Berwick-upon-Tweed	Alnwick
Newcastle-upon-Tyne	-	1:35	:15	:50	:50*
Carlisle	1:35	-	2:00	3:10	1:50*
Durham	:15	2:00	-	1:10	1:05*
Berwick-upon-Tweed	:50	3:10	1:10	-	:40*
Alnwick	:50*	1:50*	1:05*	:40*	-
Hexham	:40	:55	1:05	1:45	1:00*
Hadrian's Wall	:50	:40	1:35	2:00	1:05*
Holy Island	1:15*	2:10*	1:30*	:20*	:30*
Bamburgh Castle	1:05*	2:10*	1:20*	:30*	:20*
Farne Islands	3:30**	4:40**	3:50**	3:10**	3:10**
Dunstanburgh Castle	:55*	2:00*	1:10*	:45*	:10*
Warkworth Castle & Hermitage	:50*	1:05	1:05*	:50*	:10*

Hexham	Hadrian's Wall	Holy Island	Bamburgh Castle	Farne Islands	Dunstanburgh Castle	Warkworth Castle & Hermitage	London
:40	:50	1:15*	1:05*	3:30**	:55*	:50*	3:05
:55	:40	2:10*	2:10*	4:40**	2:00*	1:05*	4:10
1:05	1:35	1:30*	1:20*	3:50**	1:10*	1:05*	3:20
1:45	2:00	:20*	:30*	3:10**	:45*	:50*	4:25
1:00*	1:05*	:30*	:20*	3:10**	:10*	:10*	5:30*
-	:15	1:35*	1:20*	3:50**	1:10*	1:10*	4:50
:15	-	1:45*	1:35*	4:00**	1:15*	1:20*	4:40
1:35*	1:45*	-	:20*	2:55**	:35*	:45*	6:05*
1:20*	1:35*	:20*	-	2:40**	:20*	:35*	5:50*
3:50**	4:00**	2:55**	2:40**	-	2:45**	3:00**	8:30**
1:10*	1:15*	:35*	:20*	2:45**	-	:20*	5:40*
1:10*	1:20*	:45*	:35*	3:00**	:20*	-	8:30*

And that's enough of the castle bit, to say the least. Time to get back to your party roots. Get on over to Newcastle, where you'll find plenty of pals in the best nightlife city in the entire North of England. Put a pint of that famous Newcastle brown ale to your lips at one of dozens of pubs and clubs in town, and you'll soon forget all about Hadrian's Wall...and remember why a trip up North was the best idea you ever had.

And don't forget to stop by the nearby college town of **Durham,** where the pubbing is considerably cheaper than in Newcastle, and the cathedral is absolutely astonishing.

getting around the region

The gateway to England's northernmost region is **Newcastle,** the area's busiest transportation hub. You can get here by fast train from London; after that, you have to rely on secondary trains or buses. It's not too bad if you stay along the coast—which is where all the good stuff is anyway—but be prepared to spend a few extra days if you want to stop off anywhere else along the way where the transportation schedules are less regular. There's no unified system of public buses, but **National Express** *(Tel 0990/808-080),* one of the major private companies in the region, can give you information on the routes of all the bus lines that run in the area.

▶▶SUGGESTED ROUTES

Unless you're taking a topsy-turvy route, you'll probably begin your ventures in **Newcastle** itself. Take in its attractions by day and enjoy the best partying in the north at night. If you're short on time, head west to **Hexham** the next day, which makes the best base for touring Hadrian's Wall. You can also do Hexham as a day trip if you can't get enough of Newcastle.

If you have a week to spend in the north, after a few days in Newcastle with a side trip to Hexham, take a train ride south into **Durham** for a third night.

On the fourth day, head north of Durham to **Berwick-upon-Tweed,** again by train. Scotland is a stone's-throw away. If you like, you can stop in **Alnwick** as well.

On the last day, launch yourself from Berwick into some island hopping, beginning with **Holy Island,** 8 miles southeast of Berwick. After a morning there, continue south to the little fishing port of **Seahouses** for a trip over to see some of the bird colonies of the **Farne Islands.** Bamburgh Castle also is nearby.

If you've fallen in love with the North of England, you can head west from Newcastle to the city of **Carlisle,** using it as your gateway to the **Lake District National Park.**

Or you can stay longer on the northeast coast to check out more attractions, including **Warkworth** and **Dunstanburgh castles.**

NEWCASTLE-UPON-TYNE

The bustling cultural—and party—capital of the Northeast, **Newcastle-upon-Tyne** has a population of around a quarter-million people, many of whom originally came to find work in the coal mines but stayed to enjoy the freewheeling mindset and hang out in the notorious local pubs. Today the town's laissez-faire attitude is dominated by the huge **University of Northumbria,** with it's extremely diverse and eccentric student population.

Centuries ago, Romans built Newcastle as an outpost directly astride **Hadrian's Wall,** which they figured would protect them from the "savage tribes" to the north, After all, you can't be too careful when you've got hordes of skirted Scotsmen just across the border (50 miles north). But it was a thriving mining industry that truly put the town on the British map; situated on the deep-water **Tyne River** just 10 miles from the North Sea, Newcastle has been King Coal since the 1500s and a shipbuilding mecca since the 1600s. At one point, a quarter of the world's ships stayed together in or around Newcastle. By the 1850s, Newcastle was a sooty crown jewel of England's industrial revolution.

That distinction gives the city a dreary, grimy-looking patina, but make no mistake, this town is definitely on the rebound: cruddy old factories have now been converted into ultra-hip clubs, bars, and galleries. The combination of soot and chic adds a welcome down-to-earth vibe to the urban edge of the party scene. You'll stumble out of a gritty building at 3am and find yourself in front of the graceful and elegant **Tyne Bridge** (built in 1929)—just one of the beautiful old bridges that span the river here.

As in all big-city makeovers, some 'hoods have gotten distinctly yuppified: You'll see a ton of people with *way* too much money in their

newcastle-upon-tyne

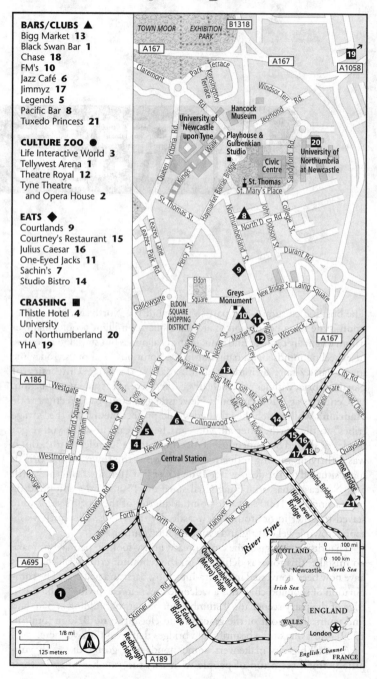

BARS/CLUBS ▲
Bigg Market **13**
Black Swan Bar **1**
Chase **18**
FM's **10**
Jazz Café **6**
Jimmyz **17**
Legends **5**
Pacific Bar **8**
Tuxedo Princess **21**

CULTURE ZOO ●
Life Interactive World **3**
Tellywest Arena **1**
Theatre Royal **12**
Tyne Theatre
 and Opera House **2**

EATS ◆
Courtlands **9**
Courtney's Restaurant **15**
Julius Caesar **16**
One-Eyed Jacks **11**
Sachin's **7**
Studio Bistro **14**

CRASHING ■
Thistle Hotel **4**
University
 of Northumberland **20**
YHA **19**

pockets, slumming and trying to pose as rich hipsters in bars like Chase in the **Quayside** neighborhood. But you'll also meet friendly working-class regulars there who seem mystified—and totally unimpressed—by it all. They are much more concerned with downing as much of the famous Newcastle brown ale as humanly possible before the traditional pub closing time of 11pm. And they'll probably duck out and hit the much more hair-down spots like Jazz Cafe before too long. There are a few hot, mainstream clubs in town, too, but be prepared to wait in line at those. Newcastle is big enough to provide choices, but not so large that it's impersonal.

In fact, the whole town is a haven for anything the staid British would ordinarily consider different, new, creative, or peculiar. Shops exhibit buttons arranged to represent the solar system [see *only here,* below]; street performers and fortune-telling Irish gypsies are a common sight; unusual characters you might tactfully label "local color" congregate around the **Monument** [see *hanging out,* below] or any street surrounding **Eldon Square** [see *stuff,* below].

neighborhoods

Newcastle is conveniently compact, so it's easy to walk between virtually every point within the inner city but be prepared for some heavy breathing as you hoof it up and down its many hills. Two of the most prominent, monument-lined boulevards are the north-south running **Grey** and **Grainger streets,** both lined with Georgian-style homes of former millionaires. Both streets originate at Eldon Square, a plaza lined with shops that forms the northern edge of Newcastle's city center. The square is presided over by a monument to Earl Grey (known simply as

only here

Twisted narrow hallways lead through various glass-encased exhibits and antique shops full of wonderfully wacky junk at **The People's Museum of Memorabilia and Newcastle Antique Center** *(42-44 Grainger Street; Tel 0191/221-15-34; 10am-6pm daily),* an eclectic collector's dream. The musty smell hits you as soon as you walk through the door. The highlight, the grand finale occurs with the discovery of the Button Solar System. Many years in the making, a million buttons from shirts, shoes, and you-name-it were color-coded and displayed in the chronological order of their birth, and arranged into a kind of celestial display to commemorate the passing of culture and fashion through the ages.

"The Monument"), a local industrialist and politico who was such a big deal they not only built this statue, they named a tea after him. Branching off to the north from the Monument is **Northumberland Street,** another toney shopping boulevard.

The River Tyne forms the southern edge of Newcastle's commercial core and is traversed by a half-dozen really cool bridges. One of them, the **Tyne Bridge,** marks the southern edge of the ritzy, revitalized Quayside district (walkable from Eldon Square but also reachable on city bus lines 34, 35, and 35B if you're coming from farther away). This is also where you'll find the old steps that lead up to the **"New Castle"** (which the city is named after) from **"the Close,"** an avenue running parallel to the Tyne's right bank. The views from this medieval Norman fortress are well worth the climb.

hanging out

Almost everywhere's a hangout in Newcastle, but when the weather's decent people tend to rush to **Leazes Park** (just west of Eldon Square), where you'll find everyone from local students pretending to study to Eurohippies and young moms pushing prams. When the weather is more inclement, as it usually is, these same folks head to the Eldon Square Shopping Center, known to locals as **Monument Mall** [see *to market,* below], which adjoins Eldon Square. A good late-night hangout is **Jazz Cafe** [see *live music scene,* below]; a great place to meet fellow travelers and locals alike is on the ever-partying **Bigg Market street** [see *bar scene,* below] or any of the bars therein. Bigg Market, a north-south street two blocks south of Eldon Square, is often overrun by a major mass of revelers.

bar scene

One of the best things about the bars in Newcastle is that no matter where you go—from trendy clubs to neighborhood pubs—you'll always find really good beer. Many of the best brews in Britain are made right here in the Tyne Brewery. The most obvious—Newcastle Brown Ale ("broon")— is nicknamed "the one and only" by loyal fans, but the same company also brews several other prizewinning lagers, ales, and stouts, including Beamish Irish Stout, McEwan's Scotch Ale, Old Peculier, McEwan's India Pale Ale, and John Courage (the official ration of the British navy). Beer is such a part of everyday life in Newcastle that an evening trip to a bar or a pub is practically mandatory; the phrase, "I'm going to walk the dog," is commonly understood to mean, "I'm off to the pub for a broon."

Bars with all the designer trimmings, including dress codes and long queues, are scattered all over the Quayside area and also along Haymarket Street, but the bouncers are a bit nicer at the latter—and the drinks are cheaper. Wherever you end up, you'll be in bed early since almost every bar in town closes long before midnight (11am-11pm Mon-Sat, noon-10:30pm Sun).

Quayside is dominated by refurbished buildings, glass exteriors, and '70s retro decor. The new—and packed—**Chase** (*13-15 Sandhill; Tel 0191/245-00-55; Noon-11pm daily; drinks £2, cocktail pitchers £7.50)* is a prime example. It hosts £1 happy hours all week till 8pm, but be prepared to dress in your slickest nightclub camo (tight black for girls, *ironed* designer shirts for guys) and stand judged by the fashion-unconscious bouncers. This is not the place to meet students, but the DJs are admittedly smokin'.

Just up the road on the waterfront (or "quayside" in Newcastle-ese) is **Jimmyz** *(48-52 Sandhill; Tel 0191/230-01-11; 5-11pm Mon-Sat; £1.90 drinks all night on Mondays),* inside the Waterside Hotel. The eclectic interior is mostly neon-free, going instead for the jungle-fever-meets-art-deco look—spears and shields mixed in with sleek, curvy sofas. It's a perfect backdrop for a James Bond–style martini, and you'll get them mixed just right here, to a world music beat played by some of the top DJs in the UK. (During the day, you'll have to settle for the jukebox, but it's got great picks.) The dress code is a little less strict than Chase's, but you still have to style it a bit to get in. (Guys, you did pack a jacket, right? OK, well, at least make sure those shoes are leather—and buffed.)

Two blocks northwest, on **Bigg Market,** you can leave the whole jacket-and-jungle-theme bit behind on a street that feels more like the Big Easy than the British Empire. Live music is everywhere—indoors and out—and the only major difference between the bars and the street is the increased tendency for punters to start a fight when they're out in the fresh air. The area's also famous for its barely clothed young women (hey, maybe *that's* what they're fighting over!) Take your pick of the bars, no one is better than the others.

One block east of Bigg Market is **FM's** *(118 Greystreet; Tel 0191/261-55-87; Mon-Sat 5pm-11pm; pub grub £2.25-4.75, drinks £1.70).* You have to hike up three flights of stairs to get here, but it's worth the climb if you're looking for the quintessential modern English pub, complete with dartboards, loads of wood trim, and posters of '60s rock stars on the walls. The crowd is friendly and talkative, but if you want some privacy for you and your group, try to score one of the large booths. If not, just settle into a conversation with the locals and take in the great third-story view.

Another block east and three more north, near the Haymarket metro station, the **Pacific Bar** *(Northumberland St; Tel 0191/245-04-40; 5pm-11pm daily, food until 10pm; £5.95-11.95 per entrée, drinks £2.50)* is easily spotted even after a few pints. Twisted, colored-metal statues cascade down its facade and the stainless steel interior is splashed with rainbows of color, all part of the makeover that has revived this former shrine to the '80s disco generation. But don't be intimidated: All the ultra-trendies now hang out along the quayside, so Pacific Bar is just unfashionable enough to make it relaxed and easily obtainable—and packed with students. The tunes are mostly FM-rock CDs cranked up real loud. Save a few quid and stick to beer here—that's what everyone else does.

LIVE MUSIC SCENE

Newcastle has its share of venues where you can tap right into the local music pulse. Jazz, funk, and salsa are far more dominant than electronic masterpieces; the musical message in this town seems to be "kick back." Jazz Cafe and Black Swan Bar are our favorite spots to soak in the Newcastle musical spirit.

Though it's not as pervasive (or as annoying) as the swing dance craze in the states, Salsa has hit it big around here. The **Salsa Club** *(91-93 Westgate Road; Tel 0191/221-10-22, 0191/241-11-41; 6pm-11pm daily; cover £3),* a block north of the main train station, offers lessons and irresistibly erotic Latin-flavored dance most nights of the week to a hip mixed crowd.

Don't miss the main venue for local artists, the **Black Swan Bar** *(Westgate Road; Tel 0191/232-24-10; 8pm-1am Thurs-Sat; £4 cover),* a block north of the main train station. It's definitely where to find up-and-coming talent. The *Saturday Salsa Night* is always a sweaty feast of shaking bodies. Local funk bands dominate the other nights. Wear black jeans or tight, colorful polyester and you'll fit right in. It's a festive, unpretentious crowd of students mixing it up with more monied folk, and they're all as friendly as it gets. The Swan opens up into the Newcastle Arts Center Courtyard, where you can easily catch a breath of fresh air between sets. The Swan also holds a small theater on its lower lever (aptly named the Basement Theater) which hosts small and unusual productions.

Jazz Cafe *(Pink Lane; Tel 0191/232-65-05; 8pm-1am Thurs-Sat; cover £3 before 8:30pm, £4 after),* just across from the station up a hidden alley, hosts nights of highly danceable jazz, Spanish style. This dark, smoky, little hole-in-the-wall feels like what New York's jazz scene must have felt like in the '50s. With a strong salsa beat Thursday through Saturday, you'll soon work up a hunger for the burger and fries included with the cover charge. And if you have one of those magic "I'm a poor student" cards (any student ID will do) the cover is dropped. Hey, free meal! Come around 11pm when it starts to heat up—Jazz Cafe has that rare license to serve booze late—and if you're a jazz lover you'll very quickly make mellow pals.

Just south of Quayside, **The Cooperage** *(32 The Close; Tel 0191/233-29-40; 11:30am-11:30pm Mon-Sat; No cover)* books live rock bands that pack huge crowds of young partiers into its three-level bar and club. The upper two levels—which feature a dance floor, lounge, and a couple bars—are called Club Xcalibur. The serious pubbers hang out on the ground floor where pints are only £1.50, and only venture upstairs, where pints are £3.50, later in the night when the dancing really heats up. All of it's jammed into a Quayside building from the sixteenth century, so atmosphere is in no short supply.

On the other end of the size spectrum from the Cooperage is the tiny **Planet Earth** *(Low Friar House, Low Friar Street; Tel 0191/230-21-86; 7pm-1am Mon-Sat; £8 cover)* the most popular dance club in town. This little hole just a block south of Eldon Square has a trio of bars surrounding a tightly packed dance floor where students and working stiffs alike blow off steam. With retro decor, the place seems trapped back in the '60s with John, Paul, George, and Ringo. The '70s nights are a blast, and Afro wigs (at least we hope they're wigs) are a hugely popular accessory.

Anchored on the south side of the river below the Tyne Bridge, **Tuxedo Princess** *(Quayside, Gateshead; Tel 0191/477-88-99; Mon, Wed-Sat 7pm-2am; beer from £2.80)* is the most bizarre place in town to go for dancing. It's a spacious two-floor club housed in a boat that floats on the Tyne. When dancers do their thing, the boat actually rocks—an ultra-dizzying experience when you're tanked up. It's *the* place to dance for the local 18-to-26-year-old crowd, who shake their groove things to the same music their parents danced to when they were dating. During the week, it serves food, which is decent and relatively cheap (£2-10 for a meal). Catch decent live jazz on Fridays and Saturdays.

club scene

For the complete dope on the club and live music scene—as well as the latest Newcastle styles and fads—take a look at *The Crack,* a hip local magazine you can pick up for free at stores, cafes, clubs, pubs, and just about every street corner in town. (They also have a great web site at *www.the-crack.co.uk*).

Serving the strongest Euro-style beers in Newcastle, **Hancock** *(2a Hancock Street; Tel 0191/281-56-53; 11am-11pm Mon-Sat; noon-10:30pm Sun; beer £2-£2.45)* attracts a young college crowd of various sexual persuasions. Good and reasonably priced traditional English food is served until 7pm. A standard rock jukebox entertains during the week but on Friday and Saturday nights the upstairs dance floor opens with a hot house DJ.

The best DJs in town can be found at **Head of Steam** *(2 Neville Street; Tel 0191/232-43-79; noon-11pm Mon-Sat, noon-10:30pm Sun; beer £1.50; No credit cards).* They're called "Rude and Reckless" and these guys play everything from northern soul (the local term for '60s schlock) to trip-hop, hip-hop, soul, jazz, funk, and reggae. There are three good local ales on tap—try the *Black Sheep.* Or, if you're in the mood for a cocktail, try a martini made with Chopin vodka; the vodka became a

boy meets girl

Looking for love, at least for the night? Guys, you'll find any number of scantily clad women along Bigg Market—though they may not quite be the kind you'd bring home to meet Mom. Still, there are nice members of both sexes to be met (not *too nice,* of course) at just about any of the big dance clubs. A proven, if blatantly superficial, method is to show up for a Latin dance lesson at Salsa Club and manage to get yourself paired off with someone interesting-looking who's also looking to "pick up" a few steps.

local legend after Roger Daltrey stopped in here and ordered it—no other pub in town stocks it. There's no food served here during the week, but as any Newcastle student will tell you, Head of Steam is *the* place to go for a cheap Sunday brunch (£2-5) of roast beef, chicken, pork, and the traditional Yorkshire pudding.

The indie scene is big in Newcastle, both on stage and on screen. You can catch more traditional stuff—Shakespeare, ballet, opera—for a little less money than in London, but it's the underground, avant-garde work that's really worth checking out.

arts scene

▶▶VISUAL ARTS

To see what local artists are up to, visit **Brown's Gallery** *(15 Acorn Rd, Jesmond; Tel 0191/281-13-15; 9am-5:30pm Mon-Sat),* in the nearby suburb of Jesmond, easily reachable via Metro. There's a wide range of oils, watercolors, and acrylics by an equally wide range of local artists.

Unless you're traveling on a major trust fund, you can't afford to buy anything from the **Corrymella Scott Gallery** *(5 Tankerville Terrace, Jesmond; Tel 0191/281-13-15)*—but looking's free! This exclusive gallery sometimes closes between exhibitions, so call to see if the doors are open. It's worth checking—this gallery showcases some of the most cutting-edge art in the northeast.

▶▶PERFORMING ARTS

Many of these theaters provide a night-out-in-a-box: a performance on one level and full restaurant (with decent-not-spectacular chow) on another. Most are conveniently concentrated right around the city center.

A great place to catch boundary-breaking, chewing-up-the-furniture performances is at the **Live Theater** *(27 Broad Chare; Tel 0191/232-12-32; 10am-6pm daily; average ticket £8; V, MC),* in a converted warehouse. It's the venue for *Rock 'n' Doris,* a monthly lesbian and gay comedy night (last Saturday of every month) that is one of the most popular—and hilarious—shows in town. Book early if possible, it usually sells out. It's a chic restaurant, Cafe Live, serves food that's pricey but not half bad.

A five-minute walk north of Eldon Square, **Newcastle Playhouse** *(Barras Bridge; Tel 0191/230-51-51; box office 10am-8pm, Mon-Sat; average ticket £6-£15, prices may vary depending on performance; V, MC)* is home to Northern Stage, a nationally known company that showcases brilliant contemporary theater. It also has a rep for attracting avant-garde touring international shows. *The Crack* calls it "an almost neo-brutalist building which shows a diverse range of productions from contemporary dance to very ambitious plays."

Leading right off Eldon Square, **Theatre Royal** *(Grey Street; Tel 0191/232-20-61; box office 10am-8pm Mon-Sat; tickets £7-£45; V, MC, AE)* features annual visits from the Royal Shakespeare Company and Opera North, both of which sell out months in advance. But when the RSC is playing at the Royal, they also perform pieces at various small venues around Newcastle, so keep tabs through *The Crack* [see *club scene,* above] and you might be able to catch England's top Shakespearean actors in a rare intimate performance. Aside from the visiting companies, the Royal features mostly mainstream musicals, many of which are on the road from London. The place is also the epitome of Victorian splendor so it's something to dress for.

The other grand old dame is the **Newcastle Opera House** *(Westgate Road; Tel 0191/232-20-61; box office 10am-8pm Mon-Sat; tickets £7.50-£18.50; V, MC).* It's five minutes south of Eldon Square, home to the renowned English Shakespeare Company, and, like Theater Royal attracts London's West End musicals and comedy stints. But the best thing about the Tyne is the building itself: It's an incredible example of prim Victorian architecture, and the crew still uses the *original* stage machinery.

Newcastle is strong on underground, indie cinema as well. For that screening of *My Life As a Dog* you keep missing, head to the **Tyneside Cinema** *(10 Pilgrim Street; Tel 0191/261-92-91; times and tickets prices vary),* five minutes southwest of Eldon Square. This is yet another building chock full o' Victorian splendor.

gay scene

You might not realize it at first—there's no organized scene to speak of, no special grapevine magazines—but Newcastle actually is the gay heart of Northeast England. Basically you find the scene through a small network of pubs and bars where the clientele is mostly gay men, with a small lesbian crowd as well. There are only about five of these bars, so don't expect a "gay village" unless you want to go as far as Manchester.

Meanwhile, you can have a gay old time in Newcastle's top queer nightlife pub, **The Powerhouse** *(21-33 George Street; Tel 0191/272-36-21; 10pm-2am daily; cover £4-8).* Located just behind the casino, near Rockies Bridge, this place is a nerve center for Newcastle gay life. Powerhouse offers serious male-to-male dancing on two floors, plus a chill-out room downstairs where you can become better acquainted with your trophy boy for the night.

One of the most enduring gay bars in town, **The Yard/Heavens Above** *(2 Scotswood Road; Tel 0191/232-20-37; 1-11pm Sun-Wed; noon-midnight Thur-Sat; No cover charge),* attracts all ages and every profession from doctor to dockworker. It's large, with a busy bar area and a dance floor that pulsates on weekends. For an escape from the frenzy, head up one flight to a cubbyhole bar, with a ceiling fresco, no less.

When you tire of the scene here, you can walk to nearby **Rockies** *(78 Scotswood Road; Tel 0191/232-65-36; 7:30-11pm Sun-Thur, 7:30-1am Fri-Sat; No cover charge),* opposite Redheugh Bridge, just west of the town center. A twentysomething crowd—that sometimes stretches into the early thirties—packs this disco, especially on weekends. On Sunday nights, you can occasionally catch a male stripper flashing "the Full

Monty." The decor is battered and the action sprawls across two floors. Rockies has a rep for a particularly horny crowd.

Outside the cruisy world of bars, there's one gay social group known as the kinder, gentler way to meet local gay men in Newcastle— **MESMAC**, or **Men Who Have Sex with Men: Action in the Community** *(11 Nelson Street; Tel 0191/233-13-33 www.mesmacnorth east.com)*. You have to be in town on a Wednesday night to go to one of their meetings, held on the third floor of an otherwise innocuous building, but you can visit their comprehensive web site 24 hours a day; check out "Scene" for listings of almost two dozen gay bars, clubs, saunas, and guest houses in Newcastle alone. If you stop by their headquarters, they'll give you copies of all the free gay papers.

CULTUre ZOO

Newcastle's ancient history scene isn't the only game in town: From the medieval ramparts of the Castle Keep and Cathedral to the DNA break-throughs on display at the high-tech Center for Life, this city has it covered. There's also serious symphonic action at the new Tellywest Arena, and you can contemplate the meaning of all this history strolling in the courtyard at Blackfriars, as good a time capsule as you'll find in any town in England.

Blackfriars *(10am-5pm Mon-Sat; free):* Just two blocks southeast of Eldon Square, this is a thirteenth-century Dominican monastery, meticulously restored, with medieval crafts like ironmongery being practiced. It makes a great place to chill and soak in the ancient vibes of Newcastle.

Castle Keep *(St. Nicholas Street; 9:30am-5:30pm Tues-Sun April-*

fESTIVALS

A celebration of the scarcely dressed crowd, the **Bigg Festival** *(July, Tel 0191/261-90-00; www.newcastle-online.co.uk)* takes over the road from which it gets its name, Bigg Market, and the neighboring streets for one weekend every summer. The whole thing's basically an extension of the bars (plus music, food from stalls, and dancing in the streets). Thoroughly fun and out of control, it's like a small-scale Mardi Gras.

Looking for a gathering with a more meaningful message than "Party Naked!"? The **Newcastle Community Green Festival** *(Tel 0191/273-65-99; www.newcastle-online.co.uk),* brings 15,000 people together in Leazes Park to celebrate preserving the environment. You'd think that that many people in a small park might damage the greenery, but apparently they're all well-behaved as they gorge themselves on veggie burgers and listen to folky bands.

Sept, 9:30am-4pm Tues-Sun Oct-March; £1.50): The "New Castle" that give this town its name is well-pedigreed. Built in 1080 by Robert Curthose, the son of William the Conqueror, it's a maze of soaring stone, but the keep (the inner tower and strongest part) is the only surviving piece of the original. Views of the city and countryside from the rooftop are stunners.

Saint Nicholas Cathedral *(St. Nicholas Street; 7am-6pm Mon-Fri, 8am-4pm Sat, 9am-noon/4-7pm Sun; free):* The tower's the thing here, with an incredible, arched, sky-high perch on which to take in your sur-roundings, as folks have since 1470.

Tellywest Arena *(Arena Way; Box Office Tel 0191/401-80-00, Info Tel 0191/260-50-00; V, MC):* This brand-spanking-new arena attracts mostly popular music, but it was built with the acoustics to handle a clas-sical concert as well. Yet with a 10,000-person capacity, it draws the biggest names in all genres. If Madonna comes to town, you'll find her here.

Center for Life *(Times Square, Scotswood Road; Tel 0191/234-82-00; 10am-5pm daily; admission £6.95 adult, £5.50 student):* This combi-nation interactive museum and biotechnology research complex, connected to the University of Northumbria, is a 10-minute walk south of Eldon Square. It's well worth a visit if you're even vaguely scientifically curious. Its clever displays actually make genetics fascinating and there are some cool hands-on games to keep visiting kindergarten classes—and your inner kid—amused.

modification

Tattoos are only too common among the residents of industrialized England—and not always the new-agey Celtic kind, we mean the anchors-and-Mom kind too. One local artist who can do either for you is Eric of **Eric's Tattoo Studios** *(239 Westgate Road; Tel 0191/232-01-05; 10am-7pm Mon-Sat; prices vary greatly; No credit cards),* who's so good he's appeared on local radio programs. But call before you show up—he's often booked solid.

city sports

It's not terribly exerting, but a Tyne cruise on a shallow-drafted barge does provide a great shot at the outdoors. **Leisure Line Cruises** *(Quay-side; Tel 0191/296-67-40; 9am-5pm Mon-Fri; prices negotiable)* launches one several times a day between June and mid-September that carries vis-itors from the Quayside piers to the mouth of the Tyne.

Swimming is possible, though the pool is none too big or modern, at **Newcastle City Pool** *(Tel 0191/232-19-81; 7:30am -7pm daily; admis-sion £2.30).*

Cycling options are great around Newcastle, even though the city itself is congested and hilly. Specially designated bike paths run along both banks of the Tyne, extending east and west from Newcastle. **Keelman's Way,** stretching along the south bank of the Tyne headed inland from the sea, offers the nicest visuals. For bike rentals you'll have to schlep out to Whickham Thorns Centre in the suburb of Dunston [see *need to know,* below].

great outdoors

To hike or bike around this area, you have to know as much about the trains as the trails. Newcastle is the gateway for the **North Pennines,** a much-eroded, sparsely populated mountain range with rugged uncrowded trails that are accessible primarily by local trains. They're located about 25 miles southwest of Newcastle. The Newcastle Tourist Information Office (see *need to know*) will give you a free leaflet, "Newcastle's Train Trails," which describes the best hiking trips—which vary from 3-hour day trips to treacherous 70-mile treks—and tells you when and where to get on and off the local trains that services the region around Newcastle. You can also contact the **Alston Moor Information Center** *(Tel/fax 01434/382-244; alston.tic@eden.gov.uk);* it's located in the town hall of Alston, a little town on the local train line that makes a great base for Pennine hikes.

stuff

For generic shopping, the horrifically large Eldon Square Shopping Center will make mall rats feel right at home while the Blackfriars crafts market may make you O.D. on olde tyme iron stuff in about 5 minutes [see *culture zoo,* above]. To get anything worth lugging around in your backpack, you have to check out the local shops around town.

▶▶**TUNES**

The town's biggest source of CDs and LPs, both new and used, is **Steel Wheels** *(60-68 Pilgrim Street; Tel 0191/261-66-71; 10am-6pm Mon-Sat, noon-6pm Sun),* where you'll probably find that copy of your brother's ancient Who album that your mom threw out.

to market

For fruit, veggies, and odd-smelling meat, head to the **Grainger Market,** an open bazaar that operates every day off this main thoroughfare just south of the city center. An old-world Victorian style marketplace—but fully covered so no worries about rain—it's full of stalls and vendors hawking everything edible you can possibly imagine—and lots of characters.

▶▶USED AND BRUISED

For secondhand ensembles that reflect everything from classic '60s to glam '20s, hit **Attica** *(High Bridge; Tel 0191/261-40-62; 10am-6pm Mon-Sat, noon-6pm Sun)*. For a funkier look, with emphasis on battered leather bomber jackets in tons of sizes, head to **Period Clothing Warehouse** *(40 Grainger Street; Tel 0191/232-55-14; 10am-6pm Mon-Sat, noon-6pm Sun)*. And for a sometimes depressing but endlessly fascinating look at the bargains to be had from other people's hardships, consider **Albemarle & Bond Pawnbrokers, Ltd** *(138 West Rd; Tel 0191/273-23-48; 10am-6pm Mon-Sat)*. You can often pick up a treasure here for just a few quid.

▶▶FOOT FETISH

Cutting-edge clubbing shoes line the walls at **Schuh** *(5/7 Sidegate Mall and Eldon Square; Tel 0191/232-87-91; 9am-5:30pm Mon-Wed, Fri; 9am-8pm Thurs, 9am-6pm Sat, 11am-5pm Sun)*. It has loads of styles in its own trendy Schuh "Clothing to Feet" brand, as well as Doc Martens, Kickers, Vans, and Bronx. **Scorpio Shoes** *(6/12 Low Friar Street, or Grainger Market; Tel 0191/232-75-48 or 0191/232-08-82)* also carries their own brand of cool—and inexpensive—shoes, as well as thigh-high boots and popular brands of club and street shoes. Their Grainger Market shop is more of a Doc Martens trip.

EATS

At least in this town every restaurant you walk into doesn't respond to your order with "you wanted that fried, right?" They actually cater to people who crave fresh flavor. You'll happen upon everything from late-night Indian to Spanish pirate food.

▶▶CHEAP

Built in the region's biggest retail behemoth, right on the city's main square, **Courtland's** *(2nd floor Eldon Square Shopping Centre, Northumberland Street; Tel 0191/233-07-38; 8am-7pm Mon-Sat; £2.50-£5 per entrée; MC)* is the everything restaurant, serving Chinese, pizzas, baked potatoes, fish & chips, or American diner food (or pretty close to it)—all of it fast. All of it's done fairly well, despite being mall food, but don't go expecting atmosphere. As for the clientele, it's anybody on the move in the heart of Newcastle.

At **Julius Caesar** *(6 Leazes Park Road; Tel 0191/222-06-59; 11am-late daily; £2.95-6 per entrée; MC)*, a block northeast of Eldon Square, the menu is varied in and of itself, but the option to create your own meal creates some intriguing options. If you *really* want Marinara sauce on your salad, this is the place. Special orders are encouraged, subject only to the availability of ingredients. They also host a happy hour (5pm-7pm, all night for students) where any pasta dish plus a pizza is only £2.95 (bring an ID, however spurious). Leave it to the Italians to stuff you silly.

Slightly more rustic, with lots of old wood trim, **One-Eyed Jack's** *(56 Pilgrim Street; Tel 0191/222-01-30; noon-1:45pm/5:30pm-11pm Tues-Thurs, until 1am Fri and Sat; under £5)*, just off Eldon Square, is more than simply a restaurant—it's a Spanish pirate experience. With a goofy nautical theme, and decent seafood offerings, the bar area is packed every weekend night with pre-bar hoppers starting things off with a few margaritas. It gets extremely busy in here on Friday and Saturday nights, but the wait at the bar is just as enjoyable as the meal itself. Don't pass up the nachos.

▶▶DO-ABLE

Worlds apart from England's many generic curry chains, **Sachin's** *(Forth Banks; Tel 0191/261-90-35; Noon-2:15pm/6pm-11:15pm Mon-Sat; £5.50-8 per entrée)*, five minutes upstream of Quayside, has developed innovative dishes that don't knock you over with too-strong spice. Focusing on gourmet Indian specialties from the Punjab, and with an elegant setting, this is the place to come for a serious lesson in Far East cuisine. One of the best is *murg makhani,* diced chicken marinated in Punjabi spices, barbecued, tossed in butter, and cooked with tomatoes.

Spanish wins again at **Cafe Sol** *(Pink Lane; Tel 0191/221-01-22; noon-2pm/6-10pm Mon-Fri, 6-10:30pm Sat; £5-10 dinner; MC)*, where the bullfight posters and cheap tapas (go for the delish ripe olives and crawfish) set the stage for Flamenco dance nights.

▶▶SPLURGE

Courtney's Restaurant *(5-7 The Side; Tel 0191/232-55-37; noon-2pm/6-10pm Mon-Fri, 6-10:30pm Sat; £5.25-27.50 two course dinner; MC)* is High Class with a capital H. Recently refurbished, the interior is decked out in Edwardian antiques from top to bottom, providing the perfect atmosphere for a grand feast. French fare, from potato and leek soup to roast duckling, makes you feel like an eighteenth-century duke.

Housed in a remodeled bank, **Studio Bistro** *(Milburn House, The Side; Tel 0191/233-11-22; Noon-10pm Mon-Sat, happy hour 6-7:30pm Mon-Fri; £5-13.50 per entrée, £4.95 two-course happy hour special; V, MC)* is swanky and smooth. The ancient wood accents and Mediterranean-style decor, along with the soft lighting, makes the great steak or grilled sea bass even better. Classy live jazz is played weekend nights.

crashing

Cheap pickins are slim in Newcastle. Unless sleeping in doorways is an option, heading outside of the town center (which, considering the size of this place, is never very far) will be your best bet—a lot of folks choose to stay in nearby Jesmond. Book reservations at the tourist information center [see *need to know,* below].

▶▶CHEAP

The **YHA** *(107 Jesmond Rd; Tel 0191/281-25-70; £11 per person, shared bath; No credit cards)* is located just outside town in Jesmond, easily reachable via Metro. It's in what used to be an old hotel, but it looks just as institutional as any other YHA. There is lockout from 10am-5pm, but no curfew, so you can stagger in at any hour you like. This is the best bang for your buck, especially if all you want is a bed. In July and August, YHA overflow is accommodated at the **Guerney House** *(7 Windsor Terrace; No phone; £15.50 per person, shared bath; No credit cards)*, right next to the main library of the University of Northumbria.

The **North East YWCA** *(Jesmond House, Clayton Rd; Tel 0191/281-12-33; £16 per person, shared bath; No credit cards)* is out in Jesmond too and about the same as the YHA, only with fewer backpackers. You can actually walk to downtown Newcastle in 15 minutes if you don't want to wait for the bus.

▶▶DO-ABLE

Those who want to relive the glory days of dorm life—or are still in the midst of them and don't know any better—can take advantage of the housing available at the **University of Northumbria** *(Ellison Terrace; Tel 0191/227-40-24; £18.75 per person, shared bath; No credit cards)*. But note that it's only available June-September—and always crawling with students, so begin the party here.

Otherwise, there's **Brighton Guest House** *(47-51 Brighton Grove; Tel 0191/273-36-00; Bus 10 or 11; £16-22 single, £32-44 double, some rooms with private bath; No credit cards)*, a mile west of the city center, a comfortable family kind of place with breakfast thrown in.

The **George Hotel** *(88 Osborne Rd; Tel 0191/281-44-42; £23-25 per person, private bath; AE, MC, V)* is a slight step up, but is basically one of those interchangeable little hotels out in Jesmond.

Also out in Jesmond, the **Portland Guest House** *(134 Sandyford Rd; Tel 0191/232-78-68; £10-30 single, £36-40 double, some rooms with private bath; No credit cards)* is another cozy little family-run spot that will serve you a hearty breakfast in the morning.

The **Westland Hotel** *(27 Osborne Ave; Tel 0191/281-04-12; £22-30 single, £40-49 double, some rooms with private bath; AE, MC, V)* is not the Ritz, but the standard-issue rooms are comfortable enough and the service is friendly. It's (you guessed it!) out in Jesmond.

▶▶SPLURGE

A nineteenth-century hotel restored to its former glory, the **Thistle Hotel** *(Neville Street; Tel 0191/232-24-71; £40 single, £80 double, private bath; MC, AE)*, on the same street as the main train station, is nothing less than extravagant. With gold-leaf ceilings and detailed carving throughout, you'll feel like visiting nobility.

need to know

Currency Exchange An easy place to exchange currency for no commission is **Marks & Spencer** *(77-87 Northumberland Street; Tel 0191/232-13-68; 9am-5:30pm Mon-Wed, 9am-8pm Thur, 9am-6pm Fri, 8am-6pm Sat, 11am-5pm Sun)*.

Tourist Information If you need help finding—or reserving—a room, definitely stop by the **Tourist Information Offices** *(132 Grainger Street; Tel 0191/277-80-00; 9:30am-5:30pm Mon-Sat, 9:30am-7:30 Thur, 10am-4pm Sun)* and *(Central Rail Station; Tel 0191/277-80-00;*

10am-8pm Mon-Fri; 9am-5pm Sat). The staff is tremendously helpful, and can give you all sorts of other information as well, including help with bike routes, local maps, etc.

Public Transportation Generally, you should skip the city buses and walk, or use the cheap and handy **Metro** *(Main station Eldon Square; Tel 0191/232-53-25; 5:30am-11:30pm),* especially if you need to get to the outskirts of the city, such as the YHA or galleries in Jesmond. Metro links to the airport and to the coast leave at least every seven minutes. You can pick up a schedule at any metro stop or at the tourist office. **Nexus** *(Tel 0191/203-33-33)* is the local inner-city bus company. Travel shops have detailed schedules, or you can pick one up at **Monument Haymarket Central Station.**

American Express Get those personal checks cashed at **AmEx** *(51 Grey Street; Tel 0191/244-50-45, 8:30am-6pm Mon-Fri).*

Health & Emergency The local hospital is **Newcastle General** *(Westgate Road; Tel 0191/273-88-11),* three blocks south of Eldon Square.

The main **police station** *(Market Street; Tel 0191/214-65-55)* is a block southeast of Eldon Square.

Pharmacies A good local pharmacy is **Boots the Chemist** *(Hotspur Way, Eldon Square; Tel 0191/232-98-44; 8:30am-5:30pm Mon-Sat, until 8pm Thur, 11am-5pm Sun).*

Airports Woolsington Airport *(Tel 0191/286-09-66)* is just a half-hour metro ride from the center of Newcastle.

Trains Central Station *(Neville Street; Tel 0345/484-950)* is a five-minute walk south of the city center. Trains run to nearly every major city in Scotland and England. Trains to Manchester, the closest major city in England, leave roughly every hour and there is an express train to London.

Bus Lines Out of the City Because of England's confusing bus system (or lack thereof) there are three separate private bus companies, often running the same routes, at three stations: **Gallowgate Coach Station** *(Gallowgate; Tel 0191/212-30-00),* a five-minute walk west of the city center; **Haymarket Bus Station** *(Haymarket; Tel 0191/212-30-00),*

wired

With one of the most comprehensive small-city websites on the Internet, ***www.tyne-online.com,*** Newcastle is definitely on top of the technological wave. A friendly little downtown hangout, **Internet Exchange** *(26 Market St.; Tel 0191/230-12-80; 9am-9pm Mon-Sat 11am-5pm Sun; membership £3, then 3-7p per hour, lower rates for mornings)* is the place to get online.

five minutes north of the center; or the **Eldon Square Station** *(Eldon Square; Tel 0870/608-26-08)*. This last is the only one with a direct daily line to Carlisle (a two-and-a-half-hour trip). Fortunately, info on all bus companies' schedules and routes is available at the tourist info center (above) and at one general number: *0870/608-26-08*.

Boats For ferries to and from Scandinavia, call the **Fjord Line** *(Tel 0191/296-13-13; www.fjordline.com)* or **DFDS Ferries** *(Tel 08705/333-000; www.dfdsseaways.co.uk)*.

Bike Rental The **Whickham Thorns Centre** *(Dunston; Tel 0191/460-11-93; 11am-10pm Mon-Fri, 11am-6:30pm Sat, noon-3pm Sun; £3.20 per hour, £17 per day)* has a good choice of mountain bikes, though it's a half-hour out of the Newcastle center via city bus N43 and N40.

Laundry Big Lamp Laundry *(13 Elswick Road; Tel 0191/272-44-65; 7am-7pm daily; £1 wash, 50p dry)* is the place to pretty up your duds before the clubs.

Postal The main **Post Office** *(St Mary's Place; Tel 0345/223-344; 9am-5pm Mon-Sat)* is a five-minute walk north of Eldon Square.

Internet See *wired*, above.

everywhere else

carlisle

Carlisle's not party central, but there is a decent vibe, thanks to a healthy student population at the University of Northumbria Carlisle campus and the Cumbria College of Art & Design. With fairly good cheap sleep options, a long and colorful history, and a nightlife flavored by artists and students of the arts, Carlisle makes a perfect base for exploring the area, including Hadrian's Wall [see **Hadrian's Wall,** below], the Roman Empire's ancient and massive attempt to defend itself from Scottish hordes.

Fought over for most of the previous millennium, the little hamlet of Carlisle is a battle-scarred testament to the hazards of life on the English frontier. Less than 10 miles south of the Scottish border (at least for now), Carlisle has been torn apart and rebuilt a dozen times as England's boundaries shifted. The narrow, cobbled lanes in the shadow of the mighty **Carlisle Castle** [see *culture zoo,* below] give you the feeling an ancient territory skirmish could flare right up again any minute.

Standing in the lowlands of the **Solway Firth estuary,** the landscape surrounding Carlisle is flat, windy and evergreen, which makes the place even more romantic. But in the sixteenth century, noble families on both sides took advantage of the political instability to plunder lands and property, stooping to murder, kidnapping, and arson. Reiving, as it became known, was common, and the words "blackmail" and "bereaved" were coined right here.

Residents these days here aren't noticeably warlike. Fortunately, the most heated it gets is a good debate at the Boardroom [see *bar scene,* below]. Young people in town regularly gather there for extremely opinionated conversation. To fill your stomach, rather than your head, the lighter conversation and fried food at Fat Fingers [see *eats,* below] should do the trick. There are some trendy places here, too, although the general mindset is a little too intellectual for such passing fancies. But even eggheads love cafe style, and you'll find it at C-A-1 [see *eats,* below]—too hip for anything more than an acronym.

The local tourist office [see *need to know,* below] publishes ***What's On in Carlisle,*** a free monthly that's the best source on what's happening. You can find it at hotels and pubs all over town.

neighborhoods

Carlisle's main thoroughfare is a north-south-running avenue called **English Street,** the northern extension of which is **Castle Street,** which leads you straight to the Castle, Carlisle Cathedral, and Tullie House Museum and Art Gallery. Streets you should know that intersect with English Street are **Lawther Street,** running off to the northeast, and two pedestrian streets, **Bank Street** and **Devonshire Street.** The swanky, prestigious hotels lie in the town center and most of the relatively cheap B&Bs are on **Warwick Road,** an east-west-running street 5 minute walk east of the center. The town's old center, nestled between the Caldew and Eden rivers, is small enough to walk across in 15 minutes, so you won't need to board a bus to get around.

hanging out

The old center of town is where you'll be hanging out, where the city's landmark **Cathedral** and castle, both crumbling, are basically right next to each other. As for gathering/chilling points, in the words of one tourist official, "We'd hang out more on the sidewalks, but alas, the weather is so

five things to talk to a local about

1. **The town's history:** Centuries of carnage make for interesting, if bloody, conversation.
2. **The Scottish:** They either love 'em or hate 'em. The younger are slightly more open-minded but many of the elders in this town have a hard time accepting anything Scottish.
3. **Americans:** For some reason, possibly the convenient location of this town between Scotland and South England, they get a lot of Americans here—and they actually *like* them.
4. **Hadrian's Wall:** Everyone who lives here is an expert on the history of the wall—just ask 'em.
5. **The cafe-revolution, and the cafe-resistance:** Possibly an after-effect of the fight against Scotland, the Carlislians are extremely resistant to cosmopolitan trends, and they'll be happy to tell you all about it.

carlisle

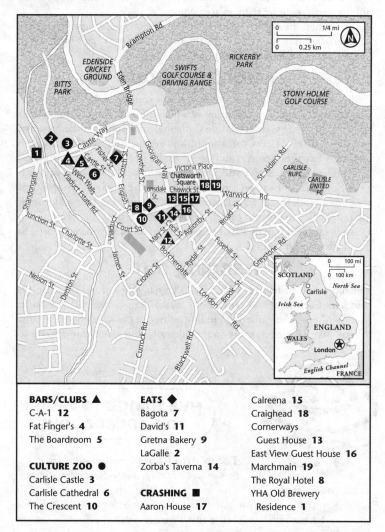

BARS/CLUBS ▲
C-A-1 **12**
Fat Finger's **4**
The Boardroom **5**

CULTURE ZOO ●
Carlisle Castle **3**
Carlisle Cathedral **6**
The Crescent **10**

EATS ◆
Bagota **7**
David's **11**
Gretna Bakery **9**
LaGalle **2**
Zorba's Taverna **14**

CRASHING ■
Aaron House **17**

Calreena **15**
Craighead **18**
Cornerways
 Guest House **13**
East View Guest House **16**
Marchmain **19**
The Royal Hotel **8**
YHA Old Brewery
 Residence **1**

bad we usually don't want to." Consequently, the main hangout zones tend to be inside pubs that are strategically scattered along **English Street,** especially near the corner of Lawther, and along the southern end of English, the increasingly trendy **Botchergate.**

bar scene

Don't expect a hot club scene in Carlisle. In fact, don't expect to find a bar where the average age is under 30. But there are a few spots where you'll find a fair share of young locals and at least some lively conversation if you want it.

Within view of the Carlisle Cathedral, **The Boardroom** *(Paternoster Row, Tel 01228/527-695; 11am-11pm Mon-Sat, noon-10pm Sun, food until 8pm; £2.50 per item, drinks £1.75; No credit cards)* is the early-evening meeting place for students and student-age locals. It's a good-sized, comfortably worn, vintage edition of the classic English pub. True to its name, the Boardroom is about spirited-but-friendly talk and deliberation that only gets more spirited as the crowd works its way toward a state of inebriation.

An excellent spot to have fun is the **Beehive** *(Warwick Road; Tel 01228/549-731; Pints £1.55-£2.12; V, MC, AE)*. With a clientele ranging in age from 18 to 80, you're bound to find someone here who wants to throw some darts or shoot snooker with you. If bar games aren't your fancy, they also have quiz night on Thursdays, live music once a month, and a giant TV screen that broadcasts all major football matches.

ARTS SCENE

Unless you have a thing for watercolor landscapes that look like they could've been painted in a senior citizens art class, you're not going to be wild about the art scene in Carlisle. Ditto the theater. But you might get lucky and catch some retro rock act that you heard on the radio when you were 10 years old. You never know.

▶▶VISUAL ARTS

One private but respected sale gallery is the **Edwin Talbot Art Gallery** *(9 Crosby Street; Tel 01228/525-231; 10am-6pm Mon-Sat; MC, V)*, which specializes in traditional English painting as well as a sampling of contemporary art, usually abstract, by local artists. Its most visible competitor is **Gray's Picture Framing Gallery** *(19 West Tower Street Tel 01228/531-837; 10am-6pm Mon-Sat; MC, V)*, where most of the inventory consists of unchallenging, bucolic depictions of the English Lake District, either in acrylics, watercolors, or oils.

▶▶PERFORMING ARTS

The town's most visible theatrical venue, inclined toward booking

RULES OF THE GAME

Carlisle is such a mellow and transient town that anything goes. The cops are mostly absent during the partying hours, leaving the streets to the punters. It seems that three centuries of war and nearly a century of lawlessness fosters a more relaxed attitude toward silly drunken escapades. There are certain areas that are held sacred, namely the cathedral and castle—although the cathedral grounds have also been known to hide restless youth looking for a toke or two.

whatever blockbuster theatrical or musical event comes into town, is **The Sands Leisure Centre** *(Hardwicke Circus, Tel 01228/625-222; Tickets £10-£25; V, MC).* Recent acts have included the exhumed version of the Temptations, lots of ballet and fairly mainstream rock concerts, and a visiting troupe from Russia that put on an ice skating version of *Phantom of the Opera* (no, we're not kidding).

Other theaters in town include **The West Walls Theater** *(West Walls; Tel 01228/533-233).* Some of the plays you'll see here are produced by the Green Room Club, a respected local theater company. The same building is also the performance venue of The Cumbrian Opera, a small but enthusiastic (caution) local opera company who in the last year launched a new production of *Faust.*

CULTURE ZOO

All the serious monuments revolve around the centuries of unbridled warfare with the Scots. Both the Cathedral and the Castle have loads of accounts of their roles in those wars etched into their walls. The castle played the obvious role of protector while the cathedral received a lot of damage during the volatile times of the sixteenth century. For a sense of just how things were actually duked-out at the castle, check out the cool town museum of ancient battle, the Tullie House Museum and Art Gallery.

Carlisle Castle *(Castle Way; Tel 01228/591-922; 9:30am-6pm daily Apr-Sep, 10am-4pm Oct-Mar; admission £3 adult, £2.30 student):* This well-preserved 12th-century castle was one of the great border strongholds of the English for its whole existence—it really brings the violent past of Carlisle to life. From the top of the Norman keep, it's possible to see into Scotland as well as the mountains of the Lake District on a clear day. Down below, the dungeon's clearly visible, giving you a chilling perspective on the trials of anyone caught on the wrong side of the old power struggle. Don't miss this one: There's a stone in the walls of one of the dungeons known as the "licking stone." It's thought that thirsty prisoners would press their tongues against it in a desperate effort to extract any condensation that formed. If the visible erosion of it is any indicator, this had to be one of the most miserable jails in the north.

A little less chilling but equally instructive is the carving visible in the sandstone walls on the third floor. Like bored soldiers anywhere, the ones stationed here resorted to copious doodling—only with medieval penknives from the look of it. Thought to date back to at least the sixteenth century, the carvings are pretty darn elaborate. Throughout the entire castle, you can almost hear the echo of long-gone bagpipes and the haunting sounds of approaching cavalry. This is one eerie place—especially on an impassive gray day (and your odds of catching one of those are always at least even).

Carlisle Cathedral *(Castle Street; Tel 01288/548-151; 7:30am-6:15pm Mon-Sat, 7:30am-5pm Sun; admission free):* Although this 12th-century cathedral was burned by the Scots and rebuilt endlessly, its 14th-century stained-glass window—one of the finest in the north—somehow survived from the fourteenth century. Its rainbow glow fills this magnificent sandstone church. A giant pipe organ divides the congregation from the entrance to the cathedral. Ornate and complex, the walls are decorated with wood carvings and marble statues topped off with a fresco of the midnight blue, star-specked, night sky of Carlisle. Located just off the pedestrian shopping area that makes up the center of town.

Tullie House Museum and Art Gallery *(Castle St.; Tel 01228/534-781, Fax 01228/810-249; 10am-5pm Mon-Sat, noon-5pm Sun; admission £3.25):* Sitting just up Abbey Road from the Castle, this is an interactive historical museum that puts the feel of catapults and stone throwers right in your hands with great re-creations of Roman battle stations.

CITY SPORTS

The area around Carlisle's three rivers—the **Eden,** the **Petteril,** and the **Caldew**—provide for great hiking and cycling routes within the town. Lots of well-maintained trails run along them and the Tourist Info Center (see *need to know,* below) has all the straight dope. The best brochure, "River Walks of Carlisle," is loaded with useful background on flora, fauna, and geology. The nerve center for cycling in Carlisle, Scotsby Cycles [see *need to know,* below], rents a decent range of mountain bikes.

EATS

This traveler-friendly town provides lots of choice for grub. Everything from quick-and-easy to romantic gourmet is available within a radius of

boy meets girl

With so many students roaming about, meeting someone should be a cinch. The best student hangout is a Mexican food place called Fat Fingers, where the £7 margarita jugs make you even more likely to find some company for the evening.

a couple of blocks. Many of the restaurants surround the pedestrian shopping area along English Street.

▶▶**CHEAP**

As always, for quick and easy, choose the cafes. Just a box on the side of Lowther Street, a block west of the city center, is **Gretna Bakery** *(4 Lowther Street; Tel 01461/338-324; 8am-4:15pm Mon-Fri, until 1:30pm Sat; 30p-£1.50 per item; No credit cards).* It is actually a Scottish company so it serves both English and Scottish food, with the ever-present meat pie a specialty of the house. Famous for its scones and cakes.

For spicier eats, head over to **Fat Finger's** *(48 Abbey Street; Tel 01228/511-774; 10am-2pm/5:30pm-11:30pm Mon-Sat, 7pm-11pm Sun; £3.25 per item, £11 cocktail jug; V, MC),* two blocks west of the Cathedral. Specializing in quasi-Mexican food (the cooks here actually use spices other than salt and pepper), you can get fajitas and tacos to fill in the spaces between margaritas. And this is one of the few places in town that will whip up a pitcher full of your favorite mixed drink (it's recommended you share the gallon-sized jug with some friends...). With a steady student crowd who seems drawn to the mail-order hacienda interior, this place gets better as the night wears on, so hit it around 10pm for the most interesting prospects.

▶▶**DO-ABLE**

Hot sauce and tequila aren't everyone's idea of a great night out, of course. There's one great cafe-bar in the up-and-coming area of Carlisle, just southeast of the railroad station. **C-A-1** *(17 Botchergate; Tel 01228/530-460l; 11am-12:30am Mon-Wed, until 2am Thur-Sat, 12noon-10:30pm Sun; meals £5-10; V, MC)* is surrounded by buildings being renovated, a sure sign this district is on the way up. There are other design-conscious bars in this hood that are also clearly aimed at the young and restless, serving food and liquor into the late hours, but C-A-1 is the only one with better than so-so food. Vegetarian and light meals are readily available, which makes a nice break for the heavy trad English fare.

Zorba's Taverna *(68 Warwick Road; Tel 01228/592-227; noon-2pm/5:30pm-10:30pm Mon-Sat; £6.25-10.25 per entrée; V, MC),* five minutes to the southwest of the city center, serves up—you guessed it—Greek. But don't groan yet—it's actually cooked by Greeks. The *spanakopita* (spinach pie) is a nice greasy delight and the lamb pitas are tangy and warming. Inside, it looks like every Greek restaurant in the world.

For something on the other side of the Adriatic, **Franco's Ristorante** *(5/6 Greenmarket; Tel 01228/512-305; 11:30am-2:30pm/5:30pm-10:30pm daily summer, Mon-Sat winter; £5.75-11.95 per entrée; MC),* a 10-minute walk south of the town center, serves up authentic and tasty Italian food with a smile as bright as the Tuscan sun. The *pasta arrabbiata* is a fiesty meld of hot peppers and fettuccini. Pizzas are also an option—and here they know to use real tomato sauce as opposed to the all-too-common English ketchup pizzas.

For gourmet that won't break the bank, it's gotta be **LaGalle** *(7 Devonshire Rd., Tel 01228/818-388; 8am-11pm Mon-Sat; £5.25 per entrée; No* *credit cards)*, two blocks east of the town center. Settle into the cozy and modern interior and be prepared for unlikely experiments with fusion. Who knew ginger went so well with traditional roasts?

▶▶SPLURGE

If you're in the mood for some high-end English food, **David's** *(62 Warwick Road; Tel 01228/523-578; £10.95-15 per entrée; V, MC, AE)*, two blocks east of the town center, is the best around. But plan on spending a bit of time here. The atmosphere is classy, a bit formal and chi-chi, but either their kitchen is in another city or the service is just really slow. The breaded salmon and roasts with beer sauces are just about worth the wait, though.

crashing

Considering the location of Carlisle, so close to both Scotland and the Lake District, it follows naturally that it's used as a stopover between destinations. Knocking on doors is actually the most efficient way of getting a place to stay for the night. Many homes have signs advertising rooms, but it really doesn't matter whether there's a sign up or not. Most locals who don't have a room to spare are still more than happy to suggest a neighbor with a room to rent. You really can just knock on doors—at a reasonable hour, of course—but if you're too shy to do that, go to the tourist information center [see *need to know*, below] and they'll help you find a bed.

There are several comfortable and affordable B&Bs along Warwick Road. The proprietors are used to people showing up at the last minute, thoroughly worn out from hiking and usually will offer recommendations on where to look next if their B&B is full or too expensive. All the B&Bs around the Warwick Road area are about £20 and offer a very similar level of accommodation. Non-meat-eaters take note: vegetarian breakfasts are not really understood in this town, so it may take you a few minutes to get it across to your B&B hosts that you don't want the bacon and sausage. Dirt-cheap beds can only be found with YHA accommodations just outside of the town center.

▶▶CHEAP

Because it is really University of Northumbria housing, the **YHA** *(Old Brewery Residences, Bridge Lane; Tel 01228/597-352; reception open 5pm July 8-Sept 9; £15 per person, shared bath; No credit cards)* here is only available during July and August. Located in a recently converted brewery a 10-minute walk west of the town center, these college dorms are some of the nicer YHA accommodations in England, with never more than seven sharing one room. Bathrooms and kitchens are, as usual, communal.

For a little more pampering than the YHA, make for the cheaper B&Bs along Warwick Road, two blocks east of the town center. Both **Marchmain** *(151 Warwick Road; Tel 01288/529-551; £16 single, £30 double, private bath in some rooms; No credit cards)* and **Calreena** *(123 Warwick Road; Tel 01228/525-020; £16 single, £30 double, private bath in* *some rooms; No credit cards)* offer basic accommodation in typical B&B houses (comfy with quaint-bordering-on-fussy decoration) for a decent price. **Craighead** *(6 Hartington Place; Tel 01228/596-767; £16 single, private bath in some rooms; No credit cards)* provides slightly more Puritan decor, with virgin white canopies covering some of the four-poster beds.

▶▶**DO-ABLE**

The accommodations at **Aaron House** *(135 Warwick Road; Tel 01228/536-728; £17.50 single, private bath in some rooms; No credit cards)* are extremely comfortable, with rooms decorated in an eclectic mix of English and classy old-Europe style.

Probably because it's just off the main shopping area, **Cornerways Guest House** *(107 Warwick Rd; Tel 01228/521-733; £18 single, private bath in some rooms; No credit cards)* charges slightly more than most. The accommodations are basic and the rooms are decorated with the usual English knickknacks.

Although it's just a few minutes' walk to all of the cheaper B&Bs on the east side of town, you may want to take the easy way out and stay at the **Royal Hotel** *(9 Lowther Street; Tel 01228/522-103; £30 single, private bath; MC),* located right next to the train and bus stations. The slightly higher price grants you a bathroom in the room and the availability of room service.

Located in one of the oldest buildings in the heart of the city center, **The County Hotel** *(9 Bothchergate; Tel 01228/531-316; £50 single, £60 double, all rooms with bath; breakfast £4.99 continental, £7.50 full English; V, MC)* is a bit pricier than some of the other options, but for good reason: All rooms have bathrooms, TVs, and free tea and coffee, and the decor and furnishings are a bit snazzier. It's a fine place to treat yourself if you feel so inclined.

nEEd To Know

Currency Exchange The best place for currency exchange here is the **tourist information center** [see below], even though it charges a £3 minimum commission. The **post office** [see below] also provides currency exchange, although that may change within the year. It charges only a 1%, £2.50 minimum commission, but the rates are better at the tourist information center. There are also a number of banks in the area, but their hours are very limited.

Tourist Info The **Tourist Information Center** is in the **Old Town Hall** *(Greenmarket; Tel 01228/625-600; 9:30am-6pm Mon-Sat summer; 10am-4pm winter),* a 10-minute walk south of the town center. It'll set you up with maps and advice galore, and help book a room if needed.

Health and Emergency Carlisle General Hospital *(Fuse Hill; Tel 01228/523-444)* is west of the castle. The **Police** *(Warwick Street; Tel 01228/528-191)* are situated right in the center of town.

Pharmacies Tesco *(Rose Hill; Tel 01228/600-400; Open 24 hrs a day from 8am Mon-10pm Sat, 10am-4pm Sun)* is your best choice for your pharmacy needs.

Trains The **train station** *(Botchergate; Tel 08457/484-950)* connects with main lines running to all areas south and east of Carlisle. There are 15 trains per day to **London Euston station,** and trains are also available to **Newcastle.**

Bus Lines Out of the City Pick up your schedules at the **main bus stop** *(Lowther Street; Tel 0870/608-26-08).* Hadrian's Wall buses 682 and 685 run between Newcastle and Carlisle daily, leaving from Newcastle's Eldon Square.

Rental Get yer wheels at **Scotsby Cycles** *(30 Bridge Street; Tel 08007/832-312; 10am-6pm Mon-Sat; £15 day; No credit cards).*

Laundry Wash and dry at **Charlie Launderette** *(Brook Street; No phone; 7am-7pm; £1 wash, 50p dry).*

Postal Send those snaps of Hadrian's Wall from the **Post Office** *(20-34 Warwick Road; Tel 01228/512-410; 9am-5:30pm Mon-Sat).*

durham

If you were kidnapped by aliens and dropped into the middle of Durham onto Silver Street—where your eardrums would likely be assaulted by the bleating noise of one of the town's infamous local characters apparently attempting to squeeze the life out of a set of bagpipes—you might not immediately guess that this charming little town is as idyllic and historical as it is lively. Populated largely by **University of Durham** students and crisscrossed with medieval cobbled lanes, Durham is squished into the oxbow of the River Wear, and overlooked by ethereal **Durham Cathedral. Durham Castle** stands upon a lovely golden-colored rise, an enduring monument to its first builder, William the Conqueror, who helped create one tough Norman military outpost here. Even the cathedral was part of it, with monks so powerful they commanded English regiments. Religious pilgrims helped build up their power base too—the remains of St. Cuthbert, a major church figure of the north, are buried in the cathedral.

The University of Durham looms large. The town's 10,000 students are everywhere—so much so that the other locals sometimes seem resentful of the benign invaders. It's really fun to party in Durham because, in addition to consistently packing the bars, the students create a friendly, laid-back vibe. No need to dress to impress in this town. Like a lot of students in Europe these days, Durham students walk around in pajama-tops.

But take a break from your alcohol-induced haze (and new best friends) to notice the exquisite craftsmanship that dominates the architecture of the town: The lampposts around **Market Place** are all carved with a variety of fantastical and real animals, as are several other buildings around town. The adjoining old-style indoor marketplace is packed with small booths and craft stands and seems a living extension of the architecture, teeming with descendents of the masons, ironmongers, and builders who created it.

durham

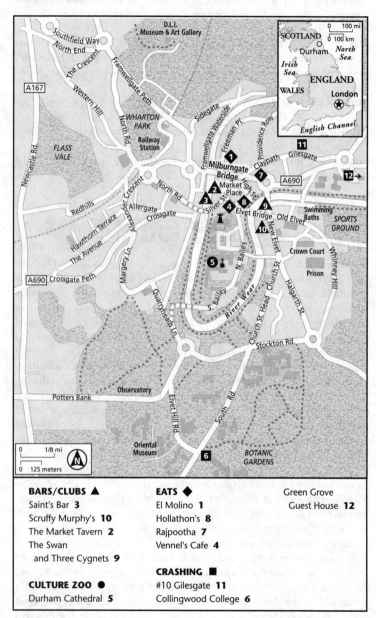

BARS/CLUBS ▲

Saint's Bar **3**
Scruffy Murphy's **10**
The Market Tavern **2**
The Swan
 and Three Cygnets **9**

CULTURE ZOO ●

Durham Cathedral **5**

EATS ◆

El Molino **1**
Hollathon's **8**
Rajpootha **7**
Vennel's Cafe **4**

CRASHING ■

#10 Gilesgate **11**
Collingwood College **6**

Green Grove
 Guest House **12**

neighborhoods

The part of Durham you'll most want to see lies within the peninsula that's created by a loop in the **River Wear,** an area that you can cross (north to south) in just 20 minutes. This is where you'll find the center-piece cathedral, and just to the north of that, **Duhram Castle** [see *culture zoo,* below, for both]. A bit farther north, at the start of the peninsula, is the town's commercial hub, **Market Place.** A very short walk to the east is **Elvet** (marked by **Elvet Bridge** and the two streets that branch off it to the east, **Old** and **New Elvet**), a small shopping neighborhood with a scattering of bars and pubs favored by students. Most of the commercial businesses that make Durham run—gas stations, garages, factories, and such—are north of Market Place, outside the peninsula.

The university itself has a few branches: One is situated in the **Bailey,** the neighborhood that surrounds the cathedral; another campus, where most of the dorms are located, is a 20-minute walk south of the cathedral, just across the river along **South Road** (reachable from the city center via bus 5 or 6). But the biggest student hangout hub is **Dunelm House** [see *bar, club, and live music scene,* below], right in the city center, in the shadow of the cathedral.

Walking is the best way to get around, although it's a steep 10-minute climb to the cathedral, so you might want to save your energy for night-time exercise instead. If it's too much for you, take one of the white-sided shuttle buses that run every 10 minutes between the parking lots just north of the Market Place and the cathedral (see *need to know,* below).

bar, club, and live music scene

Like most college towns, Durham is loaded with pubs. Students pack every one, from the average chain spots to independently owned pubs with slightly more charm. Pub crawls are commonly attempted and easily accomplished—in fact, many of these places are often jammed to capacity.

Dunelm House (*New Elvet; Tel 0191/374-33-10; 10am-11pm daily; beer £1.50; No credit cards*) is the official university gathering point, where you can start your crawl by befriending students in the bar. They will usu-ally be happy to lead you to the best dens of iniquity. It's the equivalent of a student union, complete with bar, restaurant, meeting rooms, stu-dent travel office, and innumerable bulletin boards announcing campus events.

On the corner of Old Elvet, New Elvet, and Elvet Bridge, **Scruffy Murphy's** (*84 New Elvet; Tel 0191/386-99-36; 11am-11pm Mon-Sat, noon-10:30pm Sun; beer £2, pub grub £1.50-4.00; No credit cards*) is one of far too many chain pubs characterized by the exact same decorating, style, and atmosphere as all the other "authentic Irish but somehow still part of a chain" pubs in England. Junk shop remainders straight from a catalog hang everywhere. Still, at night the place fills up with students all trying to master the Irish tradition of drinking to reach oblivion. If you're looking for a properly pulled pint of Guinness, this is the place to find it. Music is mostly rock juke tracks.

Next to the Indoor Market is Durham's best known pub, **The Market Tavern** (*27 Market Place; Tel 0191/386-20-69; 11am-11pm Mon-Sat, noon-10:30pm Sun, food until 2pm; Pint £2, food under £4; No credit cards*), serving fine ales and a featured "guest beer" that rotates almost weekly. Tradition oozes from between the dark wood panels on the walls. Basic English food—in the meat-pie mode—is available for part of the day, but it does have some great dessert pies filled with fruit and nuts, served till closing time. There's no consistent live music but things pick up the later you come.

You have to truly be an optimist—or damn lucky—to overcome the traditional Norhern English gloom and actually use its outdoor porch for warm-weather dining, but **The Swan and Three Cygnets** (*Elvet Bridge; Tel 0191/384-02-42; 11am-11pm Mon-Sat, noon-10:30pm Sun, food until 9:30pm; Pint £1.80, £4-6 per entrée; V, MC*) is still a good spot to just chill. Come here in the early evening for a breather from the rowdy student bars. You'll find plenty of students here, but they are usually in mellow mode. A traditional English pub, the Swan cooks up made-to-order meals that might as well have been cooked by your English auntie, with a vast choice of fine ales to complement them. They also serve the ultra-strong "D-Pils," a brew that's been known to leave people totally blotto after three pints and temporarily blind after six. This drink, for obvious reasons, is way popular with students.

The most inventive place in town is without a doubt the **Saint's Bar** (*Market Vaults, Back Silver Street; Tel 0191/386-77-00; 11am-11pm Mon-Sat, noon-10:30pm Sun, food until 7pm; Pint £1.80, £4-6 per entrée, £4.50 per hour internet use; MC*). Housed in the old Market Vaults and decorated with statues of saints, this two-floored bar/restaurant/internet cafe offsets its ancient castle interior with high-speed web surfing and a thoroughly modern restaurant with an open kitchen.

Students and other young people agree that for clubbing in Durham, there are basically only two choices. The first is **Klute** (*Elvet Bridge, Tel 0191/386-98-59*), a big, cheesy, three-level dance club with two separate sound systems—generally playing dance and garage/house music in the main space, funk and hip-hop in the chill-out space. This club attracts the more relaxed variety of Durham clubbers and a few students.

For wankers who like fighting, **Cafe Rock** (*15-17 North Road, Tel 0191/384-39-00*) is, according to some, *the* place to get a good thrashing. The bouncers here have a reputation for apparently holding a grudge against the entire human race.

CULTURE ZOO

The one-two punch of the Castle and Cathedral are not soon forgotten. They stand above the whole region like beacons from another age.

Durham Cathedral *(Palace Green; 9:30am-8pm Mon-Fri May-Sept, 9:30am-6pm Mon-Sat, 2:20pm-5pm Sun Oct-April; Tel 0191/386-42-66; Admission to the cathedral free, treasury £2; No credit cards):* The more details you take in here, the lower your jaw will drop. The Sanctuary Knocker, a replica of one placed on the door in 1154 A.D., is a 56-centimeter (22-inch) wide bronze lion's head that granted shelter to anyone able to touch it before their pursuing oppressors got hold of them—kinda like the safe spot in a game of tag. They then had 40 days to come up with a good story before being handed over to the local sheriff. With two towers and intricate architectural details that took a century to complete, it's tough to decide which is best: the view from the Cathedral's mighty perch atop high hill, or the architecture itself. The Romanesque Norman building featured the first ribbed vault ceilings in England—these strong arches could support all manner of heavy stone construction and allow the church to be dizzyingly vertical. In the church treasury, there are relics of St. Cuthbert's coffin, which have attracted pilgrims for centuries, as well as some incredibly ornate examples of illuminated manuscripts and phenomenally lavish priestly vestments.

Durham Castle *(Palace Green, 10am-12:30pm/2-4pm Mon-Sat, 10am-noon/2-4pm Sun July-Sept, 2-4pm Mon, Wed, Sat Oct-April; Tel 0191/374-79-11; £3; No credit cards):* This was the seat of the Princes of Durham for 800 years, until, in 1832, it became the first building of the University of Durham. You can only go in via a 45-minute tour, but it's a pretty amazing one that takes you through a huge medieval kitchen, up a very scary-looking hanging Gothic staircase, and into a vast treasure room. It's connected to the cathedral, making it easy to scrunch all your Durham sightseeing into one afternoon.

CITY SPORTS

The best hikes in town are laid out in two trail guides available from the Tourist Office [see *need to know,* below]: *Out and About from Durham* and *Discover County Durham.* Each describes really cool walking tours that take from one to eight hours, so you can let your stamina—and your desire to get back to the serious business of hanging out in the pubs—be your guide. One of the best hikes—not too long, not too short—is a 2.5-hour trek that takes you through some of the area's greatest scenery; starts near the cathedral, then follows the peninsula's inside curve through the southern edges of the old town, then breaks eastward through **Telaw Woods, Bluebell Woods,** and on to **Shincliffe Bridge,** on the eastern outskirts of Greater Durham.

EATS

No matter what you like to eat, it's easy to find good food in Durham. From trad English meals to a take-out curry, the options are good and often inexpensive.

▶▶**CHEAP**
Spanish accents flavor the menu at **El Molino** *(St Nicholas Cottage, Durham Markets; Tel 0191/383-94-44; 11am-11pm Mon-Sat, noon-10:30pm Sun;*

under £4 per item; V). Hidden in a stone alley between the tourist information center and the cathedral, this little restaurant is always packed. Spanish music flows steadily from the speakers. Come here for a full meal of the spicy chow, or enjoy a few margaritas with Spanish tapas like *patatas fritas* (fried potatoes) or calamari. It's always fiesta time in this sunshine-colored spot.

If you've got a hankering for fast food, skip Burger King and head toward **Vennel's Café** *(71 Saddler's Yard, Saddler Street Courtyard; No phone; 9:30am-5:30pm daily; Under £4 per item; No credit cards).* A whole-food restaurant, this cafe makes yummy sandwiches, including some for carnivores. Thinking about a greasy bacon cheeseburger? Try Vennel's overstuffed bacon/avocado sandwich instead. If you tend to stay away from anything that at one time had vocal chords, there are loads of delicious veggie and vegan choices to enjoy on the outdoor patio as well.

▶▶DO-ABLE

Rajpooth *(80 Claypath; Tel 0191/386-14-96; Noon-2pm/6pm-midnight daily; £8-11 per entrée; V, MC),* just north of Market Place, is a bare-bones spot that's always busy, even though most of the Indian dishes taste suspiciously similar. Catering to students, Rajpooth offers quick and tasty meals and stays open late into the night. If the vindaloo is too spicy for your taste, you can always wimp out and order one of their traditional English selections.

Open late and offering everything from salads to burgers, **Hollathan's** *(16/17 Elvet Bridge; Tel 0191/384-42-54; 10am-10pm Mon-Sat; £1.50-10.99 per entrée; V, MC),* just across the River Wear from the town center, attracts students like bees to honey. Any time of day this place is packed with people nursing a coffee or glass of wine, or filling their mouths with well-prepared English beefsteak or grilled trout. Luckily the service is excellent, so if there is a wait, it will be a short one. This isn't the place to be in a hurry—just sit back, relax, and take in the classic, conservative, dark-wood accents.

▶▶SPLURGE

A bright farm-themed eatery, **Bistro 21** *(Aykley Heads House, Aylkley Heads; Tel 0191/384-43-54; noon-2pm and 6-10:30pm Tues-Sat; Main courses £8.50-£16, fixed price lunch £12-£14.50; reservations recommended; V, MC, AE, DC)* is a hit with locals. The cuisine is precise and carefully prepared (never over-sauced) to allow the market-fresh ingredients to show off their natural essence. Though the chef borrows from all over Europe, especially the Mediterranean, the best dishes here fit into the ordinarily dubious category of English cuisine. Really. Try the deep-fried plaice (a type of large flatfish) with chips, followed by the toffee pudding with butterscotch sauce.

crashing

Considering this is the town that brought up Mr. Bean, BBC's mute rubber-faced comic character with the cartoon lifestyle, you shouldn't be too surprised by the goofy sense of humor in force around here. Besides offering a slew of reasonably cheap places to stay, the proprietors will often give you a bellyache from laughing so hard. And the tourist information center [see *need to know*, below] will help you book a room (jokes not included).

▶▶**CHEAP**

One of the cheapest places to stay—even if you don't get the funny-proprietor treatment—is the **Castle** *(Palace Green; Tel 0191/374-79-11; £11 per person; No credit cards)*. When the university is not in session, it offers basic bed-and-breakfast housing in an amazing medieval atmosphere.

Two other cheap B&Bs, both on Claypath in the northeast part of town, are those run by **Mrs. Koltai** *(10 Claypath, Tel 0191/386-20-26; £16per person, shared baths, breakfast included; No credit cards)* and **Mrs. Elliot** *(169 Claypath, Tel 0191/384-16-71; £17.50/person; shared baths; breakfast included; No credit cards)*.

▶▶**DO-ABLE**

At **#10 Gilesgate** *(10 Gilesgate; Tel 0191/386-20-26; £17 per person, shared bath; No credit cards)*, just a 5-minute walk east of Market Place, you do get a Mr. Beanesque proprietor with your clean bed. The proprietors are incredibly friendly and helpful as well as funny; they'll keep you talking for an hour after breakfast (a fact you may want to seriously consider if you're not much of a morning person), then go back to their hotel duties and do your laundry for you (for free!).

Also up on Gilesgate, the **Green Grove Guest House** *(99 Gilesgate; Tel 0191/384-43-61; £20 single, £35 double, shared bath; No credit cards)* really is situated in the middle of a green grove. With a backyard, comfortable accommodation, and close proximity to the city center, this is a perfect place for a night's stay. The rooms are like having your old bedroom from childhood back—except they're clean. A light breakfast is included.

If you cross the River Wear heading east, a half-kilometer (about a third of mile) south of Market Place, you'll find **Collingwood College** *(South Road; Tel 0191/374-45-67; £20 single, £48 suite, shared bath; No credit cards)*, which opens its dorms to travelers when school isn't in session. Although it's definitely nothing more than your average dorm—and far from the best deal in town—it is near the University Botanical Gardens, which makes for a beautiful walk into town.

▶▶**SPLURGE**

Right in the heart of town near the Elvet Bridge, the **Swallow Three Tuns Hotel** *(New Elvet, Tel 0191/386-43-26; singles £99, twins £115, executive doubles £140, luxury suites £195; all rooms with private bath; breakfast included; V, MC, AE)* offers deluxe accomodations in a former 16th-century coaching inn. While the hotel still retains many of its original features—such as oak beams, log fireplaces, and a magnificent stained glass ceiling—it has been modernized to include a pool, sauna, spa bath, plunge pool, and extensively equipped gym. Their restaurant, **Brown's**, serves traditional upscale English cuisine.

need to know

Currency Exchange The **post office** [see below] offers 1 percent commission, with a minimum of £2.50, and competitive rates.

Tourist Information Located in the Market Place, the **Tourist Information Center** *(Tel/Fax 0191/386-30-15; 10am-5pm Mon-Fri, 10am-1pm Sat)* is extremely obliging, from helping you find—and book—a place to stay to handing out free maps.

Public Transportation The town's too small to make buses worth the wait, so best to hoof it. If you have your heart set on taking a bus, you can try the Durham County Council transport inquiry line *(Tel 0191/383-33-37 for info on schedules)*.

Health & Emergency The local hospital is **Dryburn Hospital** *(Aykley Heads; Tel 0191/333-23-33)*.

The **police station** is on New Elvet Road *(Tel 0191/386-42-22)*.

Pharmacies For your legal chemical needs, try **Boots the Chemist** *(Market Place; 8:30am-5:30pm Mon-Sat, 9am-11am Sun)*.

Trains The train station (Framwelgate; Tel 0345/484-950) is at the top of a footpath off the **Milburngate Bridge** traffic circle. There are frequent trains to York, many of which continue to London via Peterborough.

Bus Lines Out of the City You can get schedules from the main **bus station** *(North Road; Tel 0191/384-3323)*. Route 724, operated by Go Northern, runs from Newcastle's Eldon Square to Durham Mon-Sat.

Bike Rental Rent bikes from **Cycle Force 2000** *(29 Claypath, Tel 0191/384-03-19, Fax 0191/386-68-17; £12 perday for city or mountain bikes)* in the center of town.

Laundry There is no public launderette in town, but you can just pretend you're a student and use the **washing machines and dryers in the student union** of the University of Durham *(Dunelm House; Tel 0191/374-33-10; New Elvet Road; 7am-9:30pm daily; 80p wash, 40p dry)*.

Postal The **post office** can post letters and change money *(33 Silver Street, Tel 0191/384-13-07; 9am-5:30pm Mon-Sat)*.

Internet Web access is available at the **Saint's Bar** [see *bar and live music scene,* above] for £4.50 per hour.

berwick-upon-tweed

Let's get this straight right off the bat: this fairytale–like little town is mainly used as a jumping-off point for travelers heading up to Scotland or out to Holy Island [see below]. As "charming" as it is, it doesn't have enough to offer to justify using it as more than a stopover point or a day trip.

Like most of the towns along the Scottish border, Berwick-upon-Tweed is what the English call "historically rich," which usually means there were a ton of bloody battles fought there—or at least that a major fort or wall was built to keep out unwelcome neighbors (in other words, *all* neighbors). Berwick has the forts (some of the best-preserved in England), ramparts that were built in the 1500s to keep the Scots and French out, and the incredibly quaint little town to go along with them. Today, walking atop the battlements, you can get an eerie sense of what it would have been like to be besieged here. There's a walkway along the entire perimeter of the old town where the wall still stands. Most people start the walk at **Scots Gate,** at the northern terminus of **Marygate,** the town's main street. Yes, it's touristy, but it's also pretty impressive.

You aren't here for the nightlife. You'll want to check out the few cafes and traditional pubs, but it'll quickly become apparent why most people travel to Newcastle or Edinburgh for a night out—except for the 13-year-olds loitering outside Boots the Chemist, the sidewalks pretty much roll up around 6pm. There isn't really any tremendously helpful news source on goings on but whatever *is* happening will probably appear in the *Berwick Advertiser,* out on Thursdays.

You should, however, *definitely* check out the beaches. They're studded with disintegrating fort walls, now only mounds of dirt and stone lining the shore, that create a romantic, kind of forlorn landscape. The terrain is so uneven there are actually warning signs advising you to watch your step. (You also need to watch out for balls sailing at you from the nearby golf course.) Take a walk out on the pier that extends waaaay out into the sea—if you sit at the very end, you'll feel fully consumed by the water.

Marygate Street runs roughly east-west, bisecting the town into two fairly equal halves. South of Marygate is Berwick's other main defining feature, the River Tweed. Most things worth seeing—and all the good pubs—lay within the ramparts to the north of Marygate. Very few visitors ever set foot in the newer residential neighborhoods to the south of the Tweed.

You can cross town on foot in about 25 minutes. Expect to spend about an hour doing that walk of the complete circumference of the wall we mentioned earlier, a good way to get your Berwick bearings—and to pick up a sense of the fanatic dedication with which these walls were built in the late sixteenth century. They took 11 years to complete and cost the English treasury £130,000, a vast fortune at the time (about $52 billion in today's money).

bar scene

For more, the place to go is **Barrel's Alehouse** *(59-61 Bridge Street; Tel 01289/308-013; 11am-11pm Mon-Sat, noon-10:30pm Sun; £1.85 drinks).* Although there are lots of pubs in the same area, they're mostly filled with an older crowd and not exactly a hopping good time. Barrel's Alehouse changes from dancehall to mellow conversational bar every few months, depending on when the owners feel like making a switch. In one year, it went from a great place to sit around with a few friends and nurse an excellent pint of ale

berwick-upon-tweed

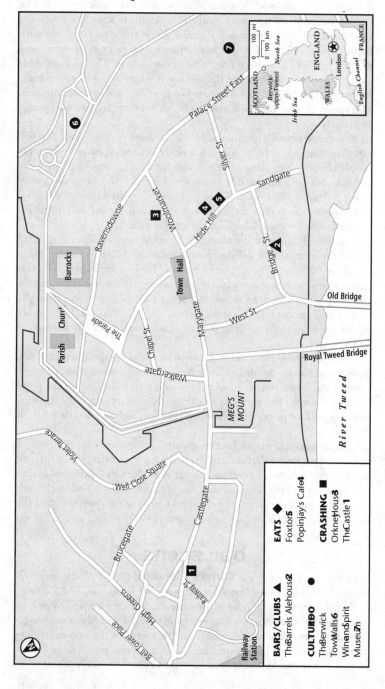

BARS/CLUBS ▲
The Barrels Alehouse **2**

CULTURE ●
The Berwick
Town Walls **6**
Wine and Spirit
Museum **7**

EATS ◆
Foxtor **5**
Popinjay's Cafe **4**

CRASHING ■
Orkney House **3**
The Castle **1**

to a mad, cramped frenzy of oldies music and cheap lighting, then back to a relaxed neighborhood bar. Keep telling yourself: Change is good.

CULTURE ZOO

Judge for yourself what it means when a town's major cultural attraction (aside from battle scars) is a museum devoted to honey wine. **Wine & Spirit Museum** *(Palace Green; Tel 01289/305-153; 9am-5pm daily; free admission):* If you've been to the wine country of France or California, you can easily skip this. But for people who haven't ever been to a winery, this museum is worth a stop, just to find out how the Lindisfarne Mead (honey liqueur) is made. Plus you get a free taste of the mead at the end of the tour, and if you're really nice to your guide, you may get a few more swigs than you expected.

EATS

Fish and chips and cafes are the common denominator in this town, though it's possible to get something Scottish as well. **Popinjay's Café** *(32 Hide Hill; Tel 01289/307-237; 9am-7pm daily; £3-7; No credit cards)* dishes out heartier fare than the standard delicate cafe offereings like cucumber sandwiches, but thankfully doesn't ignore the snack food group completely. Try the toasted teacake, an English favorite that Popinjay's is known for. Their fresh-brewed tea and coffee will keep you jumping all day. A busy sidewalk cafe that makes you feel like you're on the set of a Fellini movie, it's a great place at which to plan your day.

For something as upscale as it gets in the north, **Foxton's** *(26 Hide Hill; Tel 01289/303-939; 11am-9pm daily; £5-10; AE, MC, V)* provides color-coordinated meals with a side order of sophistication in a simple-yet-elegant modern space. Five minutes from Marygate, Foxton's melds tradition with the new century, serving mostly stylish seafood fare, plus more stolid, typically English food. Try the delicate salmon or the hearty meat pies, both plentiful and gorgeous, then relax with a glass of wine or port.

crashing

Berwick is the only town within miles that has any places to stay overnight, but it manages to keep them out of reach. Because this town attracts mostly vacationers with cars, finding something close to town that won't set you back too much is a serious challenge. The tourist office [see *need to know,* below] will help you find a bed.

▶▶**CHEAP**

Housed in what appears to be a New York City tenement building, the **Orkney House** *(37 Woolmarket; Tel 01289/331-710; £12.50 per person, private bath in some rooms; No credit cards),* just a five-minute walk east from town hall, is a good, cheap place to stay. This recently erected building sheds its low-budg appearance once you get inside. You'll be pleasantly surprised at the elegant and graceful interior, yet the owners have retained a quaint north country feel.

Another spot to crash for a while is **Four North Road** *(4 North Road; Tel 01289/306-146; £18/person; shared bath; No credit cards).* This Victorian-style house features big spacious rooms and free parking, but you certainly don't need a car to get here—it's a minute from the bus station.

▶▶**DO-ABLE**

With comfortable accommodation and private baths with every room, **The Castle** *(103 Castlegate; Tel 01289/307-900; £25 single; V, MC),* five minutes southeast of the town center, is your best bet for sleep near the center of town. It's not exactly as palatial as the name implies, but it's clean, with cool, twisting hallways that lead you to your room. Breakfast is served in the ballroom-style dining area, so you'll feel a little under-dressed if you stumble downstairs in your pajamas.

A two-story house built before 1812, **3 Scott's Place** *(3 Scott's Place; Tel 01289/305-323; £25/person; all rooms with bath; Easter-Sept; No credit cards)* is a short walk from the tourist office in the city center. It has all the perks (comfy beds, private baths, TVs) you'd expect for this price.

nEED TO KNOW

Currency Exchange The **Berwick Tourist Office** [see below] doesn't charge a commission and offers competitive rates.

Tourist Information A five-minute walk west from Marygate, **The Berwick Tourist Office** *(Eastern Lane; Tel 01289/330-733; 10am-6pm Mon-Sat, 11am-4pm Sun Jul-Aug, 10am-6pm Mon-Sat Mar-Jun, 10am-4pm Mon-Sat Nov-Apr)* will help you find a bed, and the helpful staff can load you up with trail maps.

Health and Emergency For medical emergencies, go to **Berwick Infirmary** *(Wellclose Square; Tel 01289/356/600).* For other emergencies, call on the **Police** *(Church Street; Tel 01289/307-111)* in the town center.

Pharmacies The local pharmacy is **Boots the Chemist** *(Castlegate; 10am-5pm Mon-Sat).*

Trains The **Berwick train station** *(Castlegate; Tel 0345/484-950)* is a 10-minute walk southeast of the town center. There are frequent trains to and from Edinburgh and Newcastle.

Bus Lines Out of the City Get bus schedules at the **Berwick Bus Shop** *(125 Marygate; Tel 01289/307-283),* a 10-minute walk north-west of the town center. Routes 505 and 515 run daily between Berwick and Newcastle.

Bike Rental Get your wheels at **Brilliant Bikes** *(17a Bridge Street; Tel 01289/331-476; hire@brilliantbicycles.co.uk; Mon-Sat 9am-5}30pm; £15 day),* two minutes west of Marygate. The shop rents only road bikes, but that's no problem because most of the biking around here is on paved country roads.

Postal You can take care of your postcards home at the **Post Office** *(103 Marygate; Tel 01289/307-596; 9am-5pm Mon-Fri, until 1pm Sat),* which is a 10-minute walk north of the train station (see above).

alnwick

Like most towns in this region, this beautiful little hamlet of a few thousand played a key role in defending England from the Scots for the greater part of its long history. But Alnwick (inexplicably pronounced *ANN-ick;* some locals claim it's just so they can have a good laugh at tourists) provided the backdrop for an English warrior so fearsome he was immortalized in Shakespeare's *Henry IV:* Harry Hotspur. In keeping with that warrior tradition, Alnwick's night life is notoriously rowdy (and not in a good way). Its rep is so bad *GQ* readers voted it one of the country's top 10 most likely places to get into a brawl.

As tribute to the heights of Alnwick's military fortitude, many of its strongholds are still intact, though its once impenetrable town walls are now mostly in ruins. **Alnwick Castle** is one of the greatest examples of the stately homes of England and is still occupied today by the Duke and Duchess of Northumberland—you're very unlikely to run into them in the halls, though, as they maintain a very low profile.

For news about what's on in Alnwick during your stay, pick up a copy of the local newspaper, the *Northumberland Gazette,* out on Thursdays.

neighborhoods

Many of the street-names of Alnwick date from the city layout during the Middle Ages. The main street of **Bondgate,** a north-south-running avenue lined with shops, changes its name from **Bondgate Within** (in olden days it was within the stone walls ringing the town) to **Bondgate Without** (the southern section that was outside the wall and today runs directly into Highway A1). Other focal points are **Marketplace,** just to the west of Bondgate, site of an all-day outdoor fruit and vegetable market every Thursday, between late May and late September. The town's most legendary building, Alnwick Castle, stands within an easy walk northeast of the city center along **Narrowgate,** the northern extension of Bondgate, where you'll find most of the liveliest, oldest pubs. Some great and easily overlooked ones are also on **Clayport Street,** a narrow street that is called **Market Street** by the time it runs east enough to intersect with Bondgate Within.

Because you can walk the entire length of Bondgate in less than 20 minutes, most visitors ignore the local buses for getting around town, though they are the sole links from Alnwick to surrounding towns.

bar scene

Saturday nights got so wild in Alnwick that drinking in the streets was banned long ago. But most students and local residents still take refuge from the cold northern climate by hanging out in the local pubs, and brawls remain a major pastime.

alnwick

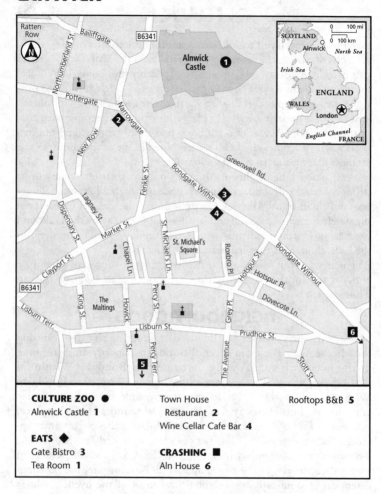

Ratten Row
Bailiffgate
B6341
Northumberland St.
Alnwick Castle **1**
Pottergate
Narrowgate
2
New Row
Fenkle St.
Greenwell Rd.
Bondgate Within
3
4
Lagney St.
Dispensary St.
Market St.
St. Michael's Ln.
St. Michael's Square
Roxbro Pl.
Bondgate Without
Chapel Ln.
Clayport St.
Hotspur St.
Hotspur Pl.
B6341
King St.
The Maltings
Howick St.
Percy St.
Grey Pl.
Dovecote Ln.
Lisburn Terr.
Lisburn St.
Prudhoe St.
The Avenue
Stott St.
6
Percy Terr.
5

SCOTLAND
Alnwick
North Sea
Irish Sea
ENGLAND
WALES
London
English Channel
FRANCE
0   100 mi
0   100 km

CULTURE ZOO ●	Town House	Rooftops B&B **5**
Alnwick Castle **1**	Restaurant **2**	
	Wine Cellar Cafe Bar **4**	
EATS ◆		
Gate Bistro **3**	**CRASHING** ■	
Tea Room **1**	Aln House **6**	

Not to worry, though; there's at least one safe spot in town where you can drink without fending off would-be warriors: **Tanner's** *(Hotspur Place; Tel 01665/602-553; 11am-11pm daily)* serves a fine ale that can be drunk at a leisurely pace. Located around the corner from the Archway, this is a dignified "olde English" kind of pub where you play darts and converse politely while, of course, waving away the cigarette smoke that clouds the room.

A block northeast of the town center, the **Wine Cellar Cafe Bar** *(Bondgate Within; Tel 01665/605-264; 8:30am-10pm Mon-Sat, 10am-9:30pm Sun; meals about £5),* spiffs up trad English food a bit by serving it in what looks like a continental-style cafe. With no angry, quick-fisted punters in sight, this is the place to gather quietly and actually taste the drink in your glass.

CULTURE ZOO

This little town is not terribly loaded with museums or galleries, but its one great attraction is a good half-day experience you won't soon forget.

Alnwick Castle *(off A1; Tel 01665/510-777; 11am-5pm daily Apr-Oct; www.alnwickcastle.com; £6.25 adult, £5.25 student admission):* Although renowned for its Victorian architecture, the town of Alnwick hosts nothing quite as spectacular as its castle. Located just northwest of the town center, it's enclosed within its own set of walls and a recently erected fence topped with daggers. Locals say the current Duke put this up because he felt the walls wouldn't be enough to keep freeloaders trying to avoid the entrance fee off the property. Locals'll tell you the entrance fee isn't worth it, but then, they aren't prisoners of strip malls. Besides, getting ripped off by a Duke makes a great story to come home with, provided you embellish it with a few creative details. Whether *you* feel ripped off depends on whether you think a tour of lavish Renaissance-era rooms and amazing views down across town are worth the price of a good lunch.

EATS

Expecting much more than trad English food will only lead to disappointment most anywhere in Northumbria, and Alnwick is no exception. Even a curry house, which is fast replacing the fish-and-chips shop as the favorite English fast-food stop, is hard to come by. As in most other small English towns, Alnwick manages to combine the restaurant and bar scene into one full-bellied drunken stop. This may be an extension of the lawlessness that was the norm here for about two centuries, but whatever the reason, the restaurants in this tiny hamlet are happy to keep pouring if that's your preference.

▶▶CHEAP

Just inside the town gates a block northeast of the town center, the aptly-named **Gate Bistro** *(14 Bondgate Within; Tel 01665/602-607; 9:30am-11pm Tue-Sun; £5.50-8 per entrée)*, attracts a steady stream of regulars by maintaining the dual booze-and-chow role. A sit-down cafe by day, it shifts to a lively restaurant by night. The rise in noise level marks the quick costume change from bistro to bar, from families devouring food to punters chugging drink.

If you'd like to chow down alcohol-free without feeling like an outcast, combine your trip to Alnwick Castle [see *culture zoo,* above] with a visit to the **Alnwick Castle Tea Rooms** *(Alnwick Castle; Tel 01665/511-131; 10am-5pm daily Apr-Oct; under £5)*. Open to the public but run by the Duke's own chef, this tea room is worth your while even if castle viewing isn't on the top of your list. The fare is excellent, with light lunches of salads, hearty soups, and scones fit for royalty. The setting is appropriately regal, if formal.

▶▶DO-ABLE

Everything is organic at the **Town House Restaurant** *(15 Narrow-gate; Tel 01665/606-336; 10:30am-4pm daily, 6:30pm-9:30 Thurs-Sat; £5-10 per entrée),* just around the corner from the castle. It serves up mostly local food but also uses fashionable ingredients new to bland English cuisine, such as Mediterranean accents and lots of fresh basil. This is a great place to take a break from heavy, smothered-in-sauce, traditional English fare. It even has a great selection of organic wine and beer. Inside it's pretty light with a groovy, new-age kind of vibe.

crashing

There are several guesthouses in the area but no real bah-gains. Alas, such is the price of beauty; so many tourists come through that innkeepers long ago learned to aim high. The friendly TIC [see *need to know,* below] can help you with bookings.

Away from crowds but just a 10-minute walk to the town center, **Rooftops** *(14 Blakelaw Road; Tel 01665/604-201; £20 single, £37 double, private bath in some rooms; No credit cards),* delivers that warm and cozy overstuffed bed to soothe a pounding head after a wild Saturday night. Quaint as all get-out with antiques and nice views, rooms also come with a breakfast of homemade bread with lots of fresh fruit to help you detox from all the beer. Short of holding your hair back as you pray to the porcelain gods, the owners will do anything to ensure your comfort. Check out the guestbook for proof.

Built in Edwardian times, the **Aln House** *(South Road; Tel 01665/602-265; £19 single, £38 double, private bath in some rooms; No credit cards)* stands out for its peaceful garden, providing fresh organic veggies for your breakfasts. The house itself is somewhat plain, which makes the eye-catching gardens stand out all the more. Rooms are pretty basic, just beds and maybe a wardrobe, but the brilliant medley of wildflowers and birds out your window goes a long way.

With a mere six rooms, the **Oronsay Guesthouse** *(18 Bondgate Without; Tel 01665/603-559; Rooms £17.50 per person, two rooms w/bath; No credit cards)* is a wee one. It's excellently located, though, on the main street of town. The house provides easy access to the Castle and the countryside. Breakfast is, naturally, included.

need to know

Currency Exchange In this little town, your best bet is the **post office** [see below] with only a 1 percent (£2.50 minimum) commission. The hours and rates are similar to those of most banks.

Travel Info Right in the city center and a 10-minute walk south of the bus station, **The Tourist Info Center** *(2 The Shambles; Tel 01665/510-665; 9am-5pm Mon-Sat, 10am-4pm Sun Apr-Oct, 10am-4pm Mon-Fri Nov-Mar; www.alnwick.gov.uk)* will help you book rooms, and load you up with free maps.

Health and Emergency There's no real hospital in town, but you can get medical services at the **Alnwick Infirmary** *(South Road; Tel 01665/626-700)*. For police emergencies, call one of Alnwick's finest at the local **police station** *(Prudhoe Street; Tel 01665/602-777), between the town center and the castle.*

Pharmacy The local drug store is **C. Wardlaw Pharmacy** *(10 Peikey Street; Tel 01665/602-142; 8:30-5:30 Mon-Sat).*

Bus Lines Out of the City Nothing but buses makes it to this town. The **bus stop** *(Lagny and Clayport Streets; Tel 0191/212-30-00 or 01665/602-182),* a 10-minute walk northwest of the city center, is connected daily to Newcastle by routes 505 and 515. The first bus to Newcastle leaves at 6am; the last bus into Alnwick arrives at 10:45pm.

Laundry Wash your dirty duds at the local **Laundromat** *(5 Clayport Street; Tel 01665/604-398; 8am-7pm Mon-Fri, 9am-5pm Sat, Sun; £1 wash, 50p dry).*

Post Office To get stamps, mail postcards, or exchange currency, go to the **post office** *(19 Market Street; Tel 01665/602-141; 8:45am-5:30pm Mon-Fri, 8:45am-12:30pm Sat).*

hexham

At first glance, Hexham appears to be just another small, boring town with a tiny but-ugly factory district and way too much air pollution for its size. The reason to visit—or live—here is all beneath the surface, literally. Hexham has become one of England's most important archeological sites; almost the entire town (16,000 people) makes its living one way or another from the excavation of Roman artifacts dating back to the building of **Hadrian's Wall** almost 2000 years ago. Those who aren't actively involved in the **Birdoswald** digs (just west of town) make big bucks off the tourists who swarm to see the site up close. (It's almost like going through celebrities' garbage.)

Hexham didn't even exist when the wall was built; it was founded about 300 years after the Romans lost Great Britain. In 674 A.D., St. Wilfred first established an abbey here. Next came the church of Hexham, partially built with stones removed from the nearby Hadrian's Wall. But the Vikings destroyed the church in 875 A.D., then the Scots virtually razed the town to the ground in 1296 and again in 1346. In 1761, when the American colonies were just getting riled, Hexham had a revolt of its own. A protest against British military conscription turned into a riot, and the militia fired into the angry crowd, killing at least 40 people and injuring about 300 others. The bitterness against the monarchy lived on for many years.

Today, Hexham is a peaceful community that is worth visiting not just for the digs, but for its location at the foot of the *Pennines* as well. Nightlife

hexham

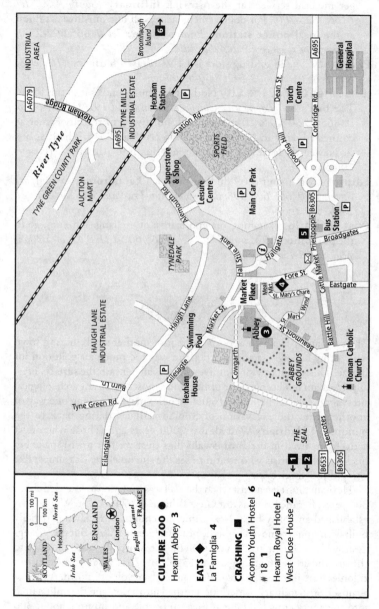

CULTURE ZOO ●
Hexam Abbey 3

EATS ◆
La Famiglia 4

CRASHING ■
Acomb Youth Hostel 6
18 1
Hexam Royal Hotel 5
West Close House 2

is definitely not what it's about—for that, save your energy for nearby Newcastle.

The **Hexham Courant,** out on Fridays, has all that's going on in it— right alongside the lists of local residents who haven't paid their parking fines and real estate taxes.

neighborhoods

The town's dominated by its medieval **Abbey.** Immediately to the east is the **Marketplace,** a square-shaped plaza filled with parked cars and home to **The Shambles,** a covered marketplace which is the site of a massive fruit and produce market every Tuesday. Just southwest of the Abbey is the **Abbey Grounds,** with green lawns, venerable trees, and a fanciful Victorian-era bandstand. To the east of the Abbey is a shopping area that's centered around **Fore Street,** a main north-south avenue that's mostly reserved for pedestrians. Fore Street's southern end leads to two interconnected streets, **Battle Hill** and **Cattle Market,** both of which run east-west. Several outlets and local crafts shops are on **Market Street,** which runs northward from the Marketplace.

Hexham is small enough to cross on foot in less than 20 minutes. Consequently, the only buses that enter the town are those coming from or going to other towns nearby [see *need to know,* below]. The local bus depot is the pavement beside **Priestpopple,** the northern extension of Cattle Market.

bar and live music scene

Nightlife's not an option, but there are a couple of traditional pubs that are kind of fun. The most popular pub in town is **The Tap and Spile** *(Battle Hill; Tel 01434/602-039; 11am to 11pm Mon-Sat; noon-3pm and 7-10:30pm Sun; beer £1.85, meals £2-5),* a well-worn-in wood-paneled classic that also serves basic pub grub. The live rock and folk on Mondays (no cover) is always fun.

Another option on the nostalgia tip is the **Heart of Olde England Pub** *(Market Street; Tel 01434/603-375; meals £4.50-5.50),* which serves up a wider array of chow to go with your pint. No live tunes here, but the crowd's so energetic you won't notice.

culture zoo

The most interesting things to see in town are the Hexham Abbey and the Birdoswald archeological site just west of town [see **Hadrian's Wall,** below].

Hexham Abbey *(Market Place; Tel 01434/602-031; 9am-7pm daily May-Sept, until 5pm Oct-Apr; admission free):* What's left of this ancient abbey, founded in 674 A.D., is mostly from the reconstruction that took place in the twelfth century. While not exceptionally ornate or complex in design, this church stands out because of a solid simplicity—and the amazing fact that it has survived so many invasions. It houses a chilling crypt made from Roman stones and has a generally dark, spooky mood, owing to the four huge Renaissance panels close to the altar depicting the Dance of Death.

eats

You'll have to settle for fairly basic, run-of-the-mill Brit food in Hexham, but some of the cheaper spots also serve as hangouts (sort of) for the local young crowd.

▶▶CHEAP

Want something with a little spice? **La Famiglia** *(20-22 St. Mary's Chare; Tel 01434/601-700; noon-2:30pm/5:30pm-11:15pm Mon-Sat; £5.25 per entrée, No credit cards)* serves a (strange but tasty) combination of Italian and Mexican, including hybrids such as pasta with quesadillas. Inside, the place looks a lot like a postcard from Baja.

When the beer is just as important as the food—as it usually is—get thee to **JD Weatherspoon** *(Market Square; Tel 01434/609-190); 10am-11pm Mon-Sat, noon-10:30pm Sun; Main dishes £3-5pm; AE, MC, V).* This chain is popular with the town's youngest pub crowd, most of them attracted by the bacon cheeseburgers, tiger prawns, and nachos. The house special is steak-and-ale pie, and the fish and chips are also truly delicious.

The most atmospheric place to eat cheap is the **Dipton Mill Pub** *(Dipton; Tel 01434/606-577; Noon-2:30pm/6-11pm Mon-Sat, noon-4:30pm/7-10:30pm Sun; Main courses £4.50-£6; No credit cards),* but it's really out of the way—1.5 miles south of the Hexham center, to be exact. The local medium-brown Hadrian's Ale is the star in this little spot that used to be a millhouse in a deep valley. Settling in to the circa-1750 building with its open fireplace and wooden beams somehow makes the home-cooked steak-and-kidney pie taste even better.

▶▶DO-ABLE:

The Hexham Royal Hotel [see *crashing,* below] provides variety, from your basic pub grub in Mr. Ant's Bar to good vintages of wine and tender steak in the much more upscale and dressy hotel restaurants.

crashing

Accommodations tend to be pricey; the only really cheap option is about 2.5 miles north of the rail station at Acomb Youth Hostel. But there are a few reasonable guesthouses, and the Hexham Royal Hotel is located right in the town center. And, of course, the tourist information center can help you out with room reservations if you're in a pinch [see *need to know,* below].

▶▶CHEAP

Actually a converted stable, **Acomb Youth Hostel** *(Main Street, Acomb; Tel 01434/602-864; Reception open 5pm-11pm Fri and Sat Nov-Mar, Wed-Sun Apr-May, Sept-Oct, daily Jul-Aug; £6.65 per person, shared bath; V, MC)* offers *very* basic accommodation. There are only 2 rooms, each with 16 beds, and the lounge has an open coal fireplace for heat, not atmosphere.

If you don't mind being out in the middle of nowhere, your other cheap option is the **Once Brewed Youth Hostel** [see **Hadrian's Wall,** below]. It's accessible via bus 185 from the end of September to the middle of May, and bus 682 from the end of May to the middle of September.

▶▶DO-ABLE

Most of the guesthouses in town are about a 10-minute walk up Hencoats Rd. west from the town center. **Number 18** *(18 Hextol Terrace; Tel 01434/602-265; £16 per person, some rooms with private bath; No credit cards)* is loaded with information on the area as well as cozy rooms decorated with the owner's homey spare furnishings.

On that very same street, **West Close House** *(Hextol Terrace; Tel 01434/603-307; £18 per person, some rooms with private bath; No credit cards)* has relaxing rooms much like Number 18's, but the real attractions here are the beautiful English gardens and the spacious grounds.

You wouldn't mistake it for the Grand Hotel, but the **Hexham Royal Hotel** *(Priestpopple; Tel 01434/602-270, Fax 01434/604-084, www.hexham-royal-hotel.co.uk/; £36.50 single, £62.00 double, £52.00 weekend rate, private bath; food 10am-10pm; No credit cards)* is pretty close to luxurious. It offers all the common features of a hotel—an in-house restaurant and bar, private baths, and the town center location make for a convenient night's stay—and rooms with comfy beds and TVs that look much like the comfy beds and TVs in hotel rooms anywhere.

The Beaumont Hotel *(Beaumont Street; Tel 01434/602-331; £66.50 single, £93 double, all rooms with baths; breakfast included; V, MC, AE)* is one of Hexham's more expensive spots. However, the breathtaking view of the Abbey and its grounds, which surround the hotel, makes it worth the price.

▶▶SPLURGE

Southwest of Haydon Bridge and about 7 miles west of Hexham, **The Langley Castle Hotel** *(Langley-on-Tyne, Hexham; Tel 01434/688-888, Fax 01434/684-019, http://dspace.dial.pipex.com/ langleycastle; £105 doubles, £155 suites; breakfast included; V, MC, AE, DC)* is set on 10 acres of woodlands at the edge of Northumberland National Park. It's the only medieval fortified castle home in England that receives paying guests. Built in 1350, the castle features a 14th-century spiral staircase, stained-glass windows, huge open fireplaces, 7-foot-thick walls, and more turrets than you'll know what to do with. Many of the hotel's luxurious rooms have their own whirlpools or saunas, and all have heavenly beds fitted with fine linens.

need to know

Currency Exchange You can change your money at all the banks along Priestpopple, but your best bet is **Thomas Cook** *(Battle Hill; Tel 01434/605-233; 9am-5pm Mon-Sat)* with its 1.5 percent commission.

Tourist Information The **Hexham Tourist Information Center** *(Wentworth Car Park; Tel 01434/605-255; 9am-5pm daily April-Oct; 9am-4pm daily Nov-Mar)*, just east of the town center, will help you find a room and load you up with maps.

Health & Emergency Call *999* for emergencies, or go to the local hospital, **Hexham General Hospital** *(Corbridge Road; Tel 01434/655-655)*, or the **police** *(Shaftoe Leazes; Tel 01434/604-111)*.

Pharmacies **Pattinson Pharmacy** *(1 Cattle Market; Tel 01434/603-080; 8:15am-5:15pm Mon-Sat)* is the only game in town; their rotating late-hours schedule is posted in the windows.

Trains The main station *(Station Road; Tel 0345/484-950)* is five minutes north of the town center. There are frequent trains to and from Newcastle, with connections available for London's King's Cross.

Bus Lines Out of the City **Stagecoach** buses arrive and leave from the **main stop** *(Priestpopple; Tel 01434/602-061)* connected by routes 602 and 685 from Newcastle, the latter of which goes on to Carlisle (1-1/2 hours).

Postal The post office is inside **Robb's Department Store** *(Fore Street; Tel 01434/602-001; 8:30am-5:30pm Mon-Sat, until 6pm Fri)*.

hadrian's wall

This 76-mile-long wall—stretching from the west to the east coast of North England—was built by the Roman emperor Hadrian, to keep out the barbarians (well, the Scots) from the north. It's not surprising that the Romans would try to keep a strong hold on their land and lifestyle (no comment on whether or not they were just a teeny bit barbarian themselves), but what is amazing is that the wall—now almost 2000 years old—is still standing in many places. In others, it has eroded into the landscape, but it invariably resurfaces somewhere nearby.

A good place to start your exploration is in **Carlisle** [see above]. Although the wall there is no longer visible, the town offers the cheapest crashing options and is just 20 minutes west of well-preserved wall and fortress ruins.

A path that will allow you to walk the length of the wall is still under construction, planned for completion in 2002. In the meantime, there are enticing walks around **Housesteads** and **Birdoswald** [see below]. There's also the **Hadrian's Wall Bus,** which Roman construction workers would surely have appreciated. It runs in the summer [see *need to know,* below] and stops at all the major attractions along the way. Another option is the scenic rail route from Carlisle to Newcastle [see *need to know,* below] though it provides fewer views of the wall and stops only in **Haltwhistle** and **Hexham.**

Spaced about a mile apart along the wall, *milecastles,* where the Roman border patrol were garrisoned, are good hike targets from these towns.

The excavated Roman fortress grounds at **Birdoswald,** 14 miles west of Hexham, contain a rustic medieval farmhouse located within its battlements—where you can actually spend the night [see *crashing,* below]. Further east at **Vindolanda Fort,** you can get in on a dig of a Roman army fort and the ruins of a small Roman town or *vicus,* which featured *hypocausts* (hot air vents) used to heat water. The dig at **Housesteads**

Fort, 3 miles north of Vindolanda Fort, has revealed the only example of a Roman hospital in England (plus ingenious latrines that actually flushed). The elevation here also provides spectacular views down the wall and wavering landscape [see *need to know,* below, for all three forts]

crashing

Most people stay in Carlisle or Hexham, but there's also a hostel nearby. A mile west of the Vindolanda Fort, the **Once Brewed Youth Hostel** *(Military Road, Once Brewed; Tel 01434/344-360, Fax 01434/344-045; open Mar-Nov; reception open 5pm-11pm daily; children under 18 £7.40, adults £10.85; breakfast, lunch, and dinner options; V, MC)* is a pretty cheap place to crash, offering modern, clean, four- and five-bedrooms with shared baths, and one room with seven beds. It's standard-issue dorm style, but it gets extra credit points for its location right at the foot of the wall. You can get here from Hexham via bus 185 from the end of September to the middle of May, and bus 682 from the end of May to the middle of September.

need to know

Tourist Information The **Once Brewed National Park Visitors Center** *(Military Rd., Once Brewed; Tel 02434/344-396; Open Mar-Oct, hours vary),* attached to the Once Brewed Youth Hostel, has all the wall dope.

Two good wall sites are ***www.hadrians-wall.org.uk*** and ***www.tynedale.gov.uk.***

If you really want to know what went down, check out a fort: **Birdoswald** *(Gilsland; Tel 01697/747-607; 10am-5:30pm Apr-Oct; admission £2.50 adult, £2 student);* **Vindolanda Fort** *10 miles west of Hexham; Tel 01434/344-277; 10am-5pm Mar-Apr, Sept-Oct, until 6:30pm May-Aug, until 4pm Nov; admission £3.80 adult, £3.20 student);* and/or **Housesteads Fort** *(Tel 01434/344-363; 10am-6pm Apr-Oct; until 4pm Nov-Mar; admission £2.80 adult, £2.10 student).*

Directions/Transportation Road A69 between Carlisle and Newcastle parallels the wall. But the **Hadrian's Wall bus** *(Tel 01434/344-777 or 01434/322-002; www.nnpa.org.uk)* does it best for non-drivers, making stops at all the attractions between Carlisle and Hexham. The bus runs about once every two hours from 9am to 5pm. Connections can be made at Hexham and Haltwhistle for the Tyne Valley rail line between Newcastle and Carlisle. You can buy a special train ticket that includes bus fare, a full-day pass, or a 2-out-of-3-day pass.

holy island

Back in the olden days (634 A.D., to be precise), Holy Island was known as **Landisfarne,** a mystic, sacred place where Saint Aidan of Iona was asked by the king to found a monastery. He did, and the monks there were such enthusiastic evangelists that they spread the gospel to much of Northern England—and created the famous *Landisfarne Gospels,* holy texts with such beautiful Celtic illuminations on the pages that they're now the pride of the British Museum in London. Landisfarne's star bishop was St. Cuthbert, so when the monks here finally decided to flee the island for fear of Viking marauders, they took his remains with them, natch. The story goes that his relics were decay-free after 10 years in the ground, a minor miracle that temporarily turned the island into a popular pilgrimage site. The Benedictines tried to revive those glory days in the ninth century; their contribution was the **Landisfarne Priory** *(Tel 01289/389-200; 10am-6pm daily Apr-Sept, 10am-5pm Oct, 10am-4pm Nov-Mar; £2.80 adult, £2.10 students),* next to the church of St. Mary the Virgin. The priory's rainbow arches give you lots to look at if you get stuck here during high tide, during which Holy Island is cut off from the shore. No great imposition, as the natural beauty of Holy Island is just as impressive as the ruins, with amazing seascapes all around and colonies of puffins frequenting the place year-round. It only takes at most a couple of hours to walk all the way around this 2 mile-square island. With sand-bars surrounding the entire island (and only 162 residents), it's impossible to reach by boat, so be prepared to drive or hike the 3-mile-long causeway connecting it to the mainland via a 1,400-year-old footpath only accessible during low tide.

EATS

You can get good local pub grub for about £6-9 at **The Ship Inn** [see *crashing,* below], a classic rollicking, wood-timbered pub and inn. Try the yummy kipper (the local specialty) and chase it with a pint of Holy Island Blessed Bitter.

crashing

The Ship Inn *(Holy Island; Tel 01289/389-311; 11am-11pm daily; double rooms £21.75-29.50 per person, private baths; V, MC)* comes complete with four-poster beds and/or views of Bamburgh Castle.

Centrally located by the village green, **The Britannia** *(Tel 01289/ 389-218; £20 per person single, £18 per person shared room; No credit cards),* provides cozy rooms with private baths, and ample breakfasts included in the price of the room. Suited to vegetarians upon request.

need to know

Directions/Transportation Bus route 477 runs twice a day Mon-Sat from Berwick-Upon-Tweed [see *need to know,* Berwick-Upon-Tweed], from mid-July to the beginning of September. In May, June, and mid to late-September there are buses only two or three times weekly, and in winter service is very limited and totally depends on weather conditions. Trip time is half an hour. From Berwick, it's a 3-mile drive or walk across the causeway to Holy Island.

bamburgh castle

Towering above the Northumberland coastline, **Bamburgh Castle** was originally built in the sixth century, but it was completely restored in 1900 and is now an amazing and elegant example of distinctive Northern English fortress-building. Filled with all of the luxury typical of turn-of-the-century England, the castle has tons of priceless armor, jade, and royal dining room silver. It also has a quintessentially Norman keep (the central tower) and juts up dramatically from the beach all around.

After a quick trip through the castle you can run down through the shaggy, grass-topped sand dunes to the shoreline. Ocean waves, a gentle breeze, and vast expanses of soothing white sand will be a welcome break from all that castle mustiness. To really clear out the cobwebs, take a walk to **Seahouses** [see **Farne Islands,** below.] Facing the ocean, take a right and amble 4 miles down the shoreline to Seahouses, where there's great seafood and a boat launch to the nature preserve just offshore.

need to know

Hours/Days Open The castle is open daily 11am-5pm, March-October.

Directions/Transportation Regular bus service from Alnwick *(Lagny Street, Alnwick; Tel 0191/212-30-00)* is the easiest way to go. The bus stops at the castle and runs about once an hour in summer.

Eats and Crashing There's no bargain accommodation in Bamburgh; the closest place to stay is **The Mizen Head** *(Lucker Road; Tel 01668/214-254; £37.50 single, £75 double, private bath; breakfast included; MC, V),* a cozy little family-run hotel set in gardens at the western edge of the village. It's also the only place for miles to get a bite to eat.

farne islands

Wildlife in industrial northern England? You betcha. A small but impressively jagged series of rocky cliffs in the seaside hamlet of Seahouses, 15 miles southwest of Berwick-upon-Tweed, provides sanctuary for dozens of bird species, from kittiwakes and terns to puffins. And just 5 miles out to sea from the cliffs are the Farne Islands, where you'll spot whole colonies of gray seals cavorting and sunning (whenever there is any noticeable sun). Since they're protected from hunting, the seals are extremely trusting, naïve souls, which means you can see them right up close. The best way is aboard one of Billy Shiel's cruise boats, which depart from Seahouses [see *need to know,* below]. During breeding season (May-July) he'll dock and let you walk around for up-close-and-personal nature appreciation. *Warning:* If you tend to get seasick, you might want to wear an acupressure wristband or pop a Dramamine an hour before boarding—these seas get pretty choppy.

eats

As you might imagine, **The Olde Ship Inn** *(9 Main St., Seahouses; Tel 01665/721-383; meals £5 to £10; MC, V)* is bristling with old sea salts. Get over the nets and tackle and dig in to the awesome kipper and chips.

crashing

A quaint two-floor brick and stone lodge, aptly named **The Lodge** *(14 Main Street, Seahouses; Tel 01665/720-158; £24.50 per room, with private bath; No credit cards),* is a 10-minute walk north of the center of town. It has five motel-style rooms that are comfy, with good mattresses and TVs, as well as a standard English-fare restaurant/pub.

need to know

Directions/Transportation Daily bus connections run from New-castle's Haymarket Street station to Seahouses, via Alnwick, run Mon-Fri, a 50-minute ride.

Rental See **Billy Shiels** *(4 Southfield Ave, Seahouses; Tel 01665/720-308; from 10am daily, Easter-Oct; £8 per person)* to arrange those up-close-and-personal cruises to the seal colonies.

dunstanburgh castle

Walk 30 minutes along the coastal dunes north of Dunstanburgh and you'll find yourself staring up at one of the most photogenic fortresses the English ever built. **Dunstanburgh Castle** *(Craster; Tel 01665/576-231; 10am-6pm daily April-Sept, 10am-5pm Oct, 10am-4pm Wed-Sun Nov-Mar; £1.80 adult, £1.40 student)* juts out against the sky in a particularly cinematic way—which is good, as you may get wind-tossed and sand-blasted on the half-hour hike up to it from the tiny harbor town of Dunstanburgh and may need inspiration to keep going. You'll be glad you put up with the obstacle course when you finally arrive at the castle and see the ocean mists blend in with the weathered gray stone of this ruined fourteenth-century castle.

Its story is pretty run-of-the-mill, just another fortification against raiders from the east without any famous battles or intrigues connected to it. But what it offers in terms of quintessential Heathcliff vibes can't be beat. Perched high, it seems to teeter above the forbidding rocks and crashing waves down below. Peer out at the vast and empty coastline checkered with jagged cliffs and just imagine trying to sack the place. And the huge entrance portal is still in pretty good shape, giving you a taste of how mighty this pile once was.

For reasonable crashing options, you'll want to head for nearby Alnwick.

need to know

Hours/Days Open The castle is open 10am-6pm daily April-Sept, 10am-5pm Oct, 10am-4pm Wed-Sun Nov-Mar.

Directions/Transportation It's a 15-minute bus ride from Alnwick to the castle. Six buses run daily. Take the 501 or 401 from Lagny Street in Alnwick *(Tel 0191/212-30-00)*.

Eats You can grab a bite to eat at **The Jolly Fisherman** *(Harbor, Dunstanburgh; Tel 01665/576-218; 11am-1pm daily; £4-6 per entrée)*, a cozy, rustic little pub with great fresh crab dishes.

warkworth castle and hermitage

On the rocks above the little town of Warkworth, **Warkworth Castle** is a moderately well-preserved castle ruin without all those safety rails and cheesy exhibitions that make visits to other ruins feel so much like an annoying elementary-school field trip. You can wander freely around the whole mess, duck into the hidden passageways, and crawl onto the windowsills to take in the view through the ornately carved stone frames. It's a fourteenth-century collection of towers, walls, and entry portals built by Henry VIII's ancestors. Though it's not especially remembered for any great battles, it has its own sort of fame: the interior has been used in many Hollywood movies, including the recent *Elizabeth*. Set high up on a rocky coast, it overlooks the tiny, enchanting town whose name it shares.

And a 15-minute walk up the River Coquet from here is one of the most unusual sights in England. Follow the **Mill Walk** signs as you walk to reach the little ferry, ride across this tiny river and you'll be deposited at the **Warkworth Hermitage,** a retreat carved out of the side of a mountain by an essentially unknown monk. He's remembered just for the amazing work that went into hollowing out two rooms by scraping away the sandstone—and for being devout enough to actually live in them afterward. He apparently wanted much better digs (pun intended) than a Flintstone studio apartment: The place is complete with ceiling beams and detailed window frames. Then, just to avoid acquiring that diner smell inside, he tacked on an outdoor kitchen built from sandstone blocks. A true Kodak moment beckons here.

need to know

Contact Info *Tel 01665/711-423.*

Hours/Days Open The Castle is open 10am-6pm daily April-Sept, 10am-5pm Oct, and 10am-4pm Nov-Mar; the Hermitage is only open 11am-5pm Wed and Sun Apr-Sept.

Cost One low price of £2.40 for adults or £1.20 for students gets you in to both the Castle and the Hermitage.

Directions/Transportation Buses from Alnwick *(Lagny Street, Alnwick; Tel 0191/212-30-00)* run twice an hour Mon-Sat, a 15-minute ride.

Eats Respectable but cheap sandwiches, cakes, and tea can be found at **The Green House** *(Dial Place, Warkworth; no phone; 11am-10pm Tue-Sat, 11am-3pm Sun)*.

Crashing The best option for those not moving on is **Roxbro House** *(Castle Terrace, Warkworth; Tel 01665/711- 416; £17.50 per person with private bath; No credit cards)*.

planning your trip

the regions in brief

England covers only 50,327 square miles (about the size of New York State), which is miniscule in comparison with the huge impact it has had on the history of the world. But we won't get into history or political debates here. The important thing to know is that within England's close borders there is so much to see and do that you may as well be in the biggest country on the planet—and there's an amazing amount of open space in terms of rural land and natural wilderness as well.

You may hear people refer to Britain, Great Britain, the UK, and a few other geographic permutations, but those terms are not alternate names for England. They refer to the United Kingdom of Great Britain and Northern Ireland (the UK), which encompasses England, Wales, Scotland, and Northern Ireland. Yet "British" definitely means "English," and people from Scotland, Wales, and Northern Ireland would almost certainly be surprised—if not utterly offended—to be called British or Brits. Even though those countries have long been under British influence, they are decidedly not English.

LONDON AND ENVIRONS You can find remnants of Merrie Olde England—and the fading, uptight British Empire—in **London,** but that's definitely not the defining character of the modern capital, where the Sex Pistols, all-night raves, and the world's wildest street fashions were born. By population alone, London is one of the world's great urban centers; some 7 million people live in the mammoth metropolis, which covers more than 609 square miles. What most people don't realize is that the city itself technically takes up merely 1 square mile, and what is commonly thought of as London is actually a cluster of separate villages, boroughs, and corporations. Within close range are the 300-acre **Kew Gardens** in the borough of Richmond-Upon-Thames, and the 13-acre **Windsor Castle,** official residence of the Queen of England, Elizabeth II, which stands on the north bank of the Thames.

OXFORDSHIRE AND CAMBRIDGESHIRE Oxfordshire and Cambridgeshire have one glaring similarity besides the ending of their names: Each county is home to one of the most famous universities in the world—**Oxford University** and **Cambridge University.** Though **Oxford** is a very modern city, its age is evident in places like the Mitre Pub, housed in a 17th-century building. Nearby are **Blenheim Palace,** where the current Duke of Marlborough lives (and Winston Churchill was born), and **Henley-on-Thames,** the stomping ground of the hatted elite during the annual summer Royal Regatta. **Cambridge** is a lot quainter than Oxford, its neighbor to the south. The rivalry between the two universities is equivalent to the Harvard-Yale feud, but it's fought out in an annual rowing competition rather than a football game. **Ely Cathedral** is 15 minutes away by train, or a brisk bike ride along a flat 15-mile path.

THE SOUTHEAST This is the land of Chaucer's *Canterbury Tales,* and the religious center of England (you remember the Archbishop of Canterbury, right?). No matter when you visit, you'll have to elbow your way through—well, that would be very un-British, so let's just say you'll have to politely queue up with—gigantic throngs of tourists making their pilgrimage to the Cathedral. The **White Cliffs of Dover** are also a major tourist spot, but they're worth a look if you're driving down the coast to East Sussex. Nearby, you can stand on the grounds of the 1066 Battle of **Hastings,** which is basically next door to a rowdy, garish seaside resort. Or skip that, and head to **Brighton,** where tons of young people escape from London for the summer and hang out in some of the hottest and trendiest clubs outside of London, including the largest gay club on the south coast. Traveling a bit west you'll hit **Hampshire,** home of the unspoiled **New Forest** (a haven for hiking and biking) and the **Isle of Wight** (immortalized in the Beatles' tune *When I'm 64*).

WILTSHIRE AND SOMERSET You have to go to **Stonehenge.** Even if it means sacrificing a day in London or some other party scene, just do it. Go there for a minute, say you saw one of the most famous prehistoric landmarks in the world, then immediately head away from the crowd to nearby **Avebury,** where the stone circles are eight times bigger than Stonehenge and you can walk among the stones and touch them, a privilege no longer allowed at Stonehenge.

Once you cross into neighboring Somerset, the undulating limestone hills of the **Mendips** begin. Hidden within is a labyrinth of caves, including the glistening grottos at **Cheddar** and **Wookey Hole.** Go to **Glastonbury** if you're into New Age healing (among ancient ruins, no less), and to **Bristol** for a party fix in a happening city with a large student population and good mix of nightspots. Then take your hangover to **Bath,** where you can soak away your symptoms in Roman-style hot springs. Somerset's largest natural attraction is **Exmoor National Park,** where 620 miles of footpaths lead through wooded valleys to stately cliffs that plunge into the Atlantic.

DEVON AND CORNWALL The neighboring counties of Devon and Cornwall share the sensational southwest coast of England. But the prettiest part of both areas is inland, where the hills are so green they look as if they've been colored in by a child's magic marker. The major natural attraction in Devon is its national park, **Dartmoor** (it also shares part of Exmoor on the north coast). When the mist clears on Dartmoor's open moorland, you can see scores of prehistoric granite formations on this bleak and isolated stretch of terrain—or head for the Lydford Gorge's 90-foot **White Lady Waterfall.**

Cornwall has its own language, which is not in common use anymore, and its own rich cuisine, which might not be in common use if the Heart Association has anything to say about it. **Polperro** is a tiny fishing village—with a history as a smugglers' port—that's still the way you would imagine a fishing port of old. Everything west from Polperro to Penzance should be explored in one swoop; the coastal drive from St. Ives to Land's End literally leads to the end of England. **St. Ives** is a must-visit town, part art colony—housing the Tate and Hepworth museums—and part surfing mecca, with miles of golden sands. Hardcore wave-hounds should proceed directly to **Newquay,** the self-proclaimed surf capital of Europe, however dubious that distinction may be. The World Surfing Championships moved to France in 1998, but you can still fulfill all your wildest surfing and clubbing fantasies here.

CENTRAL ENGLAND You may be surprised to learn that the most popular North American tourist destination in the UK—after London—isn't the *Trainspotting* Edinburgh or the religiously conflicted Belfast, but the Shakespeare Country of Central England. **Stratford-upon-Avon,** the playwright's birth town, is the country's biggest tourist trap. Pass through, get the T-shirt, and head to the nearby city of **Nottingham,** famous for Robin Hood folklore. It's got ultra-hip clubs that attract in-vogue Brits from all over the country. The region's big cities—**Birmingham,** England's second-largest, and **Leicester**—used to be drab and dreary, but now the government is spending big bucks on the arts, historical sites, and inner-city parks. The hope is that this investment will pay off in tourist dollars. The reality is that the cities are not—and never will be—London, but they do offer an amazing nightlife.

THE COTSWOLDS The Cotswolds region is actually in central England, but its unique character makes it a notable area by itself. A 2-hour drive from London, it's a perfect site for a respite from drinking and partying every night until dawn. You can literally count sheep as you mellow out among the area's grassy, rolling hills. And you may think you've drifted off into a childhood dream when you see the fairy-tale thatched-roofed cottages that dot the hills. But plan very carefully: All of the above is true only if you visit the Cotswolds during off-peak tourist season. During the summer and spring breaks, you'll find far more tourists than sheep, as throngs of middle-aged American yuppies (and their requisite 1.4 children) invade the area. What you won't find are many—if any—independent young travelers hanging out.

NORTHWEST & THE PEAK DISTRICT The Northwest is an another English odd couple: A bucolic landscape riddled with sooty industrial pockets. **Manchester** and **Liverpool** are both good party towns, especially if you like being a million light years away from the style-nazis of London, but Liverpool is definitely a notch higher on the hip scale. After all, it is the birthplace of the Beatles, as you will see and hear again and again, everywhere you go, all over town. But the endless Fab Four nostalgia—and money machine—are not the whole picture. A cool contemporary music scene makes Liverpool nightlife worth the trip.

Meanwhile, back to the bucolic: There are no peaks in the Peak District. The entire National Park is dominated by smooth, grassy, green rolling hills. (The name was adopted from the Celtic tribe that used to inhabit the area, the *Peac*.) With weather more fickle than a hormonal pre-teen, and a number of stone circles, the area holds a sort of foggy mysticism, minus the fog. Hiking through the White Peak area—the southernmost part of the Peak District—on the *Limestone Way*, you'll have plenty of opportunities for rock climbing and major doses of adrenaline.

YORKSHIRE This grand district is home to some of England's most outstanding abbeys and most rewarding cities. The party capital here is **Leeds,** a city that once slept when its workers went home at 5pm, but now rivals anyplace in England for nightlife. **York** is packed with 200 years of historic treasures, including an ancient dungeon that will simultaneously horrify and delight even the most ardent D&D freaks. Just north of York are the ruins of Rievaux Abbey, while the amazing ruins of Fountains Abbey—with inexplicably preserved arches that seem to cling to the air for support—is close to Leeds.

THE LAKE DISTRICT This is the most popular place for outdoor fun in England, a fact that becomes painfully obvious if you are in the area on any summer or holiday weekend. But it's still possible to find the idyllic beauty that inspired Wordsworth here, if you know where to look. Start where he did, around **Grasmere,** then take the beautiful **Cumbria Coastal Way** to **Ulverston** where you can pick up the **Cumbria Way.** This route will take you north into the parklands. The only way to get to many areas in the park is on foot, which helps divert bus-ridden tourists to other sights.

NORTHUMBRIA If there is one thing that you can be sure of in this part of England, it is that you will run into at least one castle, even if that is not what you are after. There are more castles in this area than any-where else in the country, and even if you are not into the fallen wonders of the past rulers of England, some of these ruins are truly a phenomenon that shouldn't be missed. In Northumbria, you can satisfy your craving for tranquility, taking a seat inside a lonesome castle with only the drum-ming of the ocean to converse with. The price you pay for this tranquility is a notable lack of public transportation, but if you like hiking and biking, you'll be in paradise. Once you get your fill of castles, move on to **Newcastle** for a few nights of beer drinking in the city known for the best nightlife in the north. From there, you can stop by **Durham,** a college town where you can catch up on student-style nightlife and a few hip shopping stops.

VISITOR INFORMATION

Before you go, you can obtain general information from **British Tourist Authority Offices:**

In The United States 551 Fifth Ave., Suite 701, New York, NY 10176-0799; Tel 800/462-27-48 or 212/986-22-00.

In Canada 111 Avenue Rd., Suite 450, Toronto, ON M5R 3J8; Tel 888/VISIT-UK in Canada.

In Australia Level 16, Gateway, 1 Macquarie Place, Sydney NSW 2000; Tel 02/93-77-44-00.

In New Zealand Suite 305, Dilworth Building, at the corner of Queen and Customs streets, Auckland 1; Tel 09/303-14-46.

The BTA also maintains a Web site at www.visitbritain.com, covering special interests, attractions, trip-planning tips, festivals, accommoda-tions, and more.

For a full information pack on London, write to the **London Tourist Board,** *(Glen House, Victoria, Stag Place, London SW1E 5LT; Tel 020/79-32-20-00).* You can also call the recorded-message service, **Visitorcall** *(Tel 01839/123-456),* 24 hours a day. Various topics are listed; calls cost 60p ($1) per minute.

You can usually pick up a copy of *Time Out,* the most up-to-date source for what's happening in London, at any international newsstand. You can also check it out online at www.timeout.co.uk.

ENTRY REQUIREMENTS & CUSTOMS

ENTRY REQUIREMENTS

All U.S. citizens, Canadians, Australians, New Zealanders, and South Africans must have a passport with at least 2 months' validity remaining. No visa is required. The immigration officer will also want proof of your intention to return to your point of origin (usually a round-trip ticket) and visible means of support while you're in Britain. If you're planning to fly from the United States or Canada to the United Kingdom and then on to a country that requires a visa (India, for example), you should secure that visa before you arrive in Britain.

Your valid driver's license and at least one year of driving experience is required to drive personal or rented cars.

WHAT YOU CAN BRING TO ENGLAND For visitors coming to England, goods fall into two basic categories: purchases made in a nonEuropean Union (EU) country (or bought tax-free within the EU), and purchases on which tax was paid in the European Union. In the former category, limits on imports by individuals (aged 17 and older) include 200 cigarettes, 50 cigars, or 250 grams (8.8 oz.) of loose tobacco; 2 liters (2.1 qt.) of still table wine, 1 liter of liquor (over 22% alcohol content), or 2 liters of liquor (under 22%); and 2 fluid ounces of perfume. In the latter category—items on which tax was paid in the EU—limits are much higher: An individual may import 800 cigarettes, 200 cigars, and 1 kilogram (2.2 lb.) of loose tobacco; 90 liters (23.8 gal.) of wine, 10 liters (2.6 gal.) of alcohol (over 22%), and 110 liters (29.1 gal.) of beer; plus unlimited amounts of perfume.

WHAT YOU CAN TAKE OUT OF ENGLAND Returning **U.S. citizens** who have been away for 48 hours or more are allowed to bring back, once every 30 days, $400 worth of merchandise duty-free. You'll be charged a flat rate of 10% duty on the next $1,000 worth of purchases. Be sure to have your receipts handy. On gifts, the duty-free limit is $100. You cannot bring fresh foodstuffs into the United States; tinned foods, however, are allowed. For more information, contact the **U.S. Customs Service,** *(1301 Constitution Ave., P.O. Box 7407, Washington, DC 20044; Tel 202/927-67-24;* www.customs.ustreas.gov) and request the free pamphlet *Know Before You Go.*

For a clear summary of **Canadian** rules, write for the booklet *I Declare,* issued by **Revenue Canada** *(2265 St. Laurent Blvd., Ottawa K1G 4KE; Tel 613/993-05-34).* Canada allows its citizens a $750 exemption, and you're allowed to bring back duty-free 200 cigarettes, 1 kilogram of tobacco, 1.5 liters of liquor, and 50 cigars. In addition, you're allowed to mail gifts to Canada from abroad at the rate of Can$60 a day, provided they're unsolicited and don't contain alcohol or tobacco (write on the package "Unsolicited gift, under $60 value"). All valuables should be declared on the Y-38 form before departure from Canada, including serial numbers of valuables you already own, such as expensive foreign cameras. *Note:* The $750 exemption can only be used once a year and only after an absence of 7 days.

The duty-free allowance in **Australia** is A$400 or, for those under 18, A$200. Personal property mailed back from England should be marked "Australian goods returned" to avoid payment of duty. Upon returning to

Australia, citizens can bring in 250 cigarettes or 250 grams of loose tobacco, and 1,125 milliliters of alcohol. If you're returning with valuable goods you already own, such as foreign-made cameras, you should file form B263. A helpful brochure, available from Australian consulates or Customs offices, is *Know Before You Go.* For more information, contact **Australian Customs Services** *(GPO Box 8, Sydney NSW 2001; Tel 02/92-13-20-00).*

The duty-free allowance for **New Zealand** is NZ$700. Citizens over 17 can bring in 200 cigarettes, or 50 cigars, or 250 grams of tobacco (or a mixture of all three if their combined weight doesn't exceed 250 grams); plus 4.5 liters of wine and beer, or 1.125 liters of liquor. New Zealand currency does not carry import or export restrictions. Fill out a certificate of export, listing the valuables you are taking out of the country; that way, you can bring them back without paying duty. Most questions are answered in a free pamphlet available at New Zealand consulates and Customs offices: *New Zealand Customs Guide for Travelers,* Notice no. 4. For more information, contact **New Zealand Customs,** *(50 Anzac Ave., P.O. Box 29, Auckland; Tel 09/359-66-55).*

money honey

The British currency is the pound sterling (£), made up of 100 pence (p), which is used throughout the United Kingdom. Notes are issued in £5, £10, £20, and £50 denominations. (A £1 note also circulates in Scotland.) Coins come in 1p, 2p, 5p, 10p, 50p, and £1.

At this writing, the price conversions in this book have been computed at the rate of $1 equals an average 61p (or £1 = $1.70). Bear in mind, however, that exchange rates can always fluctuate for a variety of reasons, so it's important to check the latest quotes before your trip so you can budget accordingly.

For the moment at least, Britain has decided not to join "Euroland," and the traditional British pound sterling is the coin of the realm. The euro, of course, is the new single European currency that officially became the currency of 11 European countries, including France, Italy, and Germany, on January 1, 1999. Euro cash will not be introduced, and the local currencies not fully replaced, however, until the year 2002.

ATMS
The ATM networks that are most widely accessible in England are **Cirrus** *(Tel 800/424-77-87; www.mastercard.com/atm/)* and **Plus** *(Tel 800/843-7587; www.visa.com/atms);* check the back of your ATM card to see which network your bank belongs to.

Call the 800 numbers above to locate ATMs in your destination, or ask your bank for a list of overseas ATMs. Be sure to check the daily withdrawal limit before you depart, and ask whether you need a new PIN (personal ID number), since ATMs in Europe usually require a 4-digit number. Keep in mind that international withdrawal fees tend to be higher in Europe than they are in the United States, and that you'll get your money in local currency (sometimes at a very good exchange rate).

TRAVELER'S CHECKS

Traveler's checks are something of an anachronism from the days before the ATM made cash accessible at any time. These days, traveler's checks seem less necessary, but you may still prefer the security of knowing you can get a refund if your wallet is lost or stolen. (Keep a record of their serial numbers—separate from the checks, of course—so you're ensured a refund in just such an emergency.)

You can get traveler's checks at almost any bank. **American Express** offers denominations of $10, $20, $50, $100, $500, and $1,000. You'll pay a service charge ranging from 1% to 4%. You can also get traveler's checks over the phone from **American Express** *(Tel 800/221-72-82);* by using this number, Amex gold and platinum cardholders are exempt from the 1% fee. AAA members can obtain checks without a fee at most AAA offices.

Visa offers traveler's checks at Citibank locations nationwide, as well as several other banks. The service charge ranges between 1.5% and 2%; checks come in denominations of $20, $50, $100, $500, and $1,000. Call **MasterCard** *(Tel 800/223-99-20)* to find out how to get traveler's checks at a location near you.

CREDIT CARDS

Credit cards are invaluable when traveling. They are a safe way to carry money and provide a convenient record of all your expenses. You can also withdraw cash advances from your credit cards at any bank (though you'll start paying hefty interest on the advance the moment you receive the cash, and you won't receive frequent-flyer miles on an airline credit card). At most banks, you don't even need to go to a teller; you can get a cash advance at the ATM if you know your PIN number.

Almost every credit card company has an emergency 800-number that you can call if your card is stolen. They may be able to wire you a cash advance off your credit card immediately, and in many places, they can deliver an emergency credit card in a day or two. Call U.S. emergency numbers: **Citicorp Visa** *(Tel 800/336-84-72);* **American Express** *(Tel 800/221-72-82)* for all Amex credit card and traveler's checks emergencies; **MasterCard** *(Tel 800/307-73-09).*

EXCHANGING YOUR MONEY

It's always wise to exchange enough money before you leave home to get you from the airport to your hotel. This way, you avoid delays and the lousy rates at the airport exchange booths. (Though ATMs *are* everywhere...) When exchanging money, you're likely to get a better rate for traveler's checks than for cash.

London banks generally offer the best rates of exchange; they're usually open Mon-Fri, 9:30am-3:30pm. Many of the "high street" branches are now open until 5pm; a handful of Central London branches are open until noon on Saturday, including **Barclays** *(208 Kensington High St., W8; Tel 020/74-41-32-00).*

Money exchange is now also available at competitive rates at major London post offices, with a 1% service charge. Money can be exchanged during off-hours at a variety of bureaux de change throughout the city, found at small shops and in hotels, railway stations (including the international terminal at Waterloo Station), travel agencies, and airports, but their exchange rates are poorer and they charge high service fees. Examine the prices and rates carefully before handing over your dollars, as there's no consumer organization to regulate the activities of privately run bureaux de change.

Time Out recently did a survey of various exchange facilities, and **American Express** *(6 Haymarket, SW1; Tel 800/221-72-82 or 020/74-84-96-00; plus other locations throughout the city)* came out on top, with the lowest commission charged on dollar transactions. American Express charges no commission when cashing travelers checks; however, a flat rate of £2 ($3.30) is charged when exchanging the dollar to the pound. Most other agencies tend to charge a percentage rate commission (usually 2%) with a £2 to £3 ($3.30 to $4.95) minimum charge.

Other reputable firms are **Thomas Cook** *(6 Mount St., W1; Tel 800/223-73-73 or 020/7707-45-01; branches at Victoria Station, Marble Arch, and other city locations);* and, for 24-hour foreign exchange, **Chequepoint** *(548 Oxford Street, W1N 9HJ; Tel 020/77-23-10-05; hours vary at other locations throughout London).* Try not to change money at your hotel; the rates they offer tend to be horrendous.

when to go

WEATHER
Yes, it rains, but you'll rarely get a true downpour. It's heaviest in November (2 1/2 inches on average). British temperatures can range from 30 to 110 degrees Fahrenheit but they rarely drop below 35 or go above 78. Evenings are cool, even in summer. Note that the British, who consider chilliness wholesome, like to keep the thermostats about 10 degrees below the American comfort level. Hotels have central heating, but are usually kept just above the goose bump (in Britspeak, "goose pimple") margin.

BARGAIN SEASON
The cheapest time to travel to England is in the off-season: November 1 to December 12 and December 25 to March 14. In the last few years, the airlines have been offering irresistible fares during these periods. Weekday flights are cheaper than weekend fares (often by 10% or more).

Rates generally increase between March 14 to June 5 and in October, then hit their peak in the high travel seasons between June 6 and September 30 and December 13 and 24. July and August are also the months when most Britons take their holidays, so besides the higher prices, you'll have to deal with limited availability of accommodations and crowds.

In short, spring offers the countryside at its greenest; autumn brings the bright colors of the northern moorlands, and summer's warmer weather gives rise to the many outdoor music and theater festivals. But winter offers savings across the board and a chance to see Britons going about their everyday lives largely unhindered by tourist invasions.

HOLIDAYS
England observes New Year's Day, Good Friday, Easter Monday, May

Day (1st Monday in May), spring and summer bank holidays (the last Monday in May and August, respectively), Christmas Day, and Boxing Day (December 26).

FESTIVALS & EVENTS

For more options, see the **Festivals and Events** sidebars throughout the book.

JANUARY

London International Boat Show. Europe's largest boat show, held at the Earl's Court Exhibition Centre, Warwick Road. *Tel 01784/473-377.*

Charles I Commemoration, London. To mark the anniversary of the execution of King Charles I "in the name of freedom and democracy," hundreds of cavaliers march through central London in 17th-century dress, and prayers are said at Whitehall's Banqueting House. Last Sunday in January. *Tel 020/87-81-95-00.*

Chinese New Year, London. The famous Lion Dancers in Soho perform free on the nearest Sunday to Chinese New Year. Either in late January or early February (based on the lunar calendar).

FEBRUARY

Jorvik Festival, York. This 2-week festival celebrates the historic cathedral city's role as a Viking outpost. *Tel 01904/621-756.*

MARCH

Crufts Dog Show, Birmingham. The English, they say, love their pets more than their offspring. Crufts offers an opportunity to observe the nation's pet lovers doting on 8,000 dogs, representing 150 breeds. It's held at the National Exhibition Centre, Birmingham, West Midlands. Tickets can be purchased at the door. *Tel 0121/780-41-41.*

APRIL

Martell Grand National Meeting, outside Liverpool. England's premier steeplechase event takes place over a 4-mile course at **Aintree Racecourse.** *Tel 0151/523-26-00.*

London Marathon. More than 30,000 competitors run from Greenwich Park to Buckingham Palace. *Tel 0161/76-20-41-17.* Mid-April.

Easter Parade, London. A memorable parade of brightly colored floats and marching bands around Battersea Park.

The Shakespeare Season, Stratford-upon-Avon. The Royal Shakespeare Company begins its annual season, presenting works by the Bard in his hometown, at the **Royal Shakespeare Theatre.** *Tel 01789/295-623.* April-January.

MAY

Brighton Festival. England's largest arts festival, with more than 400 different cultural events. *Tel 01273/292-599.*

Royal Windsor Horse Show. The country's major show-jumping presentation, held at the Home Park, Windsor, Berkshire, is attended by the queen herself. *Tel 01298/722-72.* Mid-May.

Glyndebourne Festival. One of England's major cultural events, this festival is centered at the 1,200-seat Glyndebourne Opera House in

Sussex, 54 miles south of London. Tickets cost £10-124 ($17-210). *Tel 01273/812-321*. Mid-May to late August.

Bath International Music Festival. One of Europe's most prestigious international festivals of music and the arts features as many as 1,000 performers at various venues in Bath. For information, contact the **Bath Festivals Trust.** *Tel 01225/463-362*. May 19 to June 4.

Shakespeare Under the Stars. The Bard's works are performed at the **Open Air Theatre,** Inner Circle, Regent's Park, NW1, in London. Take the tube to Baker Street. Performances are Mon-Sat, 8pm; Wed, Thur, and Sat, 2:30pm. *Tel 020/74-86-24-31*. Previews begin in late May and last throughout the summer.

Royal Academy's Summer Exhibition, London. This institution, founded in 1768, has for some two centuries held Summer Exhibitions of living painters at Burlington House, Piccadilly Circus. *Tel 020/74-39-74-38*. May 29 to August 4.

Chichester Festival Theatre. Some great classic and modern plays are presented at this West Sussex theater. For tickets and information, contact the **Festival Theatre.** *Tel 01243/781-312*. The season runs May to October.

JUNE

Vodafone Derby Stakes. This famous horse-racing event (the "Darby," as it's called here) is held at Epsom Downs, Epsom, Surrey. Men wear top hats and women, including the queen, put on silly millinery creations. *Tel 01372/463-072*. First week of June.

Trooping the Colour. This is the queen's official birthday parade, a quintessential British event, with exquisite pageantry and pomp as she inspects her regiments and takes their salute as they parade their colors before her at the Horse Guards Parade, Whitehall. Tickets for the parade and two reviews, held on preceding Saturdays, are allocated by ballot. Applicants must write between January 1 and the end of February, enclosing a self-addressed stamped envelope or International Reply Coupon to the Ticket Office, HQ Household Division, Horse Guards, Whitehall, London SW1X 6AA. Exact dates and ticket prices will be supplied later. The ballot is held in mid-March, and only successful applicants are informed in April. Held on a day designated in June (not necessarily the queen's actual birthday). *Tel 020/74-14-24-97*.

Aldeburgh Festival of Music and the Arts. The composer Benjamin Britten launched this festival in 1948. For more details on the events, and for the year-round program, write to **Aldeburgh Foundation,** High Street, Aldeburgh, Suffolk IP15 5AX. *Tel 01728/452-935*. Two weeks from mid- to late June.

Royal Ascot Week. Although Ascot Racecourse is open year-round for guided tours, events, exhibitions, and conferences, there are 24 race days throughout the year, with the feature races being the Royal Meeting in June, Diamond Day in late July, and the Festival at Ascot in late September. For information, contact **Ascot Racecourse;** *Tel 01344/622-211*.

The Exeter Festival. The town of Exeter hosts more than 150 events celebrating classical music, ranging from concerts and opera to lectures. Festival dates and offerings vary from year to year. *Tel 01392/265-200; www.exetergov.uk.* June 13 to July 16.

Lawn Tennis Championships, Wimbledon. Ever since players took to the grass courts at Wimbledon in 1877, this tournament has attracted quite a crowd, and there's still an excited hush at Centre Court and a certain thrill associated with being there. Savor the strawberries and cream that are part of the experience. Acquiring tickets and overnight lodgings during the annual tennis competitions at Wimbledon can be difficult to arrange independently. Two outfits that can book both hotel accommodations and tickets to the event include **Steve Furgal's International Tennis Tours** *(11828 Rancho Bernardo Rd., San Diego, CA 92128; Tel 800/258-36-64,* and **Championship Tennis Tours** *8040 E. Morgan Trail, no. 12, Scottsdale, AZ 85258; Tel 800/468-36-64.* Early bookings are strongly advised. Tickets for Centre and Number One courts are obtainable through a lottery. Write in from August to December to **A.E.L.T.C.** *(P.O. Box 98, Church Road, Wimbledon, London SW19 5AE; Tel 020/89-46-22-44).* Outside court tickets are available daily, but be prepared to wait in line. Late June through early July.

City of London Festival. This annual art festival is held in venues throughout the city. *Tel 020/73-77-05-40.* June and July.

Ludlow Festival. This is one of England's major arts festivals, complete with an open-air Shakespeare performance within the Inner Bailey of Ludlow Castle. Concerts, lectures, readings, exhibitions, and workshops. Shcedules are available after March from **The Ludlow Festival box office** *(Castle Square, Ludlow, Shropshire SY8 1AY; Tel 01584/872-150);* enclose a self-addressed stamped envelope. June 24 to July 9.

JULY

Kenwood Lakeside Concerts. These annual concerts on the north side of Hampstead Heath have continued a British tradition of outdoor performances for nearly 50 years. Fireworks displays and laser shows enliven the premier musical performances. The audience catches the music as it drifts across the lake from the performance shell. Concerts are held every Saturday from early July to early September. *Tel 020/83-48-12-86.*

The Proms, London. A night at "The Proms"—the annual Henry Wood promenade concerts at Royal Albert Hall—attracts music aficionados from around the world. Staged almost daily (except for a few Sundays), these traditional concerts were launched in 1895, and are the principal summer engagements for the BBC Symphony Orchestra. *Tel 020/75-89-32-03.* Mid-July through mid-September.

AUGUST

Cowes Week, off the Isle of Wight. This yachting festival takes place in early August. *Tel 01983/291-914.*

Notting Hill Carnival, Ladbroke Grove, London. One of the largest annual street festivals in Europe, attracting more than half a million people. There's live reggae and soul music plus great Caribbean food. Two days in late August. *Tel 020/89-64-05-44.*

International Beatles Week, Liverpool. Tens of thousands of fans gather in Liverpool to celebrate the music of the Fab Four. There's a whole series of concerts from international cover bands, plus tributes, auctions, and tours. **Cavern City Tours** *(Tel 0151/236-90-91),* a local company, offers hotel and festival packages that include accommodations and tickets to tours and events, starting around £75 ($127.50) for two nights. For information, contact the **Tourist Information Centre** in Liverpool *Tel 0151/709-81-11.* August 24 to 29.

SEPTEMBER

Raising of the Thames Barrier, Unity Way, SE18. Once a year, usually in September, a full test is done on this miracle of modern engineering; all 10 of the massive steel gates are raised against the low and high tides. *Tel 020/88-54-13-73* for exact date and time.

Horse of the Year Show, Wembley Arena, Wembley. Riders fly from every continent to join in this festive display of horsemanship (much appreciated by the queen). The British press calls it an "equine extravaganza." It's held at Wembley Arena, outside London. *Tel 020/89-02-88-33.* Late September to early October.

OCTOBER

Cheltenham Festival of Literature. This Cotswold event features readings, book exhibitions, and theatrical performances—all in the famed spa town of Gloucestershire. *Tel 01242/522-878 for details; 01242/237-377 to receive mailings.* Early to mid-October.

Opening of Parliament, London. Ever since the 17th century, when the English beheaded Charles I, British monarchs have been denied the right to enter the House of Commons. Instead, the monarch opens Parliament in the House of Lords, reading an official speech that is in fact written by the government. Queen Elizabeth II rides from Buckingham Palace to Westminster in a royal coach accompanied by the Yeoman of the Guard and the Household Cavalry. The public galleries are open on a first-come, first-served basis. First Monday in October.

NOVEMBER

Guy Fawkes Night, throughout England. This British celebration commemorates the anniversary of the "Gunpowder Plot," an attempt to blow up King James I and parliament. Huge organized bonfires are lit throughout London, and Guy Fawkes, the plot's most famous conspirator, is burned in effigy. Check *Time Out* for locations. Early November.

Lord Mayor's Procession and Show, The City, London. The queen has to ask permission to enter the square mile in London called the City—and the right of refusal has been jealously guarded by London merchants since the 17th century. Suffice it to say that the lord mayor is a powerful character, and the procession from the Guildhall to the Royal Courts is appropriately impressive. You can watch the procession from the street; the banquet is by invitation only. Second week in November. *Tel 020/76-06-30-30.*

Tripping Out

BIKE TRIPS

If you're planning a bike trip on your own, you can take your two wheels on passenger trains in England for a £3 ($5.10) extra charge. By 2005, a National Cycle Network will cover 8,000 miles throughout the country. The network will run from Dover in southeast England to Inverness in the Highlands. Some 3,500 miles—known as the Millennium Route—opened in the summer of 2000.

Most routes cross old railway lines, canal towpaths, and riversides. Among the more popular routes are the Sea-to-Sea cycle Route, a 140-mile path linking the Irish Sea with the North Sea across the Pennine Hills and into the north Lake District and the Durham Dales. The Essex Cycle Route covers 250 miles of countryside, going through some of the England's most charming villages; the Devon Coast-to-Coast route runs for 90 miles in southwest England, skirting the edge of Dartmoor; the West Country Way for 248 miles links the Cornish coast to the cities of Bath and Britain, and the Severn and Thames route for 100 miles links two of Britain's major rivers.

For a free copy of *Britain for Cyclists,* with information on these routes, call the **British Tourist Authority** *(Tel 800/462-27-48)* or contact the Cyclists Touring Club (see below).

The **Cyclists Touring Club** *(Cotterell House, 69 Meadrow, Godalming, Surrey GU7 3HS; Tel 01483/417-217)* can suggest routes and provide information. Memberships cost £25 ($42.50) a year for adults, £15 ($25.50) for those 26 and under. A family (three or more members) membership costs £40 ($68).

Himalayan Travel *(110 Prospect St., Stamford, CT 06901; Tel 800/225-23-80),* best known for its walking tours of England (see below), also offers a roster of roughly equivalent bike tours within England. They do cycling tours of the Cotswolds and Yorkshire. Cost for one week is $1,100 including breakfast, accommodations and some meals.

Vermont Bicycle Touring *(P.O. Box 711, Bristol, VT 05443; Tel 800/245-38-68 or 802/453-48-11),* also offers tours throughout England geared to different levels of physical ability; extra guidance, assistance, and services are always available. A van transports your luggage.

FISHING TRIPS

Fly-fishing was born here, and it's considered an art form. An expert in leading programs for fly-fishermen eager to experience the cold, clear waters of Britain is **Rod & Reel Adventures** *566 Thomson Lane, Suite B6, Copperopolis, CA 95228; Tel 800/356-69-82.* Don't expect smooth sales-manship at this place, but if you persevere, someone at this company should be able to link you up with a local fishing guide who can lead you to English waters that are well stocked with trout, perch, grayling, sea bream, Atlantic salmon, and such lesser-known species as rudd and roach. Rod & Reel Adventures has contacts in the Lake District, Scotland, and the Norfolk Broads. Such streams as the Wear, the Derwent, the Copu-quet, and the Till are especially prolific.

If you prefer to go it alone, contact the **British Salmon & Trout Association** *(Fishmonger's Hall, London Bridge, London EC4R 9EL; Tel 020/72-83-58-38)* for information about British fishing regulations.

GOLF TRIPS

Although the sport originated in Scotland, golf has been around in England since Edward VII first began stamping over the greens of such courses as Royal Lytham & St. Annes, in England's northwest, or Royal St. Georges, near London.

The unyielding reality is that golf in England remains a clubby sport where some of the most prestigious courses are usually reserved exclusively for members. Rules at most English golf courses tend to be stricter in matters of dress code and protocol than their equivalents in the United States. If, however, you just received a major inheritance which you are just dying to blow on a Bitish golf holiday, **Golf International** *(275 Madison Ave., New York, NY 10016; Tel 800/833-13-89 or 212/986-91-76)* can open doors for you. Golf packages in England are arranged for anywhere from 7 to 14 days and can include as much or as little golf, on as many different courses, as a participant wants. Weeklong vacations, with hotels, breakfasts, car rentals, and greens fees included, range from $2,735 per person, double occupancy, airfare not included.

You might be able to get by for a little less with **Adventures in Golf** *(11 Northeastern Blvd., Suite 360, Nashua, NH 03062; Tel 603/882-83-67)* or **Jerry Quinlan's Celtic Golf** *(124 Sunset Blvd., Cape May, NJ 08204; Tel 800/535-61-48)*. Each of their tours is customized, so you can cut the lodging back from a five-star deluxe manor house to a simple guesthouse.

HIKING, WALKING & RAMBLING TRIPS

In England and Wales alone, there are some 100,000 miles of trails and footpaths. The **Ramblers' Association** *(1-5 Wandsworth Rd., London SW8 2XX; Tel 020/73-39-85-00)* publishes an annual yearbook that lists some 2,500 bed-and-breakfasts near the trails; it costs £11 ($18.70). Send a check in sterling for the yearbook if you plan to order before your trip; otherwise the yearbook can be purchased in England for £4.99 ($8.50).

Alternatively, you can join an organized hiking tour—but it's definitely going to cost you. One of the longest-running tour operators is **Himalayan Travel** *(110 Prospect St., Stamford, CT 06901; Tel 800/225-23-80)*. Between April and October, they offer hiking tours within seven districts of England, for 1-2 weeks. Participants cover 8-15 miles a day within the Cotswolds, Dorset, Northumberland, Cornwall, or the Yorkshire Dales, spending the night at small inns en route. At those distances, you should be reasonably fit, but you definitely don't have to be a marathon runner to get by. All tours include breakfast daily and overnight lodging, as well as some meals. A weeklong tour costs around $900 to $1,200 per person, double occupancy.

Wilderness Travel, Inc. *(1102 Ninth St., Berkeley, CA 94710; Tel 800/368-27-94 or 510/558-24-88)* also specializes in treks and inn-to-inn hiking tours, plus less strenuous walking tours of Cornwall and the Cotswolds that combine transportation with walking sessions of 3 hours or less.

English Lakeland Ramblers *18 Stuyvesant Oval, Suite 1A, New York, NY 10009; Tel 800/724-88-01 outside New York City, or 212/505-10-20 within New York City; www.ramblers.com)* offers 7- to 8-day walking tours for the average active person. On its Lake District tour, you'll stay and have your meals in a charming 17th-century country inn near Ambleside and Windermere. A minibus takes hikers and sightseers daily to trails and sightseeing points. Experts tell you about the area's culture and history and highlight its natural wonders. There are also tours of the Cotswolds and Scotland, as well as inn-to-inn tours and privately guided tours.

HORSEBACK RIDING TRIPS

You can learn to ride or brush up on your skills at **Eastern Equation,** a facility located on the Essex/Suffolk border. British Horse Society-certified instructors teach riders at a facility with a large indoor arena, a jumping course, and 30 horses and ponies of various sizes and abilities. Many trails go directly from the farm to the countryside. You can stay in a room with a private bath at the beautiful 16th-century farmhouse (subject to availability), or find accommodation in a comfortable nearby hotel. Contact **Cross Country International** *(P.O. Box 1170, Millbrook, NY 12545; Tel 800/828-87-68).*

There are also American companies that offer horseback-riding package tours of England. **Equitour/FITS Equestrian Tours** *(P.O. Box 807, Dubois, WY 82513; Tel 800/545-00-19),* formed by the 1996 merger of two well-respected tour operators based in Wyoming and California, specializes in package tours for riding enthusiasts who want to experience the horsey traditions of the land of foxes and hounds. Two types of tours can be arranged through their auspices: stationary tours where instruction in jumping and dressage are conducted over a 7-day period at a stable beside the Bristol Channel or on the fields of Dartmoor, and "progressive" tours where treks of 4 to 10 days are conducted in Exmoor and Wales. Most riders eager to experience as wide a view of England as possible opt for the latter, spending each night at a different B&B or inn, and lodging their mounts at nearby stables. The accommodations are simple, and prices are kept deliberately low. A 4-day horseback excursion in Dartmoor that includes use of a horse and its tack, guide services, overnight accommodations, and all meals costs around $775 per person, double occupancy.

BEER & BREWERY TRIPS

A Seattle-based company, **MIR Corporation** *(85 S. Washington St., Suite 210, Seattle, WA 98104; Tel 800/424-72-89),* offers 9-day Brew Tasting and Brewery Tours that include visits to such major breweries as Samuel Smith's and Young's, outside of London; the Caledonian brewery, outside of Edinburgh; and a host of lesser-known, family-owned breweries, such as Traquair House, scattered throughout the countryside. Included are frequent opportunities to taste local brew at atmospheric pubs en route. Don't expect demure sobriety during the course of this experience. Most participants quaff their first pint at least an hour before lunch and continue sampling the merchandise throughout the course of the day and evening. Prices, without airfare, begin at $1,495 per person, double occupancy. Accommodations are in unpretentious middle-bracket hotels and inns. Each tour is limited to 20 participants, and transport throughout is by train and motor coach.

UNIVERSITY STUDY TRIPS

You can study English literature at renowned universities such as Oxford and Cambridge during the week and then take weekend excursions to the countryside of Shakespeare, Austen, Dickens, and Hardy. While doing your course work, you can live in dormitories with other students and dine in elaborate halls or the more intimate Fellows' clubs. Study programs in England are not limited to the liberal arts, or to high-school or college students.

Affiliated with Richmond College, in London, **American Institute for Foreign Study** *102 Greenwich Ave., Greenwich, CT 06830; Tel 800/727-24-37)* offers 4 weeks and up of traveling programs for high-school students, and internships and academic programs for college students. There are also programs leading to the British equivalent of an MBA.

IIE (Institute of International Education) *(U.S. Student Programs Division, 809 United Nations Plaza, New York, NY 10017-3580; Tel 212/984-54-00)* administers a variety of academic, training, and grant programs for the U.S. Information Agency (USIA), including the Fulbright grants. It is especially helpful in arranging enrollments for U.S. students in summer-school programs.

University Vacations *(3660 Bougainvillea Rd., Coconut Grove, FL 33133; Tel 800/792-01-00)* offers upmarket liberal-arts programs at Oxford and Cambridge universities. Courses usually last 7 to 12 days and combine lectures and excursions with dining in the intimate Fellows' Dining Rooms. Accommodations are in private rooms with available ensuite facilities in the medieval colleges. There are neither formal academic requirements nor pressure for examinations or written requirements. Its summer headquarters is Brasenose College, Oxford.

Worldwide Classrooms *P.O. Box 1166, Milwaukee, WI 53201, (www.worldwide.edu)* produces an extensive listing of schools offering study-abroad programs in England, and offers a directory-like catalog for $9.95.

health & insurance

STAYING HEALTHY

You're not likely to encounter many health problems while traveling in England. The tap water is safe to drink, the milk is pasteurized, and health services are good.

The mad-cow crisis is over, but caution is always advised. (For example, it's been suggested that it's safer to eat British beef cut from the bone instead of on the bone.) Other than that, traveling to England doesn't pose any health risks.

If you need a doctor, your hotel can recommend one, or you can contact your embassy or consulate. Outside London, dial *100* and ask the operator for the local police, who will give you the name, address, and telephone number of a doctor in your area. *Note:* U.S. visitors who become ill while they're in England are only eligible for free emergency care. For other treatment, including follow-up care, you will be asked to pay.

If you suffer from a chronic illness, consult your doctor before your departure. For conditions like epilepsy, diabetes, or heart problems, wear a **Medic Alert Identification Tag** *(Tel 800/825-37-85; www.medicalert.org),* which will immediately alert doctors to your condition and give them access to your records through Medic Alert's 24-hour hotline. Membership is $35, plus a $15 annual fee.

Pack prescription medications in your carry-on luggage. Carry written prescriptions in generic, not brand-name form, and bring all prescription medications in their original labeled vials. Also take along copies of your prescriptions in case you lose your pills or run out.

INSURANCE

There are three kinds of travel insurance: trip-cancellation, medical, and lost luggage coverage.

Trip-cancellation insurance is a good idea if you have paid a large portion of your vacation expenses up-front, say, by purchasing a package tour. (Trip-cancellation insurance costs approximately 6% to 8% percent of the total value of your vacation.) The other two types of insurance, however, don't make sense for most travelers. Rule number one: Check your existing policies before you buy any additional coverage.

Your existing **health insurance** should cover you if you get sick while on vacation (though if you belong to an HMO, you should check to see whether you are fully covered when away from home). If you need hospital treatment, most health insurance plans and HMOs will cover out-of-country hospital visits and procedures, at least to some extent. However, most make you pay the bills up-front at the time of care, and you'll get a refund only after you've returned and filed all the paperwork.

Members of **Blue Cross/Blue Shield** *(Tel 800/810-BLUE;* www. bluecares.com) can now use their cards at select hospitals in most major cities worldwide. For independent travel health-insurance providers, see below.

If you have renter's insurance, it probably covers stolen **luggage.** The airlines are responsible for $1,250 on domestic flights if they lose your luggage; if you plan to carry anything more valuable than that, keep it in your carry-on bag.

If you do require additional insurance, try one of the following companies: **Access America** *(Tel 800/284-83-00);* **Travel Guard International** *(Tel 800/826-13-00);* or **Travel Insured International, Inc.** *(Tel*

800/243-31-74). Companies specializing in accident and medical care include: **MEDEX International** *(Tel 888/MEDEX-00 or 410/453-63-00; www.medexassist.com);* and **Travel Assistance International** World-wide Assistance Services, Inc.; *(Tel 800/821-28-28 or 202/828-58-94).*

special needs

STUDENTS
The best resource for students is the **Council on International Educational Exchange,** or CIEE. They can set you up with an ID card (see below), and their travel branch, **Council Travel Service** *(Tel 800/226-86-24; www.counciltravel.com),* is the biggest student travel agency operation in the world. It can get you discounts on plane tickets, rail passes, and the like. Ask them for a list of CTS offices in major cities so you can keep the discounts flowing (and aid lines open) as you travel.

From CIEE you can obtain the student traveler's best friend, the $18 **International Student Identity Card (ISIC).** It's the only officially acceptable form of student identification, good for cut rates on rail passes, plane tickets, and other discounts. It also provides you with basic health and life insurance and a 24-hour help line. If you're no longer a student but are still under 26 you can get a GO 25 card from the same people, which will get you the insurance and some of the discounts (but not student admission prices in museums).

In Canada, **Travel CUTS** *(200 Ronson St., Ste. 320, Toronto, ONT M9W 5Z9; Tel 800/667-28-87 or 416/614-28-87; www.travelcuts.com),* offers similar services. **Usit Campus** *(52 Grosvenor Gardens, London SW1W 0AG; Tel 020/77-30-34-02; www.usitcampus.co.uk),* opposite Victoria Station, is Britain's leading specialist in student and youth travel.

TRAVELERS WITH DISABILITIES
A disability shouldn't stop anyone from traveling. There are more resources out there than ever before. *A World of Options,* a 658-page book of resources for travelers with disabilities, covers a number of activities. It costs $35 ($30 for members) and is available from **Mobility International USA** *(P.O. Box 10767, Eugene, OR, 97440; Tel 541/343-12-84, voice and TDD; www.miusa.org).* Annual membership for Mobility International is $35, which includes their quarterly newsletter, *Over the Rainbow.*

The Moss Rehab Hospital *(Tel 215/456-96-00* has been providing friendly and helpful phone advice and referrals to disabled travelers for years through its **Travel Information Service** *(Tel 215/456-96-03; www.mossresourcenet.org).*

You can join **The Society for the Advancement of Travel for the Handicapped (SATH)** *(347 Fifth Ave. Suite 610, New York, NY 10016; Tel 212/447-72-84; Fax 212-725-82-53; www.sath.org)* for $45 annually, $30 for students, to gain access to their vast network of connections in the travel industry. They provide information sheets on travel destinations, and referrals to tour operators that specialize in traveling with disabilities. Their quarterly magazine, *Open World for Disability and Mature*

Travel, is full of good information and resources. A year's subscription is $13 ($21 outside the U.S.).

Travelers with disabilities may also want to consider joining a tour that caters specifically to them. One of the best operators is **Flying Wheels Travel** *(143 West Bridge, P.O. Box 382, Owatonna, MN 55060; Tel 800/535-67-90).* They offer various escorted tours and cruises, with an emphasis on sports, as well as private tours in minivans with lifts. Other reputable specialized tour operators include **Access Adventures** *(Tel 716/889-90-96),* which offers sports-related vacations; **Accessible Journeys** *(Tel 800/TINGLES or 610/521-03-39),* for slow walkers and wheelchair travelers; **The Guided Tour, Inc.** *(Tel 215/782-13-70);* **Wilderness Inquiry** *(Tel 800/728-07-19 or 612/379-38-58);* and **Directions Unlimited** *(Tel 800/533-53-43.*

Vision-impaired travelers should contact the **American Foundation for the Blind** *(11 Penn Plaza, Suite 300, New York, NY 10001; Tel 800/232-54-63 or 212/502-76-00)* for information on traveling with seeing-eye dogs.

Many London hotels, museums, restaurants, and sightseeing attractions have wheelchair ramps. Persons with disabilities are often granted special discounts at attractions and, in some cases, nightclubs. These are called "concessions" in Britain. It always pays to ask. Free information and advice is available from **Holiday Care Service** *(Imperial Building, 2nd Floor, Victoria Road, Horley, Surrey RH6 7PZ; Tel 01293/774-535; Fax 01293/784-647).*

The transport system, cinemas, and theaters are still pretty much off-limits, but **London Transport** *(Tel 020/79-18-33-12)* does publish a leaflet called *Access to the Underground,* which gives details of elevators and ramps at individual Underground stations. And the **London Black Cab** is perfectly suited for those in wheelchairs; the roomy interiors have plenty of room for maneuvering.

In London, the most prominent organization for information about access to theaters, cinemas, galleries, museums, and restaurants is **Artsline** *(54 Chalton St., London NW1 1HS; Tel 020/73-88-22-27; Fax 020/73-83-26-53; 9:30am-5:30pm, Mon-Fri).* It offers free information about wheelchair access, theaters with hearing aids, tourist attractions, and cinemas. Artsline will mail information to North America, but it's even more helpful to contact Artsline after your arrival in London.

Another organization that cooperates closely with Artsline is **Tripscope** *(The Courtyard, 4 Evelyn Rd., London W4 5JL; Tel 020/85-80-70-21; Fax 020/89-94-36-18),* which offers advice on travel for persons with disabilities in Britain and elsewhere.

GAY & LESBIAN

England has one of the most active gay and lesbian scenes in the world, centered mainly around London. Gay bars, restaurants, and centers are also found in all large English cities, notably Bath, Birmingham, Manchester, and especially Brighton.

For starters, you may want to check out the new *Frommer's Gay & Lesbian Europe*. Other guides include *Spartacus Britain and Ireland* and *London Scene*. For up-to-the-minute activities in Britain, we recommend *Gay Times* (London).

The International Gay & Lesbian Travel Association (IGLTA), *(Tel 800/448-85-50 or 954/776-26-26; Fax 954/776-33-03; www.iglta.org)* links travelers up with gay-friendly service organizations or tour specialists. With around 1,200 members, it offers quarterly newsletters, marketing mailings, and a membership directory that's updated quarterly. Membership often includes gay or lesbian businesses but is open to individuals for $150 yearly, plus a $100 administration fee for new members. Members are kept informed of gay and gay-friendly hoteliers, tour operators, and airline and cruise-line representatives. Contact the IGLTA for a list of its member agencies, who will be tied into IGLTA's information resources.

General gay and lesbian travel agencies include **Family Abroad** *(Tel 800/999-55-00 or 212/459-18-00; gay and lesbian)* and **Above and Beyond Tours** *(Tel 800/397-26-81; mainly gay men)*.

There are also two good, biannual English-language gay guidebooks, both focused on gay men but including information for lesbians as well. You can get the *Spartacus International Gay Guide* or *Odysseus* from most gay and lesbian bookstores, or order them from **Giovanni's Room** *(Tel 215/923-29-60)* or **A Different Light Bookstore** *(Tel 800/343-40-02 or 212/989-48-50)*. Both lesbians and gays might want to pick up a copy of *Gay Travel A to Z* ($16). *The Ferrari Guides (www.q-net.com)* is yet another very good series of gay and lesbian guidebooks.

Out and About, *(8 W. 19th St. #401, New York, NY 10011; Tel 800/929-22-68 or 212/645-69-22)* offers guidebooks and a monthly newsletter packed with good information on the global gay and lesbian scene. A year's subscription to the newsletter costs $49. *Our World (1104 North Nova Rd., Suite 251, Daytona Beach, FL 32117; Tel 904/441-53-67)* is a slicker monthly magazine promoting and highlighting travel bargains and opportunities. Annual subscription rates are $35 in the United States, $45 outside the United States.

In London, the **Lesbian and Gay Switchboard** *(Tel 020/78-37-73-24)* is open 24 hours a day, providing information about gay-related London activities or advice in general. The **Bisexual Helpline** *(Tel 020/85-69-75-00; Tue-Wed 7:30-9:30pm, Sat 10:30am-2:30pm)* offers useful information. The best bookstore is **Gay's the Word** *(66 Marchmont St., WC1; Tel 020/72-78-76-54; Mon-Sat 10am-6:30pm, Sun 2-6pm)*, which is the largest such store in Britain.

getting there

BY PLANE
British Airways *(Tel 800/AIRWAYS; www.british-airways.com)* offers flights from 18 U.S. cities to Heathrow and Gatwick airports as well as many others to Manchester, Birmingham, and Glasgow. Nearly every flight is nonstop. With more add-on options than any other airline,

British Airways can make a visit to Britain cheaper than you might have expected. Ask about packages that include both airfare and discounted hotel accommodations in Britain.

Known for consistently offering excellent fares, **Virgin Atlantic Airways** *(Tel 800/862-86-21; www.fly.virgin.com)* flies daily to either Heathrow or Gatwick from Boston, Newark, New Jersey, New York's JFK, Los Angeles, San Francisco, Washington's Dulles, Miami, and Orlando.

American Airlines *(Tel 800/433-73-00; www.aa.com)* offers daily flights to London's Heathrow from half a dozen U.S. gateways—New York's JFK (six times daily), Newark (once daily), Chicago's O'Hare and Boston's Logan (twice daily), and Miami International and Los Angeles International (each once daily).

Depending on the day and season, **Delta Air Lines** *(Tel 800/241-41-41; www.delta-air.com)* runs either one or two daily nonstop flights between Atlanta and Gatwick. Delta also offers nonstop daily service from Cincinnati.

Northwest Airlines *(Tel 800/225-25-25; www.nwa.com)* flies non-stop from Minneapolis and Detroit to Gatwick, with connections possible from other cities, such as Boston or New York.

Continental Airlines *(Tel 800/231-08-56; www.flycontinental.com)* has daily flights to London from Houston and Newark.

United Airlines *(Tel 800/538-29-29; www.ual.com)* flies nonstop from New York's JFK and Chicago's O'Hare to Heathrow two or three times daily, depending on the season. United also offers nonstop service twice a day from Dulles Airport, near Washington, D.C., plus once-a-day service from Newark, Los Angeles, and San Francisco to Heathrow.

For travelers departing from Canada, **Air Canada** *(Tel 800/776-30-00; www.aircanada.ca)* flies daily to London's Heathrow nonstop from Vancouver, Montreal, and Toronto. There are also frequent direct services from Calgary and Ottawa.

Icelandair *(Tel 800/223-55-00; www.icelandair.com)* offers direct flights from North America to Europe via its hub in Reykjavík, Iceland. They offer service from Boston, New York, Baltimore/Washington, Minneapolis/St. Paul, Orlando, and Halifax (Canada) to London. We think they're one of the coolest ways to get to Europe, not only because of the great service, but because of their Take-a-Break program: You can make up to a 3-day layover in Iceland on any of their flights (in either direction) for no extra charge.

From Canada, **British Airways** *(Tel 800/247-92-97)* has direct flights from Toronto, Montreal, and Vancouver.

For travelers departing from Australia, **British Airways** *(Tel 800/247-92-97)* has flights to London from Sydney, Melbourne, Perth, and Brisbane. **Qantas** *(Tel 800/227-4500; www.qantas.com)* offers flights from Australia to London's Heathrow. Direct flights depart from Sydney and Melbourne. Some have the bonus of free stopovers in Bangkok or Singapore.

Departing from New Zealand, **Air New Zealand** *(Tel 800/262-12-34)* has direct flights to London from Auckland. These flights depart Wednesday, Saturday, and Sunday.

Short flights from Dublin to London are available through **British Airways** *(Tel 800/AIRWAYS),* with four flights daily into London's Gatwick airport, and **Aer Lingus** *(Tel 800/223-65-37),* which flies into Heathrow. Short flights from Dublin to London are also available through **Ryan Air** *(Tel 0541/569-569)* and **British Midland** *(Tel 0345/554-554).*

FLY FOR LESS

Here are some suggestions for getting the lowest possible airfares:

Keep your eyes peeled for **sales** in your newspaper. In the last few years, major airlines have periodically offered incredible bargains, as low as $250 round-trip from New York to London. You'll almost never see a sale during the peak summer vacation months of July and August, or during the Thanksgiving or Christmas seasons, but in spring, fall, and especially late winter, you can save a ton of money. If you already hold a ticket when a sale breaks, it may even pay to exchange your ticket, which usually incurs a $50 to $75 charge.

If your schedule is flexible, ask if you can secure a cheaper fare by staying an extra day or by flying midweek. (Many airlines won't volunteer this information, so you have to ask questions and try all the possible combinations.)

Consolidators, also known as bucket shops, are a good place to find low fares. Consolidators buy seats in bulk from the airlines and then sell them back to the public at prices below even the airlines' discounted rates. Their small ads usually run in the Sunday travel section at the bottom of the page. Among the most reliable companies are: **Council Travel** *(Tel 800/226-86-24; www.counciltravel.com)* and **STA Travel** *(Tel 800/781-40-40; www.sta.travel.com)* cater especially to young travelers, but their bargain basement prices are available to people of all ages. **Travel Bargains** *(Tel 800/AIR-FARE; www.1800airfare.com)* was formerly owned by TWA but now offers deep discounts on many other airlines, with a 4-day advance purchase. Other reliable consolidators include 1-800-FLY-CHEAP (www.1800flycheap.com); **TFI Tours International** *(Tel 800-745-80-00 or 212/736-11-40),* which serves as a clearinghouse for unused seats; or "rebators" such as **Travel Avenue** *(Tel 800/333-33-35 or 312/876-11-16).*

It's possible to get some great deals on not only airfare, but hotels and car rentals as well, via the **Internet.** Among the leading travel sites are: **Arthur Frommer's Budget Travel** (www.frommers.com); **Microsoft Expedia** (www.expedia.com); **Travelocity** (www.travelocity.com); **The Trip** (www.thetrip.com); and **Smarter Living** (www.smarterliving.com), which offers a newsletter service that will send you a weekly customized e-mail summarizing the discount fares available from your departure city.

For more information on finding travel bargains on the Web, see "Planning Your Trip: An Online Directory," the next chapter in this book.

BY TRAIN

Britain's isolation from the rest of Europe led to the development of an independent railway network with different rules and regulations from those observed on the Continent. That's all changing now, but one big difference that may affect you still remains: If you're traveling to Britain from the Continent, your Eurail pass will not be valid when you get there.

In 1994, Queen Elizabeth and French president François Mitterand officially opened the Channel Tunnel, or Chunnel, and the *Eurostar Express* passenger train began twice-daily service between London and both Paris and Brussels—a 3-hour trip. The $15 billion tunnel, one of the great engineering feats of all time, is the first link between Britain and the Continent since the Ice Age.

So if you're coming to London from say, Rome, your Eurail pass will get you as far as the Chunnel. At that point you can cross the English Channel aboard the *Eurostar,* and you'll receive a discount on your ticket. Once in England, you must use a separate BritRail pass or purchase a direct ticket to continue on to your destination.

Rail Europe *(Tel 800/94-CHUNNEL; www.raileurope.com)* sells direct-service tickets on the Eurostar between Paris or Brussels and London. A round-trip fare between Paris and London costs $438 in first class and from $218 to $298 in second class. One-way unrestricted fares for passage on the Eurostar between Paris and London cost $219 in first class and $149 in second class.

In London, make reservations for **Eurostar** by calling *Tel 0345/300-003;* in Paris, call *01/44-51-06-02;* and in the United States, it's *800/4-EURAIL.* Eurostar trains arrive and depart from London's Waterloo Station, Paris's Gare du Nord, and Brussels's Central Station.

BY FERRY/HOVERCRAFT

P&O Stena Lines *(Tel 087/06-00-06-11)* operates car and passenger ferries between Dover and Calais, France (25 sailings a day; 75 minutes each way).

By far the most popular route across the English Channel is between Calais and Dover. **HoverSpeed** operates at least 12 hovercraft crossings daily; the trip takes 35 minutes. They also run a SeaCat (a catamaran propelled by jet engines) that takes slightly longer to make the crossing between Boulogne and Folkestone. The SeaCats depart about four times a day on the 55-minute voyage.

Traveling by hovercraft or SeaCat cuts the time of your surface journey from the Continent to the United Kingdom. A hovercraft trip is definitely a fun adventure, since the vessel is technically "flying" over the water. A SeaCat crossing from Folkestone to Boulogne is longer in miles, but is covered faster than conventional ferryboats which make the Calais-Dover crossing. For reservations and information, call Hoverspeed *(Tel 0870/524-02-41.* For foot passengers, a typical adult fare, with a 5-day return policy is £24 ($40.80) or half fare for children.

BY CAR

If you plan to transport a rented car between England and France, check in advance with the car-rental company about license and insurance requirements, and additional drop-off charges before you begin.

The English Channel is crisscrossed with "drive-on, drive-off" car-ferry services, with many operating from Boulogne and Calais in France. From either of those ports, Sealink ferries will carry you, your luggage, and, if you like, your car. The most popular points of arrival along the English coast include Dover and Folkestone.

Taking a car beneath the Channel is more complicated and more expensive. Since the Channel Tunnel's opening, most passengers have opted to ride the train alone, without being accompanied by their car. The Eurostar trains, discussed above, carry passengers only; Le Shuttle trains carry freight cars, trucks, lorries, and passenger cars.

Count on at least £219 ($372.30) for a return ticket, but know that the cost of moving a car on Le Shuttle varies according to the season and day of the week. Frankly, it's a lot cheaper to transport your car across by conventional ferryboat, but if you insist, here's what you'll need to know: You'll negotiate both English and French customs as part of one combined process, usually on the English side of the Channel. You can remain within your vehicle even after you drive it onto a flatbed railway car during the 35-minute crossing. (For 19 minutes of this crossing, you'll actually be underwater; if you want, you can leave the confines of your car and ride within a brightly lit, air-conditioned passenger car.) When the trip is over, you simply drive off the flatbed railway car and drive off toward your destination. Total travel time between the French and English highway system is about 1 hour. As a means of speeding the flow of perishable goods across the Channel, the car and truck service usually operates 24 hours a day, at intervals that vary from 15 minutes to once an hour, depending on the time of day. Neither BritRail nor any of the agencies dealing with reservations for passenger trains through the Chunnel will reserve space for your car in advance, and considering the frequency of the traffic on the Chunnel, they're usually not necessary. For information about Le Shuttle car-rail service after you reach England, call *Tel 0990/353-535.*

Duty-free stores, restaurants, and service stations are available to travelers on both sides of the Channel. A bilingual staff is on hand to assist travelers at both the British and French terminals.

BY BUS

If you're traveling to London from elsewhere in the United Kingdom, consider purchasing a **Britexpress Card,** which entitles you to a 30% discount on National Express (England and Wales) and Caledonian Express (Scotland) buses. Contact a travel agent for details.

Bus connections to Britain from the continent are generally not very comfortable, although some lines are more convenient than others. One line with a relatively good reputation is **Euroways Eurolines, Ltd.,** 52

Grosvenor Gardens, London SW1W 0AU *(Tel 0990/143-219)*. They book passage on buses traveling twice a day between London and Paris (9 hours); three times a day from Amsterdam (12 hours); three times a week from Munich (24 hours); and three times a week from Stockholm (44 hours). On the longer routes, which employ two alternating drivers, the bus proceeds almost without interruption, taking occasional breaks for meals.

package deals

Package tours are not the same thing as escorted tours. They are simply a way to buy airfare and accommodations at the same time. For popular destinations like England, they are a worthwhile option to consider, because they save you a lot of money. In many cases, a package that includes airfare, hotel, and transportation to and from the airport will cost you less than just the hotel alone would have, had you booked it yourself. That's because packages are sold in bulk to tour operators—who resell them to the public at a cost that drastically undercuts standard rates.

Packages, however, vary widely. Some offer a better class of hotels than others. Some offer the same hotels for lower prices. Some offer flights on scheduled airlines, while others book charters. In some packages, your choice of accommodations and travel days may be limited. Some packages let you choose between escorted vacations and independent vacations; others will allow you to add on just a few excursions or escorted day trips (also at lower prices than you could locate on your own) without booking an entirely escorted tour. If you spend the time to shop around, you will save in the long run.

The best place to start your search is the travel section of your local Sunday newspaper. Also check the ads in the back of national travel magazines like *Travel & Leisure, National Geographic Traveler,* and *Condé Nast Traveler.*

Liberty Travel *(Tel 888/271-15-84; www.libertytravel.com),* one of the biggest packagers in the Northeast, often runs a full-page ad in the Sunday papers. You won't get much in the way of service, but you will get a good deal.

American Express Vacations *(Tel 800/241-17-00;* www.american express.com) is another option. Check out its **Last Minute Travel Bargains** site, offered in conjunction with **Continental Airlines** *(www6.americanexpress.com/travel/lastminutetravel/default.asp),* with deeply discounted vacations packages and reduced airline fares that differ from the E-savers bargains that Continental emails weekly to subscribers. **Northwest Airlines** offers a similar service. Posted on Northwest's Web site every Wednesday, its **Cyber Saver Bargain Alerts** offer special hotel rates, package deals, and discounted airline fares.

Another good resource is the airlines themselves, which often package their flights together with accommodations. Among the airline packagers, your options include **American Airlines FlyAway Vacations** *(Tel*

800/321-21-21,) **Delta Dream Vacations** *(Tel 800/872-77-86),* and **US Airways Vacations** *(Tel 800/455-01-23).* Pick the airline that services your hometown most often.

Far and away, you'll find the most options through **British Airways** *(Tel 800/AIRWAYS).* Its offerings within the British Isles are more comprehensive than those of its competitors, and can be tailored to your specific interests and budget. Many of the tours, such as the 9-day all-inclusive tour through the great houses and gardens of England, include the ongoing services of a guide and lecturer. But if you prefer to travel independently, without following an organized tour, a sales representative can tailor an itinerary specifically for you, with discounted rates in a wide assortment of big-city hotels. If you opt for this, you can rent a car or choose to take the train. For a free catalog and additional information, call British Airways before you book your airline ticket, since some of the company's available options are contingent upon the purchase of a round-trip transatlantic air ticket.

getting around by car

The British car-rental market is among the most competitive in Europe, but car rentals are still relatively expensive, unless you get a promotional deal through an airline or a tour operator.

Since cars in Britain travel on the left side of the road, their steering wheels are positioned on the "wrong" side of the vehicle, and you have to shift with your left hand; it's easier to drive an automatic, but they cost more and you have to request them at the time you make your reservation.

Most car-rental companies will accept your U.S. driver's license, provided you're 23 years old (21 in rare instances) and have had the license for more than a year. Many rental companies will grant discounts to clients who reserve their cars in advance (usually 48 hours) through the toll-free reservations offices in the renter's home country. Rentals of a week or more are almost always less expensive per day than day rentals.

When you reserve a car, be sure to ask if the price includes the 17.5% value-added tax (VAT).

Rentals are available through **Avis** *(Tel 800/331-21-12; www.avis.com),* **British Airways** *(Tel 800/AIRWAYS; www.british-airways.com),* **Budget Rent-a-Car** *(Tel 800/527-07-00; www.budgetrentacar.com),* and **Hertz** *(Tel 800/654-31-31; www.hertz.com).* **Kemwel Holiday Autos** *(Tel 800/678-06-78; www.kemwel.com)* is among the cheapest and most reliable of the rental agencies. **AutoEurope** *(Tel 800/223-55-55 in the U.S., or 0800/899-893 in London; www.autoeurope.com)* acts as a wholesale company for rental agencies in Europe.

Car rental rates vary even more than airline fares. The price you pay will depend on the size of the car, where and when you pick it up and drop it off, the length of the rental period, where and how far you drive it, whether you purchase insurance, and a host of other factors. A few key questions could save you hundreds of dollars:

Are weekend rates lower than weekday rates? Ask if the rate is the same for pickup Friday morning, for instance, as it is for Thursday night.

Is a weekly rate cheaper than the daily rate? If you need to keep the car for 4 days, it may be cheaper to keep it for 5, even if you don't need it that long.

Does the agency assess a drop-off charge if you do not return the car to the same location where you picked it up? Is it cheaper to pick up the car at the airport compared to a downtown location?

Are special promotional rates available? If you see an advertised price in your local newspaper, be sure to ask for that specific rate; otherwise you may be charged the standard cost. The terms change constantly, and phone operators may not volunteer information.

Are discounts available for members of AARP, AAA, frequent-flyer programs, or trade unions? If you belong to any of these organizations, you are probably entitled to discounts of up to 30%.

What is the cost of adding an additional driver's name to the contract?

How many free miles are included in the price? Free mileage is often negotiable, depending on the length of your rental.

How much does the rental company charge to refill your gas tank if you return with the tank less than full? Though most rental companies claim these prices are "competitive," fuel is almost always cheaper in town. Try to allow enough time to refuel the car yourself before returning it.

RENTAL INSURANCE

Before you drive off in a rental car, be sure you're insured. Hasty assumptions about your personal auto insurance or a rental agency's additional coverage could end up costing you tens of thousands of dollars—even if you are involved in an accident that was clearly the fault of another driver.

The basic insurance coverage offered by most car rental companies, known as the **Loss/Damage Waiver (LDW)** or **Collision Damage Waiver (CDW),** can cost more than $20/day.

U.S. drivers who already have their own car insurance are usually covered in the United States for loss of or damage to a rental car, and liability in case of injury to any other party involved in an accident. But coverage probably doesn't extend outside the United States. Be sure to find out whether you are covered in England, whether your policy extends to all persons who will be driving the rental car, how much liability is covered in case an outside party is injured in an accident, and whether the type of vehicle you are renting is included under your contract. (Rental trucks, sport utility vehicles, and luxury vehicles such as the Jaguar may not be covered.)

Most **major credit cards** provide some degree of coverage as well—provided they were used to pay for the rental. Terms vary widely, however, so be sure to call your credit card company directly before you rent. But though they will cover damage to or theft of your rental, *credit cards will not cover liability* or the cost of injury to an outside party and/or damage to an outside party's vehicle. If you do not hold an insurance policy, or if you are driving outside the United States, you may seriously want to consider purchasing additional liability insurance from your rental company. Be sure to check the terms, however: Some rental agencies only cover liability if the renter is not at fault.

Bear in mind that each credit card company has its own peculiarities. Most American Express Optima cards, for instance, do not provide any insurance. American Express does not cover vehicles valued at over $50,000 when new, luxury vehicles such as the Porsche, or vehicles built on a truck chassis. MasterCard does not provide coverage for loss, theft, or fire damage, and only covers collision if the rental period does not exceed 15 days. Call your own credit card company for details.

DRIVING RULES & REQUIREMENTS

In England, *you drive on the left* and pass on the right. Road signs are clear and the international symbols are unmistakable.

You must present your passport and driver's license when you rent a car in Britain. No special British license is needed. It's a good idea to get a copy of the *British Highway Code,* available from almost any gas station or newsstand (called a "news stall" in Britain).

Warning: Pedestrian crossings are marked by striped lines (zebra striping) on the road; flashing lights near the curb indicate that drivers must stop and yield the right of way if a pedestrian has stepped out into the zebra zone to cross the street.

ROAD MAPS

The best road map is *The Ordinance Survey Motor Atlas of Great Britain,* whether you're trying to find the fastest route to Manchester or locate some obscure village. Revised annually, it's published by Temple Press and is available at most bookstores, including **W & G Foyle, Ltd.** *(113 and 119 Charing Cross Rd., London, WC2 HOEB; Tel 020/74-40-32-25).*

BREAKDOWNS

If you are a member of AAA in the United States, you are automatically eligible for the same roadside services you receive at home. Be sure to bring your membership card with you on your trip. In an emergency, call the Automobile Association of Great Britain's emergency road service *(Tel 0800/887-766).* If you are not a member of AAA, you may want to join one of England's two major auto clubs—the **Automobile Association-AA** *(Norfolk House, Priestly Road, Basingstoke, Hampshire RG24 9NY; Tel 0990/500-600)* or the **Royal Automobile Club-RAC** *(P.O. Box 700, Bristol, Somerset BS99 1RB; Tel 0800/029-029).*

Membership, which can be obtained through your car-rental agent, entitles you to free legal and technical advice on motoring matters, as well as a whole range of discounts on automobile products and services.

If your car breaks down on the highway, you can call for **24-hour breakdown service** from a roadside phone. The 24-hour number to call for **AA** is *Tel 0800/887-766;* for **RAC** it's *Tel 0800/828-282.* All superhighways (called motorways in Britain) are provided with special emergency phones that are connected to police traffic units, and the police can contact either of the auto clubs on your behalf.

GASOLINE

Called "petrol," gasoline is sold by the liter, with 4.2 liters to a gallon. Prices are much higher than Stateside, and you'll probably have to serve yourself. In some remote areas, stations are few and far between, and many are closed on Sunday.

getting around by plane

British Airways *(Tel 800/AIRWAYS)* flies to more than 20 cities outside London, including Manchester, Glasgow, and Edinburgh. Ask about the British Airways Super Shuttle Saver fares, which can save you up to 50% on travel to certain key British cities. If seats are available on the flight of your choice, no advance reservations are necessary, although to benefit from the lowest prices, passengers must spend a Saturday night away from their point of origin and fly during defined off-peak times. Flights are usually restricted to weekdays between 10am and 3:30pm, whereas most night flights are after 7pm and, in certain cases, on weekends.

For passengers planning on visiting widely scattered destinations within the United Kingdom, perhaps with a side trip to a city on Europe's mainland, British Airways' **Europe Airpass** allows discounted travel in a continuous loop to between 3 and 12 cities anywhere on BA's European and domestic air routes. Passengers must end their journey at the same point they begin it and fly exclusively on BA flights. Such a ticket (for instance, from London to Paris, then to Manchester, and finally to London again) will cut the cost of each segment of the itinerary by about 40% to 50% over individually booked tickets. The pass is available for travel to about a dozen of the most-visited cities and regions of Britain, with discounted add-ons available to most of BA's destinations in Europe as well. (This Airpass is a good bargain for round-trip travel between London and Rome, but not very practical for air travel from, say, Rome to Madrid. You'd be better off traveling between points on the Continent by full-fare airline ticket, or by train, bus, or car.)

BA's Europe Airpass must be booked and paid for at least 7 days before a passenger's departure from North America. All sectors of the itinerary, including transatlantic passage from North America, must be booked simultaneously. Some changes are permitted in flight dates (but not in destinations) after the ticket is issued. Check with British Airways for full details and restrictions.

getting around by train

A Eurail pass is not valid in Great Britain, but there are several special passes for train travel outside London. For railroad information, go to Rail Travel centers in the main London railway stations (Waterloo, King's Cross, Euston, and Paddington).

Americans can obtain BritRail passes at **BritRail Travel International** (*500 Mamaroneck Ave., Suite 314, Harrison, NY 10528; Tel 800/677-85-85; 800/555-27-48 in Canada*).

BRITRAIL CLASSIC PASS This pass allows unlimited rail travel during a set time period (8 days, 15 days, 22 days, or 1 month). For 8 days, the pass costs $400 in first class, $265 in "standard" class; for 15 days, $600 in first class, $400 in standard; for 22 days, $760 in first class, $505 in standard; and for 1 month, $900 in first class, $600 in standard.

BRITRAIL FLEXIPASS This pass lets you travel anywhere on BritRail, and is particularly good for visitors who want to alternate travel days with blocks of uninterrupted sightseeing time in a particular city or region. Flexipasses can be used for 4 days within any 1-month period and cost $350 in first class and $235 in standard; ages 16 to 25 pay $185 to travel youth standard class. Also available is a Flexipass that allows 8 days of travel within 2 months and costs $510 in first class, $340 in standard; youth standard class $240. New is a Flexipass which can be used for 15 days in any 2-month period and costs $770 in first class and $515 in standard class; youth standard class $360.

SOUTHEAST PASS If you're only planning day trips southeast of London, BritRail's Southeast Pass might make better sense than a more expensive rail pass that's valid in all parts of Britain. This pass allows unlimited travel to accessible destinations throughout BritRail's "Network Southeast," which includes Oxford, Cambridge, Dover, Canterbury, Salisbury, and Portsmouth. Frequent trains—about 41 daily from London to Brighton alone—let you leave early in the morning and return to London in time for the theater or dinner.

A Southeast Pass that's good for 3 days of travel out of any consecutive 8-day period costs $100 in first class, $70 in standard class. A Southeast Pass that's good for 4 days out of any 8-day consecutive period sells for $135 in first class and $100 in standard class. A Southeast Pass that's good for 7 days out of any 15-day consecutive period costs $180 in first class and $135 in standard class. The Southeast Pass must be purchased either from your travel agent or BritRail Travel International in the United States or Canada (see phone numbers above).

getting around by bus

In Britain, a long-distance touring bus is called a "coach," and "buses" are taken for local transportation. There's an efficient and frequent express motor-coach network—run by National Express and other independent operators—that links most of Britain's towns and cities. Destinations off the main route can be easily reached by transferring to a local bus at a stop on the route. Tickets are relatively cheap, often half the price of rail fare, and it's usually cheaper to purchase a round-trip (or "return") ticket than two one-way fares separately.

Victoria Coach Station, *(Buckingham Palace Road; Tel 020/77-30-34-66)* is the departure point for most large coach operators. The coach station is located just two blocks from Victoria Station. For credit card sales

(MasterCard and Visa only), call *020/77-30-34-99* Mon-Sat 9am-7pm; for cash purchases, get there at least 30 minutes before the coach departs.

National Express runs luxurious long-distance coaches that are equipped with hostesses, light refreshments, reclining seats, toilets, and no-smoking areas. Details about all coach services can be obtained by phoning *Tel 0990/808-080* daily between 8am and 10pm. The National Express ticket office at Victoria Station is open 6am-11pm.

You might want to consider National Express's **Tourist Trail Pass,** which offers unlimited travel on their network. (This company's service is most extensive in England and Wales.) A 3-day pass costs £49 ($83.30), a 5-day pass £85 ($144.50), a 7-day pass, £120 ($204), and a 14-day pass, £187 ($317.90).

For journeys within a 35-mile radius of London, try the **Green Line** coach service *(Lesbourne Road, Reigate Surrey RH2 7LE; Tel 020/86-68-72-61).* With a 1-day £7 ($11.90) **Diamond Rover Ticket,** you can visit many of the attractions of Greater London and the surrounding region, including Windsor Castle and Hampton Court. The pass is valid for 1 day on almost all Green Line coaches and country buses Monday to Friday after 9am and all day on Saturday and Sunday.

Green Line has bus routes called Country Bus Lines that circle through the periphery of London. Although they do not usually go directly into the center of the capital, they do hook up with the routes of the Green Line coaches and red buses that do.

crashing

Reserve your accommodations as far in advance as possible, even in the so-called slow months from November to April. Tourist travel to London peaks from May to October, and during that period, it's hard to come by a moderate or inexpensive hotel room.

CLASSIFICATIONS

Unlike some countries, England doesn't have a rigid hotel-classification system. The tourist board grades hotels by crowns instead of stars. Hotels are judged on their standards, quality, and hospitality, and are rated "approved," "commended," "highly commended," and "deluxe." Five crowns (deluxe) is the highest rating. There is even a classification of "listed," with no crowns, and these accommodations are for the most part very modest.

In a five-crown hotel, all rooms must have a private bath; in a four-crown hotel, only 75% have them. In a one-crown hotel, buildings are required to have hot and cold running water in all the rooms, but in "listed" hotels, hot and cold running water in the rooms is not mandatory. Crown ratings are posted outside the buildings. However, the system is voluntary, and many hotels do not participate.

Many hotels, especially older ones, still lack private bathrooms for all rooms. However, most have hot and cold running water, and many have modern wings with all the amenities (as well as older sections that are less up-to-date). When making reservations, always ask what section of the hotel you'll be staying in if it has extensions.

All hotels used to include a full English breakfast of bacon and eggs in the room price, but today that is true for only some hotels. A continental breakfast is commonly included, but that usually means just tea or coffee and toast.

BED & BREAKFASTS

In towns, cities, and villages throughout England, homeowners take in paying guests. Watch for the familiar bed-and-breakfast (B&B) signs. Generally, these are modest family homes, but sometimes they may be built like small hotels, with as many as 15 rooms. If they're that big, they are more properly classified as guesthouses. B&Bs are the cheapest places you can stay in England and still be comfortable.

Hometours International *(Tel 800/367-46-68 or 865/690-84-84)* will make bed-and-breakfast reservations in England, Scotland, and Wales. This is the only company to guarantee reservations for more than 400 locations in Britain. Accommodations are paid for in the United States in dollars, and prices start as low as $48 per person per night, although they can go as high as $140 per person in London. The company can also arrange for apartments in London or cottages in Great Britain that begin at $800 to $900 per week for a studio. In addition, it offers walking tours of Great Britain, with prices starting as low as $650 for 7 days, including meals, guide, and accommodation.

Reservations for bed-and-breakfast accommodations in London can also be made by writing (not calling) the **British Visitor Centre** *(1 Lower Regent St., London SW1 4PQ.)* Once in London, you can also visit their office (tube: Piccadilly Circus).

In addition, Susan Opperman and Rosemary Lumb run **Bed and Breakfast Nationwide** *(P.O. Box 2100, Clacton-on-Sea, Essex CO16 9BW; Tel 01255/831-235; Fax 01255/831-437; daily 9am-6pm),* an agency specializing in privately owned bed-and-breakfasts all over Great Britain. Host homes range from small cottages to large manor houses, as well as working farms, and the prices vary accordingly. One thing you can be sure of is that owners have been specially selected for their wish to entertain visitors from overseas. Remember that these are private homes, so hotel-type services are not available. You will, however, be assured of a warm welcome, a comfortable bed, a hearty breakfast, and a glimpse of British life. Write for a free brochure.

FARMHOUSES

In many parts of the country, farmhouses have one, two, even four rooms set aside for paying guests, who usually arrive in the summer months. Farmhouses don't have the facilities of most guesthouses, but they have a rustic appeal and charm, especially for motorists, as they tend to lie off the beaten path. Prices are generally lower than bed-and-breakfasts or guesthouses, and sometimes you're offered some good country home cooking (at an extra charge) if you make arrangements in

from pudding to pies

There's a lot more to British food today than the traditional roast, which has been celebrated since long before the days of Henry VIII. Of course, parsnip soup is still served, but now it's likely to be graced with a dollop of walnut salsa verde. In contemporary England, the chef has taken on celebrity status. The creator of breast of Gressingham duck topped with deep-fried seaweed and served with a passion-fruit sauce is honored the way rock stars were in the 1970s.

But of course the traditional dishes haven't gone anywhere. On any pub menu you're likely to encounter such dishes as the **Cornish pasty** and **shepherd's pie.** The first consists of chopped potatoes, carrots, and onions mixed together with seasoning and put into a pastry envelope. The second is a deep dish of chopped cooked beef mixed with onions and seasoning, covered with a layer of mashed potatoes, and served hot. Another version is cottage pie, which is minced beef covered with potatoes and also served hot. In addition to a pasty, Cornwall also gives us "Stargazy Pie"—a deep-dish fish pie with a crisp crust covering a creamy concoction of freshly caught herring and vegetables.

The most common pub meal, though, is the **ploughman's lunch,** traditional farm-worker's fare, consisting of a good chunk of local cheese, a hunk of homemade crusty white or brown bread, some butter, and a pickled onion or two, washed down with ale. You'll now find such variations as pâté and chutney occasionally replacing the onions and cheese. Or you might find **Lancashire hot pot,** a stew of mutton, potatoes, kidneys, and onions (sometimes carrots).

Among appetizers, called **"starters"** in England, the most typical are potted shrimp (small buttered shrimp preserved in a jar), prawn cocktail, and smoked salmon. You might also be served pâté or "fish pie," which is very light fish pâté. Most menus will feature a variety of soups, including cock-a-leekie (chicken soup flavored with leeks), perhaps a game soup that has been doused with sherry, and many others.

Among the best-known traditional English meals is **roast beef** and **Yorkshire pudding** (the pudding is made with a flour base and cooked under the roast, allowing the fat from the meat to drop onto it). The beef could easily be a large sirloin (rolled loin), which, so the story goes, was named by James I when he was a guest at Houghton Tower, Lancashire. "Arise, Sir Loin," he cried, as he knighted the leg of beef before him with his dagger. Another dish that makes use of a flour base is toad-in-the-hole, in which sausages are cooked in batter.

Game, especially pheasant and grouse, is also a staple on British tables.

On any menu, you'll find **fresh seafood:** cod, haddock, herring, plaice, and Dover sole, the aristocrat of flatfish. Cod and haddock are used in making British **fish-and-chips** (chips are fried potatoes or thick French fries), which the true Briton covers with salt and vinegar. If you like **oysters,** try some of the famous Colchester variety. On the west coast, you'll find a not-to-be-missed delicacy: **Morecambe Bay shrimp.** In Ely, lying in the marshy fen district of East Anglia, it might be fenland eel pie with a twiggy seaweed as your green vegetable. Amphire also grows here in the salt marshes and along the Norfolk Coast. It's pickled in May and June and appears as a delicacy on many summer menus.

The **East End of London** has quite a few interesting old dishes, among them tripe and onions. In winter, the Cheshire Cheese on Fleet Street offers a beefsteak-kidney-mushroom-and-game pudding in a suet case; in summer, there's a pastry case. East Enders can still be seen on Sunday at the Jellied Eel stall by Petticoat Lane, eating eel, cockles (small clams), mussels, whelks, and winkles—all with a touch of vinegar.

The British call desserts "sweets," although some people still refer to any dessert as **"pudding."** **Trifle** is the most famous English dessert, consisting of sponge cake soaked in brandy or sherry, coated with fruit or jam, and topped with cream custard. A "fool," such as gooseberry fool, is a light cream dessert whipped up from seasonal fruits. Regional sweets include the **northern "flitting" dumpling** (dates, walnuts, and syrup mixed with other ingredients and made into a pudding that is easily sliced and carried along when you're "flitting" from place to place). Similarly, **hasty pudding,** a Newcastle dish, is supposed to have been invented by people in a hurry to avoid the bailiff. It consists of stale bread, to which some dried fruit and milk are added before it is put into the oven.

Cheese is traditionally served after dessert as a savory. There are many regional cheeses, the best known being cheddar, a good, solid, mature cheese. Others are the semismooth Caerphilly, from a beautiful part of Wales, and Stilton, a blue-veined crumbly cheese that's often enjoyed with a glass of port.

Britain is famous for its **breakfast** of bacon, eggs, grilled tomato, and fried bread (likely to be of the Wonder variety). Some places have replaced this cholesterol festival with a continental breakfast, but you'll still find the traditional morning meal available.

FROM PUDDING TO PIES/CONT.

Kipper, or smoked herring, is also a popular breakfast dish. The finest come from the Isle of Man, Whitby, or Lock Fyne, in Scotland. The herrings are split open, placed over oak chips, and slowly cooked to produce a nice pale-brown smoked fish.

Many people still enjoy **afternoon tea,** which may consist of a simple cup of tea or a formal tea that starts with tiny crustless sandwiches filled with cucumber or watercress and proceeds through scones, crumpets with jam, or clotted cream, followed by cakes and tarts—all accompanied by a proper pot of tea. In the countryside, tea shops abound. You'll find the best cream teas in Devon, Cornwall, and the West Country; they consist of scones spread with jam and thick, clotted Devonshire cream. It's not your Starbucks fix, but you may return stateside with a new habit. People in Britain drink an average of four cups of tea a day, though indeed, coffee is gaining.

English **pubs** serve a variety of cocktails, but their stock-in-trade is beer: brown beer, or bitter; blond beer, or lager; and very dark beer, or stout. The standard English draft beer is much stronger than American beer and is served "with the chill off," because it doesn't taste good cold. But here's the surprise—not all English beer is served warm enough to swim in. Lager is always chilled, whereas stout can be served

advance. The British Tourist Authority will provide a booklet, *Stay on a Farm,* or you can ask at local tourist offices.

The **Farm Holiday Bureau** *(Tel 1203/696-909)* publishes an annual directory in early December that includes 1,000 farms and bed-and-breakfasts throughout the United Kingdom. The listings include quality ratings, the number of bedrooms, nearby attractions and activities, and prices, as well as line drawings of each property. Also listed are any special details, such as rooms with four-poster beds or activities on the grounds (fishing, for example). Many farms are geared toward children, who can participate in light chores—gathering eggs or just tagging along—for an authentic farm experience. The prices range from £16 to £45 ($27.20 to $76.50) a night and include an English breakfast and usually private facilities. (The higher prices are for stays at mansions and manor houses.)

Another option is self-catering accommodations, which are usually cottages or converted barns that cost from £150 to £450 ($255 to $765) per week, and include dishwashers and central heating. Each property is inspected every year not only by the Farm Holiday Bureau but also either way. Beer is always served straight from the tap, in two sizes: half-pint (8 oz.) and pint (16 oz.).

One of the most significant changes in English drinking habits has been the popularity of wine bars, and you will find many to try, including some that turn into discos late at night. Britain isn't known for its wine, although it does produce some medium-sweet fruity whites. Its cider, though, is famous—and mighty potent in contrast to the American variety.

Whisky (spelled without the *e*) refers to scotch. Canadian and Irish whiskey (spelled with the *e*) are also available, but only the very best-stocked bars have American bourbon and rye.

While you're in England, you may want to try the very English drink called **Pimm's**, a mixture developed by James Pimm, owner of a popular London oyster house in the 1840s. Although it can be consumed on the rocks, it's usually served as a Pimm's Cup—a drink that will have any number and variety of ingredients (though usually involving citrus of some sort), depending on which part of the world (or empire) you're in.

Note: The English tend to drink everything at a warmer temperature than Americans are used to. So if you like ice in your soda, be sure to ask for lots of it, or you're likely to end up with a measly, quickly melting cube or two.

by the English Tourist Board. The majority of the properties, with the exception of those located in the mountains, are open year-round.

For a copy of the directory called *Stay on a Farm,* contact the **Farm Holiday Bureau** *(National Agricultural Centre, Stoneleigh Park, Warwickshire CV8 2LZ; Tel 1203/696-909);* it costs £10 ($17) and may be purchased by credit card.

NATIONAL TRUST PROPERTIES

The **National Trust of England, Wales, and Northern Ireland** *(36 Queen Anne's Gate, London SW1H 9AS; Tel 020/72-22-92-51; Tel 01225/791-199 for reservations)* is Britain's leading conservation organization. In addition to the many castles, forests, and gardens it maintains, the National Trust owns 235 houses and cottages in some of the most beautiful parts of England, Wales, and Northern Ireland. Some of these properties are in remote and rural locations, some have incomparable views of the coastline, and others stand in the heart of villages and ancient cities.

Most of these comfortable self-catering holiday accommodations are available for rental throughout the year. Examples include a simple former coast guard cottage in Northumbria, a gaslit hideaway on the Isle of Wight, a gem of a country house above the Old Brewhouse at Chastleton, a 15th-century manor house in a hidden corner of the Cotswolds, and a superb choice of cottages in Devon and Cornwall. Houses can be booked for a week or more. Many can be booked for midweek or weekend breaks on short notice, particularly in the autumn and winter months. National Trust properties can sleep from 2 to 12 guests, and range in price from £146 ($248.20) per week for a small rental in winter to £1,393 ($2,368.10) per week for a larger property in peak season. Prices include value-added tax.

Although anyone can book rentals in National Trust properties, it's worth mentioning the trust's U.S. affiliate, the **Royal Oak Foundation** (*285 W. Broadway, Suite 400, New York, NY 10013-2299; Tel 800/913-65-65 or 212/966-65-65),* which publishes a full-color 120-page booklet that describes all National Trust holiday rental properties, their facilities, and prices. Copies cost $5 for members, $7.50 for nonmembers. Individual annual memberships are $45, and family memberships are $70. Benefits include free admission to all National Trust sites and properties open to the public, plus discounts on reservations at cottages and houses owned by them, and air and train travel.

COTTAGE & APARTMENT RENTALS

Throughout England, there are fully furnished studios, houses, cottages, "flats" (apartments), even trailers suitable for families or groups that can be rented by the month. From October to March, rents are sometimes reduced by 50%.

The British Tourist Authority and most tourist offices have lists available. The BTA's free *Apartments in London and Holiday Homes* lists rental agencies such as **At Home Abroad** (*405 E. 56th St., Suite 6H, New York, NY 10022; Tel 212/421-91-65; Fax 212/752-15-91).* Interested parties should write or fax a description of their needs, and At Home Abroad will send listings at no charge.

British Travel International *(Tel 800/327-60-97 or 540/298-22-32; Fax 540/298-23-47)* represents 8,000-10,000 weekly (Saturday to Saturday) properties in the United Kingdom, and requires a 50% payment at the time of booking. A catalog with pictures of their offerings is available for a $5 fee that is counted toward a deposit. They have everything from honey-colored, thatch-roofed cottages in the Cotswolds to apartments in a British university city. The company represents about 100 hotels in London whose rates are discounted by 5% to 50%, depending on the season and market conditions, and they have listings of some 4,000 bed-and-breakfast establishments. They are also the North American representative of the United Kingdom's largest bus company, National Express.

The **Barclay International Group-BIG** *(45 Albemarle St., London W1X 3FE; Tel 020/74-95-29-86 or 800/845-66-36; Fax 020/74-99-23-12; www.barclayweb.com)* specializes in short-term apartment (flat) rentals in London, and cottages in the English countryside. These rentals can be appropriate for families, groups of friends, or businesspeople traveling together, and are sometimes less expensive than equivalent stays in hotels. Apartments, available for stays as short as 1 night (although the company prefers that guests stay a minimum of 3 nights and charges a premium if your stay is shorter), are usually more luxurious than you'd imagine. Furnished with kitchens, they offer a low-cost alternative to restaurant meals. Apartments suitable for one or two occupants begin, during low season, at around $500 a week (including tax) and can go much higher for deluxe accommodations that offer many hotel-like features and amenities. For extended stays in the English countryside, BIG has country cottages in such areas as the Cotswolds, the Lake District, and Oxford, as well as farther afield in Scotland and Wales. The company can also arrange tickets for sightseeing attractions, BritRail passes, and various other "extras."

At the cheaper end of the spectrum, there's **Hoseasons Holidays** (*Sunway House, Lowestoft, NR32 2LW; Tel 01502/500-500*), a reservations agent based in Suffolk. They arrange stopovers in at least 300 vacation villages throughout Britain. Although many are isolated in bucolic regions far from any of the sites covered within this guidebook, others lie within an hour's drive of Stratford-upon-Avon. Don't expect luxury or convenience: Vacation villages in England usually consist of a motley assortment of trailers, uninsulated bungalows, and/or mobile homes perched on cement blocks. They're intended as frugal escapes for claustrophobic urbanites with children. Such a place might not meet your expectations for a vacation in the English countryside (and a minimum stay of 3 nights is usually required), but it's hard to beat the rate. A 3-day sojourn begins from £45 ($76.50) per person, double occupancy.

HOSTELS

The **Youth Hostels Association** (*YHA, Trevelyan House, 8 St. Stephen's Hill, St. Albans, Hertfordshire, AL1 2DY; Tel 01727/855-215*) operates a network of 240 youth hostels in major cities, in the countryside, and along the coast of England and Wales. Contact their customer service department (se above) for a free map showing the locations of each youth hostel and full details, including prices.

shopping

When shopping for the best buys in England, note that British goods, even products from Wales and Scotland, may offer sensational buys even when sold in England. You will also find Irish stores and Irish departments in some stores often selling merchandise at the same good value you'd find on a shopping trip to Ireland itself. Many French brands, it may come as a surprise, are less expensive in the United Kingdom than in France!

This section is an overview of England's shopping scene, including what's hot, where to get it, and how you can save money and secure value-added tax (VAT) refunds.

When you're looking for great bargains, focus on stuff that's actually made in England and therefore is likely to cost much more if you buy it back home. That category includes anything from The Body Shop, FiloFax, or Doc Martens; many woolens and some cashmeres; most English brands of bone china; antiques, used silver, and rare books.

ANTIQUES

Whether you're looking for museum-quality antiques or simply fun junk, England has the stores, the resources, the stalls, and the markets. You can shop the fanciest of upmarket shops—mostly in London, Bath, and the Cotswolds—or browse through antiques shows, markets, fairs, buildings, centers, arcades, warehouses, jumble fairs, fetes, and car boot sales throughout the country. (A car boot sale is the British version of a yard sale. Participants set up tables at an abandoned parking lot or airfield to sell their goods.)

Actually, prices are better once you get outside of London. Entire towns and areas in Britain are known to be treasure troves for those seeking anything from architectural salvage to a piece of the Holy Grail. Whereas the Cotswolds and Bath are known as charming places to shop for antiques, there are warehouses in Suffolk, Merseyside, and in the Greater Manchester (Yorkshire and Lancashire) area that aren't glamorous but offer dealers and those in the know the best buys. Serious shoppers can head directly to the Manchester area, get a car or van and just start shopping. The best hunting grounds are Boughton (right outside Chester), Liverpool, Prestwich, and Stockport. Harrogate and nearby Knaresborough are known for antiques, but offer a far more upscale scene with prices competitive to those in the Cotswolds.

For immediate information on current antique fairs and events, check the magazine section of the *Sunday Times* where you'll find the Antique Buyer's Guide, which lists fairs all over England, not just in London.

AROMATHERAPY

The British must have invented aromatherapy—just about every store sells gels, creams, lotions, or potions made with the right herbs and essential oils to cure whatever ails you, including jet lag. Whether it works or not is secondary to the fact that most of the British brands are half the U.S. price when bought on home soil. **The Body Shop** becomes the best store in the world at prices like these. Check out drugstore brands as well. Shoppers like the Body Shop knockoffs that **Boots the Chemist** makes, as well as their own line (sold in another part of the store) of healing foot gels. Both of these are national brands available all over the United Kingdom. In addition, some small communities have homemade brands—check out **Woods of Windsor** (in the heart of downtown Windsor) for English flower soaps, lotions, and cures.

BASIC BRIT GEAR

Don't assume any bargains on woolens, cashmeres, tweeds, and the like—often British quality is much higher than similar (and less expensive) goods available in the United States. If you want the best and expect it to last forever, you can't beat British-made, especially in gear that has been fine-tuned over the last century for the weather and outdoor lifestyle: from wax coats (**Barbour** is the leading status brand) to raincoats to guns (and English roses). While we can hardly put **Doc Martens** brand of shoes in the traditional Brit category, they do cost a lot less in Britain than in America. The other quintessential English accessory is the **FiloFax,** sold in a variety of versions with inserts galore for 30% to 50% less than prices in the United States.

BEAUTY

Dime-store brands of makeup cost less than they do in the United States. The French line **Bourjois** (made in the same factories that produce Chanel makeup) costs less in London than in Paris and isn't sold in the United States; Boots, the pharmacy chain, makes its own Chanel knockoff line, Number 7.

DESIGNER STUFF

Designer clothing from any of the international makers may cost less in London than in the United States or Paris, but know your prices. Often the only difference is the VAT refund, which at 15% to 17.5% is substantial. This game is also highly dependent on the value of the dollar. While you won't get a VAT refund on used designer clothing, London has the best prices on used Chanel (and similar) clothing of any major shopping city.

ROYAL SOUVENIRS

Forget about investing in Diana memorabilia; it won't appreciate significantly because there was so much of it. Still, royal collectibles can be cheap kitsch bought in street markets or serious pieces from coronations found in specialist's shops. If you're buying new for investment purposes, it must be kept in mint condition.

TAPESTRY & KNITTING

For some reason, the English call needlepoint "tapestry." It's a passion, perhaps the seasonal flip side to gardening. Tapestry kits by the famous English designers, and Welsh queen of needles Elizabeth Bradley, cost a fraction of their U.S. prices when purchased anywhere in England or Wales. Whereas England is famous for its sweaters (jumpers), what it should be famous for are the sweater kits: do-it-yourself jobs from the major designers that come with yarn, instructions, and a photo. English knitter-designers are cult heroes in Britain and do everything but knit autographs.

STRATEGIES

Most English towns feature a main street usually called the High Street. On this one road you'll find a branch of each of what is locally called "the High Street multiples." These are the chain stores that dominate the retail scene. The leader among them is **Marks & Spencer,** a private label department store with high-quality goods at fair value prices; **Boots the Chemist** (a drugstore); **Laura Ashley** (less expensive in the United Kingdom); **The Body Shop** (the most popular politically correct bath and beauty statement of our times); **Monsoon** (hot fashion made from Far Eastern fabrics for moderate prices; they also have a dress-up division called **Twilight** and an accessories business called **Accessorize; Habitat** (sort of the English version of the Pottery Barn); and maybe (if you're lucky) **Past Times,** sort of a museum shop selling reproduction gifts and souvenirs. **Shelly's, Pied a Terre,** and **Hobbs** are all shoe stores selling everything from Doc Martens to expensive-looking cheap shoes. **Knickerbox** is usually found in train stations rather than on High Streets, but it's interesting nonetheless—the store sells fashion underwear at what the English call moderate prices.

TAXES & SHIPPING

Value-added tax is the British version of sales tax, but it is a whopping 17.5% on most goods. This tax is added to the total so that the price on a sales tag already includes VAT. Non-European Union residents can get back all, or most, of this tax if they apply for a VAT refund (see "How to Get Your VAT Refund," below).

One of the first secrets of shopping in England is that the minimum expenditure needed to qualify for a refund on value-added tax (VAT) is a mere £50 ($85). Not every store honors this minimum (it's £100 ($170) at Harrods; £75 ($127.50) at Selfridges; £62 ($105.40) at Hermes), but it's far easier to qualify for a tax refund in Britain than almost any other country in the European Union.

Vendors at flea markets may not be equipped to provide the paperwork for a refund, so if you're contemplating a major purchase and really want that refund, ask before you fall in love. Be suspicious of any dealer who tells you there's no VAT on antiques. There didn't used to be, but there is now. The European Union has now made the British add VAT to antiques. Since dealers still have mixed stock, pricing should reflect this fact. So ask if it's included before you bargain on a price. Get to the price you're comfortable with first, then ask for the VAT refund.

VAT is not charged on goods shipped out of the country, whether you spend £50 ($85) or not. Many London shops will help you beat the VAT by shipping for you. But watch out: Shipping can double the cost of your purchase. Also expect to pay U.S. duties when the goods reach you at home.

You may want to consider paying for excess baggage (rates vary with the airline), or else have your packages shipped independently. Independent operators are generally less expensive than the airlines. Try **London Baggage,** London Air Terminal, Victoria Place, SW1 *(Tel 020/78-28-24-00;* tube: Victoria), or **Burns International Facilities.** They are found at Heathrow Airport in Terminal 1 or at Terminal 4. For information, call *Tel 020/87-45-53-01.*

HOW TO GET YOUR VAT REFUND

To receive back a portion of the tax paid on purchases made in Britain, first ask the store personnel if they do VAT refunds and what their minimum purchase is. Once you've achieved this minimum, ask for the paperwork; the retailer will have to fill out a portion themselves. Several readers have reported that merchants have told them that they can get refund forms at the airport on their way out of the country. *This is not true.* You must get a refund form from the retailer (don't leave the store without one), and it must be completed by the retailer on the spot.

Fill out your portion of the form and then present it, along with the goods, at the customs office in the airport. Allow a half hour to stand in line. *Remember:* You're required to show the goods at your time of departure, so don't pack them in your luggage and check it; put them in your carry-on instead.

Once you have the paperwork stamped by the officials, you have two choices: You can mail the papers and receive your refund in either a British check (no!) or a credit card refund (yes!), or you can go directly to the Cash VAT Refund desk at the airport and get your refund in your hand, in cash. The bad news: If you accept cash other than sterling, you will lose money on the conversion rate. (If you plan on mailing your paperwork, try to remember to bring a stamp with you to the airport; if you forget, you can usually get stamps from stamp machines and/or the convenience stores in the terminal.)

Be advised that many stores charge a flat fee for processing your refund, so £3 to £5 may be automatically deducted from the total refund you receive. But since the VAT in Britain is 17.5%, if you get back 15%, you're doing fine.

Note: If you're traveling to other countries within the European Union, you don't go through any of this in Britain. At your final destination, prior to departure from the European Union, you file for all your VAT refunds at one time.

DUTY-FREE AIRPORT SHOPPING

Shopping at airports is big business, so big business has taken over the management of some of Britain's airports to ensure that passengers in transit are enticed to buy. Terminal 4 at London Heathrow Airport is a virtual shopping mall, but each terminal has a good bit of shopping, with not a lot of crossover between brands.

Prices at the airport for items such as souvenirs and candy bars are actually higher than on the streets of London, but the duty-free prices on luxury goods are usually fair. There are often promotions and coupons that allow for pounds off at the time of the purchase.

Don't save all your shopping until you get to the airport, but do know prices on land and sea so that you know when to pounce.

sightseeing passes

There are several passes available that can cut down considerably on entrance costs to the country's stately homes and gardens. If you plan to do extensive touring, you'll save a lot of pounds by using one of these passes instead of paying the relatively steep entrance fees on an attraction-by-attraction basis.

Listed below are three organizations that offer passes waiving admission charges to hundreds of historical properties located throughout the United Kingdom. Each is a good deal, as the money you'll save on visitation to just a few of the available sites will pay for the price of the pass.

The **British National Trust** offers members free entry to some 240 National Trust sites in Britain, and more than 100 properties in Scotland. Focusing on gardens, castles, historic parks, abbeys, and ruins, sites include Chartwell, St. Michael's Mount, and Beatrix Potter's House. The membership fee includes a listing of all properties, maps, and essential information for independent tours, and listings and reservations for holiday cottages located on the protected properties.

Individual memberships cost $45 annually, and family memberships, including up to seven people, run $70, so savings on the admission charges, combined with discounts on holiday cottage reservations and British Air or BritRail travel, make this especially appealing. Visa and MasterCard are accepted. Contact **The British National Trust** (*36 Queen Anne's Gate, London SW1H 9AS; Tel 020/72-22-92-51*), or **The Royal Oak Foundation** (*285 W. Broadway, no. 400, New York, NY 10013-2299; Tel 212/966-65-65*).

The **English Heritage** sells 7- and 14-day passes and annual memberships, offering free admission to more than 300 historical sites in England, and half-price admission to more than 100 additional sites in Scotland, Wales, and the Isle of Man. (Admission to these additional sites is free for anyone who renews his or her annual membership after the first year.) Sites include Hadrian's Wall, Stonehenge, and Kenilworth Castle. Also included is free or reduced admission to 450 historic re-enactments and open-air summer concerts, a handbook detailing all properties, a map, and, with the purchase of an annual membership, events and concerts diaries, and *Heritage Today*, a quarterly magazine.

A 7-day Overseas Visitor Pass runs £12.50 ($21.25) for an adult or £27.50 ($46.75) for a family of six or less. A child accompanied by an adult goes free. A 21-day pass is £28 ($47.60) for an adult (free for a child) or £40 ($68) for a family. Annual memberships are also available with rates of £26 ($44.20) for an adult, £16 ($27.20) for those between the ages of 16 and 21, and free for a child under 16, or else £45.50 ($77.35) for a family ticket. MasterCard and Visa are accepted. For visitor passes and membership, contact **Customer Services, English Heritage** (*429 Oxford St., London W1R 2HD; Tel 020/79-73-34-34*) or join directly at the site.

The **Great British Heritage Pass,** available through **BritRail**, allows entry to more than 500 public and privately owned historic properties, including Shakespeare's birthplace, Stonehenge, Windsor Castle, and Edinburgh Castle. Included in the price of the pass is *The Great British Heritage Gazetteer,* a brochure that lists the properties with maps and essential information. A pass gains you entrance into private properties not otherwise approachable. A 7-day pass costs $54, a 15-day pass is available for $75, and a 1-month pass is $102. Passes are nonrefundable, and there is no discounted children's rate. A $10 handling fee is charged additionally for each ticket issued. To order passes, contact

BritRail Travel International, Inc. *(500 Mamaroneck Ave., Suite 314, Harrison, NY 10528; BritRail's British Travel Shop, 551 Fifth Ave., New York, NY 10176; Tel 800/677-85-85; www.britrail.com).*

fast facts

AREA CODES The country code for England is **44**. The area code for London is **020**.

BUSINESS HOURS With many, many exceptions, business hours are Monday to Friday from 9am to 5pm. In general, stores are open Monday to Saturday from 9am to 5:30pm. In country towns, there is usually an early closing day (often on Wednesday or Thursday), when the shops close at 1pm.

DRUGSTORES In Britain, they're called "chemists." Every police station in the country has a list of emergency chemists. Dial "0" (zero) and ask the operator for the local police, who will give you the name of the one nearest you.

ELECTRICITY British electricity is 240 volts AC (50 cycles), roughly twice the voltage in North America, which is 115 to 120 volts AC (60 cycles). American plugs don't fit British wall outlets. Always bring suitable transformers and/or adapters—if you plug an American appliance directly into a European electrical outlet without a transformer, you'll destroy your appliance and possibly start a fire. Tape recorders, VCRs, and other devices with motors intended to revolve at a fixed number of revolutions per minute probably won't work properly even with transformers.

EMERGENCIES Dial **999** for police, fire, or ambulance. Give your name, address, and telephone number, and state the nature of the emergency.

LEGAL AID The American Services section of the U.S. Consulate (see "Embassies & High Commissions," under "Fast Facts: London," in chapter 3) will give you advice if you run into trouble abroad. They can advise you of your rights, and will even provide a list of attorneys (for which you'll have to pay if services are used). But they cannot interfere on your behalf in the legal processes of Great Britain. For questions about American citizens who are arrested abroad, including ways of getting money to them, call the **Citizens Emergency Center** of the Office of Special Consulate Services in Washington, D.C. *(Tel 202/647-52-25).*

LIQUOR LAWS The legal drinking age is 18. Children under 16 aren't allowed in pubs, except in certain rooms, and then only when accompanied by a parent or guardian. Don't drink and drive. Penalties are stiff.

In England, pubs can legally be open Monday to Saturday from 11am to 11pm, and on Sunday from noon to 10:30pm. Restaurants are also allowed to serve liquor during these hours, but only to people who are dining on the premises. The law allows 30 minutes for "drinking-up time." A meal, incidentally, is defined as "substantial refreshment." And you have to eat and drink sitting down. In hotels, liquor may be served from 11am to 11pm to both residents and nonresidents; after 11pm, only residents, according to the law, may be served.

MAIL Post offices and subpost offices are open Monday to Friday from 9am to 5:30pm and Saturday from 9:30am to noon.

Sending an airmail letter to North America costs 44p (75¢) for 10 grams (.35 oz.), and postcards require a 37p (65¢) stamp. British mailboxes are painted red and carry a royal coat of arms. All post offices accept parcels for mailing, provided they are properly and securely wrapped.

PETS It is illegal to bring pets to Great Britain—except with veterinary documents, and then most animals are subject to an outrageous 6-month quarantine.

POLICE Dial **999** if the matter is serious. Losses, thefts, and other criminal matters should be reported to the police immediately.

SAFETY Stay in well-lit areas and out of questionable neighborhoods, especially at night. In Britain, most of the crime perpetrated against tourists is pickpocketing and mugging. These attacks usually occur in such cities as London, Birmingham, or Manchester. Most villages are safe.

TAXES To encourage energy conservation, the British government levies a 25% tax on gasoline (petrol). There is also a 17.5% national value-added tax (VAT) that is added to all hotel and restaurant bills, and will be included in the price of many items you purchase. This can be refunded if you shop at stores that participate in the Retail Export Scheme (signs are posted in the window). See the "How to Get Your VAT Refund," above.

In October 1994, Britain imposed a departure tax. Currently it is £20 ($34), but is included in the price of your ticket.

PHONES To call England from North America, dial **011** (international code), **44** (Britain's country code), the local area codes (usually three or four digits and found in every phone number we've given in this book), and the seven-digit local phone number. The local area codes found throughout this book all begin with "0"; you drop the "0" if you're calling from outside Britain, but you need to dial it along with the area code if you're calling from another city or town within Britain. For calls within the same city or town, the local number is all you need.

For **directory assistance** in London, dial **142;** for the rest of Britain, **192.**

There are three types of public pay phones: those taking only coins, those accepting only phonecards (called Cardphones), and those taking both phonecards and credit cards. At coin-operated phones, insert your coins before dialing. The minimum charge is 10p (15¢).

Phonecards are available in four values—£2 ($3.40), £4 ($6.80), £10 ($17), and £20 ($34)—and are reusable until the total value has expired. Cards can be purchased from newsstands and post offices. Finally, the credit-call pay phone operates on credit cards—Access (MasterCard), Visa, American Express, and Diners Club—and is most common at airports and large railway stations.

To make an international call from Britain, dial the international access code **00,** then the country code, then the area code, and finally the local number. Or call through one of the following long-distance access codes: **AT&T USA Direct** *(Tel 0800/890-011),* **Canada Direct** *(Tel 0800/890-016),* **Australia** *(Tel 0800/890061),* or **New Zealand** *(Tel 0800/890-064).* Common country codes are: USA and Canada, **1;** Australia, **61;** New Zealand, **64;** South Africa, **27.**

If you're calling **collect** or need the assistance of an international operator, dial **155.**

Caller, beware: Some hotels routinely add outrageous surcharges onto phone calls made from your room. Inquire before you call! It'll be a lot cheaper to use your own calling card number or to find a pay phone.

TIME England follows Greenwich mean time (5 hours ahead of Eastern standard time), with British summertime lasting (roughly) from the end of March to the end of October. Throughout most of the year, including the summer, Britain is 5 hours ahead of the time observed on the East Coast of the United States. Because of different daylight-savings-time practices in the two nations, there's a brief period (about a week) in autumn when Britain is only 4 hours ahead of New York, and a brief period in spring when it's 6 hours ahead of New York.

TIPPING For cab drivers, add about 10% to 15% to the fare shown on the meter. However, if the driver personally loads or unloads your luggage, add something extra.

In hotels, porters receive 75p ($1.30) per bag, even if you have only one small suitcase. Hall porters are tipped only for special services. Maids receive £1 ($1.70) per day. In top-ranking hotels, the concierge will often submit a separate bill showing charges for newspapers and other items; if he or she has been particularly helpful, tip extra.

Hotels often add a service charge of 10% to 15% to most bills. In smaller bed-and-breakfasts, the tip is not likely to be included. Therefore, tip for special services, such as the waiter who serves you breakfast. If several people have served you in a bed-and-breakfast, you may ask that 10% to 15% be added to the bill and divided among the staff.

In both restaurants and nightclubs, a 15% service charge is added to the bill, which is distributed among all the help. To that, add another 3% to 5%, depending on the service. Waiters in deluxe restaurants and nightclubs are accustomed to the extra 5%. Sommeliers (wine stewards) get about £1 ($1.70) per bottle of wine served. Tipping in pubs isn't common, but in wine bars, the server usually gets about 75p ($1.30) per round of drinks.

Barbers and hairdressers expect 10% to 15%. Tour guides expect £2 ($3.40), although it's not mandatory. Gas station attendants are rarely tipped and theater ushers don't expect tips.

engLand onLine

TRaveL pLanning websiTes

by lynne bairstow

WHY BOOK ONLINE?

Online agencies have come a long way over the past few years, now providing tips for finding the best fare and giving suggested dates or times to travel that yield the lowest price if your plans are flexible. Other sites even allow you to establish the price you're willing to pay, and they check the airlines' willingness to accept it. However, in some cases, these sites might not always yield the best price. Unlike a travel agent, for example, they may not have access to charter flights offered by wholesalers.

Online booking sites aren't the only places to reserve airline tickets; all major airlines have their own websites and often offer incentives—bonus frequent-flyer miles or Net-only discounts, for example—when you buy online or buy an e-ticket.

The best of the travel planning sites are now highly personalized; they store your seating preferences, meal preferences, tentative itineraries, and credit card information, allowing you to plan trips or check agendas quickly.

In many cases, booking your trip online can be better than working with a travel agent. It gives you the widest variety of choices, control, and the 24-hour convenience of planning your trip when you choose. All you need is some time—and often a little patience—and you're likely to find the fun of online travel research will greatly enhance your trip.

STAYING SECURE

More people still look online than book online, partly due to fear of putting their credit card numbers out on the Net. Secure encryption and increasing experience buying online have removed this fear for most travelers. In some cases, however, it's simply easier to buy from a local travel agent who can deliver your tickets to your door (especially if your travel is last minute or you have special requests). You can find a flight online and then book it by calling a toll-free number or contacting your travel agent, although this is somewhat less efficient. To be sure you're in secure mode when you book online, look for a little icon of a padlock (in Netscape or Internet Explorer) at the bottom of your web browser.

WHO SHOULD BOOK ONLINE?

Online booking is best for travelers who want to know as much as possible about their options, those who have flexibility in their travel dates and are looking for the best price, and bargain hunters driven by a good value who are open-minded about when they travel.

One of the biggest successes in online travel for both passengers and airlines is the offer of last-minute specials, such as American Airlines' weekend deals or other Internet-only fares you must purchase online. Another advantage is that you can cash in on incentives for booking online, such as rebates or bonus frequent-flyer miles.

Business and other frequent travelers also have found numerous benefits in online booking, as the advances in mobile technology provide them with the ability to check flight status, change plans, or get specific directions from handheld computing devices, mobile phones, and pagers. Some sites will even e-mail or page passengers if their flights are delayed.

Online booking is increasingly able to accommodate complex itineraries, even for international travel. The pace of evolution on the Net is rapid, so you'll probably find additional features and advancements by the time you visit these sites. What the future holds for online travelers is ever-increasing personalization, customization, and reaching out to you.

TRAVEL PLANNING & BOOKING SITES

Below are the websites for the major airlines serving England. These sites offer schedules and flight booking, and most have pages where you can sign up for e-mail alerts for weekend deals and other late-breaking bargains.

Air Canada *www.aircanada.com*
American Airlines *www.aa.com*
British Airways *www.british-airways.com*
Continental Airlines *www.continental.com*
Delta *www.delta-air.com*
Northwest Airlines *www.nwa.com*
TWA *www.twa.com*
United Airlines *www.ual.com*
Virgin Atlantic Airways *www.fly.virgin.com*

The following sites offer planning resources and the ability to exchange opinions with fellow travelers, as well as flight and other travel-related booking, including accommodations and rental-car reservations. Free (one-time) registration is required for booking.

Frommer's. *www.frommers.com*

For booking through Frommer's website, use its online reservation system *(www.frommers.com/booktravelnow)* to access sites for booking your trip, and see Travelocity, below. For a flock of planning resources including travel tips, reviews, monthly vacation giveaways, and last-minute deals on airfares, check out *Arthur Frommer's Budget Travel Online (www.frommers.com),* subscribe to *Arthur Frommer's Daily Newsletter (www.frommers.com/newsletters),* or search the destinations archive *(www.frommers.com/destinations).* Travelocity (incorporates Preview Travel). *www.travelocity.com; www.previewtravel.com; www.frommers.travelocity.com*

Travelocity is Frommer's online travel planning/booking partner. Travelocity uses the SABRE system to offer reservations and tickets for more than 400 airlines, plus reservations and purchase capabilities for more than 45,000 hotels and 50 car-rental companies. An exclusive feature of the SABRE system is its **Low Fare Search Engine,** which automatically searches for the three lowest-priced itineraries based on a traveler's criteria. Last-minute deals and consolidator fares are included in the search. If you book with Travelocity, you can select specific seats for your flights with online seat maps and view diagrams of the most popular commercial aircraft. Its hotel finder provides street-level location maps and photos of selected hotels. With the **Fare Watcher** e-mail feature, you can select up to five routes and receive e-mail notices when the fare changes by $25 or more.

Travelocity's **Destination Guide** includes updated information on some 260 destinations worldwide—supplied by Frommer's.

Note to AOL Users: You can book flights, hotels, rental cars, and cruises on AOL at keyword: Travel. The booking software is provided by Travelocity/Preview Travel and is similar to the Internet site. Use the AOL "Travelers Advantage" program to earn a 5% rebate on flights, hotel rooms, and car rentals.

SPECIALTY TRAVEL SITES

For adventure travelers, **GORP** (Great Outdoor Recreation Pages; *www.gorp.com*) has been a standard since its founding in 1995 by outdoor enthusiasts Diane and Bill Greer. Tapping into their own experiences, they created this website that offers unique travel destinations and encourages active participation by fellow GORP visitors through the sophisticated menu of online forums, contests, and discussions.

In the same vein, **iExplore** *(www.iexplore.com)* is a great source for information and for booking adventure and experiential travel, as well as related services and products. The site combines the secure Internet booking functions with hands-on expertise and 24-hour live customer support by seasoned adventure travelers, for those interested in trips off the beaten path. The company is a supporting member of the Ecotourism Society and is committed to environmentally responsible travel worldwide.

Another excellent site for adventure travelers is **Away.com** *(www.away.com)*, which features unique vacations for challenging the body, mind, and spirit. Trips may include cycling in the Loire Valley, taking an African safari, or assisting in the excavation of a Mayan ruin. For those without the time for such an extended exotic trip, offbeat weekend getaways are also available. Services include a customer service center staffed with experts to answer calls and e-mails, plus a network of over 1,000 prescreened tour operators. Trips are categorized by cultural, adventure, and green travel.

LAST-MINUTE DEALS & OTHER ONLINE BARGAINS

There's nothing airlines hate more than flying with lots of empty seats. The Net has enabled airlines to offer last-minute bargains to entice travelers to fill those seats. Most of them are announced on Tuesday or Wednesday and are valid for travel the following weekend, but some can be booked weeks or months in advance. You can sign up for weekly e-mail alerts at airlines' sites [for their websites, see airline listings in "Travel Planning & Booking Sites," above] or check sites that compile lists of these bargains, such as **Smarter Living** or **WebFlyer** [see below]. To make it easier, visit a site that'll round up all the deals and send them in one convenient weekly e-mail. But last-minute deals aren't the only online bargains; other sites can help you find value even if you haven't waited until the eleventh hour. Increasingly popular are services that let you name the price you're willing to pay for an air seat or vacation package and travel auction sites.

Get the Deal Tip: While most people learn about last-minute weekend deals from e-mail dispatches, it can be best to find out precisely when these deals become available. Because the deals are limited, they can vanish within hours—sometimes even minutes—so it pays to log on as soon as they're available. Check the pages devoted to these deals on airlines' web pages to get the info. An example: Southwest's specials are posted at 12:01am Tuesdays (Central time). So if you're looking for a cheap flight, stay up late and check Southwest's site to grab the best new deals.

1travel.com. *www.1travel.com*
Here you'll find deals on domestic and international flights, cruises, hotels, and all-inclusive resorts like Club Med. 1travel.com's **Saving Alert** compiles last-minute air deals so you don't have to scroll through multiple e-mail alerts. A feature called "Drive a little using low-fare airlines" helps map out strategies for using alternate airports to find lower fares. And **Farebeater** searches a database that includes published fares, consolidator bargains, and special deals exclusive to 1travel.com. *Note:* The travel agencies listed by 1travel.com have paid for placement.

Cheap Tickets. *www.cheaptickets.com*
Cheap Tickets has exclusive deals that aren't available through more main-stream channels. One caveat about the Cheap Tickets site is that it'll offer fare quotes for a route and later show this fare isn't valid for your dates of travel—most other websites, such as Expedia, consider your dates of travel before showing what fares are available. Despite its problems, Cheap Tickets can be worth the effort because its fares can be lower than those offered by its competitors.

Bid for Travel. *www.bidfortravel.com*
Bid for Travel is another of the travel auction sites, similar to Priceline [see below], which are growing in popularity. In addition to airfares, Internet users can place a bid for vacation packages and hotels.

Go4less.com. *www.go4less.com*
Specializing in last-minute cruise and package deals, Go4less has some excellent offers. The **Hot Deals** section gives an alphabetical listing by destination of super-discounted packages.

LastMinuteTravel.com. *www.lastminutetravel.com*
Suppliers with excess inventory come to this online agency to distribute unsold airline seats, hotel rooms, cruises, and vacation packages. It's got great deals, but you have to put up with an excess of advertisements and slow-loading graphics.

Moment's Notice. *www.moments-notice.com*
As the name suggests, Moment's Notice specializes in last-minute vacation and cruise deals. You can browse for free, but if you want to purchase a trip you have to join Moment's Notice, which costs $25. Go to **World Wide Hot Deals** for a complete list of special deals in international destinations.

Smarter Living. *www.smarterliving.com*
Best known for its e-mail dispatch of weekend deals on 20 airlines, Smarter Living also keeps you posted about last-minute bargains on everything from Windjammer Cruises to flights to Iceland.

SkyAuction.com. *www.skyauction.com*
This auction site has categories for airfare, travel deals, hotels, and much more.

Travelzoo.com. *www.travelzoo.com*
At this Internet portal, over 150 travel companies post special deals. It features a Top 20 list of the best deals on the site, selected by its editorial staff each Wednesday night. This list is also available via an e-mailing list, free to those who sign up.

WebFlyer. *www.webflyer.com*
WebFlyer is a comprehensive online resource for frequent flyers and also has an excellent listing of last-minute air deals. Click on **Deal Watch** for a round-up of weekend deals on flights, hotels, and rental cars from domestic and international suppliers.

ONLINE TRAVELER'S TOOLBOX
Veteran travelers usually carry some essential items to make their trips easier. Following is an additional selection of online tools to help smooth your journey.

Visa ATM Locator. *www.visa.com/pd/atm/*
MasterCard ATM Locator. *www.mastercard.com/atm*
Use these to find ATMs in hundreds of cities in the U.S. and around the world. Both include maps for some locations and both list airport ATM locations. *Tip:* You'll usually get a better exchange rate using ATMs than exchanging traveler's checks at banks, but check in advance to see what kind of fees your bank will assess for using an overseas ATM.

Net Cafe Guide. *www.netcafeguide.com/mapindex.htm*
Stop here to locate Internet cafes at hundreds of locations around the globe. Catch up on your e-mail, log on to the web, and stay in touch with the home front, usually for just a few dollars per hour [also see "Internet Cafe Tips," below, and the **wired** sidebars throughout the book].

CDC Travel Information. *www.cdc.gov/travel/index.htm*
Health advisories and recommendations for inoculations from the U.S. Centers for Disease Control and Prevention. The CDC site is good for an overview, but it's best to consult your personal physician to get the latest information on required vaccinations or other health precautions.

The Travelite FAQ. *www.travelite.org*
Here you'll find tips on packing light, choosing luggage, and selecting appropriate travel wear—helpful if you always tend to pack too much or are a compulsive list maker.

Universal Currency Converter. *www.xe.net/currency*
Come here to see what your dollar or pound is worth in more than a hundred other countries.

Mapquest. *www.mapquest.com*
The best of the mapping sites lets you choose a specific address or destination, and in seconds it returns a map and detailed directions. It really is easier than calling, asking, and writing down directions. The site also links to special travel deals and helpful sites.

Tourism Offices Worldwide Directory. *www.towd.com*

This is an extensive listing of tourism offices, some with links to these offices' websites.

Intellicast. *www.intellicast.com*
Weather forecasts for all 50 states and cities around the world. Note that temperatures are in Celsius for many international destinations.

U.S. CUSTOMS SERVICE TRAVELER INFORMATION
www.customs.ustreas.gov/travel/index.htm
Wondering what you're allowed to bring in to the United States? Check at this thorough site, which includes maximum allowance and duty fees.

U.S. STATE DEPARTMENT TRAVEL WARNINGS
travel.state.gov/travel—warnings.html
You'll find reports on places where health concerns or unrest might threaten U.S. travelers. Keep in mind that these warnings can be somewhat dated and conservative.

check your E-maiL

You don't have to be out of touch just because you don't carry a laptop while you travel. Web browser-based free e-mail programs make it much easier to stay in e-touch.

With public internet access available in all of the principal cities and an increasing number of small towns, it shouldn't be difficult for you to log on regularly during your travels. In a few simple steps you can set yourself up to receive messages while overseas from each of your email accounts.

The first step to uninterrupted e-mail access is to set up an account with a freemail provider, if you don't have one already. You can find hints, tips, and a mile-long list of freemail providers at **www.email addresses.com**. The advantage of freemail is that all you need to check your mail from anywhere in the world is a terminal with internet access; since most internet cafe computers aren't set up to retrieve POP mail, this is the best option. The downside is that most web-based e-mail sites allow a maximum of only 3MB capacity per mail account, which can fill up quickly. Also, message sending and receiving isn't immediate; some messages may be delayed by several hours or even days. Most freemail providers will allow you to configure your account to retrieve mail from multiple POP mail accounts, or you can arrange with your home ISP to have your mail forwarded to the freemail account.

Internet cafes have become ubiquitous, so for a few dollars an hour you'll be able to check your mail and send messages from virtually anywhere in the world. Interestingly, these cafes tend to be more common in very remote areas, where they may offer the best form of access for an entire community, especially if phone lines are difficult to obtain. Many hostels now provide internet access for residents, as do an increasing number of hotels. If you travel with a laptop, you'll be glad to find that not only hotels but quite a few guesthouses provide a telephone jack in all rooms for dial-up access; many internet cafes also provide an Ethernet hook-up for travelers who want to surf the internet from their laptop. See the **wired** sidebars throughout the book for listings of individual internet cafes.

The Top Web Sites for England

GENERAL INFORMATION

AOL International: *Great Britain*

AOL Keyword: *Britain*
A vibrant guide to the U.K. that gives you the skinny on arts, dining, nightlife, and more. You can subscribe to a free online newsletter and participate in AOL's active chat areas to see what others are saying or pose a question of your own. To access the AOL London guide, type in the keyword, "London."

A2B Travel. *www.a2btravel.com*
This site focuses on helping travelers plan and book their trips. It has lots of nifty tools, such as bus, rail, and ferry guides, a point-to-point mileage calculator, and a guide to more than two dozen UK airports. You'll also find maps, a currency converter, and weather information.

Britannia. *www.britannia.com*
This expansive site is much more than a travel guide—it's chock full of lively features, history, and regional profiles, including sections on Wales and King Arthur.

UK for Visitors (About.com). *www.about.com/travel/gouk*
This useful gateway links to local information sites all over the country. It also offers a limited guide to hotels and restaurants, but you're better off going to a specialist for both.

GETTING AROUND

BAA: London Airports. *www.baa.co.uk*
Guides and terminal maps for Heathrow, Gatwick, Stansted, and smaller airports, with info about flight arrival times, duty-free shops, airport restaurants, and information on travel into London.
Birmingham International Airport. www.bhx.co.uk
All the information you need for navigating this airport: ground transport, facilities, flight schedules for incoming flights, and more.

Eurostar. *www.eurostar.com*
Fares, timetables, and booking for this high-speed train, which shoots through the Chunnel to France and Belgium.

London Transport. *www.londontransport.co.uk*
London Transport operates the Underground (subway), city buses, and

river ferries. This extensive and well-designed site includes maps, fare information, and advice to help you get around London as easily and cheaply as possible. You'll find schedules for the last trains and for night buses.

RailEurope. *www.raileurope.com*
This is a one-stop shopping site for European train travel, whether you're looking for fares and schedules, discount passes, or a ride through the Chunnel. Also see Rick Steves' *Europe Through the Back Door (www.rick steves.com)* for insider tips on Eurail passes.

The TrainLine. *www.thetrainline.com*
Find out schedules, book tickets, and reserve seats on trains run by all the U.K.'s privatized rail companies. This site also explains the restrictions for different ticket types.

ACCOMMODATIONS

Youth Hostel Association (YHA). *www.yha.org.uk*
Check out the comprehensive hostels appendix following this chapter or go online to view complete details. You can select hostels by location or by name, then take a look at a good-size photo of each. Reservations may be made directly from the site.

Automobile Association-UK. *www.theaa.co.uk*
This outstanding guide lists hundreds of places to stay, ranked by price and quality and with apparently objective reviews. Many of the lodgings accept online bookings. You'll also find dining information with ratings based on food, service, atmosphere, and price. Most, but not all, restaurants list typical meal prices and which credit cards are accepted.

British Hotel Reservation Centre. *www.bhrc.co.uk*
This consolidator offers hotels and apartments in London and six other popular tourist towns, publishing the rack rate, its own price and the resultant saving. You can search by hotel name, location, or closeness to attractions, and then book online.

THINGS TO SEE AND DO IN ENGLAND

Londontown.com: The Official Internet Site for London. *www.lon dontown.com*
This site from the tourist board lists events, accommodation, attractions, pubs and after dark scenes. Daily special features include discount offers. You can download mini-area maps, by Tube stop, attraction, theater, or street.

Official London Theatre Guide. *www.officiallondontheatre.co.uk*
An extensive site from the Society of London Theatres, which also runs the half-price ticket booth in Leicester Square. Search by type of show, title, theater name, or date. Or simply view everything playing in

London—listings include a brief summary, actors, times, prices, and the date a show is guaranteed to run until.

Original London Walks. *www.walks.com*
London's longest established guided walks company posts a day-by-day schedule of more than a dozen distinct tours, such as "In the Footsteps of Sherlock Holmes" or "Jack the Ripper Haunts."

This is London. *www.thisislondon.com*
This well-rounded site from the *Evening Standard* includes a frank guide to dining, drinking, and clubbing. You can search for city attractions and events. And the Hot Tickets section offers independent insider advice on theater, music, and comedy. Any kind words are well-earned.

The 24 Hour Museum. *www.24hourmuseum.org.uk*
This excellent website aims to promote Britain's thousands of museums, galleries, and heritage attractions—and, boy, does it do a good job. It is entertaining and downloads fast. You can search geographically or gear your holiday around one of its themed "trails" and tour Museums and the Macabre, Art Treasures of the North East, and so on.

Cathedrals of Britain. *www.cathedrals.org.uk*
This well-designed site features dozens of cathedrals, organized by region. Each listing includes a couple of photos, advice for getting there, and history. You could surf here to plan an entire touring vacation.

English Heritage. *www.english-heritage.org.uk*
Mouthwatering photographs and details of the hundreds of glorious historic castles, country houses, Roman sites, churches, abbeys, and ancient monuments cared for by this organization all over England. A must-visit site for pre-trip planning.

The National Trust. *www.nationaltrust.org.uk*
This charity owns over 300 historic buildings and countless acres of countryside. You can search the list by area, county, name, or theme, from film & TV to ghosts. The Surf the Coast section makes you want to pack a picnic and rush off to the seaside.

The Insider's Guide to Shopping. *www.inshop.co.uk*
Join up for free and get the latest news on promotions, events, and sales across the capital. It will also tell you where to find the hottest items of the season, from womenswear to housewares, luggage to watches and jewelry.

CITY GUIDES AND REGIONAL ATTRACTIONS

Oxford. *www.oxfordcity.co.uk*
This very user-friendly site makes it easy to learn more about lodgings, restaurants, shops, and evening entertainment. Hotel listings are divided

into price bands and link to the properties' own websites where you can see images and compare rates. It's also a nice orientation to the city itself and its prestigious university.

Stonehenge: Ancient Sites Directory. *www.henge.demon.co.uk/wilt shire/shenge.html*

Pictures of this astonishing ancient monument, directions to it, and a frank appraisal of the tourist facilities from an enthusiast. The main site lists other stone circles and barrows in England, Wales, and Scotland.

Cambridge News. *www.cambridge-news.co.uk/tourism*

This website is a great source of information about one of England's most beautiful towns. It has lots of useful links, including one to Cambridge University where you'll find a fascinating, if slightly dry, history of this ancient institution.

Peak District Tourism Online. *www.peakdistrict-tourism.gov.uk/peakdistrict*

Take a peek at some sights and find out where to go in Britain's first national park, from the White Peak to the Drowned Dales, and the Seven Wonders. There is information on wildlife, local activities such as caving and climbing, and hotel listings to search by price.

Dartmoor National Park Authority. *www.dartmoor-npa.gov.uk*

This ancient moorland is a haven for walkers and horse-riders. Check the official website for accommodation, events, fact files, and links to other local information sources.

Gloucestershire: England at its Best. *www.visit-glos.org.uk*

This handy guide to one of the most beautiful counties—it includes the Cotswolds, the Royal Forest of Dean, and Severn Vale—features attractions, activities, events, and walking tours from the local tourist information center.

Derby City Index Page. *www.derbycity.com*

Known as the Ghost Capital of the World, Derby claims haunted pubs, churches, inns, and mills; but this site is no phantom. The listings for top attractions, pubs, museums, and events are incredibly thorough and the site is nicely illustrated, offering a sense of what you can see in Derby and the dramatic Peak District.

Nottingham Tour.

www.proweb.co.uk/~lordthorpe/nottingham/notts1.htm

This site is heavy on photos and slow to load, but it's a nice introduction to Nottingham and its legendary outlaw, Robin Hood. You'll find sections on history, the local castle, inns, the Nottingham Festival, and of course Sherwood Forest, as well as local web links.

Bath.co.uk. *www.bath.co.uk*

This site attempts to round up accommodation, shopping, entertainment, attractions, and restaurants, not always successfully as some sections claim they can find no listings. The dining guide usefully allows searching by price but does not carry reviews.

Brighton & Hove: A virtual guide. *www.brighton.co.uk*
A site with everything you need to know about this seaside town, made fashionable in the late 18th century when the dissolute Prince George built the Brighton Pavilion, and now one of the funkiest places in England for shopping, clubbing, and eating out.

Bristol City Council. *www.bristol-city.gov.uk*
Unlike the various net directories serving Bristol, this site is quick and includes interesting background on the city. The hotel, restaurant, and attractions listings are nicely presented.

Canterbury: The Official Guide. *www.canterbury.co.uk*
There's everything you could need to know here from accommodation and dining to shopping, attractions, and events. It includes price, opening times, and useful links, but no reviews and the site is slow.

Stratford-upon-Avon: Shakespeare's Stratford. *www.stratford.co.uk*
This site won't win any design awards but it's a wonderful resource for exploring Shakespeare's birthplace. Click on "A Visitor's Guide" for detailed information on local attractions, including Warwick Castle *(www.warwick-castle.co.uk)*, tips for getting around, and suggestions for lodging and dining. Click on "Shakespeare" for information about local performances and background on his life.

Blackpool: Entertainment Capital of the North. *www.blackpool.gov.uk*
This site has a lovely picture of Blackpool by night—much lovelier than the daytime reality. It offers some useful listings for dining, lodging, clubs, and shows, but with no reviews or links.

Chester: An official guide. *www.chestercc.gov.uk/tourism*
Where to stay and eat out, and what to visit in this ancient town, from the biggest uncovered Roman amphitheater in Britain, the most complete city walls, the cathedral, fab shopping, and events at the local racecourse.

Hadrian's Wall. *www.hadrians-wall.org*
Take a virtual walk along the wall that stretches from Bowness-on-Solway to Wall's End (north of Newcastle upon Tyne). Use this site to find out about touring the wall (there's a link to the Hadrian's Wall bus), and to figure out where to stay nearby.

Lake District. *www.uk-north.com*
A guide to attractions, lodging, and entertainment. There are also tips on how to avoid holiday crowds and find the more secluded areas of the Lake District.

Leeds Tourism Information. *www.leeds.gov.uk/tourinfo/tourinfo.html*
An all-in-one site where you can find updated events listings, hotel information, and booking, and detailed information on more than a dozen museums and historic attractions. There are also tips on nearby places of interests, listings for parks and gardens, and local sports news.

Liverpool Guide. *www.liverpoolguide.co.uk*
An entertaining and very comprehensive site, put together by a local lad when he was still at school. He encourages input from web-surfers and city visitors, some of whom he has even met up with during their holiday in Liverpool.

Manchester Online. *www.manchesteronline.co.uk*
News, weather, sports, and what's on (events) from the *Manchester Evening News*. The paper was in the middle of creating a new tourist guide at the time of writing.

Virtual Newcastle. *www.newcastle-gov.uk*
Click through to the About Town section for very comprehensive listings, without reviews, and essential tourist information. It also has links to other useful sites.

York: This Is York. *www.thisisyork.co.uk*
This site forms the *Evening Press,* combining an extensive travel guide with local news and entertainment information.

Yorkshire Dales Online. *www.yorkshiredales.net*
Maps and guides to this 1,769 square kilometer national park, including where to stay and what to see from rare sheep breeds to ancient fortresses.

hostels appendix

YOUTH HOSTEL ASSOCIATIONS/ MAIN OFFICES

ENGLAND/WALES

YOUTH HOSTELS ASSOCIATION (ENGLAND & WALES)
Trevelyan House
8 St. Stephen's Hill
St. Albans, Hertfordshire AL1 2DY
England
Tel: 017/27-85-52-15
Fax: 017/27-84-41-26
E-mail: customerservices

Matlock Booking Centre
P.O. Box 67
Matlock, Derbyshire DE4 3HF
England
Tel: 016/29-58-14-18
Fax: 016/29-58-10-62

HOSTELS
Alston
The Firs
Alston, Cumbria CA9 3RW
Tel: 014/34-38-15-09
Fax: 014/34-38-24-01

Reservations: n/a
E-mail: n/a
Open: from 5pm
# of beds: 30

Alstonefield
Gypsy Lane
Alstonefield, Derbyshire DE6 2FZ
Tel: 013/35-35-02-12
Fax: 013/35-35-03-50
E-mail: n/a
Open: from 5pm
# of beds: 12

Ambergate
Shining Clif
Jackass Lane, near Ambergate
Derbyshire DE56 2RE
Tel: 077/88-72-59-38
Fax: 016/29-76-08-27
Reservations: 016/29-59-27-07
E-mail: reservationsyha.org.uk
Open: from 5pm
# of beds: 20

Ambleside
Hawkshead
Ambleside, Cumbria, LA22 0QD

Tel: 015/39-43-62-93
Fax: 015/39-43-67-20
Reservations: n/a
E-mail: hawkshead@yha.org.uk
Open: from 1pm
# of beds: 109

Langdale (High Close)
High Close, Loughrigg
Ambleside, Cumbria LA22 9HJ
Tel: 015/39-43-73-13
Fax: 015/39-43-71-01
Reservations: n/a
E-mail: brendling@yha.org.uk
Open: from 5pm
# of beds: 96

Waterhead
Ambleside, Cumbria LA22 0EU
Tel: 015/39-43-23-04
Fax: 015/39-43-44-08
Reservations: n/a
E-mail: ambleside@yha.org.uk
Open: 24 hours
# of beds: 245

Appleby
Dufton
Appleby, Cumbria CA16 6DB
Tel: 017/68-35-12-36
Fax: 017/68-35-37-98
Reservations: n/a
E-mail: n/a
Open: from 5pm
# of beds: 36

Arundel
Warningcamp
Arundel, West Sussex BN18 9QV
Tel: 019/03-88-22-04
Fax: 019/03-88-27-76
Reservations: n/a
E-mail: n/a
Open: from 5pm
# of beds: 60

Ashbourne
Ilam Hall
Ilam Hall, Ilam
Ashbourne, Derbyshire DE6 2AZ
Tel: 013/35-35-02-12
Fax: 013/35-35-03-50

Reservations: n/a
E-mail: ilam@yha.org.uk
Open: 24 hours
# of beds: 135

Bakewell
Fly Hill
Bakewell, Derbyshire DE45 1DN
Tel: 016/29-81-23-13
Fax: 016/29-81-23-13
Reservations: n/a
E-mail: bakewell@yha.org.uk
Open: from 5pm
# of beds: 32

Bardon Mill
Once Brewed
Military Road
Bardon Mill, Northumberland NE47 7AN
Tel: 014/34-34-43-60
Fax: 014/34-34-40-45
Reservations: n/a
E-mail: oncebrewed@yha.org.uk
Open: from 1pm
# of beds: 87

Barnard Castle
Baldersdale
Blackton, Baldersdale
Barnard Castle, County Durham DL12 9UP
Tel: 018/33-65-06-29
Fax: 018/33-65-06-29
Reservations: n/a
E-mail: n/a
Open: from 5pm
# of beds: 40

Langdon Beck, Forest-in-Teasdale
Barnard Castle, County Durham DL12 0XN
Tel: 018/33-62-22-28
Fax: 018/33-62-23-72
Reservations: n/a
E-mail: langdonbeck@yha.org.uk
Open: from 5pm
# of beds: 34

Barnoldswick
Earby
9-11 Birch Hall Lane, Earby

Barnoldswick, Lancashire BB18 6JX
Tel: 012/82-84-23-49
Fax: 012/82-84-23-49
Reservations: n/a
E-mail: n/a
Open: from 5pm
# of beds: 22

Bath
Bathwick Hill
Bath, Somerset BA2 6JZ
Tel: 012/25-46-56-74
Fax: 012/25-48-29-47
Reservations: n/a
E-mail: bath@yha.org.uk
Open: 24 hours
# of beds: 123

Beaconsfield
Jordans
Welders Lane, Jordans
Beaconsfield, Buckinghamshire HP9
  2SN
Tel: 014/94-87-31-35
Fax: 014/94-87-59-07
Reservations: n/a
E-mail: n/a
Open: from 5pm
# of beds: 22

Beverley
Beverley Friary
Friar's Lane
Beverley, East Yorkshire HU17 0DF
Tel: 014/82-88-17-51
Fax: 014/82-88-01-18
Reservations: n/a
E-mail: n/a
Open: from 5pm
# of beds: 34

Bideford
Elmscott
Elmscott, Hartland
Bideford, Devon EX39 6ES
Tel: 012/37-44-13-67
Fax: 012/37-44-19-10
Reservations: 016/29-82-59-83
E-mail: winterreservations@yha.org.uk
Open: from 5pm
# of beds: 32

Boscastle
Boscastle Harbour
Palace Stables
Boscastle, Cornwall PL35 0HD
Tel: 018/40-25-02-87
Fax: 018/40-25-06-15
Reservations: n/a
E-mail: n/a
Open: from 5pm
# of beds: 25

Bourne
Thurlby
16 High Street, Thurlby
Bourne, Lincolnshire PE10 0EE
Tel: 017/78-42-55-88
Fax: 017/78-42-55-88
Reservations: n/a
E-mail: n/a
Open: from 5pm
# of beds: 24

Brampton
Greenhead
Brampton, Cumbria CA18 7HG
Tel: 016/97-74-74-01
Fax: 016/97-74-74-01
Reservations: n/a
E-mail: n/a
Open: from 5pm
# of beds: 40

Brixham
Maypool
Galmpton
Brixham, Devon TQ5 0ET
Tel: 018/03-84-24-44
Fax: 018/03-84-59-39
Reservations: n/a
E-mail: n/a
Open: from 5pm
# of beds: 65

Bridgewater
Quantock Hills
Sevenacres, Holford
Bridgewater, Somerset TA5 1SQ
Tel: 012/78-74-12-24
Fax: 012/78-74-12-24
Reservations: 016/29-59-27-07
E-mail: reservations@yha.org.uk

Open: from 5pm
# of beds: 34

Brighton
Patcham Place, London Road
Brighton BN1 8YD
Tel: 012/73-55-61-96
Fax: 012/73-50-93-66
Reservations: n/a
E-mail: brighton@yha.org.uk
Open: from 1pm
# of beds: 84

Bristol
14 Narrow Quay
Bristol, Somerset BS1 4QA
Tel: 011/79-22-16-59
Fax: 011/79-27-37-89
Reservations: n/a
E-mail: bristol@yha.org.uk
Open: 24 hours
# of beds: 88

Broadstairs (Ramsgate)
3 Osborne Road
Broadstairs, Kent CT10 3AE
Tel: 018/43-60-41-21
Fax: 018/43-60-41-21
Reservations: n/a
E-mail: broadstairs@yha.org.uk
Open: from 5pm
# of beds: 34

Buxton
Gradbach Mill
Gradbach, Quarnford
Buxton, Derbyshire SK17 0SU
Tel: 012/60-22-76-25
Fax: 012/60-22-73-34
Reservations: n/a
E-mail: gradbach@yha.org.uk
Open: from 1pm
# of beds: 87

Hartington Hall
Hartington
Buxton, Derbyshire SK17 0AT
Tel: 012/988-42-23
Fax: 012/988-44-15
Reservations: n/a
E-mail: hartington@yha.org.uk

Open: 24 hours
# of beds: 152

Ravenstor
Millers Dale
Buxton, Derbyshire SK17 8SS
Tel: 012/98-87-18-26
Fax: 012/98-87-12-75
Reservations: n/a
E-mail: ravenstor@yha.org.uk
Open: from 1pm
# of beds: 82

Buxton
Sherbrook Lodge, Harpur Hill Road
Buxton, Derbyshire SK17 9NB
Tel: 012/982-22-87
Fax: 012/982-22-87
Reservations: n/a
E-mail: buxton@yha.org.uk
Open: from 5pm
# of beds: 56

Caldewgate
Old Brewery Residences, Bridge Lane
Caldewgate, Carlisle CA2 5SR
Tel: 012/28-59-73-52
Fax: 012/28-59-73-52
Reservations: n/a
E-mail: dee.carruthers@ynn.ac.uk
Open: from 5pm
# of beds: 56

Cambridge
97 Tenison Road
Cambridge, Cambridgeshire CB1 2DN
Tel: 012/23-35-46-01
Fax: 012/23-31-27-80
Reservations: n/a
E-mail: cambridge@yha.org.uk
Open: 24 hours
# of beds: 100

Canterbury
Ellerslie
54 New Dover Road
Canterbury, Kent CT1 3DT
Tel: 012/27-46-29-11
Fax: 012/27-47-07-52
Reservations: n/a
E-mail: canterbury@yha.org.uk

Open: from 1pm
# of beds: 85

Carnforth
Arnside
Redhills Road, Arnside
Carnforth, Lancashire LA5 0AT
Tel: 015/24-76-17-81
Fax: 015/24-76-25-89
Reservations: n/a
E-mail: arnside@yha.org.uk
Open: from 5pm
# of beds: 72

Ingleton
Sammy Lane, Ingleton
Carnforth, Lancashire LA6 3EG
Tel: 015/24-24-14-44
Fax: 015/24-24-18-54
Reservations: n/a
E-mail: n/a
Open: from 5pm
# of beds: 58

Castle Hedingham
7 Falcon Square
Castle Hedingham, Essex CO9 3BU
Tel: 017/87-46-07-99
Fax: 017/87-46-13-02
Reservations: n/a
E-mail: castlehed@yha.org.uk
Open: from 5pm
# of beds: 50

Castlefield
Potato Warf
Castlefield, Manchester M3 4NB
Tel: 016/18-39-99-60
Fax: 016/18-35-20-54
Reservations: n/a
E-mail: manchester@yha.org.uk
Open: 24 hours
# of beds: 144

Charlbury
The Slade
Charlbury, Oxfordshire OX7 3SJ
Tel: 016/08-81-02-02
Fax: 016/08-81-02-02
Reservations: n/a
E-mail: charlbury@yha.org.uk

Open: from 5pm
# of beds: 51

Cheddar
Hillfield
Cheddar, Somerset BS27 3HN
Tel: 019/34-74-24-94
Fax: 019/34-74-47-24
Reservations: n/a
E-mail: cheddar@yha.org.uk
Open: from 5pm
# of beds: 53

Chester
40 Hough Green
Chester, Cheshire CH4 8JD
Tel: 012/44-68-00-56
Fax: 012/44-68-12-04
Reservations: n/a
E-mail: chester@yha.org.uk
Open: 24 hours
# of beds: 117

Cheshunt
Lee Valley
Lee Valley Park
Cheshunt, Hertfordshire
Tel: 020/73-73-34-00
Fax: n/a
Reservations: 020/73-73-34-00
E-mail: n/a
Open: n/a
Desk hours: n/a
# of beds: 112

Cirencester
Duntisbourne Abbots
Cirencester, Gloucestershire
GL7 7JN
Tel: 012/85-82-16-82
Fax: 012/85-82-16-97
Reservations: n/a
E-mail: duntisbourne@yha.org.uk
Open: from 5pm
# of beds: 47

Cleator
Black Sail Hut, Ennerdale
Cleator, Cumbria, CA23 3AY
Tel: 041/110-84-50
Fax: 041/115-94-72

Reservations: n/a
E-mail: n/a
Open: from 5pm
# of beds: 16

Ennerdale
Cat Crag, Ennerdale
Cleator, Cumbria CA23 3AX
Tel: 019/46-86-12-37
Fax: n/a
Reservations: n/a
E-mail: n/a
Open: from 5pm
# of beds: 24

Clitheroe
Slaidburn
King's House, Slaidburn
Clitheroe, Lancashire BB7 3ER
Tel: 012/00-44-66-56
Fax: n/a
Reservations: 012/82-84-23-49
E-mail: n/a
Open: from 5pm
# of beds: 31

Cockermouth
Buttermere
Cockermouth, Cumbria CA13 9XA
Tel: 017/68-77-02-45
Fax: 017/68-77-02-31
Reservations: n/a
E-mail: buttermere@yha.org.uk
Open: from 1pm
# of beds: 70

Double Mills
Cockermouth, Cumbria CA13 0DS
Tel: 019/00-82-25-61
Fax: 019/00-82-25-61
Reservations: 016/29-58-13-99
E-mail: reservations@yha.org.uk
Open: from 5pm
# of beds: 26

Coniston
Coniston Coppermines
Coniston, Cumbria LA21 8HP
Tel: 015/39-44-12-61
Fax: 015/39-44-12-61
Reservations: n/a

E-mail: n/a
Open: from 5pm
# of beds: 28

Holly How
Far End
Coniston, Cumbria LA21 8DD
Tel: 015/39-44-13-23
Fax: 015/39-44-18-03
Reservations: n/a
E-mail: conistonhh@yha.org.uk
Open: from 5pm
# of beds: 60

Consett
Edmundbyers
Low House, Edmundbyers
Consett, County Durham DH8 9NL
Tel: 012/07-25-56-51
Fax: 012/07-25-56-51
Reservations: 018/33-62-22-28
E-mail: n/a
Open: from 5pm
# of beds: 33

Craven Arms
Clun Mill
Craven Arms, Shropshire SV7 8NV
Tel: 015/88-64-05-82
Fax: 015/88-64-05-82
Reservations: n/a
E-mail: n/a
Open: from 5pm
# of beds: 24

Daventry
Badby
Church Green, Badby
Daventry, Northamptonshire
  NN11 3AS
Tel: 013/27-70-38-83
Fax: 013/27-70-38-83
Reservations: n/a
E-mail: n/a
Open: from 5pm
# of beds: 30

Dorchester
Litton Cheney
Dorchester, Dorset DT2 9AT
Tel: 013/08-48-23-40

Fax: 013/08-48-26-36
Reservations: 016/29-59-27-07
E-mail: reservations@yha.org.uk
Open: from 5pm
# of beds: 24

Dorking
Holmbury St. Mary
Radnor Lane
Dorking, Surrey RH5 6NW
Tel: 013/06-73-07-77
Fax: 013/06-73-09-33
Reservations: n/a
E-mail: holmbury@yha.org.uk
Open: from 5pm
# of beds: 52

Tanners Hatch, off Ranmore Road
Dorking, Surrey RH5 6BE
Tel: 013/06-87-79-64
Fax: 013/06-87-79-64
Reservations: n/a
E-mail: tanners@yha.org.uk
Open: from 5pm
# of beds: 25

Dover
306 London Road
Dover, Kent CT17 0SV
Tel: 013/04-20-13-14
Fax: 013/04-20-13-14
Reservations: n/a
E-mail: n/a
Open: from 1pm
# of beds: 132

Eastbourne
East Dean Road
Eastbourne, East Sussex BN20 8ES
Tel: 013/23-72-10-81
Fax: 013/23-72-10-81
Reservations: n/a
E-mail: n/a
Open: from 5pm
# of beds: 32

Edwinstowe
Sherwood Forest
Forest Corner
Edwinstowe, Nottinghamshire NG21 9RN
Tel: 016/23-82-57-94
Fax: 016/23-82-57-96

Reservations: n/a
E-mail: serwood@yha.org.uk
Open: from 1pm
# of beds: 39

Exeter
47 Countess Wear Road
Exeter, Devon EX2 6LR
Tel: 013/92-87-33-29
Fax: 013/92-87-69-39
Reservations: n/a
E-mail: exeter@yha.org.uk
Open: from 5pm
# of beds: 88

Steps Bridge, near Dunsford
Exeter, Devon EX6 7EQ
Tel: 016/47-25-24-35
Fax: 016/47-25-29-48
Reservations: 016/29-59-27-07
E-mail: reservations@yha.org.uk
Open: from 5pm
# of beds: 24

Falmouth
Pendennis Castle
Falmouth, Cornwall TR11 4LP
Tel: 013/26-31-14-35
Fax: 013/26-31-54-73
Reservations: n/a
E-mail: n/a
Open: from 5pm
# of beds: 76

Fowley
Golant
Penquite House, Golant
Fowley, Cornwall PL23 1LA
Tel: 017/26-83-35-07
Fax: 017/26-83-29-47
Reservations: n/a
E-mail: golant@yha.org.uk
Open: from 5pm
# of beds: 94

Gillingham
Medway
Capstone Road
Gillingham, Kent ME7 3JE
Tel: 016/34-40-07-88
Fax: 016/34-40-07-94
Reservations: n/a

E-mail: n/a
Open: from 5pm
# of beds: 40

Glossop
Crowden-in-Longdendale
Glossop, Derbyshire SK13 1HZ
Tel: 014/57-85-21-35
Fax: 014/57-85-21-35
Reservations: n/a
E-mail: n/a
Open: from 5pm
# of beds: 50

Godalming
Hindhead
Devil's Punchbowl, off Portsmouth Road
Thursley
Godalming, Surrey GU8 6NS
Tel: 016/29-59-27-07
Fax: 014/28-60-42-85
Reservations: 016/29-59-27-07
E-mail: reservations@yha.org.uk
Open: from 5pm
# of beds: 16

Grasmere
Easedale Road
Grasmere, Cumbria LA22 9QG
Tel: 015/39-43-53-16
Fax: 015/39-43-57-98
Reservations: n/a
E-mail: grasmere@yha.org.uk
Open: 24 hours
# of beds: 128

Great Yarmouth
2 Sandown Road
Great Yarmouth, Norfolk NR30 1EY
Tel: 014/93-84-39-91
Fax: 014/93-85-66-00
Reservations: n/a
E-mail: n/a
Open: from 5pm
# of beds: 40

Hastings
Rye Road, Guestling
Hastings, East Sussex TN35 4LP
Tel: 014/24-81-23-73
Fax: 014/24-81-42-73
Reservations: n/a

E-mail: n/a
Open: from 5pm
# of beds: 51

Hawes
Lancaster Terrace
Hawes, North Yorkshire DL8 3LQ
Tel: 019/69-66-73-68
Fax: 019/69-66-77-23
Reservations: n/a
E-mail: n/a
Open: from 5pm
# of beds: 58

Helston
Coverack
Parc Behan, School Hill
Helston, Cornwall TR12 6SA
Tel: 013/26-28-06-87
Fax: 013/26-28-01-19
Reservations: n/a
E-mail: n/a
Open: from 5pm
# of beds: 38

Hesket Newmarket
Carrock Fell
High Row
Hesket Newmarket, Cumbria CA7 8JT
Tel: 016/97-47-83-25
Fax: 016/97-47-83-25
Reservations: n/a
E-mail: n/a
Open: from 5pm
# of beds: 20

Hexham
Acomb
Main Street, Acomb
Hexham, Northumberland NE46 4PL
Tel: 014/34-60-28-64
Fax: n/a
Reservations: n/a
E-mail: n/a
Open: from 5pm
# of beds: 36

Bellingham
Woodburn Road, Bellingham
Hexham, Northumberland NE48 2ED
Tel: 014/34-22-03-13
Fax: 014/34-22-03-13

Reservations: n/a
E-mail: n/a
Open: from 5pm
# of beds: 34

Ninebanks
Mohope, Ninebanks
Hexham, Northumberland NE47 8DQ
Tel: 014/34-34-52-88
Fax: 014/34-34-52-88
Reservations: n/a
E-mail: n/a
Open: from 5pm
# of beds: 26

High Wycombe
Bradenham
High Wycombe, Buckinghamshire
   HP14 4HF
Tel: 014/94-56-29-29
Fax: 014/94-56-47-43
Reservations: 018/95-67-31-88
E-mail: bradenham@yha.org.uk
Open: from 5pm
# of beds: 16

Holmrook
Eskdale
Boot
Holmrook, Cumbria CA19 1TH
Tel: 019/46-72-32-19
Fax: 019/46-72-31-63
Reservations: n/a
E-mail: eskdale@yha.org.uk
Open: from 5pm
# of beds: 54

Hope Valley
Bretton, near Eyam
Hope Valley, Sheffield S32 5QD
Tel: 014/33-63-18-56
Fax: 014/33-63-18-56
Reservations: 016/29-82-59-83
E-mail: winterreservations@yha.org.uk
Open: from 5pm
# of beds: 18

Castleton
Hope Valley, Derbyshire
   S33 8WG
Tel: 014/33-62-02-35

Fax: 014/33-62-17-67
Reservations: n/a
E-mail: castleton@yha.org.uk
Open: 24 hours
# of beds: 150

Edale
Rowland Cote, Nether Booth
Hope Valley, Derbyshire S33 7ZH
Tel: 014/33-67-03-02
Fax: 014/33-67-02-43
Reservations: n/a
E-mail: edale@yha.org.uk
Open: 24 hours
# of beds: 141

Eyam
Hawkhill Road, Eyam
Hope Valley, Derbyshire S32 5QP
Tel: 014/33-63-03-35
Fax: 014/33-63-92-02
Reservations: n/a
E-mail: eyam@yha.org.uk
Open: from 5pm
# of beds: 60

Hathersage
Castleton Road, Hathersage
Hope Valley, Derbyshire S32 1EH
Tel: 014/33-65-04-93
Fax: 014/33-65-04-93
Reservations: n/a
E-mail: n/a
Open: from 5pm
# of beds: 40

Hunstanton
15 Avenue Road
Hunstanton, Norfolk PE36 5BW
Tel: 014/85-53-20-61
Fax: 014/85-53-26-32
Reservations: n/a
E-mail: n/a
Open: from 5pm
# of beds: 45

Ilfracombe
1 Hillsborough Terrace
Ilfracombe, Devon EX34 9NR
Tel: 012/71-86-53-37
Fax: 012/71-86-26-52

Reservations: n/a
E-mail: ilfracombe@yha.org.uk
Open: from 5pm
# of beds: 50

Ivinghoe
High Street
Ivinghoe, Buckinghamshire LU7 9EP
Tel: 012/96-66-82-51
Fax: 012/96-66-29-03
Reservations: n/a
E-mail: n/a
Open: from 5pm
# of beds: 50

Keighley
Longlands Drive, Lees Lane
Haworth
Keighley, West Yorkshire BD22 8RT
Tel: 015/35-64-22-34
Fax: 015/35-64-30-23
Reservations: n/a
E-mail: haworth@yha.org.uk
Open: 24 hours
# of beds: 100

Kendal
118 Highgate
Kendal, Cumbria LA9 4HE
Tel: 015/39-72-40-66
Fax: 015/39-72-49-06
Reservations: n/a
E-mail: kendal@yha.org.uk
Open: from 5pm
# of beds: 54

Keswick
Borrowdale (Longthwaite)
Longthwaite, Borrowdale
Keswick, Cumbria, CA12 5XE
Tel: 017/68-77-72-57
Fax: 017/68-77-73-93
Reservations: n/a
E-mail: borrowdale@yha.org.uk
Open: from 1pm
# of beds: 88

Derwentwater
Barrow House, Borrowdale
Keswick, Cumbria CA12 5UR
Tel: 017/68-77-72-46

Fax: 017/68-77-73-96
Reservations: n/a
E-mail: derwentwater@yha.org.uk
Open: 24 hours
# of beds: 88

Honister Hause
Seatoller
Keswick, Cumbria CA12 5XN
Tel: 017/68-77-72-67
Fax: 017/68-77-72-67
Reservations: n/a
E-mail: n/a
Open: from 5pm
# of beds: 26

Skiddaw House
Bassenthwaite
Keswick, Cumbria CA12 4QX
Tel: 016/97-47-83-25
Fax: 016/97-47-83-25
Reservations: 016/97-47-83-25
E-mail: n/a
Open: from 5pm
# of beds: 20

Station Road
Keswick, Cumbria CA12 5LH
Tel: 017/68-77-24-84
Fax: 017/68-77-41-29
Reservations: n/a
E-mail: keswick@yha.org.uk
Open: 24 hours
# of beds: 91

Thirlmere
Old School, Stanah Cross
Keswick, Cumbria CA12 4TH
Tel: 017/68-77-32-24
Fax: 017/68-77-32-24
Reservations: n/a
E-mail: n/a
Open: from 5pm
# of beds: 28

King's Lynn
College Lane
King's Lynn, Norfolk PE30 1JB
Tel: 015/53-77-24-61
Fax: 015/53-76-43-12
Reservations: n/a

E-mail: n/a
Open: from 5pm
# of beds: 35

Kirkby Stephen
Market St.
Kirkby Stephen, Cumbria CA17 4QQ
Tel: 017/68-37-17-93
Fax: 017/68-37-17-93
Reservations: n/a
E-mail: n/a
Open: from 5pm
# of beds: 44

Leek
Old School, Meerbrook
Leek, Staffordshire ST13 8SJ
Tel: 015/38-30-01-74
Fax: 015/38-30-01-74
Reservations: 016/29-59-27-07
E-mail: reservations@yha.org.uk
Open: from 5pm
# of beds: 22

Leominster
The Old Priory
Leominster, Herefordshire HR6 8EQ
Tel: 015/68-62-05-17
Fax: 015/68-62-05-17
Reservations: 016/29-82-58-93
E-mail: n/a
Open: from 5pm
# of beds: 30

Lewes
Telscombe
Bank Cottages, Telscombe
Lewes, East Sussex BN7 3HZ
Tel: 012/73-30-13-57
Fax: 012/73-30-13-57
Reservations: 016/29-59-27-07
E-mail: reservations@yha.org.uk
Open: from 5pm
# of beds: 22

Leyburn
Aysgarth Falls
Aysgarth
Leyburn, North Yorkshire DL8 3SR
Tel: 019/69-66-32-60
Fax: 019/69-66-31-10

Reservations: n/a
E-mail: aysgarth@yha.org.uk
Open: from 5pm
# of beds: 67

Lincoln
77 South Park
Lincoln, Lincolnshire LN5 8ES
Tel: 015/22-52-20-76
Fax: 015/22-56-74-24
Reservations: n/a
E-mail: lincoln@yha.org.uk
Open: from 5pm
# of beds: 45

Liverpool
25 Tabley Street, off Wapping
Liverpool, Merseyside L1 8EE
Tel: 015/17-09-88-88
Fax: 015/17-09-04-17
Reservations: n/a
E-mail: liverpool@yha.org.uk
Open: 24 hours
# of beds: 100

London
36 Carter Lane
London EC4V 5AB
Tel: 020/72-36-49-65
Fax: 020/72-36-76-81
Reservations: n/a
E-mail: city@yha.org.uk
Open: 24 hours
# of beds: 193

Earl's Court
38 Bolton Gardens
London SW5 0AQ
Tel: 020/73-73-70-83
Fax: 020/78-35-20-34
Reservations: n/a
E-mail: earlscourt@yha.org.uk
Open: 24 hours
# of beds: 154

Hampstead Heath
4 Wellgarth Road, Golders Green
London NW11 7HR
Tel: 020/84-58-90-54
Fax: 020/82-09-05-46
Reservations: n/a

E-mail: hampstead@yha.org.uk
Open: 24 hours
# of beds: 199

Holland House
Holland Walk, Kensington
London W8 7QU
Tel: 020/79-37-07-48
Fax: 020/73-76-06-67
Reservations: n/a
E-mail: hollandhouse@yha.org.uk
Open: 24 hours
# of beds: 201

Oxford Street
14 Noel Street
London W1V 3PD
Tel: 020/77-34-16-18
Fax: 020/77-34-16-57
Reservations: n/a
E-mail: oxfordst@yha.org.uk
Open: 24 hours
# of beds: 75

Rotherhithe
20 Salter Road
London SE16 1PP
Tel: 020/72-32-21-14
Fax: 020/72-37-29-19
Reservations: n/a
E-mail: rotherhithe@yha.org.uk
Open: 24 hours
# of beds: 320

St. Pancras International
79-81 Euston Road
London NW1 2QS
Tel: 020/73-88-99-98
Fax: 020/73-88-67-66
Reservations: n/a
E-mail: stpancras@yha.org.uk
Open: 24 hours
# of beds: 152

Longville in the Dale
Wilderhope Manor
Longville in the Dale, Shropshire
  TF13 6EG
Tel: 019/64-77-13-63
Fax: 019/64-77-15-20
Reservations: n/a

E-mail: wilderhope @yha.org.uk
Open: from 5pm
# of beds: 70

Loughton
Epping Forest, Wellington Hall
High Beach
Loughton, Essex IG10 4AG
Tel: 020/85-08-51-61
Fax: 020/85-08-51-61
Reservations: n/a
E-mail: n/a
Open: from 5pm
# of beds: 36

Louth
Woody's Top
Ruckland
Louth, Lincolnshire LN11 8RQ
Tel: 015/07-53-33-23
Fax: 015/07-53-33-23
Reservations: n/a
E-mail: n/a
Open: from 5pm
# of beds: 22

Lydney
St. Briavels Castle
St. Briavels
Lydney, Gloucestershire GL15 6RG
Tel: 015/94-53-02-72
Fax: 015/94-53-08-49
Reservations: n/a
E-mail: stbriavels@yha.org.uk
Open: from 5pm
# of beds: 70

Lynton
Lynbridge
Lynton, Devon EX35 6AZ
Tel: 015/98-75-32-37
Fax: 015/98-75-33-05
Reservations: n/a
E-mail: n/a
Open: from 5pm
# of beds: 36

Malvern Hills
18 Peachfield Road
Malvern Wells, Worcestershire
  WR14 4AP

Tel: 016/84-56-91-31
Fax: 016/84-56-52-05
Reservations: n/a
E-mail: malvern@yha.org.uk
Open: from 5pm
# of beds: 59

Margate
3-4 Royal Esplanade, Westbrook Bay
Margate, Kent CT9 5DL
Tel: 018/43-22-16-16
Fax: 018/43-22-16-16
Reservations: n/a
E-mail: margate @yha.org.uk
Open: from 5pm
# of beds: 51

Markfield
Whitwick Road, Copt Oak
Markfield, Leicestershire LE67 9QB
Tel: 015/30-24-26-61
Fax: 015/30-24-26-61
Reservations: 016/29-58-13-99
E-mail: winterreservations@yha.org.uk
Open: from 5pm
# of beds:16

Masham
Ellingstring
Masham, near Ripon, North Yorkshire
  HG4 4PW
Tel: 016/77-46-02-16
Fax: 016/77-46-01-32
Reservations: n/a
E-mail: n/a
Open: from 5pm
# of beds: 18

Matlock
Old Hall, Main Street, Elton
Matlock, Derbyshire DE4 2BW
Tel: 016/29-65-03-94
Fax: 016/29-65-03-94
Reservations: n/a
E-mail: n/a
Open: from 5pm
# of beds: 32

40 Bank Road
Matlock, Derbyshire DE4 3NF
Tel: 016/29-58-29-83

Fax: 016/29-58-34-84
Reservations: n/a
E-mail: matlock@yha.org.uk
Open: from 1pm
# of beds: 53

Millom
Duddon Estuary
Borwick Rails
Millom, Cumbria LA18 4JR
Tel: 016/29-82-52-98
Fax: 016/29-82-45-71
Reservations: 016/29-59-27-07
E-mail: n/a
Open: n/a
# of beds: 22

Milton Keynes
Bradwell Village
Vicarage Road
Milton Keynes, Bucks MK13 9AG
Tel: 019/08-31-09-44
Fax: 019/08-31-09-44
Reservations: n/a
E-mail: n/a
Open: from 5pm
# of beds: 38

Minehead
Alcombe, Combe
Minehead, Somerset TA24 6EW
Tel: 016/43-70-25-95
Fax: 016/43-70-30-16
Reservations: n/a
E-mail: n/a
Open: from 5pm
# of beds: 36

Exford (Exmoor)
Exe Mead, Exford
Minehead, Somerset TA24 7PU
Tel: 016/43-83-12-88
Fax: 016/43-83-16-50
Reservations: n/a
E-mail: n/a
Open: from 5pm
# of beds: 51

Mold
Maeshafn
Mold, Denbighshire CH7 5LR

Tel: 013/52-81-03-20
Fax: 013/52-81-03-20
Reservations: 016/29-59-27-07
E-mail: reservations@yha.org.uk
Open: from 5pm
# of beds: 31

Newcastle upon Tyne
Byrness
7 Otterburn Green
Newcastle upon Tyne, Northumberland
  NE19 1TS
Tel: 018/30-52-04-25
Fax: 018/30-52-04-25
Reservations: 016/29-58-13-99
E-mail: winterreservations@yha.org.uk
Open: from 5pm
# of beds: 22

Newcastle
107 Jesmond Road
Newcastle upon Tyne, Tyne & Wear
  NE2 1NJ
Tel: 019/12-81-27-50
Fax: 019/12-81-87-79
Reservations: n/a
E-mail: newcastle@yha.org.uk
Open: from 5pm
# of beds: 60

Northallerton
Cote Ghyll, Osmotherley
Northallerton, North Yorkshire
  DL6 3AH
Tel: 016/09-88-35-75
Fax: 016/09-88-37-15
Reservations: n/a
E-mail: osmotherley@yha.org.uk
Open: from 1pm
# of beds: 72

Norwich
112 Turner Road
Norwich, Norfolk NR2 4HB
Tel: 016/03-62-76-47
Fax: 016/03-62-90-75
Reservations: n/a
E-mail: norwich@yha.org.uk
Open: from 5pm (from 1pm
  Mar-Oct)
# of beds: 63

Okehampton (Dartmoor)
Klondyke Road
Okehampton, Devon
  EX20 1EW
Tel: 018/375-39-16
Fax: 018/375-39-65
Reservations: n/a
E-mail: okehampton@yha.org.uk
Open: from 5pm
# of beds: 102

Oxford
32 Jack Straw's Lane
Oxford, Oxfordshire OX3 0DW
Tel: 018/65-76-29-97
Fax: 018/65-76-94-02
Reservations: n/a
E-mail: oxford@yha.org.uk
Open: 24 hours
# of beds: 105

Padstow
Treyarnon Bay
Tregonnan, Treyarnon
Padstow, Cornwall PL28 8JR
Tel: 018/41-52-03-22
Fax: 018/41-52-04-64
Reservations: n/a
E-mail: n/a
Open: from 5pm
# of beds: 41

Penrith
Helvellyn
Greenside, Glenridding
Penrith, Cumbria CA11 0QR
Tel: 017/68-48-22-69
Fax: 017/68-48-20-09
Reservations: n/a
E-mail: hellvellyn@yha.org.uk
Open: from 5pm
# of beds: 64

Patterdale
Penrith, Cumbria CA11 0NW
Tel: 017/68-48-23-94
Fax: 017/68-48-20-34
Reservations: n/a
E-mail: patterdale@yha.org.uk
Open: 24 hours
# of beds: 82

Penzance

Castle Horneck, Alverton
Penzance, Cornwall TR20 8TF
Tel: 017/36-36-26-66
Fax: 017/36-36-26-63
Reservations: n/a
E-mail: penzance@yha.org.uk
Open: from 3pm
# of beds: 80

Letcha Vean, St. Just-in-Penwith
Penzance, Cornwall TR 19 7NT
Tel: 017/36-78-84-37
Fax: 017/36-78-73-37
Reservations: n/a
E-mail: n/a
Open: from 5pm
# of beds: 43

Perranporth

Droskyn Point
Perranporth, Cornwall TR6 0GS
Tel: 018/72-57-38-12
Fax: 018/72-57-38-12
Reservations: n/a
E-mail: n/a
Open: from 5pm
# of beds: 26

Peterborough

Thorpe Meadows
Peterborough PE3 6GA
Tel: 016/29-59-27-07
Fax: n/a
Reservations: n/a
E-mail: n/a
Open: from 5pm
# of beds: 40

Pickering

Old School, Lockton
Pickering, North Yorkshire YO18 7PY
Tel: 017/51-46-03-76
Fax: 017/51-46-03-76
Reservations: n/a
E-mail: n/a
Open: from 5pm
# of beds: 22

Plymouth

Bewlmnont House
Belmont Place, Stoke

Plymouth, Devon PL3 4DW
Tel: 017/52-56-21-89
Fax: 017/52-60-53-60
Reservations: n/a
E-mail: plymouth@yha.org.uk
Open: from 5pm
# of beds: 62

Polegate

Frog Firle, Alfriston
Polegate, East Sussex BN26 5TT
Tel: 013/23-87-04-23
Fax: 013/23-87-06-15
Reservations: n/a
E-mail: alfriston@yha.org.uk
Open: from 5pm
# of beds: 68

Portsmouth

Old Wymering Lane, Cosham
Portsmouth, Hampshire PO6 3NL
Tel: 023/92-37-56-61
Fax: 023/92-21-41-77
Reservations: n/a
E-mail: portsmouth@yha.org.uk
Open: from 5pm
# of beds: 64

Richmond

Grinton Lodge
Grinton
Richmond, North Yorkshire DL11 6HS
Tel: 017/48-88-42-06
Fax: 017/48-88-48-76
Reservations: n/a
E-mail: grinton@yha.org.uk
Open: from 5pm
# of beds: 69

Keld
Upper Swaledale
Richmond, North Yorkshire DL11 6LL
Tel: 017/48-88-62-59
Fax: 017/48-88-60-13
Reservations: n/a
E-mail: n/a
Open: from 5pm
# of beds: 38

Ringwood

Cott Lane, Burley
Ringwood, Hampshire BH24 4BB

Tel: 014/25-40-32-33
Fax: 014/25-40-32-33
Reservations: n/a
E-mail: n/a
Open: from 5pm
# of beds: 36

Ross-on-Wye
Welsh Bicknor, near Goodrich
Ross-on-Wye, Herefordshire
  HR9 6JJ
Tel: 015/94-86-03-00
Fax: 015/94-86-12-76
Reservations: n/a
E-mail: welshbicknor@yha.org.uk
Open: from 5pm
# of beds: 78

Saffron Walden
1 Myddylton Place
Saffron Walden, Essex CB10 1BB
Tel: 017/99-52-31-17
Fax: 017/99-52-08-40
Reservations: n/a
E-mail: n/a
Open: from 5pm
# of beds: 40

Salcombe
Sharpitor
Salcombe, Devon TQ8 8LW
Tel: 015/48-84-28-56
Fax: 015/48-84-38-65
Reservations: n/a
E-mail: n/a
Open: from 5pm
# of beds: 51

Salisbury
Milford Hill
Salisbury, Wiltshire SP1 2QW
Tel: 017/22-32-75-72
Fax: 017/22-33-04-46
Reservations: n/a
E-mail: salisbury@yha.org.uk
Open: from 1pm
# of beds: 70

Sandown
The Firs, Fitzroy Street
Sandown, Isle of Wight PO36 8JH
Tel: 019/83-40-26-51

Fax: 019/83-40-35-65
Reservations: n/a
E-mail: n/a
Open: from 5pm
# of beds: 47

Scarborough
Burniston Road
Scarborough, North Yorkshire VO13 0DA
Tel: 017/23-36-11-76
Fax: 017/23-50-00-54
Reservations: n/a
E-mail: scarborough@yha.org.uk
Open: from 5pm
# of beds: 50

Seascale
Wastwater
Wasdale Hall, Wasdale
Seascale, Cumbria CA20 1ET
Tel: 019/46-72-62-22
Fax: 019/46-72-60-56
Reservations: n/a
E-mail: wastwater@yha.org.uk
Open: from 5pm
# of beds: 50

Seaton
Beer
Bovey Combe, Beer
Seaton, Devon EX12 3LL
Tel: 012/972-02-96
Fax: 012/972-36-90
Reservations: n/a
E-mail: beer@yha.org.uk
Open: from 5pm
# of beds: 40

Sedbergh
Dentdale
Cowgill, Dent
Sedbergh, Cumbria LA10 5RN
Tel: 015/39-62-52-51
Fax: 015/39-62-50-68
Reservations: n/a
E-mail: n/a
Open: from 5pm
# of beds: 38

Sevenoaks
Church Lane, Kemsing
Sevenoaks, Kent TN15 6LU

Tel: 017/32-76-13-41
Fax: 017/32-76-30-44
Reservations: n/a
E-mail: n/a
Open: from 5pm
# of beds: 50

Settle
Stainforth
Settle, North Yorkshire BD24 9PA
Tel: 017/29-82-35-77
Fax: 017/29-82-54-04
Reservations: n/a
E-mail: stainforth@yha.org.uk
Open: from 1pm
# of beds: 47

Sheringham
1 Creamers Drift
Sheringham, Norfolk NR26 8HX
Tel: 012/63-82-32-15
Fax: 012/63-82-46-79
Reservations n/a
E-mail: sheringham@yha.org.uk
Open: from 1pm
# of beds: 109

Shoreham-by-the-Sea
Truleigh Hill
Tottington Barn
Shoreham-by-Sea, West Sussex BN43 5FB
Tel: 019/03-81-34-19
Fax: 019/03-81-20-16
Reservations: n/a
E-mail: n/a
Open: from 5pm
# of beds: 56

Shrewsbury
Bridges Long Mynd
Ratlinghope
Shrewsbury, Shropshire SV5 0SP
Tel: 015/88-65-06-56
Fax: 015/88-65-05-31
Reservations: n/a
E-mail: n/a
Open: from 5pm
# of beds: 37

The Woodlands
Abbey Foregate
Shrewsbury, Shropshire SV2 6LZ

Tel: 017/43-36-01-79
Fax: 017/43-35-74-23
Reservations: n/a
E-mail: shrewsbury@yha.org.uk
Open: from 5pm
# of beds: 54

Skipton
Kettlewell
Skipton, North Yorkshire BD23 5QU
Tel: 017/56-76-02-32
Fax: 017/56-76-04-02
Reservations: n/a
E-mail: YHAKettlewell@compuserve.com
Open: from 5pm
# of beds: 51

Linton, near Grassington
Linton-in-Craven
Skipton, North Yorkshire BD23 5HH
Tel: 017/56-75-24-00
Fax: 017/56-75-31-59
Reservations: n/a
E-mail: n/a
Open: from 5pm
# of beds: 38

Malham
Skipton, North Yorkshire BD23 4DE
Tel: 017/29-83-03-21
Fax: 017/29-83-05-51
Reservations: n/a
E-mail: malham@yha.org.uk
Open: from 5pm
# of beds: 82

Slimbridge
Shepherd's Patch
Slimbridge, Gloucestershire GL2 7BP
Tel: 014/53-89-02-75
Fax: 014/53-89-06-25
Reservations: n/a
E-mail: slimbridge@yha.org.uk
Open: from 5pm
# of beds: 56

St. Austell
Boswinger, Gorran
St. Austell, Cornwall PL26 6LL
Tel: 017/26-84-32-34
Fax: 017/26-84-32-34
Reservations: n/a

E-mail: n/a
Open: from 5pm
# of beds: 38

Stocksbridge
Langsett
Stocksbridge, Sheffield S36 4GV
Tel: 012/26-76-15-48
Fax: 012/26-76-15-48
Reservations: 016/29-59-27-07
E-mail: reservations@yha.org.uk
Open: from 5pm
# of beds: 27

Stoke-on-Trent
Dimmingsdale
Oakamoor
Stoke-on-Trent, Staffordshire ST10 3AS
Tel: 015/38-70-23-04
Fax: 015/38-70-23-04
Reservations: n/a
E-mail: n/a
Open: from 5pm
# of beds: 20

Stow-on-the-Wold
The Square
Stow-on-the-Wold, Gloucestershire
  GL54 1AF
Tel: 014/51-83-04-97
Fax: 014/51-87-01-02
Reservations: n/a
E-mail: n/a
Open: from 5pm
# of beds: 50

Stratford
Stratford-upon-Avon, Alveston
Stratford, Warwickshire CV37 7RG
Tel: 017/89-29-70-93
Fax: 017/89-20-55-13
Reservations: n/a
E-mail: stratford@yha.org.uk
Open: 24 hours
# of beds: 132

Streatley
Streatley on Thames, Reading Road
Streatley, Berkshire RG8 9JJ
Tel: 014/91-87-22-78
Fax: 014/91-87-30-56
Reservations: n/a

E-mail: streatley@yha.org.uk
Open: from 5pm
# of beds: 51

Street
The Chalet, Ivythorn Hill
Street, Somerset BA16 0TZ
Tel: 014/58-44-29-61
Fax: 014/58-44-27-38
Reservations: n/a
E-mail: n/a
Open: from 5pm
# of beds: 28

Swanage
Cluny, Cluny Crecent
Swanage, Dorset BH19 2BS
Tel: 019/29-42-21-13
Fax: 019/29-42-63-27
Reservations: n/a
E-mail: swanage@yha.org.uk
Open: 24 hours
# of beds: 105

Taunton
Crowcombe
Crowcombe Heathfield
Taunton, Somerset TA4 4BT
Tel: 019/84-66-72-49
Fax: 019/84-66-72-49
Reservations: n/a
E-mail: n/a
Open: from 5pm
# of beds: 50

Telford
Ironbridge Gorge
High Street, Coalport
Telford, Shropshire TF8 7HT
Tel: 019/52-58-87-55
Fax: 019/52-58-87-22
Reservations: n/a
E-mail: ironbridge@yha.org.uk
Open: 24 hours
# of beds: 165

Tintagel
Dunderhole Point
Tintagel, Cornwall PL34 0DW
Tel: 018/40-77-03-34
Fax: 018/40-77-07-33
Reservations: 016/29-59-27-07

E-mail: reservations@yha.org.uk
Open: from 5pm
# of beds: 24

Todmorden
Mankinholes
Todmorden, Lancashire OL14 6HR
Tel: 017/06-81-23-40
Fax: 017/06-81-23-40
Reservations: n/a
E-mail: n/a
Open: from 5pm
# of beds: 33

Totland Bay (West Wight)
Hurst Hill
Totland Bay, Isle of Wight
  PO39 0HD
Tel: 019/83-75-21-65
Fax: 019/83-75-64-43
Reservations: n/a
E-mail: n/a
Open: from 5pm
# of beds: 62

Totnes
Dartington
Lownard, Dartington
Totnes, Devon TQ9 6JJ
Tel: 018/03-86-23-03
Fax: 018/03-86-51-71
Reservations: n/a
E-mail: n/a
Open: from 5pm
# of beds: 30

Uckfield
Blackboys
Uckfield, East Sussex TN22 5HU
Tel: 018/25-89-06-07
Fax: 018/25-89-01-04
Reservations: n/a
E-mail: n/a
Open: from 5pm
# of beds: 29

Velverton
Bellever (Dartmoor)
Bellever, Postbridge
Velverton, Devon PL20 6TU
Tel: 018/22-88-02-27

Fax: 018/22-88-03-02
Reservations: n/a
E-mail: n/a
Open: from 5pm
# of beds: 38

Wantage
The Ridgeway
Court Hill
Wantage, Oxfordshire 0X12 9NE
Tel: 012/35-76-02-53
Fax: 012/35-76-88-65
Reservations: n/a
E-mail: n/a
Open: from 5pm
# of beds: 59

Wareham
Lulworth Cove
School Lane, West Lulworth
Wareham, Dorset BH20 5SA
Tel: 019/29-40-05-64
Fax: 019/29-40-06-40
Reservations: n/a
E-mail: n/a
Open: from 5pm
# of beds: 34

Whitby
Boggle Hole
Mill Beck, Fylingthorpe
Whitby, North Yorkshire YO22 4UQ
Tel: 019/47-88-03-52
Fax: 019/47-88-09-87
Reservations: n/a
E-mail: bogglehole@yha.org.uk
Open: from 1pm
# of beds: 80
East Cliff
Whitby, North Yorkshire
  VO22 4JT
Tel: 019/47-60-28-78
Fax: 019/47-82-51-46
Reservations: n/a
E-mail: n/a
Open: from 5pm
# of beds: 60

Winchester
1 Water Lane
Winchester, Hampshire SO23 0EJ

Tel: 019/62-85-37-23
Fax: 019/62-85-55-24
Reservations: n/a
E-mail: n/a
Open: from 5pm
# of beds: 31

Windermere

Bridge Lane, Troutbeck
Windermere, Cumbria
  LA23 1LA
Tel: 015/39-44-35-43
Fax: 015/39-44-71-65
Reservations: n/a
E-mail: windermere@yha.org.uk
Open: 24 hours
# of beds: 69

Windsor

Edgeworth House, Mill Lane
Windsor, Berkshire SL4 5JE
Tel: 017/53-86-17-10
Fax: 017/53-83-21-00
Reservations: 015/29-41-34-21
E-mail: windsor@yha.org.uk
Open: from 1pm
# of beds: 68

Woodbridge

Blaxhall
Heath Walk, Blaxhall
Woodbridge, Suffolk
  IP12 2EA
Tel: 017/28-68-82-06
Fax: 017/28-68-91-91
Reservations: n/a
E-mail: n/a
Open: from 5pm
# of beds: 40

Wooler (Cheviot)

30 Cheviot St.
Wooler, Northumberland NE71 6LW
Tel: 016/68-28-13-65
Fax: 016/68-28-23-68
Reservations: n/a
E-mail: n/a
Open: from 5pm
# of beds: 52

Youlgreave

Fountain Square
Youlgreave, near Bakewell
Derbyshire DE45 1UR
Tel: 016/29-63-65-18
Fax: 016/29-63-65-18
Reservations: n/a
E-mail: n/a
Open: from 5pm
# of beds: 42

York

Carlton Lane, Helmsley
York, North Yorkshire YO62 5HB
Tel: 014/39-77-04-33
Fax: 014/39-77-04-33
Reservations: n/a
E-mail: n/a
Open: from 5pm
# of beds: 40

Water End, Clifton
York, North Yorkshire YO30 6LP
Tel: 019/04-65-31-47
Fax: 019/04-65-12-30
Reservations: n/a
E-mail: york@yha.org.uk
Open: 24 hours
# of beds: 150

aBouT THe auTHors

Dominique Herman grew up in Cape Town (hence the occasional, supremely informative South African reference in the text) and came to take a bite out of the Big Apple in 1996 where she studied journalism at NYU. These days, to the NYC work ethic borne, Dominique is a film producer by day, freelance writer by night. Since she is now an expert on Southern England, Dominique would like her next assignment to be a Frances Mayes style set-up: basking in the Italian countryside (or French, for that matter—she's not fussy). Many thanks to her wonderful family who were supportive as always, and especially her brother, Adam, without whose guidance and assistance she would have definitely floundered in a sea of pasties and teacakes (not to mention his having saved her from massive backache by disposing of half of her bulging backpack before she set off). Send questions, comments, and high praise to nickherman@hotmail.com.

Kristy Apostolides is a young and idealistic dream seeker. Since her graduation from Cornell University, she has spent her time crafting and wallowing, depending on which suits her best at the moment, trying to match the exact image seen in her sleep the night before. An avid explorer, she has managed to reach further into the folds of her own consciousness than is exactly comfortable. She now hopes to experience the intricate folds of the earth, reaching geographic and cultural areas to an extent further than is exactly comfortable. She dreams of leaving life with a firm grasp on what nothing is and how to get as far away from that as possible. Eyewitness is the only way she understands how to experience, and her objective is to see everything, at all ends of the spectrum. If it *is,* she wants to know it.

Lauren Koch is a 23-year old New York native and NYU grad who has lived in Paris, Dublin, and London before writing for *Hanging Out in England*. She is currently attending the San Francisco Art Institute for photography, and continuing to write creatively.

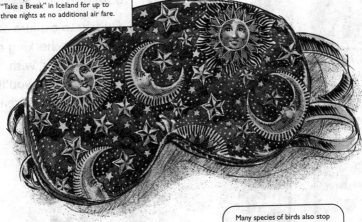